Vernacular Traditions of Boethius's *De consolatione philosophiae*

Medieval Institute Publications is a program of
The Medieval Institute, College of Arts and Sciences

Western Michigan University

Vernacular Traditions of Boethius's *De consolatione philosophiae*

Edited by

Noel Harold Kaylor, Jr. and Philip Edward Phillips

Research in Medieval Culture

MEDIEVAL INSTITUTE PUBLICATIONS
Western Michigan University
Kalamazoo

Library of Congress Cataloging-in-Publication Data are available from the Library of Congress.

Printed and bound in the United States of America

Contents

This Study is Dedicated
to
Jack Hawkins, Jr.
and
Sidney A. McPhee

Preface

THE ESSAYS AND THE EDITION of an English translation of Boethius's final work included in this collection of articles, selected from the second decade of the journal *Carmina Philosophiae: Journal of the International Boethius Society*, address a wide range of issues related to the emergence and the vitality of the vernacular traditions of Boethius's *De consolatione philosophiae* [hereafter *Consolatio*], beginning with the Old English *Boethius* and extending to the present day. This volume builds upon the studies of such scholars as Pierre Courcelle, *La Consolation de Philosophie dans la tradition littéraire: antécédents et postérité de Boèce* (1967); Richard A. Dwyer, *Boethian Fictions: Narratives in the Medieval French Versions of the* Consolatio Philosophiae (1976); Margaret Gibson, *Boethius: His Life, Thought and Influence* (1981); Alastair J. Minnis, most notably his *The Medieval Boethius: Studies in the Vernacular Translations of* De Consolatione Philosophiae (1987) and his *Chaucer's* Boece *and the Medieval Tradition of Boethius* (1993); and Maarten Hoenen and Lodi Nauta, *Boethius in the Middle Ages: Latin and Vernacular Traditions of the* Consolatio Philosophiae (1997). The collection provides an overview of the reception and influence of the *Consolatio* in the Netherlands, Italy, Poland, Byzantium, Israel, and Korea, as well as in Germany and England. The volume also introduces readers to the life and literary culture of Boethius, "the Last of the Romans, the First of the Scholastics," and encourages continued research on the several vernacular traditions of the *Consolatio*. To that end, the collection includes articles on various translation traditions, comprehensive checklists of the German and English translations, and an edition of the complete text of the heretofore-unpublished English translation by Henry Somerset, Duke of Beaufort, known as the *Comforts and Consolations of Philosophy* (1693).

The volume is introduced by two essays on Boethius: John Magee's "Boethius, Last of the Romans" and Peter King's "Boethius, First of the Scholastics," which function as a diptych, providing two important perspectives on the author of the *Consolatio*. The tradition of referring to Boethius as the "last of the Romans, the first of the Scholastics" appears to have its roots in an observation made by Lorenzo Valla, although it gained currency in the twentieth century with the appearance of new research by such noted medievalists as E.K. Rand. This pair of biographical essays reconsiders the two epithets and Boethius's place in history. Did Boethius think of himself as marking the end of an ancient tradition or as ushering in a new period? Either perspective gives a shade of difference to the way in which we understand his importance today.

The second section features essays on a broad range of too-often neglected translation traditions, including the Dutch and Italian, as well as the lesser-known Polish, Greek, Hebrew, and Korean. The translation of the *Consolatio* into the latter languages underscores the remarkable global appeal of Boethius's masterpiece across cultures. In "The Dutch Translations of Boethius's *De consolatione philosophiae*," Jefferey H. Taylor examines the rich and varied Dutch translation tradition, which stretches from the thirteenth century to our own era. Taylor views these translations as significant moments of cultural history that offer unique and important opportunities to explore the influence of Boethius's *Consolatio* upon social history and cultural development in the Low Countries and throughout Western Europe. In "Reception and Adaptation of Boethius's *De consolatione philosophiae* in Northern Italy: An Unedited Fourteenth-Century Version," Serena Lunardi focuses on a unique version of Boethius's *Consolatio* produced in northern Italy between the end of the fourteenth century and the beginning of the fifteenth century. The unedited text is preserved in a single manuscript (Bucharest, Biblioteca Academiei Române, Italian 40), and has heretofore not been included in the records of Italian translations.

The second section continues with essays devoted to Boethian translations from some unexpected regions of the world. In "Early Polish Echoes and Translations of Boethius's *De consolatione philosophiae*," Władysław Witalisz traces Boethius's direct and indirect influence on Polish literature from the *Consolatio*'s first emergence in early eleventh-century Poland—not long after the conversion of the Poles to Christianity in 966—throughout the Middle Ages and into the Renaissance, concluding with reflections on Boethian "echoes" in Jan Kochanowski's *Treny* [*Laments*] (1579–80). Leslie A. Taylor discusses the thirteenth-century Byzantine monk, teacher, diplomat, and only known translator of Boethius's *Consolatio* into Greek in her article, "Maximos Planudes and his περι παραμυθιας της φιλοσοφιας, Boethius's *De consolatione philosophiae* translated into Greek." Her essay emphasizes the value placed upon Boethius's work in the Byzantine world. In "The Hebrew Translations of Boethius's *De consolatione philosophiae*," Marina L. Gorlach, Jefferey H. Taylor, and Leslie A. Taylor discuss the two Hebrew renderings of the *Consolatio* produced in the early fifteenth century, one by Samuel Benveniste (1412, translated from Catalan) and the other by Bonafoux Bonfil Astruc (1423, translated from Latin). Because the Jewish and Christian philosophical traditions in the Middle Ages existed as separate but necessarily intersecting realms, it is interesting that Boethius, seemingly, was the only non-Jewish author whose work was translated into Hebrew during the medieval period. Finally, in "Korean Translations of Boethius's *De consolatione philosophiae*," Ji-Soo Kang examines the relatively unexplored area of Korean translations of the *Consolatio* and gives critical attention to the first Korean translator, Father Eui Chai Tjeng, whose 1964 translation remains the authoritative rendering for the Korean academic community.

The third section, devoted to the German tradition, features an article by Christine Hehle and Noel Harold Kaylor, Jr., entitled "The German Translations of Boethius's *De consolatione philosophiae*: An Inventory of Translations with Extracts from the Texts." This inventory, with samples of prose (Book I, prose 1) and verse (Book III, meter 9) passages of the *Consolatio*, provides a comprehensive listing of all the known translations into German, from Notker's Latin-Old High German text of *c.*1000 to the most recent translations, including the manuscript-translations that remain unedited and unpublished.

The fourth section of this volume focuses on the English tradition, beginning with the Old and Middle English traditions and continuing through the most recent translations. In "The English Translation Tradition of Boethius's *De consolatione philosophiae* with a Checklist of Translations," Philip Edward Phillips examines the English translations of Boethius's *Consolatio*, published and unpublished, from the ninth through the twenty-first centuries, and provides a checklist of the known English translations of the Latin *Consolatio*, organized into the following categories: Complete English Translations, Incomplete and Partial English Translations, and Occasional English Translations, as well as the Modern English Translations of the Old English *Boethius*. Jonathan Davis-Secord, in his article, "Scribal Interpretations of Genre in the Old English *Boethius*," examines the manuscript presentations of the two versions of the Old English *Boethius* in order to determine how the scribes approached generic distinctions. He indicates that each scribe highlights such distinctions through the visual presentations of the texts, showing that at least these two Anglo-Saxon readers were sensitive to variations of genre in Old English literature. In "Authorial Self-Identification in the Acrostics of Walton's Boethius and the Question of John Bonejohn," Ian Jonson examines the hermeneutic implications of Walton's acrostic signatures in the text and paratext of his 1410 translation of the *Consolatio*.

The fifth and final section of the collection features a critical edition of a seventeenth-century English translation of the *Consolatio*, with introduction—"Boethius's *Comforts and Consolations of Philosophy* by Henry Somerset, Duke of Beaufort (1693), British Library, Additional MS 40693B"—by Kenneth Hawley.

The volume concludes with a Selected Bibliography of works dealing with the vernacular traditions of Boethius's *Consolatio* that are represented in this collection—including general studies, standard editions of the *Consolatio*, translations of the *Consolatio*, and major bibliographical works—followed by an Index of Manuscripts and a General Index.

While examining this volume on the vernacular traditions of Boethius's *Consolatio*, readers will remember that Boethius is not only a significant Roman author but also a significant translator and adapter of works written originally in Greek, on logic and the mathematical sciences, which places him firmly as an important figure at the moment of transition from Antiquity to the Middle Ages. As the two introductory articles in this collection affirm, Boethius well deserves his recognition as "the last of the Romans" and "the first of the Scholastics." As the articles and the edition in this volume attest, Boethius's influence today is global in its importance, through the dissemination of his theological and scholarly works, but primarily through the vernacularizations of his final testament to the world, his *Consolatio*.

With the publication of this volume, the International Boethius Society celebrates the twentieth year of its existence and the second decade of the publication of its interdisciplinary journal, *Carmina Philosophiae*, from which all of the material for this collection was selected. Just as *New Directions in Boethian Studies* (2007) sought to highlight the work of established and emerging scholars and to encourage new approaches to the study of Boethius, the current volume seeks to expand our understanding and appreciation of the depth and range of the reception and influence of Boethius's *Consolatio* through its vernacular translations.

The editors are grateful to Simon Forde, Managing Editor of Medieval Institute Publications, Western Michigan University; Ilse Schweitzer

VanDonkelaar, Commissioning Editor; and Patricia Hollahan, former Managing Editor of Medieval Institute Publications, Western Michigan University, for shepherding this volume through the editorial process. They are indebted, as well, to Shannon Cunningham, for copyediting the book, and to Christopher Cecot, for preparing the index. The editors are grateful to Marsha Powers, Kathy Davis, and Karen Demonbreum (Middle Tennessee State University) for their helpful assistance throughout the process of preparing the manuscript for publication. The editors also acknowledge the anonymous readers and copyeditors of the manuscript of this book for their invaluable work. The editors are grateful also to John R. Vile, Dean of the University Honors College at MTSU, for his support of the project, and to Jackie Eller, Interim Vice Provost for Research and Dean of the College of Graduate Studies for approving an MTSU Office of Research Dissemination Grant to cover the cost of indexing the volume. Finally, the editors express their appreciation to Troy University and Middle Tennessee State University, and to the chief administrative leaders of these institutions, to whom this volume respectfully is dedicated.

INTRODUCTION
BOETHIUS: LAST OF THE ROMANS, FIRST OF THE SCHOLASTICS

Boethius: Last of the Romans

John Magee

For Fabio Troncarelli,
veritatis scrutator eximius

SOMETIME AROUND THE YEAR 538, at the end of his Prefecture (533–37/8) or shortly thereafter, Cassiodorus wrote his *De anima* and appended it to the recently compiled *Variae* as its thirteenth book.[1] Within about two years, Belisarius took Ravenna and Cassiodorus moved to Constantinople, the new Rome, thereby inaugurating a final phase of activity centered on his spiritual interests (ca. 540–85): the public life of his Quaestorship (507–11), his Consulship (514), his tenure as *Magister Officiorum* (523–27), and his Prefecture now lay behind him in Ravenna, the seat of Ostrogothic power. Hence, a "Roman" career at the center of Ostrogothic power followed by an extended period of exile in the center of Roman power (ca. 540–54), and a dossier of state correspondence capped by an intensely private and spiritual work emerge as a chiastic series of interconnections that point to a strange irony of Cassiodorus's life and of his age generally: What did it mean to be a member of the Roman senatorial class during a time that pitted East against West, Roman against Goth, Catholic against Arian—indeed, during a time that pitted "Rome" against *Italy*?

The first year of Cassiodorus's period as *Magister Officiorum* brings us to our theme. Cassiodorus's advancement followed upon Boethius's fall, and it is difficult to resist the *post hoc, ergo propter hoc* inference that Cassiodorus was cognizant of, perhaps even embroiled in, the machinations that led to it. The details remain mysterious, and the *Variae* above all project the sense of a conspiracy of silence.[2] The *De consolatione philosophiae* [hereafter *Consolatio*] gives a vivid, but tendentious, account, and we can hardly fail to notice how Boethius's sense of betrayal rises in intensity when it comes to the question of the involvement of members of his own class: that vicious outsiders should have attacked the Senate and all decent men is unsurprising, but that the *Senate* should have sought his head is incomprehensible.[3]

One way or another, Cassiodorus was chosen to succeed Boethius and went on to propagate on behalf of the Ostrogothic regime, as Boethius had,[4] the Platonic ideal of philosopher-kings.[5] For political as well as intellectual reasons, it was impossible for Cassiodorus simply to ape Boethius's line, and the gifted young Italian scholar Massimiliano Vitiello has even detected a note of the "anti-Boethius" in Cassiodorus's self-representation vis-à-vis the Amals.[6] For all that we do not know about the events of 523, one thing is certain: a philosophical and political ideal was never propagated by men more different in temperament than Boethius and Cassiodorus were. Cassiodorus furnishes some of the most important early attestation for the Latin word *modernus*,[7] and he is, as all would agree, along with Boethius one of the "founders of the Middle Ages." But he does not move between that description and "last of the Romans" as readily as Boethius moves between "last of the Romans" and "first of the scholastics."[8] Philosophers are as likely to take an interest in Boethius's *De hebdomadibus* as they are in his *Consolatio*, and theologians vice versa, but I have formed the impression that Cassiodorus's *Variae* and *Expositio psalmorum* tend to attract different readerships: Roman historians on the one hand, and medievalists on the other. In a sense, Boethius's premature and violent death prior to the advent of the Greco-Gothic war, coupled with the mere possibility of Cassiodorus's having lived to see the beginning of Gregory's papacy (590–604), tells the whole story: they were men whose lives pointed in different directions, or perhaps pointed in the same direction, but differently. Vitiello has put his finger on a crucial point: by about 538, the date of *De anima*, the age of Boethius and Theoderic, of Cassiodorus and Amalsuintha, was over: "l'impero romano era morto."[9]

Precisely when and how Roman civilization came to an end remain open questions, of course, and whether the fifth and sixth centuries ushered in new "techniques of accommodation" between Roman and barbarian or marked the "end of civilization" is for historians to decide.[10] Our interest is in Boethius's perceptions and their implications for his works and his cultural-political sphere generally. For what it is worth, the depressing spectacle of Western philosophy during the sixth through eighth centuries, and perhaps Cassiodorus's *De orthographia*, too, would seem to confirm suspicions voiced by Boethius in some of his more paranoid prefaces: Roman education and culture were in trouble.[11] In the *Categories* commentary Boethius at one point stops, very uncharacteristically, to ponder the current cultural implications of what he is explaining in connection with Aristotle's text. Aristotle's argument for the logical priority of the knowable to knowledge involves the example of the squaring of the circle, an (as yet) undiscovered knowable.[12] In expounding the thought that the knowable sublates knowledge but not vice versa, Boethius dutifully points out by way of illustration that what we did not know as children was nevertheless there for us to learn as adults. Then, in a moment of sudden irony, he effectively subverts Aristotle's point: remove the knowable and you remove knowledge, yes; but things have now come to such a state that knowledge is actually vanishing *despite* the continued existence of the liberal arts.[13] Some will perhaps be tempted to write this off as the standard complaint of an arrogant and reactionary aristocrat, but there is good reason for taking it as a reflection of Boethius's sober assessment of the situation. It is the only such piece of sarcasm in his extant corpus,[14] and it may well provide a unique insight into its fundamental motivation, which was, to quote Pierre Courcelle, to bring "the East to the rescue."[15] Under Theoderic, Boethius nourished hopes of both Romanizing the Ostrogoths and Hellenizing western Romans; before *De arithmetica*, he must already have formed the sense of a cultural need, and by about 515 he was contemplating the ambitious plan of translating, commenting on, and harmonizing all of Plato and Aristotle.[16] By the time of the *Consolatio*, of course, things had gone desperately wrong, and in that work Boethius (the author) is eager in the first instance to set the record straight for posterity:[17] Theoderic could not be Romanized.[18]

Here, I like to imagine, is one of the latent messages of *Consolatio* 1p4 and the ensuing poem (1m5), both of which are delivered by "Boethius" (the interlocutor):

> Theoderic, you have consistently styled yourself *rex*. King you are, of course, and since the deposition of Romulus Augustulus in 476 we Romans have adapted to both the title and corresponding political reality.[19] Nevertheless, you are known to have issued coinage in the name of the Eastern emperor Anastasius, almost as though there were still a Western one (i.e. *you*), and I myself am on record as having referred to him in the same way—but then I am a Roman.[20] It was *you* who once exhorted the Gauls to submit to Roman rather than barbarian *consuetudo*, to "don the toga" and return to the *antiqua libertas*.[21] Well then, in light of the violence you are now doing to the *libertas Romana*,[22] I will throw the title *rex* back at you.[23] Remember that we Romans once rescued our liberty from kings.[24] Read your Livy—I have, in the edition prepared by my ancestor Q. Aurelius Symmachus (cos. 391).[25] And as you reflect on the tale of Brutus and Tarquin, bear in mind that Fortune is poised to turn against you too.[26] Do unto others [. . .].[27]

It seems quite clear that one of the functions of the first book of the *Consolatio* is to position the interlocutor "Boethius" in a long line of Roman Stoics and martyrs to political despotism. Cato Uticensis, who avowed himself a Stoic and was subsequently converted by Seneca and other Romans into a sage, stands at the head of the tradition; he makes two appearances in the *Consolatio*, one alongside his nephew Marcus Brutus,[28] and his is the name that supplants that of Philo in Boethius's translation of Aristotle's *Peri Hermeneias*. Similarly, Cato and Lucius Brutus are pressed into service as *exempla* in his commentary on the same: "Cato se Uticae occidit . . . Brutus consulatum primus instituit sub rege Tarquinio."[29] Canus Iulius, Barea Soranus, and Annaeus Seneca are the three victims of Julio-Claudian despotism actually mentioned in the *Consolatio* (1p3.9), and the latter two direct us to the source that best helps to interpret Boethius's meaning. Tacitus relates the death of Soranus alongside that of Thrasea Paetus; both were, like Seneca, victims of Nero, who in the aftermath of the Pisonian conspiracy had resolved to crush the Senate. Thrasea wrote a life of Cato in protest;[30] like Seneca, he ended his life by spilling his blood and offering a libation to Jupiter *Liberator*,[31] by which he certainly meant the soul's liberation from the body,[32] but presumably also freedom from political tyranny.[33] Seneca, in addition to opening his veins, imbibed poison,[34] and Tacitus's description of the event evokes the image of Socrates,[35] whose name appears with Seneca's at *Consolatio* 1p3.9. Seneca haunts the first half of the *Consolatio* in a way that no other Roman figure except Nero does. He appears not only in the list of martyred philosophers[36] but also in 3p5, which follows hard on the heels of the second of the two Nero poems.[37] The inference is obvious: Seneca is to Nero as Boethius is to Theoderic. So too its moral: philosophy and politics are a fatal combination. If that were it, then we might be tempted to conclude that Seneca and Nero offer little more to the *Consolatio* than attractive literary embellishment of a peculiarly Roman and Senatorial sort. If, however, we consider the corollary to the analogy, something of genuine philosophical interest emerges: Theoderic is to Nero *as Boethius is to Seneca*. What did Boethius intend by inviting such a comparison?

As interlocutor, "Boethius" is given the floor twice in the *Consolatio*, at 1p4 and 5p3. Each of the two sections shows him troubling over the problem of *libertas*, that of the Senate and that of the will, respectively, and appended to each is a poem in acatalectic anapestic dimeters, again in his voice (1m5, 5m3). The first of the poems, as has long been recognized, is modeled on a choral ode in the same meter from Seneca's *Phaedra*,[38] with which it shares a pitting of celestial order against the fortuitous chaos of human affairs, as though to say that providence is hostile to humanity. A poem sung towards the end of book 4 by Philosophia effectively obliterates 1m5 by reproducing virtually all of its characteristics[39]—its meter, its number of verses, and its treatment of celestial phenomena—but removing the dualism. *Her* poem carries deep resonances of Aristotle and Neoplatonism, but none of Seneca.[40] And in the passage, apart from 1p3.9, in which Seneca is brought under consideration, the treatment is far from laudatory: in order to draw the moral implied by "Boethius's" own previous attachment to court politics, Philosophia instances Seneca's frustrated and pathetic efforts to pull free of Nero.[41] The *Consolatio* is, in a sense, an effort to come to terms with the tragic history of Roman Stoicism under the Principate; it is also a farewell to Seneca.

The *Consolatio* turns an increasingly critical eye to Roman traditions generally, and I have sometimes wondered whether the great Timaean hymn that inaugurates its second half was not meant in part as a sophisticated piece of *Kontrastimitation*.[42] Roman readers naturally would have been put in mind of the structural analogue with the invocation that inaugurates the "Iliadic" half of Vergil's *Aeneid*, and been invited thereby to contemplate the extraordinary difference between the two visions of the world:[43] a Platonic City of God, to supplant the Roman *imperium sine fine*.[44] The general direction of Philosophia's thinking is foreshadowed already in book 1: the *patria* to which she would lead "Boethius" is not of this world, its *libertas* paradoxically being an almost Pauline form of servitude—not to any body politic, but to the Good.[45] The distancing from Rome builds up in stages, by cooly noting abuses of the Consulship, an office originally founded in the name of *libertas* but subsequently vitiated by personal ambition,[46] and remarking upon the obsolescence of the Praetorship and *Praefectura annonae*.[47] The point, of course, is that their desuetude is proof that the offices carry no intrinsic worth, and also that they are confined to the narrowest spatio-temporal limitations.[48] Most memorable of all is the vanishing act performed in 2.7, where Philosophia with the help of Cicero and Macrobius[49] reduces the Roman Empire to a mere point in space and time.[50] To those inclined to think that Boethius was making a virtue of necessity, justifying in a "sour-grapes" way his anger vis-à-vis a disloyal and enervated Roman Senate, I would suggest that for him necessity had its advantages; that is, that there is much to indicate that the *Consolatio* was written in a mood of profound revaluation. For Boethius, the lesson of *libertas* was not the same as it had been for the freedman Epictetus, although to a certain extent both preached the same line on the subject. At the age of about 40 or 45, Boethius had suddenly to overcome the sense of entitlement, the freedom, that came with having been born into the Senatorial aristocracy. That he should have felt deeply embittered over the betrayal of 523 was only to be expected; the challenge lay in transcending the embitterment. In the end, the tragic *exempla* of betrayed Roman Stoics, of Soranus and Seneca, could offer low-level consolation for Boethius's sense of isolation and anger, but they could not see the *Consolatio* through to its conclusion, as *Consolatio* 5m4 makes abundantly clear. For that, Boethius had to look outside Rome, to Greece and its philosophical martyrs, above all Socrates.

That in describing Philosophia's appearance Boethius meant to evoke the dreams experienced by Plato's imprisoned Socrates is evident from the language of our text: "adstitisse mihi supra verticem visa est mulier reverendi admodum vultus."[51] Cicero and Calcidius would instantly have recognized that this comes close to being a translation of *Crito* 44a (ἐδόκει τίς μοι γυνὴ προσελθοῦσα καλὴ καὶ εὐειδής).[52] One of the more fascinating aspects of the *Consolatio* is the equilibrium it maintains between Greek and Roman *exempla*,[53] and that its general mise-en-scène is meant to recall Socrates in addition to Seneca will be obvious to most. The *Consolatio* is a thoroughly Greco-Roman work: Roman aspects tend to float on its surface, with Greek ones often moving just beneath it. The personification of Fortune in book 2 will serve to illustrate the point. Here are Fortune's opening words:

> Why, o man, do you indict me with your daily complaints? What wrong have I done you? What goods of your own have I taken from you? Before any judge you like, dispute with me concerning the possession of wealth and offices, and if you manage to show that any of them is the property of any mortal, then I will gladly concede that the things you want back did indeed belong to you.[54]

And here is Nature, as personified in Seneca's *Consolatio ad Marciam*:

> I deceive no one. Suppose you bear sons: they may well be handsome, they may well be ugly. Suppose they are many: any one of them is as likely to be the saviour of his country as its betrayer. You have every reason to hope that they will win so much esteem that no one would dare speak ill of you on their account; bear in mind, however, that they may prove so infamous as to become your curse.

> Nothing prevents their performing the last rites for you, and your being the object of their praise; but be prepared too to place your son, young or old, upon the pyre.[55]

The consolatory point is different for each work, but the tone and approach are almost identical: those to whom no promises have been made are not entitled to complain, and the gods (and Fortune) make no promises to mortals.[56] We have discovered, it seems, Boethius's source, and it is one that comports with his peculiarly Roman sense of fortune. But have we in fact discovered it? Consider briefly Fortune's *final* words:

> Well then, if [it turns out that] you have had more than your share of goods, if I have *not* completely abandoned you, if this my very mutability is good reason for you to hope for better, would you still waste away in your mind, desiring to live unto your own law though situated in a kingdom common to all?[57]

And compare now Plato's personification of the Laws, in the *Crito*:

> Suppose that as I was on the verge of running away (or call it what you will) the Laws and Commonwealth came and appeared with the questions: Tell me, Socrates, what do you have in mind to do? Are you not intending by this course of action to destroy us, the laws, and the entire state insofar as you can? Or do you think that this state can continue to exist and not be subverted once its courts have no force but are invalidated and corrupted by private individuals?[58]

The antithesis, "commune omnibus regnum . . . proprio . . . iure," runs too closely to οἱ νόμοι καὶ τὸ κοινὸν τῆς πόλεως ... ὑπὸ ἰδιωτῶν to be coincidental: Plato's sentiment was ringing in Boethius's ears. Which, then, is Boethius's "source": Seneca or Plato?—Both, or neither. Which is to say that it may be unnecessary, or indeed impossible, to decide the issue. What does matter for our understanding of the *Consolatio* is that Plato's significance grows as Seneca's gradually fades away over the course of the work.

It is tempting to imagine Boethius once having seen the famous Berlin double herm of Socrates and Seneca and unconsciously forming reflections that would later influence an unforeseen swan song.[59] Of course, there is no evidence to indicate that he ever did see it, and it is in any case unnecessary to search so far afield for an explanation of the bicultural philosophical texture of the *Consolatio*. By the time Boethius wrote the dialogue, he had invested nearly a quarter of a century in the arduous task of translating Greek into Latin. The habits built up over those decades did not die easily, and in the *Consolatio* itself we occasionally detect signs of Boethius's inability to resist the opportunity once again to assume the role of translator and glossator. For example, when Philosophia diagnoses "Boethius" as suffering from *lethargus* and immediately thereafter observes, "sui paulisper oblitus est," it looks as though she is explaining for the benefit of Greekless Romans the precise sense, the *Platonic* one, suggested to her by the Greek compound ληθαργία.[60] Similarly, when she troubles to inform us of the Greek equivalent (πόρισμα) of the Latin term *corollarium*,[61] it is difficult not to feel that she has been allowed momentarily to step out of character in order to act as her own scholiast. "Boethius," we may recall, is supposed at the start to put to her the embittered rhetorical question: "Is *this* the library in which you raised me?" She counters with an attitude of cold indifference. He is in search of books; she looks instead to his state of mind.[62] But again, such habits do not die easily, and it is unsurprising that even the *Consolatio* occasionally should breathe the arid air of the ancient schoolroom.[63] In the years immediately prior to its composition, Boethius attained perhaps his supreme achievement as a man *utriusque linguae peritissimus*, not by translating and commenting on yet another Greek work but by dedicating a monograph to harmonizing Themistius and Cicero on the theory of topical differences;[64] but his reputation as a man who could move with ease between the two languages had been well established already by ca. 505.[65]

That the *Consolatio* has always been the work to attract Boethius's largest audience is undisputable; that it is his most important work is debatable. Fortunately, we are not in a position of having to choose between it and the rest of the extant corpus, although it is probably true to say that most of us have not yet made sufficient study of the translations, commentaries, and scientific writings—not only in consideration of their own merits but as invaluable background to the *Consolatio*. It was not so in the Middle Ages, and that, we may imagine, would have pleased Boethius, who evinces a constant awareness of the significance of his work for western readers in need of guidance through the *dumeta* of Greek scientific and logical writings. His pages are crawling with Greek names; here is a brief glimpse into their "prosopography" (beyond Plato and Aristotle):[66] Pythagoras,[67] Parmenides,[68] Zeno,[69] Empedocles,[70] Anaxagoras,[71] Democritus,[72] Euclid,[73] Hippocrates,[74] Philolaus,[75] Socrates,[76] Timaeus,[77]

Speusippus,[78] Xenocrates,[79] Archytas,[80] Theophrastus,[81] Eudemus,[82] Aristoxenus,[83] Diodorus,[84] Epicurus,[85] "the Stoics,"[86] Philo,[87] Andronicus,[88] Boethos,[89] Nicomachus,[90] Aspasius,[91] Ptolemy,[92] Herminus,[93] Alexander,[94] Plotinus,[95] Porphyry,[96] Iamblichus,[97] Themistius,[98] and Syrianus.[99] This list is based only on passages that actually name individuals (or schools). There are others in which Greek authorities are anonymously cited, many by way of an "allusive" *quidam* (τινές),[100] which suggests that there is more to the story than Boethius lets on. At the same time, there is *less* than he lets on in that his knowledge of most of those named can only have been second hand. There is, for example, little or no firm evidence to indicate that Boethius read Plotinus, although he certainly read Porphyry, who is responsible for the one passage that actually mentions Plotinus;[101] and there is little chance of his having had firsthand knowledge of the Presocratics, copies of whose writings, as Simplicius informs us, were becoming difficult to procure even in the East. These two cases present very different considerations, for although few would jump at the suggestion that Boethius had direct access to the Presocratics, many have simply assumed that he had firsthand knowledge of the *Enneads*. The probability of his having read Plotinus may well be high, but again, it is remarkable how little direct *evidence* of such reading survives in the extant corpus, and even more remarkable how little attention the question has received.

Boethius, like most of the ancient commentators, tends to be imprecise and elliptical in specifying his sources: he cites and paraphrases without naming, and he names when citing or paraphrasing only on the basis of hearsay knowledge. The Roman Albinus elicits the kind of observation we most desire from him, and the resulting datum is negative: Boethius says that he managed to procure Albinus's books on geometry but not those on dialectic.[102] Moreover, reasonable guesswork as to his sources is complicated by the fact that we do not know where Boethius studied: Cassiodorus mentions Athens, evidently meaning that Boethius "entered the school" without actually having been there.[103] Pierre Courcelle votes for Alexandria, squeezing Boethius's works for evidence they either do not have or else contradict.[104] And James Shiel argues that, far from ever having been able to make use of any of the great libraries abroad, Boethius got what he did from a single heavily glossed Greek codex.[105] Given the current state of evidence, it is impossible to say where Boethius studied, and the question is probably less important than that of the sources available to him—in Athens, Alexandria, Rome, Ravenna, or anywhere else.

To repeat: most of the Greeks who figure in the list above were probably known to Boethius only indirectly. I say "probably" because the bulk of the evidence has still to be subjected to detailed scrutiny. The large commentary on Aristotle's *Peri Hermeneias* furnishes the most useful test case for investigation of the question, in that its density of doxographical material is higher than that of any Boethian work, except possibly the *Institutio Musica*. Its list of named authorities, apart from Plato and Aristotle, is as follows: Speusippus, Xenocrates, Theophrastus, Eudemus, Diodorus, Philo, the Stoics, Epicurus, Andronicus, Aspasius, Herminus, Alexander, Porphyry, Praetextatus, Themistius, Syrianus, and Albinus. Most are probably mere names as far as Boethius was concerned. He was unable to obtain a copy of Albinus, and it is unclear in any case what sort of work he meant (assuming he knew) in referring to Albinus's *dialectica*; Praetextatus had translated Themistius's paraphrases of the *Prior* and *Posterior Analytics.*[106] Andronicus never commented on the *Peri Hermeneias*, having athetized it, and neither had Speusippus or Xenocrates. Hence the list is already considerably reduced: Boethius had merely heard of some possibly relevant work by Albinus; Praetextatus's Themistius he put aside on the basis of autopsy investigation;[107] while Speusippus and Xenocrates formed part of a "bundle" of thinkers whose opinions on one very general point happened to have been transmitted as part of the commentary tradition. Andronicus was irrelevant for purposes of commentary, and Boethius's report concerning his athetization of the *Peri Hermeneias* descends from a source or tradition known also to Ammonius; it is, in other words, secondhand.

The remaining names can be grouped thus: (a) *pre-Porphyrian* authorities, either (i) *Peripatetic* (Theophrastus, Eudemus, Aspasius, Herminus, Alexander) or (ii) *non-Peripatetic* (Diodorus, the Stoics, Epicurus); and (b) the *post-Porphyrian* Syrianus. This classification is grounded in Boethius's patterns of citation, for it is almost unfailingly the case that pre-Porphyrian authorities are cited *in conjunction with Porphyry*, indeed, are often cited as his straw men, whereas Porphyry is frequently cited in their absence. Alexander occupies a unique position in that his interpretations are occasionally allowed to stand alongside Porphyry's, although Boethius places none above a Porphyrian competitor but many below them. And if we cast back to the generations immediately prior to Alexander, a similar pattern emerges. Aspasius's interpretations are occasionally tolerated, usually because they agree with Alexander's, but they are never ranked above Alexander's, although Alexander frequently has the better of Aspasius. Herminus is at the bottom of the heap: one of his interpretations is reported without comment or criticism, but the rest are roundly condemned, always by Porphyry, often by one or both of the others as well.[108]

It seems obvious that there has been considerable tampering with the evidence here, and Boethius's general interpretation of the tradition, his *prejudices* concerning it, can be summed up as follows:

> Whenever Herminus entered into the debate, progress was retarded, and Alexander could see that his teacher was not as astute a commentator as Aspasius had been.[109] Hence, Alexander often had to reiterate or develop Aspasius's interpretations in order to put Herminus's to rest. Porphyry was a better commentator than Alexander, but in a different sense. For many of Alexander's interpretations are quite acceptable but not as penetrating as Porphyry's. Hence, Porphyry will be my guide throughout, and I have found none of his interpretations to be wrong, although I have been able to make progress with *one* point where even he was "stumped."

"Sed hanc expositionem (quod adhuc sciam) neque Porphyrius nec ullus alius commentatorum vidit": this remark, I believe, is unparalleled in the extant corpus, and it says much about Boethius's understanding of both the tradition and his own place within it.[110] The list of Greek philosophers and commentators was long, essentially culminating in Porphyry, who may have been Boethius's only source apart from the one from which he culled a few passages of Syrianus. Even the dull-witted Herminus can be said to cast a long shadow to the extent that Boethius deems a number of his opinions worthy of detailed discussion owing to the confusion they stirred up. It was in the nature of the situation that Boethius should have felt obliged to take matters one step beyond Porphyry, but also that he should have conducted the task with tact and respect. For Porphyry, in Boethius's eyes, was the *excellentissimus expositor* who alone had been able to discover what all others had missed, and he was the one on whose guidance Boethius openly relied.[111] There is a strong teleological cast to the handling of doxographical material in the second *Peri Hermeneias* commentary, a relentless procession from Herminus up to Porphyry. Porphyry, in Boethius's mind, had put the final stamp on the tradition, and in that sense Boethius was left to think of himself as the last in a long line of, not Romans, but *Greeks*. Like modern scholars, the ancient commentators, Boethius included, were eager to justify the publication of yet another book on one or another text of Aristotle. Porphyry's dominance, however, did not leave a great deal of room for Boethius to move about in. How, then, was he to make his mark?

The list of Roman writers named by Boethius is short by comparison with that of the Greeks:[112] Cicero,[113] Seneca,[114] Lucan,[115] Albinus,[116] Victorinus,[117] Praetextatus,[118] Augustine,[119] and Macrobius.[120] Lucretius is quoted once, perhaps anonymously,[121] and, depending on the view one takes on the authorship of the *Geometria*, it is possible that Frontinus should be taken into account.[122] Lucan, although noteworthy for his relationship to Seneca and his entanglement in the Pisonian conspiracy, is ultimately of no philosophical consequence to Boethius. Albinus and Praetextatus too can be written off, for reasons mentioned earlier. Macrobius, although of importance, does not appear to have been a figure whom Boethius sought especially to emulate.

That leaves four: Cicero, Seneca, Victorinus, and Augustine. Augustine must have occupied a singular place in Boethius's thinking: the respect accorded him in the preface to *De trinitate*, along with the *Consolatio*'s numerous echoes of the Cassiciacum dialogues and *Confessions*, makes that very clear. It seems equally clear, however, that despite his importance—perhaps *because* of it—Boethius did not measure his own accomplishments against those of Augustine. The great theologian had been unimpressed by Aristotle's *Categories*;[123] for his part, Boethius was as eager as Augustine to demonstrate that categorical predications are inapplicable to the Trinity,[124] although his eagerness obviously was not born of any disregard for *Aristotle's work*. Indeed, one part of his famous derivation of *persona* in one of the other *Opuscula sacra* is stolen from Aristotle's *Categories*, while the other part comes directly from Porphyry's introduction to the same.[125] Boethius, I suspect, saw himself as complementing Augustine, not as competing against him. Not being a convert to Christianity, he wore his religion in a very different way than Augustine had. Where Augustine had pushed away from pagan learning, Boethius would push back towards it, but no reenactment of the struggle between his forebear Symmachus and St. Ambrose was thereby intended.

Seneca's presence within the Boethian corpus is limited to the *Consolatio* and has been discussed earlier. Boethius imitates Seneca's prose and poetry and reflects on the implications of his fate under Nero, but he essentially lets him go by the middle of book 3, as we have seen.

We come finally to Victorinus and Cicero. Victorinus may be the one whom we have to thank for Boethius's translations of Porphyry and Aristotle. If so, it is a dubious honor: Boethius had hoped to be able to work from Victorinus's translations but found his Latin version of the *Isagoge* so thoroughly incompetent, so overrun by rhetoric, that he gave up and decided to translate for himself. Here at last Boethius could see room for a significant new contribution: being *first* among the Romans as translator and commentator might add some lustre to being the last in a long line of distinguished Greek philosophers and commentators. Having reached the decision to make and comment on his own translations, Boethius began not with the *Isagoge* but with the *Categories*. He struggled with it, making two attempts before settling on a polished, complete version.[126] Only then did he return to the *Isagoge*, commenting now on his own translation. The opening words of the second commentary state what was at issue and insinuate the lesson that had been learned:

> This is [my] second effort at a commentary [on the *Isagoge*]. It follows the text of my own translation, and I will probably be criticized for having translated literally, since I have rendered and compared word for word. The reason for such an approach is that for writings the aim of which is an understanding of reality what needs to be brought out is the untainted truth rather than the elegance of refined diction. Hence, I consider myself to have made significant progress to the extent that [these] philosophical books in the Latin tongue, owing to their complete purity in translation, leave nothing more to be desired from the Greek.[127]

These words must have been composed in about 511 or 512;[128] in 510 Boethius had written of the competing demands imposed by his consular duties and his work on the *Categories* commentary:

> Although the worries that attend consular office prevent me from giving full time and attention to these studies, to instruct citizens in a subject [suitable for] the midnight oil seems nevertheless to be relevant to a certain concern for the *res publica*. I will not have done poorly by my fellow citizens if, now that the ancient virtue of men from other states (*urbium*) has transferred dominion and empire (*dominationem imperiumque*) to this one *res publica*, I at least accomplish the finishing task of instructing the character of our citizenry (*nostrae civitatis*) in the arts of Greek wisdom. And in that sense neither is *this* work exempt from a Consul's duty; for it has always been a part of Roman custom assiduously to honor through imitation what is noble and praiseworthy anywhere in the world.[129]

The point is unmistakably clear: scholarship and philosophy are matters of interest to the well-being of the *res publica*. In its balancing of public duty and private philosophical pursuits, as in its articulation of the *translatio imperii, translatio studii* theme, the second passage resonates with certain prefaces from Cicero's philosophical works.[130]

In the years immediately prior to his imprisonment (ca. 520–23), Boethius turned his attention to Cicero, writing a commentary on the *Topics* while sketching out the monograph on topical differences.[131] The commentary had the curious effect of bringing him back around to the challenge of his earliest philosophical endeavours: once again he was up against Victorinus, who had written a four-volume digest which, because of its addiction to detail, left the better part of Cicero's thought unexplained.[132] This time it was not a question of Victorinus's mistranslations, of course, but of finally getting the relationship between rhetoric and philosophy right. There was perhaps no shame in being seen as the last in a long tradition of Greek philosophers and commentators, but Boethius must have found intolerable the thought that among Romans he might go down in history as Victorinus's rather than Cicero's *Nachfolger*. By turning to the *Topics*, he would have to come to grips with both Cicero and Victorinus, although in very different ways.

In a letter addressed to Atticus, Cicero describes his philosophical works as *apographa*.[133] He was not denigrating them. Far from it: throughout his career Cicero saw it as an act of patriotism and a singular distinction to be the first Roman to bring Greek wisdom to the West. His main philosophical works, the *Topics* and a *Consolatio* in memory of his daughter among them, were written during his final years, against the background of intense political turmoil and a personal feeling of isolation. Cicero's career, his lifelong literary ambition, and especially his final philosophical works struck a chord in Boethius. Boethius would strive, alongside the great Republican orator and scholar, to be first among the Romans in matters of Greek thought, which necessarily meant clearing the ground of Victorinus's pointless (1156b) and irrational (1100a) interventions. The late engagement with Cicero's *Topics* may have arisen in connection with Boethius's reflections on the general situation between about the years 515 and 520; it may have arisen, in other words, in connection with his reflections on the cultural and political significance of his own work as against that of Cicero's. There is at any rate a noticeable change in the tone and subject matter of his prefaces from about 515 on. Boethius's obsession with *invidia* and hostility and his sense of being nearly alone among fools emerge with increasing clarity. The prefaces to *De trinitate* and *De hebdomadibus* are particularly revealing: that troublesome *brevitas* with which

Aristotle is taxed in the *Peri Hermeneias* commentaries is suddenly cultivated as a means of keeping the truth within the narrow circle of those who are capable of understanding what Boethius has to say; for wherever Boethius turns, he encounters either sluggish stupidity or cunning *livor.*[134] The paranoid mood emerges as well in the prefaces to *De hypotheticis syllogismis*, *De divisione*, and above all in the commentary on Cicero's *Topics.*[135]

Tacitus took an ambivalent view of the Stoic martyrs under Nero. Their gloomy[136] displays of independence, read as signs of sedition and intrigue,[137] and their dramatic deaths risked danger for others without thereby furthering the cause of Senatorial *libertas.*[138] That part of Tacitus's story, along with the alternative represented by Agricola—the paradigm of survival in the interest of ameliorating things[139]—was lost on Boethius. The banishments and deaths of Musonius Rufus,[140] Helvidius Priscus,[141] Seneca,[142] Lucan,[143] Soranus,[144] and Thrasea[145] had really been about *libertas* and the prerogatives traditionally held by the Senatorial aristocracy, the *res publica* as against the Caesars, and with that part of Tacitus's narrative Boethius instinctively sympathized. The fact that what is now sometimes referred to as a "Stoic Opposition" had never been a matter of philosophical creed made it possible for Boethius to identify with the "cause" without having to adopt Stoicism per se. He indeed would be the last Roman philosophical martyr to political despotism, but he was not a Stoic. At the same time, Boethius's gaze was directed toward Cicero, with whose tragic end he certainly would have identified but whose significance for him ultimately lay outside the sphere of politics *stricto sensu.* It is noteworthy that neither of the two allusions to Cicero in the *Consolatio* bears any of the political connotations attaching to Seneca's presence in the work but implicitly target him instead as the Roman interpreter of the Myth of Er and as an Academic critic of Stoic determinism.[146] In the end, Cicero's late philosophical writings would have resonated more deeply with Boethius than Seneca's Stoicism did, and Boethius could hope on the eve of his unjust death to take his place alongside the Republican statesman who had considered it an act of patriotism to be, as Cassiodorus might have said, the first to have made Greek δόγματα Roman *doctrina.*[147]

NOTES

[1] Cf. Cass., *Var.* 11, praef. 7; *Exp. ps.* 145.2 (1299.30–31. A.); *De an.* 2 (535.1–2. H.). This paper was originally published in *Carmina Philosophiae: Journal of the International Boethius Society* (16 [2007]: 1–22) as presented at a conference held at Franciscan University but with some supplementary annotation; the current version differs from its predecessor in certain minor changes and in the updating of bibliography.

[2] See now Fabio Troncarelli, "Boezio a Costantinopoli: testi, contesti, edizioni," *Litterae Caelestes* 3 (2008–09): 191–225, at 205–11; idem, "Forbidden Memory: The Death of Boethius and the Conspiracy of Silence," *Mediaeval Studies* 73 (2011): 183–255.

[3] *Consolatio* 1p4.31–32; cf. *Excerpta Vales* 2.14.85–87; Procop., *BG* 5.1.32–34.

[4] *Consolatio* 1p4.5; cf. Massimiliano Vitiello, *Il principe, il filosofo, il guerriero: Lineamenti di pensiero politico nell'Italia ostrogota*, Hermes Einzelschriften 97 (Stuttgart: Steiner, 2006), 168–83.

[5] Cass., *Var.* 10.3–4, 11.1, 11.13.4; cf. Vitiello, *Il principe*, 119–34.

[6] Massimiliano Vitiello, "Cassiodorus Anti-Boethius?" *Klio* 90 (2008): 465–86.

[7] *TLL* VIII, 1211–12, q.v.; Eduard Wölfflin, "Ueber die Aufgaben der lateinischen Lexikographie," *RhM*, n.s., 37 (1882): 83–123, at 92; John Moorhead, "The Word *modernus*," *Latomus* 65 (2006): 425–33 (I would like to thank Professor Vitiello for the latter reference).

[8] Cf. E. K. Rand, *Founders of the Middle Ages*, 2nd ed. (Cambridge, MA: Harvard University Press, 1946), 135–80; 240–48; Edward A. Synan, "Boethius, Valla, and Gibbon," *Modern Schoolman* 69 (1992): 475–91.

[9] Vitiello, *Il principe*, 15.

[10] Cf. Walter Goffart, *Barbarians and Romans, AD 418–584: The Techniques of Accommodation* (Princeton: Princeton University Press, 1980); Bryan Ward-Perkins, *The Fall of Rome and the End of Civilization* (Oxford: Oxford University Press, 2005).

[11] Cf. below, nn. 134–35.

[12] Arist., *Cat.* 7b27–33.

[13] *In Cat.* 230c.

[14] *Consolatio* 4p4.38–40 (after Plato, *Gorg.* 480b–481b) notwithstanding.

[15] Cf. below, n. 49.

[16] *In Perih.* II 79.9–80.6.

[17] *Consolatio* 1p4.25.

[18] Cf. *Consolatio* 3m2.7–16, with 2m6.4–6 and 4p3.18.

[19] John Magee, "Boethius' Anapestic Dimeters (Acatalectic), With Regard to the Structure and Argument of the *Consolatio*," in *Boèce, ou la chaîne des savoirs*, ed. Alain Galonnier (Louvain-la-Neuve: Peeters, 2003), 147–69, at 154n25; idem, "Boethius' *Consolatio* and the Theme of Roman Liberty," *Phoenix* 59 (2005): 348–64, at 355n32.

[20] *In Cat.* 264a; cf. John Moorhead, *Theoderic in Italy* (Oxford: Clarendon Press, 1992), 39–51.

[21] Cass., *Var.* 3.17.1.

[22] Cf. *Consolatio* 1p4.26.

[23] *Consolatio* 1p4.12, 17, 32.

[24] Cf. *Consolatio* 2p6.2; Livy 1.60.3; Tac., *Ann.* 1.1.1.

[25] Cf. L. D. Reynolds, ed., *Texts and Transmission: A Survey of the Latin Classics* (Oxford: Oxford University Press, 1983), 207. Symmachus's (? great-) great-grandson and

Boethius's adoptive father, Q. Aurelius Memmius Symmachus (cos. 485), for his part wrote a history of Rome in seven books.

[26] *Consolatio* 1m5.39–41; cf. 2p2.11–12, 4p4.7.

[27] Cf. *Consolatio* 2p6.9–12.

[28] *Consolatio* 2m7.16, 4p6.33. Brutus was an adherent of the Academy in its Stoicizing phase (Cic., *Brut.* 40.149; *Acad.* 1.3.12–4.18, 2.5.15).

[29] Arist., *Peri H.* 16a32–b4; *In Perih.* II 130.19f.; II 184.10–11.

[30] Plut., *Cato min.* 25.1, 37.1. The tradition went back to Cicero (cf. Tac., *Ann.* 4.34.4).

[31] Tac., *Ann.* 15.64.4, 16.35.1; cf. Dio 62.26.4.

[32] Tac., *Ann.* 16.34.1.

[33] Cf. Tac., *Ann.* 15.62.2.

[34] Tac., *Ann.* 15.64.3.

[35] Miriam T. Griffin, *Seneca: A Philosopher in Politics* (Oxford: Clarendon Press, 1976), 367–71.

[36] *Consolatio* 1p3.9.

[37] *Consolatio* 3p5.10–11; cf. 2m6, 3m4 (Nero poems).

[38] E.g., Helga Scheible, *Die Gedichte in der "Consolatio Philosophiae" des Boethius* (Heidelberg: Winter, 1972), 36; Joachim Gruber, *Kommentar zu Boethius, De Consolatione Philosophiae, 2: erweiterte Auflage,* Texte und Kommentare 9 (Berlin: Gruyter, 2006), 139.

[39] *Consolatio* 4m6.

[40] Magee, "Boethius' Anapestic Dimeters," 155–62.

[41] See above, n. 37.

[42] *Consolatio* 3m9; cf. 3p9.32–33.

[43] Verg., *Aen.* 7.41–45.

[44] Verg., *Aen.* 1.278–79, 6.817–53. With a similarly bold rhetorical gesture Augustine in the preface to the *City of God* had used a Christian text (1 Pet. 5:5 = James 4:6) to echo and (with help from Sallust, *Cat.* 2.2) subvert Vergil (*Aen.* 6.853). The motivation for his distancing himself from Rome was not, of course, the same as Boethius's.

[45] Rom. 6:22; *Consolatio* 1p5.2–5; cf. 3p12.17, 4p6.15–19; Magee, "Boethius' *Consolatio* and the Theme of Roman Liberty," 359, with n. 47. On the *patria* motif, cf. *Consolatio* 4p1.9, 4m1.25–26, 5p1.4 (etc.).

[46] *Consolatio* 2p6.2.

[47] *Consolatio* 3p4.15.

[48] Cf. *Consolatio* 2p6.3, 3p4.1, 11–16.

[49] Pierre Courcelle, *Late Latin Writers and their Greek Sources,* trans. Harry E. Wedeck (Cambridge, MA: Harvard University Press, 1969), 299.

[50] *Consolatio* 2p7.3–18; on place and time as incidental causes, cf. *In Isag.* II 174.18–19.

[51] *Consolatio* 1p1.1.

[52] Cic., *Div.* 1.25.52; Calc., *In Tim.* 254 (263.7–8. Wa.).

[53] *Consolatio* 1p3.9 (Anaxagoras, Socrates, Zeno—Canus, Seneca, Soranus), 2p2.11–12 (Croesus, Paulus), 2p6.10–11 (Busiris, Regulus), 3p5.6–10 (Dionysius, Nero).

[54] *Consolatio* 2p2.2–3.

[55] Sen., *Cons. ad Marc.* 17.6–7.

[56] *Consolatio* 2p1.12; Sen., *Cons. ad Marc.* 17.7.

[57] *Consolatio* 2p2.14.

[58] Plato, *Crito* 50a–b.

[59] Carl Blümel, *Römische Bildnisse: Katalog der Sammlung Antiker Skulpturen* (Berlin: Verlag für Kunstwissenschaft, 1933), 44 (pl. 71). See "400346: Doppelherme des Sokrates und Seneca," online at http://arachne.uni-koeln.de/item/gruppen/400346.

[60] *Consolatio* 1p2.5; cf. 3m11.15–16; John Magee, "The Good and Morality," in *The Cambridge Companion to Boethius*, ed. John Marenbon (Cambridge: Cambridge University Press, 2009), 181–206, at 191–92.

[61] *Consolatio* 3p10.22.

[62] *Consolatio* 1p4.3, 1p5.6; but note also 1p1.6 (*libellos*).

[63] Cf. *Consolatio* 1p3.3–4 ("magistra . . . alumne"), an "Epictetan" touch.

[64] Cf. *Diff. top.* 3.2.1 (1195c); 3.7.1 (1203a), etc.

[65] Cf. Cass., *Var.* 1.45.3–4; Courcelle, *Late Latin Writers*, 284, with nn. 31–32.

[66] The list and references are selective.

[67] *De arith.* 2.41 (175.9 O.-S.); *Inst. mus.* 1.1 (184.10 F.); cf. *Consolatio* 1p4.38.

[68] *In Cic. top.* 1038b; *Consolatio* 3p12.37.

[69] *In Cic. top.* 1038b; *Consolatio* 1p3.9.

[70] *Inst. mus.* 1.1 (185.23 F.).

[71] *Consolatio* 1p3.9.

[72] *Inst. mus.* 1.1 (186.6 F.).

[73] *Ars geom.* 1.1 (113.2 Fo., authorship uncertain); note as well Cass., *Var.* 1.45.4 (Archimedes).

[74] *Inst. mus.* 1.1 (186.6 F.).

[75] *De arith.* 2.32 (157.26 O.-S.); *Inst. mus.* 3.5 (276.15 F.).

[76] *Consolatio* 1p3.9.

[77] *De arith.* 2.46 (192.1 O.-S.) = Plato (as with all other references to Timaeus).

[78] *In Perih.* II 24.16.

[79] *In Perih.* II 24.16; *Diff. top.* 3.3.11 (1197b).

[80] *Inst. arith.* 2.41 (175.15 O.-S.); *Inst. mus.* 3.11 (285.12 F.); *In Cat.* 162a.

[81] *In Perih.* II 12.3; *Hyp. syll.* 1.1.3; *Syll. cat.* 814c.

[82] *Hyp. syll.* 1.1.3; *Syll. cat.* 814c; *In Perih.* II 361.9; cf. James Shiel, "Boethius and Eudemus," *Vivarium* 12 (1974): 14–17 (previously published as "From Eudemus to Boethius" [University of Sussex, 1974]).

[83] *Inst. mus.* 2.31 (265.21 F.).

[84] *In Perih.* II 234.22–23.

[85] *In Perih.* II 239.25; *Consolatio* 3p2.12.

[86] *In Cat.* 264c; *In Perih.* II 24.20; *Consolatio* 1p3.7.

[87] *In Perih.* II 234.10.

[88] *In Cat.* 263b; *In Perih.* II 11.13–14.; *De div.* 875d.

[89] *In Isag.* II 168.14.

[90] *De arith.* 2.2 (97.5 O.-S.); *Inst. mus.* 1.20 (205.28 F.).

[91] *In Perih.* II 10.4.

[92] *Inst. mus.* 1.5 (193.2 F.); *Consolatio* 2p7.4.

[93] *In Cat.* 212b; *In Perih.* II 25.22.

[94] *In Isag.* II 164.4; *In Perih.* II 3.1.

[95] *De div.* 875d.

[96] *In Cat.* 160a; *In Perih.* II 7.6; *Syll. cat.* 813c.

[97] *In Cat.* 162a.

[98] *In Cat.* 162a; *In Perih.* II 4.2–3; *Diff. top.* 2.10.1 (1194b).

[99] *In Perih.* II 18.26.

[100] E.g. *Consolatio* 1p4.30 (Epicurus).

[101] *Anicii Manlii Severini Boethii "De divisione liber": Critical Edition, Translation, Prolegomena, and Commentary*, ed. John Magee, Philosophia Antiqua 77 (Leiden: Brill, 1998), 59, ad loc. 4.5–6.

[102] *In Perih.* II 4.3–7. He must also have had access to Albinus's treatise on harmonics (*Inst. mus.* 1.12 [199.14 F.]; 1.26 [218.22 F.]), which may have perished during the Gothic wars (Cass., *Inst.* 2.5.10). Boethius's remark concerning Praetextatus's translation of Themistius is nearly as explicit (*In Perih.* II 3.7–4.3, esp. "quod qui utrosque legit facile intellegit").

[103] Cass., *Var.* 1.45.3; Courcelle, *Late Latin Writers*, 276.

[104] Courcelle, *Late Latin Writers*, 316–17; cf. John Magee, "Boethius," in *The Cambridge History of Philosophy in Late Antiquity*, ed. Lloyd P. Gerson, 2 vols. (Cambridge: Cambridge University Press, 2010), 2:788–812, at 805, and below at n. 108.

[105] James Shiel, "Boethius's Commentaries on Aristotle," in *Aristotle Transformed: The Ancient Commentators and Their Influence*, ed. Richard Sorabji (Ithaca: Cornell University Press, 1990), 349–72, at 369.

[106] Cf. Georg Pfligersdorffer, "Zu Boëthius, De Interpr. Ed. Sec. I, p. 4,4 sqq. Meiser nebst Beobachtungen zur Geschichte der Dialektik bei den Römern," *WS* 66 (1953): 131–54, esp. 151–54.

[107] See above, n. 102.

[108] John Magee, "On the Composition and Sources of Boethius's Second *Peri Hermeneias* Commentary," *Vivarium* 48 (2010): 7–54, esp. 44–50.

[109] This assumes that Boethius knew that Herminus post-dated Aspasius; if he was ignorant of that fact, then he ranked without any particular sense of the chronology prior to Alexander.

[110] *In Perih.* II 121.25–26.

[111] *In Perih.* I 132.5–6; II 7.5–9; II 106.19–20; II 219.17–18.

[112] Once again, selective.

[113] *In Isag.* II 139.20; *In Cic. top.* (pass.); *Consolatio* 2p7.8.

[114] *Consolatio* 3p5.10.

[115] *Consolatio* 4p6.33.

[116] See above, n. 102.

[117] *In Isag.* I 4.12; *In Cic. top.* 1041b.

[118] See above, n. 102.

[119] *Trin.* praef. (167.1 M.).

[120] *In Isag.* I 31.22.

[121] *Inst. arith.* 2.1 (93.11 O.-S.).

[122] *Ars geom.* 2.2.1 (146.553 Fo.).

[123] Aug., *Conf.* 4.16.28.

[124] *Trin.* 4.

[125] *C. Eut.* 2 (214.153–54 M.) = *In Cat.* 169d (Arist., *Cat.* 1a20–b9); *C. Eut.* 2 (213.135–39 M.) = *In Isag.* I 70.18–25; II 208.9–20 (Porph., *Isag.* 4.21–25 B.).

[126] Monika Asztalos, "Boethius as a Transmitter of Greek Logic to the Latin West: The *Categories*," *HSCP* 95 (1993): 367–407, at 369–77.

[127] *In Isag.* II 135.5–13 (cf. Cic., *Acad.* 1.3.12, "nihil . . . desideres").

[128] Given Asztalos's revision of the chronology of *In Isag.* II relative to *In Cat.*

[129] *In Cat.* 201b (cf. Cic., *Fin.* 1.3.7, "male . . . mererer de meis civibus").

[130] E.g., Cic., *Div.* 2.2.4–6; *Tusc.* 1.1.1–3.6; *Off.* 2.1.3–4, 3.1.1–3.

[131] Cf. *In Cic. top.* 1048d; 1050b.

[132] *In Cic. top.* 1041b–d.

[133] Cic., *Att.* 12.52.3.

[134] *Trin.* praef. (166.8–21 M.); *Hebd.* praef. (186.7–187.14 M.); cf. *C. Eut.* praef. (207.20–31 M.); *In Perih.* II 99.24–27; II 251.11; II 274.25–26 (etc.).

[135] L. M. DeRijk, "On the Chronology of Boethius's Works on Logic, I–II," *Vivarium* 2 (1964): 1–49 and 125–62, at 151–52; Henry Chadwick, *Boethius: The Consolations of Music, Logic, Theology, and Philosophy* (Oxford: Oxford University Press, 1981), 120; Magee, "Composition and Sources"; *Anicii Manlii Severini Boethii "De divisione liber,"* ed. Magee, pp. xxxi–xxxii; 61, ad. loc. 4.11–6.16.

[136] Tac., *Ann.* 14.16.2; 16.22.2.

[137] Tac., *Ann.* 14.57.3; 16.22.4.

[138] Tac., *Ann.* 14.12.1.

[139] Tac., *Agr.* 42.4.

[140] Tac., *Ann.* 15.71.4.

[141] Tac., *Ann.* 16.33.2.

[142] Tac., *Ann.* 15.63–64.

[143] Tac., *Ann.* 15.70.

[144] Tac., *Ann.* 16.33.2.

[145] Tac., *Ann.* 16.34–35.

[146] *Consolatio* 2p7.8, 5p4.1 (with Gruber, *Kommentar*, 386, ad loc. 1).

[147] Cf. Cass., *Var.* 1.45.3.

Boethius: First of the Scholastics

Peter King

BOETHIUS WAS THE FIRST of the scholastics in much more than a chronological sense. His Latin translations of Aristotle gave the medieval world something to think about, and, through his paraphrases and his word-for-word commentaries, Boethius also provided the medieval world with an object lesson in how to think about it. His theological treatises set the style for later scholastic investigations of dogma: concise, tightly reasoned chains of argument applied to matters of faith, rich enough to be commented on in their own right. His intellectual influence was so pervasive in the Middle Ages that we might be tempted to paraphrase Alfred North Whitehead's famous dictum—"The safest general characterization of the European philosophical tradition is that it consists in a series of footnotes to Plato"[1]—and declare medieval philosophy to consist in a series of glosses on Boethius.

One work, however, has been left out of this accounting. While the influence and impact in the Middle Ages of Boethius's translations, paraphrases, commentaries, and theological treatises long have been studied and are well known, the same cannot be said for his masterpiece, *De consolatione philosophiae* [hereafter *Consolatio*]. Yet it too received its "series of glosses" in the Middle Ages. In what follows, I look into this neglected history, focusing primarily on the reception of the *Consolatio* as a philosophical text by later medieval thinkers. Putting aside its literary qualities, then, we can ask: What did later scholastics make of the *Consolatio* as a philosophical treatise? What philosophical problem did they take it to address, and how did they take it to solve that problem?

I will proceed as follows. In §1, I will describe the tradition of philosophical commentary on the *Consolatio*, as far as it can be made out at present. In §2, I will discuss the interpretation of the logical structure of the *Consolatio* in the commentary tradition. In §3, I will look at the particular question of how the issues and arguments given in book 5 are related to the rest of the work, a question that has consequences for the unity of the *Consolatio* as a whole. In §4, the medicinal metaphors Boethius uses to present the "therapeutic" arguments will be looked at in detail as examples of how the commentary tradition can illuminate the logical structure of the text.

1. The Commentary Tradition

Manuscripts of the *Consolatio* can be traced from the sixth century onwards; however, the watershed seems to have been the Carolingian revival of learning in the ninth century, after which copies of the *Consolatio* can be found throughout Europe.[2] Often the text of the *Consolatio* was found along with a commentary; there are even manuscripts in which the text appears between two different commentaries. The ninth century also saw the first renderings of the *Consolatio* into the vernacular with the Anglo-Saxon version attributed to Alfred the Great and, in the tenth or early eleventh century, the bilingual Old High German edition of Notker of St. Gall. The work was translated sporadically over the next several centuries—there are versions in Catalán and Languedoc, for instance—until the series of translations into Old French began around 1100; thereafter it appears regularly in most European vernaculars.[3] Latin and vernacular traditions drew from each other: Jean de Meun translates the Latin prologue to William of Aragon's commentary to put at the beginning of his own French translation, *Li Livres de confort*, and regularly makes use of the Latin commentary of William of Conches;[4] Nicholas Trevet makes use of the Anglo-Saxon verse renderings of Boethius's poems attributed to Alfred in his Latin commentary. There are also commentaries written entirely in the vernacular, such as the Middle Dutch commentary known as the "Ghent Boethius,"[5] or the anonymous medieval French translation and commentary *Del confortement de Philosofie*.[6] Hence the text of the *Consolatio* was readily available in a variety of forms from early on in the Middle Ages.

The *Consolatio* did not simply sit on library shelves, however. There is evidence that it was used to teach proper Latinity to students in their early training, a role it played in different places and at different times.[7] In addition, the *Consolatio* seems to have figured in university education. In the first half of the thirteenth century, it is listed in the *Guide de l'étudiant* and similar manuals from the University of Paris and perhaps was recommended to students as early as 1215;[8] it was not removed from the list of books bachelors at Paris were expected to have read until sometime around the middle of the fourteenth century.[9] Elsewhere it remained on the list of required books into the first decades of the sixteenth century, particularly in central Europe. Yet the *Consolatio* does not seem to have been a text on which bachelors in the Arts Faculty were required to lecture in the same way the texts of Aristotle were. It may well be that it was a work everyone was expected to know, but not to teach or cover in detail at university. The extant commentaries do not seem to have been written for use in the classroom, even when they were written in an academic setting, as for example the commentary of Nicholas Trevet. The precise position of the *Consolatio* in the curriculum remains obscure.

There seem to have been three separate phases of commenting on the *Consolatio*.[10] The first phase begins in the middle of the ninth century, with contributions from figures such as Alcuin of York (ca. 735–804) and John Scottus Eriugena (ca. 815–ca. 877), who seem to have sparked or renewed interest in the *Consolatio*. Lupus of Ferrières (†862) wrote a short work on the meters of Boethius's poems that was used throughout the Middle Ages. The high-water mark of this first phase seems to have been the commentary of Remi d'Auxerre (ca. 841–908), composed between 902 and 908. It was widely used and widely imitated so that there are many "remigian" glosses in manuscript; even those who disagreed with Remi, such as Bovo of Corvey (†916), were indebted to his commentary.

The second phase begins at the end of the eleventh century. Like the revival of philosophy generally at this time, it shows a more technical understanding of Plato and Aristotle (the *Timaeus* and the works of the *logica uetus*, respectively). The peak of this phase is the commentary of William of Conches (1080–ca. 1150). There are many "Conchian" glosses from this time. William's commentary circulates, and remains influential, for the rest of the Middle Ages.

The third phase begins in a flurry of activity at the start of the fourteenth century, with Nicholas Trevet (1265–1334), William of Aragon, and William Wheatley (or Whetely) writing their commentaries within a few years of each other. Trevet's commentary, which makes heavy use of William of Conches, became the most popular and widely circulated of all medieval commentaries, surviving in over a hundred manuscripts.[11] From this point onwards, the *Consolatio* is the object of attention in a variety of formats: vernacular translations; literal glosses and commentaries, in the vernacular as well as in Latin; and in a new genre, namely, scholastic *quaestiones*. The latter were treatises consisting in a series of questions that were raised or inspired by a given text. In the second half of the fourteenth century, we find several such treatises, including one by Pierre d'Ailly (1350–1420/21) from around 1380.[12] The heightened attention given to the *Consolatio* in this third phase seems to have lasted for the rest of the Middle Ages. The fifteenth century, for example, saw the commentary of Denys the Carthusian (1402–71), of mixed literary genre: sections of literal commentary were interspersed with *quaestiones* and "spiritual" interpretation. Such widespread activity was responsible in part for the humanist interest in Boethius at the beginning of the Renaissance.[13]

Scholars and historians of philosophy first proposed to align these several phases doctrinally. In particular, the second phase was said to be "Platonist" and the third "Aristotelian."[14] But that simple interpretive scheme is inadequate. The patterns of borrowing from earlier commentaries are much more complicated than this scheme would allow: Bovo of Corvey in the ninth century is unsympathetic to the "Platonist" elements in the *Consolation*, and the "Aristotelian" Nicholas Trevet in the fourteenth relies extensively on the twelfth-century "Platonist" William of Conches. Better to junk this scheme altogether and look at the commentaries afresh.

When we do, a fact immediately strikes us. The commentaries on the *Consolatio* are not isolated from one another but form a continuous tradition. Later commentators read, and frequently made use of, earlier commentators. Some "Remigian" elements from the ninth century show up in Denys's fifteenth-century commentary. Naturally, each commentator had his own agenda; Trevet, for instance, seems concerned to defend positions associated with Aquinas (e.g., the unicity of substantial form) in his commentary.[15] And of course later commentators did not read all of the earlier commentators. But it is clear that the commentaries on the *Consolatio* comprise an independent tradition, and that since its inception medieval philosophers came to Boethius's text with an awareness of what their predecessors had made of it.

There is a particular advantage in recognizing that medieval commentaries on the *Consolatio* form a tradition, which it is. Rather than limiting ourselves to what any single commentator has to say, we can interrogate the tradition as a whole to see what collective wisdom,[16] or at least consensus, there may be with respect to a given question, problem, passage, or the like. Hence, we legitimately may ask: What did the commentary tradition make of the *Consolatio* as a philosophical treatise? That is, what philosophical problem did they take it to try to solve?

2. The Structure of the Argument

The literary structure of the *Consolation* makes it hard to see what the correct philosophical reading of the text could be.[17] Boethius opens the work in medias res. Its dramatic mise-en-scène is the Prisoner's lament over his fallen state, which is a problem for the Prisoner, indeed, but not obviously a philosophical problem. The point is worth a moment's reflection. As the *Consolatio* opens, there is no initial statement of a philosophical problem to be solved, theses to be defended, or a position to be held against all challengers. Indeed, the *Consolatio* offers few clues along these lines. Its separate books and chapters have no informative titles or headings, and they do not seem to divide the text in a way that articulates its logical structure. The dramatis personae, namely, the Prisoner and Lady Philosophy, are both clearly on the same side, so to speak; we do not anticipate the eventual refutation of one or the other. The *Consolatio* is a text whose philosophical meaning has to be teased out.

The commentary tradition agrees, unanimously and unhelpfully, that the aim of the *Consolatio* is, well, consolation. In the first phase, commentators generally follow Boethius in saying little or nothing more; they also tend to concentrate on biographical material in their introductions. This practice changes in the second phase. William of Conches writes a general prologue to his commentary in which he gives a succinct account of the aim of the *Consolatio* by outlining the structure of Boethius's arguments (4.39–52):[18]

> Thus Boethius deals with his subject-matter as follows: [1] he shows that temporal things are transitory and that the complete good is not among them, and so we should not be gladdened by their presence nor saddened by their absence; [2] he shows what the highest good is, and where it is situated, and how it is reached; [3] he shows that good people are always powerful and wicked people powerless, and that rewards always come to good people and punishments to evil people; [4] why some good people fare well in this life and others poorly, and likewise why some wicked people fare well and others poorly; [5] what divine providence is, as well as fate, chance, and free choice; [6] he puts forward arguments that seem to show that free choice is not compatible with divine providence, and disproves the false resolution some people offer;[19] [7] he establishes his own resolution with arguments.

William is interested in the dialectical stages of the *Consolatio*, not in its literary or expository form. His sevenfold division of its logical structure gives equal weight to unequal portions of the text. William's commentary [1] covers all of books 1–2 and the first half of book 3; [2] covers the second half of book 3; [3] and [4] treat matter in book 4; [5]–[7] deal with matter in book 5. A more inclusive amalgamation, suggested by William's division, is tempting: [1]–[4] deal with ethics, broadly speaking, including the bit of metaphysics needed to underpin the ethics, whereas [5]–[7] deal with a specific issue in philosophical theology.

The later commentary tradition seems content to follow William's analysis of the structure of the *Consolatio*. For example, Pseudo-Aquinas, writing his commentary some three to four centuries after William, not only adopts William's analysis but plagiarizes William's presentation wholesale in his preface—a good example of the kind of indebtedness found in the commentary tradition (p. 122, col. 3, lines 1–19, adding the numbers from William's presentation):[20]

> Fifth, we should generally summarize the whole book: [1] Boethius shows that temporal goods are transitory and that the whole of genuine happiness does not consist in them, and, consequently, that we should not be saddened by their absence nor pleased by their presence; furthermore, [4] that no one should exult in faring well nor be depressed in adversity. [2] He also shows in this book what the highest good is, where it is situated, and how to reach it. [3] It is also shown that good people are always powerful and wicked people powerless, and that good people always have their rewards and wicked people their punishments. After this, [5] he shows what divine providence is, as well as chance, fate, and free choice. [6] Boethius puts forward arguments by which he proves that free choice is not compatible with divine providence. He lays out a false resolution offered by some people and disproves it; thereafter [7] he establishes the genuine resolution which he confirms with arguments.

Pseudo-Aquinas's placement of [4] abstracts a step further than William from the literary details of the *Consolatio* since it groups the arguments of book 4 logically with the arguments about transitory goods rather than following Boethius's order of presentation.[21] Apart from minor variations of this sort, the later commentary tradition generally adopts William's analysis.[22]

Now William's analysis commanded widespread acceptance in the later commentary tradition because it is generally well grounded in

Boethius's text itself. Throughout the *Consolatio*, Boethius offers occasional signposts that show the direction of the argument. The first long stretch of argument is signalled by the use of medicinal metaphors introduced after Lady Philosophy's diagnosis that the Prisoner is suffering from an illness (1p2.10–12). It is a peculiarly philosophical illness, namely that the Prisoner has "forgotten himself" (1p2.12: "Sui paulisper oblitus est"); several stages of therapy are called for, each needing different medicines. Exactly how this literary metaphor plays out in philosophical terms will be discussed in §4 below. Whatever the details, the end of this stretch of the argument, corresponding to William's [1], is brought to an end when Lady Philosophy declares that she will say no more about false happiness, moving on to the task of indicating what true happiness is (3p9.2–3: "ordo est deinceps quae sit uera [felicitas] monstrare").

In line with [2], Lady Philosophy then explicitly states that she will show the Prisoner what the highest good is (3p9.2–3 and 3p9.91–92), where it is situated (3p10.3: "quonam haec felicitas perfectio constituta sit"), and how it is attained (3p10.77–86). The individual arguments under each heading are also clearly articulated, as are the several arguments that close book 3, having to do with the unity of the supreme good and God's divine governance of the world. The latter are not obviously included in William's division.

The next major signpost in Boethius's text occurs at the start of book 4. The Prisoner interrupts Lady Philosophy, and—finally!—states the fundamental problem of the *Consolatio*: not the problem of evil (4p1.9–12) but the problem of desert (4p1.13–19):[23]

> A further and greater problem looms: while wickedness rules and fares well, virtue not only goes unrewarded but is enslaved and trodden down by criminals, made to pay the penalties in place of the wrongdoers; that this happens under the reign of an omniscient and omnipotent God Who wills only good things must be the cause of astonishment and complaint from all.

Why does each person not get what he or she deserves? But each does, Lady Philosophy replies, and, given the preceding results ("si ea quae paulo ante conclusa sunt inconuulsa seruantur"), she declares in 4p1.22–30 that she will prove that good people are always powerful and wicked people always weak and that rewards always come to good people and punishments to evil people, as William describes in [3]; furthermore, she argues that good people achieve success and wicked people suffer misfortunes, as William describes in [4]. These proofs occupy the bulk of book 4.

Boethius marks the next and final major structural division of the *Consolatio* at the beginning of book 5, which William subdivides into his [5]–[7]. Lady Philosophy, about to speak of other matters (*ad alia quaedam*), is interrupted by the Prisoner, who asks about chance and Providence (5p1.6–7). Lady Philosophy replies (5p1.7–12):[24]

> She said: I am in a hurry to keep my promise[25] and to reveal to you the way by which you are to be brought back to your homeland. Although these matters you raise are quite useful to know about, they do divert us a bit from the path we have set ourselves, and I am afraid that you will be tired out by these digressions and not have enough strength to follow the proper track.

The Prisoner assures Lady Philosophy that she need not be worried on his behalf, and so they turn to chance, fate, divine providence, and free choice. But note that Lady Philosophy explicitly calls their investigations "digressions" (*deuiis*), diverting them from "the proper track" (*rectum iter*). She also describes what has yet to be done, namely, to show the Prisoner how he is to be brought back to his homeland, which seems not to happen anywhere in book 5. The material in book 5, then, seems to be only tangentially connected to the rest of the *Consolatio*, which seems not to have completed the goals it sets itself.

William's analysis, in its separating the "ethical" theses [1]–[4] from the "theological" theses [5]–[7], is in line with the ambiguous status of book 5 as seen in its introductory passages. William makes the juncture visible. But that, of course, is to raise questions about the unity of the *Consolatio* as a whole—questions that modern commentators generally ignore, preferring to take the *Consolatio* as a complete and unified work as it stands. But what did the commentary tradition make of these passages, and in general the dialectical relation between the ethical aims of books 1–4 and the technical issues in philosophical theology of book 5?

3. The Status of Book 5

Around 1480, Pierre d'Ailly summarized the whole of the *Consolatio* in two questions, one ethical and one theological, which he put as follows:[26]

> Can a philosopher arrive at a genuine understanding of human happiness, pursuing his philosophical investigation with only the natural light of reason?

> Is it compatible with God's eternal and unchangeable foreknowledge of everything future that some purely contingent event come to pass?

D'Ailly takes these two questions to be logically independent. In literary terms, we could represent this as the hypothesis that books 1–4 form a unity, to which book 5 is, essentially, an Appendix. William of Conches in the twelfth century seems inclined to the same view in his commentary on 5p1.1–2 (288.8–15):[27]

> But since treating these matters seems far removed from consolation, which is the goal of this work, [Boethius] first puts a short transition in which he shows how he comes to treat them.

The transition William refers to is the Prisoner's interruption of Lady Philosophy, which provides a dramatic, not a logical, link between the earlier books and book 5.[28] The ensuing discussion is indeed "far removed from consolation." Remi d'Auxerre, near the beginning of the commentary tradition, seems likewise to regard book 5 as an Appendix in his paraphrase of Lady Philosophy's words in 5p1.9–12 (341–42):[29]

> I have therefore proposed that you should be brought back to your former state of contemplation, which surely is close at hand. But the matters you are asking about get in your way, since while you delay me over them you cannot go to the places I have told you about.

Remi underlines the irrelevance of the discussion in book 5 for the goal of consolation, that is, for returning the Prisoner to proper contemplation of God.[30] From all phases of the commentary tradition, then, there is support for reading book 5 as a logically independent treatise appended to books 1–4.

Yet there is another hypothesis available. For book 5 might count as a digression but not as an appendix if it were embedded in a larger framework, one that made good on the repeated intention of Lady Philosophy to show the Prisoner the way back to his homeland. On this hypothesis, the *Consolatio* as we have it is missing book 6.[31]

This seems to be the view that Silk's anonymous ninth-century commentator has in mind when he turns to explain Lady Philosophy's reluctance in 5p1.7–9 (271.15–272.3):[32]

> She said: I AM IN A HURRY to fulfill the promise I made to you.

> She said this because she wanted to put an end to the work . . . [.] Lady Philosophy also said: Although these matters are useful to know, they are still remote from OUR PLAN, i.e., from our aim. Her plan was described in 4.m7.32, GO NOW YOU INTREPID ONES: with these words she exhorted him to return to his heavenly homeland. Arguing through the questions which she dismissed here got in the way of this.

To "put an end to the work" Lady Philosophy needs to carry out the rest of her plan, namely, to show the Prisoner how "to return to his heavenly homeland." The commentator explains how Lady Philosophy would accomplish this when he describes what she was up to at the time of the Prisoner's interruption in 5p1.1–2 (271.1–7):[33]

> She was ready to extend her argument further, so that mortal men would strive to attain immortality through the heights of virtue; and she WAS TURNING her discourse TO THESE OTHER MATTERS, i.e., to exhort men to practice the good.

There seems to have been consensus in the commentary tradition that the Prisoner would be shown how to return to his homeland by practicing virtue. Pseudo-Aquinas, for instance, puts it this way: "Lady Philosophy's exhortation is correct, since philosophy encourages the virtues and contempt for the goods of fortune."[34] Presumably this would have been the content of Book 6.

Nicholas Trevet has an unusual twist on this second hypothesis. He too holds that the argument of the *Consolatio* as we have it is incomplete, but that Boethius meant to resolve it in another work, as he tells us in his commentary on 5p1.7–9 (669):[35]

> The WAY through which man can arrive in reality at what he should attain are the virtues of the mind. Boethius meant to deal with them—not in this work, but at the end of his *De musica*, dealing with "human music"; this is clear from what he says at the start of *mus*. 4.2. But he never carried out his plan, since he was prevented by the death inflicted by King Theodoric.

Since the last part of the *De musica* is lost, if it ever existed, Trevet's solution cleverly combines two problems, namely the missing endings of each work. Of course, Trevet's suggestion is superfluous. If he assumes that we do not have the end of the *De musica* because of Boethius's execution, why not leave the *De musica* out of the account and simply assume that we do not have the end of the *Consolation* because of Boethius's execution? Yet whatever we may think of Trevet's solution,[36] it clearly shows that he adopted the second hypothesis and saw the *Consolatio* as incomplete.

The medieval commentary tradition, then, differs from modern interpretation in recognizing a problem with the status of book 5, although there does not seem to be consensus on whether the first hypothesis (books 1–4 are a unity and book 5 an appendix) or the second hypothesis (books 1–5 need an additional book 6) is the better. I should note, however, that in the late fifteenth century Denys the Carthusian tries to give a unified account of the *Consolatio*, breaking with the tradition in a number of respects. Closer to modern practice, Denys offers an analysis that summarizes the *Consolatio* book-by-book, rejecting William's analysis. He gives a succinct statement of his interpretation in his comments on the beginning of 4p1 (436A):[37]

> In book 1, Lady Philosophy carefully examines the causes of Boethius's sorrow. In book 2, she administers the milder remedies to him as her patient. In book 3, she administers the more effective and more sublime remedies, setting forth and arguing about in what several things happiness seems to consist (although it does not really), and again in what happiness truly is—or rather, what it is and how it may be attained. At this point, in book 4, Lady Philosophy removes from Boethius's mind anything still remaining from his former indisposition, uneasiness, doubt, and confusion, showing that the whole of the universe, and in particular the human race, is well governed in proper order by its creator: God the omnipotent, just, holy, and more than the wisest. Everything is ordered to its appropriate end, yet the providence of God does not confer necessity on human acts. This is the subject of book 4 and of the following book 5, wherein Boethius, in the role of someone not yet sufficiently illuminated, puts forward his doubts, wonderings, and confusions; Lady Philosophy answers them all wisely, or rather Boethius himself does in his role as a wise and virtuous man.

There are many differences between William and Denys: the former puts under a single logical heading what the latter sums up in each of the first three books, for instance.[38] The important move Denys makes is to understand the subject of book 4 in such a way as to make it part of a continuous enterprise with book 5, linking them through the mention of divine providence in 4.6.4. When he turns to the details of the text, though, Denys does not offer any explanation of the problems that led earlier commentators to find the status of book 5 problematic. He is often content merely to repeat and paraphrase the text rather than engage the difficulties it poses.[39] It is true that divine providence occurs in book 4 and in book 5, but that does not mean that the problems in which it plays a part are logically connected. Asserting that there is a connection does not make it so; Denys has to argue for the claim, which he does not do. For all that, Denys's extensive commentary shows that there were at least some readers who tried to take the *Consolatio* as a unified whole.

Attempting to spell out the logical structure of the *Consolatio* as a whole led us to question whether Book 5 was a proper ending, given the course of the argument. But in doing so we put off a question about whether the *Consolatio* has a proper beginning, a question to which we must now return. In particular, we need to take a look at the philosophical cash-value in Boethius's use of literary artifice: the metaphor of sickness, health, and therapeutic treatment for the Prisoner, with which the philosophical project of the *Consolatio* commences.

4. The Medicinal Metaphors

Boethius deploys the metaphor of medicines that are weaker (more gentle) and stronger (more harsh) in describing the stages that Lady Philosophy uses to make the Prisoner "healthy" again. The metaphor is introduced in 1p5.36–42 and repeated in 1p6.53–59 and 2p1.18–20. Thereafter the metaphor is exercised at intervals to signal the Prisoner's progress. The first application is at 2p1.20–24, where Philosophy's consolations are explicitly aligned with rhetoric (see also 2p3.5), and the second at 2p4, where Fortune's goods are said to be unsatisfying because ephemeral and transitory. A new stage of progress is marked at 2p5.1–2, where Philosophy offers the Prisoner stronger medicine; this seems to occupy the remainder of book 2. The third stage is reached in 3p1.7–8, where the Prisoner demands stronger remedies, including those that seem bitter indeed (3p1.13): the explanation of the forms of false happiness, as Philosophy summarizes it in 3p9.1–3—whereupon the medical metaphors are abandoned, and Boethius offers the second "signpost" for interpreting the argument (namely, "to indicate what true happiness is") as described in §2 above.

The literary metaphor serves a dialectical purpose. Roughly speaking, the "strength" of the medicines corresponds to the strength of the arguments offered by Lady Philosophy, with each successive stage dropping assumptions used in the arguments of the preceding stage. More to the point, the harsh remedies employ a different dialectical strategy, as Trevet notes in his comments on 2p1 (177–78):[40]

> After Lady Philosophy investigated Boethius's condition and the cause of his affliction sufficiently in book 1, here [in book 2] she proceeds to the business of curing him. On this score she does two things: (*a*) she administers some gentle remedies to alleviate his pain and prepare for the stronger remedies to be taken; (*b*) she gives him the stronger remedies in 3.1.1. Boethius endorsed this way of proceeding in 1p5 and at the end of 1p6. He calls "gentler remedies" the arguments derived from common use among people to remove pain; he calls "stronger remedies" the arguments directed against people's common opinion, showing what the perfect good is and where it is situated and how to reach it.

The first several stages of therapeutic medicine have this much in common: they are all more or less commonly used to console people in their miseries and do not address the root causes of their unhappiness. Trevet seems to be following William of Conches on this score, who, apropos of the Prisoner's diagnosis by Lady Philosophy in 1p6.53–59, remarks (95.30–96.37):[41]

> Lady Philosophy shows how [the Prisoner] is consoled once the cause of his sorrow is known, namely by giving first weaker medicines and then stronger ones. The weaker medicines are the rhetorical arguments in common use to take away sorrow. The stronger medicines are arguments contrary to popular opinion for showing what the perfect good is, where it is situated, and how to reach it.

William's remarks about rhetoric here show that he has an eye to the first application of mild medicine, namely the "sweet persuasiveness of rhetoric," which has to be guided by philosophy to stay on the right road (2p1.20–22). This first stage of therapy offers no arguments, strictly speaking, but rather the popular view that Fortune always involves ups and downs: the Prisoner should count his blessings (2p4.13–31); he ought to recognize that good fortune comes only with the possibility of adverse fortune (2p4.9–13); and good fortune may pass, but by the same token so does adverse fortune (2p4.34–38). Unfortunately, the Prisoner counts his misfortunes as well as his blessings and is still unhappy over his current condition. Rightly so: these consolations all boil down to the thought that

Fortune operates impersonally, and that ups and downs are inevitable. But surely that misses the point. Suffering is perhaps worse if personal (and the result of malevolence), but it is not easier to bear if it is just the roll of the cosmic dice, as it were. Likewise, while it may be true that fortunes rise and fall, it does not mean that there is not genuine suffering involved in their fall. The gambler is not consoled for his losses by the thought that sometimes you win and sometimes you lose. These popular consolations are patently inadequate for dealing with the Prisoner's tragedy.

Lady Philosophy then offers three arguments to the effect that ephemeral goods cannot provide happiness (2p4.75–96), as her second application of therapy. She immediately moves on to "stronger medicines" (2p5.1–2) wherein the ephemerality of the goods of Fortune is set aside, arguing that they are not worthwhile even apart from the fact that they can be lost, that is, arguing that the goods of Fortune are intrinsically worthless (2p5.2–5):[42]

> Suppose that the gifts of Fortune were not ephemeral and transitory: what is there in them that can ever become yours, or, once examined and weighed, is not worthless?

The transition marked at 2p5.1–5 looks back to the preceding three arguments and forward to the point-by-point arguments against wealth (2p5), honors and power (2p6), and reputation (2p7).[43] It is at this point that the commentary tradition brings the literary metaphor into alignment with its dialectical meaning, that is, by identifying the precise assumptions that are made or dropped at each "application" of medicinal reasoning. First, the Anonymous commentator of the ninth century (89.1–8):[44]

> Lady Philosophy, seeing [the Prisoner] to be a little bit improved, says: Up until now I have used weaker medicines, but now I shall use stronger ones. Above [in 2p4.75–96] I proved that earthly goods should not be pursued, since they are transitory. I prove once again the same point: If they were not transitory, they ought not be pursued; then since they are transitory so much the less ought they be pursued; but, even if they were not transitory, they ought not be pursued.

The initial round of argumentation turns on the assumption that "earthly goods . . . are transitory"; the second round of stronger medicine drops this assumption, arguing that they are not worth pursuing in their own right. So Nicholas Trevet in the fourteenth century (236–37):[45]

> After Lady Philosophy put forward [in 2p4.75–96] less forceful remedies to show that the goods of fortune should be spurned and one should not be sorrowed at their loss, here she puts to the same end more forceful remedies, which are arguments derived from the circumstances of particular goods of Fortune.

The strength of the medicines matches the dialectical power of the arguments. When the Prisoner announces that he is ready for drastic remedies in 3p1.3–14, even circumstantial features of the goods of Fortune are put aside. Instead, Lady Philosophy adopts the second dialectical strategy mentioned above, namely, "arguments contrary to popular opinion for showing what the perfect good is, where it is situated, and how to reach it." The five traditional candidates for happiness—namely, wealth, honors, power, reputation, and physical pleasure—cannot deliver on their promises but do implicitly describe the Supreme Good: it is final, in that it puts an end to all desire; complete, in that there are no goods outside it; dominant, in that there is nothing better than it. This formal specification of the Supreme Good has to be filled out, of course, but, even at this abstract level, it is enough to establish that none of the traditional candidates measure up. That brings us to the next structural division of the *Consolatio*, at which point the medicinal metaphors are dropped.

The commentary tradition explicates Boethius's literary metaphors by aligning them with strictly logical features of the arguments presented in the *Consolatio*. Modern commentators do not do as much: Joachim Gruber gives the correct cross-references for these passages, but he does not cash them out in terms of their dialectical strength. Here medieval commentators, with their eye to detail and to philosophical issues, seem to me to have it all over their modern counterparts. There is a curious "double vision" effect in books 2–3: the same issues are explored; the attractions of wealth, power, and so on take their drubbings in each book; the same sorts of considerations about happiness and the human good are mobilized. This will seem no more than pointless repetition on Boethius's part unless we see that the several arguments are of logically different strengths and are not meant to build on one another so much as to push the philosophical investigation to deeper and deeper levels. The commentary tradition makes this abundantly clear.

Conclusion

It should be apparent that if medieval philosophy is a series of glosses on Boethius, then those on the *Consolatio* deserve a place of signal honor, above all for their insight into the text as a work of philosophy, whatever its literary or other virtues might be. From the commentary tradition, we can learn to treat it with the respect it deserves, whether it is a matter of questioning the role of book 5 in the overall argument or how best to understand the initial literary introduction of the philosophical problems with which it deals. Closer attention to the commentary tradition would, I think, prove even more enlightening, questioning our contemporary assumptions and bringing us to a closer philosophical engagement with Boethius. And that, after all, is what we should be doing as philosophers and as historians of philosophy.

Appendix: Bibliography

Boethius's Commentators

The seven extensive medieval philosophical treatments of the *Consolation* readily available to us—there are many more in manuscript, and I have ignored excerpts and snippets—are, in rough chronological order, as follows:

- ANONYMOUS. From the ninth century, an anonymous commentary edited and published in Edmund T. Silk, *Saeculi noni auctoris in Boetii Consolationem philosophiae commentarius* (Rome: American Academy, 1935). Silk argues that the commentary was written by (or heavily indebted to) John Scottus Eriugena, but his case has not won general acceptance; "anonymous" seems best. Silk also includes in an appendix some extracts from the influential commentary of Remi d'Auxerre, dating from the beginning of the tenth century.
- WILLIAM OF CONCHES. From the twelfth century, the commentary by William of Conches (1080–ca. 1150), in *Guillelmi de Conchis Glosae super Boetium*, ed. Lodi Nauta, Corpus christianorum continuatio mediaevalis 158 (Turnholt: Brepols, 1999). There are many "Conchian" glosses in manuscript; no one yet has a view about their interrelations.
- TREVET. The Dominican friar Nicholas Trevet or Trivet (1265–1334) was educated at Oxford and Paris; he was a student of Thomas of York, and wrote his influential commentary around 1300. There is no critical edition, but Edmund Silk was working on an edition at the time of his death, and a typescript of his draft edition was deposited with his papers at Yale University. Trevet's commentary was the most influential at the end of the Middle Ages, being used by Jean de Meun and by Chaucer, among others. Silk notes "some eighty or ninety manuscripts" in his preface; Dean, "Nicholas Trevet, Historian," lists over a hundred.
- WILLIAM OF ARAGON. William of Aragon was a doctor and a professor of medicine, writing at roughly the same time as Trevet. Portions of this work have been edited by Charles Terbille in his unpublished doctoral dissertation,

"William of Aragon's Commentary on Boethius's *De consolatione philosophiae*" (unpublished PhD dissertation, University of Michigan, 1972), which is based on the Erfurt manuscript only. There are now five known manuscripts of Aragon's commentary: see Minnis, "Aspects," 353n15, and Atkinson and Babbi, *L'"Orphée" de Boèce*, 183–84. Crespo, "Il prologo alla traduzione," has established that Jean de Meun translated William's prologue to his commentary to preface his own French translation; Jean's death in 1305 provides a *terminus ante quem* for William's composition of his commentary.

- Pierre d'Ailly. There is a late fourteenth-century pair of questions about the *Consolatio* by the young Pierre d'Ailly (1350–1420/21). The first question has been edited in Chappuis, *Le traité*; the second is described in Chappuis, "Le traité" but has not yet been edited.
- Pseudo-Aquinas. A commentary attributed to Thomas Aquinas is found in Anton Koburger's 1473 Nürnberg edition of Boethius (the *editio princeps*); no earlier manuscript of the commentary has yet been discovered, leading some to think that it dates from the middle of the fifteenth century. This commentary was printed along with Aquinas's works for several centuries. When Busa put together his concordance to Aquinas, he attributed the commentary to William Wheatley (or Whetely) in his marked-up "edition" of the genuine and spurious works of Aquinas: R. Busa (ed.), *S. Thomae Aquinatis opera omnia*, 7:121c–172c (Stuttgart: Frommann-Holzboog, 1980). This attribution is a mistake. There is a commentary on Boethius by Wheatley that does have the same incipit as the Pseudo-Aquinas, but Wheatley's commentary was written in the first decades of the fourteenth century and is a distinct work: see Minnis, "Aspects," 354n23.
- Denys the Carthusian. Denys the Carthusian (1402–71) wrote a commentary shortly before his death: *Ennarationes seu commentaria in V libros B. Seuerini Boetii de consolatione philosophiae.* It comprises the entirety of his *Opera omnia* 26 (Tournai: Typis Cathusiae S. M. de Pratis, 1906).

Sketchy interlineal glosses are also given by Notker Labeo (a monk of St. Gall):

- *Notker der Deutsche: Boethius, "De consolatione Philosophiae" Buch IV/V.* Edited by Petrus W. Tax. Die Werke Notkers des Deutschen, n.s., 3 (Tübingen: Niemeyer, 1990).

There is a critical edition of a medieval French translation and commentary in Bolton-Hall:

- "*Del Confortement de Philosofie*: A Critical Edition of the Medieval French Prose Translation and Commentary of the *De consolatione philosophiae* of Boethius Contained in MS 2642 of the National Library of Austria in Vienna."

Edited by Margaret Bolton-Hall. Special issue, *Carmina Philosophiae* 5 and 6 (1996–97).

Primary Sources

Quaestiones communes super Timaeo Platonis et Boethium De consolatione, in *Le "Guide de l'étudiant" d'un maître anonyme de la faculté des arts de Paris au XIIIe siècle.* Edited by Claude Lafleur with Joanne Carrier, 25–324. Québec: Faculté de philosophie, Université de Laval, 1992.

William of Conches. *Guillelmi de Conchis Glosae super Boetium.* Edited by Lodi Nauta. Corpus christianorum continuatio mediaevalis 158. Brepols: Turnhout, 1999.

Valla, Lorenzo. *Elegantiae linguae.* In *Opera omnia*, ed. Eugenio Garin, 1:1–235. 2 vols. Turin: Bottega d'Erasmo 1962.

Secondary Sources

Alexander, J. J. G., and Gibson, M. T., eds. *Medieval Learning and Literature.* Oxford: Oxford University Press, 1976.

Atkinson, J. Keith, and Anna Maria Babbi, eds. *L'Orphée de Boèce au Moyen Âge.* Verona: Edizioni Fiorini, 2000.

Beaumont, Jacqueline. "The Latin Tradition of the *De Consolatione Philosophiae.*" In *Boethius: His Life, Thought, and Influence*, ed. Margaret Gibson, 278–305. Oxford: Blackwell, 1981.

Black, Robert. "Boethius at School in Medieval and Renaissance Italy: Manuscript Glosses to the *Consolation of Philosophy.*" In *Talking to the Text: Marginalia from Papyri to Print*, ed. Vincenzo Fera, Giacomo Ferraù, and Silvia Rizzo, 203–68. Messina: Centro interdisciplinare di studi umanistici, 2002.

Black, Robert, and Gabriella Pomaro. *La "Consolazione della filosofia" nel Medioevo e nel Rinascimento italiano: Libri di scuola e glosse nei manoscritti fiorentini.* Florence: SISMEL, 2000.

Chappuis, Marguerite. *Le traité de Pierre d'Ailly sur la consolation de Boèce, Qu. 1.* Bochumer Studien zur Philosophie 20. Amsterdam: Grüner, 1993.

———. "Le traité de Pierre d'Ailly sur la Consolation de Boèce, question 2: Étude préliminaire." In Hoenen and Nauta, *Boethius in the Middle Ages*, 69–86.

Courcelle, Pierre. *La Consolation de Philosophie dans la tradition littéraire: antécédents et postérité de Boèce.* Paris: Études augustiniennes, 1967.

Crespo, R. "Il prologo alla traduzione della *Consolatio philosophiae* di Jean de Meun e il commento di Guglielmo d'Aragona." In *Romanitas et Christianitas*, ed. W. den Boer, 55–70. Amsterdam: North-Holland, 1973.

Dean, Ruth. "Nicholas Trevet, Historian." In Alexander and Gibson, *Medieval Learning*, 328–52.

Denifle, Heinrich, and A. Chatelain. *Chartularium Universitatis Parisiensis*, vol. 2. Paris, 1891.

Galonnier, Alain, ed. *Boèce, ou la chaîne des savoirs*. Philosophes médiévaux 44. Louvain-Paris: Peeters, 2003.

Gibson, Margaret, ed. *Boethius: His Life, Thought, and Influence*. Oxford: Blackwell, 1981.

Grafton, Anthony. "Epilogue: Boethius in the Renaissance." In Gibson, *Boethius*, 410–15.

Gruber, Joachim. *Kommentar zu Boethius "De Consolatione Philosophiae."* Berlin: Gruyter, 1978.

Hoenen, Maarten J. M. F. "The Transition of Academic Knowledge: Scholasticism in the Ghent Boethius (1485) and Other Commentaries on the *Consolatio*." In Hoenen and Nauta, *Boethius in the Middle Ages*, 167–214.

Hoenen, Maarten J. M. F., and Stephen Gersh, eds. *The Platonic Tradition in the Middle Ages: A Doxographical Approach*. Berlin: Gruyter, 2002.

Hoenen, Maarten J. M. F., and Lodi Nauta, eds. *Boethius in the Middle Ages: Latin and Vernacular Traditions of the "Consolatio Philosophiae."* Leiden: Brill, 1997.

Jeauneau, Edouard. "La place de la *Consolation de Philosophie* de Boèce dans les 'Manuels de l'Étudiant' en la première moitié du trezième siècle." In *L'enseignement de la philosophie au XIIIe siècle*, ed. Claude Lafleur, 181–201. Studia Artistarum 5. Turnhout: Brepols, 1997.

Kaylor, Noel Harold, Jr. *The Medieval Consolation of Philosophy: An Annotated Bibliography*. New York: Garland, 1992.

Kaylor, Noel Harold, Jr., and Philip Edward Phillips, eds. *A Companion to Boethius in the Middle Ages*. Brill's Companions to the Christian Tradition 30. Leiden: Brill, 2012.

Kneepkens, C. H. *L'enseignement de la philosophie au XIIIe siècle*. With Joanne Carrier. Studia Artistarum 5 Brepols: Turnhout, 1997.

———. "The Reception of Boethius's *De consolatione* in the Later Middle Ages: The Wolfenbüttel *Quaestiones* and Buridan's *Quaestiones* on the Ethics." In Galonnier, *Boèce*, 713–39.

Lewry, Osmond. "Rhetoric at Paris and Oxford in the Mid-Thirteenth Century." *Rhetorica* 1 (1983): 45–63.

Macken, Raymond. *Denys the Carthusian: Commentator on Boethius's "De consolatione philosophiae."* Analecta Cartusiana 118. Salzburg: Institut für Anglistik und Amerikanistik, Universität Salzburg, 1984.

Minnis, Alastair. "Aspects of the Medieval French and English Traditions of the *De Consolatione Philosophiae*." In Gibson, *Boethius*, 312–61.

———, ed. *Chaucer's 'Boèce' and the Medieval Tradition of Boethius*. Chaucer Studies 18. Cambridge: Brewer, 1993.

Nauta, Lodi. "The Scholastic Context of the Boethius Commentary by Nicholas Trevet." In Hoenen and Nauta, *Boethius in the Middle Ages*, 41–67.

Nauta, Lodi. "Some Aspects of Boethius's *Consolatio philosophiae* in the Renaissance." In Galonnier, *Boèce*, 767–78.

Pattin, Adriaan. "Reinerus van St.-Truiden, rector van de Latijnse school te Mechelen (circa 1370) en commentato van Boëthius' *De Consolatione Philosophiae.*" *Tijdschrift voor Filosofie* 44 (1982): 298–319.

Palmer, Nigel F. "Latin and Vernacular in the Northern European Tradition of the *De Consolatione Philosophiae.*" In Gibson, *Boethius*, 362–409.

Patch, Howard. *The Tradition of Boethius*. Oxford: Oxford University Press, 1935.

Silk, Edmund. *Saeculi noni auctoris in Boetii Consolationem philosophiae commentaries*. Rome: American Academy in Rome, 1935.

Troncarelli, Fabio. *Cogitatio mentis: l'eredità di Boezio nell' Alto Medioevo*. Napoli: Auria, 2005.

———. *Tradizioni perdute: la "Consolatio philosophiae" nell'Alto Medioevo*. Firenze: Antenore, 1981.

Whitehead, Alfred North. *Process and Reality*. Ed. David Ray Griffin and Donald W. Sherburne, corrected ed. New York: Macmillan/The Free Press, 1974.

NOTES

*All translations are my own.

[1] Whitehead, *Process and Reality*, 39.

[2] In addition to the classic studies of Patch, *Tradition*, and Courcelle, *La Consolation de Philosophie*, see Beaumont, "Latin Tradition"; Palmer, "Latin and Vernacular"; Troncarelli, *Tradizioni perdute*; the several studies included in Hoenen and Nauta, *Boethius in the Middle Ages*; and Troncarelli, *Cogitatio mentis*. Many individual studies are also listed in Kaylor, *Medieval Consolation of Philosophy*, and several new studies are included in Kaylor and Phillips, *A Companion to Boethius.*

[3] In addition to the references in the preceding note, see also Alexander and Gibson, *Medieval Learning*; Minnis, "Aspects"; Atkinson and Babbi, *L'"Orphée" de Boèce.*

[4] See Crespo, "Il prologo alla traduzione."

[5] See Hoenen, "Transition of Academic Knowledge." This was perhaps the lengthiest commentary on the *Consolatio* in any language.

[6] See "*Del Confortement de Philosofie*," ed. Bolton-Hall.

[7] See Black and Pomaro, *La Consolazione della filosofia*, and Black, "Boethius at School," in for the use of the *Consolatio* as a teaching text in medieval Italy, for instance.

[8] See *Quaestiones*, ed. Lafleur, 71; Jeauneau, "La place de la *Consolation de Philosophie.*" Lewry, "Rhetoric at Paris and Oxford," identifies the *Consolatio* as one of the "philosophical books" mentioned by Robert de Courçon in his letter to the University of Paris in 1215: see Kneepkens, "Reception."

[9] Denifle and Chatelain, *Chartularium Universitatis Parisiensis*, 678–79: "Item quae audiuistis Boethium de Consolatione: Dispensatur."

[10] Some of the unclarity here stems from the earlier unclarity about the position of the *Consolatio* in medieval education. We need to clarify the latter to understand the circumstances in which someone would compose a commentary on the *Consolatio*. Details about editions of commentaries used here are given in the bibliography.

[11] See Dean, "Nicholas Trevet, Historian."

[12] Kneepkens, "Reception," describes some anonymous *quaestiones*. For d'Ailly, see Chappuis, *Le traité*, and Chappuis "Le traité."

[13] Lorenzo Valla particularly objects to Boethius's Latinity in his *Elegantiae linguae latinae* (*Opera omnia*, 215–16). But there were positive evaluations of Boethius in the Renaissance as well: see Grafton, "Epilogue," and Nauta, "Some Aspects."

[14] See Patch, *Tradition*, and Courcelle, *La Consolation de Philosophie*. In Courcelle, see especially Table 2, "Table des manuscrits des divers commentaires" (403–418) and the corresponding "Cinquième partie: Controverses d'écoles autour de la 'Consolation'" (241–332).

[15] See Nauta, "Scholastic Context."

[16] More exactly, we can interrogate the parts of the tradition (readily) available to us. I have listed in the bibliography the seven works that are the basis of the study here. Until more commentaries have been edited and studied, all results are only provisional. Since the commentaries are not always easy to obtain, I have provided the Latin texts cited *in extenso*.

[17] Much as in the case of another philosophical work that is also a literary masterpiece; namely, Augustine's *Confessiones*.

[18] "Agit ergo de tali materia tali modo: ostendendo temporalia esse transitoria nec in eis esse perfectum bonum, et ita non esse laetandum de praesentia eorum nec dolendum de eorum absentia; deinde ostendendo quid sit summum bonum et in quo situm et qualiter ad ipsum perueniatur. Postea ostendit bonos esse semper potentes, malos impotentes; bonis numquam deesse praemia nec malis supplicia. Deinde cur boni quidam in hac uita floreant, quidam deprimantur; similiter cur quidam mali floreant, quidam deprimantur. Deinde quid sit diuina prouidentia, quid fatum, quid casus, quid liberum arbitrium. Deinde ponendo argumenta quibus uidetur liberum arbitrium cum diuina prouidentia esse non posse, et falsam solutionem quorumdam improbando, deinde suam solutionem rationibus approbando."

[19] The "false resolution" is no doubt the one Boethius sketches in *Consolatio* 5p3.16–22.

[20] "Quinto uidendum est de generali summa huius totius libri. Ubi sciendum quod Boethius in hoc libro ostendit bona temporalia esse transitoria, et non consistere totaliter in eis totalem ueram felicitatem: et per consequens non est dolendum de eorum absentia, nec gaudendum de eorum praesentia: et neminem debere extolli in prosperis, nec deprimi in aduersis. Ostenditur etiam in praesenti libro quid sit summum bonum, ubi sit situm, et quomodo ad ipsum perueniatur. Etiam ostenditur quod boni semper sunt potentes et mali semper sunt impotentes, et quod bonis numquam desunt sua praemia, malis nunquam sua supplicia. Post haec ostenditur quid sit diuina prouidentia, quid casus, quid fatum, quid liberum arbitrium. Et ponit Boethius rationes quibus probat liberum arbitrium non posse stare cum prouidentia diuina. Et ponit quorundam falsam solutionem et eam improbat; postea ostendit ueram solutionem quam rationibus confirmat."

[21] Still, Pseudo-Aquinas may have done violence to Boethius's arguments, since the claims about desert defended in book 4 (and in [4]) seem to depend on establishing [2], and perhaps [3] as well.

[22] Denys the Carthusian is closer to modern practice in offering an overview of the *Consolation* that summarizes it book-by-book, even at the cost of doing some violence to the logical structure of Boethius's arguments. He offers a succinct statement of his interpretation in his comments on the beginning of 4p1 (436A).

[23] "At huic aliud maius adiungitur: nam imperante florenteque nequitia uirtus non

solum praemiis caret, uerum etiam sceleratorum pedibus subiecta calcatur et in locum facinorum supplicia luit. Quae fieri in regno scientis omnia, potentis omnia, sed bona tantummodo uolentis dei, nemo satis potest nec admirari nec conqueri." This is the general form of a complaint voiced by the Prisoner in *Consolatio* 1p4.113–15 (alluding to 1p4.95–97).

[24] "Tum illa: Festino, inquit, debitum promissionis absoluere uiamque tibi qua patriam reueharis aperire. Haec autem etsi perutilia cognitu tamen a propositi nostri tramite paulisper auersa sunt, uerendumque est ne deuiis fatigatus ad emetiendum rectum iter sufficere non possis."

[25] See 4p1.30–36 for Lady Philosophy's stated intent to show the Prisoner the way home and provide him with wings, which the Prisoner explicitly calls a "promise" in 4p2.1—a reference noted by Trevet ad loc. (668–69).

[26] See Chappuis, *Le traité* and "Le traité" respectively: "Utrum aliquis philosophus per inquisitionem philosophicam in naturali lumini ad ueram humanae beatitudinis notitiam ualeat peruenire" (14*), and "Utrum cum aeterna et ummutabili Dei praescientia omnium futurorum stet aliquid simpliciter contingenter euenire" (71). Chappuis, *Le traité*, 21, suggests that d'Ailly was led to this division of the text by Pseudo-Aquinas. Perhaps, but there is support in the commentary tradition, as the above sections have demonstrated.

[27] "Sed quia de istis tractare uidetur remotum a consolatione de qua intendit in hoc opere, praemittit quemdam breuem transitum quo ostendit unde tractat." William seems of two minds about the status of book 5. When Lady Philosophy claims that answering the Prisoner's questions would divert them "a bit" (*paulisper*) from reaching their goal, William explains this as a hint that answering the question isn't completely irrelevant or independent (289.29–31): "Sed ne aliquis putaret quod omnino esset aduersa et ita esset superfluum de istis in hoc loco tractare, ait: PAULISPER id est aliquantulum sed non omnino."

[28] Hence the translation of *unde* as "how he comes" in the preceding passage.

[29] "Ergo, inquit, proposui te in pristinum contemplationis statum reducendum quod utique iam prope est sed ea quae tu interrogas impediunt te, quoniam dum in his me remoraris non potes adire ea quibus a me informandus es."

[30] Silk's anonymous ninth-century commentator recognizes an ambiguity in Remi's formulation: "Et ostendit quod sit illud promissum, VIAM scilicet ei ostendere id est rationem QUA reuertatur ad PATRIAM propriam, id est ad pristinum intelligentiae suae statum, uel ad paradisum." The Prisoner is either rendered capable of contemplating God in this life, or is taken to Heaven to look upon God in the Beatific Vision.

[31] Or book 6 and book 7, and so on: the point is that there is additional material to the *Consolatio*. For the sake of simplicity, I will speak as though there were only a single book to be added.

[32] "Et illa: FESTINO tibi perficere quod promisi. Hoc ideo dixit quia finem libri uoluerat facere . . . [.] Dixit quoque Philosophia: Quamuis haec sint utilia cognitione, tamen remota sunt a PROPOSITO NOSTRO, id est ab intentione. Propositum quippe eius fuit in his quae dixit ITE NUNC FORTES; quibus uerbis hortata fuerat eum reuerti ad caelestem patriam. Ad hoc contrarium erat disputare de his questionibus quae iam amiserat." Here and throughout the essay, the text in uppercase indicates a direct citation from the text being commented upon.

[33] "Superiorem enim rationem adhuc prolongare parabat, scilicet ut mortales homines per uirtutum culmina immortalitatem consequi studerent; seriem disputationis suae VERTEBAT, ut AD ALIA QUAEDAM, id est ad bonum exercitium homines inuitarent.

[34] Pseudo-Aquinas (165, col. 3): "Notandum, quod dicit exhortationem philosophiae fuisse rectam, quia philosophia hortatur ad uirtutes et ad contemptum fortuitorum."

[35] "Via autem, per quam homo peruenit ad ipsam in re consequendam, sunt uirtutes animi, de quibus intendebat Boethius agere, non quidem in hoc libro sed in ultimis libris musicae, agendo de musica humana, ut patet ex hiis quae dicit in principio eiusdem libri musicae captulo secundo; sed non compleuit intentionem, scilicet a rege Theodorico morte praeuentus."

[36] Pseudo-Aquinas adopts Trevet's solution while correcting his grammar (165, col. 3): "Illa autem per quae homo peruenit ad ipsam, sunt uirtutes, de quibus Boethius intendebat agere non in hoc libro, sed in ultimis libris musicae suae, agendo de musica humana: intentionem autem suam non compleuit, quia a rege Theodorico morte praeuentus fuit."

[37] "Denique in primo libro Philosophia causas doloris Boethii diligenter scrutata est; in secundo autem adhibuit ei ut aegro faciliora remedia; in tertio autem efficaciora et magis sublimia, disputando et declarando in quibus beatitudo uideatur multis consistere, cum ita non sit, et item in quo uere sit: immo et quid sit, ac qualiter pertingatur ad ipsam. Nunc in hoc quarto libro remouet a mente Boethii quidquid in ea adhuc residet de sua pristina indispositione, inquietudine, dubietate et inuolutione, ostendendo totum uniuersum, praesertim genus humanum, a creatore suo Deo omnipotente, iusto, sancto ac supersapientissimo ordinate et optime gubernari, nec quidquam finaliter inordinatum relinqui, nec tamen a prouidentia Dei necessitatem actibus humanis inferri. Et haec est materia huius libri quarti, et etiam quinti sequentis: in quibus Boethius in persona hominis nondum satis illuminati, dubia sua, admirationes et inuolutiones proponit, ad quas Philosophia sapienter respondet, immo ipse idem Boethius in persona hominis sapientis ac uirtuousi." Denys offers a similar account in commenting on 5p1, in his art. 1 (562A).

[38] There seems to be an echo of Denys's account of books 1–3 in Pseudo-Aquinas's commentary on the beginning of 3p1 (143, col. 1): "Postquam Philosophia in primo libro scrutata est causas doloris Boethii, et in secundo libro adhibuit sibi remedia facilia, in praesenti libro et in sequentibus Philosophia adhibet Boethio remedia grauiora."

[39] See, for instance, Denys on 5p1.7–9, art. 1 (563A–B): "TAMEN A PROPOSITI NOSTRI TRAMITE PAULISPER AVERSA SUNT, id est aliena sunt a processu et uia nostri principalis intenti, quod fuit ea describere quae consolatoria sunt afflictis; VERENDUMQUE EST, id est formidandum, NE DEVIIS FATIGATUS, id est ne tu lassatus quaestionibus et responsionibus impertinentibus huic proposito et abducentibus a principali intento, AD EMETIENDUM RECTUM ITER SUFFICERE NON POSSIS, id est non ualeas satis fortis consistere ad pertranseundum RECTUM ITER, id est inuestigationem et apprehensionem perinentium ad principale propositum."

[40] "Postquam Philosophia in primo libro sufficienter conditionem et causam morbi Boethii inquisiuit, hic ad curationem procedit. Et circa hoc duo fecit: primo enim adhibet quaedam remedia lenia quae dolorem mitigent et ad remedia ualidiora recipienda praeparent; secundo apponit ualidiora remedia libro tertio ibi IAM CANTUM. Istum enim modum procedendi commendauit libro primo prosa quinta et sexta in fine. Et uocat 'leniora remedia' rationes sumptas <iuxta> communem usum hominum ad remouendum dolorem; 'ualidiora remedia' uocat rationes contra communem opinionem hominum, ostendentes quid sit perfectum bonum et in quo situm et qualiter ad ipsum perueniendum." Trevet offers similar remarks at the start of book 3 (297–98), and Pseudo-Aquinas copies Trevet (143, col. 1): "Postquam Philosophia in primo libro scrutata est causas doloris Boethii, et in

secundo libro adhibuit sibi remedia facilia, in praesenti libro et in sequentibus Philosophia adhibet Boethio remedia grauiora. Sunt autem remedia grauiora rationes contra communem opinionem hominum, probantes quod in bonis exterioribus non consistit uera felicitas ostendendo in quo sit felicitas uera, et quomodo ad ipsam perueniatur."

[41] "Ostendit Philosophia qualiter consoletur Boethium cognita causa doloris illius, scilicet ponendo prius leuiora medicamina, deinde grauiora. Et sunt leuiora medicamina rhetoricae rationes iuxta usum hominum ad remouendum dolorem. Grauiora medicamenta sunt rationes contra opinionum hominum ad ostendendum quid sit perfectum bonum et in quo sit situm et qualiter ad id perueniatur."

[42] "Age enim, si iam caduca et momentaria fortunae dona non essent, quid in eis est quod aut uestrum umquam fieri queat aut non perspectum consideratumque uilescat?"

[43] Boethius revises this list in book 3 by distinguishing honours and power, and by adding (physical) pleasures, to get his final catalogue of five candidates for what makes life worth living. Here, Boethius argues in each case that the supposed "good" in question is not intrinsically worthwhile, apart from its ephemeral and transitory nature.

[44] "Videns Philosophia Boethium aliquantulum esse promotum, inquit: Hactenus sum usa debilioribus medicaminibus, sed nunc utar ualidioribus. Probaui superius quod terrena non sunt appentenda, quia sunt caduca. Et adhuc idem probo: Si cum non essent caduca, non essent appetenda, tunc cum caduca sint multo minus sunt appetenda; sed, si etiam caduca non essent, non essent appetenda."

[45] "Postquam Philosophia posuit superius remedia minus mouentia ad ostendendum quod bona Fortunae sunt contemnenda nec nimis de eorum amissione dolendum, hic ponit ad idem remedia magis mouentia, cuiusmodi sint rationes sumptae ex conditionibus particularium bonorum Fortunae."

THE DUTCH, ITALIAN, POLISH, GREEK, HEBREW, AND KOREAN TRADITIONS

The Dutch Translations of Boethius's *De consolatione philosophiae*

Jefferey H. Taylor

THE DUTCH TRADITION of translating and producing commentaries on Boethius's *De consolatione philosophiae* [hereafter *Consolatio*] is rich and varied. It includes as translators some of the most important literary figures in Dutch letters, including Jacob of Maerlant, the father of Dutch Literature; D. V. Coornhert, the founder of Dutch Renaissance scholarship; and the famous poet, playwright, and novelist Willem Bilderdijk, founder of Dutch Romanticism. The tradition also includes what is perhaps the largest commentary on the *Consolatio* in any vernacular, prepared either during the medieval period or thereafter: the translation and commentary known as the Ghent Boethius. Beginning with Jacob of Maerlant's use of Boethian lines in his adaptation of Vincent of Beauvais's *Speculum Historiale*, the tradition stretches from the thirteenth century to our day. Despite the range and importance of the Dutch *Consolatio* tradition, it has received little critical attention in English and insufficient attention even among scholars in The Netherlands and Belgium. The relative obscurity of the Ghent Boethius alone demonstrates the unfortunate neglect of this tradition, since this obscurity arguably is one of the largest gaps in the study of medieval *Consolatio* traditions.

The only comprehensive survey of the Dutch *Consolatio* tradition is the dissertation of Jacobus Martinus Hoek, written for his doctorate in literature and philosophy at the University of Amsterdam in the midst of the Second World War, completed in February 1943.[1] The title of Hoek's dissertation is *De Middelnederlandse vertalingen van Boethius' "De Consolatione Philosophiae"; met een overzicht van de andere Nederlandse en niet-Nederlandse vertalingen,* which may be translated as *The Middle Dutch Translations of Boethius' "De consolatione philosophiae"; with an Overview of the Other Dutch and Non-Dutch Translations.* It does not cover either Maerlant's uses of Boethius or, of course, the two translations that appeared after its publication. It is an impressive volume that, despite any failings, represents the most thorough study of the *Consolatio* tradition in Dutch. Another impressive project is a modern critical edition of the Ghent Boethius undertaken by the University of Nijmegen. This project is far from complete, and at present it seems that it will not reach completion any time soon. Nonetheless the one published volume, the critical edition of book 2 by Mariken Goris, is stunning in its execution and reveals the incredible potential of the Ghent Boethius to enrich our understanding not only of the medieval *Consolatio* tradition in Dutch but also of the medieval translation and commentary tradition in general.[2] Information on the translation tradition is available in the introductory material of some of the translations, particularly the historic overview of the tradition in J. W. Schotman's 1924 translation and the introductory essays in R. F. M. Brouwer's 1990 translation.[3] An impressive and valuable online resource for research in any area of Dutch literature is the *Digitale Bibliotheek voor de Nederlandse Letteren* (or *DBNL*).[4]

Some information on Dutch translations of the *Consolatio* is available in English. The well-known study edited by Margaret Gibson, *Boethius: His Life, Thought and Influence*, has one page on the Dutch tradition by Anthony Grafton, which briefly mentions the Vilt, Ghent, and Coornhert translations.[5] More impressive is a volume edited by Maarten J. F. M. Hoenen and Lodi Nauta, entitled *Boethius in the Middle Ages: Latin and Vernacular Traditions of the "Consolatio Philosophiae,"* published by Brill in 1997.[6] The second part of this volume contains four essays in English on the Middle Dutch tradition, including an overview by Mariken Goris and Wilma Wissink, and an analysis by Hoenen of the commentary in the Ghent Boethius. A volume published in 1999 by Brill, *Northern Humanism in European Context, 1469–1625*, contains an article in English by Goris and Lauta which contrasts the late medieval reading of the *Consolatio* implied by the Ghent Boethius with the humanist reading of the Murmellius/Agricola commentary.[7] Another interesting analysis in English of the Ghent Boethius, also by Goris, appeared in 2001 in *The Bookshop of the World; The Role of the Low Countries in the Book-Trade, 1473–1941*.[8] Goris's edition of book 2 of the Ghent Boethius includes a summary in English.[9] Information in English on translations other than Ghent is more sparse. Of note are Gerrit Voogt's English translation of Henk Bonger's biography of D. V. Coornhert and Theo Hermans's analysis of the De Buck translation.[10] Other sources in English and Dutch are referenced throughout this study.

The Translations

Jacob of Maerlant (Thirteenth Century)

Jacob of Maerlant (ca. 1230–ca. 1299) was born in the Bruges area. Often considered the Father of Dutch literature, he produced many literary works and translations, most of which were commissioned by the nobility of Holland. The *Spiegel Historiael*, a translation/adaptation in verse of Vincent de Beauvais's *Speculum Historiale*, was Maerlant's last work, commissioned by Floris V, the count of Holland, in 1283. Maerlant completed only the first and third parts and a small portion of the beginning of the fourth part of Vincent's work. P. G. Witsen Geysbeek suggests that Maerlant stopped working on the *Spiegel Historiael* in 1296, the year Floris was murdered.[11] Maerlant's verse narrative is much reduced from Vincent de Beauvais's lengthy compilation, so that Vincent's six chapters, which include fragments from Boethius, are reduced to two chapters, totaling 166 lines.[12] These fragments from Boethius are the first translation of anything from the *Consolatio* into Middle Dutch and the only translation for another 170 years; as such, it is exceptional in the Dutch *Consolatio* translation tradition that otherwise does not begin until the closing decades of the medieval period.

The edition of the *Spiegel Historiael* by M. de Vries and E. Verwijs is available online through the *DBNL*.[13] Chapter 11 of part 3, book 6 of the *Spiegel Historiael* contains twenty-six verse lines about Boethius's life followed by sixty-three verse lines of the aphoristic selections from the *Consolatio*, Vincent's *flosculi*, which Maerlant translates as *bloemen*. The first two fragments are actually from *De syllogismo hypothetico*, which Vincent notes, though Maerlant does not.[14] Chapter 11 continues with fifty-six more lines of Boethian "flowers" and concludes with twenty verse lines, stating that these selections are from Boethius's book called *Die troost van philosophien* and that he was imprisoned by King Diederic (Theodoric) and died in the year 521. Maerlant translates in total only twenty-four fragments from the *Consolatio*: five from book 1, fifteen from book 2, three from book 3, and one from book 5, all rendered into verse and reduced to the aphoristic conclusions of Boethius's dialogues.[15]

Jacob Vilt (1466)

Jacob Vilt was a goldsmith of Bruges, living during the fifteenth century. Little else is known of him. Between 1462 and1466, Vilt produced the first complete *Consolatio* in Middle Dutch, a translation from a Pseudo-de

Meun.[16] It exists in one manuscript: Utrecht, Universiteitsbibliotheek, Cod. 1335, made by A. Drubbel in 1470. The unique manuscript contains 204 folia, 285 × 210 mm, with miniatures before books 1, 3, and 5. It is arranged in one column with wide margins that sometimes are used for commentary. The corresponding prose and meters in the *Consolatio* are indicated in the left margin; extensive Latin lemmata are in the right column.[17] There is an entry for this manuscript in Koert van der Horst's Utrecht catalog, with monochrome reproductions of five pages.[18] A description may also be found on the Koninklijke Bibliotheek's online catalog "Medieval Manuscripts in Dutch Collections," through which one may also access color scans of seven pages.[19] There is no evidence that this translation was widely circulated, and there has never been an edition made from this manuscript. Hoek supplies complete transcriptions of 1m1, 1p1, 1m7, 3m3, and scattered portions of other sections.[20] Goris and Wissink include portions of 2p5 and a marginal gloss from 1m1.[21]

Vilt translated into the Middle Dutch of fifteenth-century Bruges. By this period, the West Flemish dialect of Bruges was no longer the dominant dialect of Middle Dutch. Though Vilt claims to have consulted a Latin text along with the French, internal evidence indicates that he translated directly from the Pseudo-de Meun text. Vilt frequently uses double (and sometimes triple) renderings of words into Middle Dutch, and he occasionally adds explanations and ornamental language, resulting in an expansive translation, much longer than his French source. Vilt's meters are much more various in their rhyme schemes than those in his French source.[22]

In his introduction, Vilt says he translated the *Consolatio* for those who cannot read Latin or French, so that anyone who is depressed can find consolation, though he also excuses his translation by claiming that his poor knowledge of Latin and philosophy means that he cannot offer a good translation.[23] Hoek generally agrees with Vilt's own assessment.[24] However, despite Hoek's disparaging of this work by a mere goldsmith, Goris and Wissink consider it a good paraphrase of a paraphrase, a "faithful rendering of the Old French," and they will not "call Vilt a bad translator or unaccomplished poet, preferring to see his own introduction in the prologue as a sign of modesty."[25]

The Ghent Boethius (1485)

The identity of the translator and commentator of the Ghent Boethius is unknown, though Goris believes that the translator and commentator are the same.[26] Textual evidence indicates that the translator probably was from Ghent and likely connected with the St. Verelde Chapter, perhaps as a canon.[27] Hoek dates the original text between 1444 and 1477.[28] More recent scholarship argues for a date of either 1455 or 1456.[29] If this dating is valid, then the Ghent Boethius actually predates Vilt's translation and is therefore the first complete translation into Dutch. The translation is into the Middle Dutch of fifteenth-century Ghent, which is in the West Flemish dialect region. The translation is a careful and close rendering of the Latin, with the exception that classical allusions usually are replaced with common words.[30] The prose sections are so close to the Latin that the syntax and vocabulary are very Latinate; the meters are all rendered in rhyming couplets. The translator notes that "he could not preserve the metrical variety of the Latin meters, but translated them using the same [number] of lines as the Latin original, with a minimum of seven and a maximum of ten syllables in a line," but what then is lost from the Latin meters generally is included in the commentary.[31] Goris notes the significance of this dual-language text as the first printed edition of the *Consolatio* in the Dutch-language geographic area and comments on the vernacular emphasis of this incunable arising from the use of Middle Dutch for the table of contents, prologue, and commentary.[32]

The Ghent Boethius was printed in Ghent by Arend de Keysere in 1485 with the title *Dat weerdich bouc boecius de consolatione philosophie*. The source of de Keysere's incunable presently is unknown. The incunable is massive, giving the Latin in pericopes, each followed by a Middle Dutch translation and a Middle Dutch commentary in smaller type, though whether this structure follows the manuscript or is of Arend de Keysere's production presently is unknown.[33] The commentary of the Ghent Boethius "is probably the most extensive commentary on the *Consolatio* ever made."[34] The commentary is based mainly on Renier of St. Truiden, but it is heavily adapted, drawing from a wide range of the Latin commentary tradition and including many references to classical works from Augustine, Origen, Ovid, Cicero, Seneca, the Bible, and so on.[35] In content and execution, this incunable is an impressive achievement. Art historians Jean Michel Massing and Alain Arnould declare: "The edition of Boethius' famous text from Arend de Keyser's presses in Ghent is the most spectacular to come on the book market in late fifteenth[-]century Europe and ranks among the most impressive incunables produced in the Low Countries."[36] An incunable of this quality and length inevitably prompts the question of the intended audience or market. Goris naturally wonders whether the intended audience of the translator/commentator is the same as the intended audience for the incunable—ownership data from the early sixteenth century indicates that there were spiritual and lay owners of copies of the text (with a small majority of lay owners), but there is no conclusive evidence from marginalia that anyone read the book cover-to-cover.[37] Goris and Nauta argue that this incunable, appearing at a time of overlap between late medieval and early humanist approaches to the *Consolatio*, has qualities that indicate "a late-medieval context for this fifteenth-century work rather than a humanist one."[38]

There are two manuscripts based on the incunable. A complete version in manuscript form completed in 1492 by Jan of Kreckenborch for Lodewijk of Bruges, the lord of Gruuthuse, is known as the Gruuthuse Boethius, an impressive book of 392 folia, 510 × 380 mm, with elaborate illuminations, miniatures and ornately decorated margins.[39] Though Hoek supposes that Kreckenborch and de Keysere followed a common earlier manuscript, Goris and Wissink argue effectively that Kreckenborch copied from the incunable.[40] There is also a manuscript of excerpts from the Ghent Boethius in the city library of Antwerp with an owner mark of S. Mechteld Rombouts, a "simple and small manuscript with excerpts from the Ghent Boethius," 225 folia, 145 × 107 mm, known as the Antwerp Boethius, and a devotional book made up "of fragments of Books I and II and a few from Book IV."[41]

In 1557, an edition of the Ghent Boethius without the Latin or commentary was produced by D. V. Coornhert, who adapted the language to the Northern Dutch dialect. It was published in Deventer by Symon Steinberghen. Perhaps the changes in this text are sufficient to consider it a translation in its own right since the differences are not only between dialects but also across a century of much change in the language. Much later Coornhert translated the *Consolatio* directly from Latin (see Coornhert entry below). In the preface to his later translation, Coornhert characterizes the language of the Ghent Boethius as "oude ende duystere vlaamsche tale" [old and dark Flemish language].[42] Hoek's side-by-side comparison of the Ghent Boethius and Coornhert's "Dutching" of it reveals texts that vary from each other considerably, despite the obvious connection between the two.[43]

Goris and Wissink claim that "at least fifty copies of the incunable are extant."[44] There never has been a complete modern critical edition made of the Ghent Boethius, which according to Goris and Wissink would "cover approximately 3000 pages."[45] In his dissertation, Hoek provides transcriptions of scattered passages and complete transcriptions of 1m1, 1p1, 1m2, 1m3, 1p6, 2m1, 2m3, 2m4, 2m5, 2m7, 3m1, 3m2, 3m9, and

5m1.[46] In 2000, Mariken Goris published a critical edition with extensive introduction and commentary of book 2 of the Ghent Boethius.[47] Wilma Wissink's much anticipated edition of book 1 is well overdue. Plans for the other three books "await funding."[48] A critical edition of 5p3 produced by Bregje van Dommelen and Dirk-Jan Dekker is published in Hoenen and Nauta, *Boethius in the Middle Ages*.[49] The Ghent Boethius is a monument of the medieval *Consolatio* tradition and the studies on it so far produced have made significant contributions to several fields of study, yet it is readily apparent that there has been insufficient work on this remarkable text.

D. V. Coornhert (1557 and 1585)

Dirck Volkertszoon Coornhert (1522–90), a playwright, philosopher, and translator, was one of the greatest Dutch Renaissance scholars and writers. His 1562 translation of the first twelve books of the *Odyssey* is considered the first major poetic work of the Dutch Renaissance. He also translated Cicero, Boccaccio, and Seneca. Coornhert actively supported religious tolerance during this time of great religious conflict, which led to his imprisonment and exile. His 1557 *Consolatio* edition, *Der vertroestringhe der Wyßheyt* (Deventer, 1557), is an adaptation of the Ghent Boethius, adjusting it to the Northern dialect (see entry above). However, in some respects, Coornhert's 1557 edition may be considered a new translation. Henk Bonger writes:

> [Bruno] Becker concluded that this was truly a translation, because Coornhert changed spelling and pronouns, replaced numerous Flemish, French and Latin words with northern Dutch ones, added synonyms and gave a new form to the poems.[50]

Coornhert, however, was displeased with this book because of the poor job of printing, which resulted in many errors and omissions, and in his later translation he disparages the 1557 edition and derides the printers who produced it. Hoek, however, through his careful analysis, concludes that, though the printer bore some blame, some of the errors were Coornhert's.[51]

Almost thirty years later, in 1585, Coornhert published a completely new translation of the *Consolatio* into Dutch, *Boethius vande Vertroosting der wijsheyd: uijt 't Latijn op nieus vertaalt*, translated directly from the Latin. Hoek declares that this is a reliable and sound translation, but on careful analysis he notes that, though Coornhert claims to have made this translation wholly new and directly from the Latin, there is evidence that he consulted his 1557 edition for this new translation.[52] Schotman describes Coornhert's 1585 translation favorably, characterizing the verses as set in majestic melodies and the prose as conscientiously conveyed in fine language.[53] Indeed, the meters from the first two books and the first two meters of the third book are accompanied by musical settings. Anthony Grafton claims that Coornhert only undertook this translation at the request of the Amsterdam rhetoric chamber in order to demonstrate that the Dutch language "was as ancient, regular, and capable of expressing high thoughts and deep emotions as Greek or Latin" and that Coornhert's preface demonstrates that his efforts constituted only "an exercise de style rather than anything more lofty."[54] Certainly, Dutch scholars at this time were intent on putting forth their language as capable of conveying high culture, a practice paralleled for many European vernaculars during the Renaissance. Yet, the personal context of this publication suggests less superficial motivations. In 1584 Coornhert lost his wife of forty-five years and, though just recently returned from exile, was threatened with imprisonment by leaders of the Reformed movement after the assassination of Prince William, who had protected him.[55] Indeed, the cavalier attitude expressed in the preface toward this carefully wrought work in the socially charged context of the day is more likely a typical literary device. Bonger perceives a more personal connection to this text for Coornhert and claims that he chose the *Consolatio* for this task because it was "one of his favorite books" and that he "was pleased that Plantin was willing to print the work."[56] W. P. Gerritsen's study of Coornhert's 1585 translation also makes a strong case for the seriousness of the work, stating that for Coornhert translating the *Consolatio* was a "labour of love, for he was fond of it and had long been in the habit of reading it through several times a year," and he "reverenced the work" and had a "high opinion of its moral value."[57] Indeed, Gerritsen sees Coornhert's 1585 translation as an important contribution to Dutch Renaissance letters and argues that the translated meters form a key text for appraising the development of Dutch "syllabo-tonic" verse.[58] Further, Brouwer notes the obvious influence of the *Consolatio* on Coornhert's *Zedekunst dat is Wellevenskunste*, published in 1586.[59] Moreover, in light of Coornhert's bitter dispute with Lipsius in the last years of his life, a dispute centered on Coornhert's rejection of any doctrine of strict predestination that might encumber a belief in free will, his bringing forth a new Dutch *Consolatio* at this time well may have been a riposte to the arguments favoring predestination in Lipsius's *De constantia* (1584), marking this new Boethius as a significant moment in the religious disputes of the sixteenth century. Indeed, the bitter conflict between Coornhert and Lipsius over human agency, Lipsius's overt use of Boethian dialogue to structure *De constantia*, and the Boethian flavor of Coornhert's *Zedekunst dat is Wellevenskunste* place Coornhert's 1585 translation in the midst of a significant dispute over the very ideas central to Boethius's text.[60] Surely Coornhert's widely disseminated translation of the *Consolatio* was much more than an *exercice de style*.

The original 1585 edition was published by Christoffel Plantyn in Leyden (eight volumes, 219 pages). It was reissued in 1616 by Pieter Jascobszoon in Amsterdam, and in 1630 in volume 1 of *Coornherts Werken*. In 1654, F. van Hoogstraten reworked and published Coornhert's translation with his own translation of the meters (see the van Hoogstraten entry below). In 1610 the meters from Coornhert's 1585 Boethius were published in *Recht Ghebruyck ende Misbruyck van tijdlicke Have: Door D.V. Coornhert . . . t' Amersteram*, by Dirck Pieterszoon.[61] An edition of Coornhert's 1585 translation was published in 1945 by A.A. Balkema, Amsterdam.[62]

Adrianus de Buck (1653)

Nobertijn Adrianus de Buck was a Canon and much-loved poet of Veurne in West Flanders (Belgium). In 1653 he issued his translation of the *Consolatio* under the title *Troost-Medecijne-vvynkel der zedighe Wysheyt*, published in Bruges by Lucas vanden Kerchove. The book contains "a dedication to a numbler of local dignitaries" and "a number of other liminary texts including the usual approbations and laudatory poems."[63] One unique feature of de Buck's translation is that many of the meters are translated twice, but in different modes. Hoek reports that this translation was much praised by Flemish scholars in the nineteenth century.[64] Despite its literary merit, it only saw one printing and does not seem to have had wide success. Hoek reports that, due to the war, he was unable to examine a copy of this book for his dissertation, though he had examined a copy in the National Library in Brussels before the war, so he relied on a description and analysis of the book published by Prudens van Duyse in 1853 that praises its bold, poetic style.[65]

The de Buck translation has received a fascinating treatment by Theo Hermans, professor of Dutch and comparative literature at University College London, in his article "Translation and Normativity."[66] Hermans also reprints the dedication from de Buck's volume in *Door eenen engen hals*.[67] Hermans analyzes de Buck's translation as an illustration of the cultural and political choices made by translators and in doing so offers interesting insights into the context and execution of this *Consolatio* translation. The title itself, *Troost-Medecijne-vvynkel der zedighe Wysheyt,* is unique. Hermans renders the title into English as "Comforting Medicine Shop of Moral Wisdom" and notes that this "expansive rendering stresses the aspect of healing and the practical usefulness of moral philosophy."[68] The title highlights one of the three interwoven purposes that Hermans sees in this translation: that of offering "consolation to his compatriots who have suffered at the hands of the French," de Buck's hometown of Veurne having been "overrun a few years earlier by the armies of Louix XIV." Yet Hermans also discerns two other important purposes of this translation: to claim "Boethius for the Counter-Reformation" and to show that southern (i.e., Flemish) culture can compete with the flourishing Protestant north.[69] In his preface, de Buck assumes Boethius is not being translated in the north because "the references to free will are unacceptable to Calvinist doctrine."[70] De Buck presents Boethius "emphatically [. . .] as a Catholic writer" and fashions his translation as "one small move [. . .] in support of the militant Counter-Reformation."[71] Hermans further notes:

> That is why his vocabulary here borrows directly from the terminological and discursive resources of Catholic theology and liturgy. In so doing de Buck also helps to consolidate the hegemony of Catholic discourse in the vernaculars of Counter-Reformation Europe.[72]

De Buck's third purpose, to vindicate the culture of the south, is also explicitly stated. Hermans notes that de Buck's dedication "leaves us in no doubt that he is green with envy at the miracle of Dutch culture in the Northern Netherlands" and that he is "acutely aware of living in what [. . .] was rapidly becoming a cultural backwater."[73] Hermans also sees this cultural sparring as a primary motivation for de Buck's unusual practice of rendering meters twice, arguing that "they serve as displays of virtuosity to underscore a claim to professional equality *vis-à-vis* the translators of the North." Hermans further notes that this practice of double-translating the meters functions to emphasize the social appropriation of Boethius through translation since it "clearly undermines the illusion that we are reading Boethius [. . .] thus drawing attention to the translator's presence as a discursive subject."[74]

De Buck's *Consolatio* translation is arguably one of the least influential treatments of the text in the Dutch language. Yet Hermans's analysis of de Buck's translation highlights the importance of studying all renderings in the translation traditions of the *Consolatio*, in Dutch or any language. Translations occur within specific social and cultural contexts, and the qualities of each translation reveal much about that context and the many uses that have been made of Boethius's powerful text throughout the centuries.

François van Hoogstraten (1654)

In 1654, François (or Frans) van Hoogstraten (1632–96) reworked and reissued Coornhert's 1585 translation. The prose passages are only slightly altered; however, the meters are substantially different and can be considered new translations. The book was published in Dordrecht by Nicolaes Geerlingh with the title *Boethius van de verstroostingh der philosophie. Eerst vertaelt deur D.V. Coornhert: Nu op Nieuws oversien en in sijn Gedichten verandert.* Reprints were produced by François van Hoogstraten in 1655 and 1680.

François van Hoogstraten was from a distinguished family of booksellers and was himself a bookseller in Dordrecht and Rotterdam. He composed poetry in Dutch and Latin and translated More's *Utopia* and Erasmus's *In Praise of Folly* among other works in Latin, French, and Spanish. His brother Samuel was a well-known painter, and his sons David and Jan also were known as scholars and humanists. Hermans, in developing his reading of de Buck's translation, notes François van Hoogstraten's Erasmian and Catholic sympathies as further evidence that in the seventeenth-century interest in Boethius in the Low Countries was limited to Catholic circles.[75] Hoek does not see van Hoogstraten's book as any improvement over Coornhert's.[76] Schotman seems unaware of either of these seventeenth-century translations, of de Buck and van Hoogstraten, noting only a long pause between the 1616 reprint of Coornhert's translation and Gargon's version of 1703.[77]

Mattheus Gargon (1703 and 1722)

In 1703, Mattheus Gargon published his translation of the *Consolatio* under the title *Vertroostinge der wijsgeerte*. Gargon was a preacher who translated the *Consolatio* to comfort his wife, who was suffering from terminal cancer.[78] His first edition sold very well, prompting a second edition, new and improved, in 1722, under a slightly different spelling of the title: *Vertroostinge der wysgeerte*. The 1703 edition was published in Amsterdam by Adriaan Braakman and in Gouda by Lucas Kloppenburg. The 1722 edition was published in Amsterdam by Hendrik Bosch and Salomon Schouten. A careful examination of the two editions reveals significant emendations in the new edition, though the major portion of the text is the same. The 1703 edition includes a verse dedication to "Hermanus van de Putte, Rentemeester der Heeren Staaten van Zeeland" and praise poems by Johannes Ulaeus, W. Keuchenius, M. Bode, and Johannes van Nieuwland. The first three are in Dutch, the last in Latin. It also contains five engravings, each accompanied by an explanatory verse, called a *klink-dicht* or "sound-poem," and an extensive index. Indeed, this volume, though nowhere near the level of quality attained in the 1485 incunable, is an impressive piece of material culture. The 1722 edition adds to these features a second dedication to van de Putte, this time in prose, a poem of praise to Gargon from his daughter Agneta, a sixth plate with accompanying *klink-dicht*, and a new foreword to the reader.[79]

Gargon claims that he had heard rumors of three earlier translations but had never seen them, and so Hoek, believing Gargon, as a minister, to be truthful, concludes that his translation is independent of all earlier ones.[80] Hoek considers Gargon's two translations to be of good quality, both in style and accuracy.[81] An article appearing in 1940 in the journal *Hermeneus* also praises Gargon's translation, declaring his style to be clear and melodious while discerning well the sense of the original text, and characterizing the meters as "fluently rhymed" and "written with apparent ease" though not always equal to the skill of Boethius.[82]

In the new foreword for the 1722 edition, Gargon asserts the belief that the *Consolatio* was an unfinished work, that Boethius would have added a sixth book expressing a Christian consolation if his life had not been cut short, though Hoek notes that modern critics find this claim untenable.[83] An interesting side-note to this discussion is a relatively obscure translation of the *Octavius* of Minucius Felix, which Gargon published in 1712. However, Gargon's choice of title for this translation alone is quite telling: *Octavius, dienende als tot Vervolg op de Vertroostinge van Boethius*, which may be rendered into English as "Octavius, Serving as a Continuation of the *Consolation* of Boethius." Minucius Felix lived in the late second and early third centuries, and it is unlikely that Gargon could have mistaken this book as an actual continuation of Boethius in ancient times. Instead, Gargon must have offered this book as a Christian continuation for the reader seeking religious consolation.

Willem Bilderdijk (Meters 1809)

Willem Bilderdijk (1756–1831), famous poet and playwright, was the founder of Dutch Romanticism and one time tutor to Louis Bonaparte, brother of Napoleon. He authored many books, notably the incomplete epic *De ondergang der eerste wareld* (The Destruction of the First World) and an early work of science fiction, *Kort verhaal van eene aanmerklijke luchtreis en nieuwe planeetontdekking* (A Short Account of a Remarkable Aerial Voyage and Discovery of a New Planet). Because of poor health, Bilderdijk spent much of his youth as an invalid, which allowed him time for much study. He was trained as a lawyer in Leiden but practiced only a few years in The Hague, having been exiled in 1795 due to the troubles of the times, which exile he spent mainly in England. Hoek supposes that Bilderdijk identified with Boethius due to his exile, which led him to translate all the meters of the *Consolatio*. He first selected twenty-three meters, which he translated between 1790 and 1800, but eventually he translated all thirty-nine meters, published in 1809 as a part of the book *Verspreide Gedichten*.[84] They were reprinted in volume 4 of *De Dichtwerken van Bilderdijk*, published by A. C. Kruseman, Haarlem in 1857. In *De Dichtwerken*, 3m9, "Aan God," is misidentified as 3m8—this is obviously a typographical error, since the preceding poem also is identified as 3m8.[85] Hoek offers much praise for Bilderdijk's translation of the meters, noting that he was an excellent Latinist and supreme poet and that his sensitivity to the poetry of the *Consolatio* allowed him to produce highly original translations that nonetheless express almost every feature of the original meters.[86]

J. W. Schotman (1924)

Johan Wilhelm Schotman (1892–1976) was a doctor, poet, scholar, and psychiatrist who lived and worked in many places in the world, including China and Portugal. He was a prolific translator from many languages, ancient and modern, and produced an eclectic variety of translations into Dutch during his lifetime, including works from authors as various as Julius Caesar, Diogenes, Democritus, Calderón de la Barca, Cervantes, Balzac, Lord Byron, Martin Buber, Immanuel Velikovsky, Winston Churchill, Albert Camus, Bertolt Brecht, Agatha Christie, Lawrence Durrell, the Dalai Lama, and Daphne Du Maurier, among others. His 1924 translation of the *Consolatio*, entitled *Der vertroosting der wijsbegeerte*, was published by Wereld-Bibliotheek, Amsterdam. Produced while Schotman was working as a doctor in China, the volume includes an introduction to Boethius's life and to the *Consolatio*, with an overview of the medieval European translation traditions and the Dutch translation tradition (Ghent, Coornhert, and Gargon only), and a commentary. Schotman's Boethius was reissued in 1945 in a flawed edition by De Nederlandsche

Boekhandel, Antwerpen. A new edition with a new foreword by Schotman was issued by Wereld-Bibliotheek, Amsterdam, in 1952.

In the introduction, Schotman considers Gargon's discussion of Boethius's Christianity and argues that no rational person today can believe that Boethius was Christian. Schotman argues that "[d]e Boethius, die we uit de Vertroosting leren kennen is geen christen, hij is volbloed Romein end geheel een kind van de grote tijden vóór hem" [the Boethius we come to know from the *Consolation* is no Christian; he is full blooded Roman and entirely a child of the great eras before him].[87] Hoek is highly critical of Schotman's bold assertion, noting that many scholars such as E. K. Rand and F. Klinger make sound arguments that Boethius was Christian.[88] Hoek's main point is that Schotman's attitude is neither critical nor grounded in the scholarly debate over the question, and this reflects a general weakness of the translation in that, though it is well written, it is not scholarly. The strength Hoek sees in Schotman's translation lies in his masterful command of the Dutch language, calling his prose "helder and vloeiend, fris and lenig" [clear and flowing, fresh and agile] and noting Schotman's achievement as the first Dutch translator to render the meters in the original measures. However, Hoek is critical of much of the content of the translation, noting that though Schotman boldly defends his liberal rendering of the text, a close analysis of the translation reveals that much of the freedom taken with the prose stems from an uneven command of the Latin original and occasional ignorance of cultural and even geographical contexts. Hoek concludes that Schotman's considerable literary craft makes it all the more regrettable that he did not put more effort into resolving the typical problems inherent in translating a classical text in order to ensure a translation as accurate as it is well written.[89]

S. J. Suys-Reitsma (1953)

Dr. Sophia Jacomina Suys-Reitsma, a classicist, was born in Surabaia, Indonesia, and received her doctorate in letters and philosophy from the University of Amsterdam in 1955. Her 1953 translation of the *Consolatio*, entitled *Vertroosting der Wijsbegeerte*, was published in Amsterdam by N.V. de Arbeiderspers.[90] Her translation is careful and well written and includes interesting commentary. Her admiration for Boethius and his book is obvious. Bonger writes:

> In her commentary the translator explains why so many admired and still admire this book. Philosophers found in it a lucid explanation

> of cardinal philosophical questions. Literati encountered a plastic Platonic style and poems written in all known Classical meters. Wise men in positions of power or wealth were taught the lesson of the vicissitudes of fortune. Those suffering injustice found consolation in the notion that what matters most could not be taken from them. "[B]ut all recognized in him the master, the man who was more than they because he had managed to triumph over death and pain, because he had vanquished his gruesome fate."[91]

This sentiment is recognizable from centuries of *Consolatio* translation and commentary in many languages. Suys-Reitsma's succinct expression of this sentiment underscores her sensitive and insightful handling of the text. Obviously her translation, appearing two years before her doctoral dissertation on Homer, was a labor of love.[92]

R. F. M. Brouwer (1990)

The most recent translation of the *Consolatio* into Dutch was brought forth by R. F. M. Brouwer in 1990, entitled *Der vertroosting van de filosofie*, and published by Ambo/Baarn.[93] Brouwer is a teacher of classical languages at Vossius-gymnasium in Amsterdam. His translation is a carefully prepared critical edition and includes a thorough introduction with sections on the life of Boethius, the political and cultural history of his times, philosophy in late antiquity, the framework of the *Consolatio*, the use of allegory, the philosophical tradtions in the work, and a quick overview of its reception and translation traditions. Each of the five books is preceded by a short summary. The annotations in the endnotes are extensive and thorough. Brouwer's is certainly the most scholarly translation of the *Consolatio* into Dutch. A second edition was published in 2000 with slight emendations and very few changes in wording. A third edition was published in 2010. Brouwer analyzes his own role as translator in an article in 1992 in which he notes that Boethius himself "was moved by a strong and explicit consciousness of the value of that tradition and of his own role and pretensions in the transmission of classical culture."[94] The Boethian scholar Lodi Nauta lauds Brouwer's book as a beautiful translation, noting that he reproduces the various measures of the meters in Dutch, and he praises the introductory material and explanatory notes—Nauta concludes that this high-quality translation will be the standard Dutch *Consolatio* for many years to come.[95]

Two Minor Translations: J. Vollenhove (1686) and Samuel I. Wiselius (1833)

Patrick De Rynck and Andries Welkenhuysen credit two authors with translating a few meters of the *Consolatio*: J. Vollenhove and Samuel I. Wiselius.[96] Joannes Vollenhove (1631–1708), son of the mayor of Vollenhove, studied theology in Utrecht and Groningen, was a preacher for ten years and was awarded an honorary doctorate from Oxford in 1675. Vollenhove was a prolific poet who actively wrote for fifty years. He translated 2m5 in 1685 or 1686 for his book *Poëzy*.[97] Samuel Iperuszoon Wiselius (1769–1845), born in Amsterdam, was a lawyer, businessman, and writer. His writing was stimulated by the struggle against imperial France. He translated three meters from the *Consolatio*, 1m6, 2m3, and 5m2, which are included in the book *Nieuwe Dichtbundel van Samuel Iperuszoon Wiselius*.[98]

Conclusion

The Dutch translation tradition of Boethius's *Consolatio* ranges over more than seven centuries and includes some of the most prominent authors of the Dutch literary world. Studying this tradition reveals the extensive influence of the *Consolatio* in the Lowland countries, yet it also discloses the insufficient attention that has been given to this extensive and complex tradition. The not-yet-fully edited Ghent Boethius alone reveals a considerable gap in the understanding of Boethian translation and commentary with potential impact well beyond just the Dutch tradition. Similarly, the immense importance of D. V. Coornhert in the intellectual conflicts of the early modern period sets his translations within a greater discourse affecting the development of Western European society in general. We have yet adequately to assess the transmission of Boethian thinking through Coornhert into the development of the Arminian religious movement that subsequently affected much of the Protestant world, including the religious and political conflicts of seventeenth-century Britain. Later translations map the cultural struggles that still divide the Netherlands from the Flemish communities in Belgium. In particular, Theo Hermans's analysis of the de Buck translation reveals the process of translation as a culturally embedded act, replete with the dramatism of any rhetorical performance. In the eighteenth century, the book as a multifaceted cultural product emerges in Gargon's successful renderings of the text. The Romantic era finds the prodigious Dutch author Bilderdijk turning his considerable poetic talent to Boethius's meters. In turn, each of the three twentieth-century translations marks the considerable power of Boethius's text still growing in our day. Indeed, the study of the Dutch translation tradition reveals the immense importance of examining the many translation traditions of the *Consolatio*, for in this study we find much more than a curious catalog of translations—we find a significant tracing of meaning as an inheritance and the integral role of the *Consolatio* in the development of that inheritance in the Western world and beyond.

Appendix

Presented here are translations of 3m9, "*O qui perpetua*," from six of the Dutch translations of Boethius's *Consolatio*.

1. GHENT (1485)[99]
O Du heere diet al regiers
Hemel aerde ende tijd bestiers
Onroerlic zijnde roers al dat leift
Niet vreimders dij eerst bedwonghen heeft
Alle dijnc te maken maer eyghen deught.
Du hebs de weereld vut eewigher vreught
Ghevormet schone na dijn ghelijke
Vut hoghen exemplen vulcommelijke.
zulc wilstu wesen al hare deele
De elemente voughstu gheheele
Tcoude ten heeten theete ten couden
zo dat zij gherechte reghel houden
Der sielen tusschen [tusschhen] drien nateuren
Hebstu den middel doen ghebeuren
zou deelt haer bij ghelijken leden
Ende keert tot harer eerster steden
Rondomme naer des hemels wijse
Du voerdse mettij ten hooghsten prise
Ghelikelic voughdij dneder leuen
Vut rechter minnen hebstu gheheuen
Dat zou ooc wederkeert tot dij
Och vader den wegh wilt leiden my
Vul van deughden ter fonteyne
Ghef dij te siene met oghen reyne
Jaeght daerdsche lastighe deimsterheit
Licht ruste die bes ghef paeyselicheit
Dij schauwen es dhende dat ic meen
Beghin/ wegh/ middel/ in dij zijn een.

2. COORNHERT (1585)[100]

O Schepper ghoed van Hemel en van Aarde
Diet al bestiert zeer wyslyck elck na waarde:
Die eeuwigh zyt en zendt den tyd op weghen,
Zelf onbeweeght, doer ghyt hier al beweghen.
Gheen óórzaack vreemd en deed u krachtigh scheppen,
Dit gróte werck, vant stóf dat ghy doer reppen:
Maar liefde ghoed, u eyghen zelfs nature,
Dient weldoen lust, ghy nyd tót gheender ure.
Ghy alderschóónst hebt schóón en wel gaan maken,
De schóne werld na t'schóónst van alle zaken,
Na t'hóghe beeld, daar uyt dit is ghenomen:
In elcken deel, volmaackt en ghants volkomen.
Ghy bindt met tal de Elementen viere,
Zó dat de koud' met óóck het hete viere,
Het nat en dróógh eendrachtelyck verzamen,
Op dat het vier niet jeghen zyn betamen
Vervliegh' opt hóógh, en d'aarde zwaar doer zincken,
Ontzielt en dóód, ghy draaghtse met u wincken.
Ghy hebt gheknóópt de ziel van drie naturen,
Diet al beweeght door leden licht om sturen.
Als ghy die deylt, en weder wilt ontbinden,
Zó zwermt zy weer tót haar aan beyden inden
Om t'diep ghemoed en draayt het Aartryck spoedigh
Na s'Hemels beeld, zó voert ghy Heer óóck ghoedigh.
De zielen en de kleynder ledens mede,
Op waghens licht, in d'hóghe Hemels vrede:
Die ghy bekeert door Wet zeer ghoedertierigh,
En t'uwaart ruckt' als vlammen snel en vierigh.
Laat Vader ghoed ons hert ter hogher steden
Opstyghen, om te zien dyn moghentheden
Met óghen klaar, en die op u zó vesten,
Dat wy versmaan de last van d'Aartsche nesten.
Neemt wegh den damp vant snóde lyfs bezórghen,
Dyn glans verschyn van dyn oneyntlyck mórghen.
Want ghy zyt klaar, de zoete en stille ruste,
Der zielen reyn, ghy zyt alleen haar luste.
Het zien van u is heyl heyligh regierder,
Ghy zyt beghin en eynd de wech en stierder.

3. GARGON (1722)[101]

O Schepper, die 't heel-al bind aan al-wyze wetten,
En aarde, en Hemel grond door eindelooze kracht,
Die eeuwig zyt, en hebt den tyd zyn loop doen zetten,
En onbeweeglyk, al aan het beweegen bragt,
Die door geen oorzaak zyt van buiten aangedreeven,
Om uit de vloeib're stof te brengen 't konst-werk voort,
Maar om als 't hoogste goed van godeheid blykte geeven,
En dat uw' wysheid mogt daar in zyn nagespoord!
De schoone waereld hebt gy, Schoonste! voort doen spruiten,
Na 't schoon ontwerp, dat gy had by u zelf gemaakt.
De deelen slaan tot een, en volgen uw besluiten,
Waardoor het groot gebouw tot zyn volmaaktheid
raakt.
Gy hebt het tal bepaalt der sirydige Elementen,
Getemperd koude, en gloed, verzamelt nat en droog,
Om ons de maatigheid zo leevend in te prenten,
En dat het vlugge vuur niet al-te snel vervloog,
Of de aarde door gewigt niet neder wierd getogen.
Ge zond een wonder-kracht door 's waerelds wonder-
leên.
Waar door zy leven, en ordentlyk zyn bewogen,
En die zich heerlyk spreid door 's hemels kringen heen,
De geesten, die om hoog voor uwen heil troon zweeven,
De menschen, die zich hier onthouden op der aard',
Dien geeft gy wezen, kracht, gezwindheid, licht, en
leven:
En voerd de zuivre ziel weêr gunstig hemelwaart.
Gun, Vader van het licht ! dat wy uw licht beschouwen,
Gun, dat wy goedheids bron ontdekken, en uw heil,
Gun, dat wy onze hoop op uwe waarheid bouwen,
Op dat de ziel verblind door aardschen zorg niet feil.
Verdryf de nevelen van onkund door uw' waarheid
En laat uw' hemel-glants zyn onze wensch, en luft.
In u, in u alleen is aller vroomen klaarheid,
Gy zyt begin, en eind, bestierder, weg, en rust.

4. BILDERDIJK (1809)[102]
"AAN GOD"

ô Gy, die 't wareldrond naar één bestendige orden
Bestiert; die aarde en zee en hemel hebt doen worden;
Den tijd uit de eeuwigheid hervoortriept, en zijn baan
Afbakende om zijn' weg onstoorbaar af te gaan;
Die, zelf onwrikbaar, 't al beweging sehenkt en leven!
Wien niets bewegen konde om iets bestaan te geven
Dan uwe goedheid; zelf het opperst goed alleen,
Van vlekken zuiver! Gy, die uw volkomenheên
U zelv' ten voorbeeld stelt, en, door geen macht te omperken,
Zelf schoonheid, 't schoon bevat en uitdrukt in uw werken!
Die, aan u-zelv' gelijk, in alles ongewraakt,
't Volmaakte van 't geheel door ieder ded volmaakt!
Gy legt de hoofdstof vast aan 't snoer der samenstemming,
In duurzaam evenwicht, 't geen schokken vreest noeh stremming;
Dat koude en gloed, en droogte en vloeistof onderling
Zich schragen; 't fijner vuur niet aan den band ontspring',
Noch 's aardrijks logge klomp ter neêr zink' door zijn zwaarte.
Gy vormde tusschen geest en 't redenloos geäarte
De menschelijke ziel van middelbaren stand,
En bracht haar met het stof in 't wonderbaarst verband;
Niet om door 't lichaam sleehts haar leven te verspreiden,
Maar ziec door beider kring by beurten uit te breiden ,
En in zich-zelv gekeerd, haar eigen vatbaarheên
Te zien, en 't groot heelal te schildren in het kleen.
Gy-zelf, gy voert de ziel, als op een' wolkenwagen,
Door aarde en hemel, en uw godlijk welbehagen
Roept ze eenmaal weêr te rug tot uw genoegzaamheid.
Gy, oorsprong van 't heelal, en oppenmjesteit!
Gy, geef gy dat mijn ziel uw' zetel moog genaken;
Geef haar, de bran van 't goed, die zuivre bron, te smaken;
Het licht te ontdekken; en het schemerend gezicht
Onafgewend op u te vesten, zee van licht!
Verdrijf de nevels en des aardrijks zwarte dampen,
Die om ons zweven en dien heldren glans bekampen;
En straal ons toe! Want gy, gy zijt het, die verkwikt;
Gy, kalmte en rust van hun op wie uw aanschijn blikt!
In u, in u te zien, bestaat het eind des levens,
Die einde en aanvang zijt, en weg en leidsman tevens.

5. SUYS-REITSMA (1953)[103]

Gij die de wereld regeert naar altijd durende wetten,
Stichter van aarde en hemel, die vanuit het eeuwig de tijd doet
Gaan, en die zelf onbeweeglijk het Al aanzet tot bewegen.
U niet hebben uitwendige krachten gedreven tot scheppen
Uit de vloeiende stof, maar de u eigen vorm van het hoogste
Goede, dat vrijf is van afganst. Gij nu ledit af maar uw hoge
Voobeeld de dingen, als schoonste bestiert ge de wereld schoon met uw
Geest en ge vormt haar gelijk naar uw eigen beeld; ook beveelt ge
Aan wat volmaakt is om van zich to laten volmaakt zijnde delen.
Gij houdt in maat d'elementen en zorgt dat er evenwicht kome
Tussen het koude en warme, het droge en 't natte, opdat niet
't Puurdere vuur omhoog vliegt, haar massa de aarde omlaag drukt.
Driedelig is de natuur en het alles bewegende midden, de
Ziel, maakt ge los haar verknopend met harmoniserende leden.
En wanneer zij, verdeeld, wat beweegt, heeft gevoegd tot twee kringen
Keert z'in zichzelve terug en doorloopt ze de diepten des geestes.
En naar hetzelfde principe beweegt zij tevens de hemel.
Gij brengt ook aan het licht, om gelijke oorzaak, , het kleine
Dat ook bezield is en leeft; en op luchtige wagens hen heffend
Zaait ge hen uit over hemel en aarde en doet gij hen keren
Volgens genadige wetten als 't vuur weer terug tot uw aanschijn.
Vader, vergun onze geest de verhevene plaats 't bereiken,
Geef ons de bron te aanschouwen van 't goede; als 't licht is gevonden,
Geef dat gescherpt dan het oog van degeest zich op u mag richten.
Jaag uiteen al de nevels der aarde, hef op alle zwaarte.
Glans met d'u eigene stralen, want gij zijt immers het klare,
Gij zijt kalmerende rust voor de vromen, uw aanblik ons streven,
Gij zijt tevens begin, bestierder, gids, pad maar ook einde.

6. BROUWER (2000)[104]

Gíj die 't heelál bestúurt volgens dúurzaam géldende wétten,
hemel en aarde verwekt, die de tijd, haar op eeuwigheid entend,
voortgang gelast en die, zelf roerloos, 't heelal doet bewegen,
Gij die, door niets vanbuiten genoopt, van de deinende oerstof
't werk van Uw handen gemaakt hebt, geleid door de wezensvorm ín U,
Hoogste Goed en de gulheid zelve: Gij kiest voor 't Al tot Uw voorbeeld
't hoog steeds prijkende oerbeeld, als Uw denkbeeld draagt ge, O Schoonste,
't schone heelal in U om; naar dat beeld, die gelijkenis schept ge,
dwingt ge volmaakte elementen tot louter volmaaktheid tezamen.
Gij vereent ze door tal en maat, opdat hitte en koude,
droogte en vocht een verbond aangaan, dat het zuiverder vuur niet
opstijgt slechts, en 't gewicht niet de aarde diep doet verzinken.
Gij hecht de ziel, van drievoudige aard, die 't heelal doet bewegen
middenin vast, en verdeelt haar, tot samenklank voegend de leden.
Eerst, in twee repen gesplitst, rolt ze op zich tot draaiende cirkels,
dan keert ze in tot zichzelf, met haar kringloop omvattend de diepe
peilloze geest: naar dat beeld modelleert ze de hemelbeweging.
Gij, uit dezelfde beginselen puttend, schenkt zielen her aanzijn,
mindere levens ook; hoog wijst ge wendbare wagens hun toe en
zaait hen in hemel en aarde; dan, door de wet van Uw goedheid,
wendt ge ze weer naar U toe door her vuur dat hen laaiend terugvoert.
  Geef, Vader, dat mijn geest naar 't verheven oord weer mag stijgen,
  geef dat hij schouwt de bron van het goede, geef dat hij weervindt
't licht dat hem U doet zien, op wie gretig zijn blik is gevestigd;
jaag wat de aarde omwolkt uiteen, doe haar zwaarte teniet, dat
doorbreekt Uw stralende glans, want Gij zijt de heldere hemel,
Gij zijt de rust die de vromen verkwikt, U te zien is het oogmerk,
Gij die 't begin zijt, ons draagt en ons gidst, die de weg zijt en 't einde.

NOTES

*The author wishes to thank Jeff Alton, Dr. Theo Hermans, Karen Simmering, Dr. Leslie A. Taylor, and Dr. Wendolyn Weber for providing assistance during this project.

[1] Jacobus Martinus Hoek, *De Middelnederlandse vertalingen van Boethius' "De Consolatione Philosophiae"; met een overzicht van de andere Nederlandse en niet-Nederlandse vertalingen* (Harderwijk: FLEVO, 1943).

[2] Mariken Goris, ed., *Boethius en het Nederlands: Studie naar en tekstuitgave van de Gentse Boethius (1485), Boek II* (Hilversum: Verloren, 2000). This volume contains an extensive bibliography.

[3] Johan Wilhelm Schotman, "Inleiding," in Boethius, *Der vertroosting der wijsbegeerte*, trans. Johan Wilhelm Schotman (Amsterdam: Wereld-Bibliotheek, 1924), vii–xxvi; R. F. M. Brouwer, "Inleiding," in Boethius, *Der vertroosting van de filosofie*, trans. R. F. M. Browuer, 2nd ed. (Amsterdam: Ambo, 2000), 9–62.

[4] *Digitale Bibliotheek voor de Nederlandse Letteren* (hereafter *DBNL*) (Leiden: Stichting *DBNL*, 2008), accessed September 8, 2015, http://www.dbnl.org/.

[5] Nigel F. Palmer, "Latin and Vernacular in the Northern European Tradition of the *De Consolatione Philosophiae*," in *Boethius: His Life, Thought, and Influence*, ed. Margaret Gibson (Oxford: Blackwell, 1981), 362–409. Anthony Grafton is the author of Appendix II of this article, "The Dutch Tradition," 398. Grafton's analysis is sparse and, in the case of Coornhert, problematic. See the Coornhert entry in this essay.

[6] Maarten J. F. M. Hoenen and Lodi Nauta, eds., *Boethius in the Middle Ages: Latin and Vernacular Traditions of the "Consolatio philosophiae"* (Leiden: Brill, 1997).

[7] Mariken Goris and Lodi Nauta, "The Study of Boethius's *Consolatio* in the Low Countries Around 1500: The *Ghent Boethius* (1485) and the Commentary by Agricola/Murmellius (1514)," in *Northern Humanism in European Context, 1469–1625: From the "Adwert Academy" to Ubbo Emmius*, ed. F. Akkerman, A. J. Vanderjagt, and A. H. van der Laan (Leiden: Brill, 1999), 109–30.

[8] Mariken Goris, "Boethius's *Consolatio Philosophiae* and the Early Printing Tradition," in *The Bookshop of the World: The Role of the Low Countries in the Book-Trade, 1473–1941*, ed. Lotte Hellinga et al. ('t Goy-Houten: HES & De Graaf, 2001), 49–54.

[9] Goris, *Boethius en het Nederlands*, 403–05.

[10] Henk Bonger, *The Life and Work of Dirck Volkertszoon Coornhert*, trans. Gerrit Voogt (Amerstdam: Rodopi, 2004); Theo Hermans, "Translation and Normativity," *Current Issues in Language and Society* 5, no. 1/2 (1998): 51–72.

[11] P. G. Witsen Geysbeek, *Biographisch anthologisch en critisch woordenboek der Nederduitsche dichters: Deel 4, JAC–NYV* (Amsterdam: C. L. Schleijer, 1823), 291. This reference is available online at the *DBNL* (see n. 4 above).

[12] Mariken Goris and Wilma Wissink, "The Medieval Dutch Tradition of Boethius' *Consolatio Philosophiae*," in Hoenen and Nauta, *Boethius in the Middle Ages*, 127–28.

[13] Jacob van Maerlant, *Spiegel Historiael*, ed. M. de Vries and E. Verwijs (Leiden, 1863); the Boethian portions are in part 3, book 6, 360–62. See *DBNL*, accessed September 8, 2015, http://www.dbnl.org/tekst/maer002spie03_01/maer002spie03_01_0007.php.

[14] Goris and Wissink, "Medieval Dutch Tradition," 128n24.

[15] Ibid., 128–29.

[16] Though Vilt's rendering is considered the first Middle Dutch *Consolatio*, some scholars believe the lost manuscript of the Ghent Boethius was completed earlier than Vilt's. See Goris and Wissink, "Medieval Dutch Tradition," 139n40. For information on the Pseudo-de Meun used by Vilt, see Glynnis M. Cropp, "The Medieval French Tradition," in Hoenen and Nauta, *Boethius in the Middle Ages*, 249–50.

[17] Goris and Wissink, "Medieval Dutch Tradition," 130–31.

[18] Koert van der Horst, *Illuminated and Decorated Medieval Manuscripts in the University Library, Utrecht: An Illustrated Catalog* (Cambridge: Cambridge University Press, 1989), 40–41.

[19] "Medieval Manuscripts in Dutch Collections," Koninklijke Bibliotheek, accessed September 8, 2015, http://www.mmdc.nl/.

[20] Hoek, *De Middelnederlandse Vertalignen*, 82–83, 101–02, 212, 214.

[21] Goris and Wissink, "Medieval Dutch Tradition," 132–33, 137.

[22] Ibid., 132–34.

[23] Ibid., 132.

[24] Hoek, *De Middelnederlandse Vertalignen*, 103–04.

[25] Goris and Wissink, "Medieval Dutch Tradition," 135–36.

[26] Goris, *Boethius en het Nederlands*, 404.

[27] Goris and Wissink, "Medieval Dutch Tradition," 140; Goris, *Boethius en het Nederlands*, 35.

[28] Hoek, *De Middelnederlandse Vertalignen*, 36–37.

[29] Goris and Wissink, "Medieval Dutch Tradition," 138–39.

[30] Goris, *Boethius en het Nederlands*, 403.

[31] Goris and Wissink, "Medieval Dutch Tradition," 140–41.

[32] Goris, "Boethius's *Consolatio Philosophiae*," 50–51.

[33] Goris and Wissink, "Medieval Dutch Tradition," 138–39.

[34] Ibid., 145.

[35] Ibid., 145–50.

[36] Alain Arnould and Jean Michel Massing, *Splendours of Flanders* (Cambridge: Cambridge University Press, 1993), 168.

[37] Goris, *Boethius en het Nederlands*, 35; Goris, "Boethius's *Consolatio Philosophiae*," 52.

[38] Goris and Nauta, "Study of Boethius's *Consolatio*," 109–18.

[39] Goris and Wissink, "Medieval Dutch Tradition," 157–58.

[40] Hoek, *De Middelnederlandse Vertalignen*, 37–38; Goris and Wissink, "Medieval Dutch Tradition," 158.

[41] Goris and Wissink, "Medieval Dutch Tradition," 159–60.

[42] D. V. Coornhert, "Aande Gildebroeders des Rederycx Kamer tót Amsterdam: In Liefd Bloeyende," in Boethius, *Van de Vertróósting der Wysheyd*, trans. D. V. Coornhert (1585; repr., Amsterdam: Balkema, 1945), 6.

[43] Hoek, *De Middelnederlandse Vertalignen*, 40–43.

[44] Goris and Wissink, "Medieval Dutch Tradition," 138–39. Goris and Wissink (139) also report that of the extant incunables "only twelve contain miniatures and penwork in the open spaces provided by the printer," and further, that there are "two types of the edition of the Ghent Boethius: one on heavy paper in excellent type and one on paper of a lesser quality and with a somewhat careless execution."

[45] Goris and Wissink, "Medieval Dutch Tradition," 123n 5.

[46] Hoek, *De Middelnederlandse Vertalignen*, 173–74, 179–85, 188–89, 210, 212, 214, 216–17.

[47] See n. 2.

[48] Goris and Wissink, "Medieval Dutch Tradition," 123n5; Goris, *Boethius en het Nederlands*, 405.

[49] Bergje van Dommelen and Dirk-Jan Dekker, "Edition of the Ghent Boethius, Book V Prose 3: Latin Text, Middle Dutch Translation and Commentary," in Hoenen and Nauta, *Boethius in the Middle Ages*, 305–25.

[50] Bonger, *Life and Work*, 282.

[51] Hoek, *De Middelnederlandse Vertalignen*, 40–43.

[52] Ibid., 44–48.

[53] Schotman, "Inleiding," xxiii.

[54] Palmer, "Latin and Vernacular," 398. Theo Hermans reproduces Coornhert's 1585 preface in *Door eenen engen hals: Nederlandse beschouwingen over vertalen 1550–1670* (The Hague: Bibliographia Neerlandica, 1996), 61–63.

[55] Bonger, *Life and Work*, 122–23.

[56] Ibid., 282.

[57] Willem Pieter Gerritsen, "Coornhert and Boethius: A Side-Light on the Genesis of Dutch Renaissance Verse," in *From Wolfram and Petrarch to Goethe and Grass: Studies in Literature in Honour of Leonard Forster*, ed. D. H. Green, L. P. Johnson, and Dieter Wuttke (Baden-Baden: Koerner, 1982), 307–08.

[58] Ibid., 310–19.

[59] Brouwer, "Inleiding," 52.

[60] Gerrit Voogt, "Primacy of Individual Conscience or Primacy of the State? The Clash between Dirck Volckertsz. Coornhert and Justus Lipsius," *Sixteenth Century Journal* 28, no. 4 (1997): 1231–33; Brouwer, "Inleding," 52.

[61] Hoek, *De Middelnederlandse Vertalignen*, 44.

[62] See n. 42.

[63] Hermans, "Translation and Normativity," 52.

[64] Hoek, *De Middelnederlandse Vertalignen*, 225.

[65] Hoek, *De Middelnederlandse Vertalignen*, 50. Hoek's reference is to P. van Duyse, *Een lettervond, Het Taelverbond, Tijdschr. voor Geschiedenis, Tael-, Oudheid-, en Letterkunde* (1853), 23–38. However, I have been unable to find this source or any reference to it elsewhere.

[66] See nn. 10 and 63.

[67] Hermans, *Door eenen engen hals*, 121–22.

[68] Hermans, "Translation and Normativity," 56.

[69] Ibid., 53–54.

[70] Ibid., 59.

[71] Ibid., 55.

[72] Ibid., 57.

[73] Ibid., 53.

[74] Ibid., 57.

[75] Ibid., 70.

[76] Hoek, *De Middelnederlandse Vertalignen*, 53.

[77] Schotman, "Inleiding," xxiv.

[78] Ibid.

[79] The 1703 edition is more widely available than the reworking of 1722. I was able to obtain a microfilm of the 1722 version from the Beinecke Rare Book and Manuscript Library at Yale University. I am grateful to Eric White, curator of Special Collections at Bridwell Library, Perkins School of Theology at Southern Methodist University, for supplying scans from the 1703 edition.

[80] Hoek, *De Middelnederlandse Vertalignen*, 56–57.

[81] Ibid., 225.

[82] F. M., "Gargon's vertaling van Boethius' *De Consolatione Philosphiae*," *Hermeneus* 13 (1940): 63–64. The author is listed only by the initials "F. M."; however, Hoek identifies these initials as "F(ehr)-M(eerwaldt)" in Hoek, *De Middelnederlandse Vertalignen*, 57, 221.

[83] Hoek, *De Middelnederlandse Vertalignen*, 56.

[84] Ibid., 58–59.

[85] Willem Bilderdijk, *De Dichtwerken van Bilderdijk*, vol. 4 (Haarlem: A. C. Kruseman, 1857), 403–05. Note that 1m5 is also titled "Aan God," 386–87.

[86] Hoek, *De Middelnederlandse Vertalignen*, 59.

[87] Schotman, "Inleiding," xx.

[88] Hoek, *De Middelnederlandse Vertalignen*, 61–62.

[89] Ibid., 62–67.

[90] Boethius, *Vertroosting der Wijsbegeerte*, trans. Sophia Jacomina Suys-Reitsma (Amsterdam: Arbeiderspers, 1953). This translation is available in several libraries in The Netherlands. The only copy in North America of which I am aware is the one in my possession.

[91] Bonger, *Life and Work*, 281.

[92] Sophia Jacomina Suys-Reitsma, *Het Homerisch Epos; als Orale Schepping van een Dichter-Hetaire* (Amsterdam: H.S. Paris, 1955). This dissertation contains a summary in English.

[93] Boethius, *Der vertroosting van de filosofie*, trans. R. F. M. Brouwer (Amsterdam: Ambo, 1990). A second edition was issued in 2000 by Ambo/Amsterdam; See note 3. There are many copies of this book throughout The Netherlands. In North America there is one copy of the 1990 edition at the Library of Congress in Washington, DC. I have a copy of the 2000 edition in my possession.

[94] R. F. M. Brouwer, "Boethius Vertalen," *Lampas* 25, no. 2 (1992): 136.

[95] Lodi Nauta, "Boethius, *Trost der Philosophie*. Herausg. und übers. von E. Gegenschatz und O. Gigon mit einer Einf. von O. Gigon. Artemis Verlag, München / Zürich 1990. 210 p. ISBN 3760818927. Prijs: DM 29,50. Boëthius, De vertroosting van de filosofie. Vert., inl. en aant. R. F. M. Brouwer. Ambo, Baarn 1990. 272 pp. ISBN 9026309775. Pfijs : f69—," *Theoretische geschiedenis* 20 (1993): 462–64.

[96] Patrick De Rynck and Andries Welkenhuysen, *De Oudheid in het Nederlands* (Amsterdam: Ambo, 2003), 125. See *DBNL*, accessed September 8, 2015, http://www.dbnl.org/tekst/rync001oudh01_01/rync001oudh01_01_0011.php.

[97] Joannes Vollenhove, *Poëzy* (Amsterdam: H. Boom en de weduwe van D. Boom, 1686).

[98] Sameul I. Wiselius, *Nieuwe Dichtbundel van Samuel Iperuszoon Wiselius* (Amsterdam: Garman, 1833).

[99] Hoek, *De Middelnederlandse Vertalignen*, 188–89.

[100] Boethius, *Van de Vertróósting der Wysheyd*, trans. Coornhert, 103–04.

[101] Boethius, *Vertroostinge der wysgeerte*, trans. Mattheus Gargon (Amsterdam: Adrian Braakman, 1722), 91–92.

[102] Bilderdijk, *De Dichtwerken*, 404–05.

[103] Boethius, *Vertroosting der Wijsbegeerte*, trans. Suys-Reitsma, 82–83.

[104] Boethius, *Der vertroosting van de filosofie*, trans. Browuer (2nd ed.), 124–25.

The Reception and Adaptation of Boethius's *De consolatione philosophiae* in Northern Italy: An Unedited Fourteenth-Century Version*

Serena Lunardi

THE SUCCESS of Boethius's *De consolatione philosophiae* [hereafter *Consolatio*] during the Christian Middle Ages was extensive: in terms of space, the work was transmitted in manuscripts (in addition to the standard commentaries and glosses) through the whole of Western Europe; in terms of time, its diffusion in manuscripts spread until the beginning of the Renaissance (with several remarkable examples from subsequent centuries as well). The rich and complex history of the reception and adaptation of Boethius's last work within these spatial and temporal parameters is only partly written: a catalogue of the existing manuscripts is still a work in progress, and great effort needs to be exerted to edit all of the texts;[1] in fact, of the most important Latin commentaries written between the tenth and the fifteenth centuries, only the *Glosae super Boetium* by William of Conches is available in a modern critical edition.[2] Robert Black and Gabriella Pomaro's groundbreaking work on school manuals in Florence recently has revealed compelling new information about the use of the *Consolatio* as a textbook.[3] This has called into question earlier interpretations (such as those advanced by Pierre Courcelle[4]) that consigned the work to the lowest part of the *curriculum studiorum* during the fourteenth and fifteenth centuries and suggested that it was used as a mere instrument to teach grammatical and rhetorical rules to students with no knowledge of Latin.[5] Indeed, recent and probing studies of early medieval commentaries (including those of Nicolas Trevet and William of Aragon) have highlighted the considerable hermeneutic value of the commentaries. In recent decades, analyses of vernacular commentaries, glosses, and translations have become more important, showing the diffusion of Boethius's work beyond clerical and pedagogical contexts and demonstrating the breadth of the diffusion of the *Consolatio*, even among less educated readers, often wrongly defined as *illitterati*.[6] Perhaps, the greatest value of recent studies, however, is their focus not only upon the most famous authors and translators into the vernacular but also upon a number of less well-known or anonymous translators involved in the wide diffusion of the *Consolatio*, and upon the continuous vitality of its reception.[7]

The exhaustive analysis of the reception of the *Consolatio* in Italy is complicated by three factors: first, there is a persistent lack of concrete knowledge of the works in Latin; second, the category of *volgarizzamento* itself has yet to be defined within specific parameters;[8] third, many versions of the *Consolatio* have not yet been edited.[9] Thus, more thorough inquiry is required to determine the relationship between the Latin tradition, vernacular production, iconography, and medieval popular traditions.[10]

Nonetheless, the inventory of the Italian versions recently has been enriched thanks to new discoveries.[11] Among these discoveries, a new vernacular translation dating back to the late fourteenth century has been identified in a single codex (MS Italian 40), heretofore not included in the records of Italian translations.

The codex is housed in the Biblioteca Academiei Române at Bucharest.[12] This parchment manuscript of small format (the handwriting measures 200 mm × 140 mm) contains exclusively the vernacular Italian version of Boethius's work, written full-line in a studied *littera textualis.* The manuscript comprises 108 folios divided into twelve whole quires; neither the author's name nor the names of the three copyists are inscribed. The first change in hand occurs at *Consolatio* 3m9 (fol. 55r), whereas the second appears halfway through *Consolatio* 3m12 (fol. 69r). The three different hands can be dated to between the end of the fourteenth and the beginning of the fifteenth century; specifically, the first two (hereafter, α and β) seem to date from the end of the fourteenth century, whereas the third (handwriting γ) is more recent (beginning of the fifteenth century), as attested by the considerable presence of pre-humanistic graphic elements and by later decorations, *tituli*, and rubrics. The Bucharest manuscript is definitely not an autograph, and, indeed, it clearly betrays the presence of a vernacular antigraph. Scribal errors abound, among which there are two occurrences of "saut du même au même," the inversion of *Consolatio* 2p4, 2m4, and 2p5, probably due to an erroneous rebinding of quires in the antigraph. There is also a double transcription of lines 1–16 in *Consolatio* 3m9, occurring in the section between α and β (the two versions introduce different variants, attesting both their independence and their link to an antecedent). Linguistic analysis confirmed the dating of the Bucharest version to around the fourteenth century, and one could reasonably argue for a Venetian provenance, though a small number of Trevisan traits have yet to be considered fully. The manuscript does not appear to be a school textbook, given the small format and the nearly total absence of glosses, inclusions, or other handwritten notes (with the exception of two instances: two very short interventions by a humanist, corresponding to two corrupted parts of the transcription). Judging from the elements briefly described above, the codex was not the possession of a scholar but rather that of a lay person. The manuscript features the *ex-libris* of Marco Antonio Borghese's, and it seems to have reached Romania quite recently (probably following the auction of the Burghesiana Collection, which occurred during the last decade of the nineteenth century).[13]

The Italian version of the *Consolatio* present in the Bucharest manuscript is complete (with the exception of a few omissions),[14] and it is divided into five books like the Latin original. The scansion in both the prose and the metres also replicates the original, as the paratextual aspects (rubrics, paragraph signs, etc.) demonstrate.[15] One exception to the system imposed is the absence of separation between 2p4, 2m4, and 2p5 (corresponding to the anomaly inversion described above); another occurs between 3m3 and 3p4. Both exceptions are located in the section copied by α. The vernacular version adds a *prohemium* and a *conclusio* (the latter in Latin hexameters) to the canonical five books.

This is the scheme of sectioning in the work:

PROHEMIUM (1r–5v); *titulus*: *Prohemium translacionis Boecii de Consolacione Philosophie*; *incipit*: *Boecio nobele citadino de Roma . . .*; *explicit*: *. . . E così la raxon è formada da la inteligencia, pò iudegare, etcetera* [fols. 6r and 6v are left blank].
BOOK I (7r–37v); *tit.*: *Boecius De Consolacione Philosophie*; *inc.*: Carmina qui quondam *etcetera. Questo Boetio, voiando tractare de la consolacion de la Filosofia . . .*; *expl.*: *. . . Caça via lo dolor imperçò che là che queste quatro cose regna non può esser la Filosofia, ché la mente no può arecordarse del suo Creator.*
BOOK 2 (37v–46r); without *tit.*; *inc.*: Post h<ec> paulisper obutivit. *E l'è usança de li antisi che, quando eli comple algun lebro . . .*; *expl.*: *. . . lo qual dixe La mia paxe e lo mio ben voler sia sempre con vui.*
BOOK 3 (46r–69v); without *tit.*; *inc.*: Iam cantu<m> illa. *En questo terço libro l'autor amaistra tuti li dotori . . .*; *expl.*: *. . . e dise che elli sente quella de plu de cento mia lonci. E fi ponidi unde elli hanno pecado.*
BOOK 4 (70r–87v); *tit.*: *Veni et vidimus que sit vera beatitudo et ubi sit posita . . .*; *inc.*: Hec cum Philosophia. *Conplide le doe parte de la beatitudene o del sovran ben . . .*; *expl.*: *. . . E plu non vuole le moralitade per singolo, e basti l'oficio esenplificativo cum plena entenzione.*

> BOOK 5 (87v–106v); *tit.*: *Quintus liber continet primi naturaliter duo tantum scilicet de causa et de libero albitrio . . .*; *inc.*: Dixerat orationisque cursum. *Dicto è en quella sesta prosa del quarto libro çoè* Ita est inquam . . .; *expl.*: . . . *Adonca caçando letargo gracia a Dio de la sanitade. Deo gracias. Amen.*
> *CONCLUSIO* (107r); *inc.*: *Scriptor erat liber. Explicit iste liber*; *expl.*: . . . *Regulat iste bona corporis ac anime. Amen. Amen. Amen.* [fols. 107v–108v are left blank].

In the Bucharest manuscript, the translation is always preceded by the corresponding Boethian lemma; the structure is similar to the lemmatic (or "continuous") one used by William of Conches, Nicolas Trevet, and William of Aragon, but it also is present in some editions of Remigius of Auxerre's commentary and in some schoolbooks.[16] Thus, it is likely that the structure of the Bucharest version derives from the Latin tradition, although atypically if compared to other vernacular versions: the lemmatic structure presupposes that the vernacular version is subordinated to the original Latin text, but the absence of lemmata here could indicate that the translator intended to create an independent work, capable of being read independently of Boethius's original version.

The *prohemium* placed at the beginning of the Bucharest manuscript also bears greater similaritiy to the Latin *accessus ad auctores* than to the prefaces of other vernacular translations.[17] For example, there are no programmatic statements by the author.[18] The translator appears to follow the Latin tradition, as the commentator in an *accessus* does not reveal his motives for commenting on the text, focusing instead on the *intentio* presented in the original text by the *auctor*. My analyses of the Latin comments have not yet revealed any direct sources of the Bucharest *prohemium*, since the latter includes neither the typical six-part model nor the Aristotelian four-cause structure. Nonetheless, the pivotal focus in the *intentio*, the *materia*, and the *ordo* seems to derive from the Latin tradition, and in particular from the prologue-paradigm C, classified by Richard W. Hunt.[19] The absence of the remaining parts (*titulus*, *cui parti philosophiae supponitur*) does not appear anomalous, however, for the Latin *accessus* does not follow strict rules in choosing which parts to include.[20] Similarly, the absence of the biography of the *auctor* is not completely uncharacteristic, being absent in other vernacular versions as well (for instance, it is missing in those of Bonaventura of Demena).[21] The preface displays a tight connection with the vernacular version present in the subsequent parts of the manuscript: the linguistic and stylistic movement is uniform, as in the lemmatic structure, and many intertextual links can occur between the prologue and the vernacular version. It is even probable, looking carefully at the content, that the prologue was composed after the vernacular version already had been completed, and perhaps in the same translator's hand.

It is fair to assume, therefore, that the Bucharest version derives, at least in part, from the Latin tradition. It remains to identify the purpose of the translation. First, one should note that the vernacular text is not an exact translation of the Boethian original: the translator does not adhere fatihfully to the original work. Some passages are mere summaries of the original: there are several intentional omissions and paraphrases (such as, for instance, changes between direct and indirect discourse). Moreover, the vernacular text tends to modernize the original Latin, and to overlook allusions to historical facts; it seems as if the translator tried to turn the Boethian work into a moral tale, devoid of any historical allusion (according to the moral *intentio* put forward in the prologue).[22] This stance is similarly adopted in other versions of the *Consolatio*, which is probably due to the fact that the translator meant to address an audience unschooled in historical facts long forgotten by that time.

One specific passage (1p4) effectively illustrates the way the *Consolatio* is adapted to address its implied audience. Boethius, at the request of Philosophy, explains his conduct and the false accusations leading to his condemnation. In the vernacular version, the historical events are shortened and summed up roughly; in addition, the Boethian monologue is turned into a dialogue that does not include the same arguments that Boethius employed. These are the original Latin and the vernacular texts in parallel columns:

***Consolatio*, 1p4.2–22**[23]	**MS Ital. 40, sec. 3–18**[24]
2 Tum ego collecto in uires animo: [. . .] **3** Haecine est bibliotheca, quam certissimam tibi sedem nostris in laribus ipsa delegeras, in qua mecum saepe residens de humanarum diuinarumque rerum scientia disserebas? **4** Talis habitus talisque uultus erat, cum tecum naturae secreta rimarer, cum mihi siderum uias radio describeres, cum mores nostros totiusque uitae rationem	*Heccum est biblioteca.*[26] **3** "È questa la grande casa di libri in la qual io te è amaistrado quando tu me designavi le vie de le stelle co un baston e tuti li cursi di planeti?"[27] [. . .][28] E imperçò la Filosofia arecorda a Boecio la ca' de li libri, quasi a dir: **11** "Io te amaistrei: se tu vos esser libero, de le richeçe no te soperbir, e per povertade no te desperar; e questo è lo raxonevole motu. Mo tu non a fato quello che

ad caelestis ordinis exempla formares? Haecine praemia referimus tibi obsequentes? **5** Atqui tu hanc sententiam Platonis ore sanxisti beatas fore res publicas, si eas uel studiosi sapientiae regerent uel earum rectores studere sapientiae contigisset. **6** Tu eiusdem uiri ore hanc sapientibus capessendae rei publicae necessariam causam esse monuisti, ne improbis flagitiosisque ciuibus urbium relicta gubernacula pestem bonis ac perniciem ferrent. **7** Hanc igitur auctoritatem secutus, quod a te inter secreta otia didiceram, transferre in actum publicae amministrationis optaui. **8** Tu mihi et qui te sapientium mentibus inseruit deus conscii nullum me ad magistratum nisi commune bonorum omnium studium detulisse. **9** Inde cum improbis graues inexorabilesque discordiae et, quod conscientiae libertas habet, pro tuendo iure spreta potentiorum semper offensio. **10** Quotiens ego Conigastum [. . .].[25] **19** Quid igitur? Nostraene artes ita meruerunt an illos accusatores iustos fecit praemissa damnatio? Itane nihil fortunam puduit si minus accusatae innocentiae, at accusantium uilitas? **20** At cuius criminis arguimur summam quaeres. Senatum dicimur saluum esse uoluisse. **21** Modum desideras? Delatorem, ne documenta deferret, quibus senatum maiestatis reum faceret,

io te dixi, e, se tu vos coreçer, io te fa."[29] *Heccum.*[30] Responde Boecio a la Filosofia e dixe: **12** "Io confermo, mandona, tuto çò che tu dis; anpoi io no deverave aver tanto mal per questa cosa, ché vu savé che vu me amaistrase de defender li boni e no li lasar tormentar a li potenti, e io l'è fato sempre, io son stà solicito de lo comun ben e sempre lasie star lo proprio. **13** Onde, per lo vostro amaistramento, reçevo questo mal?" Responde la Filosofia e dixe: "Ti te crì esser in una grande aversità per quel ben che ti às fato, e questo è lo to eror, ché questa non è aversità, **14** ananti è prosperitade. Li to nimisi te fa questo per invidia: ma no save che lo invidioso brusa dentro e di fuora? Vu savé la vostra pena, mo no savé quella de li invidiosi: non a mè possa nì requia. Sapiè che, quel che vu avé soferto, no lo avé soferto per amor che vu avé mantegnù li boni, **15** me' per invidia de lo bon stado, la qual tera à cresudo per la tua çustixia e per la tua bontade."[31] Dixe Boecio: "Ampoi io me comporterave tuto questo, ma per questo no me torberave, çoè per la invidia, la qual me porta li mie' contrarie; **16** mo lo mio grando dolor è che elli me à acusado inçusta e falsamente, e io son [33v] sentenciado no fiando clamado, nì açitado de verme scusado.[32] E, açò che onnio homo sepa che inçustamente io impedisse criminamur. **22** Quid igitur, o magistra, censes?

son sententiado, io clamo varente vu e lo Signor Dio, **17** li qual no dixe altro ca veritade. Tunca se io no receve merito de ben far, no deverave per lo men recever mal. Ampoi, se li acusadori fose homini de fé, io non deverave <aver> ampoi tanta grameça. **18** A vu, madona Filosofia, laso lo çudixio di questo eror."[33]

Not only does the translator offer only a loose translation of the original text, as one can see in the passage quoted above, but he also introduces several heterogeneous glosses into the vernacular version, that is, within the Boethian lemma and the corresponding erroneous translation. As a result, the translation is continually and purposefully interspersed with didactic-encyclopedic digressions, similar to the glosses often included in the manuscripts of the Latin *Consolatio*.[34] For example, sections 3–10 in the vernacular version (omitted in the section previously quoted) consist of a long digression concerning the astrolabe and the firmament's movement, taken from the *Glosae super Boetium* by William of Conches:

> Devé saver che questo baston è un instrumento co lo qual li astrologi designa lo firmamento; e vien dito questo baston astrolabio; e lì dentro fie depinto li planeti e tuti li signi. E co'l zè lo dito astrolabio? È quasi una rigola, e in cavo de quella è do pignolo, over ponte, sotilemente forade. E quando quelli astrologi vol saver alguna cosa d'alguna stella, çoè in qual luogo sia, over in che segno, over in qual grado del segno, alora leva su e basa çó quelle ponte de quel astrolabio tante fiade in fin ch'el vé quella stella e li so raçi; e, po' che l'à veçuda, elo mostra co' la sta in cielo; e per cotal modo la Filosofia mostra a Boecio l'astrologia. Ancora devé saver che è do movimenti in cielo: l'un è de lo firmamento, e questo è raxionevole, l'altro è di planeti, e questo vien dito eratico. Lo firmamento se muove da oriente e passa per occidente e torna in oriente. Li planeti fa tuto lo contrario: ei se muove de occidente e passa per oriente e torna in occidente; e questo motu vien dito eratico inperçò che una fiada monta e un'altra fiada desmonta. Ma lo motu de lo firmamento sta sempre in un corso, e perçò fi dito firmamento, ché sta sempre in un raxonevole motu. Un simele motu è in l'omo: e 'l sarà plusor homini i qual scomençerà una bona ovra per onor del Signor Dio

> e serà tuto di- [33r] -sposto a servir e cognoscere lo Signor Dio. E, stagando in questo deleto de cognoser lo Creator, adeso se lasarà inganar a le prosperitade, a li deleti del mondo e a le richeçe, le qual li creserà. E per quel richeçe se levarà in superbio. E, quando le perde, elo se mete a desperacio', e per cotal modu perde lo cognosimento del so Creator. E questi homini se move da oriente e va in occidente, çoè in le tenebrie.[35]
>
> [You must know that this stick is an instrument with which the astrologer draws the sky; this stick is called an astrolabe; and inside it all planets and signs have been drawn. And what is this astrolabe? It is like a staff, and on the top of it there are two punched bits. When the astrologers want to know something about a star, where it is, in which sign, in which phase of that sign, they raise those bits many times until they see that star and its rays; and then, when they have seen it, the astrolabe shows how it is in the firmament; and in this way Philosophy demonstrates astrology to Boethius. In addition, you must know that there are two movements in the firmament: the first one is the movement of the firmament, and this is reasonable; the second one is the movement of planets, and it is said to be erratic. The firmament moves from the east, transits through the west, and returns to the east. For planets, it is the contrary: they move from the west, pass through the east, and return to the west. This movement is termed erratic because it goes up once and goes down once. But the movement of the firmament always stays on the same trajectory, [and] that is why it was called firmament, because it always remains in a reasonable movement. A similar movement is inside man: there will be several men who begin a good action to honour God, and they will be willing to serve and know God. But, while they enjoy knowing God, they will deceive themselves by their prosperity and wealth, in which they will be rich. And for these riches they will become supercilious. And, when they lose them, they will become desperate, leaving in that way the knowledge of God. These men move from east to west, that is, towards the darkness.][36]

The inclusion of such extraneous material within the text prevents us from describing the Bucharest version as a mere translation of the *Consolatio*. Indeed, the incidence of the digressions is such that one can label the Bucharest version variously as a remaking, a rewriting, or a commentary.

Given the current state of research, it is difficult to evaluate exactly what part (and to what extent) the changes in the vernacular translation are to be ascribed to the translator, and what parts are the legacy of the consolidated Latin tradition of commentary on Boethius's work. Given the deficiency of detailed information, I could not identify the direct sources of some of the glosses; however, in the first two books, I noticed similarities with the *Glosae* by William; however, comparisons with other Latin commentaries (those of Remigius of Auxerre, Nicolas Trevet, and William of Aragon[37]) and with other vernacular translations have yielded no conclusive results.[38] A systematic comparison of the relationship between the vernacular version and Conches's commentary indicates, nevertheless, that the Bucharest version reveals influence from William's commentary. More specifically, the comparison also revealed that the extraneous material does not always derive directly from the *Glosae* by William but also from the so-called "Pseudo-William" redaction, dated by Nauta from the late thirteenth or early fourteenth century.[39] For example, note the following quotation from *Consolatio* 1 m 1:

Glosae super Boetium, ll. 1–39[40]	**Ms. Ital. 40, sec. 1–17**
CARMINA. Boetius tractaturus de philosophica consolatione primitus se talem ostendit qui indigeat consolatore, scilicet se ostendens miserum. Miser est ille cuius animus mutatur mutatione temporalium extollendo si fiant prospera, deprimendo si fiant aduersa. (rr. 1–7)	**1** *Carmina qui quondam, etcetera.*[41] Questo Boetio, voiando tractare de la consolacion de la Filosofia, imprimeramente mostra la raxon perché illo vol tractare de la dicta consolation. **2** E la cason si sè perché illo sè misero, e li miseri abisogna sempre de consolation. Imperçò che ogno homo non intende propriamentre che cosa è a dire misero, io lo explano:[42] **3** quillo fo dicto misero lo qual laga mutar lo so animo per la piccola stabilitate delle cose temporali, levandose in superbia in lo tempo delle richeçe e di li guadagni, e desperandosi quando fi perse per alcuna acason.
Deinde introducit Philosophiam ad se consolandum, quod non est aliud nisi, cum caro doleret de temporalium amissione, sapientia docebat non esse dolendum inde.	**4** Ed imperçò introduxe Boecio la Filosofia a consolar, la qual cosa no sè oltro a dire che l'omo, ovir la humana carne, non debia aver grameça de la perdicion delle cose

Caro enim concupiscit aduersus spiritum, spiritus autem aduersus carnem. (rr. 7–10)

Et ostendit se miserum competenti genere carminis, id est elegiaco metro. Elegiacum metrum est ubi est hexameter et pentameter uersus, id est uersus sex pedum et uersus quinque pedum. Et dicitur elegiacum, quia ad miseriam describendam inuentum fuit, quamuis hodie eo aliud describatur. Elegia est miseria. Vnde Horatius: Versibus impariter iunctis querimonia primum
post haec inclusa est uoti sententia compos. (rr. 11–18)

Littera sic legatur et continuetur: EGO QVI QVONDAM PEREGI CARMINA. Carmen est scriptum de aliquo delectabili cum metro. FLORENTE STVDIO. Studium est uehemens applicatio animi ad aliquid agendum cum magna uoluntate. Sed studium aliud floret, aliud arescit: floret tempore prosperitatis, arescit tempore aduersitatis. (rr. 19–24)

temporali; **5** e questa è la raxon che, segondo lo dicto de lo savio Salamon, lo spirito grameçoso seca le ossa, onde se genera e nasse la morte.[43]

Imperçò che lo colore naturale s'à studà, ancora se mostra essere misero questo Boetio, per continuare lo so dire.[44] **6** E mostra per çeneration de versi, li quali versi fi dicti Elegiaco. E per dare li meio a cognoser, dixe che questi versi è di se' pie' e de cinque pie', e fi dicti pentametri ed exametri: **7** penta in gresesco è a dire cinque i' latin, exametri in gresesco è a dir se' in latino.[45] E questa çeneration di versi è acatadi da li autori a scriv<e>re le miserie e le aversitade de la çente. Imperçò che dixe Elegiaco, è da intendire che Elegia in gresesco è a dir miseria in latin.[46]

8 E in questo modo devimo intendire la lettera so: Boecio, lo qual, in lo tempo passado, siando lo studio florido, çoè fervente, fi dolci versi e deletevoli. Anançi che segua lo sequente verso, devemo intendire che cosa è studio.[47] **9** Lo studio, secondo lo dir dei savi, è una solicitudine d'animo, lo qual se move a fare una cosa con una spontanea e firma voluntade; emperçò se dixe che lo core de lo homo, çò che se mecte in animo de far, sì fa per lo grande studio che dé.[48] **10** E questo vol dir lo savio quando dise che la gotta de l'acqua cava la piera.[49]

COGOR INIRE MODOS. Boetius uero studio florente carmina peregerat, quia tempore prosperitatis uehementi animi applicatione cum magna uoluntate de aliquo delectabili scripserat. FLEBILIS in tempore aduersitatis, INIRE id est incipere, MAESTOS MODOS id est uersus de mea miseria et aduersitate. Qui dicuntur "modi", quia metro modulantur; "maesti", quia sunt de aduersitate.
Notandum quod isti duo uersus dicti sunt per antithesim, id est contrariam positionem: anti enim est contra, thesis est positio.
Contra hoc quod in primo uersu dicitur "quondam peregi", dicitur in secundo uersu "cogor inire"; proprium est enim dolentis multa incipere et nichil perficere.
Contra hoc quod ibi dicitur "fiorenti studio", hic dicitur "flebilis"; contra "carmina", "maestos modos". Et haec est antithesis, id est contraria positio. (rr. 24-39)

Devimo ancora intendire che quando lo homo no sè agravado de le quatro qualitate, le qual sè dicte le quattro passion de lo corpo, **11** sta in bona disposicion, e lo so studio allo' pò ben florir: allora disimo lo homo eser in bona prosperitate. E, siando Boecio in cotal studio, fé' dolxi versi e delectevili, imperçò che lo so animo non era impaçado da le dicte quatro qualitade del corpo, né signoriçado. **12** Imperçò dise un savio: "Coluy è verasio re lo qual sa ben signoriçare lo so regnamo."[50] E, siando Boetio in cotal stado, illo fé' deletevili versi. **13** E quando illo se laga signoriçare alle quatro qualitade de lo corpo, così l'alegreça, la spirança, la paura e lo dolore, ello fé' un'altra man di versi, e dixe: *Heu flebilis.*[51] Çoè a dir: "Io so' forte gramo, imperçò che so' constrieto a fare grami versi." **14** E questa grameça è venuda a Boecio imperçò che se laga signoriçare allo dolore, lo qual è una de le quatro pasion del corpo. E continua dicando: "So' constrito."[52] **15** Lo primo verso dixe che Boecio avea facto per spacio de un tempo versi multo deletevoli, ed avevali facti spontaneamente, e lo secondo versu dixi che illo è constrictu di fare versi di miseria per la grande grameça che avea de le so cose, **16** e di versi bon li qual àve perduti. Ancora è plu manifesto che Boecio era forte plen de dolori, ché e primeramente dixe dolci versi, e po' adesso dixe grameçosi. **17** Anzi, non è da maraveigiar, on po' che è usança che, quando l'omo è abastioso, dixemo una cosa, mo' un'altra, inperçò che la inbastia de lo cor no lo lassa continuar lo so dire.[53]

As noted earlier, the vernacular version in the Bucharest manuscript does not present a close translation of the *Consolatio*. Despite its title (*Prohemium translacionis Boecii De Consolacione Philosophie*), the vernacular version does not aim simply to render the original text, but rather to offer a complete *corpus* of glosses alongside a serviceable translation (albeit inaccurate and free) of the original Latin; in addition, the synoptic comparison with William's *Glosae* corroborates the proposition that the vernacular version does not represent a direct translation of the commentary of Conches. The Latin text indeed is often either abridged or expanded in the vernacular version (see above, sec. 2, 5, 7, 8, 10); moreover, the quotations within the Latin commentary frequently are changed (as in sec. 5 and 9–10), or thoroughly left out (as occurs with the Horace quotation mentioned by William in lines 17–18), and quotations missing in the *Glosae* are added *ex novo* (see sec. 10 and 12).

The sources used by the translator, as well as the ways in which they are presented, suggest further that the implied audience/readership did not have an "élite" classical education. If one is to except the sources deriving from the *Glosae*, the translator includes Eberardo Alamanno, the *Disticha Catonis*, Salomon's proverbs, the Holy Bible (above all Psalms and the New Testament). Also, there are cases in which the quotations introduced in the *Glosae* are contextualized, so to speak, within a narrating frame, probably to help an audience ignorant of the sources, who otherwise would not be able to recognize the connection. An example of this practice is found in meter 1 of the translation:

Glosae super Boetium, lines 55–63[54]
Sed notandum est quod dicit "ueris fletibus". Sunt enim quidam ex adulatione et non ueri, ut ait Iuuenalis, cum de adulatore loqueretur: *Flet,*

MS Ital. 40, sec. 23–26
Dé notar che Boecio dise verase planti. Ello è in do manier planti. Fa una generacion d'amisi, li qual è amisi a tempo. **24** Dixe Juvenal che illo era uno lo qual era vicario

si lacrimas conspexit amici, nec dolet. Sunt alii et ueri qui ex dolore uel pietate proueniunt. Aliter potest legi uersus iste, scilicet quod "elegi" sit genitiuus hoc modo: CAMENAE LACERAE DICTANT MICHI SCRIBENDA ET RIGANT MEA ORA ELEGI id est miseri.[55]	de un re de corona, lo qual era sì giunto de grande amore co·llo re, che quello re ne feva negocta sença parola del suo vicario. Caçi caso che lo re se infirma, e fé' testamento, e lassa lo rignamo al suo vicario. **25** E morì lo re. Lo vicario, videndose re, continenti scomença a plançire: no che avesse grameça de lo re che era morto, ma per grandi alegreça de lo regnamo che l'era romaso. **26** E questi planti no è simili a quelli de Boecio, imperçò che quelli de Boecio proçedea da lo cor di grandi dolor che illo avea.[56]

This comparison suggests that the vernacular version was produced for use in primary schools. However, other features differentiate it from typical school handbooks; for instance, the translation presents only a few grammatical and rhetorical annotations, sporadic and short.[57] The vernacular version also omits William's explanations regarding the Latin phrases: in the fragment quoted above, lines 32–39 of the Latin commentary have no corresponding lines in the Bucharest version, which instead develops the description of Boethius's state of mind (sec. 15–17). Note also, in the sections 23–26 the Italian version omits William's gloss on the possible variations of a Latin sentence (lines 61–63). In sum, the Bucharest version seems to prefer those passages from the Latin commentary that deal with moral, encyclopedic, and content issues, while omitting the formal elements of the *Consolatio*, which were widely available in school textbooks.

Furthermore, the vernacular version also introduces digressions absent from the Conchian commentary. A striking case is represented by *Consolatio* 2p4, in which the vernacular version completely discards William's commentary;[58] in Boethius's text, Philosophy urges Boethius not to yield to desperation, arguing that he still has the benefit of the love and faithfulness of his father-in-law Symmachus, and the honesty and virtue of his wife Rusticiana;[59] the translator identifies Boethius's wife erroneously as "madona Erpes" (sec. 5) and an often-quoted epitaph ascribed to her is included in its entirety:

Misera la mia vita plena de dolor:
Nata sum in Sicilia, nobele region,
Lonçe son arivada da la mia maxon
Per conservar integro lo mio amor,
Lo qual a torto reçeve condanaxon
Di star per sempre in scura bandiçaxon.
Lo mio spirito non è çença dolor,
Remebrandome de sì nobele signor.
La mia luxe me è forte smarida,
Siandome da là di<s>tolta[60] la mia vita.
Longa demorança de la morte
Me fa star confusa intro le porte.
La mia posança, che era plena d'oro,
D'arçento, de palaxii e dignitate,
La è desmetuda e versa in povretade.
E dimoro me<n>dicando in porticali
De li templi, i qual reçeta
Ognunca persona che caçe en defeta.
Di çò me reclamo a lo Fiiol de Dio,
Che conserve e salve lo corpo mio,
Che omo vivente no posa contaminar
Quel che apartien al matrimonio natural. (lines 6–11)

[Unfortunate my painful life
I was born in Sicily, noble region,
from my home I went far away
to preserve intact my love
that unfairly is condemned
to be forever banned.
My soul is not without pain
remembering that lord so noble.
I lost my light
because they took away my life.
The long permanence of death
makes me stay confused at home.
My richness, full of gold, silver, palaces, and nobility,
is declined and in misery.
Now I live begging in front of the temples
that house all persons who fell into difficulties.
I ask the Son of God
to preserve and to save my body.
That nobody can contaminate
what belongs to the natural marriage.]

This epitaph (thought by some earlier scholars to have been the first wife of Boethius), written in Latin, can be found in some manuscripts of the *Consolatio* and in some of the schoolbooks registered and described by Gabriella Pomaro.[61] In this case, therefore, the anonymous author of the Bucharest version relies on traditional sources (of modest level, comparable to those used in introductory school manuals).

As mentioned previously, the relationships between the Bucharest version and the Conchian *Glosae* merely involve the first two books. As for the last three books, the Bucharest version seems to rely on another source, while following the Boethian text more closely (without, however, offering a direct translation of the original) but while analyzing the moral content of the work (such as the question of the existence of evil, the relationship between providence and fate, the analysis of the essence of true bliss and how the human being can attain it, and the relationship between divine prescience and free will).[62]

Consideration of a passage from the beginning of Book 3, prose 12 in the vernacular version is instructive:

> *Tum ego: Platoni.*[63] En la ultima prosa del primo libro son proponude quattro question sovra le quale sè profundado tuto lo libro: l'una chi reze questo mundo, l'oltra qual sia la fine de le cose, la terça che cosa sia homo, la quarta en che modo Deo reze questo mondo. E questa quarta, grevissima, resta mo' principalmente a declarare. A la quale question respose Boecio ello non l'atendeva,[64] ed emperçò non ge saveva respondere; e non serà ben declarada se non complido tuto lo libro, e terço, e quarto, e quinto. Ed en questa prosa se contene una sola cosa principale, e compagnada de quatro cose. La principale è en che modo Deo reze questo mundo zeneralmente. La compagna èn la prima: che Deo fese [65v] lo mundo, lo quale non pode esser da sé enstesso. La seconda che Deo reçe lo mundo per bene, çoè per sé ensteso, chi è lo bene, non per far bene. La terça è che Deo reze lo mundo soavemente per amor e per utilità, non per tirania. La quarta recoçe sumariamente tuto quello chi è dicto da ochi in perpetua in qua,[65] recomandando lo modo de procedere. Adonqua dise Boecio a Filosofia: "Io consento a la opinion de Plato che la anima fo creada en celo plena de siencia e de virtù, e non sì como carta nuda e rasa, e perdeva en elo corpo lo particulare e reteniva lo universale." Mo' propone Filosofia: "Io te voio redure a memoria, e mostrare en questo modo Deo reçe questo mundo, la qual cosa tu disisti de sovra, en la ultima prosa del primo libro, che tu non entendivi. Ma, en prima, io te voio provare che questo mondo non

fo da sé, inançi fo creado da Deo. E po' serà plu leve cosa credere lo rezimento. E che lo mundo non sia da sé, io lo provo così: questo mondo è componudo de parte contrarie e inimige entro sé; la tera è frida e seca, l'aqua è freda e humida, lo aero è coldo e humido, lo fogo è coldo e seco; sì che queste cose non serìa vignude a compagnia ensemel, se posança e virtude de oltri non avese constrete quele, e per soa sapiencia non avesse temperade, ordena- [66r] –de, ed apasade quelle. Ancora, queste cose contrarie non regnarav'e<n> pase ensemel, se la posança, e la sapiencia, e la bontade <d>e alcuno non constrenzese quelle. Ancora, lo ordene de la natura non procederìa sì certo, e non averìa sì certi movimenti per loci, per tempi, per operacion, per quantità, per qualità, per ordene, sença posança e sença rezimento de alcun. E questa cosa de tanta posança fi dicta Deo per usado vocabolo de tuta zente." (sec. 1–10)

[In the last prosa of the first book, four issues are proposed, and the entire book is founded on them: the first one, who holds this world; the second one, what is the end of the things; the third one, what is man; the fourth one, how God holds this world. And this forth one, so important, still has to be defined. Boethius said that he could not understand this issue and so he could not answer it. It will be clarified when the entire book, and the third, the fourth, and the fifth ones will be finished. In this prosa there is a principal issue, accompanied by four secondary issues. The principal one is how God holds this world generally. The first secondary issue is that God created the world, that it could not be created on its own. The second one, that God holds the world for good, that is for himself, that is good and not to do good. The third one, that God holds kindly the world, for love and usefulness, not for tyranny. The fourth one, a summary of what has been said from the beginning until here, indicating the way to proceed. Boethius said to Philosophy: "I agree with the opinion of Plato that the soul was created in the sky full of science and virtue, and in the body it lost the particular and kept the universal." Now Philosophy answered: "I want to show you how God holds this world, the issue in the last prosa of the first book that you said you could not understand. But, first of all, I want to demonstrate to you that this world is not made on its own but was created by God. And then it will be easier to understand how God holds the world. I will demonstrate it to you in this way: this world is made up of opposing and inimical things: earth is cold and dry, water is cold and wet, air is warm and wet, fire is warm and dry; so that all these things would not have been able to stay together if the power and virtue of someone else did not force them. And if the wisdom of someone else did not make them softer, arrange, and reconcile them. Again, all these things would not have been able to reign together if the power, the wisdom, and the goodness of someone did not oblige them to do so. Furthermore, their nature would not have followed places, times, actions, quantities, and qualities without the power and the soverignty of someone. And this so powerful thing is commonly called God."]

The introduction, which occupies sections 1–5, is missing; sections 6–10, in turn, represents a nonliteral translation of the original text.[66] As one can see, the vernacular version displays different styles of translation, possibly because it draws on different sources.

In general, the translator's viewpoint does not differ from the traditional christianising exegesis of the *Consolatio*, already present in the commentary of Remigius of Auxerre.[67] For instance, in *Consolatio* 4p3, the commentator exposes Boethius's doctrine, according to which men, once having achieved bliss, become gods themselves. The commentator quotes from the Sacred Scriptures to show the agreement between Boethius and Revealed Truth (although the Boethian concept of "bliss through partaking" was largely questioned by exegetes, since it seemed to follow only partially Christian orthodoxy):

> Dicto è de sovra che lo bene e la biadança è una medema cosa, e così tuti li boni eno biadi, e che tuti li biadi erano dei. Ma uno era Dio per natura, ed erano plusor dei per participasone. Unde Psalmista: "Ego dixi: dii estis, et filii Excelsi omnes."[68] (sec. 7–8)
>
> [As mentioned above, good and beatitude are one and the same, so that all good men are blessed, and all blessed men are gods. But one of them was God by nature, and all the other ones were gods by participation. According to the Psalmist: "*Ego dixi: dii estis, et filii Excelsi omnes.*"]

Usually, when the translator is confronted with the doctrines in Boethius that are at odds with Christian orthodoxy, he merely underlines the discrepancy without expressing his own opinions about it. For instance, at 3m9, which was the fulcrum of the philosophical exegesis of the *Consolatio* in the Latin commentaries,[69] in the Bucharest manuscript, *α transcribes two different renderings to highlight the famo*us meter (the first part of the second rendering is copied by β, up to the comment to line 16, due perhaps to an anomaly that occurred during the change in hand). The first rendering concerns only the first three lines, while the second relates to the whole metre; sections 5–8 (quoted below) illustrates the contradiction between ancient philosophers and the Church about the concept of the eternity of the world:[70]

> Ché entencion de Arestotele, e de Plato, e de Boecio, e de tuti li filosofi antisi, fo ch'el mondo fose eterno, sença scomençamento e sença fine, ch'eli non podi vedere nì scomençamento né fine. E pareti a quelli che lo mundo pode sempre essere stado e sempre podere durare per natura. Ma, per revelacion, Deo ha mostrado altre cose. Unde se dirà en la tridera prosa de questa opinion. Ed è da redure li vocabili a le cose, e non le cose a li vocabili, ché la verità e la falsità è da parte de le cose e non de li vocabili. Unde eli dirà così: "Se nu volemo enponere digni nomi a le cose, sequando opinion de Plato, nu deremo <Deo> essere eterno e'l mondo essere perpetuo. Mo questa opinion è contra la Clesia, dicando: "In principio creavit Deus celum et terram, et iudicabit Deus seculum per ignem."[71] (sec. 5–8)
>
> [The opinion of Aristotle, Plato, Boethius, and all the ancient philosophers was that the world is eternal, without beginning and end, and that they could not see any beginning or end. They thought the world has always been and can last forever. But God revealed many things about which it will be written in the third prosa. The words have to be brought back to the things and not the things to the words, because truth and falsity arrive from the things and not from the words. So he will say: "If we want to give adequate names to the things, following the opinion of Plato, we will say that God is eternal and the world is perpetual. This opinion goes against the Church, which says: '*In principio creavit Deus celum et terram, et iudicabit Deus seculum per ignem.*'"]

In other passages, the translator underlines discrepancies between Boethius and Revealed Truth (above all while commenting on books 4 and 5). This dispute proves that he was neither completely ignorant of the philosophical questions the work engages nor unaware of the traditional exegetic dispute concerning it, even if he disregarded compelling criticism. In fact, he apparently was attempting to distill moral teachings useful for the readers.

To conclude, the Bucharest rendering of the *Consolatio* appears to be similar to translations mentioned by Thomas Ricklin in a compelling essay on the reception of the *Consolatio* in Italy;[72] their authors were active in northern Italy in the fourteenth century, and they too offered a moral and Christian interpretation of the work and an appraisal of its traditional Latin exegesis with the purpose of educating a humble and poorly schooled audience.[73]

My analysis indicates that the translator used matter from the tradition, borrowed from various sources, or, more likely, already merged within some previous text.[74] At this preliminary stage of research, it is not possible to trace back more accurately the trajectory of the text. However, it seems that the cultural environment from which the glosses and the quotations originate is of a primary school level. As such, both the didactic exposition and the introduction of the glosses (that provide the readers with ideas barely related to the *auctor*'s reasoning) may be explained. However, I believe that Ital. 40 does not derive only from a school manual, given the nearly total absence of grammatical notes; it is possible that the elimination of such a typology of glosses, systematic even when it strictly adheres to the Conchian *Glosae*, is to be ascribed to the translator, who was little interested in Latin sentence structures. Rather, he is interested in providing an analysis of the moral scope of the *Consolatio*.

This hypothesis is confirmed both by the setting of the *prohemium* and the *tituli* and by the lemmatic structure, all customary elements in the Latin tradition. Moreover, the digressions reveal great heterogeneity from a structural viewpoint: hence, one might suppose that they have been taken from the glosses of another tradition, which often accompanied the manuscripts of the work by Boethius. The structure is, in fact, fragmented in the vernacular version; the consistency of the original argument dwindles, and no other coherent structure emerges. Indeed, the continuity in the expositions depends primarily upon the lemmata, and by cross-references to the original text: thus, the vernacular version needs the support of the original text and shows its proximity to the Latin glosses.

The discrepancy between the first two books (in which the digressions are more frequent and draw from William's *Glosae*) and the last three has yet to be elucidated; from the sections analyzed previously, it appears that William's commentary and the "Pseudo-William" redaction were not the sole sources of the Bucharest version, and not even for the first two books. The difference between the first and the second parts of the vernacular version could be due to the fact that the translator resorted to a previous text in which different materials already were present rather than to different sources. In fact, at the structural level, the reciprocal relationships between the prologue and the commentary, and the intertextual references between the various books (essential to the description), prove an original unity, not a late addition.

Therefore, this Italian version should be viewed as an indeterminate, transitional version—between commentary and translation, remaking and vernacularization. Its complex structure proves the success and popularity that the *Consolatio* continued to hold towards the end of the fourteenth century, to belie the opinion of Philosophy in 2p7 about the transience of the memory of human writings: "Quid ipsa scripta proficiant, quae cum suis auctoribus premit longior atque obscura uetustas?" (*Consolatio* 2p7.13, p. 33).

NOTES

[*]I am very grateful to Professor Anna Maria Babbi and Professor Alfonso D'Agostino for their scholarly guidance during the development of this study; Dr. Roberto Tagliani for his editorial advice regarding Italian quotations; my friends Maurizio Vito and Scott Millspaugh for their help in translating my article into English; and Professor Dario Brancato, who helped me with the final revision of this article.

[1] The systematic census of the manuscripts of the *Consolatio* began in 1995 under the aegis of the Warburg Institute. To date, the following volumes have been published: Margaret T. Gibson, Lesley Smith, and Joseph Ziegler, eds., *Great Britain and Ireland*, vol. 1 of *Codices Boethiani: A Conspectus of Manuscripts of the Works of Boethius* (London: Warburg Institute, 1995); Lesley Smith and Theodore Christchev, eds., *Austria, Belgium, Luxembourg, The Netherlands, Sweden, Switzerland*, vol. 2 of *Codices Boethiani* (London: Warburg Institute, 2001); Marina Passalacqua et al., eds., *Italy and the Vatican City*, vol. 3 of *Codices Boethiani* (London: Warburg Institute, 2001); Lesley Smith, ed., *Portugal and Spain*, vol. 4 of *Codices Boethiani* (London: Warburg Institute, 2010). The methods used by these authors have drawn some criticism; see for example Fabio Troncarelli's review published in *Cahiers de Civilisation médiévale* 41 (1998): 305–07, and by Robert Black's assessment in Robert Black and Gabriella Pomaro, *La "Consolazione della filosofia" nel Medioevo e nel Rinascimento italiano: Libri di scuola e glosse nei manoscritti fiorentini* (Florence: SISMEL-Edizioni del Galluzzo, 2000), xxi and 36n18. See also: Fabio Troncarelli, *Tradizioni perdute: la "Consolatio philosophiae" nell'Alto Medioevo* (Florence: Antenore, 1981); idem, *"Boethiana aetas": Modelli grafici e fortuna manoscritta della "Consolatio Philosophiae" tra IX e XII secolo* (Alessandria: Edizioni dell'Orso, 1987).

[2] William of Conches, *Guillelmus de Conchis Glosae super Boetium*, ed. Lodi Nauta (Turnhout: Brepols, 1999).

[3] See Black and Pomaro, *La Consolazione della filosofia.*

[4] See Pierre Courcelle, *La "Consolation de Philosophie" dans la tradition littéraire: antécédents et postérité de Boèce* (Paris: Études augustiniennes, 1967), 317–44, especially 318, 336–37, 318–19, and 321–22.

[5] The following scholars sustain the hypothesis of an exclusively rhetorical and grammatical use of the *Consolatio* in the fourteenth and fifteenth centuries: Gabriella Federici Vescovini, "Due commenti inediti del XIV secolo al *De Consolatione Philosophiae* di Boezio," *Rivista critica di storia della filosofia* 13 (1958): 384–14; Courcelle, *La Consolation*

de Philosophie, 317–44; the Florentine documents analyzed by Black and Pomaro show instead that the *Consolatio* was used midway through the *curriculum studiorum*, precisely after studying *auctores minores* and before devoting attention to the *maiores*: Black and Pomaro, *La Consolazione della filosofia*, 32. On this specific issue, see Black on Gabriella Federici Vescovini's assessment on the exclusively grammatical character of the commentary of Giovanni Travesio to the *Consolatio*: ibid., 45n199.

[6] For the reception of the *Consolatio* in vernacular literature, see Fabio Troncarelli, "Boezio," in *Lo spazio letterario del Medioevo, 2: Il Medioevo volgare*, vol. III, *La ricezione del testo*, ed. Piero Boitani, Mario Mancini, and Alberto Vàrvaro (Roma: Salerno, 2003), 315–16, and Fabio Troncarelli, "Afterword: Boethius in Late Antiquity and the Early Middle Ages" in *A Companion to Boethius in the Middle Ages*, ed. Noel Harold Kaylor, Jr. and Philip Edward Phillips, Brill's Companions to the Christian Tradition 30 (Leiden: Brill, 2012), 519–49; on the difficulty to define the users of vernacular translations, see Loris Sturlese, *Filosofia in volgare, Filosofia in volgare nel Medioevo*, Atti del convegno della S.I.S.P.M (Lecce, 27–9 settembre 2002), ed. Nadia Bray and Lorisf Sturlese (Louvain-La Neuve: Fédération internationale d'études médiévales, 2003), 9.

[7] Glynnis M. Cropp, for example, published a critical edition of the anonymous *Livre de Boece de Consolacion*, which has been transmitted by a great number of witnesses and in two different redactions (the older of which, without glosses, was ascribed previously to Jean de Meun because it included his prologue to the *Livres de Confort*); the second redaction, anonymous, seems to be the most popular among the French versions in the fourteenth and the fifteenth centuries. This case shows how anonymous versions have often assumed a fundamental role in the history of the vernacular reception of the *Consolatio*. See *Le Livre de Boece de Consolacion*, ed. Glynnis M. Cropp (Genève: Droz, 2006).

[8] See, for example: Cesare Segre, "I volgarizzamenti del Due e Trecento," in *Lingua, stile e società* (Milano: Feltrinelli, 1963), 49–78; and idem, "I volgarizzamenti," in *Lo spazio letterario del Medioevo, 1: Il Medioevo latino*, vol. III, *La ricezione del testo*, ed. Guglielmo Cavallo, Claudio Leonardi, and Enrico Menestò (Roma: Salerno, 1995), 271–98. An important overview of the most recent studies on vernacular translations in Italy is that of Alessandra Coco and Riccardo Gualdo, *Enciclopedismo ed erudizione nei volgari italiani: una panoramica sugli studi recenti, Filosofia in volgare nel Medioevo.* Atti del Convegno della Società Italiana per il Pensiero Medievale (SISPM), Lecce, 27–29 settembre 2002 (Louvain-la-Neuve: Fédération Internationale des Instituts d'Etudes Médiévales, 2003), 265–317. See also Alfonso D'Agostino, "Itinerari e forme della prosa," in *Storia della letteratura italiana*, vol. 1 (Roma: Salerno, 1995), 574.

[9] See Carlo Milanesi, *Il Boezio e l'Arrighetto: Volgarizzamenti del buon secolo, riveduti su' codici fiorentini* (Florence: Barbera, 1864); Troncarelli, "Boezio," 325–26; Giuseppina Brunetti, "Guinizzelli, il non più oscuro Maestro Giandino e il Boezio di Dante," in *Intorno a Guido Guinizzelli*, Atti della Giornata di Studi (Università di Zurigo, 16 giugno 2000), ed. Luciano Rossi and Sara Alloatti Boller (Alessandria: Edizioni dell'Orso, 2002), 181–83; Silvia Albesano, *"Consolatio Philosophiae" volgare: volgarizzamenti e tradizioni discorsive nel Trecento italiano* (Heidelberg: Universitätsverlag Winter, 2006), 45–53.

[10] See Thomas Ricklin, "... *Quello non conosciuto da molti libro di Boezio*: Hinweise zur *Consolatio Philosophiae* in Norditalien," in *Boethius in the Middle Ages: Latin and Vernacular Traditions of the "Consolatio philosophiae,"* ed. Maarten J. F. M. Hoenen and Lodi Nauta (Leiden: Brill, 1997), 267–85, on the reception of the *Consolatio* (and on the legend of Boethius).

[11] For example, see the works by Giuseppina Brunetti on the unpublished vernacular translation by Giandino of Carmignano: Brunetti, "Guinizzelli," 155–91, and "Preliminari all'edizione del volgarizzamento della *Consolatio Philosophiae* di Boezio attribuito al maestro Giandino da Carmignano," in *Studi sui volgarizzamenti italiani due-trecenteschi*, ed. Paolo Rinoldi and Gabriella Ronchi (Roma: Viella, 2005), 9–45. For the most recent study on the reception of Boethius's *Consolatio* in Italy between the fourteenth and sixteenth centuries, see Dario Brancato, "Readers and Interpreters of the *Consolatio* in Italy, 1300–1550," in *A Companion to Boethius in the Middle Ages*, ed. Noel Harold Kaylor, Jr. and Philip Edward Phillips, Brill's Companions to the Christian Tradition 30 (Leiden: Brill, 2012), 357–411.

[12] See Serena Lunardi, "Un inedito commento italiano trecentesco alla *Consolatio Philosophiae*," *ACME* 57 (2004): 297–321.

[13] As for the format and the identification of the *ex-libris*, I consulted Giambattista di Crollalanza, *Dizionario storico-blasonico delle famiglie nobili e notabili italiane estinte e fiorenti*, vol. 1 (Pisa: Presso la Direzione del Giornale Araldico, 1886), 110; Achille Bertarelli and David H. Prior, *Gli Ex Libris Italiani* (Milano: Hoepli, 1902), 112–13; and Carlo Frati, *Dizionario bio-bibliografico dei bibliotecari e bibliofili italiani dal sec. XIV al XIX* (Firenze: Olschki, 1933), 34. The sales catalogue of Burghesiana collection, edited by Vincenzo Menozzi (*Catalogue de la Bibliothèque de S.E.D. Paolo Borghese prince de Sulmona* (Roma: Menozzi, 1892), 689, includes the Bucharest manuscript in the list of the fifteenth-century manuscripts, labelled number 4583. A brief description by the author reads: "Traduction en langue vulgaire du livre 'De Consolatione Philosophiae' d'Anicio Manlio Severino Boezio. Sur parchemin, in-4°, du XV siècle, de 106 ff. non numerotés, en format in-8°, avec très belle écriture minuscule; reliure en cuir du XVIII siècle." The manuscript was auctioned in June 2, 1893. The sample I consulted, which is held in the Catholic University Library in Milan, is not the original used by Menozzi during the auction, and therefore it does not offer information about the buyers. Nonetheless, it is safe to assume that the manuscript left Italy following that event. See Lunardi, "Un inedito commento italiano," 309–10.

[14] It overlooks 1m6, 2m1, 2m2, 2m5, 2p8, 3m3 (of which only the incipit is mentioned), 3p5, and 3m5; it is worth noting that all these shortcomings are in section α, not in β or γ.

[15] For the situation of *tituli* and rubrics in Ital. 40, see Lunardi, "Un inedito commento italiano," 307. For the analysis of the relationships between text and paratext in the manuscripts, see *Intorno al testo: Tipologie del corredo esegetico e soluzioni editoriali*, Atti del Convegno (Urbino, 1–3 ottobre 2001) (Roma: Salerno, 2003), especially Furio Brugnolo's essay on the relationships between text and paratext in the manuscripts that preserve the translation by Alberto della Piagentina: Furio Brugnolo, "Testo e paratesto: la presentazione del testo fra Medioevo e Rinascimento," 41–60.

[16] For the use of the "lemmatic" commentary in William of Conches, see William of Conches, *Glosae*, ed. Nauta, xxvi–xxx; for the redactions of the commentary by Remigius of Auxerre composed in the form of "continuous" commentary, see Colette Jeudy, "L'oeuvre de Remi d'Auxerre: État de la question," in *L'école carolingienne d'Auxerre: de Murethach à Remi (830–908) (Entretiens d'Auxerre 1989)*, ed. Dominique Iogna-Prat, Colette Jeudy, and Guy Lobrichon (Paris: Beauchesne, 1991), 374–80; see also Lodi Nauta, "The Scholastic Context of the Boethius Commentary by Nicholas Trevet," in Hoenen and Nauta,

Boethius in the Middle Ages, 41–67; Black and Pomaro, *La Consolazione della filosofia*, 14–23; Carmen Olmedilla Herrero, "Commentaire de Guillaume d'Aragon sur *De Consolatione Philosophiae* de Boèce," in *L'"Orphée" de Boèce au Moyen Âge*, ed. J. Keith Atkinson and Anna Maria Babbi (Verona: Fiorini, 2000), 181–95.

[17] I treat the *prohemium* in the Bucharest manuscript in Serena Lunardi, "Il prologo di un volgarizzamento inedito della *Consolatio Philosophiae*: ipotesi sull'*intentio operis*," *Studi mediolatini e volgari* 53 (2007): 181–226.

[18] In her article, "The Medieval French Tradition," in Hoenen and Nauta, *Boethius in the Middle Ages*, 254, Glynnis M. Cropp explains:

> Prologues were either derived and translated from Latin prologues to the *Consolatio* or a commentary [. . .], or composed by the translator as a preface [. . .]. The conventional components are a short biography of Boethius, a summary of the moral purpose and the development of the philosophical argument in dialogue form and the explanation of Boethius's alternation of verse and prose. Some or all these elements normally accompany a statement on the translation process. Translators aimed to translate into a vernacular a Latin text which lay readers and sometimes clerics found difficult to understand [. . .]. The translators express an almost conventional concern about *mot a mot* translation and the increased number of words required to convey clearly the full meaning of Boethius's complex thought.

Personal statements by the translators are visible in many versions (for example, in those by Jean de Meun, Alberto della Piagentina, and Bonaventura da Demena). An analysis of the reciprocal similarities or differences would be helpful in defining the landscape of vernacular reception and reinterpreting of the *Consolatio.* See Venceslas L. Dedeck-Héry, "Boethius *De Consolatione* by Jean de Meun," *Mediaeval Studies* 14 (1952): 168; Salvatore Battaglia, *Il Boezio e l'Arrighetto nelle versioni del Trecento* (Torino: Unione Tipografico—Editrice Torinese, 1929), 5; Anna Maria Babbi, *"Consolatio Philosophiae," una versione veneta: Verona, Biblioteca Civica, ms. 212* (Milano: Franco Angeli, 1995), 91. Furthermore, one should account for the omission of the *prologo d'autore* in other versions, which instead include forewards taken directly from the Latin commentaries or from the most famous vernacular versions in the translation. This case is visible, for example, in *Livre de Boece de Consolacion*, quoted previously. See Glynnis M. Cropp, "Le Prologue de Jean de Meun et *Le Livre de Boece de Consolacion*," *Romania* 103 (1982): 278–98; *Le Livre de Boece de Consolacion*, ed. Cropp, 15–17, and, more recently, "Boethius in Medieval France: Translations of the *De Consolatione Philosophiae* and Literary Influence," in *A Companion to Boethius in the Middle Ages*, ed. Noel Harold Kaylor, Jr. and Philip Edward Phillips, Brill's Companions to the Christian Tradition 30 (Leiden: Brill, 2012), 319–55.

[19] Richard W. Hunt, "The Introduction to the *Artes* in the Twelfth Century," in *Studia mediaevalia in honorem admodum reverendi patris R. J. Martin* (Bruges: De Tempel, 1948). Concerning *accessus ad auctores*, see Alastair J. Minnis, "The Influence of Academic Prologues on the Prologues and Literary Attitudes of Late-Medieval English Writers," *Mediaeval Studies* 43 (1981): 342–83; Alastair J. Minnis and A. B. Scott, *Medieval Literary Theory and Criticism, c. 1100–c. 1375: The Commentary-Tradition* (Oxford: Clarendon Press, 1991), 12–36; also, see Maria Luisa Meneghetti, *Il pubblico dei trovatori: Ricezione e riuso dei testi lirici cortesi fino al XIV secolo*, 2nd ed. (Torino: Einaudi, 1992), 209–44. For a general overview, see

Jacqueline Hamesse, ed., *Les prologues médiévaux*, Actes du Colloque international organisé par l'Academia Belgica et l'École française de Rome avec le concours de la F.I.D.E.M. (Roma, 26–28 mars 1998) (Turnhout: Brepols, 2000), and, in particular, the essays by Barbara Faes De Mottoni, "I prologhi dei Commenti al Vangelo di Luca di Giovanni della Rochelle e di Bonaventura," 471–513, and Jacques Dalarun, "Épilogue," 639–61.

[20] See: Meneghetti, *Il pubblico*, 231–32.

[21] Babbi, *"Consolatio Philosophiae,"* 91.

[22] The prohemium of Ital. 40 is divided into two main sections: the first one concerns the main issue of *Consolatio,* according to the anonymous author, after briefly treating Boethius's exile and captivity: Boethius wants to show how it is possible, in a world governed by Divine Providence, that secular goods are given to the wicked, while good people endure injury. The second one concerns the content of each book, above all with Boethius's methodology in treating the above-mentioned question in his work.

[23] Hereafter, Consolatio stands for the following critical edition of the Consolatio: *Boethius, De Consolatione Philosophiae: Opuscula theologica, Editio altera*, ed. Claudio Moreschini, Bibliotheca Teubneriana, 2nd ed. (Munich: Saur, 2005).

[24] The transcription given here of the text is from the critical edition of MS Ital. 40 on which I am working. I proofread the text, separated the words, standardized spelling variants where they were not motivated by etymological reasons or other well-documented causes; moreover, I added capital letters, punctuation marks, quotation marks (to mark direct discourse), and I have expanded all abbreviations. The bold numbers stand for the paragraphs in which I have divided the text to ease its consultation. My interventions in case of lacunae are marked by angled brackets (<. . .>), while I use square brackets ([. . .]) in case of corrections due to an incorrect transmission of the text, and to show the leaf number, followed by r (recto) and v (verso). To avoid a lengthy discussion on language and spelling of the manuscript, here is a provisional list of my editorial choices to distinguish homographs: a «to» (prep.), *à* «he has» or «you have»/ ca «than» *(sec*ond term of comparison), ca' «house»/ co «with», co' «like»/ de «of», de' «must, has to», dè «gave»/ è «is», but also «I have», e' «he», e «and» (conjunction)/ en «*in», èn «they a*re» (third plural person of "to be")/ fé «faith», fé' «he did»/ me «mi», mè «never», me' «but»/ mo «but», mo' «now»/ po' *and puo'* «*then», pò and* può «can» / se «if» (conj.), «si» (reflexive pronoun), sè «it is», sé «itself»/so «his/her», so' «I am / they *are» (f*irst singular and third plural of "to be")/ çò «this», çó «down».

[25] Here, I omit a long part of Consolatio (sec. 10–18), in which Boethius addresses the accusations for which he was condemned, producing a detailed self-defense that is completely overlooked by the translator. Compare this episode with what Alberto della Piagentina, who closely translates Boethius's argument, writes: Battaglia, *Il Boezio e l'Arrighetto,* 24–32.

[26] See *Consolatio* 1p4.3, *Haecine est bibliotheca.* I have left uncorrected the mistaken lemmata I found in Ital. 40 because they could derive directly from errors found in the antigraph or in possible sources. The correct version of the lemma, according to Bieler's edition, is in the footnotes. A systematic comparison of the variants in the transcriptions of the Boethian lemmata within the entire manuscripts tradition (including commentaries and vernacular versions included) could prove to be pivotal in the definition of the relationships among the manuscripts of the original by Boethius, the quotations of which represent themselves an indirect tradition.

[27] In *Consolatio,* Boethius poses this question to Philosophy; in the vernacular version, Philosophy herself addresses Boethius.

[28] Here, I omit a digression (missing in Consolatio) about the astrolabe and the firmament's movement (see *below).*

[29] This is a moralizing explanation by Philosophy completely missing in the corresponding section of the Latin text, in which Philosophy does not speak, permitting Boethius to express the causes of his wretchedness.

[30] See above, n. 26; the lemma is the same.

[31] In this case, too, Philosophy's reply is completely absent in Consolatio, which entirely constructs this prose as a monologue. The introduction of Philosophy's comment in the vernacular version is intended to be moralizing.

[32] The interpretation of this section (which is, in all likeliness, corrupted) is uncertain.

[33] In the second part of the vernacular version of this prose (sec. 18–26), there is a brief mention of the accusations his detractors moved to Boethius, with particular attention to the one of sacrilege (sec. 22–26).

[34] A convincing essay on the techniques of introduction of glosses in the Italian translations is Valentina Pollidori, *La glossa come tecnica di traduzione: Diffusione e tipologia nei volgarizzamenti italiani della Bibbia*; *La Bibbia in italiano fra Medioevo e Rinascimento,* Atti del Convegno internazionale (Firenze, 8–9 novembre 1996), ed. Lino Leonardi (Firenze: Edizioni del Galluzzo, 1998), 93–118.

[35] Here, I quote the section in *Glosae*:

> Habent astrologi instrumentum quod uocant astrolabium ad modum rotulae, in quo depicti sunt planetae et signa. Et est in postica eius astrolabii quasi quaedam regula, in cuius capitibus sunt duae pinnulae subtiliter perforatae. Quando illi astrologi uolunt aliquid de aliqua stella scire, scilicet in quo signo uel in quo gradu signi sit, eleuant praedictam regulam uel deprimunt tam diu quod per duo foramina, quae sunt in duabus pinnulis, uideant radios illius stellae et ipsam. Et tunc uident super quod signum uel partem signi in eodem instrumento descripti, sit caput ipsius regulae. Et sic dicunt illam stellam in caelo esse. Ita Philosophia describit radio uias siderum. [. . .] Duo motus sunt in caelestibus: firmamenti et planetarum. Et mouetur firmamentum ab oriente per occidentem ad orientem, planetae uero e contrario ab occidente per orientem in occidentem. Et dicitur motus planetarum erraticus, quia modo ascendunt, modo descendunt; motus firmamenti rationabilis, quia semper eodem modo et eodem loco uoluitur. Sed erraticus motus retorquetur cottidie rationabili motu firmamenti. Similiter est in homine. Sunt enim qui a creatore existentes ad cognitionem et dilectionem eius tendunt, sed tamen quasi tendunt per occidentem, quia de necessariis carnis aliquando cogitant; sed parum ibi inhaerentes moram ad creatorem quasi ad orientem tendunt. Sunt alii qui ab occidente ad orientem tendunt, qui scilicet de una cura temporalium ad aliam tendunt. Sed nullus est ita obstinatus in nequitia quin aliquando de creatore cogitet; sed parum immorans ibi reuertitur ad curam temporalium, quasi per orientem transiens tendit ad occidentem. Sed ut iste erraticus motus planetarum retorquetur rationabili motu firmamenti, ita iste erraticus motus carnis illo rationabili spiritu refrenari debet. (William of Conches, *Glosae*, ed. Nauta, pp. 80–82, lines 21–56)

Clearly, the vernacular version is not a close translation of the Conchian text.

[36] Unless otherwise indicated, all translations are my own.

[37] The comment by Remigius has been studied primarily through the *excerpta* published by Courcelle (Courcelle, *La Consolation de Philosophie*, 244–48), which has failed to find meaningful confirmations; obviously, it is only a provisional assessment, given the wide *mouvance* of the textual transmission of Remigius's glosses, extant in various manuscripts and in multiple redactions. Concerning the Remigian commentary, see also Edmund T. Silk, *Saeculi noni auctoris in Boethii "Consolationem Philosophiae" commentarius* (Rome: American Academy in Rome, 1935); H. F. Stewart, "A Commentary by Remigius Autissiodorensis on the *De consolatione philosphiae* of Boethius," *Journal of Theological Studies* 17 (1916): 22–42. The commentary by William of Aragon has been compared to the extracts published by Olmedilla Herrero, "Commentaire de Guillaume d'Aragon"; see also eadem, "Edición crítica de los comentarios de Guillermo de Aragón al *De Consolatione Philosophiae* de Boecio" (Madrid, Universidad Complutense, 1997). For Trevet's commentary, I used, instead, two important manuscripts held in Biblioteca Ambrosiana of Milan: MS A. 222. inf. of the fourteenth century and MS A. 58 inf. of the fifteenth century, which contains the letter to Paolo da Pisa. I can therefore rule out an even partial use of Trevet's commentary in the Bucharest version; this datum seems interesting because, at the end of the fourteenth century, the work by the Dominican friar had a massive influence on the vernacular translations, the Italian ones above all, and on school manuals. See Ricklin, "... *Quello non conosciuto da molti libro di Boezio*," 270–71; Brunetti, "Guinizzelli," 155–91; eadem, "Preliminari all'edizione"; Otto Löhmann, "Boethius und sein Kommentator Nicolaus Trevet in der italienischen Literatur des 14. Jahrhunderts," in *Bibliothekswelt und Kulturgeschichte, eine internationale Festgabe für Joachim Wieder zum 65. Geburtstag dargebracht von seinen Freunden*, ed. Peter Schweigler (München: Dokumentation, 1977), 28–48. However, one cannot rule out the fact that our author did not know other contemporary productions, such as the well-known case of Pierre de Paris, whose commentary, which dates back to 1309, seems to be composed "in a virtual vacuum": see Richard A. Dwyer, *Boethian Fictions: Narratives in the Medieval French Versions of the "Consolatio Philosophiae"* (Cambridge, MA: Medieval Academy of America, 1976), 11. Moreover, one cannot exclude the possibility that he intentionally chose his materials from the tradition available to him, or that he used the only sources he had.

[38] I made systematic comparisons between all the available versions in critical edition. For the French tradition, see: Dedeck-Héry, "Boethius *De Consolatione*," 165–275; Rolf Schroth, *Eine altfranzösische Übersetzung der "Consolatio Philosophiae" des Boethius (Handschrift Troyes Nr. 898)* (Bern: Lang, 1976); Béatrice Atherton, "La version longue du *Roman de Fortune et de Félicité* de Renaut de Louhans, édition critique" (PhD diss., Université de Queensland, 1994); J. Keith Atkinson, *Boeces, De Consolation: Édition critique d'après le manuscrit Paris, Bibl. Nationale, fr. 1096* (Tübingen: Niemeyer, 1996); Margaret Bolton-Hall, ed., "*Del Confortement de Philosofie*: A Critical Edition of the Medieval French Prose Translation and Commentary of the *De consolatione philosophiae* of Boethius Contained in MS 2642 of the National Library of Austria in Vienna," special issue, *CarmP* 5 and 6 (1996–97), 1–128; Marcel Noest, "*Böece de Confort*: A Critical Edition of a Late Fourteenth Century Verse Translation of Boethius' *De Consolatione Philosophiae*," *CarmP* 8–9 (1999–2000): 1–331; 11 (2002): 9–15; *Le Livre de Boece de Consolacion*, ed. Cropp; as for the Italian tradition, see: Ernesto Giacomo Parodi, "Studi liguri," *Archivio Glottologico Italiano* 14 (1898): 49–97;

Battaglia, *Il Boezio e l'Arrighetto*; Grazia di Meo, *Il libro di Boeçio de chonsolazione (1343)*, ed. Helmuth W. Heinz (Frankfurt am Main: Lang, 1984); Babbi, *"Consolatio Philosophiae"*; Alessandra Favero, "Nuovi studi sulla tradizione manoscritta e sul testo del volgarizzamento di Alberto della Piagentina del *De Consolatione Philosophiae* di Boezio" (PhD diss., Università degli Studi di Padova, 2002); as for the sections quoted in the following essays, I used the the unedited translations in Atkinson and Babbi, *L'"Orphée" de Boèce*; Anna Maria Babbi, ed., *Rinascite di Ercole*, Atti del Convegno Internazionale (Verona, 29 maggio–1 giugno 2002) (Verona: Fiorini, 2002) 377–490. See also Brunetti, "Preliminari all'edizione"; Albesano, *"Consolatio Philosophiae" volgare*, 38–53, 68–82. See also: Serena Lunardi, "'La victuoria de la terra dona lo cielo': l'interpretazione del metro IV, VII in un volgarizzamento italiano inedito alla 'Consolatio Philosophiae," *La parola del testo* 12 (2008): 117–63.

[39] William of Conches, *Glosae*, ed. Nauta, lxxiii–lxxxv; Alastair J. Minnis and Lodi Nauta, "'More platonico loquitur,'" in *Chaucer's Boece and the Medieval Tradition of Boethius*, ed. Alastair J. Minnis (Cambridge: Brewer, 1993), 1–33; *Le Livre de Boece de Consolacion*, ed. Cropp, 13–15; Glynnis M. Cropp, "Les Gloses du *Livre de Boece de Consolacion*," *Le Moyen Âge* 92 (1986): 367–81. I have seen the "Pseudo-William" redaction in the manuscript Città del Vaticano, Biblioteca Apostolica Vaticana, Ottoboni lat. 612.

[40] To transcribe the sections of G*losae,* I adopted the criteria of Lodi Nauta edition (already mentioned, see above, note 2); the numbers between brackets correspond to the lines in the edition; as for the sections quoted here, see William of Conches, *Glosae*, ed. Nauta, 9–10.

[41] See *Consolatio* 1m1.1.

[42] This short introduction to the gloss of *miser* is not in the Latin commentary.

[43] The quotation that appears in the *Glosae* is replaced by one taken from Salomon's Proverbs *(Proverbi*a, 14, 30).

[44] In this case, also, the brief introduction to the gloss is missing in William.

[45] He should simply write *exa*. The explanation of the Greek words *penta* and *exa* is missing in William, who merely comments on the metrical structure of the elegiac verse. It is remarkable that Boethius, in order to provide a better explanation for the kind of verse used, exposes its metrical structure. However, this explanation is in William's gloss and not in metre 1 of *Consolatio.* How did the translator fail to distinguish the gloss from the original text? Perhaps by assuming that he was using a text in which the *Glosae* were completely blended in Boethius's work, and not in margin or in line spacing.

[46] The quotation of Horace that is present in the *Glosae* is taken away, and substituted with an *amplificatio* on the meanings of the word el*egia.*

[47] New enlargement of the Conchian text.

[48] Doubtful.

[49] The vernacular version lingers more on the gloss of the word *studium* and introduces a quotation (absent in William) of a proverb recorded by Hans Walther (8087a); see Hans W*alther, Proverbia sententiaeque latinitatis medii aevi: Lateinische Sprichwörter und Sentenzen des Mittelalters in alphabetischer Anordnung,* 6 vols. (Göttingen: Vandenhoeck & Ruprecht, 1963–69).

[50] See the repertoire of Walther (see previous note), who quotes two proverbs similar to the one in the vernacular version (26844 and 26846).

[51] See *Consolatio* 1m1.2.

[52] This passage differs considerably from the *Glosae*, in which there is a paraphrase of

the first two lines of the Latin metre; the vernacular version instead indicates Boethius's state of mind, also introducing an original element, namely, the theme of desperation ruling over the human being insofar as it is a bodily passion (hence, irrational), which diverts from study and discipline. Also, a proverb is introduced, one missing in William (see Walther 26844 and 26846).

[53] William's rhetorical note, which highlights the antithesis in the construction of the first two lines of Boethius's metre, is completely discarded; once again, the translator prefers to dwell on the content of the *Consolatio*, and not on the *forma tractandi.*

[54] William of Conches, *Glosae*, ed. Nauta, 11.

[55] The vernacular version overlooks the analysis made by William about possible constructions of the Latin sentence.

[56] This part reveals the translator's skills as a narrator and a storyteller; the quotation introduced in the Latin commentary is completely changed, but I could not find the source of the short tale present in the unpublished version. As opposed to the French versions (above all the poetry ones), the anonymous mostly overlooks the narrative points that Boethius offers, or he tends to use the allegorical interpretations that are traditional in the Latin commentaries.

[57] On the other hand, it is known that the main grammatical interest of the fourteenth-century school textbooks about the *Consolatio*, an interest concerning above all the analysis of rhetoric and syntax of the Latin work, aims to make clear the content for those pupils basically ignorant of the language and style of the classics (Black and Pomaro, *La Consolazione della filosofia*); see also Tommaso Raso, *Il "Boezio" abruzzese del XV secolo* (L'Aquila: Edizioni Libreria Colacchi, 2001).

[58] William of Conches, *Glosae*, ed. Nauta, 110–13.

[59] Here is the transcription of the part in *Consolatio* 2p4.4–6:

> "Igitur si quod in omni fortunae tuae censu pretiosissimum possidebas id tibi diuinitus inlaesum adhuc inuiolatumque seruatur, poterisne meliora quaeque retinens de infortunio iure causari? Atqui uiget incolumis illud pretiosissimum generis humani decus Symmachus socer et, quod uitae pretio non segnis emeres, uir totus ex sapientia virtutibusque factus: suarum securus tuis ingemescit iniuriis. Viuit uxor tua ingenio modesta, pudicitia pudore praecellens et, ut omnes eius dotes breuiter includam, patri similis; uiuit, inquam, tibique tantum uitae huius exosa spiritum seruat, quoque uno felicitatem minui tuam uel ipsa concesserim, tui desiderio lacrimis ac dolore tabescit."

[60] Doubtful passage; the manuscript version is *siandome daladi tolta* (fol. 41v), which I have changed, as indicated.

[61] Black and Pomaro, *La Consolazione della filosofia*, 137; the scholar also quotes *incipit* and *explicit* of the Latin epitaph in the manuscript Florence, Biblioteca Centrale Nazionale, Conv. Soppr. J. X. 22: "*inc.*. Elpes dicta fui, Siculle regionis alumpna; *expl.* Iungat uterque cinis. Expleta sunt carmina facta/a uxore <magistri> Boetii que dicta Elpes"; see also: *Patrologia Latina*, 64:1421C, in which there is the full version of the Latin text; in 63:537–38 see the section entitled: "*ELPIS UXOR BOETII: Hymni duo in honorem ss. Apostolorum Petri et Pauli, anno Domini DXXV*"; similarly, in Ital. 40, the anonymous author claims: "Devé saver che questa mandona Erpes fo una savia dona e fé' un imno de san Piero e de sen Pollo, lo qual

començа: *Felix per hoċ festum mundi cardines*" (section. 5). However, the *incipit* quoted in the vernacular version does not coincide with the two ascribed to Elpis in *Patrologia*; on the other hand, it is in other two *loci* of the *corpus*: see *Patrologia Latina*, 94:0495D, in the section devoted to the *opera omnia* by Venerable Beda (*Homilia XCIV*), and see 99:484A, the section devoted to hymns works by Paolino d'Aquileia (*Hymnus II*). About the diffusion of the epitaph in Italy, see: Albesano, *"Consolatio Philosophiae" volgare*, 28, 48.

[62] For a history of the exegesis of these important conceptual themes in Boethius's works, see, among others, Luca Obertello, *Severino Boezio*, vol. 1 (Genova: Accademia Ligure di Scienze e Lettere, 1974), 572–707 and 727–30; Courcelle, *La Consolation de Philosophie*, 204–25; William of Conches, *Glosae*, ed. Nauta, lxiii–lxxiv.

[63] See *Consolatio* 3p12.1.

[64] Doubtful; the manuscript reads: *non la tendeva* (fol. 65r).

[65] Hard to be interpreted.

[66] I quote the correspondent section in *Consolatio* 3p12.1–8:

> Tum ego: Platoni, inquam, uehementer assentior; nam me horum iam secundo commemoras, primum quod memoriam corporea contagione, dehinc cum maeroris mole pressus amisi.—Tum illa: Si priora, inquit, concessa respicias, ne illud quidem longius aberit quin recorderis quod te dudum nescire confessus es—Quid? Inquam.—Quibus, ait illa, gubernaculis mundus regatur.—Memini, inquam, me inscitiam meam fuisse confessum, sed quid afferas, licet iam prospiciam, planius tamen ex te audire desidero.—Mundum, inquit, hunc deo regi paulo ante minime dubitandum putabas.—Ne nunc quidem arbitror, inquam, nec umquam dubitandum putabo, quibusque in hoc rationibus accedam breuiter exponam. Mundus hic ex tam diuersis contrariisque partibus in unam formam minime conuenisset nisi unus esset qui tam diuersa coniungeret. Coniuncta uero naturarum ipsa diuersitas inuicem discors dissociaret atque diuelleret nisi unus esset qui quod nexuit contineret. Non tam uero certus naturae ordo procederet nec tam dispositos motus locis, temporibus, efficientia, spatiis, qualitatibus explicarent nisi unus esset qui has mutationum uarietates manens ipse disponeret. Hoc, quicquid est, quo condita manent atque agitantur usitato cunctis uocabulo deum nomino.

[67] For example, in the unpublished version, the pursuit of bliss is identified with the pursuit of Christian God, He who bestows punishment and reward, and Philosophy is often identified with Divine Wisdom, and at times with the Holy Spirit; this kind of exegesis fully partakes the traditional medieval interpretation of Boethius; see: Courcelle, *La Consolation de Philosophie*, 161–84; Obertello, *Severino Boezio*, 1:674–99; Troncarelli, *Boezio*, 306–17.

[68] Quotation from Ps. 81.6.

[69] See Courcelle, *La Consolation de Philosophie*, 161-84; Troncarelli, *Boezio*, 303–29.

[70] See Lunardi, "Un inedito commento italiano," 316–18.

[71] The same quotation (from the *Genesis*) is in the *Glosae* by William, although the unpublished translation uses the Latin commentary neither to illustrate the metre nor to interpret it: William of Conches, *Glosae*, ed. Nauta, p. 146, lines 44–45.

[72] Ricklin, "... *Quello non conosciuto da molti libro di Boezio*," 267–85.

[73] Thomas Ricklin argues that there is no clean break between traditional philosophical interpretation and religious one, which is mainly interested in celebrating Boethius as martyr and saint; it is a little studied facet, above all the intertwining of commentaries, literary products, and popular beliefs; however, these interrelations are important, at least as far as the Italian reception of Boethius is concerned. See ibid., 181–82, and Troncarelli, *Boezio*, 303–04:

> Vi è sempre stato un rapporto stretto fra commenti, rifacimenti e traduzioni dei testi boeziani, al punto che è impossibile affrontare separatamente i problemi di queste tre forme di diffusione delle idee boeziane [...]. Quest'impostazione è particolarmente valida se esaminiamo il fenomeno della diffusione dei testi boeziani e della creazione di un vero e proprio mito di Boezio nella prospettiva di analizzare il problema dei volgarizzamenti.

[74] For an analysis of the genesis and layering of glosses and commentaries, see Violetta De Angelis, concerning Latin commentaries to Statius's *Thebiad*: Violetta De Angelis, *I commenti medievali alla "Tebaide" di Stazio: Anselmo di Laon, Goffredo Babione, Ilario d'Orléans*; *Medieval and Renaissance Scholarship, Proceedings of the Second European Science Foundation Workshop on the Classical Tradition in the Middle Ages and the Renaissance* (London, The Warburg Institute, 27–28 November 1992), ed. Nicholas Mann and Birger Munk Olsen (Leiden: Brill, 1997), 82–84. For the constant return of this exegetic issues in the vernacularized *Consolatio*, see Gianfelice Peron, "Cultura e pubblico del Boèce franco-italiano (Paris, B.N. ms. fr. 821)," in *Testi, cotesti e contesti del franco-italiano*, Atti del I Simposio franco-italiano (Bad Homburg, 13–16 aprile 1987), ed. Günther Holtus, Henning Krauss, and Peter Wunderli (Tübingen: Niemeyer, 1989), 145–46.

Early Polish Echoes and Translations of Boethius's *De consolatione philosophiae*[1]

Władysław Witalisz

THE ACCEPTANCE of Roman Christianity in the year 966 brought Poland within the influence of Western Latin culture. During the eleventh and twelfth centuries, cathedral schools and libraries were founded in important political and religious centers such as Gniezno, Poznań, Wrocław, Płock, Sandomierz, and Kraków. From the very beginning, the libraries acquired major works of theology, philosophy, and Latin literature. A catalog of the cathedral school of Kraków from the year 1110 survives.[2] Among works by Ovid, Terence, and Gregory the Great, the catalog lists "Boecius de consolacione."[3] This is the first mention of Boethius in Polish sources. We shall never know whether the book in the library was copied in the cathedral's own scriptorium or whether it was a Western manuscript acquired by the bishop. In the early years of the thirteenth century, the cathedral treasury suffered an extensive fire,[4] and this early Boethian manuscript most probably was lost in it.

Another early bit of Boethian trace evidence was identified by Professor Marian Plezia in an early twelfth-century letter written by Bishop Matheus of Cracow to St. Bernard of Clairvaux.[5] The bishop reports to St. Bernard the progress of Christianization among the Ruthenians in the eastern territories of Poland and invites the abbot of Clairvaux to visit Kraków. A few verbal parallels between the letter and Boethius's *De consolation philosophiae* [hereafter *Consolatio*] show that the bishop knew Boethius quite well.[6] It is possible that he himself taught Boethius's works in the cathedral school of Kraków.

A later and much better known scholar, Mathew of Cracow (born 1335), professor at Prague University, rector of the University of Heidelberg, and bishop of Worms in Germany, also should be included among Polish Boethian links. His contacts with Kraków did not cease when he moved to Heidelberg and Worms. In the last years of the fourteenth century, Mathew returned to reorganize the Kraków Academy. His Latin

De Consolatione Theologiae is a well-known example of Boethian influence. It is possible that Mathew encouraged the teaching of Boethius in the reorganized Academy. We know for certain that the *Consolatio* was taught at the Kraków Academy around the year 1490 by Professor Laurentius Rabe, known also as Corvinus. Rabe truly must have been fascinated by Boethius, for in his textbook on descriptive geography, *Cosmographia*, he imitates Boethius and intersperses the prose text of the book with verse passages.[7]

Of course, all of the above echoes of Boethius in the early Polish scholarship are in Latin. Polish started developing as a literary language in the middle of the twelfth century. The first Polish words appearing in an extant manuscript date back to 1136 (*The Bull of Gniezno*, including four hundred Polish place-names). The earliest recorded sentence in Polish dates back to 1270. The fourteenth century saw many biblical translations and paraphrases into Polish, but it was only in the latter part of the fifteenth century, especially after the first printing press was established at Kraków in 1473, that the vernacular became the dominant literary language in Poland. It was not until 1535 that Boethian ideas were expressed in Polish for the first time.

The first Boethian echo in Polish can be found in a translation, not yet of the works of Boethius, but of Walter Burley's fourteenth-century *Life of Ancient Philosophers and Poets*, which includes a life of Boethius. The author of the translation, an educated Polish nobleman, Marcin Bielski (1495–1575),[8] works from two texts: Burley's original and a shorter Czech version of 1514 by Mikulas Konac (known also as Finitor).[9] Bielski follows Konac in the choice of most passages for translation, but he checks the sentences he translates against the original, which allows him to avoid some of the mistakes found in the Czech version.[10] The life of Boethius in the Polish version of Burley is narrated on the last five pages of the book and features a simple drawing of the philosopher with a walking stick in his hand. The figure is positioned between two pillars, and he has a rather stern look on his face. The chapter on Boethius is divided into three sections. The first presents the philosopher as a defender of justice and propagator of the common good, outlines briefly his conflict with Theodoric, mentions the *Consolatio* as his main work, and closes with a paragraph explaining the other names by which Boethius was known. Section 2, entitled, "Domysły jego przykładne" ("Examples of his ideas"), is a collection of *sententiae* focusing mainly on the importance of wisdom, justice, and perseverance in pursuing wisdom through regular and diligent study. There is also a warning against the danger of excessive wine drinking. Section 3 discusses the proximity of wisdom and virtue, the fleetingness of mortal existence, and the reassurance man finds in God. The chapter ends with a mention of Boethius's wife.

The language used by Bielski in the Polish adaptation of Burley and Konac shows that the book was meant for the popular reader: the sentences are short, often of epigrammatic conciseness and curtness; Polish rather than Latinate vocabulary is used; and the rhetoric is simple.

A sophisticated reader, who sought more detailed and first-hand knowledge of Boethius, would still, for another 150 years, have to turn to the Latin original, as the first translation of the *Consolatio* appeared in Toruń only in the year 1694.[11] It was a work by Father Jan Alan Bardziński, abbot of the preaching order of Łęczyca and a well-known translator of Lucan and Seneca. In the title of the Polish version, Bardziński describes the *Consolatio* as "an effective remedy against all misfortunes offered to those with a troubled mind."[12] In the introduction, he explains further why he chose Boethius's *Consolatio* for translation. He brings the book to the Polish reader to warn him "against the Politicians of today's world, who smack of atheism."[13] His interest in the *Consolatio* is clearly not that of an antiquarian dusting off an old classic but rather that of an educator and preacher for whom the message of Boethius is still meaningful in the modern world. The introduction clearly emphasizes the Christian aspects of the *Consolatio*, and this is quite understandable if one remembers the translator's background (he was an abbot of a preaching order), and the time in which the book was published: seven years after the publication of Newton's *Principia,* the time when the deistic and agnostic ideology of the Enlightenment started to reach Poland.

Bardziński's translation is very close to the original. In the introduction he makes it his aim to be a "faithful translator."[14] He asks readers' forgiveness for not always being able to please their taste and explains that he "had to follow the style and the thought of the Principal himself."[15] Still, he appropriates the meaning of the Latin to naturally-sounding Polish sentence structures and achieves an effect of clarity and cohesion of style.

In translating the meters, Bardziński skillfully and consistently uses thirteen-syllable couplets. The number of verses in the meters is exactly the same as it is in the original, such as this rendering from Boethius's *Consolatio* 1m1.1–4:

Ja, którym przed tym pisał wiersz pilnując Xsiegi,
Muszę się na płacz zbierać y frasunek tęgi.
Ot co mam pisać szepcą strapione Kameny,
A wiersz smutny poddają pod płaczliwe treny.
(Bardziński 1694, leaf 9, recto)[16]

In 1738, only forty-four years after the completion of the first Polish *Consolatio,* another translation was attempted by Count Karol Wielopolski,[17] a nobleman with large estates in the south of Poland. As we learn in his preface to the second edition of the book (1751),[18] Wielopolski was not aware of the existence of an earlier Polish translation. He learned about Bardziński's rendering when he was already quite advanced with his own; still he continued his work. He chose the *Consolatio* for translation because he believed, just as Bardziński had, that the reader "finds in it a thorough, effective and a well-proven consolation that will relieve his sorrows."[19] But it is a very different translation from the one produced by Bardziński. First of all, Wielopolski lacks the skill, the experience, and—it must be said—the talent of Bardziński. Secondly, he works from a French text, which he admits in his preface. The French translation he used is published alongside his Polish version on a *pagina fracta*. The French *Consolatio*, whose author is never mentioned by Wielopolski, is itself far from faithful, especially in the meters.[20] Since Wielopolski follows the French almost slavishly, his translation also turns out to be quite removed from the original in the shape of rhetoric and the choice of images. In the preface, he speaks of the difficulties he faced in his work, pointing out that the French translator had an easier job, as French and Latin are related languages while Polish and French are not. He is aware of the potential dangers of mistranslation, yet he does not find it necessary to compare the French text with the Latin original. He even tells the reader of the pains to which he went in trying to keep the French versification of the songs.[21] The opening fragment of the first meter (*Consolatio* 1m1.1–8) shows how the prosody differs from the Latin original and how it imitates the French translation:

Moy qui fis autrefois des Verse si pleins de charmes
En ma prosperité,
Je n'en compose plus que baignes de mes larmes
En mon adversité.
Ma Muse me dictant ce que je veux ecrire
Pour plaindre mon malheur,

Fait voir en ses habits, qu'elle-même dechire,
L'exces de sa douleur.
[. . .]

Ja com niegdy wiersz pisał, pełny uciechami,
W mego szczęścia chlubie,
Ten tylko teraz składam, co oblany łzami,
Będąc prawie w zgubie,
Muza, która mi to co mam pisać, obiera,
Na mój los opaczny,
Daje poznać przez swój strój, który sama zdziera,
Zal swój znaczny.
(Wielopolski 1751, 1–2)

What Bardziński expressed in a couplet is here expanded into a curious quatrain of alternating thirteen- and six-syllable lines, rhyming *abab*. On the whole, Wielopolski's translation of both the meters and the prose is less exact, more verbose, and employs more elaborate sentence structures, which often makes his text tedious to read. However critical one can be of it today, Wielopolski's *Konsolacya Philozophyi* must have found readers in the eigtheenth century, as it was published again in 1750 and then in 1751.

The two editions briefly characterized above remained the only Polish versions of the *Consolatio* until 1926, when the book was translated by Tadeusz Jachimowski and published together with a Polish version of Boethius's *Theological Tractates*.[22] The Latin text of the *Consolatio* used for this translation came from Migne's *Patrologia Latina* (vol. 63). Another modern translation, by Witold Olszewski,[23] appeared in 1962 and, as textual references in footnotes suggest, was based on Bieler's 1957 edition of the *Consolatio*, in volume 94 of Corpus Christianorum, Series Latina.[24] The most recent rendering of the *Consolatio* into Polish was done by Gabriela Kurylewicz and Mikołaj Antczak,[25] who identify the Loeb edition of 1978 as their source text.[26]

One significant echo of the *Consolatio* can be found in a celebrated classic of Polish elegiac poetry, the *Laments* (*Treny*), written in 1579–80 by the master of Polish Renaissance poetry Jan Kochanowski (1530–84),[27] a renowned Polish humanist and a secretary to the deputy chancellor of King Sigismund II Augustus of Poland. The *Laments* were not mentioned in the survey above, as they do not contain any direct reference to Boethius, and a case for substantial verbal parallels would be rather difficult to prove. Yet, looking at the consolatory argument of his poetry, the reader soon realizes Kochanowski must have had Boethius in the back of his mind while he was writing the sequence of nineteen lyrics on the death of his little daughter Ursula.[28] He may have studied Boethius in Latin either at the Kraków Academy or later at the University of Padua. It also would have been quite natural for a humanistic man of letters like Kochanowski to turn to Boethius for consolation when his youngest daughter, not quite two years old, died suddenly.

Even though the *Consolatio* and the *Laments* belong to two different genres of literature, they both express personal sorrow and the authors' search for consolation. Parallels between them are numerous, especially in the themes they explore. Both Boethius and Kochanowski open their complaints as poets, and they invoke the muses (Boethius, *Consolatio* 1m1) and the dirge poetry of Heraclitus and Simonides (Kochanowski, *Lament* 1) to help them bewail their grief (transcribed, here and below, from the translation into English by Heaney and Barańczak).

> All Heraclitus tears, all threnodies
> And plaintive dirges of Simonides,
> All keens and slow airs in the world, all griefs,
> Wrung hands, wet eyes, laments and epitaphs,
> All, all assemble, come from every quarter,
> Help me to mourn my small girl, my dear daughter.
> (*Lament* 1, lines 1–6)

Such an invocation is, of course, common to many elegiac poems, but in *Lament* 2 the link with Boethian thought becomes more distinct. The greater part of *Lament 2* sounds like a variation, however distant, on the opening lines of the *Consolatio* (1m1), which contrast the pleasant songs of yesterday with the tearful refrains of today. The poet in the *Lament* makes it still more emotional by admitting that he did not write the pleasant songs while it was time for them:

> If my vocation had been children's rhymes
> And my true art the one that mimes and calms
> The rhythm of the cradle, then my verse
> Might have made dangling songs for the wet nurse
> To sing to her new charge until at last
> Its tears would stop and its small woes be past!
> Such jingles would have been of much more use

Than what misfortune forces me to choose.

[. . .]

The lullaby, to a grown man like me,
Seemed far too childish; now the epitaph
Looms like a cliff above some wild and rough
Shore, where I'm cast by fate and where I sing
Oblivious to my fame, to everything
Except my grief. And I who never wrote
To court a living ear, have tuned my note
To appease the dead.
(*Lament* 2, lines 1–8, 11–18)

Trying to deal with the injustice of his fate, Kochanowski echoes the traditional Boethian complaint of book 1 about the fickleness and cruelty of Fortune: "All is in vain! We play at blindman's buff / Until hard edges break into our path. / Man's life is error" (*Lament* 1, lines 17–19). The unavoidable and unpredictable misfortunes of one's life, of which Kochanowski speaks in *Lamant* 2, receive an even more outspokenly Boethian coloring in the English translation of Heaney/Barańczak: "man is Fortune's fool" (*Lament* 2, line 20).

Boethius's questions addressed to Philosophy, indeed his initial doubts on the benefits of Philosophy, are paralleled in *Lament* 9 by the poet's address to Wisdom:

I'd buy you, Wisdom, with all the world's gold—
But is there any truth in what we are told
About your power to purge our human thought
Of all its dread, and raise up the distraught
Spirit to heaven, to the highest sphere
Where angels dwell beyond distress and fear?
(*Lament* 9, lines 1–6)

At this point, Kochanowski sees no remedy in Wisdom:

To think that I have spent my life in one
Long climb towards your threshold! All delusion!
Wisdom for me was castles in the air;
I'm hurled, like all the rest, from the topmost stair.
(*Lament* 9, lines 17–20)

The Renaissance scholar and humanist has lost his hope in learning and wisdom: his equanimity is gone. The Boethian complaint—"Is this the recompense of my obedience?" (1p4)[29]—seems to be looming all the time over the speaker's thoughts in the *Laments*. At one point, he clearly rejects the humanist stoicism he pursued all his life:

> Reason, once adequate
> To weigh and arbitrate
> What God and life allow,
> Is no help to me now.
> Philosophers who claim:
> Loss? Loss is a mere name,
> No more. Laugh at your lot!"
> They just tighten the knot.
> (*Lament* 17, lines 25–32)

Before Lady Philosophy offers consolation to Boethius, she chides him for allowing himself to be "reft of reason's light" (*Consolatio* 1m2, line 27), even though "once he ranged the open heavens, / The sun's bright pathway tracked" (*Consolatio* 1m2, lines 7–8). In the *Laments*, the chiding and consolation also are brought by an apparition, the ghost of the poet's mother.[30] In *Lament* 19, the maternal apparition turns to her son with a similar reproach:

> What profit have you reaped for all that cost,
> That foolishly, irretrievably lost
> Time you spent poring over books, those years
> Of study that still leave you in arrears?
> By now your grafting should have yielded fruit:
> Windfalls of wisdom, comfort, resolute
> Self-mastery. When others were in pain,
> You've helped them over it, time and again;
> Now, master, you will have to heal yourself.
> (*Lament* 19, lines 137–45)

The consolation that the poet's mother offers to him is far from being a philosophical treatise, but it is a very forceful recommendation of Christian stoicism. Rational acceptance of fate by a balanced mind is the remedy she prescribes:

> So dry your tears. Believe. Take comfort. Rest.

Weigh up your losses, ponder each mistake,
Yet never overlook what is at stake:
Your peace of mind, your equanimity!
However robbed of these you seem to be,
However little of a help they are
Be your own master. Every evil star
Shines with impunity and as of right:
No matter how it hurts, we must abide,
We must obey.
[. . .]
Proud Fortune's ways
Are not to be contested.
(*Lament* 19, lines 106–15, 129–30)

Further on, Kochanowski's vision of Paradise is reminiscent of Lady Philosophy's discourse on God being the utmost happiness and good, and on the workings of God's Providence:

Heavenly joys are boundless. Paradise
Exists forever, crystalline, secure.
There happiness is absolute and pure;
There tragedy, disease, death have no place;
There tears are wiped away from every face.
We live our endless lives in endless bliss.
We know the cause of each thing that exists.
Our Sun will never set; our days don't end,
The dark and fear of night never descend
Upon our realm, where we unceasingly
Witness our Maker in His majesty.
You mortals cannot see Him. Still, dear son,
Turn your thoughts toward Him, try to live on
Consoled by changeless heaven's certainty.
(*Lament* 19, lines 66–79)

She concludes her consolation on a strongly humanist note:

He who has grasped this accepts what has been
And what will be with equal steadfastness,
Resigned to suffer, glad to suffer less.
Bear humanly the human lot. There is—
Never forget—one Lord of blight and bliss.
(*Lament* 19, lines 152–56)

It would be difficult to find in Kochanowski any direct verbal borrowings from the *Consolatio*, yet I believe that the examples above allow us to accept the *Laments* as having been written consciously in the spirit of Boethius. The two works share much: the stoical attitude, the comfort of God, the philosophical tone, the consolatory aim, the consolation coming from an apparition of a wise woman, and common classical allusions (e.g., to the story of Orpheus: Boethius in the closing meter of book 3 [3m12] and Kochanowski in *Lament* 14). The *Laments* would certainly not be what they are without the *Consolatio*.

NOTES

[1] A version of this paper was presented at the Thirty-Fifth International Congress on Medieval Studies in Kalamazoo, Michigan, in May 2000, subsequently published as "Early Polish Echoes and Translations of Boethius" in *CarmP* 11 (2002): 17–26, and has been reedited for this volume.

[2] Marian Plezia, "Księgozbiór katedry krakowskiej wedle Inwentarza z r. 1110," in *Silva Rerum Seria Nova*, ed. Władysław Berbelicki, Tadeusz Ulewicz (Kraków: Wydawictwo Literackie, 1981), 16–29; see also Adam Vetulani, "La bibliothèque de l'Eglise Cathédrale de Cracovie d'après le catalogue de 1110," in *Mélanges Joseph de Ghellinck*, vol. 2 (Gembloux: Duculot, 1951), 489–507.

[3] Plezia, "Księgozbiór katedry krakowskiej," p. 20.

[4] Ibid., p. 28.

[5] Marian Plezia, "List Biskupa Mateusza do Św. Bernarda," in *Prace z dziejów Polski feudalnej ofiarowane Romanowi Grodeckiemu w 70 rocznicę urodzin* (Warsaw: Państwowe Wydawnictwo Naukowe, 1960), 123–40.

[6] For example, compare "legemque pati coegit" (line 110 in Matheus) and "legemque pati sidera cogis" in Boethius, *Consolatio* 1.5.4: Boethius, *The Theological Tractates; The Consolation of Philosophy*, trans. H. F. Stewart, E. K. Rand, and S. J. Tester, Loeb Classical Library 74 (Cambridge, MA: Harvard University Press, 1973; repr. 1978, 1990).

[7] Kazimierz Morawski, *Historya Uniwersytetu Jagiellońskiego*, vol. 2 (Kraków, 1900), 170.

[8] *Żywoty Filozofów, to jest mędrców nauk przyrodzonych, I też inszych mężów cnotami ozdobionych ku obyczajnemu nauczaniu człeka każdego krótko wybrane* (Kraków, 1535).

[9] *Zivotovee a mravnaa Nauceny Mudrtzuo przyrozenych a muzuo cztosty oswyetzenych kratcze wybrany. Renandantur Pragae a Nicolae Impressore in Lacu* (Prague, 1514).

[10] See Ignacy Chrzanowski, *Marcin Bielski: Studjum historyczno-literackie* (Warsaw: Książnica-Atlas, 1926).

[11] *Skuteczny na wszelkie przygody nieszczęśliwe sposób, wszystkim w utrapieniu zostajacym podany, to jest, Pociecha Filozofiey, niegdy od An. Man. Torq. Seweryna Boecyusza napisana, teraz przez W. X. Jana Alana Bardzińskiego, S. Theologiey Lektora, Przeora Łęczyckiego Zakonu Kaznodziejskiego, przetłumaczona* (W Thoruniu: nakladem Jana Christiana Laurera, 1694). Hereafter cited as Bardziński 1694.

[12] All translations from Bardziński are mine.

[13] "[...] przeciwko teraźniejszym Świata tego Atheizmem trącącym Politykom

przestrogi," Bardziński 1694, leaf 7 (recto) of unpaginated, original edition available at Wrocław University Library.

[14] Bardziński 1694, leaf 8 (verso).

[15] Bardziński 1694, leaf 8 (verso).

[16] See Boethius, *Consolatio* 1m1.1–4:

> Carmina qui quondam studio florente peregi,
> flebilis heu maestos cogor inire modos.
> Ecce mihi lacerae dictant scribenda Camenae
> et ueris elegi fletibus ora rigant.

[17] *Konsolacya Philozophyi Boecyusza* (Warszawa: Collegium Scholarum Piarum, 1738); the translator's name is given neither in the first (1738) edition nor in the reprint of 1750. Only in the edition of 1751 (given as second edition on the title page) do we find the name of Wielopolski. This edition is hereafter cited as Wielopolski 1751.

[18] The title page of the 1751 edition reads:

> Boethius Anicius Manlius Torquatus Severinus. Consolation de la philosophie de Boece. Traduite du françois par monseigneur Charles Comte de Zywiec et Pieskowa Skała Wielopolski, Marquis de Mirow et Pinczow Gonzaga Myszkowski, Grand ecuyer de la Couronne: Staroste de Cracovie, general de la Petite Pologne. Dediée à ses illustres Fils. Seconde edition. à Varsovie, dans l'imprimerie Royalle, et de la Republ. aux Peres des ecoles pieuses. 1751. — Konsolacya Filozofij Boecyusza z francuzkiego wytłomáczona. Przez Jáśnie Wiel. J. Mci Pááá Karola Hrábię ná Zywcu, y Pieskowey Skále Wielopolskiego Márgrábię na Mirowie y Pińczowie Gonzagę Myszkowskiego. Koniuszego koronnego, Starostę krakowskiego, Generała Máło-Polskiego. Przypisana. Zacnym synom Jego. Druga edycya.w Warszawie w Drukárni J. K. Mći y Rzeczyp. XX. Scholarum Piarum 1751.

[19] Wielopolski 1751, p. A2 (translation mine).

[20] The translation Wielopolski uses is F. N. Regnier's *Böece console par la philosophie: Traduction nouvelle* (Paris: Loyson, 1676).

[21] Preface of the translator, Wielopolski 1751, p. A2.

[22] *Boecjusz: O pociechach filozofji ksiąg pięcioro oraz Traktaty teologiczne*, Pisma Ojców Kościoła 5 (Poznań: Fiszer i Majewski, 1926).

[23] *O pocieszeniu jakie daje filozofia* (Warsaw: PWN, 1962).

[24] *Anicii Manlii Severini Boethii Philosophiae Consolati*, ed. Ludovicus Bieler, Corpus Christianorum Series Latina 94 (Turnholt: Brepols, 1957).

[25] *Boecjusz: O pocieszeniu, jakie daje filozofia* (Kęty: Wydawnictwo Marek Derewiecki, 2006).

[26] Boethius, *The Theological Tractates*, trans. Stewart, Rand, and Tester.

[27] All quotations from Kochanowski come from Jan Kochanowski, *Laments*, trans. Seamus Heaney and Stanisław Barańczak (London: Faber and Faber, 1995).

[28] Boethian influences on Jan Kochanowski have been noticed before, mostly as a possible source of the poet's Neoplatonic attitudes; see I. Richter, "Boecjusz a Kochanowski," *Przewodnik Naukowy i Literacki XV*, 40, no. 7 (Lipiec [July] 1912): 1142–56.

[29] Quotations from the *Consolatio* in this chapter follow the translation of H. R. James in *The Consolation of Philosophy of Boethius* (London: Stock, 1897).

[30] For a discussion of Kochanowski's use of the comforting female figure as an echo of Latin literary conventions, see Grażyna Urban-Godziek, "*De consolatione somni*—figura Pocieszycielki: Jan Kochanowski w nurcie łacińskiej literatury europejskiej (Boecjusz, F. Petrarca, G. Pontano, J. Secundus)," online at "Biblioteka Literatury Staropolskiej i Nowołacińskiej," accessed September 16, 2015, http://neolatina.bj.uj.edu.pl/.

Maximos Planudes and his περι παραμυθιας της φιλοσοφιας: Boethius's *De consolatione philosophiae* Translated into Greek

Leslie A. Taylor

MAXIMOS PLANUDES (ca. 1255–ca. 1305), the thirteenth-century Byzantine monk, teacher, and diplomat, is the only known translator of Boethius's *De consolatione philosophiae* [hereafter *Consolatio*] into Greek. Planudes possessed a rich knowledge of Latin, and his translation of the *Consolatio* is among the most excellent and attentive of all translations. Until recently, very few editions of Planudes's rendering of the *Consolatio* have been published, but a considerable amount of scholarly work has focused on the history and/or quality of this translation. The first edition of Planudes's translation was compiled by C. F. Weber in 1832, but this edition contains only the verses.[1] In 1871, É.-A. Bétant brought forth the first complete edition, but it is not a critical edition.[2] It is based on one manuscript and contains only a brief introduction (three pages in French) and limited notes. A facsimile edition of Bétant was issued in 1964. In the late 1990s, two very important editions were published: Anastasios Megas's 1996 bilingual edition, with notes and introductory materials in modern Greek; and Manolis Papathomopoulos's 1999 bilingual edition with notes and introductory materials in French.[3] Also of interest are the stylistic analyses of Planudes's translation presented by D. Ceoletta, B. Kopanos, and Marco Galdi.[4]

To appreciate Planudes's translation of the *Consolatio*, one should understand the historical and personal context in which Planudes completed this work. At a time when knowledge of Latin was not highly valued in Byzantium, Planudes acquired a good working knowledge of the language, primarily through self-education but also through the assistance of Papal envoys.[5] Because of his good working knowledge of Latin, Planudes often was called upon to serve as a diplomat. In 1274, he was present at the Council of Lyons, which resulted in the reunification of the Eastern and Western Churches from 1274–1281. In order to help his countrymen understand the differences between the Eastern and Western Churches' concepts of the Trinity, Planudes translated the *De trinitate* of St. Augustine into Greek. Planudes's translation of Augustine's work, completed *verbum e verbo,* is inferior to his work on the *Consolatio*, but one must consider the context in which it was produced and the need for a highly literal translation. Nearly two decades later, in 1296, Planudes was sent to Venice "in the capacity of imperial envoy."[6] Although Planudes's assignment was sensitive in reestablishing good relations between these two communities, he was well received by the Venetians, and they even bestowed upon him honorary citizenship of their city.[7]

In *The Early Palaeologan Renaissance (1261–1360)*, Edmund Fryde praises Planudes as "the greatest Hellenic scholar of his time."[8] Planudes was involved in a variety of scholarly projects throughout his lifetime, and his output was phenomenal: he was an author, translator, compiler, editor, and commentator. According to L. D. Reynolds and N. G. Wilson, "He is generally thought to have been responsible for the production of a large volume (preserved in Florence as Laur. 32.16) containing a collection of classical poetry."[9] Fryde, having worked directly with this manuscript, confirms that while Laur. 32.16 was only partially written by Planudes, Planudes checked and annotated all contributions to the manuscript. The collection was begun in 1280, when Planudes was a layman, and finished after he had become a monk (ca. 1283). It is a selection of "choice Greek hexametric verse" that includes works of Hesiod, Pindar, Apollonius of Rhodes, Theocritus, and St. Gregory of Nazianzus, to name a few.[10] Planudes is also widely known for his revision of the Greek anthology, a collection of epigrams, the earlier version of which is known as the Palatine manuscript.[11]

Planudes also conducted a successful search for Plutarch's works and compiled an edition of Plutarch's *Lives of the Illustrious Greeks and Romans* and *Moralia*. In a later copy, which Planudes made in 1301, "he also included an ancient list of Plutarch's works, probably a catalogue from some ancient library [. . .] which contained many treatises not available to Planudes." After his death, his students continued the search for Plutarchian works, and later copies of the manuscript contained additional materials, although not all authentic.[12]

Planudes devoted much time to searching for and editing Ptolemy's *Geography*, and according to Reynolds and Wilson, "he may have been responsible for reconstructing the maps in Ptolemy's *Geography.*"[13] Fryde provides convincing evidence that Planudes was fully capable of and indeed did reconstruct the maps. An exceptional manuscript of Planudes's edition of Ptolemy's *Geography* was brought to Florence by Manuel Chrysoloras in

1397.[14] This manuscript had profound influence on the history of Western civilization.[15] Planudes's interest in mathematics is evidenced in his compilation of books 1 and 2 (out of six) of Diophantos's *Arithmetica*, and he is "known to have lectured on Euclid's *Elements*."[16] He also is known to have written a pamphlet supporting the adoption of Arabic numerals because the Greeks at this time continued to use the alphabetic system of numerals.[17]

Planudes possessed a strong appreciation of Latin literature, and during his lifetime he translated significant works into Greek. Fryde remarks: "his delight in literary variety and in distinguished writing is confirmed by his choices of works that merited translation. Some had high spiritual quality like Cicero's *Somnium Scipionis* [. . .], with the 'Commentary' on it by Macrobius, and the *Consolation of Philosophy* by Boethius, but it is possible that Planudes was also attracted by the literary artistry of Cicero and Boethius."[18] Fryde notes that Planudes also translated the anonymous *Disticha Catonis*, another work with "a high moral message," as well as the *Heroides* and *Metamorphoses* of Ovid. His work with Ovid evidences a gradual improvement, which may indicate an interest in this author over a period of time.[19] According to Deno J. Geanakoplos, he also translated into Greek some works of the grammarian Donatus, the medieval physician and philosopher Petrus Hispanus, and possibly Boethius's *De dialectica*.[20]

As a translator and/or editor, Planudes did have the tendency at times to "over-edit." When editing Ovid, he made "moral" changes in terms such as *amor* or *Venus*, and when revising the Greek anthology he omitted epigrams he thought unsuitable.[21] However, Fryde notes "[t]hat he had avoided classical texts that were plainly immoral is intelligible in a sincerely pious monk and a teacher of young pupils."[22] In editing Aratus's didactic poem on astronomy, the *Phaenomena*, he simply removed the inaccurate parts and composed corrections.[23]

The date when Planudes acquired a Latin manuscript of the *Consolatio* and began his translation is not clear. Reynolds and Wilson suggest that Planudes may not even have acquired a good working knowledge of Latin until his stay in Venice in 1296.[24] Geanakoplos, however, implies that Planudes had already translated the *Consolatio* before his arrival in Venice.[25] Papathomopoulos sets the date of translation at around 1293–96, based on the date of Planudes's famous letter no. 5 to his friend Leon Vardalis. This letter to Vardalis is believed to have been composed sometime between 1297 and 1300, and in this letter Planudes states that he has lent out the manuscript of the translation and wants it returned.[26]

Planudes's autograph copy has not been located, but the Ur-text (Romanus Angelicus) is believed to have been taken directly from his copy.[27]

Analyzing the Ur-text and the additional thirty-four manuscript copies that are known to have been made, we do acquire an understanding of Planudes's autograph copy. Scholars believe that Planudes must have been working with manuscript T, one of the oldest Latin manuscripts of the *Consolatio.* It also has been noted that the *vita*, which he translated into Greek, contains sections of three of the six Latin *vitae*; thus the Latin manuscript (or possibly manuscripts) used by Planudes probably contained at least three of these versions.[28] Papathomopoulos also believes that the *scholium* was not composed by Planudes, but probably by Loup de Ferrieres and/or another anonymous commentator in the ninth century. Papathomopoulos believes that Planudes found it in the one or more Latin manuscripts to which he had access and included it in his translation.[29] Papathomopoulos and Megas include the *scholium* in their recent editions of the translation; Bétant does not.

The quality of Planudes's translation of the *Consolatio*, completed *sensum de sensu*, is exceptional. Although Planudes used the Attic style of Greek for the prose sections, the language and vocabulary of the meters have what Papathomopoulos refers to as a "caractère composite." He elaborates: "Ce caractère reflète la curiosité intellectuelle et la vaste érudition de l'auteur qui n'hésite à puiser son bien là où il le trouve: poésie épique, lyrique, tragique, etc." [This character reflects the intellectual curiosity and vast erudition of the author who did not hesitate to use his strength where he found it: epic poetry, lyric, tragedy, etc.]. In composing his translation of the *Consolatio*, Planudes used a mixture of vocabulary from Plato, Aristotle, and the Neo-Platonists (Plotinus, Proclus, Iamblichus, Damascius). He also borrowed vocabulary from poetic language, Christian language, and popular language. According to Papathomopoulos,

> Ce vocabulaire riche et de provenance variée reflète l'intention de Planude de s'adapter, à travers la langue, à l'esprit de l'oeuvre de Boèce, où se rencontrent harmonieusement de multiples influences philosophiques.
>
> [This rich vocabulary derived from various sources reflects the intention of Planudes to adapt through language the spirit of Boethius's work which reconstructed harmoniously the multiple philosophical influences].[30]

Several scholars have studied the specific style that Planudes used in his translation of the *Consolatio*. Both Ceoletta and Kopanos have noted that Planudes tended to use multiple Greek words for the same Latin word when he found the Latin word to be vague, and he chose a more specific Greek word, depending on the context. According to Ceoletta, Planudes used ten different words for the term *mens*; eight for each of the terms *forma, animus, effectus*; seven for the term *condicio*; six for the term *felicitas*. Kopanos notes that for the Latin term *potens* (mighty, powerful, capable) Planudes would use three possible Greek terms, depending on the context: δυνατος (strong, mighty, able); δυναμενος (powerful, mighty); ισχυρος (strong and mighty, but also, stiff, stubborn, severe). According to Papathomopoulos,

> [C]ela montre la profonde connaissance que Planude avait de la langue latine et marque son effort pour rendre les nuances de sens des mêmes mots dans des contexts différents.
>
> [This shows the profound knowledge that Planudes had of the Latin language and demonstrates his effort to render the nuances of sense of the same words used in different contexts.]

In his analysis of the style of Planudes's translation of the *Consolatio*, Galdi notes Planudes's tendency to use new words, which he probably invented himself, his preference for terms that had fallen into limited usage (i.e., antique or obsolete terms), and his tendency to render Boethius's text into more poetic terms where he found it too prosaic. Papathomopoulos's analysis of the translation notes that it is often characterized by preciosity, amplification, and periphrasis. He also cites Kopanos's observation that doubling is more common in the *Consolatio* than in many of Planudes's other translations: doubling appears 90 times in the *Consolatio*, compared to 32 in the *Metamorphoses*, five in the *Heroides*, and twice in the *Dream of Scipio*.[31]

Planudes's translation of the *Consolatio* has survived in an abundant and rich manuscript tradition. We know of thirty-five manuscripts that were completed between the fourteenth and seventeenth centuries.[32] Only three of these manuscripts are not complete, and six of the manuscripts contain both the Latin and the Greek. Papathomopoulos states:

> Le nombre relativement élevé des manuscripts témoigne de l'intérêt qu'avait suscité la Traduction de Maxime Planude et du succès du *De Consolatione* dans le monde byzantin.

> [The relatively high number of manuscripts testifies of the interest that was aroused by Planudes's translation and the success of the *Consolatio* in the Byzantine world.][33]

Over the years, six of the manuscripts have disappeared. Five were lost in fires. The sixth to disappear was the manuscript acquired by Bétant from Greece for his edition. Papathomopoulos and Megas both agree that Manuscript O from the fourteenth century, Romanus Angelicus, is the source text of all the existing manuscripts. According to Papathomopoulos, it was copied from a manuscript of "qualité exceptionnelle, peut-être l'autographe même de Maxime Planude" [of exceptional quality, perhaps Maximos Planudes's autograph copy].[3435]

Planudes's translation of Boethius's *Consolatio* is the work of a scholar who truly understood and appreciated Boethius's work, and, as Papathomopoulos has commented, the abundant manuscript tradition testifies to the value that was placed on Planudes's translation in the Byzantine world. Although the translation remained apart from print culture for many centuries, the recent editions of the translation by Megas and Papathomopoulos—in addition to the amount of scholarly work that has focused on a stylistic analysis of the translation—support its position as one of the more brilliant translations of Boethius's work.

NOTES

[1] C. F. Weber, ed., *Carmina Anicii Manlii Torquati Severini Boethii graece conversa per Maximum Planudem* (Darmstadt: Leske, 1832).

[2] Boethius, *De la Consolation de la Philosophie: Traduction Grecque de Maxime Planude*, ed. É.-A. Bétant (Geneva: Carey, 1871; fasc. repr., Amsterdam: A. M. Hakkert, 1964).

[3] Boethius, *Boethii De Philosophiae Consolatione in Linguam Graecam Translati*, trans. Maximos Planudes, ed. Anastasios Megas (Thessalonicae: University Studio Press, 1996); Boethius, *Anicii Manlii Severini Boethii De Consolatione Philosophiae: Traduction Grecque de Maxime Planude*, ed. Manolis Papathomopoulos (Athens: Academy of Athens, 1999).

[4] D. Ceoletta, "Planude Traduttore di Boezio," in *Scritti in Onore di Caterina Vassalini*, ed. Luigi Barbesi (Verona: Fiorini, 1974), 157–64; B. Kopanos, "Παραταχτιχα ζευγη στις μεταφράσεις του Μαξιμου Πλανουδη," *ΕΕΦΣΘ* 13 (1974): 21–34; Marco Galdi, *Saggi Boeziani* (Pisa: Giardini, 1938).

[5] Deno J. Geanakoplos, *Interaction of the "Sibling" Byzantine and Western Cultures in the Middle Ages and Italian Renaissance (330–1600)* (New Haven: Yale University Press, 1976), 111.

[6] Ibid., 110.

[7] Deno J. Geanakoplos, *Greek Scholars in Venice: Studies in the Dissemination of Greek Learning from Byzantium to Western Europe* (Cambridge, MA: Harvard University Press,

1962), 24. According to Geanakoplos, Planudes's "mission was to mollify the Venetian anger over the murder of Venetians in Constantinople" (24n48).

[8] Edmund Fryde, *The Early Palaeologan Renaissance (1261–c.1360)* (Leiden: Brill, 2000), 89.

[9] L. D. Reynolds and N. G. Wilson, *Scribes and Scholars: A Guide to the Transmission of Greek and Latin Literature*, 3rd ed. (Oxford: Clarendon Press, 1991), 74.

[10] Fryde, *Early Palaeologan Renaissance*, 229-36.

[11] Reynolds and Wilson, *Scribes and Scholars*, 74. See also Fryde, *Early Palaeologan Renaissance*, 244–46.

[12] Fryde, *Early Palaeologan Renaissance*, 241–44.

[13] Reynolds and Wilson, *Scribes and Scholars*, 75.

[14] Fryde, *Early Palaeologan Renaissance*, 254-7.

[15] Pollard and Reid create a fictitious account of Planudes discovering the *Geography* in the great market of Constantinople as the frame for their study on the importance of Alexandria: Justin Pollard and Howard Reid, *The Rise and Fall of Alexandria: Birthplace of the Modern Mind* (New York: Viking, 2006).

[16] Fryde, *Early Palaeologan Renaissance*, 339–41.

[17] Reynolds and Wilson, *Scribes and Scholars*, 75.

[18] Fryde, *Early Palaeologan Renaissance*, 257.

[19] Ibid., 260–66.

[20] Geanakoplos, *Interaction*, 110.

[21] Reynolds and Wilson, *Scribes and Scholars*, 74.

[22] Fryde, *Early Palaeologan Renaissance*, 228.

[23] Reynolds and Wilson, *Scribes and Scholars*, 74. See also Fryde, *Early Palaeologan Renaissance*, 157-8.

[24] Reynolds and Wilson, *Scribes and Scholars*, 73.

[25] Geanakoplos, *Greek Scholars*, 27.

[26] Manolis Papathomopoulos, "Introduction," in Boethius, *Anicii Manlii Severini Boethii De Consolatione Philosophiae*, ed. Papathomopoulos, xlvii; Maximus Planudes, *Maximi monarchi Planudis Epistulae*, ed. Leone, 15.

[27] For Papathomopoulos's illustration of the relationship of manuscripts, see Papathomopoulos, "Introduction," lxvii.

[28] Ibid., xlviii. Papathomopoulos's discussion of the six Latin *vitae* cites Peiper's 1871 edition of the *Consolatio*. Peiper includes these six *vitae* in his introductory materials. See: Boethius, *Anicii Manlii Severini Boetii Philosophiae Consolationis*, ed. Rudolfus Peiper (Leipzig: Teubner, 1871), xxix–xxxv.

[29] Papathomopoulos, "Introduction," xlviii–xlix.

[30] Ibid., xlix–l. As an example of the exceptional of quality of Planudes's versification, I include his translation of 3m9 from Papathomopoulos, 48–49:

> Βιβλίον Γ, ποίημα 9
> Ὦ κόσμοιο κυβερνητὴρ μονίμοισι λόγοισι,
> γῆς τε πόλου τε δομῆτορ, ὅτις χρόνον ἐξ αἰῶνος
> πέφραδας ἐξιέναι, στάσιμός τ' ὢν πάνθ' ἅμα κινεῖς,
> ὅν γ' οὔκουν ἐξώτεραι αἰτίαι ὤτρυνον ἔρδειν
> ἔργα ῥοώδεος ὕλης, ἀλλ' ἡ ἔμφυτος εἰκών
> τοῦ ἀγαθοῖο και ἄφθονος, ἀενάοιο σὺ πάντα

ἐκ παραδείγματος ἱστᾷς, κάλλιστος μάλα καλὸν
νῷ κόσμον φορέων και ὁμοίῃ εἰκόνι μορφῶν,
καί μιν ἀνώγων ἄρτιον ἄρτια καὶ μέρη αὐχεῖν.
σὺ στοιχεῖ' ἀριθμῷ συνδεῖς, ψύχος ὄφρα φλόγεσσι,
ξηρά θ' ὑγροῖς συνίοιεν, ὅπως μὴ εἰλικρινὲς πῦρ
ἐκπετάσῃ, χθόνα δ' ἄχθος ἐπιβρῖσαν καταδύσῃ.
σὺ τριπλῆς φύσιος μεσάτην κινοῦσαν ἅπαντα
ψυχὴν ζευγνὺς συμφώνοις μέλεσιν διαλύεις,
ἥτις ἀποστᾶσ' ἐν δυσὶ κυκλεύσασά τ' ὀπωπαῖς
εἰς αὐτὴν αὖ ὑποστρέφει, ἐν δὲ νόον γε βάθιστον
κύκλοῖ, καὶ στρέφετ' ἴκελον οἴκοθεν εἶδος Ὀλύμπῳ.
σὺ ψυχὰς ζωάς τε ἐλάττους αἰτίῃ ἴσῃ
κραίνεις, καὶ ταύτας ἀναείρων ἅρμασι κούφοις
σπείρεις ἐς χθόνα καὶ πόλον, ἅς νόμῳ εὐμενέοντι
πρὸς σὲ παλινδρομέειν πολιτευσαμένας πυρὶ τεύχεις.
Δός, πάτερ, ἠγάθεον ποτὶ θῶκον νοῦν ἀναβῆναι,
δὸς πηγὴν ἀγαθοῦ λεύσσειν, δὸς κύρματι φωτὸς
εἰς σὲ τιμαλφέσι πάντοτε νοῦ βλεφάροις ἀτενίζειν.
ῥῆξον ἐπιχθονίου πάχεος βάρος ἠδέ τ' ὀμίχλην,
σῷ τε φάει κατάλαμπε. σὺ γὰρ σέλας αἴθριον ἐσσὶ
λῆξίς τ' ἠρεμέουσ' ἐσθλῶν, ἵνα σ' ἀθρῶ, τέρμα,
ἀρχή, ὁδός, προσαγωγεῦ, ὁδηγέ, ὅρος τε ὁ αὐτός.

[31] Papathomopoulos, "Introduction," xlix–l.

[32] For a division of these manuscripts into the different centuries, see Ibid., liv.

[33] Ibid., liv.

[34] Ibid., lviii.

The Hebrew Translations of Boethius's *De consolatione philosophiae*

Marina L. Gorlach, Jefferey H. Taylor,
and Leslie A. Taylor

ALTHOUGH BOETHIUS'S *De consolatione philosophiae* [hereafter *Consolatio*] had a tremendous influence on the literary and cultural tradition of medieval and early modern Europe, its role in the cultural history of Judaism is less significant. Nonetheless, the *Consolatio* entered some scholarly circles of medieval Judaism, "especially among Spanish and Italian Jews," mainly because of the Jewish philosophical interest in Neoplatonic thought and the text's emphasis on many of the moral values inherent in Judaism.[1] Richard Gottheil and S. Kahn claim that Boethius was the only non-Jewish author whose work was translated into Hebrew during the medieval period.[2]

Two Hebrew translations of the *Consolatio* are known to be extant: the one produced by Samuel Benveniste in 1412, and the more easily accessible one performed by Bonafoux Bonfil Astruc in 1423 CE (or 5183 by the Jewish calendar). The modern edition of Bonafoux's text was edited by Joseph Sierra and published in 1967 with Sierra's Hebrew introduction translated into Italian.[3] Yet there is little information about the Hebrew *Consolatio* tradition available to the English-speaking world. In his book, *Boethius*, John Marenbon mentions Bonafoux's Hebrew translation in passing; however, both the endnote and the bibliographic entry in his book misspell Sierra's name as "Siena," an error that made the preliminary phase of this research much more difficult.[4] In addition, Marenbon references Sierra's edition with the Italian title, *Boezio: De Consolatione Philosophiae, traduzione ebraica di 'Azaria ben r. Joseph ibn Abba Mari, ditto Bonafoux Bonfil Astruc*, whereas WorldCat mainly references it by its Hebrew title transliterated into the Roman alphabet, *Sefer Di Konsolasioni Filosofya* (also *Konsulasioni*)—a confusion exacerbated by the fact that the main part of the book, being in Hebrew, opens in the opposite direction from the Italian title page and translation of the Introduction into Italian. With this information in hand, however, one may easily find libraries in the United States, the United Kingdom, and elsewhere that own this title, but these very difficulties speak to the relative obscurity of this fascinating piece in the *Consolatio* translation tradition.

The earlier Hebrew translation of the *Consolatio* was produced by Samuel Benveniste in 1412 in Catalonia. An extant manuscript of this text has only recently resurfaced in modern scholarship, though evidence of its existence had been discussed in earlier studies. When Sierra produced his edition of Bonafoux's text, he did not know of an extant manuscript of the Benveniste translation, but he did note that several prominent bibliographers had argued for its existence: G. Bartolocci, Giovanni Bernardo De Rossi, Jo. Christophori Wolf, Johannes Henricus Hottinger, and Isaac Ben-Yakov.[5] In particular, Ben-Yakov's convincing argument for the Benveniste translation left little doubt about its existence. However, the one manuscript known at the time that was associated with the Benveniste translation does not seem to have been the actual text of the translation; this is the almost illegible scattered parts of a text found on pages 71B–82B of the Hebrew Code of the Neophyte House in the Vatican Library. Most of these barely preserved notes constitute an introduction to the Benveniste translation accompanied by an analytical summary of its parts. The pages are severely damaged with ink, rendering most of the manuscript illegible, though perhaps technological enhancements might reveal the text. The few legible passages are obviously drawn from one or more of the traditional *vitae Boethianae* attached to many Latin manuscripts. It can also be discerned that the Latin *prosa* is translated into Hebrew as *sipur* ('story'), while *canto* is represented by the Hebrew word *melitsa*, meaning rhetorical, flowery language. The text is handwritten in Rabbinical-Sephardic script, and according to several sources, for example, Ben-Yakov (1880), it was produced by Benveniste. Ben-Yakov claimed that the final lines of the manuscript's conclusion constituted good evidence of the existence of a full translation.[6] Other evidence of this earlier Hebrew translation from different scholarly circles includes a text listed in appendix 4 of Adrian Fortescue and George Smith's 1925 edition of the *Consolatio*—"Facta est uersio a Rabbi Samuel ben Banšath (Banàst)"; Fortescue and Smith ascribe it to Iulius Bartoloccius de Celeno (1675), who claimed that the manuscript was in the Vatican Library, and Pierre Daniel Huet (1683).[7] A similar entry appears in the translation list in Peiper's Latin edition of the *Consolatio* (1871), though with a spelling closer to 'Benveniste": "hebraice quoque expressa esse dicitur a R. Samuel Benbenaste. Banastum dicit Bartoloccius bibl. rabbin. I 503 Hottinger bibl. orient. p. 28. eius operis exemplar extat inter libros Vaticanos."[8] These references suggest two different traditions that mention this translation, though the fact that they do not reference each other speaks volumes about the social and political distance and intellectual disconnect between them, an operative cultural segregation. Finally, an extant manuscript of the Benveniste translation surfaced, not in the Vatican but in St. Petersburg. Francesca Ziino reports that the Benveniste translation "is preserved in an unique MS (S. Petersburg, Oriental Institute, B 18)." Ziino discusses the Benveniste translation in connection with the Catalan translation tradition and refers the reader to a study in Italian of the Hebrew translations that was published by Mauro Zonta in a 1998 Festschrift dedicated to Sierra. Zonta notes a Russian paper published in 1965 by I. Ginzburg that verifies the existence of this manuscript in St. Petersburg, and a further mention of it appears in *Revue des études juives* by G. Vajda in 1969.[9] However, these reports seem to have remained unnoticed by most scholars for several decades. A reprint of Zonta's study in 2010 includes a short summary stating that the Benveniste translation is "based upon the 14th century Catalan version [. . .] made by Pere Saplana (1360 ca.), as revised by Antoni Ginebra (1390 ca.)" and that the Benveniste text "is still unpublished."[10]

Presently, the only easily accessible version of the *Consolatio* in Hebrew is Bonafoux's translation via Sierra's edition. As Benveniste worked from the Catalan tradition, Bonafoux's is also the only known Hebrew translation produced directly from the Latin. The Bonafoux translation in the Sierra edition is the focus of the rest of this study.

In his introduction, Bonafoux says that he began the work in 5183 (or 1423 CE) and finished it in the same year.[11] This translation is extant in two known manuscripts, one at the National Library in Paris (catalog number 895), the other at the Moscow State Library, known as the Ginzburg manuscript (catalog number 181, previously 188). The Paris manuscript, previously in the possession of Eliezer Askenazi, is slightly damaged, missing the end of *Consolatio* 1m1 and part of 5p2. It is a clean manuscript in Spanish rabbinic script without glosses and few obvious errors. The Hebrew *Consolatio* in Moscow is inscribed on leaves 39b–74b of the Ginzburg manuscript, written in an Italian rabbinic hand. It is a less legible document than the Paris manuscript, but it is complete and contains glosses and other marginalia. It also contains the name of the copyist, Meshullam ben Izhak of Lucca, and a completion date of 5223 (or 1463 CE). Similar errors in both manuscripts, though more common in the Paris copy, indicate a shared provenance.[12] The one printed edition of Bonafoux's translation, edited by Sergio Joseph Sierra, was brought forth by the S. H. Margulies-Disegni Institute for Jewish Studies and the Rabbinical School of Turin, published in 1967 in Jerusalem. Sierra's preface and introduction are given both in Hebrew and Italian, though beyond the preface, introduction and an index of names, the text and apparatus are in Hebrew. The edition is based primarily on the Paris manuscript (P) with missing passages and some corrections supplied by the Ginzburg manuscript (G), indicated in the text by brackets.[13] The text is not normalized, containing neither punctuation nor paragraph breaks, and is presented in the often problematic Hebrew of manuscripts that abound in orthographic and grammatical inconsistencies. The apparatus is minimal, with endnotes mainly noting biblical references added to the text by Bonafoux and indicating differences between the two manuscripts.

In modern times, Bonafoux's translation of the *Consolatio* was brought to the attention of Hebrew scholars by Adolf Neubauer and the great Hebrew bibliographer and scholar Moritz Steinschneider, who documented the Jewish philosophical and cultural activity of the European Middle Ages.[14] Nonetheless, our knowledge about the life of Bonafoux Bonfil Astruc comes solely from his introduction to his translation of the *Consolatio* and from the introductions to his translations of two medical texts: the second book of the *Simplicia* (*Temurat ha-samim*) of Dioscorides Pedanius of Anazarbos, and part of the twenty-eighth book of the *Liber practicæ* (*Mesharet ha-rofim*) of Abu al-Qasim Khalaf ibn 'Abbas al-Zahrawi. Bonafoux was cast out from Perpignan in French Catalonia during a persecution of Jews who refused baptism, which occurred either in 1414, according to Neubauer,[15] or 1420, according to the *Gallia Judaica* of Heinrich Gross.[16] In either case, in 1423 Bonafoux and his son settled in Italy, where he had connections with local Jewish scholars.[17] Among the people he met in Italy was a young man to whom he became strongly attached—Rabbi Joseph Abigdor, who devoted his life to studying the Torah.

In his preamble to the Hebrew version of *Consolation*, Bonafoux states that since Christians often supported their theological claims by referring to Boethius's book, Bonafoux decided to translate the *Consolatio* into Hebrew as an aid for his young friend's studies.[18] Bonafoux apologizes for translating a book written by a Christian, anticipating that some will scorn him for this, but he reminds the reader that the great rabbi Maimonides himself translated numerous works by non-Jewish philosophers and contends that truth from any source is valuable and should be accepted. The apologetic tone of Bonafoux's introduction contrasts greatly with the commentaries and translations into European languages, since for centuries Boethius was accepted as a great authority by the Christian world. He claims that one reason for his work of translating the *Consolatio* was his personal need for consolation stemming from his own plight in a cruel world.[19] In defense of his work, Bonafoux emphasizes the unity of God and reveals a number of points of contact between Boethius's work and Jewish religious principles. For example, the neo-Platonic concept in the *Consolatio* of the inner light filling the soul becomes for the Hebrew translator an inner light reflecting the intuition and the faith in God, which serves as a vision of the Universe matching the monotheistic message and harmonizing with the mythical-religious traditions of medieval Judaism. Sierra writes that several Jewish communities in the fourteenth and fifteenth centuries, especially in Italy and Greece, expressed interest in Boethius's neo-Platonic views and accepted them while rejecting the rationalist or naturalistic doctrines drawn from Aristotle.[20] This article aims at preliminary analysis of the linguistic and semantic aspects of the Hebrew translation of the *Consolatio* by Bonafoux.

Bonafoux's translation follows the original structure of five books, but with each book containing an equal number of prose and verse passages; however, all the meters are translated into Hebrew prose. The translation begins with a preamble in the form of a song praising the Jewish faith in monotheism in contrast to the Christian Trinity. Each verse and prose passage is introduced with a brief summary, and these are gathered together at the beginning as a summary of the whole manuscript. Each book also ends with an added song praising God and introducing the next book.[21]

Bonafoux's text is not a literal *verbum e verbo* translation from Latin text but rather *sensum de sensu*. Numerous expressions are translated freely, making the translation rather interpretational and circumlocutory. However, though the wording of many passages differs from the Latin original, the translator succeeds in preserving the basic meaning. In some cases, Bonafoux intentionally omits lines that contain ideas alien or contrary to Jewish philosophy; in others, he adds explanatory lines for classical references unfamiliar to a Jewish audience. He often intertwines words and idioms from the Old Testament or words reminiscent of biblical situations.[22] In addition, there are whole sections added throughout that serve a similar function: to make the book comprehensible and palatable to a Jewish audience, in particular, his intended reader, the young Rabbi Abigdor. For example, in 3m2, the first six lines are missing from the translation entirely, while the rest of the poem is translated paraphrastically and freely.

In 3p2, the wording of the final paragraph in Hebrew is very different from the corresponding Latin text, but the central idea is preserved:

> מינפואב שרדנו שקובמ היהי הזו תויהבו .םתרובגו םחכ יצמאמ לכב םישנאה
> ריכהל ףסכנה תילכתה הז לא אבל םיצור םלוכ הנה םיפלחתמו םיבר םיכרדבו
> לעופ אוה יכ םישנאה לע ותרובגו וחכ תא הרוי עבטהו .טלחומה בוטה הז עדלו
> ןפוא ןתונ עבטהו .םירישהו םירמאמה הלאב הרוי הזו .םירחאה םינינעה לכ לע
> הז רחא ךשמיש המ יפכ םינינעהו םירבדה לכל רודיסו.
>
> [Because the ultimate happiness contains in itself all the good that can be and can be reached. And to reach this ultimate good men will try with all their power and effort. And if this is desired and required in multiple and alternating ways and avenues, everybody wants to arrive to this desired goal to learn and experience this ultimate good. And the Nature will exercise its power and might upon people since it controls all the other matters. And it will rule over the stories and songs. And the Nature gives order and form to all things and matters according to what will transpire later.]

The original text differs significantly in its wording:

> Atqui haec sunt quae adipisci homines uolunt eaque de causa diuitias, dignitates, regna, gloriam uoluptatesque desiderant quod per haec sibi sufficientiam, reuerentiam, potentiam, celebritatem, laetitiam credunt esse uenturam. Bonum est igitur quod tam diuersis studiis homines petunt; in quo quanta sit naturae uis facile monstratur, cum licet uariae dissidentesque sententiae tamen in diligendo boni fine consentiunt.

The same phenomenon is observed in book 3p3, in which the free verbal representation of the Latin original leaves intact the core meaning—that wealth is not going to satisfy all human needs and make people happy and self-sufficient.[23] The dialogue form, preserved in many translations, is absent from Bonafoux's translation. It is hard to determine the reason for the avoidance of dialogue by the translator and whether it is typical of the Judaic narrative in general. We may assume that the need for many digressions and expansions could make it difficult to follow the elegant conversational format of the *Consolatio* prose.

> ותוא ףוסכיו קקותשיש רבדה ותוא םדאל ךירצ הנה ןכ םא .יל הרמא איהו
> אלו ונוצרו וצפח תמלשה ודיב ןיא הנה רבד הז יאמ ךירצ אוהש יכ ןכ םא ךשמי
> םדאל תתל םירשפיא םניא םירשועה יכ רוריבב ראבתי ןכ ומכו .ובל תולאשמ

> ונתי אל םגו ושעי אל םירשועה יכ הארת הזבו .וניע ידמחמ לכו ויצפח לכ תא םירשועל ןיא יכ תאזמ תרחא הלוח הער הז םגו םינימאמ םהש המ םישנאל .םהילעמ םאמצ תא תוורלו םקלחב םישנאה חומשל ולכויש םעבטמ
>
> [And she told me: If a man really lacks something that he wants and desires, he will continue pursuing it because he needs this, although it cannot satisfy his desires or the longings of his heart. And it will also become clear that wealth cannot give a man everything his eye desires. And he will see therefore that wealth will not do or give people what they believe in, and it also brings evil and trouble with it because wealth, due to its nature, cannot make people happy with what they have and satisfy their thirst for it.]

Compare with the Latin text:[24]

> —Eget vero, inquit, eo quod quisque desiderat?—Eget, inquam.—Qui vero eget aliquo non est usquequaque sibi ipse sufficiens.—Minime, inquam. —Tu itaque hanc insufficientiam plenus, inquit, opibus sustinebas?—Quidni? inquam.—Opes igitur nihilo indigentem sufficientemque sibi facere nequeunt, et hoc erat quod promittere videbantur. Atqui hoc quoque maxime considerandum puto, quod nihil habeat suapte natura pecunia ut his a quibus possidetur invitis nequeat auferri.—Fateor, inquam. (3p3.22–32)

Although not technically accurate, this example reveals a translation that is skillful and strives to provide a creative Hebrew version of the original text. Being faithful to the meaning of the original, Bonafoux expands his translation, drawing on the rich commentary tradition to facilitate the understanding of the text by a reader who not only was unfamiliar with Latin but also unfamiliar with the European cultural inheritance from the classical world.[25]

Some of Bonafoux's changes are simple substitutions. Sierra notes that in 3p8, the original "tiger" in "num enim elephantos mole, tauros robore superare poteritis, num ***tigres*** velocitate praeibitis?" (3p8.14–16, emphasis added) is translated into Hebrew as *tzvi*—"deer."[26] Of greater interest is the frequent translation of *fortuna* as *maaraxa*, which means "system." This choice relates to the need to eschew any concepts that might be offensive to Jewish sensibilities either because they smack of paganism or refer to parts of Christian doctrine directly contrary to Jewish traditions. These concerns probably lie behind Bonafoux's choice to translate the *Consolatio* in a paraphrased manner, adding occasional Judaist interpretations to Boethius's text and eliminating names of pagan deities and natural forces, presenting them in a Jewish guise.[27] This may be illustrated in the translation of book 3m12.[28] The famous tale of Orpheus and Eurydice is retold without mentioning any of the Greek deities and referring to the Furies impersonally as "the devils of the Hell" to eliminate any section potentially at odds with monotheism. It is less clear why the translator also decides to replace the word *amor* in 3m12 with *heshek* ("desire", "longing"). Furthermore, where Boethius says: "Quis legem det amantibus? / maior lex amor est sibi" (3m12.47–48), the Hebrew translation uses "those led by desire" or "the desiring":

> ומצע קשחה תמאב הנה .םיקשוחה לא תדו טפשמו קוח תתל לוכי רשא אוה ימו
> .קוחו טפשמו תדל םהל אוה
>
> [And who can impose rules, law and judgment on those led by desire? In reality, the desire itself is their rule, law, and judgment.]

In the closing paragraph of the meter, the conclusion is modified so as to increase its comprehensibility for the Jewish reader. It also acquires significantly more far-reaching implications and surpasses the Latin text in the degree of generalization:

> םימשל תולעל םתלאש רשא םדא ינב םכילא עיגמ לשמה הז התעו
> .םיאורב םתא ונממש
>
> [Here is the lesson coming to you people who aspire to go to Heaven where you were created.]
>
> .וינדעמלו ויגונעתל םכמצע חצנל ובזעתו םלועה הזל דאמ ובשחתשכו
>
> [And if you think too much of this world, you will leave yourselves forever without its joys and pleasures.]
>
> רשא בוט לכ ודבעת םג ורזחתו ודיספת םכירחאמ םכטיבהבו םכפיקהב רשא
> .ותושעל ידכ םיארבנ םתא עבטב
>
> [And if you turn around and glance back, you will lose and forfeit everything good that there is in nature and what you are created to accomplish.]

Compare with the Latin text:

> Vos haec fabula respicit
> quicumque in superum diem
> mentem ducere quaeritis;
> nam qui Tartareum in specus

victus lumina flexerit,
quicquid praecipuum trahit
perdit dum videt inferos.
(3m12. 52–58)

Sometimes expansions extrapolate a Jewish context from a classical source. One example, noted by Sierra, appears in 1p4, in which Boethius claims to quote Pythagoras. The injunction to "follow God" [1p4.134] is expanded greatly in the Hebrew, stemming from the religious nuances of Judaism:[29]

"אין ראוי להשתחוות ולעבוד רק לאל האחד המיוחד ולו לאחר זולתו.."

[Don't bow down and work for anybody but the God, the only and the unequalled, and for nobody else.]

While paying tribute to the translator's expertise in finding sophisticated ways of rendering the philosophical meaning of the Latin text into Hebrew, we should also mention the numerous grammatical errors and inconsistencies of the text. Sierra notes many such tendencies in this translation, including violating the noun-verb and noun-adjective agreement in gender, word forms used in the wrong syntactic slot, misuse of subjunctives, misspellings, and so on—too many problems to attribute them all to scribal miscopies.[30] Sierra footnotes many examples of these errors. Here we flesh out several of these to demonstrate the effect.

Agreement errors are obvious from the very beginning of the translation. In 1p1 we find:[31]

ועיניה דולקים ובהירים יוצאים

ve ejneja dolkim u-behirim jotsim

[and her eyes *(plur. fem.)*; glow *(3rd pers. plur. masc.)*; are clear *(plur. masc.)*]

This should be:

ועיניה דולקות ובהירות יוצאות

ve ejneja dolkot u-behirot jotsot

[and her eyes *(plur. fem.)*; glow *(3rd pers. plur. fem.)*; are clear *(plur. fem.)*]

Another example:

הזה לודגה תוירזכאה	*should be*	תאזה הלודגה תוירזכאה
ha-axzarijut ha-gadol' ha-ze		ha-axzarijut ha-gdola ha-zot
[The cruelty (*sing. fem.*) big (*sing. masc.*) this (*sing. masc*)]		[The cruelty (*sing. fem.*) big (*sing. fem.*) this (*sin. fem.*)]

Sierra notes many other instances of misused word forms such as using participles as nouns and prepositions as adverbs. One of the more frequent problems is using adjectives as nouns: תחלצומה *ha-mutslaxat* (successful) is used for לזמה *ha-mazal* (luck), or םיערה *ha-rajim* (bad) for םיעשרה *ha-rashajim* (criminals) (4m2 and 4p4). Another example noted by Sierra is placing demonstratives before nouns, violating the phrase structure rules of Hebrew which require that demonstratives follow the noun:[32]

םלועה הזב	*instead of*	הזה םלועב
ba-ze ha-olam		ba-olam ha-ze
[in this world]		[in world this]

A typical spelling problem noted by Sierra is the inaccurate use of the Hebrew letter *yod*: it is generally doubled unnecessarily, contradicting the correct pronunciation and spelling of numerous words. For example, in book 4p4 we find:[33]

ייצרא יינידמ,	*should be*	יצרא ,ינידמ
artsii, medinii		artsi, medini

In book 4p6:

ייחצנ ,ייינמז	*should be*	יחצנ ,ינמז
zmanii, nitsxii		zmani, nitsxi

The spelling is also remarkably inconsistent throughout the translation, and even the word 'philosophy' that occurs on every page is spelled differently. The cover of the Jerusalem edition has איפוסוליפ, and this spelling appears in most places in the translation, but in the table of contents and the introduction, it is spelled האיפוסוליפ. On page 35 of the Jerusalem edition the word 'pholosophy' is spelled in a third way — היפוסוליפ.

Sierra footnotes other typical errors and even more may be easily located in the text of the translation. A full accounting of these problems is well beyond the scope of this article, but the foregoing illustrates the general condition of the translation, which Sierra reports as being typical of the translators of the Tibbonidi family.[34] These errors, however, do not negate the cultural value of this fascinating text, a translation that reveals both the Jewish interest in the *Consolatio* and the need to adapt it to a significantly different worldview.

To illustrate this basic analysis of the translation, we present word-for-word English renderings of the Hebrew translations from 4p7 and 4m7 and compare these to the Latin text. The translation of 4p7 opens, as noted above, with a brief summary of its contents added by the translator.[35]

> המוד אוה קידצ םדא לכש איפוסוליפה חיכותו הרות הפ **יעיבשה רובידה**
> .תומהבה לא םימוד םה םירסחה םישנאהו םיהלאל
>
> [**Prose Seven** where the philosophy will show and prove that every righteous man is like God and deficient people are like animals.]

The next passage given corresponds to the first twenty-six lines of the Latin text, followed by a word-for-word English rendering:

> םא תכרעמ לכש הלעמל םירמאנה םירבדה לישכהלו עדיל **לכות התע הנה**
> הז תויהל ןכתי ךיאו .הבוט איה זא הקוצמו הרצ עיפשת וא החלצהה עיפשתש
> הנה הער וא הבוט וא הכרעמ לכ הנה הרמאו התנע איהו .יסיאוב ינא יתרמא
> ותוא ןכ םא .םיעשרה רסילו שנוע תתל האב וא םיבוטל לומג תתל האב איה
> ותויה יניעב הארי םעטה הז הנה ינא יתינע .בוט אוה ליעומ וא קדוצ אוהש רבדה
> לעופהמו איסנידיוורפ ארקנה יבשחמה לעופהמ הלעמל רמאנש המ יבשחב יתמא
> ראב רתוי שורדה הז ראבנו ליבגנש ךינפ הלחמ ינא םנמא .וטאפ ארקנה יחרכהה
> וא הער הכרעמ םירמואה ןומהה תאמ יללכה רובידה הז והמ עדנש ידכ בטיה
> יפב םירוגשה םיללכה םירבדהמ רבדנ ונחנאש התא הצרתש הרמא איהו .הבוט
> ישע הל יתינע .ישונאה עבטה לכו לכמ ונחנהו ונבזעש הארתי אלש ידכ ןומהה
> ביטיי רשא רבדה ותואש ךיניעב הארי אל יל רמאת הרמא איהו .ךיניעב בוטכ
> לדתשיש ותוא םגו .ינא יתרמא תמא יניעב הארי הז בוט אוהש המ שיא יניעב
> הרמא איהו .ךל הדומ ינא הז הל יתרמא בוט השוע ונניאה רישייהלו רסייל לעפיו
> לבקל ןלבס היהש םלש אוהש םדאל הלענ דאמ רבד אוה הנה ךל תרמוא יכנא
> תבסב ויתובשחמ ןוא שיאו עשר בוזעיש לודג בוט אוה םגו .תורצה תוכפהתה
> .םימעפל םיברל הז הרקיש ומכ וילע םיאבה ןירוסיה
>
> [**Now you'll be able** to acknowledge and connect the aforesaid that every <u>system</u>, whether causing success or suffering and misery, is good. And how can that be, said I, Boethius. And she replied and said that every <u>system</u>, either good or bad, is intended to either reward the

> good or punish and correct the evil. If so, whatever is fair or helpful is good. I answered that it seems true to me, taking into consideration what has already been said about the abstract concept of Providence and the essential concept of Fate. However, I would like to ask you to delimit and clarify the most required things very clearly for us to know why it is common and frequent for people to talk about good system and bad system. And she asked whether you want us to talk about the general things that are common in conversation of common folks lest we should seem to abandon and forget human nature. I told her to do whatever she thought was best. And she said, "Tell me, wouldn't you think that helpful things are good?" "This is what I would think," I said. "And that which is striving to exercise and correct would not be good?" I told her that I admit it. And she said, "I tell you that it is excellent for a virtuous man who suffers to get his troubles reversed. And it is also a great good when a man leaves his vices and turns to virtue due to the punishment he gets."]

Compare with the Latin text:

> Iamne igitur vides quid haec omnia quae diximus consequatur? — Quidnam? inquam. — Omnem, inquit, bonam prorsus esse fortunam. —Et qui id, inquam, fieri potest? —Attende, inquit. Cum omnis fortuna vel iucunda vel aspera tum remunerandi exercendive bonos tum puniendi corrigendive improbos causa deferatur, omnis bona, quam vel iustam constat esse vel utilem. —Nimis quidem, inquam, vera ratio et, si quam paulo ante docuisti providentiam fatumve considerem, firmis viribus nixa sententia. Sed eam, si placet, inter eas quas inopinabiles paulo ante posuisti numeremus. —Qui? inquit. —Quia id hominum sermo communis usurpat, et quidem crebro, quorundam malam esse fortunam. —Visne igitur, inquit, paulisper vulgi sermonibus accedamus, ne nimium velut, ab humanitatis usu recessisse videamur? —Ut placet, inquam. — Nonne igitur bonum censes esse quod prodest? —Ita est, inquam. —Quae vero aut exercet aut corrigit, prodest? —Fateor, inquam. —Bona igitur? —Quidni? —Sed haec eorum est qui vel in virtute positi contra aspera bellum gerunt vel a vitiis declinantes virtutis iter arripiunt. —Negare, inquam, nequeo. —Quid vero iucunda, quae in praemium tribuitur bonis, num vulgus malam esse decernit? (4p7.1–24, emphasis added)

The translation is rather close to the original text, but it uses dialogue less frequently, replacing the direct speech of both the author and Philosophy with reported speech. This passage contains an interesting feature of the translation referred to earlier in that it translates the Latin *fortuna* by the Hebrew word *maaraxa*, which has the meaning of "system," "order," "structure." We can assume that "fortune" would not be perceived adequately by the Hebrew reader, who would respond better to the familiar and neutral notions of "system" and "order" than to a concept derived from a Graeco-Roman philosophical concept. One might also note the handling of the phrase "tum remunerandi exercendive bonos tum puniendi corrigendive" (4p7.5–6), in which Fortune is either "rewarding or disciplining the good" or "punishing or correcting the wicked." The simplification of these parallel structures in the Hebrew to "reward the good or punish and correct the evil" may seem minor, but to the astute Boethian scholar the difference is rather significant. The original text clarifies that Fortune does not always reward good people, but when it fails to do so, the good should see their adversity as useful discipline. To the wicked, punishment does not necessarily entail correction; the Latin text indicates one or the other instead of the two conjoined.

The translation of book 4m7 further illustrates Bonafoux's creative approach to his task.[36] The passage again is prefaced by a summary:

> מדאהש דמלמו תוימלש לועפל םדא לכ איפוסוליפה ארקת הפ **יעיבשה רישה**
> .םלועל םייק היהישו הכרעמה תונתשהב ומצע הנתשי אלש ותוא אוה דבל םכחה
>
> [**Verse Seven** where the philosophy calls every man to realize his fullest potential and teaches that a clever man is the one who won't change himself with the change of the system and will exist forever.]

Next we give the Hebrew passage that corresponds with the Latin meter, followed by a literal English rendering:

> אצמי אל םלועה הזבש ונל תורוהל איפוסוליפה הצור םיירישה םירמאמה **הלאב**
> הרצ וז יא םהל היהי אלשו העגיו למעב אלא גשומ היהי אלש חלצומ רבד םוש
> יסירג רקנה םינויה תומוא אבצ רש היהש ןונימאגאמ לשמה איבמו .ותגשהב
> גישהש תויה םעו םימש הרשע ןמזל תידימת תמחלמ םע אייורטל רוצמב דמעו
> רחא אייורטמ עסיל וצרשכ ויחא ינשש הקוצמו רעצ ול היה הנה לודג דובכ
> לוכי היה אל הז תלוזו .ותבמ ןברק בירקהל וילא ךירצ היה םהיביוא תא וחצניש
> עסנשכ ישילוא םגו הנממ ןברק בירקהו ותב תא גרה וידיב ומצעב הנהו .לצנהל
> יאל םעיגהב ויעירמ תזוחא לודג קלח דבאו רסח הבה הלודג החלצהב אייורטמ
> רד היה רשא קנעה ומיפילופ ידי לע חבטל םיחצרנו םיגורה ויה המשו .שיסריש
> הוקו ליחוה ול תראשנה הרובחת םע ישילוא לבא .אוהה יאב תחא הרעמב ונועמ
> וניעמ ותוא רועו רקנ אוהו תחא ןיע םא יכ ול היה אלו קנעה ותוא ןשיש תעה
> ול היהש תויה םע ילוקריא םגו .אוהה יאה ןמ עסנו לוצנ היה ןפואה הזבו דחאה

תא עינכה תמאב אוהו .בורל למעו העיגי ול התיה הנה הבר החלצהו לודג ןוחצנ
םגו היראה תא גרה וחכ בוטב םגו .םיבר םיללח םהמ וגרהב שורבאטניס ןואג
רתוי דאמ דע םיקזח םה רשא יאיפרא םיארקנה תופועהמ םיבר גרה ויצח םע
המש ויהש בהזה יחופת םישחנהו םיפרשה דימ קשעו חקל םגו .םישנאה ןמ
הצילמהו רישה ימכח ובתכש המ יפכ וריבריס בלכ רשק םגו .םרמשל םיחנומ
וחקלו לזרב תואלשלש השלש םע ותוא רשק רובגה הזו םניהג רעוש אוהש
היה אוהו דאמ דע רובגו קזח היהש ידירישרוב גרה םגו .הצוח ואיצוהו םשמ
דחא ףרש גרה םגו .םיסוסל םרשב לוכאל ןתונ היהו םישנאה בנוגו קשועו גרוה
הזו ותויסרא שופיעמ תחא הלסמו קנחמ היהו אילישא ארקנ היהש ייסרא דאמ
םחלנ םגו .ותלבנ תא ףרשו רצק דאמ רחא ףוחב חורבלו תכלל וחירכה רובגה
ץראל לפונ היהשכש הלוגסה תאז ול התיהו דאמ קזח היהש קנעה ואיטניא םע
ילוקריא הארשכו .הלחתב רשאמ שלש םימעפ ותרובגו וחכ ףסותיו לדגי זא
ריואה ןמ הלעמל והיבגה הנה לידגהש ץראל ולפנב וחכ לדוג תא תאזה הלוגסה
םישנאה תומהב לזוגו בנוג היהש קנעה וקאק שיאהו .וגרהו והזחב ותוא רצו
בורב םגו .וגרה ילוקריא הזו רד היה אוה רשא םיכרדבו תורבעמב םכילומ היהט
הזו הצילמהו רישה ימכח ובתכש המ יפכ ולופי לבל םימש ךמס ותרובגו וחכ
תושעל לטומ היה אוה רשא םתוא ךומסלמ ףיעו עגי היה שאלאטא רשאכ היה
ותוא דיפקהו ילוקריא ארק זא .םימשה ךומסלו דימעהל הכאלמה תאזל חנומו
.תאזה הדובעה דובעלו תושעל רובגו קזח אוהש ותוארב םכמסיו םדימעי אוהש
וראוצ תקלח םעו ומע םתוא ךומסל ושאר םימשל עיגמ ונניאש ותוארב הנהו
חרוטהו למעה הז ומכו .םתכמס אוה ועבצא םע וילגר ינהוב לע ומצע היבגה זא
םילצעה לבא .גשומ דובכה היהי למעו העיגי המכ םע הארת ןכ םא דובכה גישה
.בוטה םשהמ רכשו דובכ גישהל םהל רשפיא יא למעלו עגיל םיצור םניאש

[In these poetic passages the philosophy wants to show us that in this world no success is ever achieved without hard work and a good deal of suffering and misery during its achievement. And she brings a fable of Agamemnon who was the chief commander of the Greek armies and endured the siege of Troy during the continuous ongoing ten-year war, and although he gained great respect, he had to suffer sadness and misery when his two brothers fled and left Troy, and in order to defeat their enemies, he had to sacrifice someone from his family. And nobody else could perform it. And he killed his daughter with his own hands and sacrificed her, and also Ulysses when he left Troy with great success, lost most of his comrades when they arrived at the Isle of Cyrcis. And there they were killed and slain by the giant Polyphemus who lived in one of the caves on this island. But Ulysses with his remaining companions waited for the time when the giant who had only one eye was asleep, and they blinded him, cutting out his only eye, and this way they were saved and left the island. And also Hercules has won a big victory and enjoyed success due to his hard work. And he indeed tamed the genius Centaurs who murdered many of his people. And also in his might he killed the lion and also killed with his arrows many birds named harpies that were much stronger than men. And also took from the serpents and snakes the golden apples they guarded. He also tied Cerberus, the dog who guarded the gates of the Hell, according to what great poets and rhetoricians wrote, and this hero tied him up with three metal chains, and dragged him out. He also killed Bursiridis who was very strong and very brave, and who killed, subdued and robbed people and fed their meat to his horses. He also killed a very poisonous serpent called Achelous by making him escape to a very narrow river bank where Hercules burned his corpse. He also fought the great Antaeus, who was very strong and had such a feature that when he fell to the ground, his strength and courage grew two or three times bigger than before. And when Hercules saw this ability of his to multiply his strength after falling to the ground, he lifted him into the air, hit him in the chest, and killed him. And the giant named Cacus stole and smuggled cattle and people, leading them by the paths and roads to where he dwelled, and Hercules killed him. He was so strong and brave that he even supported the heavens and did not let them fall down, according to what the great poets and rhetoricians wrote. And this was when Atalash refused to hold them and ran away, while it was his duty and task to stand and support the heavens. He called Hercules and gave him the job to lift the heavens and bear their burden when he saw how strong and courageous Hercules was. And when Hercules saw that he could not reach the heavens to support them with his head and neck, he raised himself on his toes and stood on them. And his labors and sacrifice have earned him respect, and this respect was achieved by his work. But the lazy who do not want to work hard cannot gain any respect and reward from the good God.

We end the fourth Book
And begin the fifth Book
Praised be the God shepherding me
And bringing me joy. [

Compare with the Latin text:

Bella bis quinis operatus annis
ultor Atrides Phrygiae ruinis
fratris amissos thalamos piavit;
ille dum Graiae dare vela classi
optat et ventos redimit cruore,
exuit patrem miserumque tristis

foederat natae iugulum sacerdos.
Flevit amissos Ithacus sodales,
quos ferus vasto recubans in antro
mersit immani Polyphemus alvo;
sed tamen caeco furibundus ore
gaudium maestis lacrimis rependit.
Herculem duri celebrant labores:
ille Centauros domuit superbos,
abstulit saevo spolium leoni,
fixit et certis volucres sagittis,
poma cernenti rapuit draconi
aureo laevam gravior metallo,
Cerberum traxit triplici catena,
victor immitem posuisse fertur
pabulum saevis dominum quadrigis,
Hydra combusto periit veneno,
fronte turpatus Achelous amnis
ora demersit pudibunda ripis,
stravit Antaeum Libycis harenis,
Cacus Evandri satiavit iras,
quosque pressurus foret altus orbis
saetiger spumis umeros notavit;
ultimus caelum labor inreflexo
sustulit collo pretiumque rursus
ultimi caelum meruit laboris.
Ite nunc, fortes, ubi celsa magni
ducit exempli via. Cur inertes
terga nudatis? superata tellus
sidera donat. (4m7.1–35)

One can see the paraphrastic rendering of this text and understand that this is Bonafoux's strategy for preparing the text for a reader with insufficient knowledge of the cultural contexts of the Latin world. Translating this passage, in which each line contains at least one mythological reference, demanded a great effort, and results in a text that is at least double the length of the Latin original. The underlined parts are passages added by the translator, who feels obligated to provide a short background for every reference made by Boethius, including the need even to retell stories of Ulysses and Hercules. This well illustrates the complete separation between Roman and Jewish philosophical thought in the Middle Ages. Even living in Italy, Rabbi Joseph Abigdor, the immediate audience for Bonafoux's translation, must have been unaware generally of the philosophic and cultural legacy of the land.

NOTES

* We dedicate this article to our colleague and friend, Naomi Lester, who passed away in October of 2006 (Tishri 5767). We also wish to thank the following people who have provided assistance during this project: Rinna Kirshenbaum, Librarian of the Hebrew University in Jerusalem; Marshall Ryan Beck; and Katherine A. Fehr. We express our gratitude to Francesca Ziino and Mauro Zonta for providing valuable information on both the Benveniste and Bonafoux translations.

[1] Sergio Joseph Sierra, "Introduzione," in Boethius, *Sefer Di Konsolasioni Filosofya / Boezio De Consolatione Philosophiae: Traduzione Ebraica di 'Azaria Ben R. Joseph Ibn Abba Mari detto Bonafoux Bonfil Astruc 5183–1423*, trans. Bonafoux Bonfil Astruc, ed. Sergio Joseph Sierra (Turin: Instituto di Studi Ebraici Scuola Rabbinica, 1967), xv–xvii. Note that Roman numeral references to Sierra are from the Italian preface and introduction; Arabic numeral references are to the Hebrew text.

[2] Richard Gottheil and S. Kahn, "AZARIA BEN JOSEPH IBN ABBA MARI (also called Bonafoux or Bonfos Bonfil Astruc)," in *The Jewish Encyclopedia: A Descriptive Record of the History, Religion, Literature, and Customs of the Jewish People from the Earliest Times*, ed. Cyrus Adler, et. al., 12 vols. (1901–06; repr., New York: Ktav, 1964), 2:362. This reference is also available online: http://www.jewishencyclopedia.com/articles/2196-azaria-ben-joseph-ibn-abba-mari [accessed September 17, 2015].

[3] Boethius, *Sefer Di Konsolasioni Filosofya/Boezio De Consolatione Philosophiae; Traduzione Ebraica di 'Azaria Ben R. Joseph Ibn Abba Mari detto Bonafoux Bonfil Astruc 5183–1423*, trans. Bonafoux Bonfil Astruc, ed. Sergio Joseph Sierra (Turin: Instituto di Studi Ebraici Scuola Rabbinica, 1967).

[4] John Marenbon, *Boethius* (New York: Oxford University Press, 2003), 180, 217, 233.

[5] Sierra, "Introduzione," xxiv–xxvii. Sierra includes references for Bartolocci, De Rossi, Wolf, Hottinger, and Ben-Yakov as follows: G. Bartolocci, *Biblioteca magna rabbinica = Hebraice et latine digestis*, vol. 1 (Roma, 1675–93); Giovanni Bernardo De Rossi, *Dizionario storico degli autori ebrei* (Parma, 1802); Jo. Christophori Wolf, *Bibliotheca hebraea* (Hamburg, 1715–33), No. 2051; Johannes Henricus Hottinger, *Promtuarium sive Bibliotheca Orientalis.* (Heidelberg, 1658); Isaac Ben-Yakov, *Otzars HaSeforim* (Vilna, 1880). He also references: M. Steinschneider, *Die Hebrais Uebers* [sic], Hebraische Bibliographie 8 (Berlin, 1865).

[6] Sierra, "Introduzione," xxv–xxvii.

[7] Boethius, *De consolatione philosophiae libri quinque*, ed. Adraianus a Forti Scuto and Georgius D. Smith (London: Burns Oates & Washbourne, 1925; repr., New York: Olms, 1976), 198. Interestingly, Fortescue and Smith make no mention of Bonafoux's translation.

[8] Boethius, *Anicii Manlii Severini Boetii Philosophiae Consolationis*, ed. Rudolfus Peiper (Leipzig: Teubner, 1871), lvi. Peiper also does not mention the Bonafoux translation.

[9] Francesca Ziino, "The Catalan Tradition of Boethius's *De consolatione*: A New Hypothesis," *CarmP* 10 (2001), 31–38; Mauro Zonta, "Le origini letterarie e filosofiche delle versioni ebraiche del *De Consolatione philosophiae* di Boezio," in *Hebraica: Miscellanea di studi in onore di Sergio J. Sierra*, ed. F. Israel, A. M. Rabello, and A. M. Somekh (Turin: Instituto di Studi Ebraici Scuola Rabbinica, 1998), 571–604. Two years earlier, Zonta had published brief analyses on both the Benveniste and Bonafoux translations in Mauro Zonta, *La Filosofia Antica nel Medioevo ebraico* (Brescia: Paideia, 1996), 262–67.

[10] Mauro Zonta, "Le origini letterarie e filosofiche delle versioni ebraiche del *De*

Consolatione philosophiae di Boezio," in *Boethius Christianus? Transformationen der "Consolatio Philosophiae" in Mittelalter und Früher Neuzeit*, ed. Reinhold F. Glei, Nicola Kaminski, and Franz Lebsanft (Berlin: Gruyter, 2010), 397. There are also brief references in English to the two Hebrew translations in: Mauro Zanto, *Hebrew Scholasticism in the Fifteenth Century: A History and Source Book* (Dordrecht: Springer, 2006), 21, 27.

[11] Sierra, "Introduzione," xiii–xiv.

[12] Ibid., xxvii–xxx.

[13] Ibid., xxviii, 158.

[14] Sierra, "Introduzione," ix; Joseph Jacobs and Goodman Lipkind, "NEUBAUER, ADOLF," in *The Jewish Encyclopedia*, 9:234–35; Isidore Singer, "STEINSCHNEIDER, MORITZ," in *The Jewish Encyclopedia*, 11:545–47 (see n. 2 above): see http://www.jewishencyclopedia.com/articles/2196-azaria-ben-joseph-ibn-abba-mari [accessed January 7, 2016].

[15] In Ernst Renan (with Adolf Neubauer), *Les Rabbins français du commencement du quatorzième siècle*, Histoire littéraire de France 27 (Farmborough: Gregg, 1969), 649.

[16] Heinrich Gross, "Notice sur Abba Mari de Lunel," *Revue des Études Juives* 4 (1882): 192–207 (p. 192).

[17] Gottheil and Kahn, "AZARIA BEN JOSEPH IBN ABBA MARI," 362; Sierra, "Introduzione," ix–xiii.

[18] Sierra, "Introduzione," xiii.

[19] Ibid., xiv–xv.

[20] Ibid., xv–xvi.

[21] Ibid., xix.

[22] Ibid., xix–xx.

[23] Hebrew passages are from Boethius, *Sefer*. For easier reference, notes will give page numbers to this edition. So, this Hebrew passage from 3p3: Boethius, *Sefer*, 73–74.

[24] Latin passages are from: Boethius, *De consolatione philosophiae: Opuscula theologica, Editio altera*, ed. Claudio Moreschini, Bibliotheca Teubneriana, 2nd ed. (Munich: Saur, 2005).

[25] Sierra, "Introduzione," xviii. For a more detailed analysis of Bonafoux's expansions, see Zonta, "Le origini letterarie" (in *Hebraica*), 586–604, and Zonta, *La Filosofia Antica*, 265–67.

[26] Sierra, "Introduzione," xviii–xix.

[27] Ibid., xix–xx.

[28] Boethius, *Sefer*, 98.

[29] Sierra, "Introduzione," xx, 42.

[30] Ibid., xx–xxii.

[31] Ibid., xxi.

[32] Ibid., xxi–xxii.

[33] Ibid., xxi.

[34] Sierra, "Introduzione," xxi. The Tibbonidi family was one of famous Hebrew translators from Spain and Provence active in the twelfth through the fourteenth centuries. See Max Schloessinger, Isaac Broydé, and Richard Gottheil, "IBN TIBBON," in *The Jewish Encyclopedia*, 6:544–50 (see n. 2 above); see http://www.jewishencyclopedia.com/articles/2196-azaria-ben-joseph-ibn-abba-mari [accessed January 7, 2016].

[35] Boethius, *Sefer*, 121–22.

[36] Boethius, *Sefer*, 122–24.

Korean Translations of Boethius's *De consolatione philosophiae*

Ji-Soo Kang

THE FIRST KOREAN TRANSLATION of Boethius's *De consolatione philosophiae* [hereafter *Consolatio*], as for many other translations of this work, was inspired by the *Consolatio*'s "serious outlook on life" and its "flowing style and rich poeticism."[1] It was fortunate for Korean readers that such an inspiration came to Father Eui Chai Tjeng, an eminent scholar and teacher of medieval philosophy and theology and a renowned translator of writings by Thomas Aquinas. Born in 1925 and educated in Korea and Italy, Father Tjeng taught theology at the Catholic University of Korea for thirty years, until 1985, when he joined the faculty at the department of philosophy at Sogang University, another Catholic institution in Korea, where he subsequently became a professor, holding an endowed chair. Father Tjeng's translation of the *Consolatio* still is considered to be the authoritative text in the Korean academic community for its philosophical integrity and literary style.

In 1964, at a time when Korean translations of writings from the West depended heavily on Japanese translations of the original texts, and when first-hand, scholarly translations of classical works were even rarer, Father Tjeng introduced Korean readers to his own translation of the *Consolatio* from the Latin, informed by Italian, English, German, and Japanese translations, as mentioned in "The Translator's Note." His accomplishment may be more fully appreciated if one considers the fact that a second Korean translation of the *Consolatio,* which first came out in 1990 and was revised in 2011, by Byung Duk Park, is merely a retranslation of V. E. Watts's English version.[2] Little is known about Park except for the brief information given by the publisher in the back of the first edition: that he is a professional translator educated at Korea University, and that he has published translations of works by Marcus Aurelius, Leo Tolstoy, and Friedrich Nietzsche, among others. Even this short biography altogether disappears in the second edition. Without any acknowledgement of the base text, Park's translation presents the first few pages of Watts's introduction, rendered, often inaccurately, as its own, and offers the same footnotes as Watts's but with long notes often truncated. Occasionally the English words and phrases from Watts's edition are provided in parentheses adjacent to Korean words, as from an original source text. The only difference between Park's translation and Watts's seems to be that Watts's glossary at the end of the book is incorporated into the footnotes and redistributed on relevant pages with the contents slightly changed. Park even keeps the same number of lines for the poems as in Watts's translation. The revised edition has a new look, with a different cover and a much better page layout, but this and the slight improvement in the phrasing of some awkward passages in the Korean cannot change or resolve the fundamental problem related to this translation. Korean readers who come into contact with the *Consolatio* for the first time through this translation may very well get the impression that the original work was composed in English. Since such a practice is unethical in the world of publishing and indicative of this translator's evasion of responsibility for the quality of the translation, I shall focus my critical attention mostly on Father Tjeng's work.

Father Tjeng's translation had gone through nine printings since its original publication, before the same publisher, St. Paul Editions (Seoul), brought out a revised edition in 1993.[3] However, the extent of the revision was minor, as much of the translation was maintained, and the footnotes remained unaltered. Most of the changes to the actual text pertain to transcribing Greek and Roman names so that they adhere to common Korean pronunciation. Nevertheless, a book with a publication history that extends through almost fifty years is bound to reflect changes in readers' preferences and consequent changes in the publisher's marketing strategy. Earlier printings were replete with Chinese characters, appearing without transcription in Korean letters, *Hangul*. This reflected the concerns of the older generation of scholars and readers who were sensitive to the capacity of Chinese characters to convey more precise meanings. The newly revised pages are almost entirely in *Hangul* script, and they contain only a few Chinese characters, which appear in parentheses following the corresponding Korean words. This practice reflects the concerns of younger Koreans, who typically perceive Chinese characters to be burdensome and aiding little in understanding a text. This social trend started in the 1980s: and as this generation ages, they become the major book buyers. As the revised edition purports to be more accessible to readers, without any significant change to the main text of the translation, I will limit myself to discussing the revised edition.

Father Tjeng's translation is preceded by a four-page preface, only a half-page of which comprises the preface to the revised edition, and a list of Boethius's writings. A brief life of the author is presented in the preface, followed by a short explanation of the philosophical affiliations and background that inform the *Consolatio*, such as Neoplatonism, Aristotelianism, Stoicism, and Augustinianism. The translator concludes with the assertion that even though this work is of purely philosophical argument, evincing no explicit relation to Christian faith, it can be understood that "underneath Boethius'[s] thinking lie meditations of a Christian."[4] In closing, the translator outlines the principles and practices employed in this translation, including the facts that the primary Latin text he used was volume 63 of "Patrologiae, accurante J.-P. Migne," from which he translated the summary of each section, and that he also consulted Ludwig Bieler's Corpus Christianorum edition along with translations in other languages, as mentioned above.[5]

Father Tjeng's translation labels each prose and verse passage separately and begins each section with the summary taken from his base text. The summaries are quite helpful because this volume has very little introductory information about the subject matter of the *Consolatio*. However, because each summary is distinguished from the main text only by the insertion of an additional blank line, the layout is rather confusing and forces the reader consistently to isolate mentally the first four to five lines, which are visually very much a part of the work, when they are followed by a prose section. I am curious about the rationale behind the publisher's decision in the revised edition to use the same font and size of letters for summaries without introducing any means of demarcation, unlike the practice in the earlier edition in which each summary paragraph was preceded by an appropriate section heading.

As soon as the reader turns to the first prose section of book 1, it immediately becomes recognizable that the distinct speech forms in Korean work to an advantage in this text. Following the paragraph on the mysterious and dignified appearance of Lady Philosophy, her first speech addressed to the poetic muses is aptly in a familiar form, a form used by a person of authority to someone of equal or inferior social status:

> 도대체 누가 이 어릿광대들을 앓는 이 사람 옆에 가까이 하였느냐 (*sic*)? 이 여자들은 결코 이 사람의 고통을 약으로 덜어주는 것이 아니라 오히려 달디단 독으로 고통을 더 길러주는 것이다. 이 자들이 하는 짓이란 감정이라는, 열매도 없는 가시로써 풍성한 결실을 맺는 이성의 수확

을 말살하며 인간의 정신을 병에서 해방시키는 것이 아니라 병에 만성이 되게 하는 것이다.[6]

Quis [. . .] has scenicas meretriculas ad hunc aegrum permisit accedere? quae dolores ejus non modo nullis remediis foverent, verum dulcibus insuper alerent venenis? Hae sunt enim quae infructuosis affectuum spinis uberem fructibus rationis segetem necant, hominumque mentes assuefaciunt morbo, non liberant.[7]

[Who let these clowns near this man who is sick? These women would never reduce his pains with medicine but rather increase them with the sweetest poison. What these creatures do is to destroy with barren thorns of passion the harvest of reason that bears much fruit, and to make the minds of men accustomed to the sickness instead of liberating them from it.]

The difference in speech form establishes the relationship between Lady Philosophy and Boethius. Philosophy is acknowledged as the one with more power and authority in her relative status, and she consistently uses the same familiar form, though less severe in tone, as in the following speech to Boethius in 1p2:

너는 지난날 나의 젖으로 자라고 나의 음식으로 길리워져 씩씩하고 든든한 정신을 지녔던 바로 그 사람 아니냐…. 너는 나를 알아보느냐? 왜 말이 없느냐? 부끄러워서냐, 놀라서 그러느냐. 부끄러워서라면 차라리 괜찮지만 너를 보아하니 아주 놀라 얼이 빠진 것 같구나.

Tune ille es [. . .] qui nostro quondam lacte nutritus, nostris educatus alimentis, in virilis animi robur evaseras? [. . .] Agonoscisne me? Quid taces? pudore, an stupore siluisti? Mallem pudore; sed te, ut video, stupor oppresit.

[You are the one, are you not, who used to have a courageous and strong spirit as you were brought up on my milk and raised on my food? [. . .] Do you recognize me? Why are you silent? Is it because you are ashamed, or is it because you are astonished? It would be okay if you are ashamed, but from the way you look you must be utterly stupefied.]

On the other hand, Boethius's address to Lady Philosophy is always in an honorific form, as in the first words he speaks to her in 1p3:

오오, 모든 덕의 스승이신 당신께서 어찌 이 쓸쓸한 귀양

> 살이 땅 위에 내려 오셨습니까, 혹시 당신께서도 나 모양 무고를 당하여 유형을 당하신 것은 아니십니까?
>
> Et quid [. . .] tu in has exsilii nostri solitudines, o omnium magistra uirtutum, supero cardine delapsa venisti? an ut tu quoque mecum rea falsis criminationibus agiteris?
>
> [Oh, why have you, Teacher of all virtues, descended to this lonely land of exile? Have you by any chance been banished by false accusations like me?]

It is as though Boethius's form of speech already signals his respect for her superiority, even when he is questioning her status or ideas. As can be seen, the relative status and attitudes of the characters are immediately and clearly marked by the forms of speech.

It is interesting to note, also, from a cultural perspective that the most often-invoked relationship between Boethius and Lady Philosophy is one of teacher and disciple. While such a relationship is obviously found in the Latin original, the Korean translation emphasizes it more consistently. As can be seen above, Boethius addresses Lady Philosophy as "Teacher of all virtues." Such a translation is anticipated by Father Tjeng's footnote on the word *laribus*, appearing just before this quotation. While many English translations, for example, render it as "house," Father Tjeng chooses to repeat the note in Migne's edition, indicating that the word is supposed to refer to "schoolhouse" or "the state of being under someone's instruction." Whereas English translations render *magistra* in a number of ways, including "Queen," "Mistress," and "Lady," the same Korean word for teacher is used throughout this translation. *Alumne*, when used by Lady Philosophy to address Boethius, in the same vein, is translated as "disciple," as in 1p3, 3p9, and 3p11.[8] The translator's decision may not be unrelated to the Confucianism-based Korean custom according to which a person of authority and respect is addressed as the speaker's "teacher," even for those who are not in the teaching profession.

The translator stated in the preface that his goal was to be faithful to the original Latin text, given its significance and value as a classic and important philosophical treatise, rather than to observe the conventions of decorum in the target language. While footnotes are sparse and refer only briefly to some historical or mythical names and events, a few of them discuss the meanings of the original Latin. These enhance the value of the translation as a literary project and as an academic tool for those with a basic knowledge of or interest in linguistic aspects of the original.

In addition, one may assume that Father Tjeng attempted to be faithful to the original in a rather extraordinary way. It is obvious that he wanted to convey the poetic force of the verses and impress the readers with real poetry. Since I regard the *prosimetric* nature of the *Consolatio* and the literary and philosophical significance that stems from this formal feature to be at least as important as the book's discussion of *fortuna* or *providence*, I appreciate Father Tjeng's achievement. Of course, the translation does not concern itself much with preserving the look of the Latin form as, for instance, none of the meters have the same number of lines as the source text. I dare to think such an attempt is impossible in a Korean translation. Instead, Father Tjeng opted for a free verse form for all of the thirty-nine poems. Some of them are good enough to be read like original Korean poetry, for there is little of the syntactical or lexical awkwardness that typifies some translations. Contrary to the translator's cautious remark that his intention was to render the Latin as accurately and, therefore, as literally as possible, which may have been achieved at the cost of sacrificing the readability in Korean, I think Father Tjeng has given us a fine piece of Korean writing through some of the poems.

To assist him in translating the verses—probably one of the most difficult tasks facing a translator of the *Consolatio* into any language—Father Tjeng asked for and received assistance in revising the translated text, with special emphasis on the verses, from one of the best-known Catholic poets of his generation, Sang Ku (1919–2004). With a career that spans over half a century, Ku had lived through and written during the periods of the Japanese occupation, the ideological confrontations after Korea's independence, the Korean War, and the industrialization and modernization endeavors that characterize the recent history of Korea. Ku has figured into many of his poems his insights on human folly, antagonism, and absurdity. A sharp sense of anxiety and anguish over the symptoms of intrinsic flaws in human nature often has distinguished him as an outspoken critic of society as well. However, as the majority of his poems treat religious issues pertaining to the essential meaning of life and experiences of truth and beauty, and they conclude with his meditation on God and eternity, Ku may have been a valuable assistant, providing the necessary literary force—thematic as well as formal—characterizing the *Consolatio*. Take, for instance, 1m5, in which the narrator praises God for ruling the physical world according to reason, in the form of a hymn:

오오, 별들이 반짝이는 창공의 창조자시여

구원의 왕좌에 좌정하시는 이여
당신은 천체를 신속히 선회케 하며
성신은 일정한 법칙을 따르도록 명하셨도다.
찬란히 비치는 만월로써
작은 별들, 그 빛을 그늘지게 하셨고
달도 또한 태양에 더 다가서면
그 빛을 잃어 창백케 하셨네.
밤의 어둠이 질어오면
헤스페루스는 차디찬 맑은 빛을 뿜으며 떠올랐다가는
루치페르로 다시금 길을 바꾸어
희멀건 빛을 띄우면서
아침 해를 떠오름을 알려주네.
당신은 낙엽을 모조리 지우는
추운 겨울날 해를 짧게 하시고
더운 여름이면 밤을 당겨놓으시니
당신의 능이 사계의 변화를 조절하고 있도다.

O stelliferi conditor orbis,
Qui perpetuo nixus solio,
Rapido coelum turbine versas
Legemque pati sidera cogis,
Ut nunc pleno lucida cornu,
Totis fratris et obvia flammis,
Condat stellas luna minores;
Nunc obscuro pallida cornu,
Phoebo propior lumina perdat,
Et qui primae tempore noctis
Agit algentes Hersperus ortus,
Solitas iterum mutet habenas,
Phoebi pallens Lucifer ortu.
Tu frondifluae frigore brumae
Stringis lucem breviore mora:
Tu, cum fervida venerit aestas,
Agileis noctis dividis horas.
Tua vis varium temperat annum.

[O the Maker of the starry heavens,
The One seated on the throne of salvation,
You have spinned the heavens rapidly
And ordered the heavenly bodies to obey the fixed laws.
With the brilliant reflection of the full moon
You shadowed the lesser stars, their light,
And then when the moon nears the sun
Made it, in turn, pale against it losing its light.

When the darkness of the night thickens
Hesperus rises exuding cold and clear light
Then changes its path as Lucifer
With its white and glossy light
Informing the rise of the morning sun.
You make the cold winter strip the trees of leaves
And draw in the short day's light,
And in summer hasten the night.
Indeed Your power controls the changing year.]

Here, some lines are more boldly figurative than in other parts of the translation, starting with the second line, where the Maker is seated "on the throne of salvation" instead of the "eternal throne," thus complicating Boethius's complaint in the latter part of the poem in a more Christianized context. Overall, the words of adoration come alive in the remarkably natural vocabulary and structure of Korean religious poetry, especially as found in the Christian hymn.[9]

In spite of the merits of Father Tjeng's work, there are a few shortcomings that ultimately undermine his claim to be faithful to the original. First, there is a lack of metrical variety, and the uniformly short lines in the poems fail to render accurately the spirit of Boethius's experiments with various forms of verse. While individually they are admirable, taken together the translated poems give a limited impression of the scope of the original writing, and, more seriously, they are monotonous to read. One of the greater disappointments is 3m9. Given the philosophical and literary importance that has been ascribed critically to this meter, anyone familiar with the *Consolatio* would turn to this poem with heightened expectation. However, after twenty-three poems showing little metrical variation, the majestic words in the fifty-one short lines, expanded from the original twenty-eight longer lines, fail to carry the poetic and philosophical weight. The first four-and-a-half lines of this prayer of adoration and supplication to the omnipotent Creator and Father read as follows:

오오, 영원한 법칙으로
세상을 다스리시는 자여!
천지의 창조자이신 당신은
시간을 영원에서 이끌어내시며
당신 스스로는 부동으로 계시면서
만물을 움직이시고
유동하는 물질세계를 만드실 적에

당신 이외의 원인이란 없었네.

O qui perpetua mundum ratione gubernas
Terrarum coelique sator, qui tempus ab aevo
Ire jubes, stabilisque manens das cuncta moveri;
Quem non externae pepulerunt fingere causae
Materiae fluitantis opus.

[O with everlasting law
You rule the world!
You, who created the heaven and earth,
Bring forth time from eternity,
And while staying fixed
Move all
And there was no cause except you
When creating the fluid world of matter.]

The efforts at versification seem disappointingly forced. For whatever formal or thematic reasons, the translator has decided to cut most of the original lines in the middle and thereby double the total number of lines, many of which seem to end abruptly. It appears to be a random choice that eventually diminishes the power of this piece as an ecstatic hymn and elaborate petition. It would have been much better had the translator kept the same longer lines of the original, even though it might have appeared a bit awkward or unusual in Korean, from a purely literary perspective.

Uncertainty about the exact audience that Father Tjeng intends to address raises another issue. In 1964, when the translation first came out, the book must have offered to the general public an enjoyable read, even though it was in an unfamiliar genre. Yet readability has its detriments as well, depending on the intended audience. The uncluttered pages with generally brief footnotes and the lack of an extensive introduction, glossary, or cross-references might appeal to someone who needs only a rough guide to understanding the *Consolatio*. However, if Father Tjeng intended to address a more educated and even academic audience, as is evidenced by his footnotes on the Latin, his work may disappoint that audience through the absence of other indications of scholarly concerns. The effort to produce a more modern edition, which was indicated in the preface to the revised edition, needs to be more substantial than in simply eliminating the Chinese characters appended to the Korean words.

The Korean vocabulary employed, as well as the style of writing, have become dated, as the greater part of the translation has not been changed in the last forty-seven years. It would better serve Korean readers and scholars alike if Father Tjeng's valuable translation were updated, incorporating a more modern vocabulary and style. Furthermore, it is about time that Korean readers should expect other translations by Korean scholars, which would include comprehensive and detailed introductions, bibliographies, footnotes, glossaries, and cross-references.[10] Experiments with the verse forms are another pleasure to which we should look forward.

In 2001, when Father Tjeng was asked by a colleague to provide his own words about his translation, to be used as reference for this review, he wrote as follows:

> The life of Boethius as it appears in the book raises a great sympathy in the minds of Korean people. Traditionally the people of Korea have conceived loyalty to Heaven and have worshipped Heaven with much awe. Such a tradition explains over ten thousand martyrs of Catholic faith during the persecution that lasted more than one hundred years covering the nineteenth and twentiety centuries. 103 of them were canonized by Pope John Paul II in 1984 in Seoul, outside Rome for the first time in the history of Catholic Church. The biographical facts that appear in the *Consolatio philosophiae* must have appealed to the Korean readers because since its initial publication in 1964 it went through ten printings before a revised edition came out in 1993.[11]

According to his assessment, the enduring interest in Boethius's *Consolatio* in Korea assures, to a certain degree, its marketability. The *Consolatio* has a universal appeal, both as a religious and a secular meditation on human suffering and mortality. As a statement of both scholarly and popular philosophy on the ways of God and destiny, it has confirmed itself in Korea as well, which perhaps should be recognized by more publishers.

NOTES

[1] Boethius, *The Consolation of Philosophy*, trans. Father Eui Chai Tjeng (Seoul: St. Paul, 1993), 4.

[2] Boethius, *The Consolation of Philosophy*, trans. Byung Duk Park (Seoul: Yookmoonsa, 1990); *The Consolation of Philosophy*, trans. V. E. Watts (New York: Penguin, 1969).

[3] Since 1994, the two divisions of St. Paul Edition—Pauline and St. Paul's—publish independently. For this reason, the new printings of Father Tjeng's translation in 2003 and, most recently in 2007, have been published under the name Pauline.

[4] Boethius, *Consolation*, trans. Tjeng, 4.

[5] *Anicii Manlii Severini Boethii Philosophiae consolati*, ed. Ludovicus Bieler, Corpus Christianorum Series Latina 94 (Turnholt: Brepols, 1957).

[6] The Chinese characters that appear in parentheses next to the Korean words in order to distinguish them from homonyms have been omitted in my citations. Throughout this chapter I have tried to be as literal as possible when rendering Father Tjeng's Korean text into English.

[7] All Latin citations of the *Consolatio* are taken from Father Tjeng's base text, *Manlii Severini Boethii Opera omnia*, in *Patrologiae cursus completus, series latina*, ed. Jacques-Paul Migne, vol. 63 (Paris, 1882).

[8] The same Korean word for "disciple" is used when referring to what English translations would render as "follower" or "devotee." This teacher-pupil designation is also consistent with P. G. Walsh's translation, most likely motivated by different circumstances. See Boethius, *The Consolation of Philosophy*, trans. P. G. Walsh (Oxford: Clarendon Press, 1999).

[9] The *Consolatio* was Ku's recommendation in a 1986 Korean publication called *One-Hundred Selections by One-Hundred Celebrities: Great Books for Youth*, compiled by Korea Book and Magazine Ethics Commission.

[10] About half a dozen research papers and another half dozen MA theses on the *Consolatio* have been written and archived or published during last twenty-five years in Korea according to my search of the databases at the National Assembly Library and the Korea Education and Research Information Service as well as my knowledge of information missing from their list. An updated and/or more extensive translation can be expected to raise the number and quality of the scholarly papers on the subject. It may be added as a note of interest that the list of essays on Boethius in Korea expands considerably if the discussions on Boethius's music theory are included.

[11] This is my translation from Korean.

THE GERMAN TRADITION

The German Translations of Boethius's *De consolatione philosophiae*: An Inventory of Translations with Extracts from the Texts[1]

Christine Hehle and Noel Harold Kaylor, Jr.

Introduction

BOETHIUS'S *De consolatione philosphiae* [hereafter *Consolatio*] has been translated into German frequently during the last thousand years. The earliest translation, by Notker of St. Gall, is a monument in Old High German letters, and it was prepared as a bilingual text about AD 1000.

The German tradition comprises a variety of translations and adaptations of the Latin original: all prose, verse-prose, full renderings, translations of the meters only, scholarly or popular renderings, and even a translation presented as a dramatization for the stage. As in all the linguistic traditions, much German *Consolatio* translation is fairly direct, aiming to convey the philosophical content of the work, but there are occasional moments of striking literary quality, especially in renderings of the meters.

Where possible, two sample passages are transcribed from each German translation: a prose passage (book 1, prose 1) and a verse passage (book 3, meter 9). Each has commanded particular scholarly attention in the work as a whole—the scene in which Lady Philosophy makes her first appearance in the Prisoner's cell, and the central Platonic hymn to the governor of the universe.

Translations that remain in unedited manuscripts are registered here, and the known manuscripts containing each translation are listed, in order to indicate one important need for future editorial work in the German tradition, but no attempt has been made to transcribe passages heretofore unedited for inclusion here.

Some of the more scholarly translations contain notes on various aspects of the text, and the notes on all passages transcribed from the translations in this inventory are included as footnotes, as they usually appear as footnotes (sometimes as endnotes) in the translations themselves. The notes are part of the general conception guiding the translations, or of editions of the translations, in which they appear, and they tell much about the translator's or editor's attitude toward the *Consolatio*. Some translators consulted commentaries, and some consulted earlier translations made into German or into other linguistic traditions. Such information generally is mentioned in the introductions, but specific information often is presented in the notes, which are transcribed here. However, standard editorial notation on the collation of manuscript variations, provided in the notes in modern critical editions of the manuscripts, are omitted. As the footnotes in the editions signal variations in readings of the *Consolatio* by the translators or editors, they thus represent points for comparison between the individual German translations, and between German translations and translations in other linguistic traditions. In order to distinguish footnote numbering from endnote numbering in this inventory, footnote numbers appear with a superscripted "fn" and a hyphen prior to the footnote number [ex.: fn-#]. Endnote numbers appear without any prefix.

This inventory of German translations is presented not only to assist scholars interested in Boethius's final work and its reception by German-speaking audiences, but also to assist students interested in the history of the development of the German language and the history of German prosody. The *Consolatio* presents a base-text in Latin, with prose passages alternating with meters that are written in a variety of Latin verse forms. The German translations represent efforts, in a more-or-less continuous sequence, period by period, to render the Latin content, and often the Latin verse forms, into the German of their time.

The earlier translators use standard abbreviations for recurring endings and letters or groups of letters within words, and these abbreviations, where marked by diacriticals in the translations, have been quietly expanded to their full form. Other orthographic features such as spelling peculiarities are maintained, and no standardization has been imposed upon the texts.

The twenty-five known or attested *Consolatio* translations into German are included in this inventory:

Notker of St. Gall	ca. 1000
Peter von Kastl	ca. 1401
Münster Fragments	ca. 1450–1500
Lemgo Translation	ca. 1463/64
Erfurt Translation	ca. 1465
Anonymous [Koberger printing]	1473
Niklas (Niclas) von Wyle	1477
Konrad Humery	ca. 1462/63 or ca. 1500
Anonymous [Schott, editor]	ca. 1500

Johann Hellwig [Helwig]	1600
Christian Knorr von Rosenroth	
and	
Franciscus Mercurius van Helmont	1667/97
Friedrich Roth-Scholz [F.R.]	1717
Johann Just. Fahsius	1734
Johann Gottfried Richter	1753
Friedrich Karl Freytag	1794
L[ambert] I[gnaz] Wortberg	1826
Johann Hilarius Weingärtner	1827
Richard Scheven	1893
Eberhard Gothein	1932
Johannes Zimmermann	1934
Karl Büchner	1939
Konrad Weiss	1956
Ernst Neitzke	1959
H[ermann] M[artin] Endres	1961
Ernst Gegenschatz	
and	
Olof Gigon	1981

* * *

Notker of St. Gall

(d. 1022)

Translation: ca. 1000

Notker's translation of the *Consolatio* is the earliest into German and one of the earliest into any vernacular [a unique, complete manuscript: Sankt Galler Codex 825]. It is an all-prose, bilingual work, prepared in syntactically simplified Latin with Old High German "paraphrase with commentary"[2] for use in monastic schools. As in the edition by Tax, the Latin of the Boethian text is presented here in italics and Notker's Latin and Old High German is in non-italic type.

Book 1, prose 1

De Ingressu Philosophiae. Et Eius Habitu.

Haec dum mecum tacitus reputarem ipse. Únz íh tíz suîgendo in mînemo mûote áhtota. *Et signarem lacrimabilem querimoniam . officio stili.*

Únde íh sús âmerlicha chlága scréib mít temo gríffele. *Uisa est mulier astitisse mihi supra uerticem.* Uuâr sáh íh . éin vuîb stân óbe mír. *Reuerendi admodum uultus.* Êr-uuírdigero tâte hárto. *Ardentibus oculis.* Mít érnestlichên óugôn. *Et perspicacibus . ultra communem ualentiam hominum.* Únde dúrnóhtor séhentên . tánne îoman ménniskôn séhen múge. Ióh profunda dei gesíhet philosophia. *Colore uiuido.* Mít iúnchlichero uáreuuo. Sî neáltêt nîeht. *Atque inexhausti uigoris.* Únde mícheles mágenes ! únde úngebróstenes ! quia pertingit a fine usque ad finem fortiter. *Quamuis ita plena esset ęui.* Tóh si sô ált uuâre. *Ut nullomodo crederetur nostrę ętatis.* Táz síh nîoman íro negelóubti . uuésen ébenált. Uuánda sî uuás îo. *Staturę discretionis ambiguę.* In íro geuuáhste zuîueligero mícheli. Íh nemáhta uuízen . uuîo míchel si uuâre. *Nam nunc quidem cohibebat sese ad communem mensuram hominum.* Uuánda éina uuîla . kezúhta si síh hára ze únsermo méze . uuánda si uuîlôn humana áhtot. *Nunc uero uidebatur pulsare cęlum . cacumine summi uerticis.* Ándera uuîla tûohta si mír den hímel rûoren . mít óbenáhtigemo hóubete . uuánda si astronomiam uuéiz. *Quę cum altivs extulisset caput . etiam ipsum cęlum penetrabat.* Sô si daz hóubet hô ûf erbúreta . sô úber slûog iz ten hímel . táz tûot sî diuina scrutando. *Et frustrabatur intuitum respicientium.* Únde sô tróug si déro sîa ána uuártentôn óugen.

De Amictu Eius.

Vestes erant perfectę tenuissimis filis . subtili artificio . indissolubili materia. Íro uuât uuás chléine . únde uuáhe . únde féstes kezívges. Tíu uuât íst tíure . târ díu dríu ána sínt. Íro uuât . táz sínt artes liberales. Táz sî chléine íst . táz máchônt argumenta . táz sî uuáhe íst . táz máchônt figurę dianoeos únde lexeos. Táz sie uéste sínt . táz máchôt tiu uuârhéit. Sô uuâriu sumptis uuâríu inlatio fólget . sô nemág tára uuídere nîoman nîeht ketûon. Fóne díu íst îo in uuârhéite fésti. *Quas ipsa textuerat manibus suis . uti post cognoui eadem prodente.* Tîa uuât sí íro sélbiu uuórhta . sô íh áfter dés fóne íro uernám. Uuánnân máhtîn dîe artes chómen . âne uóne dei sapientia? *Quarum speciem obduxerat . quędam neglectę uetusatatis caligo . ueluti solet fumosas imagines.* Íro bílde uuâren fóre álti uersáleuuet . sámo so rúcchegíu gemâle. Uel sic. Áltiu sûmhéit hábeta uertúnchelet íro uuáhi. Uuánda sô die artes nîoman neûobet . sô uuírt iro geâgezôt. *Harum in extremo margine . legebatur intextum π grecum.* Ze níderôst án dero uuâte . stûont kescríben taz chrîecheska p. Táz pezéichenet practicam uitam . táz chît Actiuam. *In superiore uero legebatur θ.* Ze óberôst stûont theta. Tíu bezéichenet theoreticam uitam ! dáz chît contemplatiuam. *Atque inter utrasque literas uidebantur insigniti quidam gradus in modum scalarum.* Únde únder zuískên pûohstaben . stûonden sámo so léiter-sprózen gezéichenet . álde stégôn stûofâ. *Quibus esset ascensus . ab inferiori ad superius elementum.* Áfter dîen man stîgen máhti . fóne demo níderen pûohstabe ze demo óberen. Uuánda sancti únde sapientes . fárent fóne actiua vita . ad contemplatiuam. *Eandem tamen uestem . sciderant quorundam uiolentorum manus.* Tîa sélbûn uuât hábeton ferbróchen súmeliche nôt-núnftara. *Et abstulerant particulas quas quisque poterat.* Únde uuâren sie ána-uuert mít íro stúcchen . dîe îogelicher besuérben máhta. Uuánda epicurei únde stoici . únde achademici stríten . únde téiltôn síh in mísseliche sectas. *Et gestabat quidem dextra libellos . sinistra uero sceptrum.* Án dero zéseuuûn trûog si búoh . târ liberales artes ána uuâren . án dero uuínsterûn sceptrum ! uuánda si chúningen íst. Sî chád . per me reges regnant . et thronus meus in columna nubis.

De Expulsione Blandientium Musarum.

Quę ubi uidit poeticas musas . assistentes nostro thoro. Sô sî gesáh fóre mînemo bétte stân . tîe mêter-uuúrchûn. *Et dictantes meis uerba fletibus.* Únde mír trâne récchende . mít íro uuórten. *Commota paulisper.* Sâr dés éin lúzzel zórneg uuórteníu. *Ac toruis inflammata luminibus.* Ióh trôlicho séhentíu. *Inquit.* Frâgeta si. *Quis permisit has skenicas* . i. theatrales *meretriculas accedere ad hunc ęgrum?* Uuér lîez hára in ze dísemo sîechen . tíse geuuéneten hûorrâ ze theatro? In fornicibus theatri . uuúrten meretrices prostratę . dánnan íst fornicatio gehéizen. Álso dîe den man mít íro lenociniis árgerotôn . sô tâten óuh tíse mít íro âmerên uuórten. Fóne díu héizet er sîe meretrices. Álde skenicas meretriculas . héizet er skenicas musas . álso comedię uuâren . únde tragędię . dîe óuh mánne scádotôn . uuánda comedię ráhtôn ímo risum . tragędię luctvm. *Quę non modo nullis remediis fouerent . dolores eius . uerum insuper alerent dulcibus uenenis.* Tîe ímo sîn sêr nîeht éin nehéillent . núbe ióh mêront . mít sûozemo éitere íro uuórto. *Hę sunt enim quę necant / infructuosis spinis affectuum . uberem segetem fructibus rationis.* Tíz sínt tîe dén uuûocher únde dén ézisg tero rationis ertémfent . mít tîen dórnen uuíllônnes. Táz chît mít íro uuíllechôsonne . ergézzent sie mán sînero rationis. *Hominumque mentes assuefaciunt morbo . non liberant.* Únde ménniskôn mûot stôzent sie ín dia súht . sîe nelôsent siæ nîeht. *At si quem profanum detraherent blanditię uestrę . uti uulgo solitum uobis.* Áber infûortînt ir mír éinen uréiden . mít íuuermo zárte . sô ir díccho tûont. *Minus moleste ferendum putarem.* Táz neuuâge mír sô nîeht. *Nihil quippe lederentur in eo operę nostrę.* Án démo neinfûore mír nîeht mînero árbéito. *Hunc uero innutritum eleaticis studiis . atque achademicis . s . non patior mihi subtrahi.* Áber dísen chrîechiskero méisterskéfte . únde achademiskero dúrh-lêrten. *Sed abite potius sirenes . usque in exitium dulces.* Rûment sirenes . lúst-same únz án dia uerlórnísseda. Sirenes sínt mére-tîer . fóne déro sánge intslâfent tie uérigen . et patiuntur naufragium. *Et relinquite eum curandum sanandumque meis musis.* Únde lâzent míh ímo sîn mûot néren . únde héilen *!* mít mînên carminibus. *His ille chorus increpitvs . deiecit humi mestior uultum.* Tô snífta níder dáz sús erstóuta gezuâhte. *Confessusque rubore uerecundiam . tristis limen excessit.* Únde uóre schámôn irrôtende . gelîez iz síh. *At ego cuius acies caligarat . mersa lacrimis . nec dinoscere possim . quęnam esset hęc mulier tam imperiosę auctoritatis . obstipui.* Áber íh erchám míh tô dés . uuér dáz uuîb uuâre sô geuuáltîgo uárentíu . íh nemáhta sia bechénnen . uuánda mír daz óuga tímbereta . fóllez trâno. *Uisuque in terram defixo.* Únde íh fúre míh níder séhende. *Quid deinceps esset actura . explorare tacitus coepi.* Pegónda íh suîgendo chîesen . uuáz sî dára nâh tûon uuólti. *Tum illa propius accedens . consedit in extrema parte lectuli mei.* Tô hítemon náhôr gânde . gesáz si ze énderôst mînes péttes. *Et intuens meum uultum grauem luctv.* Únde ána séhende mîn ánalútte . trâglichez fóne vuûofte. *Atque deiectum in humum merore.* Únde fóne trûregi níder gehángtez. *His uersibus conquesta est . de perturbatione nostrę mentis.* Chlágeta si síh mít tísên uérsen . mînes únmûotes.[3]

Book 3, meter 9

Oratio Philosophiae Ad Deum . Ut Summum Bonum Ipse Demonstret.

O sator terrarum cęlique. Tû sképfo hímeles únde érdo. *Qui gubernas mundum perpetua ratione.* Tû dísa uuérlt órdenôst . únde scáffôst . únde ríhtest . mít tînemo êuuîgen uuîstûome. *Qui iubes tempus ire ab ęuo* . i . qui iussisti tempora incipere ab exordio mundi. Tû die zîte hîeze íro férte begínnen . sáment tero uuérlte . uuánda êr neuuâren zîte . núbe êuuighéite. *Stabilisque manens . das cuncta moueri.* Únde sélbo stâtêr . állíu díng uuérbest . únde uuéhselôst. Uuánda der hímel uuárbelôt . únde állíu díng uuándônt. *Quem non pepulerunt externę causę . fingere opus fluitantis materię* . i . informis et indiscretę. Tíh nehéiniu ánderíu díng nescúntôn . daz scáffelôsa zímber ze máchônne . ûzer démo dísiu uuérlt uuárd . Sî méinet tîa sámentháftigûn mássa . dîa er ze êrest téta . an déro nîeht keskéidenes neuuás. *Uerum* . i . nisi *insita forma boni . carens liuore.* Âne dîn sélbes ínniglicha gûoti . nîeht nîdes hábentíu. *Tu gerens mente pulchrum mundum . pulcherrimus ipse.* Tû in dînemo mûote íu trágende dísa scônûn uuérlt *!* scônero sélbo. *Ducis cuncta ab ęterno exemplo.* Scûofe dû iz ál nâh téro uuîsûn . únde nâh témo êuuigen bílde dînes mûotes. *Similique imagine formans* . i . formasti. Únde démo gelîh tâte dû iz . sô dir in mûote uuás.

Tír nebíldôta . nîoman fóre. *Iubensque* . i . iussisti *perfectas partes absoluere perfectum* . s . opus. Únde hîeze dû uuóla getânív stúcche máchôn uuóla getân uuérh. Uuánda álso uuâlliche líde máchônt uuâllichen mán . sô geskáh óuh táz . táz állero téilelîh tero uuérlte dúrh-skáffenêr . sîa máchôta dúrh-skáffena. Prâste íro téilen . sô brâste íro sélbûn. *Tu ligas elementa . numeris* . s . certis. Quasi diceret ! quatuor elementa ligas. Fîer elementa bíndest tu sô zesámine. *Ut conueniant frigida flammis . arida liquidis.* Táz héiz únde chált . sô fíur únde uuázer íst . únde dúrre . únde náz . sô érda únde lúft íst . nîeht nestrîtên. *Ne euolet purior ignis.* Sô fásto . dáz fóre lîehti hína ûf neflîege daz lîehtera fíur . in démo nehéin trûobi neíst . uuánda iz ze óberôst íst. *Aut pondera . deducant mersa terras.* Nóh tiu suâri . tia érda níder nesénche. *Tu conectens mediam animam . resoluis per consona membra* . i . conectis et resoluis animam per consona membra. Tû gehéftest tia sêla zûo dîen íro gemínnên líden ! únde zetéilest sia áfter dîen . íh méino dia súnnûn gânda an míttemo hímele . únde in míttemen gânda déro septem planetarum. Tîa philosophi hîezen animam mundi . uuánda ál dáz-tir grûet . únde uuáhset . táz túrh kât sî . álso diu sêla die líde tûot. *Triplicis naturę.* Tíu drískero naturę íst ! uuánda si skînet . prûotet . únde brénnet. Ánderíu fíur brénnent óuh . síu nebrûotent áber nîeht. *Mouentem cuncta* . s . ad crescendum. Állíu díng chícchenta . álso únseren lîchamen diu sêla chícchet. *Quę cum glomerauit motum secta in duos orbes* . i . quę cum circumducit cursum sectum in duo hemisperia . *meat reditura in semet* . i . in suum ortum. Únde sô sí gechrúmbet íro fárt . ketéilta in zuêne bógen . éinen óbe érdo . ánderen únder érdo . sô gât si uuídersínnentíu . ze íro ortu. *Circuitque mentem profundam . et conuertit* . i . conlustrat *cęlum simili imagine.* Únde náhtes erstrîchet si dîa tóugenûn fárt . únder dero érdo . únde ze sámolichero uuís . erstrîchet si táges ten hímel óbe dero érdo. *Tu prouehis* . i . producis *animas . uitasque minores paribus causis* . hoc est his causis . ut essent qui deo gratis obedirent. Úmbe gelîchíu díng scûofe du ángelos . únde dîe ín hínderôren ménnisken. Uuáz uuás tíu causa? Táz sie díh íro sképfen bechénnên . únde êreên. Uel sic. Mít kelîchên díngen hábest tu ángelos únde homines fúre gezúcchet fúre ánderíu tîer . íh méino . ratione . et intellectu. *Et aptans sublimes . leuibus curribus.* Únde sîe hóho erhéuende in spûotigên sínnen. *Seris in cęlum terramque* . Sézzest tu sie in hímele . únde in érdo. Angelos in hímele . homines in érdo. *Quas* . s . animas . et uitas . *facis tu conuersas . benigna mente . conuerti ad te reduci igne.* Tîe tûost tû uuíder / sínnen ze dír . án díh keuuánte . mít tînero uuóla-uuílligi. *Da pater menti* . s . eius . *conscendere augustam sedem.* Tû dáz tûost . kíb sînemo mûote . dáz iz hína ûf kestîgen múge . ze dînemo chéiserlîchen stûole . táz iz hímeliskíu díng fernémen múge. *Da lustrare* . i . inuenire *fontem boni.* Ketûo sînen sín fínden gûotes úrspríng. *Luce reperta.* Únde sô er dáz lîeht fínde. *Da defigere in te conspicuos uisus animi.* Sô getûo ín fásto háben an dír . clátíu óugen sînes sínnes. *Dissice nebulas et pondera terrenę molis.* Zeirfûore dîa blíndi . únde dîe súndâ des írdisken lîchámen. *Atque mica tuo splendore.* Únde skîn ín ána mít tînemo skîmen. *Tu namque serenum.* Tû bíst tiu héiteri. *Tu tranquilla requies piis.* Tû bíst tiu kemáchíu râuua dien gûot-uuílligên. *Te cernere finis.* Sô man díh kesíhet . táz íst taz énde. *Idem principium . uector . dux . semita . terminus.* Tû bíst taz ána-génne . tû bíst tér únsih fûoret . s . ze demo énde . tû bíst uuégo-uuîso . únde sélbêr der uuég . únde daz énde . ze démo uuír râmeên.[4]

* * *

Peter von Kastl

(fl. late 1300s–early 1400s)
Translation: ca. 1401

Peter von Kastl was a Benedictine cleric, educated at Prague, associated with the Kastl Benedictine reform movement, and in residence at Cloister Reichenbach on the Regen River in Bavaria during the late 1300s and early 1400s. His translation of the *Consolatio* is first noted by Andreas von Regensburg.[5] Bernhard Pez later makes the suggestion that Peter is the translator of the work printed as anonymous at Nürnberg in 1473.[6] This proposition generally is rejected as speculative.

The Peter von Kastl translation, once in the library at Reichenbach, supposedly is lost.

* * *

Münster Fragments

Anonymous Translator
Translation: ca. 1450–1500

The unique manuscript containing these fragments is lost. It burned in a fire of 1945, which destroyed many of the Münster Library's holdings. Three fragments of this verse translation of the 1400s survive in a transcription published by Alois Bömer in 1908.[7]

Universitätsbibliothek Münster, MS [lost]
Fragment A: from book 1, meter 4

Fragment B: from book 4, prose 3
Fragment C: from book 5, prose 6

* * *

Lemgo Translation

Anonymous Translator
Middle Low German Translation
Translation: ca. 1463/64

This translation, written by Gerhard Folle in Lemgo, survives in one (unedited) Manuscript:

MS Gießen, Universitätsbibliothek, Cod. 863, fols. 229r–244v

The extant prose translation covers book 1. Books 2–4 have been lost, and book 5 was never translated.[8]

* * *

Erfurt Translation

Translator Unidentified
Translation: ca. 1465 [Books 3–5][9]

This translation survives in one (unedited) manuscript from Erfurt, presumably from the Charterhouse of St. Salvator:

Oxford, Bodleian Library, MS Hamilton 46

* * *

Anonymous Translator

Anton Koberger, publisher
(ca. 1440–1513)
Nürnberg Publication: 1473

The Koberger printing contains both the Latin and the German texts, and it is the first printed *Consolatio* in northern Europe. It also contains a commentary, the "Pseudo-Aquinas," which is the earliest known appearance of this commentary. The German provides an all-prose translation, with the Latin verse and prose passages appearing prior to the German rendering of each. The printing of 1473 is transcribed here. Later printings show some orthographic variation from this text.

Book 1, prose 1

Prosa prima

Und da ich die geticht mit mir selber betracht still schweýgent • vnd ein bewainliche chlag oder zeherkich mit dem schreibampt beczaichet • da ward mir gesehen ein frau peýstend auff der schaýtel • gar erwirdiges antliczes • mit prinnenden augen • vnd über die gemain krafft der menschen durchplickend • mit roter varb • vnd was auch vnzergencklicher kraft. Und wiewol sie doch was vols alters • das sie in keinerlay weis würd gelaubt das sie vnsers alters wer. So was sie doch an der größ czweiuelhafftiger erkentnüß • Wann ýezund beweiset sie sich • oder hielt sich zusammen • nach der gemainen maß der menschen • Aber nun wart sie gesehen • das sie an der höch der öbersten schaitel den hýmel züret. Vnd da sie das haupt höher auf hub • da durchgieng sie auch oder anzürt den himel • vnd machet das die menschen ir nimmer gesehen mochten. Vnd ýre klaider die warn gar von dünnen faden • vnd mit behender maisterschaft • vnd von vnaufzulösenlicher materi verpracht • die sie mit iren henden selber geweben het • als sie mir selber darnach offenwart • da ich sie erkant • Vnd der selben klaider gestalt het ein vinster der altschaffenkeit umbzogen • sam die rauchuarben pild • die da helfenpainen oder güldein sein • vnd tunckel werden. Vnd in dem ausser tail der selben klaider was ein krichisch P vnd an dem oberen tail las man ein T das drein geweben was • vnd peý dem P sol man vernemen • das wörtlin practica scientia • das zu teusch haist die würckelich kunst. Aber das T wedeut • als vil sam theorica scientia • das ist die wescheülich kunst • Vnd zwischen ýedwedern puchstaben • sach man etlich staffel wezaichent • in der weis sam ein laitter • Vnd an den selben staffeln • was ein aufgang • von dem vndern puchstaben pis zu dem obern • Vnd auch dasselb klaid • heten die hendt etlicher freuenlicher menschen zuschniten • vnd het ýedlicher die stück hin getragen • die er wegreiffen mocht • Vnd in der rechten handt trug sie püchlein • vnd in der lincken trug sie ein scepter • Vnd da sie ersach • das die göttin der puchtichter in stunden peý vnserm pett • vnd von mir tichteten mein klagwort • da ward sie ein wenige weil erzürnet vnd sach sie mit prýnnenden augen greulichen an vnd sprach • P • Wer hat die vnfletigen pulerin her zulassen geen zu disem krancken • die im nun nicht allein seinen schmerzen nit püssent • sunder sie nern in auch dar zu mit susser vergift. Wann das sind die dý mit vnfruchparn dörnen der wegerung • erdzückent die volkummen frucht • der sat der weschaidenheit • vnd machent der menschen gemüt • das sie ir gewonent • vnd erlösent sie doch nicht von den süchten • Wann het ir mit eurem liebkosen • mir einen gar eýteln oder werntlichen enzogen •

als es gemainglichen vnter dem volk gewon ist • so het ich es nit als gar verübel • Wann so wirt nichznit vnsers fleiß an im versert • Aber ir habt vns den enzogen der da genert ist worden • in der krichischen stat Elida do Arestotiles gelert hat • vnd in dem dorff academia da Plato gelert hat • vnd dauon get nun pillicher hin ir süssingenten sirenen • die mit eurem gesang pringt die hörer pis in den tod • vnd last mir in meinen maistern & künsten hail und gesundt zumachen • B • Vnd da die schar der selben sirenen oder göttin der puchtichter • wart mit solchen worten also gestrafft • da hielt sie das antlütz trawriglichen nider zu dem ertrich • vnd wekant die röt irer scham • vnd gieng über das trischeufel trawrig hin aus • Aber ich • des augen mit zebern wegossen vnd tunckel waren • das ich nicht erkennen mocht • wer die fraw wer • als gar gewaltiger bewerter maisterschaft • da erschrack ich vnd hielt das gesicht nider gegen dem ertrich • Vnd wegunt stillchweigent paiten • was sie denn darnach wolt tun • Da gieng sie neher her zu • vnd sas an das aussertail meins pettleins • vnd sach mein antlütz an das mit schwerer klag in herczenlaid gegen dem ertrich genigen was • vnd klagt von der trübsal vnsers gemütes • mit den versen die man zu teutsch also mag außsprechen •[10]

Book 3, meter 9

Metrum nonum

O Got der du mit ewiger vorschickung außrichst die werlt • vnd bist ein scöpfer des ertrichs vnd des himels • der du die zeit haissest geen von ewig • vnd stet beleiben&[11] machest das alle ding bewegt werden • Den nit frömbde sachen betzwüngen haben zu machen das werck der hinfliessenden materig • Sun& von & innwesenden forme des hösten gutes • die neides mangelt bringest du alle ding von dem obersten ebenpild • Vnd du selber der allerschönst hast getragen die schönen werlt in dem gemüte • vnd bist sie pildent mit gleichem pilde • Vnd du hast gehaissen das volkomen • ledig zumachen die volkomen teýle der element • vnd dieselben element pindest du mit der zal • Also das die kelte mit dem feür • vnd die dürren mit den feüchten beqweme werdent • vnd das das lauter feür nicht außfliege • oder das die schwerikeit nicht vnderdrücke das gesenckt ertrich • Auch bis du zusamen besstend vnd zerlösend mit mithellenden gelidern die mitteln sele der trifaltigen natur • die alle ding beweget • Vnd so sie getailt ist worden • so hat sie die bewegung umbgefürt in zwen umbkreis • vnd geet denn widerkerend in sich selber • vnd umbgeet das tieffe gemüte • vnd mit geleicher pildung bekeret sie den himel • Vnd mit gleichen sachen fürest du die sele vnd das mýnder leben • vnd bist zufügend die hohen sele auff geringen wägen • vnd die mýndern seest du auff das ertrich • vnd die sele die mit gütwilligem gesetze zu dir gekert sind • die machst du das sie widerkeren in dem widertragenden feüre • O vater gib dem gemüte aufzesteigen zu dem engen stul • gib vns durchsehen den prunnen des guten • gib vns das wir finden das liecht • vnd in dich hefften das bescheülich gesichte des gemütes • Vnd zertreib die nebel • vnd die pürden der irdischen schwerheit • vnd scheine mit deinem glantz • wann du bist unsere heitere zeit • vnd bist ein stille rwe [*sic*] den gütigen • vnd ein ende dich zesehen • Du bist der anfang • der fürer • der laitter • der steig • vnd auch das zil • Darnach sprach die weißheit •[12]

* * *

Niklas (Niclas) von Wyle

(ca. 1415–79)
Translation: 1477

Niklas von Wyle earned his BA degree in Vienna in 1433. He was "the leading figure of early Humanism in Southern Germany. [...] In accordance with his theoretical view that Latin was the best model for German style, he aspired in his translations to render the Latin as closely as possible."[13]

The Wyle translation, attested only in his own writings, supposedly is lost. Another earlier German translation, as yet unidentified, is mentioned in his writings.

* * *

Konrad Humery

(ca. 1403–prior to 1478)
Translation: ca. 1462/63 or ca. 1500[14]

Konrad Humery's *Consolatio* translation is very free, with many comments upon the text inserted throughout.

The translation survives in three (unedited) manuscripts:

Berlin, Staatsbibliothek, MS theol. lat. fol. 490, fols. 109r–176v (1476)
Mainz, Staatsbibliothek, Cod. III 44, fols. 2r–71r (1472)
Tübingen, Universitätsbibliothek, Cod. M. d. 124, fols. 2r–115v (*c.*1475)

* * *

Anonymous Translator of the 1473 Koberger Publication

Reedited by Johann Schott

Publication: ca. 1500

This all-prose text is a reediting of the Koberger Printing of 1473. The dialect of this version differs slightly from that of the Nürnberg publication. It is for linguistic interest that the following passages from this reediting are transcribed here.

Book 1, prose 1

Die erst Prosa.

Vnnd da ich die gedicht mit mir selber betracht stillschweigent : vnd ein bewäinliche klag oder zeherlich mit dem schreibampt bezeichet / do ward mir geschen ein fraw beystend uff &[15] schäytel / gar erwirdiges antlützes / mit prinnenden augen / vnd über die gemein krafft der menschen durchplickend : mit roter varb : vnd was auch vnzergencklicher krafft : vnd wie wol sy doch wz vols alters dz[16] sy in keiner läy weis würd gelaubt dz sy vnsers alters were / so was sy doch an & größ zweifelhafftiger erkentnuß. Wann yetzund beweiset sie sich oder helt sich züsammen nach der gemeinen masz & menschen : aber nun ward sy gesehen dz sy an der höhe & öbersten schäitel den himel rüret. Vnd do sy dz haupt höher auff hüb / do durchgieng sy auch oder anrürt den hymel / vnd machet dz die menschen jr nimmer gesehen mochten. Vnd jre kläider die waren gar von dünnen fäden / vnd mit behender mäisterschaft / vnd von vnauffzulösenlicher materig verpracht : die sy mit jren henden selber geweben het : als sye mir selber darnach offenbart da ich sy erkant • Vnd & selben kläider gestalt het ein vinster & altschaffenheit vmbzogen • sam die rauchfarben pild die do helfenbeinn o& guldin seinn / vnd tunckel werden. Vnd in dem aussertäil der selben kläider was ein kriechisch P. vnd an dem öberntäil las man ein T. dz dar eingeweben was. Vnd bey dem P. sol man vernemen dz wörtlin practica scientia : das zü teütsch häißt die würckenlich kunst : aber dz T. bedeut als vil sam theorica scientia : das ist die beschaulich kunst. Vnd zwischen yetwedern büchstaben sach man etlich stapfel vezeichent in & wets sam ein läiter. Vnd an den selben stapflen was ein auffgang von dem vndern büchstaben biß zü dem öbern. Vnd auch das selb kläid hetten die hend etlicher freuenlicher menschen züschniten : vnd het yegklicher die stuck hin getragen die er begreiffen mocht. Vnd in & rechten handt trüg sye büchlein / vnd in der lincken trüg sye ein scepter. Vnd do sy ersach dz die göttin & büchtichterin stunden bey vnserm bett / vnd von mir tichteten mein klagwort / do ward sy ein wenige weil erzürnet von sach sy mit brinnenden augen greülichen an vnd sprach. P. Wer hat die vnfletigen bülerin her zülassen geen zü disem krancken: die jm nun nit allein seinen schmertzen nit püssent / sun& sye nerit jn auch dar zü mit süssem vergifft. Wann dz sind die die mit vnfruchparn dörnen der wegerung / erdruckent die volkommen frucht des sats & beschäidenheit : vnd machent & menschen gemüt dz sye jr gewonent / vnd erlösent sy doch nit von den füchten. Wann hett jr mit eürem liebkosen mir einen gar eyteln o& werntlichen entzogen / als es gemeinglichen vnder dem volk gewon ist / so het ich es nit als gar für übel : wann so wirt nichtz nit vnsers fleisz an jm versert • Aber jr habt vns den enzogen & da genert ist worden in der krichischen stat Elida do Arestotiles gelert hat : vnd in den dorff Academia do Plato gelert hat : vnd dauon geet nun billicher hin jr süssingenden Syrenen / die mit eurem gesang bringent die hörer bisz in den tod : vnnd laßt mir jn meinen mäistern der künsten heyl vnd gesund zümachen. B. Vnd do die schar & selben Syrenen o& göttin der büchtichter / wardt mit sölichen worten also gestrafft / do hielt sy dz antlütz trawriglichen nider zü dem ertrich : vnd bekant die röt jrer scham : vnd gieng über dz trischheüfel trawrig hin auß. Aber ich / des augen mit zehern begossen vnd tunckel waren / das ich nicht erkennen mochte wer die fraw wer / als gar gewaltiger bewerter mäisterschafft / do erschrack ich vnd hielt dz gesicht nider gegen dem ertrich. Vnd begund stilschweigent beiten was sye denn darnach wolt tün. Do gieng sy neher her zü / vnd saß an das aussertäil meins betleins : vnd sach mein antlütz an das mit schwerer klag in hertzenläid gegen dem ertrich genigen waß : vnd klagt von der trübsal vnsers gemütes / mit den versen die man zü teütsch also mag ausssprechen.[17]

Book 3, meter 9

Das neündt Metrum.

O got der du mit ewiger vorschickung außrichst die werlt : vnd bist ein schöpfer des ertrichs vnd des hymels : der du die zeit haissest geen von ewig : vnd stet beleiben&[18] machest dz alle ding bewegt werden : den nit frömde sachen betzwüngen haben zü machen das werck der hinfliessenden matery : sunder von der inwesenden forme des höchsten güts : die neides mangelt : bringest du alle ding von dem obersten ebenpild. Vnd du selber der aller schönst hast getragen die schönen werlt in dem gemüte : vnd bist sie pildent mit gleichem pilde. Vnd du hast gehaissen das volkommen ledig zümachen die volkomen teyle & element : vnd die selben element pindestu [*sic*] du mit der zal : also das die kelte mit dem feür / vnd die dürren mit den feüchten beqweme werdent : vnd das das lauter feür nicht außfliege : oder das die schwerigkeit nicht vn&trücke dz gesenckt ertrich. Auch bistu du züsamen hefftend vnd zerlösend mitt mithellenden geli&n die mitteln sele der trifaltigen natur : die alle ding beweget. Vnnd so sie getailt ist worden / so hat sie die bewegung vmbgefürt in zwen vmbkreis : vnd geet denn widerkerend in sich selber : vnd vmbgeet das tieffe gemüte : vnd mit geleicher pildung bekeret sie den himel. Vnd mit gleichen sachen fürest du die sele vnd das myn& leben : vnd bist züfügen die hohen sele auff geringen wägen : vnd die myndern seest du auff das ertrich : vnd die sele die mit gütwilligem gesetze zü dir gekert sind / die machst du das sie widerkeren in dem wi&tragenden feüre. O vater gib dem gemüte aufzesteigen zü dem engen stül : gib vns durchsehen den prunnen des güten : gib vns das wir finden das liecht / vnd in dich hefften das beschawlich gesichte des gemütes. Vnd zertreib die nebel vnd die pürden & jrdischen schwerheit : vnd scheine mit deinem glantz : wann du bist vnsere haitere zeit : vnnd bist ein stille rüe den gütigen vnd ein ende dich zeschen. Du bist & anfang / der fürer / & laiter / & steig vnd auch dz zil. Darnach sprach die weyßheit:[19]

* * *

Johann Hellwig [Helwig]

Printing: 1600

This verse-prose translation is complete. The intent of the translator is indicated in a prefatory note:

Severini Boethii
Christlich vernünftiges
Bedenken /
Wie man sich bey vordrin-
gendem Gewalt und Wohler
gehen der Gottlosen / auch unrecht-
mässigem Leiden und Ubelgehen
der Frommen zu trösten habe /
In fünf Bücher verfasset /
Dem Liebhaber der
Teutschen Sprache zu Nu-
tzen aus dem Latein übergesetzt;
benebenst richtiger
Beschreibung des Boëthii
Lebenslaufes. (title page)

This statement is followed by a poem of nine eight-line stanzas, which, begins with these two opening verses:

Wo sind die guldnen Zeiten?
Wie sind sie worden Bley? (n.p.)

Book 1, prose 1

Als ich solchem stillschweigend bey mir nachsanne / und meine erbärmliche Klage aufzeichnete / bedunket mich mir oben zum Haubt stehen ein Weibsbild eines herzlichen Ansehens / mit stralenden und über aller gemeinen Menschenweise scharfichtigen Augen / lebhafftem Angesichte / und wohl vermöglicher Kräften / wiewohl sie schiene solches Alters seyn / das wohl nicht glaublich mit Menschlichem Alter eintrafe / wie auch einer unersinnlichen Leibsgestalte. Dann sie bald eines gemeinen Menschen Länge habend / bald aber mit dem Haubt an den Himmel reichend / vorkame / ja so sie das Haubt etwas höher erhube / auch durch den Himmel selber drange / und sich gleichsam der Nachschauenden Augen entzoge. Die Kleider waren von zarten Gewirke / subtiler Arbeit / und von unauflößlichem Gezeuge gemacht / welche / wie ich nachmals von ihr gehöret hab / sie selber mit eignen Händen gewirket hatte. An deren End oder Saum unten das Griechische Л. oben aber das Θ. eingewirket zu sehen gewesen / und zwischen beeden Buchstaben scheineten etliche Staffel einer Stiege gleich verzeichnet seyn / auff welchen man von dem untern zu dem obern Buchstab steigen konte. Jedoch hatten ihrer etliche solches Gewand ihr gewaltsamer Weise gerissen / und die Stuklein / was ein ieder vermocht / mit hinweggenommen. Und truge sie zwar in der rechten Hand Bücher / in der linken aber einen Scepter. Da solche nun die dichteriche Musen bey meinem Bette stehende / und sich auch mit mir kläglich geberdende erblikket hat / ist sie mit versteltem Angesicht in diese Worte herausgebrochen. Wer hat diese kurtzweilige Dirnen zu diesem Kranken eingelassen? welche ihm seine Schmertzen durch keinerley wege mildern / sondern vielmehr durch süssen Gifft vermehren. Sintemal diese die jenige seyn / welche mit den dörnichten Gedanken die reiche Saat der fruchtbaren Vernunfft erstekken / und das menschliche Gemüth zur Krankheit nur angewöhnen / aber nicht erledigen können. Wann ihr dann nur / wie ihr sonsten pfleget / einen unberichten durch eure Schmeichell ist uns entzöget / so were etwan dieses noch zu gedulten / und geschehe uns hiemit ein ringer Abbruch; nun aber habt ihr einen in guter Lehre und Platonischen Ubungen erzogenen angegriffen. Weichet demnach von hinnen ihr sußvergallte Sirenen / und überlasset ihn meiner Musen Warte und

Heilung. Woraus jene solcher massen bescholten gantz traurig zur Erden geschauet / und mit ihres Angesichts Röte die Schand bekennende zu der Thür hinaus gewichen. Ich aber / dessen Augen durch die Threnen also vertrunklet gewesen / daß ich nicht wohl erkennen könte / was heroisches Weibsbilt doch gegenwärtige were / bin hierüber sehr erstaunet / und mit nidergeschlagenem Anlitz stillschweigend erwartet / was sie doch ferners thun würde. Da sie dann näher zu mir getretten / sich auf das äuserste meines Betts gesetzet / und meine traurige und nidergeschlagene Gestalt betrachtend / mit folgenden Wörten über menschlicher Gemüthsverwirrung ihre Klag geführet:[20]

Book 3, meter 9

O Schöpfer des bunten und runden Gebäude /
vorsichtig und richtig du leitest die Zeite /
        regirest und führest den hohen Gewalt /
        im Handel und Wandel bleibt deine Gestalt.
Nichts kunte / begunte von aussen anlassen
diß Werke zu werken / zusammenzulassen;
        Dann ohne Mißgunste der Künsten betracht
        beruhet im Guten des Höchsten Allmacht.
Ohn Ende dein' Hände hier alles erfüllen /
Du rufest / und schufest ein iedes nach Willen:
        Das schönste Geschöpfe du Schönster gestellt /
        diß reichlich vergleichlich dein Bildniß vorhält
Den Samen der Dingen auch artest und parest /
der einig vereinigten Stifter du warest /
        daß Frost und die Flamme zusammengemischt /
        das Trokne durch feuchte gar leichtlich sich frischt.
Die reine Glut über die Schranke nicht schwanke /
die Schwere der Erde mit Gfährden[21] nicht wanke:
        Du leitest / bereitest den seeligen Geist /
        der iedem Bewegung und Regung anweist.
Durch dich er zertheilet gleich bleibet und treibet /
gar mächtig und prächtig gesondert umscheubet
        den obersten Kreise / nach Weise sich kehrt
        in seiner selbsteigenes Eigenschaft / lehrt
verstehen und sehen die Göttliche Gstalte[22] /
so gleichend bezeugend den obern Gewalte.
        Bemeistert / begeistert ingleichen von dir /

was lebet und schwebet im grossen Rund' hier.
Beseelet von fernen der Sternen Liecht prachtet /
dein Gegen der Erde Vermögenreich machet;
was hägend und regend die Gnade gereicht /
solchs billich und willig zu dir wiedrum weicht.
Gib Vatter / gib günstig / daß brünstig verehre
die Seel dich / gebührlich dein' Ehre vermehre:
Die Sinnen gewinnen den glaubigen Schein /
dir trauen ohn Schmertzen des Hertzen allein /
verachten / verlachen diß Leidengewümmel:
erleuchte / bereiche sie / Vatter vom Himmel!
Den frommen dein Wille die stille Ruh' ist /
der Anfang und Außgang der Zeiten du bist.
Ein starker Beleiter auf Wegen und Stegen /
ein Schutzer und Trutze den feinden entgegen:
Den Blöden in Nöthen ein tröstlicher Bot /
ohn welchen alls nichtig / hinflüchtig / und tod.[23]

* * *

Christian Knorr von Rosenroth
(July 15 or 16, 1636–May 4, 1689)
and
Franciscus Mercurius van Helmont
(1614–99)
(Printings: 1667 [Sulzbach, 268 pages]
and
1697 [Lüneburg, 255 pages])

Christian Knorr von Rosenroth rendered the meters and Franciscus Mercurius van Helmont rendered the prose passages into German for this verse-prose *Consolatio* translation. The printing of 1697 is transcribed here.

Book 1, prose 1

Indem ich dieses stillschweigend bey mir bedachte, und eben solche meine Jammer-Klag in Schrifften verfassen wolte, erzeigte sich zu meinen Haupten ein Weibsbild, in einer gar ehrwürdigen Gestalt: Ihre Augen waren wie glânzend und scharffsichtiger, als andere Menschen insgemein. Sie war auch gar lebhaffter Farb, und noch vvol bey leib und vermôglicher Krâfften, unerachtet sie eines so grossen Alters vvar, dasz man nicht glauben konte, dasz sie bey diesen unseren Zeiten gebohren wâre: Ihr Grôsse mochte man nicht gevvis absehen oder eigentlich ermessen, Dann bald vvar sie einer gemeinen Menschen-Lânge, bald schiene sie mit ihrer Hôhe an den Himmel zu reichen, und wann sie das Haupt recht auffhube, durchdrunge sie den Himmel gar, also, dasz wann man ihr nachsahe, sie nicht mehr zu erkennen war. Ihre Kleider waren von zartem gespûnft subtiler Arbeit, und solchem Zeug verfertigt, vvelchen man nicht Aufflôsen konte, die sie (vvie ich nachmal von ihr verstanden) mit eigenen Hânden gevvûrcket hatte, deren schône Gestalt und Ansehen, vvegen vervvarlosten Alters und lânge der Zeit, vvie die alten beraucherten und bestaubten Bilder der Vorfahren pflegen, etvvas dunckel und gleichsam überzogen und unscheinlich: An deren Ende oder Saum unten das Griechische π, oben das θ, eingevvûrckt zu lesen, und zvvischen beyden Buchstaben etliche Staffeln angezeichnet zu sehen vvaren, auff vvelchen man von dem unteren zu dem oberen Buchstaben gelichsam steigen solte. Dieses Kleid aber hatten etliche ihr mit Gevvalt zerrissen, und einer hier der ander dort, vvie ein jeder gekunt, ein Stûcklein davon hinvveg genommen. In der rechten Hand trug sie einige Büchlein, in der lincken aber einen Scepter. Da sie nun die Verstichtende oder *Poêtischen Musen*, bey meinen Bett stehen erblicket, in acht genommen, dasz dieselben mit ihrem Klagen mein Leyd nur vermehreten, und mir zu Beschreibung meines Schmertzens ihre anmuthige Wort gleichsam darliehen, fieng sie, etvvas entrüstet, und mit einem sauren Gesicht, an; Wer hat diese *Comediantische* Dirnen zu diesem Krancken herein gelassen? Die doch seinem Schmertzen nicht allein keine Artzney und Hûlff bringen, sondern selben noch durch ihr süsses Gifft und Schmeichlen vermehren. Dann eben diese sinds, vvelche durch die unfruchtbahre Dôrner der Affecten und unordentlichen Zuneigungen die sonst gar fruchtreiche Erndte tôdten und ersticken, indem sie dem menschlichen Gemuth seine Kranckheit und Mângel nur angenehm machen, keines vvegs aber es davon entledigen. Und zvvar wann ihr vvie sonst zugeschehen pflegt, nur irgend einen gemeinen und hôherer Sachen unerfahrnen Menschen durch euer Schmeichel-Geschvvâtz von mir abzôget, môchte man sich darûber vveniger beschvveren; Sintemalen hierdurch mein Fleisz und angevvendte Arbeit keinen Schaden oder Abbruch litte. Nun habt ihr aber diesen Mann, so in des *Zenons* von *Eleate* Unterred-Kunst und in des *Plato* Academischer Weisheit-Schul aufferzogen vvorden, angefasst: Darum vveichet von dannen, ihr schâdliche *Sirenen* und susgiftige Zauberinnen, und lasset ihn meinen tugendhafften rechtschaffenen *Musen* und Kunst-lehrerinnen seiner zu pfegen und ihn gesund zu machen; Auff vvelchen Vervveis und Ausscheltung dann jene das Angesicht traurig zur Erden schlugen, und gantz beschâmt sich aus dem Zimmer davon machten. Ich aber, vveiln mir das Gesicht durch die Thrânen ûbergossen und verduncklet vvar, dasz ich nicht wol erkennen konte, vver dann dieses Weib, die sich einer so meisterhafften Autoritât und Bottmâssigkeit gebrauchte, seyn müsse, vervvunderte mich hierüber hoch, und vvolte mit neidergeschlagenen Augen stillschweigend ervvarten, vvas sie vveiters anfangen vvurde. Darauff sie dann nâher zu mir trat, sich an das End meines Bettleins satzte, und nachdem sie meine traurige und von schmertzhafften Gedancken gantz verfallene Gestalt betrachtet, über solche meine Gemüts-Vervvirrung mit folgenden Reimen klagte:[24]

Book 3, meter 9

Schôpffer Himmels und der Erden, dessen Hand die gantze Welt
In bestândig-schôner Ordnung hoch-vernûfftig unterhâlt,
Der du aller Zeiten Lauff heissest auff dein Wort entstehen,
Daß er aus der Ewigkeit stracks beginnt herfûr zu gehen:
Der du ewig-unbeweget bloß in einem Stande bist,
Und doch gleichwol machst, daß alles immer in Bewegung ist.

Dich, Herr, trieb des hôchsten gutes wesentliche Neigung an,
Die, sich selber mitzutheilen, keine Mißgunst hindern kan,
Den zerfliessend-dûnnen Zeug bildend in ein Werck zu bringen,
Daß dich nicht von aussen erst etwas anders dorffte zwingen.
Und da hast du nach dem Muster, das sich in dir selbst befindt,
Alle Sachen ausgewûrcket, wie sie nun erschaffen sind.

Denn du, als der allerschônste, trâgst die wunder schône Welt
Wûrcklich selber im Gemûte, und was du dir vorgestellt,
Hat des Bildes Æhnlichkeit stracks von aussen angenommen,
Und so hat das gantze Rund auch die Stûcke gantz bekommen.
Daß der Elementen wesen, und zugleich, was daraus entsteht,
Nach den eingetheilten Zahlen gleichsam als in Schnûren geht.

Dannenhero kômt die Kâlte mit den Flammen ûberein,
Und das wâßrig-feuchte Wesen kan wol um das trockne seyn,
Daher muß das reine Feur nicht aus seinen Schrancken fliegen,
Noch der schweren Erden Last tieff-versenckt im Wasser liegen.

Und so haben alle Sachen ihr gewisses Maß und Ziel,
Daß sie nicht zu wenig würcken, und doch auch nicht gar zu viel.

Du vertheilst die Mittel-Seele, welche dreyfach ist von Art,
Und den grossen Bau zu regen, keine Mûh noch Sorge spart
Gar genau in Glieder ein, die sich trefflich zu ihr schicken,
Und so wunderbar verknûpft die Natur mit Ordnung schmûcken.
Diese, wenn sie nun zwey Kreisse wol-getheilt durchwandert hat,
Kômmt denn wieder zu sich selber, und vollbringt ihr grosses Rad.

Denn sie lâufft um das Gemûte, das so tieff verborgen steht,
Und bewegt also den Himmel, daß er auch im Cirkel geht.
Du siehst auch in gleicher Art fleissig auff der Seelen Schaaren,
Und lâsst nicht die Grossen nur, sondern auch die Kleinen fahren,
Jene zwar auff leichten Wagen, als erhôht ins Himmels Feld,
Aber diese tieff herunter auff den Unterkreiß der VVelt;

Die du doch nach deiner Gûte wieder lâsst zurûcke gehn,
Daß sie wieder zu dir kehren, und sich auch im Feur erhôhn.
Und nun, Vater, gieb doch auch, daß mein seuffzendes Gemûte
Steig auff jenen hohen Thron: und beschau den Brunn der Gûte,
Laß mich mit Vergnûgung finden, deines Liechtes Glantz und Schein,
Und mit des Verstandes Augen bloß auff dich gerichtet seyn.

Komm, zertreib des Côrpers Nebel, und der schweren Erden-Last,
Scheine selbst mit deinen Stralen, die du mir gezeiget hast,
Denn du bist die Heiterkeit, und die stille Ruh der Frommen,
Dich zu schauen ist der Zweck, in dem alles ist vollkommen.
Hôr, O Anfang aller Sachen, Trâger dem nichts wird zu viel,
Fûhrer, und zugleich die Strasse, und denn selber auch das Ziel.[25]

* * *

Friedrich Roth-Scholz [F.R.]

(September 17, 1687 [Herrnstadt/Lower Silesia]—
January 15, 1736 [Nürnberg])
Publication: 1717[26]

This translation is attested in: Luca Obertello, *Severino Boezio II*. Accademia Ligure de Scienze e Lettere Collana di Monograph 1 (Genova: Accademia

Ligure de Scienze e Littere, 1974). For this inventory, no copy has been be located. The translator was the proprietor of the Tauber'sche Buchhandlung at Nürnberg.

* * *

Johann Justus Fahsius

(d. 1734)
Publication: 1724

Johann Fahsius's work is one of the more unusual renderings of the *Consolatio*, into any vernacular. The translator builds upon dramatic features inherent in the *Consolatio* to present the work as a play. The biographical information on Boethius, given in book 1 after the opening sections of the Latin original, is moved to the beginning of the play and presented as acts 1–2. The content of book 1, meter 1, of the *Consolatio* then opens act 3, as scene 1. Then, book 1, prose 1, follows as act 3, scene 2.

[Prior to act 1, Fahsius lists the characters.]

Personæ Dramatis.

Theodoricus, *Der Ost-Gothische König in Italien.*
Cassiodorus, *dessen Cantzler und vornehmster Staats-*Minister.
Triguilla, *ein königlicher* Financen-*Rath.*
Coniastus, *ein alter Hof-*Procurator.
Gaudentius, Opilio, Basilius, *3. abgesetzte Hof-Bediente des* Boethii *Angeber.*
Symmachus, *Bürgermeister zu Rom*, Boëthii *Schwieger-Vater.*
Boëthius, *Bürgermeister zu Rom und zugleich königlicher* Minister.
Philosophia, *die Weltweißheit.*
Fortuna, *die Göttin des Glücks.*
9. Musæ Lugubres.
Arrogante, *ein königlicher* Mignon.
Satyrique, *sein Diener.*
Cajoleur, *dessen* Secretair.
Harpax, *des* Coniasti *Diener.*[27]

Book 1, prose 1

[As noted above, the content of Book 1, prose 1 is delayed in this translation until a dramatically appropriate point in the translator's play.]

Actus III. Scen 2.

Boëth. Lib.I. Pros.I. (Die *Philosophia* erscheinet in Gestalt einer ansehnlichen *Dame* und in der *Positur*, wie sie von *Boëthio* selbst beschrieben wird.)

PHILOSOPHIA

Wer hat diese unzeitigen und zärtlichen Klage-Weiber zu diesen Patienten herein geführet, welche seinen Schmertz nicht allein gar nicht lindern, sondern auch noch darzu mit dem sussen Gifft ihrer beweglichen Stimmen vermehren? Diese sind es eben, welche durch unzeitige Erregung der zärtlichen Affecten *alle vernünfftige Vorstellung gantz unterdrücken, und das menschliche Gemüth nur zur Kranckheit gewöhnen, nicht aber davon befreyet. Wenn es eine von denen gemeinen und niedrigen Seelen wäre, die Ihr mir durch eure Schmeicheley entziehen woltet, so wolte ich den Verlust mit Gedult ertragen, denn dabey gieng keine von mir angewandte Mühe verlohren; dieser aber ist meiner geheiligten Schule erzogen, und an denen Brüsten meiner Weißheit ernähret worden. Drum so packt euch von ihm weg, ihr* Sirenen, *die ihr den Menschen biß in dem Tod süß und angenehm schmelz thelt. Uberlasset mir dieses Hertz, welches ich mit meinen* Musen *und vernunfft mässigen Mitteln curiren will. Eylet, sag ich, geschwinde von hinnen und erscheinet in dieser unanständigen Trauer-Gestalt nicht mehr an diesem Ort. (Die* Musen *reteriren sich hinter die* Scenen, *drauf setzet sich die* Philosophie *vor dem* Boëthio *aufs Bette, und nachdem Sie, ihn mittleydig beschauet, fängt sie an:)*[28]

Book 3, meter 9

PHIL.

Du hast recht. Laßt uns derohalben folgende Seuffzer gen Himmel schicken.

Met. 9. *O Gott, dessen weise Hand das gantze Rund der Welt*
Erschaffen, und noch stets in schönster Ordnung hält,
Der alles samt der Zeit beweget, reget, treibet,
Und doch selbst unbewegt und ohne Aendrung bleibet:
Daß du so wunderbar aus deiner Gottheit Macht
Das fliessend-dünne Zeug hast in ein Werck gebracht,
Dazu hat dich, O HERR, von aussen nichts beweget,
Nur deine Gütigkeit, die keine Mißgunst beget,
Und nach den Muster nun, das sich dort oben findet,
Ist alles eingericht, was Zeit und Ordnung bindet.
Du bist der Schöneste, und hast die schöne Pracht

Der Welt, aus deinem Witz und Bilde hergebracht,
Und wie du alles bist, und ein vollkommen Wesen,
So ist sie auch durch dich vollkommen und genesen.
Die Elementa sind so ordentlich gefast,
Daß alles wunderschön und recht zusammen past,
Die Kälte mischet sich gar artig mit den Flammen,
Das Trockne kömmt gar offt mit dem, was Naß zusammen.
Geht, wie das leichte Feur nicht gar zu hoch auffleigt,
Und auch der Erden-Last, nicht gar in Abgrund weicht.
Du hast den edlen Geist, der alles hier beseelet,
Als in dreyfacher Krafft, mit Leib und Seel vermählet,
Wie sichs zu jeden schickt. Und wenn er seinen Lauff
Vollendet, nimmstu ihn zu dir einst wider auf.
Ja jede Seele kehrt, die grossen und die kleinen
Einst wieder in sich selbst, und muß vor dir erscheinen,
Die grossen fliehen hoch an dem gestirnten Plan,
Die kleinen zeigen sich auf niedrer Erden-Bahn,
Biß sie doch alle einst in dich zurücke gehen,
Und durch der Reingung-Feur erhöht und prangend stehen.
Ach Vater! gib doch Krafft, daß sich mein armer Geist
Aufschwinge, wenn er sich der Eitelkeit entreist.
Laß mich in deinem Licht die Segens-Quelle finden;
Und meiner Seelen Aug an dich alleine binden.
Vertreib aus meiner Brust den eitlen Erden-Dunst,
Und strahle starck hinein mit deiner Gottheit Brunst.
Du bist allein die Ruh, der Himmel aller Frommen,
Wer sich mit dir vereint ist selig und vollkommen.
Dich dermahleins zu sehn ist aller Seelen Zweck,
O Anfang unsres Wohls, O Ende, Führer, Weg.[29]

* * *

Johann Gottfried Richter

(1713–58)
Publication: 1753

Book 1, prose 1

Als ich diese Gedanken in der Stille bey mir hegte, und meine Thränenklage aufzeichnete, kam mir vor, als stünde oben zu meinem Haupte eine Weibsperson, von sehr ehrwürdigem Ansehen, mit stralenden und für Menschen ganz ungewöhnlich scharfsehenden Augen, von lebhafter Farbe und muntern Kräften; ob sie gleich von einem solchen Alter war, daß sie nicht zu unserer Zeit gebohren zu seyn schiene. Desgleichen war auch ihre Grösse und Länge nicht genau zu bestimmen. Denn bald gliche sie hierinnen andern Menschen, bald aber schien sie auch mit ihrem Haupte bis an die Wolken zu reichen; Ja, wenn sie dasselbe noch höher erhub, so drange sie damit so gar bis in den Himmel, und entzog es den Augen derer, die ihr nachsahen. Ihre Kleidung war von zartem Gewebe, künstlicher Arbeit, und unauflöslichem Stoffe, die sie sich, wie ich hernach von ihr selbst erfahren habe, mit eigenen Händen gemacht hatte. Die eigentliche Tracht aber war, wie ein beräuchertes Bild, durch die Länge der Zeit unkennbar worden; Auf den untersten Saum war ein griechisches π, auf den obersten aber ein θ, gesticket;[fn-1] *und zwischen diesen beyden Buchstaben waren, gleich einer Leiter, einige Stuffen zu sehen, auf welchen man von dem untern Buchstaben bis an den obern steigen konnte. Doch hatten einige Grausame dieses Kleid zerrissen, und Stückchen davon mitgenommen, soviel ein jeder vermocht hatte. In der rechten Hand trug sie etliche Bücher; in der linken aber ein Zepter. Da sie nun die dichterischen Musen an meinem Bette stehen sahe, die mit mir kläglich thaten, und meineten, wurde sie ganz unwillig, und sprach mit ernsthaften und drohenden Minen: Wer hat diesen theatralischen Schwestern den Zutritt zu diesem Kranken erlaubt, die nicht nur seine Schmerzen durch keine Mittel lindern, sondern sie noch vielmehr durch einen süssen Gift unterhalten? Denn diese sind es, welch durch die unfruchtbaren Dornen der Leidenschaften die Früchte einer reichen Saat der Vernunft ersticken, und der Menschen Gemüther nur zur Krankheit gewöhnen, aber nicht davon befreyen. Ja, wenn ihr durch eure Schmeicheleyen mir nur einen unweisen Mann entzöget, wie gemeiniglich geschiehet: so würde der Verlust eher zu ertragen seyn; denn mit einem solchen verlieren meine Bemühungen nichts. Aber, so habt ihr euch an einen gemacht, der in der Weltweisheit der Eleater und Akademiker von Jugend auf unterrichtet worden ist. Darum weichet, ihr bis zum Verderben schmeichelnden Syrenen, und überlasset ihn meiner Weisheit und Hülfe. Hierauf schlugen jene die Augen traurig nieder, verriethen durch die Röthe des Gesichts ihre Beschämung, und giengen betrübt*

[fn-1] Da durch dieß Bild die ganze Weltweisheit vorgestellet wird: so theilet Boethiüs die dahin gehörigen Wissenschaften überhaupt ein, 1) *in theoreticas, siue contemplatiuas*, als die vornehmsten und höchsten, dergleichen sind: die Metaphysik, Physik, Mathematik, u.s..f. und diese zeigt der Buchstabe θ an; 2) *in practicas*, welche von der Einrichtung des menschlichen Thuns und Lassens handeln, und durch den Buchstaben π bezeichnet werden. Jene sollen die Vollkommenheiten des Menschen verschaffen, in Absicht auf Gott und die Geister; diese, in Ansicht der menschlichen Gesellschaft.

hinweg. Ich aber gerieth in die äusserste Bestürzung, als ich wegen meiner durch Weinen verdunkelten Augen nicht genau erkennen konnte, wer denn dieses Weib, von so gebieterischem Ansehen, seyn möchte, und erwartete mit niedergeschlagenen und unbewegten Augen stillschweigend, was sie ferner thun würde. Sie trat hierauf näher zu mir, setzte sich auf den Rand meines Bettes, und sahe auf mein trauervolles und vor Betrübniß auf die Erde gerichtetes Gesicht, und beklagte sich über die Vewirrung meines Gemüths also:[30]

Book 3, meter 9

Gott, dessen Allmachtshand den ganzen Kreis der Welt
Durch ewigweise Kraft erschaffen und erhält;
Du bist der Wesen Grund im Himmel und auf Erden;
Du machst, daß Zeiten sind, vergehen, und auch werden;
Bleibst aber, wie du bist, wenn alles sich bewegt.
Du hast aus freyer Macht den Grund der Welt gelegt,
Und aus dem leichten Stoff ein solches Werk erbauet,
An dem man selbst dein Bild des höchsten Gutes schauet.
Von deiner Schönheit zeugt der Schöpfung Glanz und Pracht,
Denn auf dein hohes Wort ist alles schön gemacht.
Ein jeder Theil bezeugt das Wirken deiner Hände.
Wie weislich hast du nicht der Dinge Elemente
Vereint, daß sich das Feur oft mit der Kälte mischt,
Und das verdorrte Land ein Regenguß erfrischt,
Damit die leichte Glut nicht allzuhoch aufsteige,
Und auch der Erden Last nicht in den Abgrund weiche.
Den dreyfachregen Geist, der alles hier beseelet,
Hast du nach jeder Art mit einem Leib vermählet.
Du machst ihn wieder frey, und nach vollbrachtem Lauf
Nimmst du ihn, in sich selbst gekehrt, einst wieder auf.
Denn jede Seele muß, die grossen, wie die kleinen,
Erst in sich selbst zurück, und dann vor dir erscheinen.
Die hohen stellest du an den gestirnten Plan,
Die niedern, die noch nicht nach ihrer Pflicht gethan,
Verweilen sich, gestraft, so lange noch auf Erden,
Bis alle durch das Feur mit dir vereinigt werden.
Verleih, o Vater, mir die Kraft, damit mein Geist,
Eh noch des Todes Macht das Lebensband zerreißt,
Durch dich schon hier beglückt in deiner Liebe lebe,
Und seinen Blick allein zu deinem Thron erhebe!

Vertreibe selbst aus mir die Macht der Finsterniß,
Und mach durch deinen Glanz im Guten mich gewiß!
Denn nur durch dich kann man zum wahren Gute kommen,
Du bist das letzte Ziel, Licht, Heil und Weg der Frommen.[31]

* * *

Friedrich Karl Freytag
(d. after 1805)
Publication: 1794

[The notes that accompany this translation are rife with typographical errors, but the errors are left, unnoted, as they stand in the text.]

Book 1, prose 1

Indem ich mich noch mit diesen Ideen beschäftigte, und meine Klagen unter Vergiessung vieler Thränen niederschrieb, erblickte ich über mir ein Weib, dessen Anblick die tiefste Ehrfurcht einflößte. Nie sah' man bei einem Menschen einen so feurigen und durchdringenden Blick. Ihre Farbe war lebhaft, und ihre Gesundheit schien unzerrüttet zu seyn, ob man gleich ein Alter an ihr wahrnahm, dessen Anfang nicht in unser Zeitalter gesetzt werden konnte. Ihre Statur war nicht zu bestimmen. Denn jetzt zwang sie sich in die gewöhnliche menschliche Form, jetzt schien sie mit ihrem Scheitel den Himmel zu berühren, ja, wenn sie ihr Haupt höher erhob, ihn selbst zu durchdringen, daß die Menschen sich vergeblich bemühten, sie mit ihren Blicken zu erreichen. Ihr Gewand war das feinste künstlichste Gewebe, aus unverwüstlichem Stoffe verfertigt. Ich erfuhr nachher von ihr, daß sie es selbst gewebt hatte. Durch die Länge der Zeit, auf die sie keine Rücksicht nahm, war es grau und unscheinbar geworden, gleich den Gemälden, auf die sich der Staub gelegt hat. Unten am Saum desselben war ein π oben ein θ eingewebt[fn-2], und

[fn-2] Durch diese beiden Buchstaben wird die Eintheilung der ganzen Philosophie angezeigt; durch das π der praktische, und durch das θ der theoretische Theil derselben. Plato, dem Boethius beinahe in allen Stücken folgt, ward auf diese Eintheilung durch die Vergleichung der ersten Gründe des Denkens und Handelns gebracht. Ihre Unentbehrlichkeit und Richtigkeit hat sie allen Wahrheitsforschern bis auf den heutigen Tag wichtig gemacht. Um so mehr ist es zu verwundern, daß der neuste englische Übersetzer Ridpath von dieser Erklärung abgegangen ist, und dem θ die Bedeutung Gott, und dem π die der Philosophie beigelegt hat, besonders da das griechische π zur Bezeichnung der Philosophie meines Wissens nie gebraucht worden ist. [Note: the translator acknowledges here his reading or knowledge of the English translation by Philip and George Ridpath, published in 1785.]

zwischen beiden Buchstaben bemerkte man einige Stufen, in Gestalt einer Leiter, die anzuzeigen schienen, dass man von dem Untern zu dem Obern steigen müsse. Doch hatten einige Gewaltthätige dieses Gewand zerrissen, und davon so viel Theile, als sie deren konnten habhaft werden, mit sich genommen. In ihrer Rechten trug sie Bücher, in ihrer Linken ein Scepter.

Als sie an meinem Lager die Göttinnen der Dichtkunst erblickte[fn-3], die meinen Schmerz in Worten auszudrücken beschäftigt waren, wurde sie unwillig, warf einen verächtlichen und zornigen Blick auf sie, und rief: Wer gestattete diesen Theaterbuhlerinnen den Zutritt zu diesem Schwermüthigen? Unfähig, auch nur das geringste zur Linderung seiner Schmerzen beyzutragen, geben sie denselben im Gegenheil neue Nahrung. Sie sind es, die durch Erregung der Leidenschaften, gleich unfruchtbaren Dornen, die geseegnete Saat der Vernunft ersticken, und das Gemüth der Menschen an Krankheiten gewöhnen, nicht davon befreien. Wenn, wie gewöhnlich, eure Lockungen einen Ungeweihten irre geführt hätten, dann könnt ich gelassener seyn, denn ich würde an einem solchen nichts verliehren; aber diesen Eingeweihten in der Weisheit der Eleatiker[fn-4] und Akademiker[fn-5] –

[fn-3] Die Philosophie vertreibt die Musen der Dichtkunst, weil, wie Plato *1.X. de repub.* sagt: eine alte Feindschaft zwischen der Philosophie und der Dichtkunst obwaltet. Denn fast alle Dichter schmeicheln den Leidenschaften, die die Philosophie der Vernunft unterwerfen will. Aus dieser Ursache verstattet auch Plato der Dichtkunst in seiner Republik keinen Zutritt. Wenn du, sagt er, die Muse aufnimmst, deren Gesänge und Gedichte nur Wollust athmen, so werden Wollust und Schmerz, statt des Gesetzes und der Vernunft in deinem Staate herrschen. Deswegen nennt sie auch unser Autor Theaterbuhlerinnen (*scenicae meretriculae*), weil mehrentheils in theatralischen Vorstellungen von den Dichtern hierinne gesündigt wurde; und wo denn auch die Kleidung der Aktricen der Schlüpfrigkeit des Stücks entsprach. Daß Plato aber nur die wollüstige Muse meinte, erhellet daraus, daß er ausdrücklich der Dichtkunst, die sich auf Lobgesänge der Götter und Preisung der Thaten berühmter Männer einschränkt, seinen Beifall giebt, und sie in seinem Staate zuläßt.

[fn-4] Xenophanes war der Stifter der Eleatischen Schule in Unteritalien. Seine Geburt fällt ungefähr in das 584 Jahr vor Christum. Er griff die Volksreligion an, und lehrte eine unendliche Weltsubstanz. Einer seiner Nachfolger war Zeno aus Elea in Lucanien gebürtig. Dieser war der Erfinder der Dialektik (oder Logik). Er lebte lange vor Zeno, dem Vater der Stoiker. Man sehe *Diogen. Laert. in proem.* Daß Boethius einer der größten Dialektiker seiner Zeit war, kann man schon aus dieser Schrift sehen, wenn man auch nicht wüßte, daß er die Dialektik des Aristotels [*sic*] übersetzt, kommentirt, und bereichert hat.

[fn-5] Als Plato von seinen Reisen nach Athen zurückkehrte, eröffnete er seine Schule in der Akademie, einem zu Leibesübungen bestimmten Platze vor dem Thore, wovon anfänglich Platos Sekte, hernach öffentliche Anstalten für höhere Wissenschaften, endlich jene neuere Einrichtungen, wodurch Gesellschaften von Gelehrten, Kenntnisse erweitern und berichtigen, zu Platos ewigem Andenken Akademie genannt wurden. Um den gemischten Zulauf von seinen Lehrstunden zu entfernen, hatte er über seinen Hörsaal schrei

Doch, fliehet bis zum Verderben, angenehme Sirenen[fn-6], überlaßt es meinen Musen, ihn zu warten und zu heilen.

Bei diesen Worten entfernten sich die Göttinnen. Ihr zur Erde gesenkter Blick, ihre Traurigkeit, die Röthe, mit der ihre Wangen überzogen wurden, alles verrieth ihre Schaam und ihre Bestürzung.

Voller Erstaunen, mit gesenktem Blick, und ohne ein Wort zu reden, erwartete ich, was dies Weib ferner beginnen würde, das so stolz befahl, und das ich wegen meiner durch Thränen geschwächten Augen nicht erkennen konnte.

Sie näherte sich mir, ließ sich auf dem äussersten Rande meines Bettes nieder, betrachtete meine schwermüthige und niedergeschlagene Miene, und beklagte die Verstörung meines Geistes in folgenden Versen:[32]

Book 3, meter 9

Du, dessen ewiger Verstand das Weltall[fn-7]

---

ben lassen: kein in der Geometrie Unbewanderter komme herein. Er war unter Sokrates Schulern der berühmteste und unstreitig der größte philosophische Schriftsteller seiner Zeit m.s. *Remarks on the Life and Writings of Plato. Edinb. 1760. 8.* Tidemann's Geist der spekulativen Philosophie. Th. I. Von den alten Akademikern sind zu unterscheiden die neuern. Arcesilaus, der fünfte Lehrer nach Plato in der Akademie, war ihr Stifter. Er verließ das System seiner Vorgänger; er behauptete nichts, und zweifelte an allem. Cicero sagt *Orat. 3. 18.* seine Lehre war: *nihil esse certi, quod aut sensibus aut animo percipi possit.* Man sehe *Middleton's Life of Cicero*. Th. III. p. 327. ff.

[fn-6] Die Sirenen waren Töchter des vom Herkules im Kampf bezwungnen Acheolous. Ihre Anzahl, ihre Namen und ihre Gestalt werden verschieden angegeben. Als Ceres, sagt Hyginus, ihre geraubte Tochter Proserpina suchte, kam sie unter andern auch nach Sicilien, und verwandelte die Sirenen zur Strafe, daß sie derselben nicht beigestanden hatten, in Vögel mit weiblichen Köpfen. Das Orakel hatte ihnen verkündiget, daß sie so lange leben würden, als sie Vorbeireisende anlocken und an sich fesseln könnten; wenn aber nur einer von diesen ihnen entgienge, müßten sie sterben. Keiner von denen, die sich ihnen näherten, könnte ihrem reizenden Gesange widerstehn; man vergaß Essen und Trinken, und verschmachtete. Daher der Fuß des Felsen, worauf sie saßen, ganz mit Gebeinen bedeckt war. Nur Ulysses entkam dieser Gefahr. Von der Circe gewarnt, gab er seinen Gefährten den Rath, sich die Ohren mit Wachs zu verstopfen; er selbst ließ sich an den Mast seines Schiffes anbinden, mit dem Befehl, ihn nicht los zu machen, er möchte bitten oder drohn. Dies geschah, und als er vorbey war, stürzten sich die Sirenen ins Meer. Sie sind das Bild der Verführung. Die Musen werden deshalb hier von der Philosophie, wegen ihrer moralischen Aehnlichkeit mit ihnen, sehr passend Sirenen genannt. *L'Antiquité expliquée par Montfaucon. Part. II. T.I.*

[fn-7] Auslegern und Uebersetzern hat dieses Gedicht unendlich viel zu schaffen gemacht und keiner ist, meinem Bedünken nach, ganz aufs reine damit gekommen. So, zum Beispiel

Regiert, des Himmels und der Erde Schöpfer,
Auf deinen Wink entströmet den Aeonen
Die Zeit: unwandelbar und bleibend
Bist du die einz'ge Quelle der Bewegung.
Nicht äußrer Zwang, des höchsten Gutes Form
Die wesentlich, und keines Neides fähig

---

hat der neueste deutsche Uebersetzer, (um bei den Uebersetzungen stehen zu bleiben) die Stelle, *Tu triplicis mediam* u.s.w. ohne allen Sinn so übersetzt:

Den dreifach regen Geist, der alles hier beseelet,
Hast du nach jeder Art mit einem Leib vermählet.
Du macht ihn wieder frei, und, nach vollbrachtem Lauf
Nimmst du ihn, in sich selbst gekehrt, einst wieder auf, u.s.w.

Nicht viel glücklicher ist der Franzos Cerizier gewesen. Er übersetzt diese nehmliche Stelle also:

C'est la puissante main qui contraint et referre [*sic*]
Cet immortel esprit qui dans tout l'univers
Anime également tant de membres divers,
Esprit, qui partagé dans deux globes spheriques
De qui le movement fait ses retours obliques
Ioignant le même endroit d'ou son point est parti, u.s.w.

Mit mehrerm Erfolg, obschon auch nicht ganz befriedigend übersetzt Regnier:

Tu places au milieu de ce grand univers
Un esprit composé de trois etres divers
Et cet esprit second répand par tout le monde
Les trois divers effets de sa vertu seconde
Il partage ses soins aux deux pôles des cieux
Dont ton bras a fixé les solides essieux.
Et toujours agité par sa vitesse extrême
Comme un globe de flamme; il entre dans lui-même,
Et sans cesse occupé, pendant ce movement,
Des objets figurés par son entendement.
Il fait mouvoir des cieux la machine éternelle
Comme il la voit mouvoir en ce premier modèle
Qu'il ne peut regarder sans en faire un portrait,
Ou tout est exprimé jusques au moindre trait.

Die neusten englischen und französischen Uebersetzer haben diese Stelle unübersetzt gelassen. *The 12 lines*, sagt der erstere, und mit ihm stimmt der Franke überein, *that follow in the original refer to some of the mort* [*sic*] *subtile, abstruse parts of Plato's philosophy; and are very obscure. I have not translated them, as I despaired of making any version of them, that would be satisfactory to myself, or agreeable to my readers.* Auch mir scheint es unmöglich, daß ein Uebersetzer, bei der Dunkelheit und Verworrenheit, die selbst in Platos Timäus über Weltschöpfung und Weltseele herrscht, und folglich auch hier bei seinem Epitoma

Bewog zur Bildung dich der regellos–
Bewegten Masse der Materie.
Dein Werk entspricht dem hohen Ideale,
Das in Dir ist! Du selbst die höchste Schönheit,
Trägst im Verstand das Bild der schönen Welt
Und formst nach diesem Bild sie ausser dir.

---

tor herrschen muß, die nachdruksvolle, bis zur Verwunderung wohlklingende Kürze, mit der Boethius diesen Theil der speculativen platonischen Philosophie in diesem Meisterstücke der Poesie vorgetragen hat, erreichen kann. Nur an den Sinn kann er sich halten, die eigenthümlichen Schönheiten des Originals muß er fahren lassen. In wie ferne ich jenen erreicht habe, mögen [*sic*] mein Leser beurtheilen.

In nachstehender Erklärung dieses Gedichts bin ich dem Herrn Hofrath Tidemann gefolgt, der in die Ideen des Plato über diese Gegenstände im 2. Buch es seines Geistes der speculativen Philosophie am tiefsten eingedrungen zu sein scheint.

Unter der Gottheit, oder dem göttlichen Verstande, tobte vor der Weltbildung die ewige Materie — deren Ewigheit Plato auf den, von allen Physikern angenommenen Grundsatz gründete: Aus Nichts wird Nichts — in wüsten Bewegungen. Als Masse betrachtet und im Gegensatz der Form und Gottheit, bestand sie aus zwey verschiedenen Wesen, einem würksamen, und einem unthätigen und formlosen. Jene thätige Qualität ist die vernunftlose bewegende Kraft der Materie. Durch diese wurden die, aus ihr zufällig entstandnen Elemente Erde, Wasser, Feuer, Luft aus und durch einander geworfen, weil ihre Schwingungen regellos waren, und sie sich hin und her bewegten. Weil aber Gott gütig ist, und alles Gute will, und Ordnung für besser denn Unordnung hält, so suchte er, ohne durch etwas ausser sich dazu bewogen worden zu sein, durch die schönste Ordnung die Unordnung zu endigen, und die Spuren von Elementen, die die Materie bei sich führte in die vier Elemente zu formen. Wer aber ein Kunstwerk hervorbringen will, muß einen Plan, ein Muster vorher entworfen haben. Gottes Weisheit hatte also gleichfalls ein Muster der künftigen Welt vor Augen, oder in seinem Verstande, und zwar das beste, das vollkommenste, weil das Werk vortreflich und schön, und der Werkmeister vollkommen und gütig ist. Er, von allem Neid entfernt, wollte, daß alles ihm so ähnlich sei, als möglich. Nach angestellter Ueberlegung, fand Gott, daß aus der Materie kein verstandloses Ganze entstehen dürfe, weil ein Verständiges für einem Unverständigen den Vorzug hat, fand, daß Verstand ohne Seele niemals statt haben könne; desshalb mischte er einen Theil von sich, oder die Form, oder den Verstand, mit der ganzen Qualitätenlosen Materie zu gleichen Theilen, um der Form dadurch Verkörperung zu verschaffen. Darauf fügte er noch einen Theil von den thätigen Materienkräften oder vernunftlosen Seele hinzu, damit die Materie ihrer Natur gemäß wirken könne; so daß die Weltseele, aus einem Theile der Gottheit, einem Theile grober Masse, und einem Theile thätiger Materienkräfte oder der vernunftlosen Seele besteht, die der Materie wesentlich beiwohnt. Hierauf ward diese Masse in zwei Haupttheile zerlegt, deren oberster, unmittelbar unter der Gottheit kreisförmige Bewegung um seinen Mittelpunkt; der untere, neben dieser, Fortschreitung erhielt; erstere ist die Bewegung des unveränderlichen, letztere die des veränderlichen Wesens.

Du spricht und ein vollkommenes Ganze gehet
Aus der Vereinigung vollkommner Theile
Hervor: du einigst die Elemente
Durch Harmonie, daß sich mit Trockenheit
Das Wasser gattet, und der Frost mit Flammen:
Daß nicht das reinere Feuer in die Lüfte
Verfliegет, oder die gesenkte Erde
Durch ihre Schwerkraft fortgerissen werde.
Der allbelendenden, aus drei Naturen
Gemischten Weltenseele, weisest Du
Den Mittelpunkt der Welt an und ertheiltest
Die ihr entsprechenden Organe ihr.
Getheilt bewegt sie sich in zweien Kreisen,
Kehrt in sich selbst zurück, und von der Gottheit
Begrenzet bildet sie göttlichen
Verstand in der Gestirne sphärlicher
Bewegung nach. Du schufst aus gleichem Stoffe
Die höhern Geister, und die niedern Seelen,
Und kleidest die zur Höhe strebenden
In leichte, feingewob'ne Körper, giebest
Den Himmel ihnen und die Erd' zur Wohnung
Und läßest einst die, die zu dir sich wandten,
In dich zurück nach gütigen Gesezzen
Als reines Feuer kehren. –[fn-8] Laß, o Vater,

Der Weltseele oberer Theil demnach ist reinerer, der untere gröberer Natur, jener ist zum Aufenthalt der Fixsterne, dieser zum Wohnplatz der Planeten bestimmt. Die unveränderliche Bewegung der erstern, heist Dauer (αιων, *aevum.*) Die Fortschreitung der letztern die aus der Dauer hervorgeht, Zeit, (χρονος) Die Weltseele verbreitet sich demnach aus dem Mittelpunkt des Weltalls durch das ganze Universum; und ihre Bewegung ist ähnlich der Bewegung des sie umgehenden göttlichen Verstandes, der sich durch sich selbst in vollkommer Ordnung und Regelmäsigkeit bewegt, wie es einem denkenden Wesen zukommt. [Note: the translator acknowledges here his reading or knowledge of the French translation by one Cerizier (i.e., P. R. de Ceriziers), published in the 1630s; he also acknowledges here his reading or knowledge of the French translation by one Regnier (i.e., Nicolas Régnier), published in 1676.]

[fn-8] Die höhern und niedern Geister, die sich theils in der Luft, theils auf der Erde aufhalten, sind alle, nach der Meinung der Platoniker, aus gleichem Stofe (*causis paribus, εχ τον αντον χρατῆϱος*) Nur ihre Körper machen ihren Unterschied, die theils aus Aether, theils aus Luft, theils aus Wasser theils aus Erde gebildet sind. Die Seelen der aus Erde gebildeten Thiere haben, ausser ihrem thierischen Körper, noch ein feineres Organ (*leves currus,*

Den Geist zum Sitz der Gottheit sich erheben!
Laß ihn den Quell des höchsten Guts erblicken,
In deinem Anschaun nur sich seelig fühlen![fn-9]
Zerstreu der Erde Nebel, löß die Fesseln
Des läst'gen Körpers! strahl' in deinem Glanze!
Du bist das reine Licht, du nur allein
Bist heit're, seel'ge Ruh dem Tugendfreunde.
In dir ist unser Ursprung, unser Ende;
Zu dir führt alles, Allerhalter, Du
Des Ganzen Grenze, – laß uns dich betrachten![33]

* * *

L[ambert] I[gnaz] Wortberg
(1756–1829)
Publication: 1826

Only the meters of the *Consolatio* are translated by L. I. Wortberg. The prose passages, however, are summarized in their proper place and their proper order. Even-numbered pages [left] contain the Latin text; odd-numbered pages [right] contain the German renderings. The translator's footnotes all begin on the even-numbered pages, from notes placed by the translator upon the Latin text, but they continue at the bottom of the odd-numbered pages.

Book 1, prose 1

[As noted above, the prose passages were not translated, but summaries of their content is provided.]

---

aetherius sensus, θειοτερον ταν χαλὄμενων ϛοιχεων, Nervengeist) wodurch sie fähig gemacht werden, sich zur Erkenntniss Gottes aufzuschwingen, da sie durch den thierischen Körper zur Erde herabgezogen werden.

> Die Seelen, die sich von aller irdischen Begierde losgemacht haben, werden mit der Gottheit, aus der sie hervorgegangen sind, wieder vereinigt. Gott ist aber, nach Plato, das reinste Feuer, ein Lichtwesen, daraus folgt, daß unsre Seelen, die göttlich sind, wenn sie von allem Irdischen befreit sind, als reines Feuer in die Gottheit zurükkehren.

[fn-9] Nach Plato ist ein Weltweiser, der sich von allen Vergnügungen zurückziehet, der sich mit sinnlichen Empfindung nicht im mindesten befast, weil sie theils trüglich sind, theils den Verstand im Denken hindern, ein Mensch, der schon hier fast ganz Geist ist. Ihm ist das höchste Gut oder Glückseeligkeit Betrachtung und Anschauung der Gottheit, die jenseits des Himmels Grenze ist.

[page] 7
Inhalt der Prose.

Hier erscheint die Philosophie unserm B. Dieser schließt die überaus schöne Prose, worin er die Umstände der Erscheinung erzählt, mit folgenden Worten: "Sie näherte sich mir, betrachtete meine schwermüthige und niedergeschlagene Miene, und beklagte die Zerrüttung meines Geistes in folgenden Versen:"[34]

Book 3, meter 9

[page] 69
Neuntes Lied

O, du Beherrscher der Welt nach immer besteh'ndem Gesetze,
Schöpfer der Himmel und Erden, der Du die Zeiten von Anfang
Fortgehen läßt, und unbewegt selbst giebst Allem Bewegung!
Den nicht Drang von äußeren Wesen zur Bildung des rohen
Wogenden Chaos vermogt' – Nein – sondern nur inneren Wesens

[page] 71

Güte, des Neides unfähig: du bildetest Alles nach deinem
Hohen Muster, denn selbst der Schönste trugst du in Gedanken,
Diese so schöne Welt, und schufst sie nach deinem Bilde,
Daß vollendet nun sie, auch ihre Theile vollende.
Die Elemente band'st du nach Verhältniß, daß Kaltes mit Warmem,
Trock'nes mit Flüss'gem sich paar', daß nicht das reinere Feuer
Aufflög', noch ihre Last die schwerere Erde hinabsenk'.
[*][fn-10] Mit der dreifachen Natur verband'st du das Mittelding, Seele,
Allbewegende Seele, vertheilst sie durch schicklich Glieder

[fn-10] [The translator placed this note upon the Latin text (on the even numbered page 70), but it also applies to the corresponding German translation on the facing (odd numbered) page (71). Here, as the Latin text (upon which the footnote begins in the book) is not transcribed, the asterisk appears on the German line that corresponds to the line in the Latin text. The Latin (on the even numbered page 70) reads:

Tu triplici mediam naturae cuncta moventem*
Connectens animam per consona membra resolvis.]

[page] 73

[*] fn-11 Diese nun, hat sie getheilt, sich in zweifachem Kreise gewunden
Kehrt in sich selber zurück, umschwebt des göttlichen Wesens
Hohe Tiefen, und schwingt nach ähnlichem Bilde den Himmel.
Höhere Seelen und ringere Leben, desselbigen Ursprungs,
Schieb'st du in's Dasein: den höher'n gieb'st du ätherische Wagen,
Streu'st durch Himmel und Erde sie, zieh'st durchs Gesetz deiner Liebe

---

[note beginning on page] 70

*) Ganz erbärmlich quält diese Stelle alle Uebersetzer und Commentatoren. Inzwischen haben alle Ausgaben, die mir zu Gesicht gekommen sind, *Triplicis mediam naturae connectens animam*. Muß man da nicht fragen: *Connectens*? *Cui*? verbinden? womit? Lies't man dagegen *Triplici mediam* u.s.w.; so ist die Stelle grammatisch richtiger, und die Schwierigkeit großentheils gehoben.

[same note, but continuing on page] 71

*) Setzt man Gott außer der Natur oder vielmehr über dieselbe, so bleibt für diese *Intelligenz organisierte* und *unorganisierte* Materie (*ὑλη* oder *αωμα*) übrig.

Ward nun die Weltseele mit der organisierten Materie verbunden: so enstand in der mitleren Categorie das *νοητον*, *εμψνχον* und *σωματοειδες* und zugleich das dreifache Leben, *vita rationalis*, *sensiliva* und *vegetativa*. So viel, vor der Hand, zur Rechtfertigung meiner Leseart: *Tu triplici naturae* u.s.w. *connectens* u.s.w.

fn-11 [The translator placed this note upon the Latin text (on the even numbered page 72), but it also applies to the corresponding German translation on the facing (odd numbered) page (73). Here, as the Latin (upon which the footnote begins in the book) is not transcribed, the asterisk appears on the German line that corresponds to the line in the Latin text. The Latin (on the even numbered page 72) reads:

Quae cum secta duos motum glomeravit in orbeis* [*sic*], ...]

[note on page] 72

*) Hat mir's geträumt? oder habe ich es würklich gelesen, daß die geometrische Aufgabe: Eine Linie dergestalt zu theilen, daß der kleinere Theil zu dem größern sich verhalte, wie dieser größere zu der ganzen, von Plato herrühre, und deswegen *Sectio divina Platonis* genannt worden sey. Dies wäre nun so was für die Herren Mystiker. Uebrigens wär' es zu wünschen, daß in der Weltregierung der kleinere Theil der Intelligenz sich zu dem größren Theile derselben verhalte, wie der größere Theil zu derjenigen Intelligenz, die alles regieret. Doch wir wollen nicht witzeln, son-

[same note, but continuing on page] 73

dern von dem 18ten Verse mit der Philosophie und dem B. herzlich bis zu Ende des hochliedes beten, denn von jenem Verse an wird uns die Sprache wieder verständlicher. So viel ist's: Plato geometrirte gerne; ja er soll sogar auf die Frage: was Gott mache? geantwortet haben: *γεωμετϱει*, *κοσμομτϱει* wäre wohl schicklicher gewesen; ob aber auch *μετϱει* zu dem hohen Begriffe paßte, den Plato von dem göttlichen Wesen hatte? Doch, wie gesagt, wir wollen nicht klügeln; wir werden ja bald wissen, wie es dort oben aussieht.

Sie zu dir, dann lodern empor die Flammen zum Urquell.
Vater! gieb dem Geiste jenen hehren Sitz zu besteigen,
Laß die Quelle des Guten ihn schau'n, nach gefundenem Lichte

[page] 75

Fest auf Dich heften, die helleren Augen der Seele.
Scheuche doch weg die Nebel; entheb' uns der irdischen Bürde
Und mit Deinem Lichte leucht'uns, denn Du bist die Klarheit,
Du, der Frommen sanfteste Ruh', Dich schau'n ist der Endzweck,
O! Du Anfang, Beförderer, Führer, Weg, Ziel miteinander![35]

* * *

Johann Hilarius Weingärtner
(January 13, 1784–June 9, 1842)
Publication: 1827

Book 1, prose 1

Erste Prose

[The translator's prefatory note on Book 1, prose 1:]

Die Philosophie erscheint in einer ehrwüdigen Frauengestalt, entfernt die Musen als unfähig, den Kranken zu heilen, und verspricht ihm eine bessere Arzeney aus ihrem Heilichtume zu geben.

Einst, als ich dieß bey mir selbst überdachte, und meinen Kummer dem Papiere anvertraute, schien es mir, als erblickte ich über meinem Haupte eine Frauengestalt von ausnehmend ehrwürdigem Antlitze, mit einem durchdringenden Blicke von übermenschlicher Klarheit; ihre lebhafte Farbe zeugte von unerschöpfter Kraft, obschon sie so reich an Jahren schien, daß sie keineswegs unserer Zeit angehören konnte. Die Gestalt ihres Körpers war nicht genau zu bestimmen; denn bald hielt sie sich im Maße gewöhnlicher Menschen, bald schien ihr Scheitel den Himmel zu berühren; erhob sie ihr Haupt höher, so drang es in den Himmel selbst, und kein menschlicher Blick konnte es mehr erreichen. Ihr Kleid war vom zartesten Gewebe, von der feinsten Kunst, aus unzerreißbarem Stoff gemacht; ich erfuhr später von ihr selbst, daß sie es mit eigenen Händen verfertigt hatte. Die Form dieser Hände aber hatten Alter und Verwahrlosigkeit mit Dunkelheit umhüllt, wie Bilder, die vom Rauche geschwärzt sind.[fm-12] Am untern Saume war ein π, am obern aber ein θ eingewoben zu sehen. Zwischen beyden Buchstaben waren einige Stufen angezeigt, auf denen man von unten nach oben aufsteigen konnte. Gewaltthätige Hände hatten das Kleid zerrissen, und einige kleine Stücke davon geraubt. Ihre rechte Hand trug Bücher, die linke einen Zepter. Als diese Frauengestalt die Musen der Dichtkunst um mein Bette stehend, und in meine Klagen einstimmend erblickte, ward sie etwas unwillig, und sprach mit tief glühendem Blicke: "Wer ließ diese Buhlerinnen der Bühne zu diesem Kranken kommen? die seinen Schmerz nicht nur durch keinen Beystand lindern, sondern vielmehr mit süßem Gifte nähren. Denn sie sind es, die die fruchtreiche Saat der Vernunft durch die unfruchtbaren Dornen der Leidenschaften ersticken, und das menschliche Gemüth an die Krankheit gewöhnen, anstatt es davon zu befreyen. Zwar wenn eure schmeichelnden Töne nur einen Ungeweihten uns entzögen, wie dieß gewöhnlich ist, so hielte ich es für minder beklagenswerth. Denn an einem solchen wären unsere Bemühungen nicht verloren. Ihr aber habt in diesem einen Menschen angegriffen, der in eleatischen[fm-13] und akademischen Kenntnissen[fm-14] auferzogen worden. Entfernt euch, ihr Sirenen! Ihr verführerischen Schmeichlerinnen! und überlaßt ihn meiner Muse zur heilenden Pflege. "Beschämt durch diese Verweise senkten jene ihren Blick zur Erde nieder, gestanden erröthend ihre Bestürzung, und entfernten sich traurig. Ich aber, dessen Blick Thränen verdunkelten, erkannte noch nicht, wer diese Frauengestalt von so gebiethendem Ansehen war, und erwartete mit niedergeschlagenem Auge, staunend und stumm, was sie beginnen würde. Sie trat näher, setzte sich am Ende meines Lagers, schaute mir ins ernste,

[fn-12] Die beyden Buchstaben θ und π bedeuten nach einigen Uebersetzern θεος, Gott, und πὶλοδορὶα, Weltweisheit. Wahrscheinlicher aber nach Freytags Bemerkung θεορια und πραξις, den theoretischen und practischen Theil der ganzen Philosophie.

[Note: the translator acknowledges here his reading of the earlier German translation by Friedrich Karl Freytag, published in 1794.]

[fn-13] Der Stifter der eleatischen Schule war Xenophanes. Er griff die Volksreligion an, und lehrte eine unendliche Weltsubstanz. Ihren Nahmen aber hat diese Schule von Zeno, einem Nachfolger des Xenophanes, der aus Elea gebürtig war. — Er erfand die Logik.

[fn-14] Die Akademie war zu Athen ein offener, zu Liebesübungen bestimmter Platz. Plato eröffnete dort seine Schule, als er von seinen Reisen nach Athen zurückkehrte. Daher der Nahme Akademiker.

trübe Angesicht, das kummervoll den Boden anstierte, und beklagte die Verwirrung meines Geistes mit folgenden Worten.[fn-15] [36]

Book 3, meter 9

Neuntes Metrum.

[Translator's prefatory note on book 3, meter 9:]

Anrufung des Urhebers alles Guten, daß er die Augen des Geistes eröffne, und zur Erkenntniß der wahren Glückseligkeit vorbereite.
O, der du mit ewiger Weisheit die Welt regierest,
Schöpfer des Himmels und der Erde; Ewiger! der du
Schufst die Zeit, und, selbst unwandelbar, alles bewegest!
Den kein äußerer Grund bewog, die vergänglichen Stoffe
Zu erzeugen, nur die höchste unendliche Güte
Deines Wesens, in dem kein Haß ist. Alles nach einem
Himmlischen Urbild schaffend trugst du, unendliche Schönheit,
Diese schöne Welt in ähnliche Wirklichkeit über.
Ordnend zum vollkommenen All die herrlichen Theile;
Du gebeutst den Stoffen, daß sich die Kälte mit Flammen,
Trocknes mit Flüssigem sich vereine: Daß nicht des Feuers
Urstoff entflieh', und dann die Last der Erde versinke.
Du erhältst die Seele der Welt in der Mitte der Wesen,
Daß sie die dreyfache Natur belebend durchkreise;

[fn-15] Die Philosophie verscheucht von dem Philosophen, zur Zeit der Leiden, alle eitle Kraft: und werthlose Zerstreuungen, und ermahnt ihn, nur bey ihr Hülfe zu suchen. Der fromme Glaube aber ruft den Chriften in jedem Leiden kräftiger auf, seinen Trost nur in dem zu suchen, der da allein vermag, wahrhaft zu helfen und zu trösten. Siehe da! ruft ihm die Stimme seines Gewissens zu: "Dein Zeuge ist im Himmel, und der dich kennet, ist in der Höhe." Hiob 16, 19. — Erwacht von der Betäubung des Schmerzens, antwortet der Gläubige: "Ja, ich weiß, daß mein Erlöser lebt, er wird mich einst aus der Erde auferwecken." Hiob 16, 22. — Jetzt aber will ich meine Leiden tragen, denn der Herr spricht: "Wer sein Kreuz nicht auf sich nimmt, und mir nachfolgt, der ist meiner nicht werth." Matth. 10, 38. — Ich weiß, daß ich nach dem blicken muß, der da sprach: "Ich bin der Weg, die Wahrheit und das Leben. Niemand kommt (zur Erkenntniß Gottes) zum Vater (in dem das wahre Leben ist), als durch mich." Joh. 14, 6 "Und die Leiden dieser Zeit sind nicht zu vergleichen mit der Herrlichkeit, die künftig an uns wird offenbar werden." Rom. 8, 18 — Matth. 5, 3–12.

Wenn sich diese theilt, und in zwey Kreisen beweget,
Kömmt sie zur Selbsterkenntniß, und zum Begriffe des höchsten
Geistes, und macht sich ein ähnliches Bild von des Himmels Bewegung.
Menschenseelen und thierisches Leben erschufst du mit gleicher
Allmacht, und bestimmst die höhern und niedern Naturen
Für den Himmel und für die Erde, und führest sie endlich
Wieder zu dir zurück durch das Feuer der unendlichen Liebe.
Vater, laß meinen Geist zu deinem Throne sich schwingen;
Laß mich den Urquell des Guten schauen, laß meine Seele
Liebend auf dich im hellern Lichte die Blicke heften.
Theile die dunkelen Nebel des schweren irdischen Körpers;
Zeige deinen vollendeten Glanz, du ewig Klarer!
Du, der Frommen friedliche Ruh! O laß dich erkennen,
Anfang und Ende, Leiter und Herr, und Ziel aller Wesen![37]

* * *

Richard Scheven

(b. May 12, 1867 [Malchin])
Publication: 1893

Book 1, prose 1

Während ich solche Gedanken still für mich im Herzen bewegte und meine jammernde Klage mit dem Schreibgriffel aufzeichnete, da erschien mir zu Häupten eine Frauengestalt von ehrfurchtgebietender Hoheit, mit glühenden Augen von so durchdringender Kraft, wie sie sonst den Menschen nicht eigen ist. Frisch war ihre Geschichtsfarbe und unerschöpft ihre Körperkraft, obgleich sie schon ein so langes Leben hinter sich zu haben schien, daß man sie kaum noch unserem Zeitalter zurechnen konnte. Ihre Gestalt war eine wechselnde. Bald nämlich schrumpfte sie auf das gewöhnliche Maß der Menschen zusammen, bald wieder schien sie mit der Höhe des Scheitels die Wolken zu berühren. Hätte sie das Haupt noch höher erhoben, so wäre sie in den Himmel selbst eingedrungen und den Blicken der Menschen entschwunden. Ihre Kleider waren von den dünnsten Fäden, aber aus unverwüstlichem Stoff, mit der feinsten Kunstfertigkeit gewebt und zwar, wie sie mir später erzählte, das Werk ihrer eigenen Hände. Äußerlich zeigten sie indes die Verschossenheit eines vernachlässigten Alters, verwitterten und bestaubten Gemälden vergleichbar. Im untersten Saum war der griechische Buchstabe π, im obersten ein θ

eingewirkt[fn-16] zu lesen und zwischen beiden wurden gewisse, in Form einer Treppe angeordnete Stufen sichtbar, mittelst deren, wie es schien, ein Aufstieg von dem unteren zu dem oberen Buchstaben stattfinden sollte. – Gewaltthätige Hände hatten übrigens das ganze Gewand zerrissen und einzelne Teile davon, deren sie habhaft werden konnten, mit sich fortgenommen.

In der rechten Hand trug sie Gestalt Bücherrollen, in der linken ein Scepter.

Als sie nun die Musen der Dichtkunst, die meinen Klagen die Worte liehen, an meinem Lager stehen sah, da begann sie erregt zu werden und sprach mit finster funkelnden Augen: "Wer hat diese Theaterdirnen zu diesem Kranken zugelassen, um seine Leiden nicht nur durch kein Heilmittel zu lindern, sondern durch süßes Gift nur noch mehr zu entfachen? Denn sie sind es, die mit den unfruchtbaren Dornen der Affekte die fruchtschwangere Saat der Vernunft töten und den Geist der Menschen an die Krankheit gewöhnen, statt ihn davon zu befreien! Erträglicher würde mir ihre Missethat noch erscheinen, wenn sie, wie gewöhnlich, irgend einen untergeordneten Geist durch ihre Lockungen auf Abwege gebracht hätten. Aber nun diesen Mann, der in eleatischen und akademischen Studien aufgezogen ist!

"Nun aber fort mit euch, ihr Sirenen, die ihr eure Opfer bis an den Rand des Verderbens so süß umschmeichelt! Überlaßt diesen Mann mir und meiner Muse zur Pflege und zur Heilung!"

So gescholten senkte der Chor der Musen traurig das Antlitz zur Erde und als diese falschen Trösterinnen die Schwelle verließen, zeugte ihr Erröten von ihrer tiefen Beschämung.

Ich aber, dessen Gesicht noch von den strömenden Thränen verdunkelt war, so daß ich noch nicht erkennen konnte, wer denn dieses Weib von so majestätischer Hoheit sei, ich erwartete staunend, mit zu Boden gesenktem Blick, was sie nun weiter beginnen werde. Sie aber trat näher herzu, ließ sich auf dem äußersten Ende meines Lagers nieder, blickte mir in das tieftraurige, von Schmerz zu Boden geneigte Antlitz und beklagte dann in folgenden Versen die Verwirrung meines Geistes:[38]

Book 3, meter 9

Der du die Welt regierst nach ewigen, weisen Gesetzen,
Der du die Erde, den Himmel erschufst, und aus ewigem Urquell

[fn-16] π (P) für πραζις (praxis) und Θ für θεωρια (theoria).

Führtest die Zeiten, des Alls unwandelbarer Beweger!
Bildner des flüchtigen Stoffs, befreit von äußerem Antrieb,
Aus deinem eigensten Ich, der makellosen, erhabnen
Güte, befolgend allein das leuchtende, himmliche Vorbild,
Schufst du das All! – Der Schönste du selbst, die schönste der Welten
Hast du, sie schauend im Geist, in den herrlichsten Formen gestaltet,
Hast zu vollendetem Ganzen verknüpft die vollendeten Teile,
Einst die Stoffe mit festem Band, daß Kälte zu Wärme,
Trocknes zu Feuchtem sich fügt, daß nicht das reinere Feuer
Schwebe davon, und lastende Wucht versenkte den Erdball!
Siehe, die Seele der Welt, sie thront in der innersten Mitte
Dreifach geteilter Natur,[fn-17] das Einzelne rhythmisch bewegend,
Teilt ihre Kraft und beherrscht die zweifach kreisenden Welten.[fn-18]
Immer sich selber getreu, durchströmt vom göttlichen Geiste,
Führt sie, wie du es gedacht, im Kreise das Himmelsgewölbe.
Leitend aus gleichem Quell die hohen, die niederen Geister,
Läßt du die höchsten frei in des Äthers Räume sich schwingen,[fn-19]
Läßt an dem Himmel, auf Erden die anderen wohnen, und gnädig
Führst zu deinem Feuer zurück, die zu dir sich bekannten!
Vater, auch unseren Geist in des Lichts Regionen erhebe!
Zeige des Guten Quell, gieb gnädig völlige Klarheit!
Zeige dein eigenes Ich dem trunkenen Blicke des Geistes!
Nimm uns hinweg den Wahn und die Bande des irdischen Daseins!
Strahle mit himmlischem Glanz! Denn du, der Tröster der Frommen,
Du giebst Frieden und Ruh'! So gieb dich auch uns zu erkennen,
End' und Beginn, und Führer und Pfad, und Ziel alles Wissens![39]

* * *

Eberhard Gothein

(October 29, 1853–November 13, 1923)
First Published: 1932
[First published as a bilingual text, with the Latin original facing the German edition]

[fn-17] Vergl. die Einleitung.

[See pages 1–8 of the translator's book, in which the translator discusses in brief the Platonic aspects of the meter.]

[fn-18] Die höhere himmlische und die niedere irdische.

[fn-19] Vergl. die Einleitung. [Note pages 1–8 of the translator's book, in which the translator discusses in brief the Platonic aspects of the meter.]

Between 1932 and the present, the Gotheim rendering of the *Consolatio* has undergone many reprintings or reeditings. For historical interest, the 1932 version is transcribed here. That edition contains, on facing pages, the Latin [left] and German [right] texts. It also contains an introduction by Marie Luise Gothein.

Book 1, prose 1

Während ich solches schweigend bei mir selbst erwog und meine tränenvolle Klage mit Hilfe des Griffels aufzeichnete, schien es mir, als ob zu meinen Häupten ein Weib hinträte von ehrwürdigem Antlitz, mit funkelndem und über das gewöhnliche Vermögen der Menschen durchdringendem Auge, von leuchtender Farbe und unerschöpfter Jugendkraft, obwohl sie so bejahrt war, daß sie in keiner Weise unserem Zeitalter anzugehören schien. Ihr Wuchs war von wechselnder Größe; denn jetzt zog sie sich zum gewöhnlichen Maß der Menschen zusammen, jetzt aber schien sie mit dem Scheitel den Himmel zu berühren; und als sie noch höher ihr Haupt emporhob, ragte sie in den Himmel selbst hinein und entzog sich so dem Blick der Menschen. Ihr Gewand war von feinstem Gespinst und mit peinlicher Kunstfertigkeit aus unlösbarem Stoff gefertigt: sie hatte es, wie ich später aus ihrem eignen Munde erfuhr, mit eigner Hand gewebt. Seinen Glanz hatte wie bei rauchgeschwärzten Bildern ein trüber Anflug von Vernachlässigung und Alter überzogen. An seinem untersten Rande las man eingewebt ein griechisches π, an seinem obersten aber ein θ. Und zwischen beiden Buchstaben schienen wie an einer Leiter etliche Stufen eingezeichnet, die von dem unteren zum oberen Schriftzug emporstiegen. Doch hatten dieses selbe Kleid die Hände einiger Gewalttätiger zerfetzt, und jeder hatte ein Stückchen nach Vermögen weggeschleppt. Ihre Rechte endlich trug Bücher, ihre Linke aber ein Szepter.

Als sie die Dichtermusen, die mein Lager umstanden und meiner Tränenflut Worte liehen, erblickte, sprach sie etwas erregt, entflammt mit finsteren Blicken: "Wer hat diesen Dirnen der Bühne den Zutritt zu diesem Kranken erlaubt, ihnen, die seinen Schmerz nicht nur mit keiner Arzenei lindern, sondern ihn obendrein mit süßem Gifte nähren möchten? Sind sie es doch, die mit dem unfruchtbaren Dorngestrüpp der Leidenschaften die fruchtreiche Saat der Vernunft ersticken, die der Menschen Seelen an die Krankheit gewöhnen, nicht sie davon befreien. Wenn eure Schmeichelreden einen Uneingeweihten, wie es gemeinhin durch euch geschieht, ablenken, so würde ich das für minder lästig halten. In diesem aber darf unser Werk nicht verletzt werden: denn er ist mit den Studien Eleas und der Akademie ernährt worden. Drum hinweg ihr Sirenen, die ihr süß seid bis zum Verderben, überlaßt ihn meinen Musen zur Pflege, zur Heilung![”]

So gescholten senkte jener Chor tief bekümmert die Blicke, Erröten verriet ihre Scham, so gingen sie traurig über die Schwelle hinaus. Ich aber, dessen tränenüberströmtes Antlitz ein Nebel hüllte, so daß ich nicht unterscheiden konnte, wer diese Frau von so gebietender Würde sei, verstummte, heftete mein Auge auf die Erde und begann schweigend abzuwarten, was sie nun weiter tun werde. Da trat sie näher an mich heran, setzte sich auf das Ende meines Bettes, blickte auf mein tränenschweres, auf die Erde geneigtes Antlitz und klagte in folgenden Versen über die Verwirrung meines Geistes:[40]

Book 3, meter 9

Der du lenkest die Welt nach dauernden festen Gesetzen,
Schöpfer des Himmels, der Erden, der du von Ewigkeit wandeln
Hießest die Zeit, selbst nimmer bewegt, bewegend das Weltall!
Keine äußere Macht trieb dich aus wogenden Massen
Deine Schöpfung zu formen; in dir nur trägst du des höchsten
Guten Gestalt, des fleckenlosen. Das All vom Urbild
Leitest du her; die herrliche, Herrlichster selber,
Trägst du im Geiste, die Welt, nach deinem Bilde geschaffen,
Von der vollendeten löst dein Befehl vollkommene Teile.
Bindest mit Zahlen die Elemente, daß Hitze und Kälte,
Regen und Dürre ihr Maß einhalten; die reinere Flamme
Nicht emporflieh', die Last nicht abwärts zöge die Erde.
Aus der Mitte der Drei-Natur entläßt du die Seele,
Die das Weltall bewegt, hüllst sie in harmonische Glieder.
Wenn sie getrennt, ballt sie das Bewegte in zwiefache Kreise,
Kehrt sie wieder in sich zurück, umschreitet des Geistes
Tiefen sie und verwandelt nach ähnlichem Bilde den Himmel.
Auch den geringeren Wesen hast du abwägenden Sinnes
Seelen verliehn, und die Hohen, anpassend dem leichten Gefährte,
Säest du aus in Himmel und Erde; nach güt'gem Gesetze
Rufst du sie wieder dir zugewandt zurück von dem Feuer.
Vater, verleih seinem Geist, den himmlischen Sitz zu ersteigen,
Gib ihm zu schauen die Quelle des Guten, gib du ihm wieder
Licht des Geistes, daß er auf dich nur richte die Augen.
Scheuche die irdischen Nebel, zerstöre die wuchtenden Lasten.
Leuchte du auf mit deinem Glanz; denn du bist die Helle,

Du beseligende Ruh den Frommen, dich schauen ist Ende,
Ursprung, Führer, Erhalter und Weg und Grenze du selber.[41]

* * *

Johannes Zimmermann
Publication: 1934

Only selected sections of Boethius's text were translated by Zimmermann. These selected prose and verse passages are from books 1, 3, 4, and 5, and only certain lines from each selected passage were extracted by the translator for translation. Of Boethius, the translator writes in his introduction, "Zu den Männer, die in hervorragender Weise den Grund legten zu einer ausgedehnten Beschäftigung des Mittelalters mit der antiken Philosophie und damit zu einer Verschmelzung ihrer Ewigkeitswerte mit der christlichen Wahrheit, gehört Anicius Manlius Severinus Boethius" (3).[42]

Book 1, prose 1

So überdachte ich schweigend mein Unglück und zeichnete mit meinem Griffel meine tränenvollen Klagen auf. Da schien es mir, als träte zu meinen Häupten eine Frau von ehrfurchtgebietendem Antlitz. Ihre Augen leuchteten und blickten durchdringender, als Menschenaugen vermögen. Ihr Aussehen war blühend und zeugte von ungebrochener Kraft, wenngleich sie so alt war, daß man unmöglich glauben konnte, sie gehöre unserer Zeit an.

Als sie die Musen der Dichtkunst sah, die an meinem Lager standen und meinen Klagen Worte verliehen, rief sie etwas unwillig mit zornigem Blick: ". . . Hinweg mit euch, ihr Sirenen, die ihr mit süßen Reden den Kranken ins Verderben lockt, überlaßt ihn meinen Musen zur Pflege und zur Heilung!" So gescholten, senkten die Musen allesamt betrübt den Blick zur Erde und schritten traurig über die Schwelle, während die errötenden Wangen ihre Beschämung verrieten. Ich aber, dessen Augen vor Tränen verdunkelt waren, so daß ich nicht zu erkennen vermochte, wer denn diese Frau von so gebietender Hoheit sei, wußte kein Wort hervorzubringen und erwartete schweigend mit gesenktem Blick, was sie jetzt tun werde. Da trat sie näher heran, setzte sich auf das äußerste Ende meines Lagers, schaute mir in das traurigernste, vor Kummer zu Boden geneigte Antlitz und erhob Klagen über die Verwirrung meines Geistes.[43]

Book 3, meter 9

This meter was not translated.

* * *

Karl Büchner

(1910–81)
Publication: 1939

The often-cited introduction to this translation is by Friedrich Klingner [pp. 5–39].

Book 1, prose 1

Während ich dies bei mir schweigend bedachte und die tränenreiche Klage durch des Griffels Arbeit aufzeichnete, da zeigte sich, daß mir zu Häupten eine Frau getreten war von sehr ehrwürdigem Aussehen, mit feurigen und über die gemeine Kraft der Menschen hinaus durchdringenden Augen, von lebhafter Farbe und unerschöpflicher Frische, mochte sie auch so hoch in Jahren sein, daß man sie keineswegs für eine Zeitgenossin gehalten hätte – , von einer Größe, die man nicht klar erkennen konnte. Denn bald hielt sie sich in dem gewöhnlichen Maße der Menschen, bald aber schien sie mit dem Gipfel ihres Scheitels an den Himmel zu rühren. Wenn sie aber ihr Haupt höher erhoben hätte, wäre sie selbst in den Himmel eingedrungen und hätte des Blickes der nachschauenden Menschen gespottet. Ihr Gewand war aus ganz dünnen Fäden, in feiner Arbeit und aus unzerstörbarem Stoff vollendet hergestellt. Sie hatte es, wie ich später – sie verriet es selbst – erfuhr, mit ihren eigenen Händen gewebt. Sein Äußeres hatte, wie gewöhnlich rauchgedunkelte Bilder, der Schatten vernachlässigten Alters überzogen. Auf seinem unteren Rand konnte man ein griechisches π, auf dem oberen ein θ eingewebt lesen. Und zu beiden Buchstaben hin schienen nach Art von Treppen Stufen eingewebt zu sein, so daß auf ihnen vom untern Buchstaben zum oberen ein Aufstieg vorhanden war. Dies Gewand aber hatten Hände brutaler Menschen zerrissen, und jeder hatte die Teile weggeschleppt, die er vermochte. Und ihre rechte Hand hielt Bücher, die linke ein Szepter. Als sie nun die Musen der Dichtkunst an meinem Lager stehen und meinen Tränen Worte eingeben sah, sagte sie ein wenig erregt und finster mit den Augen blitzend: Wer hat diese Bühnendirnen zu diesem Kranken gelassen, daß sie seine Schmerzen nicht nur durch Heilmittel nicht lindern, sondern mit süßem Gift noch nähren? Sind sie es doch, die durch das unfruchtbare Gestrüpp der Leidenschaften die früchtereichen Saaten der Vernunft ertöten und den Geist der Menschen an die Krankheit gewöhnen, nicht von ihr befreien. Indes, wenn euer Schmeicheln, wie gewöhnlich, einen aus der uneingeweihten Masse verlockte, so brauchte man sich, glaube ich, weniger zu grämen. Denn bei ihm würden meine Mühen nicht verletzt. Aber diesen Mann, der in der Beschäftigung mit den Eleaten und der Akademie aufwuchs?! – Geht lieber davon, ihr Sirenen, süß bis zum Untergang, und laßt ihn meinen Musen zur Behandlung und Heilung!

Mit solchen Worten gescholten, senkte die Schar den Blick traurig zu Boden und schritt betrübt über die Schwelle. Durch Erröten gestand sie ihre Beschämung. Aber ich, dessen Auge in Tränen getaucht und beschattet war und der deshalb nicht unterscheiden konnte, wer denn diese Frau von solcher Macht des Befehls war, erstaunte, heftete den Blick auf die Erde und begann schweigend darauf zu warten, was sie denn nun tun würde. Da kam sie näher heran und setzte sich an den Rand meines Lagers. Sie betrachtete mein Antlitz, wie es von Trauer schwer und in Trübsal zu Boden gesenkt war, und klagte über die Verwirrung meines Geistes in folgenden Versen:[44]

Book 3, meter 9

Du, der das Weltall in ewiger Satzung beherrschet, des Himmels[fn-20]
und der Erden Schöpfer, der du von Ewigkeit wandeln
hießest die Zeit und in Ruh selbst, gibst, daß sich alles bewege,
den nicht äußere Gründe getrieben, aus flutendem Stoffe
auszuformen das Werk, sondern eingeborene Form des
höchsten Guten, das frei von Mißgunst: du leitest alles
ab vom Vorbild droben, im Geist das herrliche Weltall
tragend, selber am schönsten, es formend in ähnlichem Abbild,
und befiehlst dem Vollkommnen vollendete Teile zu bilden.
Du erbändigst durch Zahlen den Urstoff, daß sich die Kälte
schickt in die Flamme, das Trockne dem Flüssigen, daß nicht das Feuer
zu rein entfliege oder die Massen die Erde versenken.
Du bist's, der füget als Mitte[fn-21] die alles bewegende Seele
dreigeteilter Natur und sie löset in einträcht'ge Glieder;
da sie zerteilt die Bewegung in doppeltem Kreise geballt hat,

[fn-20] *Neuntes Gedicht:* Hexameter.

[fn-21] Zwischen Geist und Körper steht die "Seele", das Lebenspendende, in der Mitte.

läuft sie ins Selbst sich zu kehrn und umkreiset die Tiefe des Geistes,
dreht auch herum zugleich nach ähnlichem Bilde den Himmel.
Du führst geringere Seelen und Wesen hervor durch gleichen
Grund und die flüchtigen fügend an leichte Gefährte, verteilst du
diese der Erde, jene dem Himmel; nach gütiger Satzung
dir zugewendet läßt du sie heimkehrn geleitet durchs Feuer.
Gib dem Geiste, o Vater, den erhabenen Sitz zu erklimmen;
gib die Quelle des Guten zu schaun; wenn das Licht so gefunden,
gib, daß von Angesicht auf dich das Auge des Geistes sich hefte!
Schlage entzwei Gewicht und Nebel der irdischen Schwere!
Strahle in deinem dir eigenen Glanze; denn du bist das Heitre,
Du bist ruhige Rast allen Frommen, dich sehen ist Endziel,
Anfang, Beweger du, Führer und Pfad und Ende im gleichen![45]

* * *

Konrad Weiss

(May 1, 1880 [Rauenbretzingen bei Schwäbisch Hall]–
January 4, 1940 [Munich])
Publication: 1956

Konrad Weiss translated only the metra of Boethius for this bilingual edition, which bears the subtitle: *De consolatione philosophiae: Metra/Trost der Philosophie: Verse*. The Nachwort is by Joseph Pieper [pp. 111–30].

Book 1, prose 1

Only the meters were translated.

Book 3, meter 9

O der steuert die Welt nach alles durchdauerndem Ratschluß,
    Urvater du von Himmel und Erde, die Zeit aus der Urzeit
setzest in Lauf und alles bewegst du, du Gleicher vom immer;
    keinem Grunde gefolgt, der außer dir, bildest das Werk du
fern dem gestaltlosen Stoff, allein nach der Form, die dir einwohnt
    höchsten Gutes, mit keinerlei Neid; du vom obersten Beispiel
nimmst dies alles, was ist; die schöne Welt, selber du Schönster,
    führst du sinnvoll und formst sie dir ähnlich im Bilde, so daß in
Teilen vollendeter Art sie selbst sich vollende; das willst du.
    Du Elementen gibst Zahlen und Halt, daß Fröste und Flammen

walten zugleich, auch Dürre und Feuchte, daß reiner das Feuer
weder entflüchte, noch hemmungslos sinke durch Schwere die Erde.
Du gibst das waltende Band der Natur, der dreifachen, gibst ihr
all zur Mitte die Seele und zeigst sie im Wohllaut der Glieder.
Sie geteilt hat Bewegung vollbracht in ihren zwei Welten,
kommt doch und will zu sich selber zurück, und die Tiefen des Geistes
nun umschreitend hebt auf sie zum Bilde, das gleich ist dem Himmel.
Du lässest so die Seelen gedeihn und geringeres Leben
gleichen Grundes, du hebst mit dem Fahrzeug hinauf die erhabnen,
säest sie aus in Himmel und Erde, du guten Gesetzes
gönnst, wenn sie Heimkehr suchen zu dir, durch das Feuer Zurückkunft.
Gib du, Vater, dem Geist, den hohen Sitz zu ersteigen,
gib die Schauung des Guten am Quell, laß wieder zum Licht ihn,
gib, daß mit leuchtenden Augen der Geist an dir seinen Halt hat.
Scheuche die Nebel hinweg, die Schwere, die irdische Mühsal,
zücke aus deinem Glanze den Blitz; du bist ja der Lichtraum,
du die Rast und der Friede der Frommen, dich sehen ist Endziel,
Ausgang, Beweger, Führer und Weg und Abschluß du alles.[46]

* * *

Ernst Neitzke
Publication: 1959

Ernst Neitzke's translation is a complete verse-prose rendering of the *Consolatio.*

Book 1, prose 1

Während ich dies schweigend bei mir selbst überdachte und die tränenreiche Klage mit dem Griffel niederschrieb, dünkte es mich, daß mir zu Häupten eine Frau erschien: von sehr verehrungswürdigem Aussehen mit funkelnden und über die gewöhnliche Fähigkeit des Menschen hinaus durchdringenden Augen, von frischer Farbe und unverbrauchten Kräften, obwohl sie doch in so vorgerücktem Alter stand, daß man keinesfalls eine Angehörige unseres Zeitalters in ihr sehen konnte, und von nicht klar erkennbarem Wuchs. Denn bald begnügte sie sich mit dem gewöhnlichen menschlichen Maß, bald aber schien sie oben mit ihrem Scheitel den Himmel zu berühren. Und wenn sie ihr Haupt noch höher erhoben hätte, so wäre sie bis in den Himmel selber vorgestoßen und hätte sich den Blicken der ihr nachschauenden Menschen völlig entzogen. Ihr Gewand war aus den zartesten Fäden und mit sauberster Kunstfertigkeit aus unzerstörbarem Material gefertigt und, wie ich später durch ihr Geständnis erfuhr, von ihren eigenen Händen gewebt; sein Äußeres war, was bei verräucherten Ahnenbildern gewöhnlich ist, wie infolge von Alter und Unachtsamkeit nachgedunkelt. In seinem unteren Rande war ein griechisches π, im oberen aber ein θ eingewebt zu sehen; und zwischen beiden schien eine Art von treppenförmig angelegten Stufen angedeutet zu sein, auf denen ein Aufsteigen vom unteren zum oberen Buchstaben erfolgen könnte. Dasselbe Gewand hatten jedoch die Hände gewisser gewalttätiger Menschen zerrissen und die Teile, soviel jeder nur konnte, davongeschleppt. Auch trug sie in der rechten Hand Bücherrollen, in der linken ein Zepter.

Als sie nun die Musen der Dichtkunst neben meinem Lager stehen und mir den Text für meine Klageweisen vorschreiben sah, da ergrimmte sie und sprach mit finster blickenden Augen: Wer hat diesen Huren vom Theater den Zutritt zu diesem Kranken gestattet, die seine Schmerzen nicht nur mit kleinerei Heilmitteln lindern, sondern durch ihr süßes Gift obendrein vermehren wollen? Sie sind es nämlich, die durch das unfruchtbare Gestrüpp der Leidenschaften die Saat der fruchtverheißenden Vernunft vernichten und den Geist der Menschen an die Krankheit gewöhnen und nicht ihn von ihr befreien. Ja, wenn eure Schmeichelreden einen Unwissenden, wie bei euch üblich, verführten, so würde ich das für weniger bedenklich halten. Denn bei einem solchen würde meinen Bemühungen nicht zu nahe getreten werden. Nun aber diesen Mann, der mit dem Studium der Eleaten[fn-22] und der

[fn-22] Durch Xenophanes aus Kolophon um die Mitte des 6. Jahrhunderts v. Chr. in Elea in Unteritalien begründet und durch seinen bedeutenderen Schüler Parmenides (vgl. Anm. III, 23 und IV, 8) weiter entwickelt, stellt die Schule der Eleaten die erste der später so zahlreichen griechischen Philosophenschulen dar. Xenophanes bemüht sich, die Religiosität seiner Zeit zu veredeln, und ist ein abgesagter Feind der homerischen Mythologie. Für ihn ist es ein Sakrileg, daß man den Göttern irdische Unzulänglichkeiten zuschreibe; und die ihm unverständliche Tatsache, daß die Menschen ihren Gottheiten menschliche Gestalt verleihen, veranlaßt ihn zu der bissigen Folgerung, daß sich die Ochsen, wenn sie Götter hätten und ihnen Gestalt geben wollten, entsprechend verhalten müßten. Die höchste Gottheit ist für ihn das ewige, unbewegliche Sein, unentstanden und unwandelbar; ihrem Wesen ist nicht durch mystisches Schauen, sondern allein durch rationales Denken beizukommen, und auch dann nur annäherungsweise: denn alle irdische Wahrheit kommt über Scheinwahrheit nicht hinaus.

Parmenides, um 540 geboren, setzt in einem in Fragmenten erhaltenen Lehrgedicht "Die Natur" die Gedanken seines Lehrers fort. Er unterscheidet eine auf trügerischer Sinneswahrnehmung und Meinung beruhende

Akademie[fn-23] groß geworden ist? Verschwindet also, ihr Sirenen,[fn-24] deren Süße nur Verderben bringt, und überlaßt ihn meinen Musen zur Pflege und zur Heilung.

Derart ausgescholten, senkte die Schar den Blick betrübt zu Boden, und durch Erröten ihre Beschämung verratend, verließ sie traurig die Schwelle. Ich aber, dessen Gesicht von vielen Tränen umflort war und der nicht erkennen konnte, wer denn diese Frau von so gebieterischer Würde wäre, erstaunte und schickte mich mit zur Erde gesenktem Blick an, schweigend darauf zu warten, was sie wohl weiter tun werde. Da trat sie näher heran, setzte sich auf das untere Ende meines Ruhebettes, betrachtete mein trauervolles und im Schmerz zum Boden gesenktes Gesicht und klagte über die Verwirrung meines Geistes in dem folgenden Gedicht:[47]

Book 3, meter 9

Du bist es, der die Welt regiert nach ewigem Ratschluß,
Erde und Himmel erschuf und die Zeit seit ältesten Tagen
fortschreiten läßt und voll Festigkeit sorgt, daß das All sich bewege;
denn nicht äußerer Antrieb vermochte, aus flüchtigem Stoffe
auszugestalten sein Werk, sondern nur das Urbild des eignen,
lautersten Guten. Und so allein von dem himmlischen Muster
leitest das Ganze du her; und selber der Herrlichste, hast du,
ganz wie dein Geist es erschaut, das herrliche Weltall geschaffen
und zum vollkommenen Ganzen vollkommene Teile verbunden.
Du gibst den Grundstoffen Regel und Maß, daß die Kälte der Hitze,

---

Scheinwelt von dem alleinigen, wahren Sein, das durch das Denken erkennbar, ja mit ihm identisch ist. Dieses höchste Sein ist für ihn, wie schon für Xenophanes, unentstanden und unvergänglich, und er vergleicht es, gleichsam als könne er in seiner subtilen Gedankenwelt ohne eine plastische Vorstellung doch nicht auskommen, einer "allseitig wohlgerundeten Kugelgestalt": wir werden im dritten Buche sehen, wie dieses alleinige, höchste Seiende der alleinigen höchsten Gottheit von Boëthius gleichgesetzt wird.

[fn-23] Die Akademie Platons [. . .] hat ihren Namen daher, daß Platon seine Schule nahe dem heiligen Hain des athenischen Heros Akademos gründet. Aus dieser Schule geht Aristoteles als ihr nächst dem Gründer angesehenstes Mitglied hervor; er wird Erzieher Alexanders des Großen und gründet später in Athen die philosophische Schule der Peripatetiker (384-322).

[fn-24] Die Sirenen sind Fabelwesen mit Vogelleibern und Jungfrauenköpfen. Sie locken die vorüberfahrenden Schiffer durch verführerischen Gesang an und saugen ihnen die

Trocknes dem Nassen entspreche, daß nicht die Reinheit des Feuers
sich verflüchtige, nicht seine Schwere den Erdball versenke.
Du beläßt die bewegende Seele der Welt in der Mitte
dreifach gestufter Natur[fn-25] und gliederst die Kräfte im Gleichmaß.
Also geteilt, verstärkt sie des zweifachen Kreises Bewegung,
strebt dann zurück zu sich selbst, umwandelt die Tiefen des Geistes
und verändert die himmlische Welt nach ähnlichem Bilde.
Du aus gleichem Grunde bringst mindere Wesen und Seelen
wie auch erhabne hervor und gibst ihnen luftige Schwingen,
teilst die einen dem Himmel zu, der Erde die andern;
gnädig führst du erleuchtet zurück, die zu dir sich bekennen.
Vater, vergönne dem Geist einen Sitz in den seligen Höhen,
weise den Urquell des Guten, erneue die frühere Klarheit,
daß nur auf dich allein sich richten die Blicke des Geistes.
Laß vergehen die irdischen Nebel und drückenden Lasten,
und deinen Glanz laß strahlend leuchten; denn du bist das Leichte,
bist den Frommen friedvolle Ruhe; du bist ihnen Ende,
Anfang und Förderer, Führer und Pfad und Markstein in einem.[48]

Lebenskraft aus; weshalb Odysseus, als er auf der Heimreise von Troia die gefährliche Stelle passiert, seinen Gefährten die Ohren zustopft und sich selbst am Mastbaum festbinden läßt. (Vgl. Odyssee 12, 36 ff.)

[fn-25] Diese Stelle zeigt ganz besonders deutliche Ankläge an neu-platonische Gedankengänge, und zwar vorzüglich an die berühmte Emanationslehre Plotins: Das höchste, unwandelbare Wesen, das Ur-Eine, strahlt, ohne selbst an seiner unausschöpfbaren Substanz zu verlieren, in immer abgeschwächterer, weil weiter von ihrem Ursprung sich entfernender Kraft alles Bestehende aus. Die nächstliegende und somit höchste Emanationsstufe stellt den Nous, den Weltgeist dar, unter dem man sich, wenn man es platonisch ausdrücken will, die Gesamtheit und den Inbegriff der Ideen zu denken hat. Die zweite und somit wertmäßig mindere Emanationsstufe bringt die Weltseele hervor, die die Einzelseelen umfaßt. Diese bilden die psychische Welt und stehen als solche immer noch hoch aber der materiellen. (In einem anderen Zusammenhange, aber durchaus im Sinne Plotins, drückt Boëthius dies im fünften Buche so aus: "Die menschlichen Seelen . . . sind zwar ziemlich frei, solange sie in der Betrachtung des göttlichen Geistes verharten; weniger dann, wenn sie in die Substanz abgleiten* usw.) Die dritte und unterste Stufe wird also durch die physische, materielle Welt gebildet. Wird ihr zwar ein wirklicher Wert abgesprochen, so ist sie dennoch nach Plotins Ansicht, in die kosmische Harmonie eingegliedert, und der in sie abgesunkenen Seele bleiben Möglichkeit und Fähigkeit erhalten, zum Ur-Einen zurückzufinden, wozu ihr die Ekstase, d.i. die Verzückung, die mystische Versenkung, verhilft. "Gnädig führst du erleuchtet zurück, die zu dir sich bekennen", sagt Boëthius.

* * *

H[ermann] M[artin] Endres

Publication: 1961

Book 1, prose 1

Indem ich schwieg, gingen mir solche Gedanken durch den Sinn, und ich schrieb die leidvolle Klage mit meinem Griffel nieder. Da war mir, als erschiene zu meinen Häupten eine Frau, gar ehrwürdig anzusehen; ihr Auge funkelte, und mehr, als sonst es Menschen vermögen, durchdrang es mich; lebendig leuchtete ihre Farbe, unverdorben dünkte mich ihre Jugendkraft, obgleich sie bejahrt schien; nein, daß sie unserer Zeit zugehörte, war nicht zu glauben. Ihre Größe ließ sich nicht klar unterscheiden; denn bald war sie nicht größer, als Menschen gewöhnlich sind, bald aber schien sie mit ihrem Scheitel an den Himmel zu reichen. Und hätte sie ihr Haupt noch höher erhoben, so hätte sie wohl selbst in den Himmel geragt, und vergeblich hätte man nach ihr geblickt. Gar fein war ihr Kleid gesponnen, mit viel Kunst war es aus unzerstörbarem Gewebe gefertigt; später hörte ich von ihr selbst, daß sie es war, die es mit eigener Hand gewebt hatte. Wie bei alten rauchgeschwärzten Bildern hatte sich durch das Alter und durch mangelnde Sorgfalt ein dunkler Schatten darauf gelegt. Am unteren Rand war ein griechisches Pi, am oberen ein Theta eingewebt zu sehen; dazwischen schienen irgendwie in Gestalt einer Treppe Stufen dargestellt zu sein, die von unten nach oben emporstiegen. Dieses Kleid hatten aber die Hände gemeiner Frevler zerschlissen, und jeder hatte, so gut er konnte, ein Stück davon mit sich genommen. In der Rechten hielt sie Buchrollen, in der Linken aber ein Zepter.

Als sie nun sehen mußste, wie die Musen der Dichtkunst mein Lager umstanden und meine Tränen in Worte faßten, sprach sie in einiger Erregung und grimmig mit düsteren Blicken: Wer hat diese Theaterdirnen zu diesem Kranken gelassen? Sie, die nicht nur kein Mittel kennen gegen seinen Schmerz, die ihn nur mit ihrem süßen Gift zu steigern suchen? Ja, sie sind es, die mit dem unfruchtbaren Dickicht der Leidenschaften die fruchtreife Saat der Vernunft zerstören, die des Menschen Seelen an die Krankheit gewöhnen, statt ihn davon zu befreien. Wäre es ein Unwissender, den ihr wie sonst verführt, ich fände weniger Schlimmes daran; denn an ihm wäre meine Mühe nicht gefährdet. Der aber ist doch mit den Lehren der Eleaten und der Akademie großgezogen worden! So hebt euch hinweg, ihr Sirenen, ihr süßen Verderberinnen, laßt ihn meinen Musen, daß sie ihn pflegen und heilen!

Auf solchen Schimpf senkte die Schar die Augen leidvoll zu Boden; errötend verrieten sie ihre Scham, und traurig zogen sie ab über die Schwelle. Doch ich, das tränenfeuchte Antlitz wie von einem Nebel umhüllt, unfähig zu erkennen, wer diese hoheitsvolle Frau sein mochte, ... ich fand kein Wort, senkte meinen Blick und begann stillschweigend zu warten, was sie wohl täte. Da trat sie näher zu mir, ließ sich unten an meiner Lagerstatt nieder, sah auf mein kummervolles, nach unten geneigtes Antlitz und klagte also in Versen über die Verwirrung meines Geistes:[49]

Book 3, meter 9

Der Du die Welt regierst nach ewigem unwandelbarem Gesetz,
Schöpfer der Erde, Schöpfer des Himmels, der du [*sic*] der Zeit von Ewigkeit an befiehlst,
selbst in Ruhe verharrst, obgleich Du das All in Bewegung hältst,
der keiner von außen wirkenden Kraft bedurfte, um aus dem wogenden Urstoff
das Werk der Schöpfung zu bilden; Deinem Wesen zu eigen ist
des allerreinsten Guten Gestalt, nichts trübt sie; und aus dem himmlischen Urbild
leitest Du her das All; und Du selbst als das herrlichste Wesen
schufest die Welt ganz nach dem Bild Deines Geistes
und heißest das vollkommene Ganze gleich vollkommene Teile erzeugen.
Die Elemente ordenest Du durch die feste Bindung der Zahlen,
auf daß Kälte und Wärme, Trockenes und Nasses einander entsprechen,
daß nicht nach oben entschwinde das reinere Feuer oder ihr eignes Gewicht die Erde versinken macht.
Du machst zur Mitte der Dreinatur
die alles bewegende Seele und sorgst für den Einklang der Teile.
Ist sie geteilt, so ballt sie, was sie bewegt, in doppeltem Kreise,
strebt wieder in sich zurück und umkreist des Geistes Tiefen,
um schließlich den Himmel nach gleichem Vorbild zu wandeln.
Genauso läßt Du geringeres Leben und mindere Wesen entstehen
wie auch die hohen, die Du leichthin schweben lässest,
weisest sie Himmel und Erde zu, und nach freundlicher Satzung
holst Du sie wieder zurück zu Dir mit Hilfe des Lichtes.
Vater, gib, daß mein Geist sich erhebe zu Deinem strahlenden Throne,
gib, daß er den Quell alles Guten erschaue
und, wenn er zum Lichte gefunden, den Blick nimmer wende von Dir!

Verteile die irdischen Nebel, die drückende Last zerschlage,
laß strahlen Deinen Glanz, Du bist ja die heitere Helle,
Du schenkst allen Guten Ruhe und Frieden; Dich schauen zu dürfen,
ist Ende und Anfang; Du bist die bewegende Kraft; Geleiter und Weg
zugleich,
und Du auch bist unser Ziel![50]

* * *

Ernst Gegenschatz
(1914–98)
and
Olof Gigon
(1912–98)
Translation copyright: 1981
(Düsseldorf: Patmos/Artemis & Winkler)

The 1981 printing of the Gegenschatz and Gigon translation is in bilingual format, with the Latin text on the even pages and the German rendering facing, on the odd pages. Later printings and editions present the German translation alone. The introduction is by Olof Gigon [pp. vii–lxiii]. An edition of 2010, edited and with a Nachwort by Kurt Flasch, contains only the German text [Munich: Deutscher Taschenbuch Verlag, 2010 (also 1995 and 2005)].

Book 1, prose 1

Während ich solches schweigend bei mir selbst erwog und meine tränenvolle Klage mit Hilfe des Griffels aufzeichnete, schien es mir, als ob zu meinen Häupten ein Weib hinträte von höchst ehrwürdigem Antlitz, mit funkelnden und über das gewöhnliche Vermögen der Menschen durchdringenden Augen, von frischer Farbe und unerschöpfter Jugendkraft, obwohl sie so bejahrt war, daß sie in keiner Weise unserem Zeitalter anzugehören schien. Ihr Wuchs war von wechselnder Größe; denn bald zog sie sich zum gewöhnlichen Maß der Menschen zusammen, bald schien sie mit dem Scheitel den Himmel zu berühren; und als sie noch höher ihr Haupt emporhob, ragte sie über den Himmel selbst hinaus und entzog sich so dem Blick der Menschen. Ihr Gewand war von feinstem Gespinst und mit peinlicher Kunstfertigkeit aus unzerstörbarem Stoff gefertigt; sie hatte es, wie ich später aus ihrem eignen Munde erfuhr, mit eigner Hand gewebt. Seinen Glanz hatte wie bei rauchgeschwärzten Bildern ein trüber Anflug von Vernachlässigung und Alter überzogen. An seinem untersten Rande las man eingewebt ein griechisches π, an seinem obersten aber ein θ. Und zwischen beiden Buchstaben schienen wie an einer Leiter etliche Stufen eingezeichnet, die von dem unteren zum oberen Schriftzug emporstiegen. Doch hatten dieses selbe Kleid die Hände einiger Gewalttätiger zerfetzt, und jeder hatte die Stückchen, die er gerade fassen konnte, an sich gerissen. Ihre Rechte endlich trug Bücher, ihre Linke aber ein Zepter.

Als sie die Dichtermusen, die mein Lager umstanden und meiner Tränenflut Worte liehen, erblickte, sprach sie etwas erregt und mit finster flammenden Blicken: Wer hat diesen Dirnen der Bühne den Zutritt zu diesem Kranken erlaubt, ihnen, die seinen Schmerz nicht nur mit keiner Arznei lindern, sondern ihn obendrein mit süßem Gifte nähren möchten? Sind sie es doch, die mit dem unfruchtbaren Dorngestrüpp der Leidenschaften die fruchtreiche Saat der Vernunft ersticken, die der Menschen Seelen an die Krankheit gewöhnen, nicht sie davon befreien. Wenn eure Schmeichelreden einen Uneingeweihten, wie es gemeinhin durch euch geschieht, ablenken, so würde ich das für minder betrüblich halten, denn bei ihm würden unsere Mühen nicht verletzt. Doch dieser, ist er nicht mit der Wissenschaft der Eleaten und Akademiker ernährt worden? Drum hinweg ihr Sirenen, die ihr süß seid zum Verderben, überlaßt ihn meinen Musen zur Pflege und zur Heilung!

So gescholten senkte jener Chor tief bekümmert die Blicke zu Boden, Erröten verriet ihre Scham und traurig gingen sie über die Schwelle hinaus. Ich aber, dessen Auge von strömenden Tränen umschleiert war, so daß ich nicht unterscheiden konnte, wer diese Frau von so gebietender Würde sei, verstummte, heftete mein Auge auf die Erde und begann schweigend abzuwarten, was sie nun weiter tun werde. Da trat sie näher an mich heran, setzte sich auf das Ende meines Bettes, blickte auf mein kummerschweres, auf die Erde geneigtes Antlitz und klagte in folgenden Versen über die Verwirrung meines Geistes:[51]

Book 3, meter 9

Der du lenkest die Welt nach dauernden, festen Gesetzen,
Schöpfer des Himmels, der Erden, der du von Ewigkeit ausgehen
Hießest die Zeit, selbst nimmer bewegt, bewegend das Weltall!
Keine äußere Macht trieb dich, aus wogenden Massen
Deine Schöpfung zu formen; in dir nur trägst du des höchsten

Guten Gestalt, bist frei von Mißgunst. Das All vom Urbild
Leitest du her; die herrliche, Herrlichster selber,
Trägst du im Geiste, die Welt, und formst sie zu ähnlichem Bilde,
In der vollendeten schafft dein Befehl vollkommene Teile.
Bindest mit Zahlen die Elemente, daß Hitze und Kälte,
Regen und Dürre ihr Maß einhalten; die reinere Flamme
Nicht emporflieh, die Last nicht abwärts ziehe die Erde.
Aus der Mitte der Drei-Natur entläßt du die Seele,
Die das Weltall bewegt, hüllst sie in harmonische Glieder.
Wenn sie getrennt, ballt sie das Bewegte in zweifache Kreise,
Kehrt sie wieder in sich zurück, umschreitet des Geistes
Tiefen sie und verwandelt nach ähnlichem Bilde den Himmel.
Auch die geringeren Wesen und Seelen aus gleichem Grunde
Führest hervor du; und die in der Höhe fügend an leichte Gefährte,
Teilst du sie aus in Himmel und Erde; nach gütgem Gesetze
Rufst sie wieder dir zugewandt mit rückführendem Feuer.
Vater, verleih meinem Geist, den himmlischen Sitz zu ersteigen,
Gib ihm zu schauen die Quelle des Guten, gib du ihm wieder
Licht des Geistes, daß er auf dich nur richte die Augen.
Scheuche die irdischen Nebel, zerstöre die wuchtenden Lasten.
Leuchte du auf mit deinem Glanz; denn du bist die Helle,
Du besel'gende Ruh den Frommen, dich schauen ist Ende,
Ursprung, Führer, Erhalter und Weg und Erde du selber.[52]

Annotated Bibliography of Selected General Works

Gibson, Margaret, ed. *Boethius: His Life, Thought and Influence.* Oxford: Blackwell, 1981.

- This volume was assembled to commemorate the fifteen-hundredth anniversary of Boethius's birth (481–1981). It is comprehensive in scope, covering all major areas of Boethius's scholarly work. Of interest for the study of the German *Consolatio* translation tradition is Nigel Palmer's chapter, "Latin and Vernacular in the Northern European Tradition" (362–409) and particularly two subsections in that chapter, "The Münster Fragments" (372–81) and "MS Hamilton 46" (381–91). Appendix 1 (392–97) contains two extracts from the text of Hamilton 46, 4m1 and 4p6.

Glei, Reinhold F., Nicola Kaminski, and Franz Lebsanft, eds. *Boethius Christianus?* Berlin: Gruyter, 2010.

- This is a very challenging collection of articles, partly because they are written variously in English, French, German, and Italian. Of particular significance here are several chapters: Reinhold Glei's contribution, "Einleitung: Boethius Christianus?" (1–17), in which the German *Consolatio* translations are noted briefly (6–10); Stephan Müller's contribution, "Boethius im Klassenzimmer: Die Bearbeitung der *Consolatio Philosophiae* durch Notker den Deutschen" (333–54); Bernd Bastert's contribution, "Boethius unter Druck: Die *Consolatio Philosophiae* (35–69); Yvonne Dellsperger's contribution, "Die Erfurter Übersetzung der *Consolatio Philosophiae* (1465) im Spannungsfeld von Jenseitsfurcht und Sündenvergebung" (95–127), containing two important subsections, "Die deutsche Boethius-Tradition" (97–101) and "Die Übersetzung der *Consolatio Philosophiae* in MS Hamilton 46" (101–02); Manfred Eikelmann's contribution, "Boethius für Laien: Konrad Humerys deutsche Übersetzung (vor 1467)" (129–56); and Nicola Kaminski's contribution, "Hellwig–Villinus–van Helmont/ Knorr von Rosenroth: Boethius' *Consolatio Philosophiae* im Fadenkreuz einer konfessionalisierten Philologie" (261–301).

Gruber, Joachim, "Boethius 1925–1998." *Lustrum* 39 (1999): 307–38, and 40 (2001): 199–259.

- A very comprehensive annotated bibliography on Boethius, on all aspects of his life and works up to 2000.

Hoenen, Maarten J. F. M., and Lodi Nauta, eds. *Boethius in the Middle Ages: Latin and Vernacular Traditions of the "Consolatio philosophiae."* Studien und Texte zur Geistesgeschichte des Mittelalters 58. Leiden: Brill, 1997.

- This volume presents studies of three traditions of *Consolatio* influence during the Middle Ages: the Latin tradition; the Middle Dutch tradition; and the English, French Italian, and German traditions. Of particular interest here is Nigel Palmer's contribution, "The German Boethius Translation Printed in 1473 in Its Historical Contest" (287–302).

Kaylor, Noel Harold, Jr. *The Medieval "Consolation of Philosophy": An Annotated Bibliography*. Garland Medieval Bibliographies 7. New York: Garland, 1992.

- This volume annotates all books and articles on the Old English, medieval German, medieval French, and Middle English *Consolatio* translation traditions up to the year of publication. Of interest here is the chapter "The Medieval German Tradition" (71–97).

Kaylor, Noel Harold, Jr., and Philip Edward Phillips, eds. *A Companion to Boethius in the Middle Ages*. Brill Companions to the Christian Tradition 30. Leiden: Brill, 2012.

- This volume is comprehensive, with chapters on all aspects of Boethius's scholarly work and thought and on his influence upon the Middle Ages. Of particular interest for the study of the German *Consolatio* translation is the contribution by Christine Hehle, "Boethius's Influence on German Literature to *c.* 1500" (255–318). The medieval *Consolatio* translations are addressed in part 5 (299–314).

Marenbon, John, ed. *The Cambridge Companion to Boethius*. Cambridge: Cambridge University Press, 2009.

- This volume is divided into two parts, "Before the *Consolatio*" and "The *Consolatio*," and they examine the logical and theological works by Boethius as well as the *Consolatio*. Of interest here is the contribution by Winthrop Wetherbee, which gives brief discussion of some of the major medieval *Consolatio* translations (279–302).

Stewart, Hugh Fraser. *Boethius: An Essay*. London: Blackwood, 1892; repr. New York: Franklin, 1974.

- This is a classic study of all aspects of Boethius and his works. Of particular interest here is the chapter "On Some Ancient Translations of Boethius's Last Work" (160–240).

NOTES

[1] Several scholars have contributed significantly to the identification and collection of translations listed in this article: at the beginning of the project, Karl Heinz and Jutta Göller helped locate German scholars knowledgeable on the Boethian tradition in Germany; Susanne Gärtner did preliminary researched in German libraries; Hans Sauer arranged for us to access translations held at the Ludwig-Maximilian University at Munich; Anne Aschenbrenner found important translations online and via interlibrary loan in Munich; Florian Schleburg accessed materials at the University of Regensburg; Johannes Weber accessed materials in archives at Bamberg; Christoph Houswitschka arranged for us to access translations held at the University of Bamberg; Brian Donaghey shared his collection of *Consolatio* translations with me during a visit in Sheffield, England.

[2] Nigel F. Palmer, "Latin and Vernacular in the Northern European Tradition of the *De Consolatione Philosophiae*," in *Boethius: His Life, Thought and Influence*, ed. Margaret Gibson (Oxford: Blackwell, 1981), 363.

[3] *Notker der Deutsche: Boethius, "De consolatione Philosophiae," Buch I/II*, ed. Petrus W. Tax, Die Werke Notkers des Deutschen 1, Altdeutsche Textbibliothek 94 (Tübingen: Niemeyer, 1988), 7–11.

[4] *Notker der Deutsche: Boethius, "De consolatione Philosophiae," Buch III*, ed. Petrus W. Tax, Die Werke Notkers des Deutschen 2, Altdeutsche Textbibliothek 100 (Tübingen: Niemeyer, 1988), 148–51.

[5] Andreas von Regensburg, *Sämtliche Werke*, ed. Georg Leidinger (Munich: Rieger, 1903; repr. Aalen: Scientia, 1969), 119.

[6] Pez (Pezius), Bernard (Benedictine), *Thesarus Anecdotorum Novissimus*, vol. 4 (Augsburg: Augustae Vindelicorum and Gracii, 1723), xxiv.

[7] Alois Bömer, "Fragmente einer gereimten deutschen Boethiusübersetzung," *Zeitschrift für deutsches Altertum und deutsche Literatur* 50 (1908): 149–58.

[8] For a description, see Christine Hehle, "Boethius's Influence on German Literature to *c.* 1500," in *A Companion to Boethius in the Middle Ages*, ed. Noel Harold Kaylor, Jr. and Philip Edward Phillips, Brill's Companions to the Christian Tradition 30 (Leiden: Brill, 2012), 303–05.

[9] For a description, see Yvonne Dellsperger, "Die Erfurter Übersetzung der *Consolatio Philosophiae* (1465) im Spannungsfeld von Jenseitsfurcht und Sündenvergebung," in *Boethius Christianus?*, ed. Reinhold F. Glei, Nicola Kaminski, and Franz Lebsanft (Berlin: Gruyter, 2010), 95–127. See also Nigel F. Palmer "Latin and Vernacular in the Northern European Tradition of the *De Consolatione Philosophiae*," in *Boethius: His Life, Thought and Influence*, ed. Margaret Gibson (Oxford: Blackwell, 1981), 381–91.

[10] *Hic liber Boecii de consolatione philosophiae in textu latina alemannicaque lingua refertus ac translatus una cum apparatu & expositione beati Thome de aquino ordinis praedicatorum finit feliciter*, trans. Anonymous (Nürnberg: Anton Koberger, 1473), n.p.

[11] In this text, a symbol resembling an ampersand represents "der."

[12] *Hic liber Boecii de consolatione philosophiae*, n.p.

[13] Hehle, "Boethius's Influence," 300.

[14] For information on Humery and extracts from his translation (Berlin MS), see Hehle, "Boethius's Influence," 305–10; see also Michael Mommert, "Konrad Humery und seine Übersetzung der *Consolatio Philosophiae*. Studien zur deutschen Boethius-Tradition am Ausgang des Mittelalters (PhD diss., Westfälische Wilhelms-Universität, 1965).

[15] In this text, a symbol resembling an ampersand represents "der."

[16] *Boethius der Hochberumpt meister vnd poet von dem trost der weissheit,* trans. Anonymous, ed. Johann Schott (Strassburg, ca. 1500; orig. pub. Nürnberg: Anton Koberger, 1473), n.p. In Schott's edition, "daz" is reduced to "dz," and this reduction is maintained in this transcription.

[17] Ibid.

[18] In this text, a symbol resembling an ampersand represents "der."

[19] Ibid.

[20] Johann Hellwig (Helwig), *Des Annici Manlii Torquatii Severini Boethii: V Bücher von Trost aus der Vernünft Lehre* (Nürnberg: Gedruckt bey Christoph Gerhard / In Verlegung Johann Taubers, 1660) 15–18.

[21] The "e" of this word apparently is omitted for the sake of even scansion. There are other occurrences of this practice in this translation.

[22] The "e" of this word apparently is omitted for the sake of even scansion. There are other occurrences of this practice in this translation.

[23] Johann Hellwig (Helwig), *Des Annici Manlii Torquatii Severini Boethii: V Bücher von Trost aus der Vernünft Lehre* (Nürnberg: Gedruckt bey Christoff Gerhard/In Verlegung Johann Taubers, 1660), 134–38.

[24] Christian Knorr von Rosenroth and Franciscus Mercurius van Helmont, *Des Fûrtrefflichen Hochvveisen Severini Boetii, Weil. Bûrgermeisters zu Rom, Consolatio Philosophiae, oder Christlich-vernunfft-gemesser Trost und Unterricht in Widerwertigkeit und Bestûrtzung ûber dem vermeinten Wohl-oder Ubel-Stand der Bösen und Frommen: Verteutschet, und mit beygefügten kurtzen Anmerckungen ûber etliche dunckele Ort desselben zum andernmahl auffgeleget 1697* (Lüneburg: Johann Georg Lippern, 1697), 17–20.

[25] Ibid., 127–28.

[26] Friedrich Roth-Scholz [F.R.], *Fünf Bücher vom Troste der Weisheit in Widerwertigkeit aus dem Lateinischen übersetzt und mit kurzen Anmerkungen ans Licht gestellt von F.R.* (Nürnberg, 1717), n.p.

[27] Johann Just Fahsius, *Der in seinem Gefängniss philosophirende Boëthius, das ist: des im 6ten Seculo hochberühmten römischen Bürgermeisters und königl. Ost-Gothischen Staats-Ministers Anicii Manlii Torquati Severini Boethii V. Bücher "De Consolatione Philosophiæ," oder Tröstung aus der Welt-Weissheit, usw* (Goslar: Johann Christoph König, 1724), n.p.

[28] Ibid., 32–33.

[29] Ibid., 146–47.

[30] *Des Anicius Manlius Troquatus Severinus Boethius: Fünf Bücher vom Philosophischen Troste aus dem lateinischen vom neuen übersetzt,* trans. M. Johann Gottfried Richter (Leipzig: Johann Michael Teubner, 1753), 3–5.

[31] Ibid., 96–98.

[32] Friedrich Karl Freytag, *Trost der Philosophie aus dem Lateinischen des Boethius mit Anmerkungen und Nachrichten die Geschichte des Originals und das Leben des Verfassers betreffend von Friedrich Karl Freytag* (Riga: Johann Friedrich Hartknoch, 1794), 2–7.

[33] Ibid., 106–11.

[34] Lambert Ignaz Wortberg, *Des römischen Consuls Anicius Manlius Torquatus Severinus Boethius Gesänge im Kerker (De Consolatione philosophiae) nachgebildet von L[ambert] I[gnaz] Wortberg* (Greifswalt, Barlini, Gesellius: Mauritius in Commission in der Mauritusschen Buchhanlung 1826), 7.

[35] Ibid., 69–75.

[36] *Des Manlius Torquatus Severinus Boethius: Fünf Bücher vom Troste der Philosophie: prosaisch und metrisch übersetzt und mit Anmerkungen eines Christen begleitet, von J.H. Weingärtner, Pfarrer,* trans. J. H. Weingärtner (Linz: Verlag der k.k. priv. academischen Kunst-, Musik- und Buchhandlung, 1827), 1–3.

[37] Ibid., 68.

[38] *Die Tröstungen der Philosophie des Anicius Manlius Torquatus Severinus Boethius. Senator und Mitglied der obersten Rangklasse, gewesener ordentlicher römischer Konsul und Chef der Civilverwaltung, Patricius von Rom,* übersetzt von Richard Scheven, trans. Richard Scheven (Leipzig: Philipp Reclam jun., 1893), 10–11.

[39] Ibid., 79.

[40] *Anicius Manlius Severinus Boethius: Trost der Philosophie: Übersetzt von Eberhard Gothein,* trans. Eberhard Gothein (Köln: Verlag die Runde, 1932), 7 and 9.

[41] Ibid., 93 and 95.

[42] In the introduction to his translation (*Boethius: Trost der Philosophie: Ausgewählt und Übersetzt von Dr. Johannes Zimmermann: Studienrat am Dreikönigsgymnasium in Köln,* trans. Johannes Zimmermann [Düsseldorf: Schwann, 1934], 6), Zimmermann writes:

> "Bemerkungen zu dieser Auswahl: Wenngleich die Consolatio fast ausschließlich Gedanken der griechischen, insbesondere der neuplatonischen und stoischen Philosophie vermittelt und spezifisch christliche Färbung nur leicht durchschimmern läßt, so wird doch schon aus dieser kurzen Auswahl deutlich werden, daß sie einen tieffrommen Gottesglauben eindringlich und überzeugend in edler Sprache predigt und auf letzte Lebensfragen Antworten gibt, die ihres Gehalts und ihrer Fassung wegen Aufnahme in diese Sammlung religiöser Quellenschriften verdienen.
>
> Den größten Teil der ausgesonderten Texte lieferten die Bücher IV und V. Aus Buch III wurde nur ein Abschnitt übernommen. Das erste Buch, das die Rahmenerzählung und wichtige Aufschlüsse über Anklage und Prozeß unseres Autors bringt, durfte nicht unberücksichtigt bleiben, wohl aber konnten die dann folgenden Eröterungen über die Nichtigkeit irdischer Güter übergangen werden; an solchen Betrachtungen ist ja kein Mangel. Bei der Übersetzung der ausgewählten Verseinlagen war die Überzeugung wegweisend, daß schöne Gedanken durch eine klare Sprache nicht an Wert verlieren."

[43] Ibid., 7.

[44] *Boethius: Trost der Philosophie: Deutsch von Karl Büchner,* trans. Friedrich Büchner, intro. Friedrich Klingner (Stuttgart: Philipp Reclam jun, 1971), 41–43.

[45] Ibid., 101–02.

[46] *Die Gedichte aus der Tröstung der Philosophie des Boethius: Deutsch von Konrad Weiss,* trans. Konrad Weiss, epilogue by Jofseph Pieper, Tausenddrucke 2 (Berlin: Suhrkamp, 1956), 63.

[47] *Boethius: Trost der Philosophie,* trans. Ernst Neitzke (Stuttgart: Reclam-Verlag, 1959), 21–23.

[48] Ibid., 89–90.

[49] *Boethius: Trost der Philosophie: Ins Deutsche übertragen und eingeleitet von H.M. Endres*, trans. H. M. Endres (Munich: Wilhelm Goldmann, 1961), 18–19.

[50] Ibid., 82-83.

[51] *Boethius: Trost der Philosophie*, ed. and trans. Ernst Gegenschatz and Olof Gigon (Munich: Deutscher Taschenbuch Verlag, 1981), 3, 5, and 7.

[52] Ibid., 129 and 131.

THE ENGLISH TRADITION

The English Tradition of Boethius's *De consolatione philosophiae* with a Checklist of Translations[1]

Philip Edward Phillips

IN THE CENTURIES IMMEDIATELY FOLLOWING the death of Anicius Manlius Severinus Boethius in Pavia ca. 524/25, his most famous work, *De consolatione philosophiae* [hereafter *Consolatio*], remained relatively obscure, while his *trivial* and *quadrivial* works, including his *Opuscula sacra,* were used widely in medieval schools. Alcuin of York (735–804) is credited with having brought the *Consolatio* from Italy to the Carolingian court, where he Christianized Boethius's masterpiece and first included it in the academic curriculum.[2] The *Consolatio* became one of the most widely studied texts in the Middle Ages, as attested by numerous surviving manuscripts, glosses, and commentaries that followed thereafter, which have been the subject of much scholarly attention.[3] Although fourteenth- and fifteenth-century France witnessed the greatest proliferation of vernacular translations of the *Consolatio* during the Middle Ages, King Alfred of the West Saxons is recognized as the first translator to render Boethius's *Consolatio* into a vernacular language or to "authorize" its translation as part of his educational reform program in England. However, as Paul E. Szarmach recently has observed, despite internal and external "references to Alfred's involvement in the influence of Boethius, there has always been an uneasiness about Alfred's personal participation in the renaissance/revival that otherwise bears his name."[4] Indeed, Malcolm Godden and Susan Irvine argue that the Old English *Boethius*—traditionally believed to have been translated by King Alfred ca. 890, but whose personal authorship they doubt—actually appeared sometime between 885–950.[5] Regardless of its authorship,[6] however, the Old English *Boethius* inaugurated the vernacular translation tradition of the *Consolatio* in Europe.

A venerable tradition of English translations followed in the fourteenth and fifteenth centuries, beginning with the appearance of Geoffrey Chaucer's prose *Boece* and John Walton's verse *Boethius: De Consolatione Philosophiae*, both influenced by the French tradition.[7] During the Renaissance and beyond,[8] the humanist interest in Horace, Vergil, and Boethius prompted the rendering of their Latin texts into contemporary English prose and poetry. Among those classically educated figures whose fortunes changed during such events as the English Civil Wars, the Restoration, and the American Revolutionary War, Boethius found some empathetic translators. In the nineteenth century, which witnessed a general decline in Latin education in the English-speaking world, Boethius's *Consolatio* was not wholly forgotten. This was true, in part, because of the nationalistic interest in Alfred during the millennial celebrations of his birth and death and the establishment (later in the century and early in the next) of libraries of classics, intended to make Latin and Greek works available not only to educated but also to monolingual readers.

This article provides an overview of the English translations of Boethius's *Consolatio*, published and unpublished, from the ninth to the twenty-first centuries. It also provides a checklist of those translations for the purpose of stimulating further research on the English translation tradition of the *Consolatio*. By examining selected translators within their literary historical contexts, one can appreciate the various reasons why and the ways in which Boethius's *Consolatio* was translated, adapted, and refashioned through the centuries.

I. The Old English *Boethius*

As previously noted, the tradition of vernacular translations of Boethius's *Consolatio* began in England ca. 885–950 with an Old English translation attributed to King Alfred the Great (r. 871–99). Alfred was a monarch and a man justly to be admired.[9] In addition to his fame as a military and a political leader, Alfred was responsible for instituting a series of ecclesiastical and educational reforms, which were intended to repair the sorry condition of the clergy and to revitalize his country by reintroducing learning—once available in the past and then lost—to his people. In his preface to Gregory the Great's *Regula Pastoralis*, Alfred proposed a series of Old English translations of significant works meant to educate and to strengthen the Christian faith of his people. According to Simon Keynes and Michael Lapidge, King Alfred is alleged to have been primarily responsible for translating Gregory's *Pastoral Care*, Boethius's *Consolatio*, St. Augustine's *Soliloquies*, and the first fifty prose psalms of the Psalter.[10] Mary P. Richards includes the *Laws of Alfred and Ine* in this list of works traditionally attributed to Alfred.[11] Several scholars associate Gregory's *Dialogues*, Orosius's *Histories Against the Pagans*, and Bede's *Ecclesiastical History* with Alfred's educational reform program, but they do not necessarily attribute their translation to Alfred himself.[12] These titles, in which Boethius's work figured prominently, were ones that Alfred considered "most necessary for all men to know."[13]

According to Godden and Irvine, there are two extant Old English versions of Boethius's *De consolatione philosophiae*: "a prose version, and one alternating prose and verse in the fashion of the Latin text. The latter evidently is derived from the first, and both begin with prefaces claiming King Alfred the Great (849–899) as author."[14] These versions appear in two separate manuscripts: MS Bodley 180 (prose only), in the Bodleian Library, and MS Cotton Otho A.vi. (prose and verse), in the British Library.[15] According to Alfred's biographer, the Welsh bishop Asser, Boethius's *Consolatio* was a work that appealed to Alfred as a king and as a Christian because it offered spiritual comfort in adversity. With instruction from his team of scholars, that included Asser, Grimbald the Frank, and John the Saxon, Asser attests that Alfred learned to read Latin. Godden and Irvine, however, question whether Alfred would have had either the necessary skill in Latin or the time to complete the work, especially during years fraught with constant warfare with the Vikings, to complete so ambitious a project as the translation of Boethius's *Consolatio*.[16]

The introductory verse narrative on Boethius and the Goths preceding the Old English adaptation casts Boethius as a Christian martyr, and the text refers to the narrator as Mind (*mod*) and Lady Philosophy as Wisdom (*wisdom*). Nicole Guenther Discenza argues that "Alfred had Christian precedent for his program, both in the Old Testament wisdom books and in the recent Carolingian Renaissance."[17] Some readers through the ages have been troubled or perplexed that the author of the *Consolatio* presents the Divine in the Platonic form of the *summum bonum* without making any overt appeals to Christianity in his moment of crisis; however, the ideas presented in the work are not incommensurate with Roman Christianity as it was understood by Boethius and his sixth-century contemporaries. The author of the Old English *Boethius* believed correctly that the themes presented in the *Consolatio*—God as unity, *summum bonum*, and the final end of humanity; the insufficiency of worldly goods; the soul's need to remember its true origin; the role of free will in a world governed by an all-knowing God; the Augustinian belief that evil is merely a negation of the Good, not an equal and opposite force; and consolation itself—are indeed Christian themes.

The Old English *Boethius* goes further by including a "Gregorian sense of duty towards others, although this sense of responsibility directly conflicted with the text's emphasis on personal responsibility and turning away from the world."[18] According to Discenza, the author of the Old English *Boethius* "works in the vernacular context both linguistically and at higher levels in the text: he injects Anglo-Saxon images and references to make his text more acceptable to his audience."[19] Moreover, the Anglo-Saxon adaptor of Boethius's *Consolatio* resolved the "tension between rejection of the world and good stewardship of its gifts [. . .] in favor of the latter, making the text more palatable to Anglo-Saxons, who highly valued wealth, honor, and position."[20] If it was authored, adapted, or authorized by Alfred, it would represent personal support of his own vision of educational, ecclesiastical, and military reform in Anglo-Saxon England. The Old English prose *Boethius* and a subsequent rendering of most of the meters into alliterative verse constitute the first and the only Anglo-Saxon renderings of Boethius's Latin *Consolatio*.

II. The *Consolatio* in German, French, and Middle English

Notker III of St. Gall (ca. 950–1022), also known as Notker Laebo ("thick-lipped"), produced an Old High German translation of Boethius's *Consolatio* sometime around the year 1000, making it the second oldest known vernacular translation after the Old English *Boethius*,[21] or perhaps the third oldest, depending upon the dating of the Occitan *Boecis* [*c.*1000], which is an adaptation of the first meter and prose of Boethius's *Consolatio*.[22] Also known as Notker the German (*Teutonicus*), he was a devoted scholar and teacher who wrote translations and produced commentaries for the benefit of his students.[23] Notker's interlinear translation of the *Consolatio*, which combined text and commentary, soon was followed elsewhere on the continent by other vernacular translations of Boethius.

At least thirteen Old French translations of the *Consolatio* followed during the thirteenth, fourteenth, and fifteenth centuries. According to Glynnis M. Cropp, "In no other country than France, in no other language than French, did so many vernacular translations of the *Consolatio* exist in the Middle Ages."[24] Cropp notes that "France also contributed significantly to the Latin commentary tradition by the commentary (*c.* 1120) of William of Conches (*c.* 1080–1154/60), which together with the commentaries of Nicholas Trevet (*c.* 1258–after 1334) [. . .] and his near contemporary William of Aragon, provided the main source of explanation and interpretation of Boethius's text for the translators."[25] According to Noel Harold Kaylor, Jr., "The medieval French translations formed the 'richest and most complex' vernacular translation tradition of the *Consolatio*."[26] Both the German and the French translation traditions would influence the reception and translation of Boethius's *Consolatio* into English during the Middle Ages.

Geoffrey Chaucer (ca. 1343–1400), the author of *The Canterbury Tales* and *Troilus and Criseyde*, was the first writer to translate Boethius's masterpiece into English after the translator of the Old English *Boethius*. Chaucer's prose translation, produced ca. 1380–85, was indebted to the French prose translation of Jean de Meun (*ante* 1250–1305)[27] and to the Latin commentary on the *Consolatio* by Nicholas Trevet, completed before 1307. Trevet seems to have been more concerned with "historical and literal exposition" than with the use of pagan allegory to "clothe profound moral doctrine," as was the case with other commentators, such as William of Conches.[28] According to Alastair Minnis, "[b]oth Jean de Meun and Chaucer seem to have been indebted to Boethius-commentaries for basic character-sketches and plot-summaries[,] which they filled out with materials from other sources and, of course, with their own imaginative touches."[29]

It may seem ironic that Chaucer, the "father of English poetry," would produce an all-prose translation of Boethius's prosimetric *Consolatio*; however, it can be argued that his primary goal was accuracy and fidelity to the content of the text. Given his interest in mathematics, science, and philosophy, as evidenced especially by his publication of *A Treatise on the Astrolabe*, it is not difficult to imagine that Chaucer was interested in understanding Boethius's work as literally as possible. Larry D. Benson goes a step further by suggesting that "Chaucer[,] by translating it[,] was fulfilling a clearly perceived need, making the work available to his contemporaries, not [. . .] merely writing out a pony for his own use."[30] Chaucer's prose rendering of Lady Philosophy's meter of petition in book 3, meter 9 ("*O Qui Perpetua*"), reads, in part:

> O Fadir, yyve thou to the thought to steyen up into the streyte seete; and graunte hym to enviroune the welle of good; and, the lyght ifounde, graunte hym to fycchen the clere syghtes of his corage in the; and skatere thou and tobreke the weyghtes and the cloudes of erthly hevynesse; and schyn thou by thi bryghtnesse, for thou art cleernesse, thow art pesible reste to debonayre folk; thow thiself art bygynnynge, berere, ledere, path, and terme; to looke on the, that is our ende.[31]

Chaucer produced a complete, all-prose, literal rendering of Boethius's *Consolatio* that survives in eleven manuscripts, plus an incunabulum published by William Caxton in ca. 1478. The number of extant manuscripts, according to Larry D. Benson, suggests a "reasonably broad" readership for the *Boece*.[32] Benson defends Chaucer's choice of prose over poetry for the meters of Boethius on the grounds that Chaucer sought not simply to translate the work accurately but also to "provide a definitive guide to the work" by imitating Jean de Meun's use of prose and seeking clarification from Trevet's commentary.[33] This having been said, it seems that readers can admire the faithful clarity of Chaucer's generally accurate translation and still wish that the "father of English poetry" had not rendered the metrical sections of the *Consolatio* into prose. It is worth noting, as well, that although Chaucer's *Boece* is not as well known or as highly regarded as many of his other works, Chaucer himself identified it in his *Retractions*—regardless of how scholars may choose to interpret that piece—as one of the works by which he wished to be remembered.

Though Chaucer's *Boece* was the first Middle English translation of the *Consolatio*, John Walton's (fl. 1410) verse translation of 1410, which is extant in more than twenty manuscripts, apparently was "more popular."[34] Walton was an Augustinian canon of Osney Abbey, Oxford. Aside from these few details, little is known about his life. What is known about him as a translator comes from the preface to his translation of Boethius's *Consolatio*, which he dedicated to Elizabeth Berkeley (d. 1422). Although he may have produced also a prose translation of Vegetius's *De re militari* for Sir Thomas Berkeley in 1408, Walton is best known for his verse translation of Boethius's *Consolatio*. Unlike Chaucer and Jean de Meun, Walton chose to write an all-verse translation of the five books of the *Consolatio*, with the first three books in eight-line stanzas and the last two in rime royal. Interestingly, Walton signed his name in the form of an acrostic anagram in the 1525 edition published by Thomas Richard, monk of Travistock—of which three copies survive—and he indicates his patron, or dedicatee.[35] Walton's patrons, the Berkeleys and the Beauchamps, likely owned copies of the Latin *Consolatio* as well as Chaucer's *Boece*.[36]

Walton seems to have drawn simultaneously upon three main sources when producing his verse translation of Boethius's *Consolatio*: the Latin Vulgate original, Chaucer's *Boece*, and Nicholas Trevet's glosses.[37] Walton's verse rendering of the concluding lines of *Consolatio* 3m9 ("*O Qui Perpetua*"), written in octaves, reads:

> Thow fairest fadire, grau*n*te hym of thi grace
> Þat souereyn see to serchen and atteyne,

[W]here perfite goodenesse haþ his p*ro*pre place.

8. The welle of wisdom fo to seke *and* fynde
Thow graunt hym lord be lemyng of þi light,
Clerly in þe þat he may sette hys mynde
To fecchen [þere] þe vigour of his sight.
Breek þou dow*n* þe pays of heuy wight
Of erþely bondes þat him sore annoyeth,
And hym beschyne þow wiþ þi bemes bright
Þat all clowdes skaturep *and* distroyeth.

9. Thow art cleernesse, þere may none be so faire;
Thow art pesible rest of mannys mynde;
To hertes þat ben meke *and* debonaire,
The to beholde it is þaire p*er*fit ende;
Thow p*r*incipal begynner of þaire kynde,
Þow berist all, þow ledest hem full even;
Þow art the wey in wiche þat man schal wende,
And þou þi-self art all þe blisse of heuen.[38]

Overall, Walton's verse translation compares favorably with Chaucer's prose rendering, having the added benefit of containing many eloquent renderings of the Boethian meters.

Although A. Van de Vyver and Brian Donaghey list only two English translations of the *Consolatio*—those by Chaucer and Walton—from the fourteenth and fifteenth centuries,[39] an anonymous cleric produced an incomplete adaptation with commentary of the *Consolatio*, which remained as a unique manuscript at the Bodleian Library, Oxford, until it was edited and published in 1993, then reedited and republished in 2007.[40] The anonymous translator probably was a monk associated with a monastic school northwest of London, who flourished between ca. 1380 and 1420. The translation, which was likely produced near the end of the fourteenth century, has no title, but the translator's introduction contains the sentence: "Here begynneth *The Boke of Coumfort of Bois* of Anyce of Manle of Severyne of Bois." Therefore, the translation can be designated best as *The Boke of Coumfort of Bois*.

The language of *The Boke of Coumfort of Bois* is not remote from Chaucer's Middle English. Certain features in the manuscript suggest that the text was composed or dictated in the dialect of the southeast Midlands. Because of the predominance of interpolated commentary, which is encyclopedic in scope, the translation probably was intended as a textbook for students in a monastic school. The commentary attempts to expand and contextualize various ideas alluded to in the *Consolatio* in order to conform to the worldview of late fourteenth-century or early fifteenth-century science, theology, and philosophy. The reliance by the anonymous translator upon Chaucer's earlier *Boece* is evident throughout the work. According to Ian Johnson, *The Boke of Coumfort of Bois* "repurposes Chaucer's words, brings further Latin commentary materials into expository vernacular play, and [. . .] reslants the Boethian text devotionally."[41] Indeed, many passages in *The Boke of Coumfort of Bois* echo both the diction and the syntax of Chaucer's translation, and the Anonymous adaptor follows Chaucer in rendering his partial translation completely into prose. Nevertheless, as Johnson asserts, "for all its vernacularity, [*The Boke of Coumfort*] is first and foremost another *Consolatio*."[42]

III. English Translations from the Early Modern Period to the Enlightenment

The Renaissance brought with it a humanistic interest in studying and translating the classics that would extend well into the Age of Enlightenment. Among those works studied and translated was, of course, Boethius's *Consolatio*, which the eighteenth-century historian Edward Gibbon famously termed "a golden volume not unworthy of the leisure of Plato or Tully, but which claims incomparable merit from the barbarism of the times and the situation of the author."[43] Gibbon's laudable assessment of "the senator Boethius [. . .] [,] the last of the Romans whom Cato or Tully could have acknowledged for their countryman,"[44] contributed to the popularity of his *Consolatio* during the period. And, indeed, the proliferation of English translations between 1500 and 1800 is remarkable.[45] Between the end of the sixteenth century and the beginning of the nineteenth century, there were no fewer than eleven complete translations and eight incomplete or partial translations of Boethius's Latin *Consolatio*.[46] In addition, there were several known occasional renderings from Boethius's meters.[47]

According to Donaghey, translators during the sixteenth and seventeenth centuries, especially those who chose to render selected verses into English verse, enjoyed participating in the translation traditions of Homer and Vergil, in which "there is a challenge of outdoing others in skill, or of putting a different slant or emphasis on the work."[48] Many translators during this period, in general, "preferred to bring out the moral values they saw encapsulated in the book [the *Consolatio*], seeking therefore to adapt their style and register to the current religious and devotional literature of their day."[49]

In 1556, George Colvile (or Coldewel) published a complete translation of the *Consolatio* with facing Latin text under the oddly ungrammatical title, *Boethius de Consolationae Philosophiae*.[50] Colvile's translation of the *Consolatio*, dedicated to Queen Mary, was printed by John Cawood in London in 1556. While there are references to editions of 1561, 1566, and a later undated edition, it appears that they no longer are extant. Colvile's translation of the *Consolatio* generally is clear and accurate, although some of his parenthetical explanations of the text stray from the meaning of the original. This tendency is most apparent in his prose renderings of Boethius's meters, where Colvile explains the poetic metaphors, often pointing out the moral implications of mythological references.[51] Both Colvile's preface and his dedication to Queen Mary suggest the author's view of Boethius as a Catholic martyr.

Better known today, but known during her lifetime only to her immediate circle in the final years of her reign, is the complete, but unpolished, first-draft (but for a few fragmentary reworked sections) prose and verse translation made by Queen Elizabeth I (1533–1603). Her translation of the *Consolatio*, undertaken at Windsor in 1593, was later bound up with her translations of Plutarch's *De curiositate* and Horace's *De arte poetica* in 1598 in a kind of "scrapbook," which later was deposited in the Public Record Office, London. It would not be published until 1899.[52] According to the Computation of Days included within the manuscript, Elizabeth is reported to have translated all five books of Boethius's *Consolatio* between October 10 and November 8, 1593, spending no more than *twenty-six* or *twenty-seven* hours total on translation.[53] Although one is tempted to regard these figures as hyperbolic, it must be kept in mind that Elizabeth had been a pupil of the famous humanist and educator Roger Ascham, author of *The Scholmaster*, who taught a "dual-translation" method of learning Latin, based on the example of Pliny the Younger,[54] at Hatfield to Henry VIII's children: Prince Edward (later Edward VI), Princess Mary (later Mary I), and Princess Elizabeth (later Elizabeth I). Ascham notes proudly in his treatise that Queen Elizabeth I, "who never took yet Greek nor Latin grammar in her hand after the first declining of a noun and a verb, but only by this double translating [. . .] for the space of a year or two, hath attained to such a perfect understanding in both the tongues."[55] In particular, Ascham commends Elizabeth on having attained "such a ready utterance of the Latin, and that with such a judgment as they be few in number in both the universities, or elsewhere in England, that be in both tongues comparable with Her Majesty."[56]

While clearly a first-draft version, Elizabeth's 1593 complete translation of Boethius reveals her exceptional sight-reading skills, perfected much earlier under Ascham's instruction, and her affinity for poetic language in her own italic inscriptions of the meters:

Graunt that the my'd O father Clime to thy hiest Seat
And On thy vew the clirest Sigh may Set
Away Cast erthely Cloude and Waight of this mold
do thou with Lustar then them Grace
Thou art the Cleare and quiet rest for best folke
The to admire is first last helpe Gide
pathe and stedy Last[.][57]

No one close to Queen Elizabeth I would have doubted her linguistic skills in ancient or modern languages. That she produced her translation of Boethius in her sixtieth year is an indication that her Latin skills never declined.

Although Elizabeth I was one of England's greatest monarchs and has therefore received considerable scholarly attention, her translation of Boethius's *Consolatio* has been largely neglected until recently. Some who have written about her translation have tended to perpetuate the assumption that she translated Boethius to console herself over the conversion of Henry IV to Roman Catholicism in 1593, in order to win the favor of his people.[58] Although she almost certainly was disappointed by Henry IV's conversion, it is unlikely that Elizabeth would have sought personal consolation through the process of translating an author viewed by many to have been martyred for his Roman Catholic faith. It is more likely that during the thirty-fifth year of her reign Elizabeth would have been reflecting upon her life—upon her superlative education at Hatfield under the instruction of Ascham (wondering if her skills were still sharp), or upon those dark days in the Tower of London on the orders of her Catholic sister, Queen Mary, fearing that her very life was in danger—finding parallels in the *Consolatio* as motivation for translating Boethius's masterpiece.[59]

Before becoming queen, Princess Elizabeth had been imprisoned both at Woodstock and later in the Tower of London under suspicion of treason against Mary. An early verse evinces traces of Boethian influence:

O Fortune, thy wresting, wavering state
Hath fraught with cares my troubled wit,

Whose witness this present prison late
Could bear, where once was joy flown quite.[60]

Elizabeth wrote these lines, dated from 1554–55, during her imprisonment at Woodstock when her own future was uncertain. Though accused of treason, Elizabeth ("a prisoner") denied it in her signature following the poem: "Much suspected by me, but nothing proved can be."[61] Later, in a prayer written in the Tower of London, Elizabeth implored God in a time of great fear for her life: "Grant, O God, that the wicked may have no power to hurt or betray me; neither suffer any such treason and wickedness to proceed against me. [. . .] [I] am thy servant and at Thy commandment, trusting by Thy grace ever so to remain, amen."[62]

Perhaps the aging Queen Elizabeth, recalling the vicissitudes of her own reign, would have returned with appreciation to Boethius's *Consolatio*—as well as to the circumstances of its composition—and translated his text with "like eloquence" and "true understanding," to apply Ascham's terms.[63] Elizabeth's rough but literal translation is the product of one whose time for such pursuits necessarily was limited by her greater responsibilities to the state. One can only wish that Elizabeth had enjoyed the leisure to polish her translation to the full extent of her talents.

Aside from Colvile and Elizabeth, other thoughtful individuals demonstrated an interest in translating the *Consolatio*—several of them connected to the court. Thomas Chaloner, who served for a time as Elizabeth's ambassador to Spain, translated the meters in 1563. Donaghey has noted a complete but unpublished manuscript in the archives of the Yorkshire Archeological Society by "T.R.," who otherwise remains unidentified, dated from Hackney, January 1, 1584.[64] In 1602, John Bracegirdle, who was newly appointed vicar of Rye, dedicated a manuscript-translation to his patron, Thomas Sackville, earl of Dorset.[65] After Sackville's death in 1608, another translator, designated simply as "I.T.," dedicated a highly successful translation, called *Five Bookes of Philosophicall Comfort* (London, 1609), to Sackville's widow.[66] Throughout the seventeenth century, many other translations were produced, including a scholarly summary of the *Consolatio* by "S.E.M." (Sir Edward Spencer), *Boethius De Consolatione, Anglo-Latinae* (Wing B3431), with commentary, and with some translations from "I.T." facing the Latin texts.[67] Other complete, partial, and occasional translations would appear during the period of the English Civil War and its aftermath, including those by translators such as Harry Coningsbye (1664); Anonymous (1674); Henry Somerset, first duke of

Beaufort (1693);[68] and Sir Richard Graham, Viscount Preston (1695).[69] A complete text of the Duke of Beaufort's translation, introduced and edited by Kenneth Hawley, is included in this volume.

Donaghey perceptively notes that there was an increasing awareness of "the uncomfortable amount of Platonism, and the lack of reference to Christian doctrine" in the *Consolatio* during the Renaissance.[70] Nevertheless, translators of the work, both Protestant and Catholic, remained sympathetic to Boethius and the equanimity with which he faced Fortune's blows, and they found ways to adapt his prose and verse for their own audiences. One notable example is Alexander Pope's translation of Boethius's *Consolatio* 3m9. Like many classically educated writers of the Renaissance and Enlightenment, Pope (1688–1744) admired Boethius's *Consolatio* both for its philosophical and literary qualities as well as for its compatibility with his own Roman Catholicism. Like Samuel Johnson, who, in collaboration with Heather Thrale Piozzi, translated several of Boethius's meters, and like other poet-translators of the period, Pope rendered a portion of Boethius's famous "*O Qui Perpetua*" into English verse around 1710, and his translation was published in 1717 in his *Poems on Several Occasions*. Pope's translation, which he likely undertook at the urging of his friend and mentor Sir William Trumbull, omits the Platonic content in the center of Boethius's Latin meter and focuses instead upon the elements in lines 1–3 and 22–28 of the poem, which are more compatible with Christianity.

The complete text of Pope's verse adaptation of Boethius's *Consolatio* 3m9 reads:

> O thou, whose all-creating hands sustain
> The radiant Heav'ns, and Earth, and ambient main!
> Eternal Reason! Whose presiding soul
> Informs great nature and directs the whole!
> Who wert, e're time his rapid race begun,
> And bad'st the years in long procession run:
> Who fix't thy self amidst the rowling frame,
> Gav'st all things to be chang'd, yet ever art the same!
> Oh teach the mind th'aetherial heights to rise,
> And view, familiar, in its native skies,
> The source of good; thy splendor to descry,
> And on thy self, undazled, fix her eye.
> Oh quicken this dull mass of mortal clay;
> Shine through the soul, and drive its clouds away!

For thou art Light. In thee the righteous find
Calm rest, and soft serenity of mind;
Thee they regard alone; to thee they tend;
At once our great original and end,
At once our means, our end, our guide, our way,
Our utmost bound, and our eternal stay![71]

A hymn or prayer in form, Pope's translation captures the spirit of Christian stoicism, the private moral virtues, and the rational basis for belief in God expressed in the Latin original.[72] Pope's translation of Boethius is only one example of a poet accepting the challenge of translating and refashioning individual Boethian meters, as so many writers had done before with the verses of Horace and Vergil.

As for the complete translations of the *Consolatio* penned or published near the end of the eighteenth century, three writers undertook the challenge of rendering the work into prose and verse. Little is known about the first, William Causton (1730). The second, however, was the Rev. Philip Ridpath, minister of Hutton, who published a translation of Boethius's *Consolatio* with notes and illustrations in London in 1785. Like Alexander Pope, Ridpath chose not to translate the Platonic content in the middle of *Consolatio* 3m9, largely because of his desire to emphasize the work's affinities with (rather than its departures from) Christian thought. Ridpath mentions some degree of collaboration with his brother, George Ridpath, on parts of the translation of 3m9.[73] The third, Rev. Robert Duncan, was an ordained minister of Dundonal, Scotland, who intended for his translation, *The Five Books of Anicius Manlius Torquatus Severinus Boethius, on the Consolation of Philosophy* (Edinburgh, 1789), to serve "a school-book, both in Latin and English schools."[74] Another effort to translate the Latin *Consolatio* would not come until 1897, over a hundred years after Duncan's work. Instead, attention would be directed towards the founder of the vernacular translation tradition, who was believed to be King Alfred the Great.

IV. Translating the Old English *Boethius* for the Alfred Millennial Celebrations

During the mid- to late nineteenth century in Britain, there was renewed popular and scholarly interest in King Alfred, "the father of the English nation" and the "father of English prose."[75] This interest coincided with the millennial celebrations planned for 1849 and 1901 to celebrate Alfred's birth and death, respectively.[76] The first of these celebrations was conceived and organized by Martin F. Tupper (1810–89), the well-known author of *Proverbial Philosophy* (1838), who envisioned for October 25, 1849 a "great" and "unprecedented" patriotic celebration in Wantage of the thousandth anniversary of the birth of Alfred, "perhaps, the Greatest Man,—Certainly the Best King,—that ever lived."[77] The second, and much larger, celebration of Alfred's life, this time in Winchester, was the brainchild of Frederic Harrison, who long had admired and lectured on Alfred. As a result of these two major events, as well as of a growing movement to preserve and study Anglo-Saxon literature and culture, efforts were made to assemble and to translate the works of Alfred into modern English for the benefit of scholars and the general reading public. Because Boethius's *Consolatio* was widely believed to have been one of the books King Alfred had identified as being "most necessary for men to know," and included as a central text in his educational reform program, it was therefore one of the works to which Anglo-Saxon scholars gave special attention during the nineteenth century.

Prior to the twenty-first century, there were four translators of the Old English *Boethius*: J. S. Cardale, Rev. Samuel Fox, Martin F. Tupper, and Walter John Sedgefield. Their role in the transmission of knowledge, however, was comparable in intention to that attributed to Alfred's educational reform program: just as the king, with the assistance of his advisors, was believed to have adapted Boethius to appeal to his Anglo-Saxon audience, Alfred's Victorian translators produced modern English versions of the Old English *Boethius*, largely for the benefit of those who could not read Old English, or for the benefit of students who were just beginning to learn to read the original language.[78]

The first translator of the Old English *Boethius* was J. S. Cardale, who published *King Alfred's Anglo-Saxon Version of Boethius De Consolatione Philosophiae: With an English Translation and Notes* in London in 1829. His "paraphrastical" translation offers facing Anglo-Saxon and modern English texts, provides a sound translation of Alfred's all-prose version of the *Consolation* with a sample meter (4m3), and includes notes on the Old English text. The translation seems intended both for students of Anglo-Saxon literature and for scholars interested in Alfred's language and the history of the manuscript.

The second complete, all-prose translation of the Old English *Boethius* was published by the Rev. Samuel Fox (1801–70), longtime rector of St. Matthew Parish, Morley.[79] Rev. Fox published a "literal version" of *King*

Alfred's Anglo-Saxon Version of the Metres of Boethius in 1835 that attempts, according to its preface, to preserve in the translation a semblance of the Anglo-Saxon rhythm found in the original. Fox's translation remained the standard one from the time of its publication until 1899, despite the fact that his prose translations were virtually identical to those of Cardale. In addition, Fox's edition also includes the verse translations of M. F. Tupper, previously published as *King Alfred's Poems: Now First Turned into English Metres* (London, 1850), in place of his own 1835 verse translations. Tupper's meters, however, are rather free translations into modern English verse, and as such they are generally not as literal as Cardale's or Fox's prose translations.

Walter John Sedgefield, of Melbourne and Christ College, Cambridge, was the fourth person to translate the Old English *Boethius* into Modern English. In 1899, he published the first scholarly edition of the Old English *Boethius*, which takes into account the work's complex and fragmentary manuscript history.[80] The translation is not without its share of problems for scholars, however, as it is a composite text based upon the Cotton and Bodleian versions of the Anglo-Saxon original. In 1900, the following year, Sedgefield's complementary translation of the Old English *Boethius* was published by Oxford, just in time for the Alfred Millennial. *King Alfred's Version of the "Consolations" of Boethius, Done into Modern English, with an Introduction*, dedicated to the renowned Anglo-Saxon scholar W. W. Skeat, presents itself clearly as a scholarly edition of Alfred's *Boethius* and refers enthusiastically to the preparations underway to celebrate the Alfred Millennial. Sedgefield no doubt sought to "cash in" on the national celebration in his own way by preparing his volume in time for the national festivities. Like the translators before him, whom he does not mention, Sedgefield praises Alfred, as a king, but more importantly as a translator and as an educational reformer. Sedgefield duly acknowledges the Old English masterpiece for "head[ing] the roll of English philosophical writings [. . .] [and] likewise heading[ing] the roll of English translations."[81] Sedgefield's introduction attempts to inform his audience about Alfred's life and career and to provide a survey of the English tradition of Boethius's *Consolatio*, beginning with the Old English translation attributed to Alfred.

The most recent and authoritative Modern English translation of the Old English Boethius is included in *The Old English Boethius: An Edition of the Old English Versions of Boethius's De Consolatione Philosophiae*, ed. Malcolm R. Godden and Susan Irvine, with Mark Griffith and Rohini

Jayatilaka, 2 vols. (Oxford: Oxford University Press, 2009). Malcolm Godden, fellow of the British Academy, is the Rawlinson and Bosworth Professor of Anglo-Saxon at Oxford University, and Susan Irvine is professor of English at University College London. The Godden-Irvine edition contains critical texts of both versions, a translation, an introduction, detailed commentary exploring the relationship to the Latin text and to the early medieval commentary tradition, textual notes, and a glossary. Based on the two-volume 2009 Godden-Irvine edition, the one-volume edition, *The Old English Boethius, with Verse Prologues and Epilogues Associated with King Alfred*, ed. and trans. Susan Irvine and Malcolm R. Godden, Dumbarton Oaks Library (Cambridge, MA: Harvard University Press, 2012), makes the Old English text with a facing-page English translation available to a broader range of readers, doing for medieval texts what the Loeb Classical Library volumes do for classical texts.

V. Boethius's *Consolatio* and the Modern English Reader

The millennial celebrations of Alfred's death in 901 (actually in 899) witnessed not only a growing interest in King Alfred the Great but also a gradually increasing interest in reading classical authors (including Boethius) in translation. The interest in Boethius is attested by the publication of two new English verse and prose translations of his Latin *Consolatio*: one by H. R. (Henry Rosher) James and the other by W. V. Cooper. H. R. James (1862–1932), MA, Christ Church College, Oxford, translated the *Consolatio* in 1897; a second edition was published in 1906. James, who served as principal of Presidency College, Calcutta, from 1907 to 1916, later published *Education and Statesmanship in India, 1797–1910: Our Hellenic Heritage* in two volumes (London: Macmillan, 1921; 2nd ed., 1927), and *Mary Wollstonecraft: A Sketch* (London: Oxford University Press, 1932).

James's translation of Boethius into English—with preface, proem [on Boethius's life and career], index of verse interludes, references to quotations in the text, as well as book summaries and prose and verse descriptive titles—seems to have been part of his larger vision of making classical learning more widely available. Labeling Boethius's *Consolatio* as "the scholar's familiar companion" from the Middle Ages into the sixteenth century, James writes: "[t]he belief that what once pleased so widely must still have some charm [was his] excuse for attempting the present translation." James's rendering of *Consolatio* 3m9 ("*O Qui Perpetua*") reads, in part:

Oh, grant, almighty Father,
Grant us on reason's wing to soar aloft
To heaven's exalted height; grant us to see
The fount of good; grant us, the true light found,
To fix our steadfast eyes in vision clear
On Thee. Disperse the heavy mists of earth,
And shine in Thine own splendour. For Thou art
The true serenity and perfect rest
Of every pious soul—to see Thy face,
The end and the beginning—One the guide,
The traveller, the pathway, and the goal.[82]

James's translation of Boethius seems to have been intended for readers perhaps unfamiliar with Boethius or simply unable to read the Latin original; nevertheless, he notes that "[t]hose who can go to the original will find their own reward."[83]

James calls attention to the venerable tradition of the various European translations of the *Consolatio* in his Preface, especially the efforts of such English translators as King Alfred, Lord Preston, Causton, Ridpath, and Duncan. James sets his translation apart from other more recent renderings by his choice of a frontispiece depicting a diptych of the father of Boethius, rather than an image of Boethius himself, on the grounds that earlier portraits, purportedly based upon a bust of Boethius in Rome and used by other English translators, were untraceable and probably "apocryphal." James's frontispiece, however, based upon a plaster cast in the Hope Collection in the Ashmolean Museum, Oxford, taken from the original in the Bibliotheca Quiriana at Brescia, was chosen to give readers a more authentic representation of "the consular dress and insignia of the time."[84]

James's prose and verse translation, based upon the 1874 Pieper edition,[85] is clear, accurate, and written with the reader's ease of understanding in mind. The translation provides summaries and descriptive head-notes (as well as scattered footnotes) for the reader's convenience. Aware of his place within the English translation tradition of the *Consolatio*, James seems intent upon making accessible to readers of his age this masterpiece once known only by learned people of previous ages. In the preface, James writes, concerning his translation in relation to previous translations (and future translations), "[t]here may be room also for a new translation in English after an interval of close on an hundred years."[86] James sought to do for his age what Duncan, Ridpath, and Causton had done for the preceding age, and what Lord Preston had done for his. One can only imagine what James's response to the many fine English translations of Boethius in the twentieth and twenty-first centuries would be. It had been a century since Duncan's English translation of Boethius; James, therefore, could imagine that it would be nearly as long before another English translation would be needed.

A subsequent readable and textually reliable modern translation was produced by W. V. (Wilbraham Villiers) Cooper (b. 1876), released as part of the Temple Classics series.[87] Cooper's all-prose translation of the *Consolatio* was undertaken during the millennial celebrations at Winchester in 1901 and published the following year. Over fifty years after the second printing of James's translation, a virtual renaissance of translating Boethius's *Consolatio* occurred, largely in the United States and Great Britain, and principally for the purpose of supplying humanities courses with modern versions of classical texts. These translators include Richard Green, 1962 (prose);[88] V. E. Watts, 1969 and revised in 1999 (prose and verse);[89] S. J. Tester, 1973 (prose and verse with facing Latin text);[90] Sanderson Beck, 1996 (prose and verse on the web);[91] P. G. Walsh, 1999 (prose and verse);[92] Joel C. Relihan, 2001 (prose and verse);[93] David R. Slavitt, 2008 (prose and verse);[94] and, most recently, Scott Goins and Barbara H. Wyman, 2012 (prose and verse).[95] These translations, and the introductions and notes that many of them contain, have contributed significantly to the general knowledge of Boethius, his life, times, and influence. The publication of the 1973 Loeb Classical Library volume, containing Tester's translation of the *Consolatio*, in particular, has secured Boethius's place within the canon of classical writers in the minds of modern English-speaking readers, and it continues to provide Boethian scholars with a generally authoritative Latin text (in the absence of the editions of Ludwig Bieler or Claudio Moreschini)[96] and a dependable translation.

Conclusion

In total, there are at least *twenty-four* complete English translations (see Appendix I.A) and at least *thirteen* incomplete or partial English translations (see Appendix I.B) of Boethius's *Consolatio*, although the number of translations continues to increase. There are at least *eleven* known occasional renderings of portions of Boethius's *Consolatio*,[97] which generally appear as individual meters translated into English verse, and probably many more that have not yet come to light. For this reason, the occasional renderings are more difficult to catalogue with any degree of accuracy (see Appendix I.C). These English translations are attested from the prose and verse Old English adaptation traditionally attributed to King Alfred the Great in the late ninth–early tenth century to the modern English translations of the twentieth and twenty-first centuries. In addition, there are five translations of the Old English *Boethius*: four nineteenth-century English translations of King Alfred's Anglo-Saxon *Boethius*, all produced between the years 1829–1900, and one twenty-first century translation and edition in two volumes by Malcolm Godden and Susan Irvine, which replaces the one-hundred-year-old Oxford edition by Walter J. Sedgefield as the standard scholarly text (see Appendix II).[98] These English translations of the Latin *Consolatio* and of the Old English *Boethius* represent a sustained tradition of rendering Boethius's greatest work into English, throughout the centuries. Although the tradition includes many distinguished translators, comparable in scope to the French and German *Consolatio* traditions, it remains insufficiently appreciated and studied. This essay, therefore, provides a *vade mecum* for scholars interested in pursuing new and deeper investigations into the many and varied relationships between these translations and their translators and between these English translations and the translations of other linguistic traditions.

Appendix 1

A Checklist of English Translations of Boethius's Latin *Consolatio*

A. Complete Translations

Translator	*Year*	*Mode*
King Alfred (traditional attribution)	ca. 885–950	separate prose and prose and verse versions
Geoffrey Chaucer	1380–85	all prose
John Walton	1410	all verse
George Colville (*alias* Coldewel)	1556; 1561	prose and verse with facing Latin
"T.R."	1584	unpublished MS; all prose
Queen Elizabeth I	1593	prose and verse
John Bracegirdle	ca. 1602	prose and verse
"I.T." (Michael Walpole or John Thorpe)	1609	prose and verse
Harry Coningsbye (or Coningsby)	1664	all verse
Henry Somerset, duke of Beaufort	1693	prose and verse
Sir Richard Graham, viscount Preston	1695; 1712	prose and verse
William Causton	1730	prose and verse
Philip Ridpath (with George Ridpath)	1785	prose and verse
Robert Duncan	1789	prose and verse
H. R. James	1897; 1926	prose and verse
W. V. Cooper	1902	all prose
Richard Green	1962	all prose
Victor E. Watts	1967	prose and verse
S. J. Tester	1973	prose and verse with facing Latin
Sanderson Beck	1996	prose and verse
P. G. Walsh	1999	prose and verse
Joel C. Relihan	2001	prose and verse
David R. Slavitt	2008	prose and verse
Scott Goins and Barbara H. Wyman	2012	prose and verse

B. Incomplete or Partial English Translations

Translator	*Year*	*Mode*
Oxford Anonymous	mid-/late 1400s	prose translation of book 1 with commentary
William Baldwin	1547	four books of selected maxims
Sir Thomas Chaloner	1563	selected meters from book 1
Richard Fanshawe	ca. 1626–31	meters only
John Polwhele	ca. 1649	unpublished MS; meters only
Sir Nicholas Bacon and John Hobart	1664	meters only
Anonymous (attributed to Edmund Elys)	1674	prose and verse (books 1–4)
William Warburton	1724	prose translation of book 1 only
John Skinner	ca. 1789–1802	unpublished MS, selected meters
Paul Preston	1808	incomplete verse and prose translation
James J. Buchanan	1957	abridged, all-prose translation
Peter Glassgold	1994	meters only
James Harpur	2007	meters only

C. Some Occasional English Translations

Translator	*Year*	*Mode*
Sir Thomas Wyatt the Elder	ca. 1530s?	verse adaptation of 3m5, 3m6, and 3m3
Owen Feltham	1623?	some quotations with translations of meters
Phineas Fletcher	1631	verse (selected meters)
Henry Vaughan	1651; 1678	verse (selected meters)
Alexander Pope	1717	verse (3m9 only)
Sir William Trumbull	1717	verse (selected meters)
Elizabeth Tollet	ca. 1756	verse (3m5 only)
Samuel Johnson and Hester Thrale Piozzi	ca. 1765; publ. 1788	verse (selected meters)
Robert Proud	1776	verse (selected meters)
William Cullen Bryant	1866; publ. 1876	verse (2m8 only)
Helen Waddell	1929	verse (selected meters)

Appendix 2

A Checklist of Modern English Translations of the Old English *Boethius*

Translator	*Year*	*Mode*
J. S. Cardale	1829	prose with facing Old English text
Samuel Fox	1835	meters with facing Old English text
Martin F. Tupper	1850	meters only
Samuel Fox	1864	prose and verse
Walter J. Sedgefield	1900	prose and verse
Malcolm Godden and Susan Irvine	2009; 2012	Old English texts with modern prose translations

NOTES

[1] Originally published as "The English *Consolation of Philosophy*: Translation and Reception," *CarmP* 17 (2008), 97–126, this article has been substantially revised and updated by the author to take into account recent developments in the scholarship on the English translations of Boethius's *Consolatio*. The author is especially grateful to Professors Glynnis M. Cropp and Paul E. Szarmach for reading and offering valuable comments on this article, to Noel Harold Kaylor, Jr. for his careful proofreading, and to Nicole Guenther Discenza for graciously providing additional bibliographical citations related to the issue of the "authorship" of the Old English Boethius.

[2] P. G. Walsh, "Introduction," in Boethius, *The Consolation of Philosophy*, trans. by P. G. Walsh (Oxford: Oxford University Press, 1999), xliii–xliv.

[3] See, most recently, Rosalind C. Love, "The Latin Commentaries on Boethius's *De consolatione philosophiae* from the 9th to the 11th Centuries," in *A Companion to Boethius in the Middle Ages*, ed. Noel Harold Kaylor, Jr. and Philip Edward Phillips, Brill's Companions to the Christian Tradition 30 (Leiden: Brill, 2012), 75–133.

[4] Paul E. Szarmach, "Boethius's Influence in Anglo-Saxon England: The Vernacular and the *De Consolatione Philosophiae*," in Kaylor and Phillips, *A Companion to Boethius*, 224. Szarmach makes a convincing point when he suggests,

> Perhaps the royal stamp on *Boethius* is best understood as a contribution by a staff or court ghostwriter whose hand may be traceable in several works connected by its apparent presences. When John F. Kennedy announced to the cheering multitudes in Berlin that he was a kind of doughnut ("Ich bin ein Berliner"), many chortled at this presidential error in idiomatic German, but it was long-time aide Theodore Sorensen who wrote the speech. Nevertheless, Kennedy took all the linguistic barbs.

[5] See *The Old English Boethius: An Edition of the Old English Versions of Boethius's "De Consolatione Philosophiae,"* ed. Malcolm R. Godden and Susan Irvine, 2 vols. (Oxford: Oxford University Press, 2009), 1:8.

[6] The "authorship" of the Alfredian or Old English *Boethius* long has been the subject of debate, especially in recent years. In his article, "Did King Alfred Write Anything?" *Medium Ævum* 76, no. 1 (2007): 1–23, Malcolm R. Godden asserts that Alfred "did not 'write' anything" and concludes, "there is no real evidence for authorship." On the other hand, in her article, "Did King Alfred Actually Translate Anything? The Integrity of the Alfredian Canon Revisited," *Medium Ævum* 78, no. 2 (2009): 189–215, Janet Bately challenges Godden's position and maintains that "it is reasonable to conclude" that there was ultimately "one mind" behind the translations or renderings of *Pastoral Care*, *Consolatio*, *Soliloquies*, and *Psalms*, "and that that mind was King Alfred's," a position that is supported as well by Szarmach in "Boethius's Influence," 221–54.

I am grateful to Nicole Guenther Discenza for supplying the following list of additional citations, which illustrates clearly that the Alfredian authorship question remains unresolved: Janet M. Bately, "The Alfredian Canon Revisited: One Hundred Years On," in *Alfred the Great*, ed. Timothy Reuter (Aldershot: Ashgate, 2003), 107–20; Nicole Guenther Discenza, "Alfred the Great and the Anonymous Prose Proem to the *Boethius*," *JEGP* 107 (2008): 57–76; Paramjit S. Gill, Tim B. Swartz, and Michael Treschow, "A Stylometric Analysis of King Alfred's Literary Works," *Journal of Applied Statistics* 34, no. 10 (2007): 1251–58; Malcolm R. Godden, "The Alfredian Project and its Aftermath: Rethinking the Literary History of the Ninth and Tenth Centuries," Sir Israel Gollancz Memorial Lecture, January, 15 2009, *Proceedings of the British Academy* 162 (2009): 93–122; idem, "King and Counselor in the Alfredian Boethius," in *Intertexts: Studies in Anglo-Saxon Culture Presented to Paul E. Szarmach*, ed. Virginia Blanton and Helene Scheck (Tempe: Arizona Center for Medieval and Renaissance Studies, 2008), 191–208; idem, "The Latin Commentary and the Old English Text: Authorship and Kingship," paper presented at the fourth annual symposium of The Alfredian Boethius Project, University of Oxford, August 4, 2006, http://www.english.ox.ac.uk/boethius/Symposium2006.html, accessed September 18, 2015; idem, "The Player King: Identification and Self-Representation in King Alfred's Writings," in *Alfred the Great*, ed. Reuter, 137–50; idem, "Stories from the Court of King Alfred," in *Saints and Scholars: New Perspectives on Anglo-Saxon Literature and Culture in Honour of Hugh Magennis*, ed. Stuart McWilliams (Cambridge: Cambridge University Press, 2012), 123–40; David Pratt, *The Political Thought of King Alfred the Great*, Cambridge Studies in Medieval Life and Thought, 4th ser., 67 (Cambridge: Cambridge University Press, 2007); idem, "Problems of Authorship and Audience in the Writings of King Alfred the Great," in *Lay Intellectuals in the Carolingian World*, ed. Patrick Wormald and Janet L. Nelson (Cambridge: Cambridge University Press, 2007), 162–91; Timothy Reuter, ed., *Alfred the Great: Papers from the Eleventh-Centenary Conferences* (Aldershot: Ashgate, 2003); and Michael Treschow, Paramjit Gill, and Tim B. Swartz, "King Alfred's Scholarly Writings and the Authorship of the First Fifty Prose Psalms," *Heroic Age* 12 (May 2009), accessible at http://www.heroicage.org/issues/12/treschowgillswartz.php, accessed September 18, 2015. Issues related to the Alfredian or Old English *Boethius* are treated further by articles included in *A Companion to Alfred the Great*, ed. Nicole Guenther Discenza and Paul E. Szarmach, Brill's Companions to the Christian Tradition 58 (Leiden: Brill, 2014).

[7] For the most recent studies of the medieval English and French traditions, respectively, see Ian Johnson, "Making the *Consolatio* in Middle English," in Kaylor and Phillips, *A Companion to Boethius*, 413–46, and Glynnis M. Cropp, "Boethius in Medieval France: Translations of the *De Consolatione Philosophiae* and Literary Influence," in Kaylor and Phillips, *A Companion to Boethius*, 319–55.

[8] For a treatment of the English translations of Boethius's *Consolatio* that extends from the medieval to include early modern translations, see Kenneth Carr Hawley, "The Boethian Vision of Eternity in Old, Middle, and Early Modern English Translations of *De Consolatione Philosophiae*" (PhD diss., University of Kentucky, 2007).

[9] For the traditional account of Alfred's life and works, see Simon Keynes and Michael Lapidge, "Introduction," in *Alfred the Great: Asser's Life of King Alfred and Other Contemporary Sources* (London: Penguin, 1983), 9–58.

[10] Ibid., 29.

[11] See Mary P. Richards, "The Manuscript Context of Old English Laws," in *Studies in Earlier Old English Prose: Sixteen Original Contributions*, ed. Paul E. Szarmach (Binghamton: State University of New York Press, 1986), 171–92.

[12] See Keynes and Lapidge, "Introduction," 29.

[13] Simon Keynes and Michael Lapidge, "From the Translation of Gregory's *Pastoral Care*," in Keynes and Lapidge, *Alfred the Great*, 126.

[14] Godden and Irvine, *Old English Boethius*, I:8.

[15] For a comprehensive treatment of the manuscripts of the Old English *Boethius*, see Godden and Irvine, *Old English Boethius*, 1:9–139.

[16] On the question of Alfredian authorship, see Godden and Irvine, *Old English Boethius*, 1:140–51.

[17] Nicole Guenther Discenza, *The King's English: Strategies of Translation in the Old English* Boethius (Albany: State University of New York Press, 2005), 124.

[18] Ibid.

[19] Ibid., 3.

[20] Ibid., 125.

[21] Noel Harold Kaylor, Jr., *The Medieval Consolation of Philosophy: An Annotated Bibliography* (New York: Garland, 1992), 71.

[22] Cropp, "Boethius in Medieval France." According to Cropp, "[f]ound in a manuscript dating from the early 11th century, Orléans, Bibliothèque municipale 444, fols 269–75, the *Boecis* is an anonymous, untitled fragment of 257 decasyllabic assonance lines in *laisses* of varying length. It is the oldest Occitan text, as well as the oldest example of the vernacular tradition of the *Consolatio* in the Gallo-Roman area." Cropp notes, however, that the *Boecis* is an "incomplete work" that "offers a Christian rather than philosophical vision" (320–21); as such, it more properly may be regarded as a fragmentary adaptation rather than as a "translation." For more on the Occitan *Boecis*, see Glynnis M. Cropp, "The Occitan *Boecis*, the Medieval French Tradition of the *Consolatio Philosophiae* and Philosophy's Gown," in *Etudes de langue et de literature médiévales offertes à Peter T. Ricketts à l'occasion de son 70e anniversaire*, ed. D. Billy and Ann Buckley (Turnhout: Brepols, 2005), 255–66.

[23] Christine Hehle, "Boethius's Influence on German Literature to c. 1500," in Kaylor and Phillips, *A Companion to Boethius*, 257.

[24] Cropp, "Boethius in Medieval France," 320.

[25] Ibid.

[26] Kaylor, *Medieval Consolation of Philosophy*, 107. For additional treatments of the French *Consolatio* tradition, see Antoine Thomas and Mario Roques, "Traductions françaises de la *Consolatio Philosophiae* de Boèce," *Histoire Littéraire de la France*, vol. 31, 419–88 (Paris: Klincksieck, 1938); A. Van de Vyver, "Les Traductions du *De consolatione philosophiae* de Boèce en Littérature Comparée," *Humanisme et Renaissance* 6, no. 3 (1939):

247–73; and Richard A. Dwyer, *Boethian Fictions: Narratives in the Medieval French Versions of the "Consolatio Philosophiae"* (Cambridge, MA: Medieval Academy of America, 1976)—available in HTML and PDF formats through Medieval Academy Books Online on the Medieval Academy of America website at http://www.medievalacademy.org.

[27] See *Sources of the "Boece,"* ed. Tim Machan (Athens: University of Georgia Press, 2005), in which Machan seeks to reconcile the *Boece* and Jean de Meun's *Li Livres de Confort.*

[28] Alastair Minnis, "Aspects of the Medieval French and English Traditions of the *De Consolatione Philosophiae*," in *Boethius: His Life, Thought, and Influence*, ed. Margaret Gibson (Oxford: Blackwell, 1981), 312–61 (314–15).

[29] Ibid, 315.

[30] Geoffrey Chaucer, trans. "Boece," in *The Riverside Chaucer*, ed. Larry D. Benson, 3rd ed. (Boston: Houghton Mifflin, 1987), 396.

[31] Chaucer, "Boece," 431.

Cf. Chaucer's rendering with the concluding lines of Boethius's *Consolatio* 3m9 ("*O Qui Perpetua*"):

> Da, pater, augustam menti conscendere sedem,
> da fontem lustrare boni, da luce reperta
> in te conspicuos animi defigere visus.
> Dissice terrenae nebulas et pondera molis
> atque tuo splendore mica; tu namque serenum,
> tu requies tranquilla piis, te cernere finis,
> principium, vector, dux, semita, terminus idem.

From Boethius, *De Consolatione Philosophiae: Opuscula theologica, Editio altera*, ed. Claudio Moreschini, Bibliotheca Teubneriana, 2nd ed. (Munich: Saur, 2005), 80.

[32] Benson, "Boece," 396.

[33] Ibid., 396–97.

[34] Ian Johnson, "Placing Walton's Boethius," in *Boethius in the Middle Ages: Latin and Vernacular Traditions of the "Consolatio philosophiae,"* ed. Maarten J. F. M. Hoenen and Lodi Nauta (Leiden: Brill, 1997), 217. See, more recently, Ian Johnson, "Making the *Consolatio* in Middle English," in Kaylor and Phillips, *A Companion to Boethius*, 413–46, especially 423–39.

[35] Johnson, "Placing Walton's Boethius."

[36] Ibid., 218.

[37] For a detailed discussion of Walton's links with earlier sources, see ibid., 219–28.

[38] *Boethius: De Consolatione Philosophiae*, trans. by John Walton, ed. Mark Science, Early English Text Society o.s. 170 (London: Oxford University Press, 1927), 173–74.

[39] See Brian Donaghey, "The Post-Medieval English Translations of the *De Consolatione Philosophiae* of Boethius, 1500–1800," in *The Medieval Translator/Traduire au Moyen Age*, ed. Roger Ellis and René Tixier (Turnhout: Brepols, 1996), 302–21, and Van de Vyver, "Les Traductions."

[40] The translation exists as the last of seven texts bound up in MS Auct. F.3.5., held since about 1602 by the Bodleian Library of Oxford University. The manuscript was first edited and published as "The Boke of Comfort of Bois (Oxford MS AUCT.F.3.5.)," ed. Noel Harold Kaylor, Jr., Jason Edward Streed, and William H. Watts, in *CarmP* 2 (1993), 55–104; it has been reedited and published as "*The Boke of Coumfort of Bois* [Bodleian Library, Oxford Manuscript AUCT.F.3.5]: A Transcription with Introduction," reed.

Noel Harold Kaylor, Jr. and Philip Edward Phillips, in *New Directions in Boethian Studies*, ed. Noel Harold Kaylor, Jr. and Philip Edward Phillips, Studies in Medieval Culture 45 (Kalamazoo: Medieval Institute Publications, 2007), 223–79.

[41] Johnson, "Making the *Consolatio* in Middle English," 440–41.

[42] Ibid, 441.

[43] Edward Gibbon, *The History of the Decline and Fall of the Roman Empire: A New Edition, in Twelve Volumes*, vol. 7 (London, 1813), 48.

[44] Ibid., 43.

[45] For the most detailed discussion and checklist up to 1996 of the early modern English translators of the *Consolatio*, see Donaghey, "Post-Medieval English Translations."

[46] See Appendices I.A (Complete Translations) and I.B (Partial and Incomplete English Translations) for a listing of translations with publication dates and translation modes.

[47] See Appendix I.C (Some Occasional English Translations) for a listing of renderings with publication dates and translation modes.

[48] Donaghey, "Post-Medieval English Translations," 304–05.

[49] Ibid., 305.

[50] The full title is much longer: *Boetius de Consolationae Philosophiae. The Boke of Boecius, called the comforte of philosophye, or wysedome moche necessary for all men to read and know, wherein suche as be in aduersitie, shall fynde muche consolation and comforte, and suche as be in great worldly prosperitie may knowe the vanitie and frailtie therof, and consequently fynde eternall felycytie. And this boke is in maner of a dialoge or communication between two persones, the one is Boecius, and the other is Philosophy, whose disputations and arguments do plainly temporall, and transistory thynges. Translated out of latin into the Englyshe tongue by George Coluile, alias Coldewel, to thintent that such as be ingnoraunt the mergentes is added to the Latin, accordynge to the boke of the translatour, whiche was a very olde prynte* (London: In Paules churche yarde at the sygne of the holy Ghost, by Ihon Cawoode, printer to the Kynge and Quenes Maiesties, 1556).

[51] See P. Botley, "Colvile, George (fl. 1556)," in *Oxford Dictionary of National Biography* (Oxford: Oxford University Press, 2004), available online at http://www.oxforddnb.com/view/article/6003, accessed February 3, 2005.

[52] See *Queen Elizabeth's Englishings of Boethius, De Consolatione Philosohiae, Plutarch, De Curiositate, Horace, De Arte Poetica (part)*, ed. Caroline Pemburton, Early English Text Society o.s. 113 (London: Kegan Paul, Trench, Trübner, 1899). Until 2009, Pemburton's edition was the standard edition of Elizabeth's translation of Boethius's *Consolatio*. Although Pemburton's text provides a generally smooth reading of the translation for the purpose of conveying content, it does not maintain the textual integrity of the manuscript, collating first draft inscriptions and later fair copy inscriptions and supplying orthographic normalization not present in the manuscript. Pemburton's edition has been superseded recently by two editions of Elizabeth's translation of Boethius's *Consolatio*: "1593: Boethius's *De Consoltione Philosophiae*," in *Elizabeth I: Translations, 1592–1598*, ed. Janel Mueller and Joshua Scodel (Chicago: University of Chicago Press, 2009), 45–365, and *The Consolation of Queen Elizabeth I: The Queen's Translation of Boethius's "De Consolatione Philosophiae"* (Public Record Office Manuscript SP 12/289), ed. Noel Harold Kaylor, Jr. and Philip Edward Phillips, introduction by Quan Manh Ha, Medieval and Renaissance Texts and Studies 366 (Tempe: Arizona Center for Medieval and Renaissance Studies, 2009).

[53] See "[The Computation of Days and Hours]" in *The Consolation of Queen Elizabeth I*, ed. Kaylor and Phillips, 41.

[54] Roger Ascham, *The Schoolmaster (1570)*, ed. Lawrence V. Ryan, Folger Shakespeare Library (Charlottesville: University Press of Virginia, 1967), 85. Ascham bases his "dual-translation" method upon Pliny the Younger's method of translating from Greek to Latin and from Latin to Greek.

[55] Ibid., 87.

[56] Ibid.

[57] *The Consolation of Queen Elizabeth I*, ed. Kaylor and Phillips, 92.

[58] See, for example, A. Van de Vyver as well as Janel Mueller and Joshua Scodel.

[59] See Quan Manh Ha, "Introduction," in *The Consolation of Queen Elizabeth I*, ed. Kaylor and Phillips, 22–23.

[60] Poem 1 ("Written on a Window Frame at Woodstock"), in *Elizabeth I: Collected Works*, ed. Leah S. Marcus and Mary Beth Rose (Chicago: University of Chicago Press, 2000), 45.

[61] Ibid, 46.

[62] Prayer 2 ("Princess Elizabeth's Prayers in the Tower of London"), in Marcus and Rose, *Elizabeth I: Collected Works*, 48.

[63] Ascham, *The Schoolmaster (1570)*, 86.

[64] Donaghey, "Post-Medieval English Translations," 316.

[65] See *John Bracegirdle's "Psychopharmacon": A Translation of Boethius's "De Consolatione Philosophiae" (MS BL Additional 11401)*, ed. Noel Harold Kaylor, Jr. and Jason Edward Streed, Medieval and Renaissance Texts and Studies 200 (Tempe: Arizona Center for Medieval and Renaissance Studies, 1999).

[66] This translation by "I.T." was later used in the first Loeb Classical Library edition of the *Consolatio*.

[67] See the entry for this translation in Donaghey, "Post-Medieval English Translations," 317.

[68] Donaghey identifies the 1693 translator as Henry Somerset, the first Duke of Beaufort, noting that the translator "may have had publication in mind but never achieved it." The first volume contains an autograph preface and translation of Petrus Bertius's Latin preface, while the second volume contains a fair copy of the Duke's complete translation, written by another scribe. See Donaghey, "Post-Medieval English Translations," 317.

[69] For a checklist of English translations and their translators, see the appendices at the end of this chapter.

[70] Donaghey, "Post-Medieval English Translations," 306.

[71] "From Boetius, de cons. Philos.," in *The Poems of Alexander Pope*, ed. John Butt (New Haven: Yale University Press, 1963), 115.

[72] Philip Edward Phillips, "Boethian 'Happiness' in Alexander Pope's *An Essay on Man*, Epistle IV," in *Vitality of Literature*, ed. An Sonjae (Seoul: Han-Ul Academy, 2002), 389–402. For an earlier treatment of Pope's Boethian adaptation, see B[rian] S. Donaghey, "Alexander Pope's and Sir William Trumbull's Translations of Boethius," *Leeds Studies in English*, n.s., 1 (1967), 71–82.

[73] See *Boethius's "Consolation of Philosophy,"* trans. Rev. Mr. Philip Ridpath, Minister of Hutton, Berkwickshire (London: Printed for C. Dilly, in the Poultry, 1785).

[74] See *The Five Books of Anicius Manlius Torquatus Severinus Boethius, on the Consolation*

of Philosophy, trans. Robert Duncan (Edinburgh: Printed for the Translator; and Sold by William Creech, 1789).

[75] Because of his military and political achievements, King Alfred is the only English monarch to be recognized by the epithet "The Great."

[76] When the organizers were planning the millennial celebration, King Alfred was believed to have died in 901. Much to the consternation of the same organizers, Anglo-Saxon scholars discovered that King Alfred, in fact, had died in 899, too late for the event to be rescheduled.

[77] For a magisterial treatment of Alfred mania, see Simon Keynes, "The Cult of King Alfred the Great," *Anglo-Saxon England* 28 (1999), 225–356. For a discussion of Alfred's nationalistic significance during the nineteenth and the early twentieth centuries, see Barbara Yorke, "Alfredism: The Use and Abuse of King Alfred's Reputation in Later Centuries," in *Alfred the Great*, ed. Timothy Reuter, Studies in Early Medieval Britain (Aldershot: Ashgate, 2003), 361–80. For an account of the modern English translations of the Old English *Boethius* that arose from the Alfred millennial celebrations, see Philip Edward Phillips, "King Alfred the Great and the Victorian Translations of His Anglo-Saxon *Boethius*," in *Global Perspectives on Medieval English Literature, Language, and Culture*, ed. Noel Harold Kaylor, Jr. and Richard Scott Nokes (Kalamazoo: Medieval Institute Publications, 2007), 155–73. For an overview of the tradition and reception of Alfred in the popular imagination, see David Horspool, *King Alfred: Burnt Cakes and Other Legends* (Cambridge, MA: Harvard University Press, 2006).

[78] Phillips, "King Alfred the Great," 162–70.

[79] See F. Boase, *Modern English Biography*, 6 vols, 1892–1921 (*BBA* I:347), and J. F. Kirk, *A Supplement to Allibone's Critical Dictionary of English Literature*, 2 vols, 1891 (*BBA* I:345).

[80] See *King Alfred's Old English Version of Boethius "De Consolatione Philosophiae": Edited from the MSS., with Introduction, Critical Notes and Glossary*, ed. Walter Sedgefield (Oxford: Clarendon Press, 1899).

[81] Walter J. Sedgefield, "Introduction," in *King Alfred's Old English Version of Boethius "De Consolatione Philosophiae"*, viii.

[82] Boethius, *The Consolation of Philosophy of Boethius*, trans. H. R. James (London: Elliot Stock, 1897), 130–32. James's translation was later published in a second edition for the New Universal Library in London by George Routledge & Sons and in New York by E. P. Dutton & Company, 1906. A full-text, electronic version of James's translation is available courtesy of Project Gutenberg at http://www.gutenberg.org/files/14328/14328-h/14328-h.htm, accessed September 22, 2015.

[83] James, "Preface," in James, *The Consolation of Philosophy of Boethius*, vi.

[84] Ibid., vii.

[85] Boethius, *Anicii Manlii Severini Boetii Philosophiae Consolationis*, ed. Rudolfus Peiper (Leipzig: Teubner, 1871).

[86] James, "Preface," vi.

[87] Boethius, *The Consolation of Philosophy*, trans. W. V. Cooper, Temple Classics (London: Dent and, 1902). A full-text, electronic version of Cooper's translation is available online courtesy of the Electronic Text Center, University of Virginia Library, at http://etext.lib.virginia.edu/toc/modeng/public/BoePhil.html, accessed September 22, 2015.

[88] Boethius, *The Consolation of Philosophy*, trans. Richard Green, Library of Liberal Arts (Indianapolis: Bobbs-Merrill, 1962).

[89] Boethius, *The Consolation of Philosophy*, trans. V. E. Watts (New York: Penguin, 1969; rev. edn. 1999).

[90] Boethius, "The Consolation of Philosophy," trans. S. J. Tester, in Boethius, *The Theological Tractates; The Consolation of Philosophy*, trans. H. F. Stewart, E. K. Rand, and S. J. Tester, Loeb Classical Library 74 (Cambridge, MA: Harvard University Press, 1973; repr. 1978, 1990), 130–435.

[91] Boethius, *The Consolation of Philosophy*, trans. Sanderson Beck (1996), published online: http://www.san.beck.org/Boethius.html, accessed September 22, 2015.

[92] Boethius, *The Consolation of Philosophy*, trans. Walsh.

[93] Boethius, *Consolation of Philosophy*, trans. by Joel C. Relihan (Indianapolis: Hackett, 2001).

[94] Boethius, *The Consolation of Philosophy*, trans. David R. Slavitt (Cambridge, MA: Harvard University Press, 2008).

[95] Boethius, *The Consolation of Philosophy*, trans. Scott Goins and Barbara H. Wyman, Ignatius Critical Editions (San Francisco: Ignatius, 2012).

[96] See Boethius, *Philosophiae consolatio*, ed. Ludwig Bieler, Corpus Christianorum Series Latina 94 (Turnhout: Brepols, 1984); Boethius, *De Consolatione Philosophiae*, ed. Moreschini.

[97] There are probably more extant occasional renderings by prominent historical figures. This is a fruitful area for scholars and graduate students to pursue as other examples surface.

[98] See *The Old English Boethius: An Edition of the Old English Versions of Boethius's "De Consolatione Philosophiae,"* ed. Malcolm Godden and Susan Irvine, 2 vols. (Oxford: Oxford University Press, 2009), and *The Old English Boethius, with Verse Prologues and Epilogues Associated with King Alfred*, ed. and trans. Susan Irvine and Malcolm R. Godden, Dumbarton Oaks Library (Cambridge, MA: Harvard University Press, 2012).

Scribal Interpretations of Genre in the Old English *Boethius*

Jonathan Davis-Secord

TWO OLD ENGLISH TRANSLATIONS of Boethius's *De consolatione philosophiae* [hereafter *Consolatio*] were produced in the late ninth or early tenth century, one in prose and one in alternating verse and prose, both presented as the work of King Alfred (871–99).[1] The two versions share nearly identical prose translations of Boethius's original prose sections, but they diverge in their treatments of Boethius's poetry. One version (Oxford, Bodleian Library, MS Bodley 180) translates Boethius's *metra* into Old English prose, and the other (London, British Library, MS Cotton Otho A. vi) renders them as Old English poetry.[2] The full extent of the generic differences between the two versions, however, remains unclear, with some scholars finding "prosaic" vocabulary in the *Meters* and other scholars finding "poetic" devices in the prose version. In this chapter, I explore how an original Anglo-Saxon audience—the scribes—reacted to the texts and to what degree they recognized the generic mixture of the two versions.

The topic of genre itself is elusive and contested: not only are genre scholars challenged to define the characteristics of any individual genre, but even the validity of generic grouping is a tendentious topic. Opponents of genre studies sometimes have stereotyped the field as "border control"—the creation of an ahistorical organizing taxonomy simply for taxonomy's sake. Jacques Derrida attacks the approach that treats genre as a teleological construct that institutes norms and limits at its very conception: he decries the concept that the genre defines the text.[3] An alternative approach that avoids the pitfalls highlighted by Derrida is to treat the concept of individual genres not as fundamental paradigms but as historical constructs, as Ralph Cohen suggests;[4] genres are not Platonic ideals but messy, on-the-ground accidents. Cohen writes:

> [G]enre groupings arise, change and decline for historical reasons. And since each genre is composed of texts that accrue, the grouping

> is a process, not a determinate category. Genres are open categories. Each member alters the genre by adding, contradicting or altering constituents, especially those of members most closely related to it.[5]

Thus, a genre is not an entity of itself but a product of its constituents at any given time. Interestingly, Cohen's approach agrees with Derrida's call to action on one important point: both scholars call for the examination of texts, not genres. While genres, according to Cohen, can guide interpretation, the foundation of any individual genre is a group of texts; understanding a genre involves understanding its texts.

Approaching genre as a historically specific process naturally problematizes the application of anachronistic modern terminology, even such an apparently basic distinction as that of prose and verse. Indeed, the difference between verse and prose in Old English, which some modern scholars often take as an essential given, is not entirely clear.[6] Of course, recovering the Anglo-Saxon understanding of the genre of, say, Ælfric's homilies is not entirely necessary: modern theories and approaches, although in a sense anachronistic, reveal a great deal that might not have been recognized by a contemporary audience. Nonetheless, determining an original understanding of genre helps to elucidate the literary culture of the time, and it can open up our understanding of individual texts.

In an excellent example of determining contemporary ideas of genre, Karl Reichl has examined the resonances of the Old English genre term *giedd* [song, poem] for Anglo-Saxons.[7] He finds that *giedd* can denote four different types of text: (1) proverbs, (2) utterances of the prophets, (3) New Testament parables, and (4) poetry and song, including the psalms. Ultimately, he concludes that *giedd* means, at its base, "'poetic utterance,' ranging from 'proverb' to 'heroic lay,'" with some specialized meanings. He reaches this conclusion through an exhaustive appraisal of the occurrences of the term *giedd* in Old English texts, one of which (or two of which, depending on one's point of view) is found in the Old English *Boethius*. Based on the terms used to translate Latin *cantus* in the *Boethius*, Reichl claims that "[i]t can be assumed that the translator thought of the *metra* as sung poetry."[8] Although his definition of *giedd* is necessarily wide ranging, Reichl thus provides some insight into the contemporary understanding of genre.

Textual content, with which Reichl works, is one fundamental and important source of information on genre terms and conceptions, but so too is manuscript presentation. The lexical choices of the OE *Boethius*, as Reichl shows, reveal the translator's understanding of *giedd*, but I argue that the manuscripts reveal the two scribes' reception of the mixture of prose and poetry (or pseudo-poetry, as I discuss below). In this essay, I examine the manuscript presentations of the two versions of the Old English *Boethius* in order to determine how those scribes approached literature in terms of generic distinctions. While neither of the two manuscripts of the Old English *Boethius* presents marginal notes or overt commentary from the scribes, each one's *mis-en-page* can be taken, I argue, as an interpretation of the text. Both manuscripts are in fact quite spare, presenting very little decoration, but the placements of those decorations are quite telling. The only decorations that the Bodleian manuscript has are spartan initial capitals that indicate the division of the text into various sections; the Cotton manuscript does not even have actual capitals, leaving only the blank spaces left for initial capitals that no one ever returned to fill in.[9] The choices of where to divide the texts and which sections to call out indicate how the scribes interpreted the structure of the texts they copied. Although this information provides very limited access to their understandings of the texts, it elucidates their responses to the issue of genre, since the structure of the *Consolatio* intrinsically is tied to genre.

Indeed, the Old English *Boethius* presents an excellent case study for exploring the reception of genre, given, first, the prosimetric structure of the Latin original and, second, the two different versions of the Old English translation. The actual extent of the differences between the two versions of the *Boethius*, however, remains unclear, with (as noted above) some scholars finding so-called "prosaic" vocabulary in the *Meters* and other scholars finding so-called "poetic" devices in the prose text. Godden and Irvine point out that the prose versions of Boethius's poetry display an "elevated" style appropriate for verse, employing alliteration, two-stress phrases, and repetition—all standard elements of Old English poetry.[10] They consider these characteristics to be signals that the Bodley 180 version attempts to distinguish linguistically between the translations of Boethius's poetry and the translations of his prose, even though the entire text is rendered as Old English prose. Indeed, such elements should stand as sufficient linguistic signals, as Katherine O'Brien O'Keeffe points out, for "literate" Anglo-Saxons approached written texts with great sensitivity to their discursive characteristics, at least as regards Old English poetry.[11] The comparative dearth of pointing and the orthographic irregularity in the manuscripts of Old English poetry required Anglo-Saxon readers to read such texts more actively and to provide more contextual information than is required of modern readers with access to modern editions of the same texts. Anglo-Saxon readers required prior knowledge of the "rules" and traditions of Old English poetry to compensate for the lack of visual cues in the manuscripts. As a result of this approach to engaging texts, an Anglo-Saxon audience presumably should have been sensitive enough to the characteristics noted by Irvine to recognize the poetic character of the prose translations of Boethius's poetry. The degree of difference between prose and prosimetric versions is further diminished by the so-called "prosaic" vocabulary of the *Meters*; as E. G. Stanley puts it, the *Meters* "freely admit prose words."[12] Thus, just as the Old English prose *metra* employ devices of poetic style, the actual poetic translations employ prose vocabulary.

Here is an example of these overlapping generic traditions: portions of the translations of Boethius's *Consolatio* 2m5:

Prose:
Æala, hwæt se forma gitsere wære, þe ærest þa eorþan ongan
delfan æfter golde, and æfter gimmum?[13]
[Alas, who was the earliest miser that first began to dig into the
earth after gold and after gems?]

Verse:
Eala, hwæt se forma feohgitsere
wære on worulde, se þas wongstedas
grof æfter golde and æfter gimcynnum?[14]
[Alas, who was the first money-miser in the world that dug up
the pasture-places after gold and after precious gems?]

A large number of elements from the prose text are repeated in the verse text, showing that the prose already fulfilled some requirements of poetry: it provides some appropriate rhythms and some alliteration. Many of the changes in the process of versification simply supply additional alliteration. The prose version is much like poetry, and the poetic version is much like prose. Thus, it seems that, in an Anglo-Saxon audience's perception, the difference between the prose and verse versions would have been far less significant than the difference our modern editions offer with their distinctive lineations and page presentations.

Nonetheless, the existence of the two versions of the *Boethius* implies that Anglo-Saxon readers did recognize a difference of some sort; otherwise there would have been no reason to create the prosimetric version. Someone felt that it was important to create a version of the text with full-fledged poetry, and not just poetic prose.[15] One clue to the motivation for versification comes in the form of mistakes: three Latin *metra* that were translated into Old English prose were not subsequently versified in the prosimetric version—1m6, 2m2, and 4m7. This failure on the part of the versifier raises the question of why these three *metra* were left unversified. Perhaps the versifier considered the poetic diction of these three sections close enough to actual poetry; perhaps he forgot them. It is quite possible that the versifier simply missed them, failing to recognize that they were prose-*metra* that needed to be versified.

In the all-prose text, these three *metra* have no signposting statement—that is, there is no statement marking them as a separate section consisting of translations of poetry. For all other prose-*metra* but one (1m7, discussed below), the Old English *Boethius* introduces each *metrum* with a reference to Wisdom finishing a speech and beginning to sing a song. Janet Bately describes these markings as "sign-posting" statements included to mark the transition between prose and prose-*metrum*.[16] For example,

> Ða ongan se wisdom hreowsian for þæs modes tydernesse and ongan þa giddian and þus cwæð[17]
>
> [Then Wisdom began to be sad for Mind's weakness and then began to sing and said the following]

> *Ongan ða giddien, and þus singende cwæð*[18]
>
> [Then (Wisdom) began to sing and, singing, said the following]

> Þa se Wisdom þa ðis spel asæd hæfde, þa ongan he eft singan and ðus cwæð.[19]
>
> [When Wisdom had finished this story, then he began to sing again and said the following]

These statements mark a distinct transition between sections, indicating in particular the presence of poetic elements with the word *giedd*. As a result, these statements point out textually the difference between prose and verse, something that Old English manuscripts rarely did visually. Thus they most likely served as an important aid to the versifier, indicating which sections needed full verse treatment. In addition to the fact that the three unversified sections lack these statements, their manuscript presentation also hinders the recognition of these three sections as different from the surrounding prose. In Bodley 180, the three unversified *metra* are presented as continuations of the preceding prose sections.[20] The prose translation of 1m6 begins on line 3 of 6v with "þonne þære"; that of 2m2 begins on line 7 of 10v with "ðeah feohgitsere"; and that of 4m7 begins on line 6 of 87v with "*wella*" (see Figures 1–3). Visually, the prose appears simply to continue on with no indication of any transition or section break at all three of these locations. In fact, the large Þ marking a section break on 87v at line nineteen indicates not the beginning of 4m7 but the transition from book 4 to book 5, further emphasizing the lack of any marking for 4m7.

Without the aid of visual cues or signposting statements, it seems likely that the versifier failed to recognize the change from prose to prose-*metrum* in these cases. There is, of course, the issue of the prose translation of 1m7, which also lacks a signposting statement but was nonetheless versified. That prose-*metrum*, however, is visually marked off as a distinct chapter in Bodley 180, as shown in Figure 4, with 1m7 beginning on line 16 with the space left for an enlarged *L* to begin chapter 6. Thus, the translation of 1m7 was not lost amid the prose translation, as 1m6, 2m2, and 4m7 seem to have been.

The versifier's lack of recognition of the three prose-*metra* suggests either that he was not paying close attention to the text—perhaps only skimming for statements of "singing" or for chapter breaks—or that he did not recognize the supposed stylistic change from prose to prose-*metrum*. Given the probable nature of Anglo-Saxon reading practices, skimming is an unlikely possibility.[21] With the dearth of visual cues in manuscripts of Old English, the need to subvocalize the text while reading most likely precluded the ability to skim.[22] Particularly in Old English manuscripts, elements such as unsystematic word division and letter spacing required a form of reading closer to aural than visual comprehension. As a result of the persistent need to reinterpret the visual information into auditory forms, an Anglo-Saxon reader would have been unable to skim-read a text, unless it had been memorized previously (suggesting at least an attentive first reading). Moreover, although the versifier recognized 1m7 as a prose meter most likely due to its chapter status, he also was not simply versifying alternating chapters. Several of the prose-*metra* are subsections of chapters, and several chapter breaks do not correspond to a transition between prose and verse. Nonetheless, the versifier was not misled by these inconsistencies: apart from the three missing *metra*, the other correct sections were versified. Consequently, skimming in any form can explain neither the versifier's successes nor his failures; he must have been paying fairly close attention to the text.

This situation suggests that the poetic elements found in the prose-*metra* were insufficient by themselves to mark those sections as special; only in conjunction with visual cues and/or signposting were those elements notable. As sensitive as Anglo-Saxon readers must have been, the versifier apparently was not sensitive enough to recognize that the poetic rhythms, alliteration, and repetitions in these three sections indicated poetic prose. Thus, for at least one reader, the prose version of the *Boethius* did not accurately recreate the structure of the original Latin: it did not have enough generic variation.

Cotton Otho A. vi, on the other hand, matches the prosimetric nature of its text with visual indications of the alternation between verse and prose.[23] For example, even in the face of the significant damage suffered by the manuscript, a blank space for an enlarged initial capital and an enlarged *v* are still visible, marking the beginning of *Meter 5*, the first *Meter* now extant (see Figure 5). These blanks occur throughout the manuscript, and each one marks either a transition between genres (prose to verse or verse to prose) or between books.[24] The scribe (or the scribe of an earlier exemplar) clearly must have recognized the generic alternation and highlighted the structure visually. (Table 1 indicates all the *Meters* and points where I found spaces left for capitals in the manuscript.) As a result of the fire damage and subsequent neglect, the first leaves of the manuscript are missing, so the first verse section is now *Meter* 5, and there are several damaged or missing leaves throughout. Nonetheless, each beginning and end of a verse section that remains is marked with a blank space for an initial capital. This pattern holds throughout the manuscript, and any uncertainty due to the genre transitions lost in the fire should be outweighed by the remarkable regularity of the marking in the rest of the manuscript. Visual indications of the difference between Old English prose and Old English verse are highly rare, but in Cotton Otho A. vi we find repeated, accurate markings of such distinctions.

This same pattern does not hold for Bodley 180. For the first half of the text, the markings follow the guidance of the prose structure, leaving space for enlarged initials at the beginning of each chapter, as seen in Figure 4, for the beginning of chapter 6 on line 16. This practice leaves the prose-*metra* unmarked initially, thus obscuring visually any possible generic distinctions the text might have. Approximately halfway through the text, however, the placements of enlarged initials change significantly.

Table 2 summarizes the locations of enlarged initial capitals and blank spaces left for enlarged initial capitals in Bodley 180. The scribe continued to mark chapter breaks but began to add many more capitals at points that are not breaks between chapters. In chapter 26, the breaks apparently begin marking transitions between speakers, although these transitions appear to have no structural significance. In chapter 29, the markings take on important generic significance: specifically, they begin to mark the beginnings of the passages that translate Boethius's Latin poetry into Old English prose. Even when the beginning of a prose-*metrum* does not coincide with a chapter division, the scribe still calls it out. In fact, he also begins marking the mid-chapter ends of prose-*metra* in the final chapters of the translation. So, from marking only prose chapter divisions in the first half of the text, the scribe of Bodley 180 moves to marking the beginnings and ends of prose-*metra* in the final portion. The scribe seems finally to have recognized a distinction between the prose translations of Boethius's prose and the prose translations of Boethius's poetry. This constitutes a significant change of presentation method: the scribe had begun copying and visually formatting a prose text divided into chapters, but he eventually recognized obscured generic alternations.

Perhaps the scribe eventually noticed the various elements of poetic discourse in the prose-*metra*. Perhaps the repeated appearance of those elements in conjunction with the signposting statements finally did their job, leading this reader/scribe finally to recognize some sort of generic variation in the text. Whatever the motivation, the scribe moved away from marking chapter divisions solely to marking generic variation in addition. Note, however, that it took forty folios for the Bodley 180 scribe to begin marking the generic distinctions, whereas the Otho A. vi scribe was doing so from the very first.

So, in one manuscript (Otho A. vi), the scribe overtly marked generic differences, and in the other manuscript (Bodley 180), the scribe began to mark generic differences very late in the text. This situation complicates modern scholars' understanding of exactly which elements actually differentiate prose from verse in these two versions. As I noted earlier, the two versions of the text are fairly similar, and, given this mixed generic identity, there seems to have been little to instill an immediate sense of differentiation. The poetic elements identified by Irvine in the Bodley 180 text seem to have worked only slowly on its scribe, warranting acknowledgment late in the copying process. The alternations between prose and verse apparently were more readily noticeable in the prosimetric text than in the solely prose text, even though it shares many of the elements highlighted by Irvine. There are, however, other features associated with Old English poetry that may help explain this conundrum. In particular, the characteristics of the compound words differ greatly between the two texts, providing strong associations with either prose or verse within each version that are much more clear-cut than those provided by alliteration and rhythm.[25] It appears that this distinction in compound words may explain the lag in the Bodley 180 scribe's recognition of the prose-*metra*.

In terms of a general understanding of genre, the manuscript presentations also show that, at the very least, both scribes noted generic alternation—thus, it is clear that they did conceive of generic difference. Like good structuralist critics, they had at least a basic taxonomy of Old English genres. Although "genres leak" in Old English literature,[26] as John Miles Foley puts it, the visual cues in the *Boethius* manuscripts demonstrate that at least these two scribes still felt that the prose sections were distinct from the verse, and ultimately even from the verse-like prose in the case of Bodley 180.

Such recognition on the part of the scribes is especially interesting since the prosimetric structure of Boethius's Latin text was probably quite foreign to an Anglo-Saxon audience and therefore not something that was likely to have been expected by the scribes. Combining verse and prose was not completely unknown to Anglo-Saxons literate in Latin, given, for example, their attraction to Latin *opera geminata* [twinned works] such as Aldhelm's *De virginitate*.[27] An *opus geminatum*, however, combines two complementary versions of a work, one in prose and one in verse; it does not entail repeated alternation between the two genres. As other possible parallels to the generic mixture in the *Boethius*, verse sections are interspersed among prose sections both in the Vercelli Book and the *Anglo-Saxon Chronicle*, but the natures of those two works are very different from that of the Old English *Boethius*. The Vercelli Book comprises not a unified, sustained work but a series of separate works in a compilation; the alternation of prose and verse then is not a work-internal phenomenon as it is with the *Boethius*. Moreover, the poems of the *Anglo-Saxon Chronicle* do not create the same sense of internal alternation, although one could take the *Chronicle* as a single, sustained work.[28] The *Chronicle* presents a somewhat unified account of one royal line (the Cerdicings) with some narrative vignettes spanning several year-entries, but it has a very different character from the *Boethius*. The *Boethius* clearly is conceived as a long, sustained conversation, while the individual *Chronicle* narratives are much more self-contained.

The fact that the scribes ultimately did recognize and highlight the generic alternations in the Old English *Boethius* displays a sensitivity to genre and an interest in matching linguistic difference with visual difference. The scribes clearly read and copied with an awareness of genre, and with the presumption that generic difference is significant. Had it been otherwise, the Otho A. vi scribe would not have recognized the structure of his text as he did, and the Bodley 180 scribe certainly would not finally have noticed the distinction of the prose-*metra*.[29] Furthermore, the creation of visual differentiation in reaction to generic difference suggests that the scribes felt that future readers also would share their interest in genre, and they therefore provided visual guides that reinforce the generic distinctions for those readers. The two scribes of the Old English *Boethius* thus were quite aware of the issue of genre, and their decisions in presenting the texts that they copied reveal their interest in highlighting that issue. Their decisions also make it clear to today's readers that our modern distinctions between Old English verse and Old English prose do indeed mark a difference that was recognized at the time. While prose and verse may have been on a continuum, with Ælfric and late Old English poetry perhaps somewhere in the middle, the two ends of that spectrum indeed were different at least to these two readers.

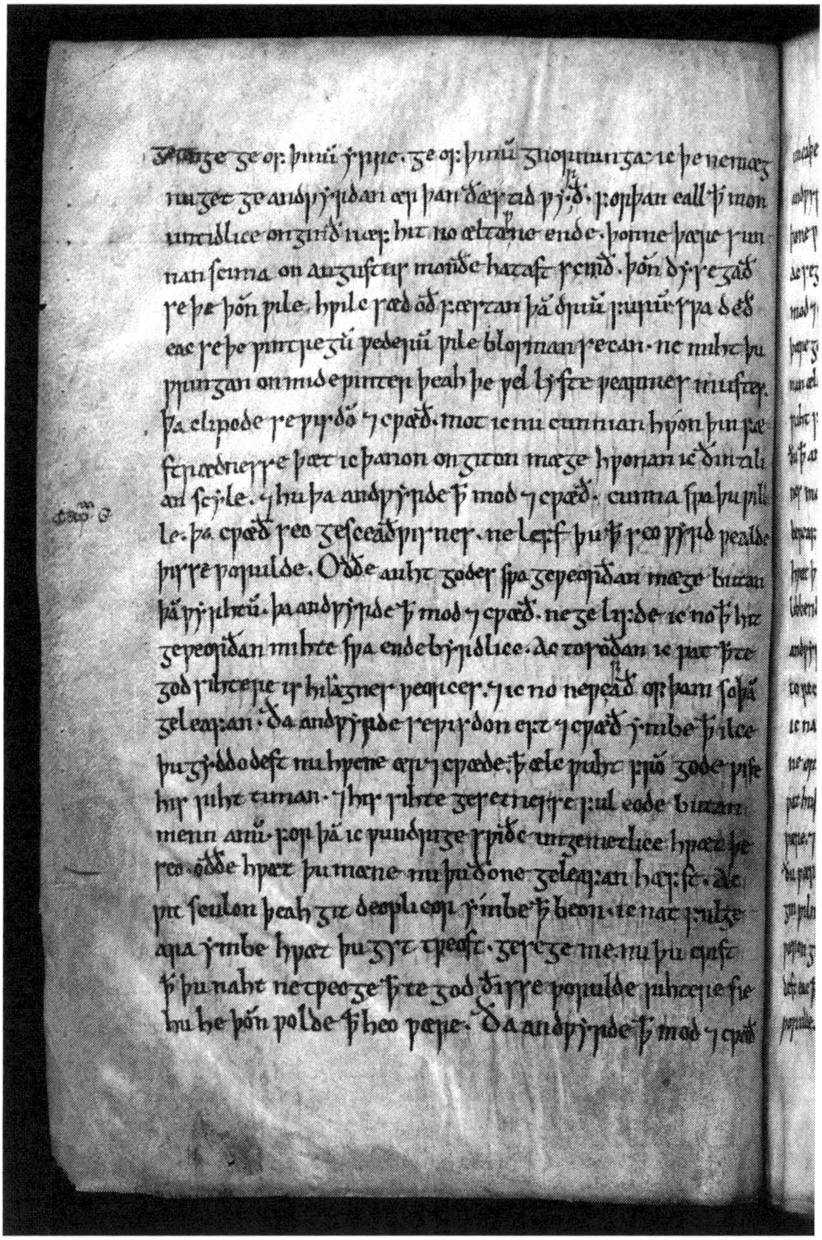

Figure 1: Bodley 180, fol. 6v
Reproduced with permission from The Bodleian Libraries, University of Oxford

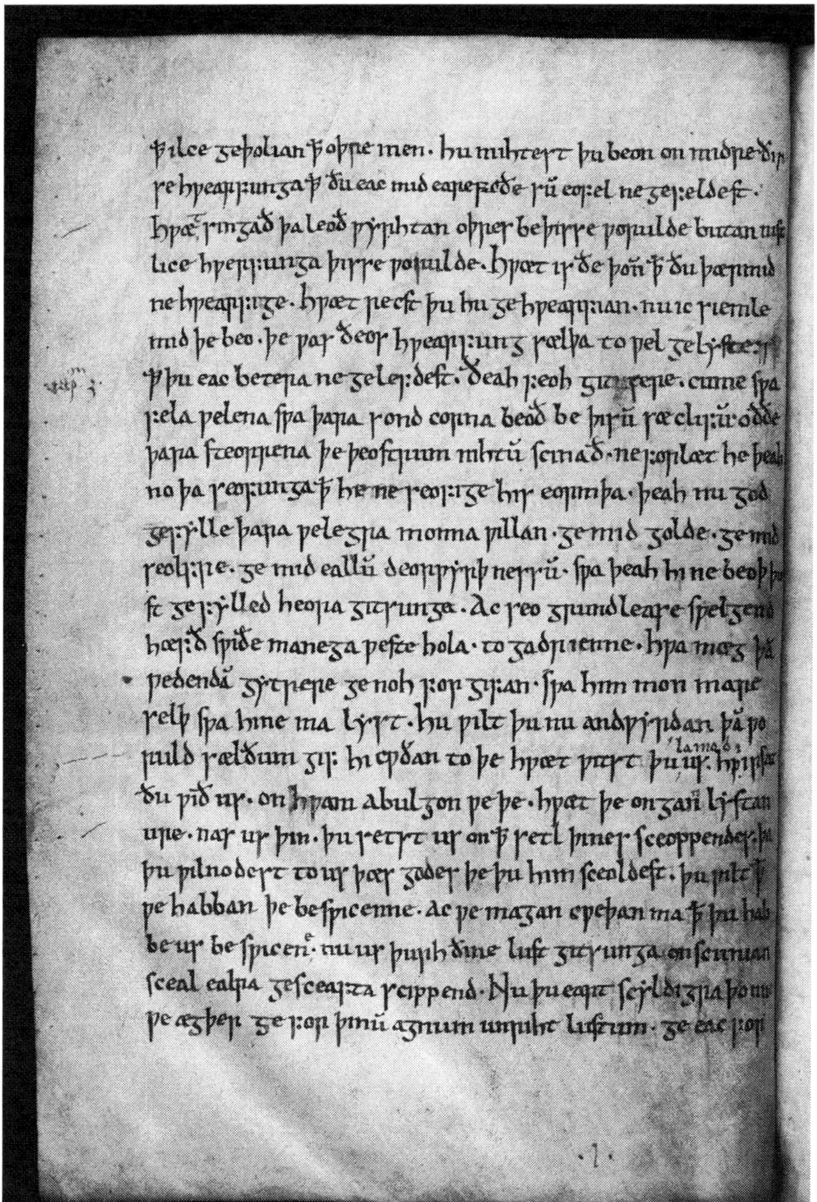

Figure 2: Bodley 180, fol. 10v
Reproduced with permission from The Bodleian Libraries, University of Oxford

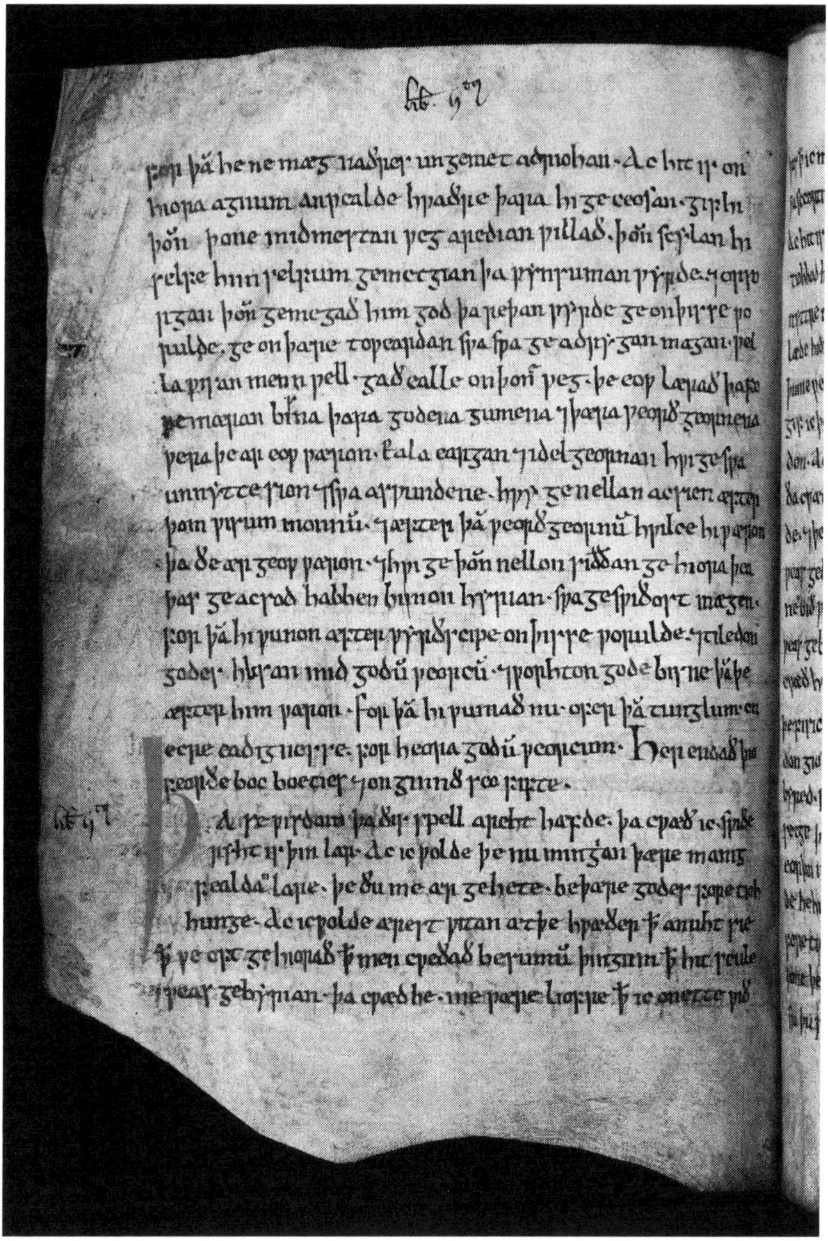

Figure 3: Bodley 180, fol. 87v
Reproduced with permission from The Bodleian Libraries, University of Oxford

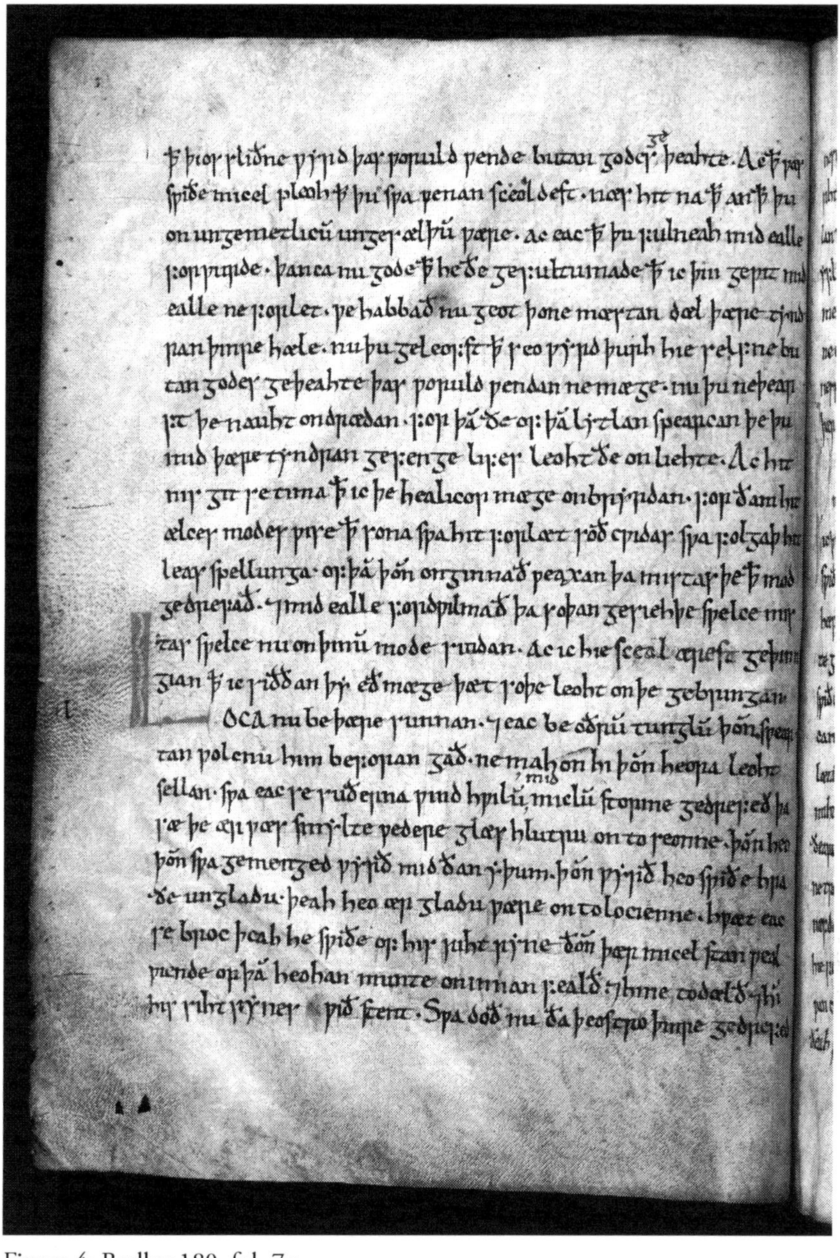

Figure 4: Bodley 180, fol. 7v
Reproduced with permission from The Bodleian Libraries, University of Oxford

Figure 5: Cotton Otho A. vi, fol. 3r

Table 1:
Locations of Space for Enlarged Initials in Cotton Otho A. vi

Meter	Beginning	End
5	marked (3r)	marked (4r)
6	marked (9r)	marked (10v)
7	marked (14r)	marked (15r)
8	*damaged* (20v)	*damaged* (21v)
9	*damaged* (27v)	marked (28r)
10	*damaged* (34r)	marked (35r)
11 (and Book 2)	marked (36v)	marked (38v)
12	marked (40r)	marked (40v)
13	*damaged* (44v)	marked (46r)
14	*damaged* (48v)	marked (48v)
15	marked (52r)	marked (52r)
16	marked (54v)	marked (55r)
17	marked (56r)	*damaged* (56v)
18	marked (57v)	marked (58r)
19	marked (59v)	marked (60v)
20	marked (64v)	marked (69r)
21	marked (75r)	marked (75v)
22	*missing*	*missing*
23	*missing*	*missing*
(Book 4)	marked (86v)	
24	marked (88v)	marked (93v)
25	marked (93v)	marked (95r)
26	marked (97v)	marked (99v)
27	marked (106r)	marked (107r)
28	marked (108r)	marked (109v)
29	marked (117v)	marked (119v)
(Book 5)	marked (121v)	
30	marked (123r)	marked (123v)
31	*missing*	marked (128r)

Table 2:
Locations of Enlarged Initials and Blank Spaces in Bodley 180

Chapters Marked	Non-chapters Marked[30]
2	
4	
5	
6	
7	
8	
9	
10	
	Anticipate c. 11 (scribal error?): 13r, line 8 [Ð] (1:260, line 55)
11	
12	
13	
14	
15	
16	
	Begin 2m6: 23r, lines 21–22 [Ð] and 23 [space for H] (1:276, line 147)
17	
18	
19	
20	
21	
22	
	Dialogue transition?: 31r, lines 13–14 [Ð] (1:287, line 30)
23	
24	
25	
26	
	Dialogue transition?: 36r, lines 3–4 [Þ] (1:295, line 23) Dialogue transition?: 36r, lines 8–9 [Ð] (1:295, line 27) Dialogue transition?: 36r, line 22 [Þ] (1:295, line 42) Dialogue transition?: 36r, line 23 [Ð] (1:295, line 44) Dialogue transition?: 36v, lines 4–5 [Þ] (1:296, line 48) Dialogue transition?: 36v, lines 11–12 [Ð] (1:296, line 54 [second Ða]) Begin 3m3: 37r, lines 11 [Ð] and 13 [H] (1:296, lines 77 and 78)

Table 2 (*continued*)

27	
	Dialogue transition?: 38r, lines 7–10 [Þ] (1:298, line 41) Dialogue transition?: 38r, lines 11–12 [Ð] (1:298, line 45)
28	
29	
	Begin 3m5: 41r, penultimate line [Ð], and 41v, lines 1–2 [Ð] (1:303, lines 77 and 78)
30	
	Begin 3m6: 42v, lines 8–10 [H] (1:305, line 38)
31	
	Begin 3m7: 43v, lines 9–12 [Þ] (1:307, line 30)
32	
	Begin 3m8: 45r, lines 15–16 [space for W] (1:309, line 67)
33	
	Begin 3m9: 49r, lines 7–8 [E] (1:315, line 142)
34	
	Begin 3m10: 55v, lines 18–19 [Ð] and 19–22 [W] (1:324, line 189)
35	
	Begin 3m12: 63v, lines 4–5 [open space for G] (1:336, line 195)
36	
	Begin 4m1: 65v, lines 10–11 [Ð] and 11–13 [I] (1:339, lines 40 and 41)
37	
	End 4m2: 70r, lines 13–14 [G] (1:346, line 33)
39	
	Begin 4m5: 78v, final line [Ð], and 79r, lines 1–4 [space for H] (1:359, lines 50 and 51) End 4m5: 79v, lines 8–9 [Ð] (1:360, line 79) Begin 4m6: 85r, lines 16 [Ð] and 17–18 [G] (1:368, lines 331 and 332)
40	
	End 4m7 and Book 4: 87v, lines 17 [H] and 16–22 [Þ] (1:372, lines 72 and 73)
41	
	End 5m2: 89r, lines 13–15 [Ð] (1:374, line 10) Begin 5m5: 92v, lines 5–8 [H] (1:379, line 163)

NOTES

[1] After a long period of incomplete editions, both versions of the Old English translation receive full and masterful treatment in *The Old English Boethius: An Edition of the Old English Versions of Boethius's De Consolatione Philosophiae*, ed. Malcolm R. Godden and Susan Irvine, with Mark Griffith and Rohini Jayatilaka, 2 vols. (Oxford: Oxford University Press, 2009). Although Alfred is presented as the translator of the *Boethius*, that claim has been questioned and debated recently; however, the claim's verity or falsity has no bearing on my discussion in this article. For notable, recent work on the authorship of the "Alfredian canon," see Paul E. Szarmach, "Boethius's Influence in Anglo-Saxon England: The Vernacular and the *De Consolatione Philosophiae*," in *A Companion to Boethius in the Middle Ages*, ed. Noel Harold Kaylor, Jr. and Philip Edward Phillips, Brill's Companions to the Christian Tradition 30 (Leiden: Brill, 2012), 221–54; Sharon M. Rowley, *The Old English Version of Bede's "Historia Ecclesiastica"* (Cambridge: Brewer, 2011), esp. 37–46; Janet Bately, "Did King Alfred Actually Translate Anything? The Integrity of the Alfredian Canon Revisited," *Medium Ævum* 78, no. 2 (2009): 189–215; Malcolm R. Godden, "Did King Alfred Write Anything?," *Medium Ævum* 76, no. 1 (2007): 1–23; David Pratt, "Problems of Authorship and Audience in the Writings of King Alfred the Great," in *Lay Intellectuals in the Carolingian World*, ed. Patrick Wormald and Janet L. Nelson (Cambridge: Cambridge University Press, 2007), 162–91; Nicole Guenther Discenza, *The King's English: Strategies of Translation in the Old English "Boethius"* (Albany: State University of New York Press, 2005), esp. 139–40n1; Janet Bately, "The Alfredian Canon Revisited: One Hundred Years On," in *Alfred the Great: Papers from the Eleventh-Centenary Conferences*, ed. Timothy Reuter (Aldershot: Ashgate, 2003), 107–20; Malcolm R. Godden, "The Player King: Identification and Self-Representation in King Alfred's Writings," in *Alfred the Great: Papers from the Eleventh-Centenary Conferences*, 137–50; Simon Keynes, "The Power of the Written Word: Alfredian England 871–899," in *Alfred the Great*, ed. Reuter, 175–97; and Ross Smythe, "King Alfred's Translations: Authorial Integrity and the Integrity of Authority," *Quaestio Insularis* 4 (2003): 98–114.

[2] For a description of the two *Boethius* manuscripts and the related fragment and transcript, see Godden and Irvine, *Boethius*, 1:9–44.

[3] Jacques Derrida, "The Laws of Genre," trans. Avita Ronell, *Critical Inquiry* 7, no. 1 (1980): 55–81, at 57.

[4] Ralph Cohen, "History and Genre," *Neohelicon* 13, no. 2 (1986): 87–105.

[5] Cohen, "History and Genre," 88.

[6] See E. G. Stanley, "Studies in the Prosaic Vocabulary of Old English Verse," *Neuphilologische Mitteilungen* 72 (1971): 385–418; Mark Griffith, "Poetic Language and the Paris Psalter: The Decay of the Old English Tradition," *Anglo-Saxon England* 20 (1991): 167–86; Roberta Frank, "Poetic Words in Late Old English Prose," in *From Anglo-Saxon to Early Middle English: Studies Presented to E. G. Stanley*, ed. Malcolm R. Godden, Terry Hoad, and Douglas Gray (Oxford: Clarendon Press, 1994), 87–107; and Tiffany Beechy, *Poetics of Old English* (Farnham: Ashgate, 2010).

[7] Karl Reichl, "Old English *giedd* and Middle English *yedding* as Genre Terms," in *Words, Texts, and Manuscripts: Studies in Anglo-Saxon Culture Presented to Helmut Gneuss on the Occasion of His Sixty-fifth Birthday*, ed. Michael Korhammer, Karl Reichl, and Hans Sauer (Cambridge: Brewer, 1992), 349–70. Reichl acknowledges that he follows a line of scholars investigating OE *giedd*: Reinhold Merbot, "Ästhetische Studien zur angelsächsischen (altenglischen) Poesie" (PhD diss., University of Breslau, 1883), pp. 25–28; Andreas

Heusler, "Dichtung," in *Reallexikon der germanischen Altertumskunde*, ed. Johannes Hoops, 4 vols. (Strassburg: Trübner, 1911–19), 1:439–62; Roscoe E. Parker, "*Gyd, Leoð*, and *Sang* in Old English Poetry," *University of Tennessee Studies in the Humanities* 1 (1956): 59–63; Richard North, "The Pagan Inheritance of Egill's *Sonatorrek*," in *Atti del 12° Congresso Internazionale di Studi sull'Alto Medioevo. Poetry in the Scandinavian Middle Ages. The Seventh International Saga Conference* (Spoleto: Centro Italiano di Studi sull'Alto Medioevo, 1990), 147–67, at 161–64. See also Beechy, *Poetics of Old English*, 31–38, and John D. Niles, *Homo Narrans: The Poetics and Anthropology of Oral Literature* (Philadelphia: University of Pennsylvania Press, 1999), 26–30.

[8] Reichl, "Old English *giedd* and Middle English *yedding* as Genre Terms," p. 356.

[9] For a description of the capitals and spaces, see Godden and Irvine, *Boethius*, 1:14–16 and 23.

[10] Godden and Irvine, *Boethius*, 1:72, 103–5, and 185–88; these passages concentrate on vocabulary. Susan Irvine was also kind enough to provide me with a copy of her paper, "The Authorship of the Alfredian Versions and the Relationship of Prose and Verse," presented at the third annual symposium of the Alfredian Boethius Project in 2005, in which she discusses two-stress phrases and repetition in addition to vocabulary (page 6). For definitions of "poetic," see Mark Griffith, "Poetic Language and the Paris Psalter: the Decay of the Old English Tradition," *ASE* 20 (1991): 167–86; and Frank, "Poetic Words in Late Old English Prose." Essentially, both scholars take a corpus-based approach, requiring various proportions of prose-text occurrences to poetic-text occurrences. If not performed rigorously, this approach to defining "poetic" can come close to tautology in that it seeks to characterize words by terms that are themselves sometimes based on the presence of the words being studied. We must be careful not to conclude, for example, that a word is poetic because it appears in texts that we define as poetic partially because they contain that word.

[11] Katherine O'Brien O'Keeffe, *Visible Song: Transitional Literacy in Old English Verse* (Cambridge: Cambridge University Press, 1990), 21: "[A]t whatever level one wishes to examine reading activity for Old English verse, the written text is relatively rich in orthographic surprise. The implication of this statement is that a reader of Old English necessarily brought a great deal of predictive knowledge to the text to be read, precisely because the manuscripts were low both in orthographic redundancy and in graphic cues. This knowledge came from a deep understanding of the conventions of Old English verse, marked as it is by formula, generic composition and repetition."

[12] Stanley, "Studies in the Prosaic Vocabulary of Old English Verse," at 387 and 390. See also Godden and Irvine, *Boethius*, 1:103–5 and 191–92.

[13] Godden and Irvine, *Boethius*, 1:271, lines 21–22. Translations are my own, unless otherwise noted.

[14] Godden and Irvine, *Boethius*, 1:413, lines 55–57.

[15] I follow the current consensus, summarized in Godden and Irvine, *Boethius*, 1:80–82, that the prosimetric Old English text is dependent upon the entirely prose text. In other words, the prose-*metra* were a source for the *Meters*, not the other way around.

[16] Janet Bately, "Book Divisions and Chapter Headings in the Translations of the Alfredian Period," in *Early Medieval English Texts and Interpretations: Studies Presented to Donald G. Scragg*, ed. Elaine Treharne and Susan Rosser, Medieval and Renaissance Texts and Studies (Tempe: Arizona Center for Medieval and Renaissance Studies, 2002), 151–66 at 159.

[17] Godden and Irvine, *Boethius*, 1:245, lines 21–22.

[18] Godden and Irvine, *Boethius*, 1:246, lines 40–41.

[19] Godden and Irvine, *Boethius*, 1:293, lines 1–2.

[20] It is unlikely that the versifier was working with Bodley 180 itself, but he was most likely working with a similar text that would have shared its *mis-en-page*.

[21] See O'Brien O'Keeffe, *Visible Song*, 14–21; and H. J. Chaytor, "The Medieval Reader and Textual Criticism," *Bulletin of the John Rylands Library* 26 (1941–42): 49–56.

[22] The versifier also could not have succeeded in locating all the *metra* that he actually did by looking for forms of a single word, such as *singan*, which is present in most of the sign-posting statements introducing prose-*metra*. Not all of the prose-*metra* are introduced with a form of *singan*; specifically, 2m4, 2m6, 3m1, and 3m4 are introduced in manners very similar to the other meters, but without *singan*. All four of these meters were versified, making it impossible that the versifier searched simply for forms of *singan*. Although fairly regular, the "signposts" marking transitions between prose and verse are variable enough that searching for a single word would not have sufficed.

[23] O'Brien O'Keeffe suggests that the arrangement of the space between prose and verse and the space left for large initial capitals in Cotton Otho A. vi may stem from breaking up the running prose of a manuscript similar to Bodley 180, representing simply a break in the copying and not necessarily an overt acknowledgment of the distinction between prose and verse (*Visible Song*, 2). However, the deliberate use of the breaks to mark section changes and the interest in providing enlarged initial capitals argues against that interpretation: it seems unlikely that the scribe would squander space and routinely insert capitals each time he paused to change his copy source. Moreover, the consistent placement of visual breaks at every genre transition and nowhere else, as discussed below, further supports the interpretation of the breaks as intentional markers of generic change.

[24] Occasional enlarged letters occur at other points in the text, but never on the scale or with the accompanying blank space interrupting the text of those marking section breaks.

[25] I will discuss the nature of the compound words in the two versions and the implications for generic associations in more detail in a future publication in my forthcoming monograph: *Joinings: Compound Words in Old English Literature* (Toronto: University of Toronto Press, forthcoming 2016).

[26] John Miles Foley, "How Genres Leak in Traditional Verse," in *Unlocking the Wordhord: Anglo-Saxon Studies in Memory of Edward B. Irving, Jr.*, ed. Mark C. Amodio and Katherine O'Brien O'Keeffe (Toronto: University of Toronto Press, 1998), 76–108.

[27] On *opera geminata*, see Peter Godman, "The Anglo-Latin *Opus Geminatum*: From Aldhelm to Alcuin," *Medium Ævum* 50 (1981): 215–29.

[28] Thomas Bredehoft argues that the genealogies in the *Chronicle* represent a shift toward verse, but that shift is a product of visual presentation of columnar material in running prose not of actual composition in verse genre (*Textual Histories: Readings in the Anglo-Saxon Chronicle* [Toronto: University of Toronto Press, 2001], 36 and 15). Moreover, the genealogies would not create the sense of an organizing, prosimetric structure as is found in Boethius's work.

[29] Assigning significance to generic difference further complicates late Old English texts that seem to blend verse and prose, such as those by Ælfric and Wulfstan.

[30] Letters in square brackets indicate the capitals in the manuscript. All volume, page, and line numbers in parentheses refer to Godden and Irvine, Boethius; in the interest of clarity, I have not reiterated the editors and title for every citation.

Authorial Self-Identification in the Acrostics of Walton's *Boethius* and the Question of John Bonejohn

Ian Johnson

IN THIS ESSAY, I examine the hermeneutic implications of the apparently authorial acrostic signatures in the text and paratext of John Walton's 1410 verse translation of Boethius's *De consolatione philosophiae* [hereafter *Consolatio*].[1] I start with the acrostic anagrams woven into the first (**NWLOTA**) and penultimate (**WTALVN**) stanzas of his rendering of the Vulgate *Boethius* text:

> Allas I wrecche þat whilom was in welthe
> And lusty songes vsed for to write
> **N**ow am I set in sorowes and vnselthe.
> **W**iþ mournyng now my merþe I most respite;
> **L**o rendyng muses techiþ me to endite,
> **O**f wo wiþ wepyng weteþ þay my face.
> **T**hus hath my disese distroyed al my delyte
> **A**nd broght my blisse and my bone cheefe all bace. (stanza 32)
>
> **W**iþstonde þou vice and ȝif þe to vertue;
> **T**o rightwys hope þou lifte vp þi corage;
> **A**nd for þy nedes if þou wilt pursue,
> **L**o humble prayer send on thi message
> **V**p to þi god; hit fayleth not his wage.
> **N**e doute þe noght þou schalt be sped full sone,
> For he refuseth neuere a lowely bone. (stanza 1001)

More than presenting just good evidence that Walton wrote Walton's *Boethius*, these acrostics also can be probed for their significance to our critical understanding of this very important Middle English work.[2] But first, however, a new question about signatures and authorship, arising from these selfsame stanzas, requires discussion.

It is odd that in each of these two acutely signatory stanzas a highly aware translator imposes the word *bone* onto the text when it is by no means necessitated by the source. The last two lines of stanza 1, 1m1, "Thus hath my disese distroyed al my delyte / And broght my blisse and my bone cheefe all bace," are the lament of a hapless Boethius-persona in the midst of his unenlightened woes. *[B]one cheefe* (good fortune), the opposite of *mischeefe*, is written as two words, thereby heightening each element. Then, at the close of the work, the end of stanza 1001 reads, "Ne doute þe noght þou schalt be sped full sone, / For he refuseth neuere a lowely bone." *Bone* here means "prayer," not to be refused by the Almighty, though it also carries a sense, perhaps, of a request to be granted by favor of a patron. In Walton's case, this patron was Elisabeth Berkeley, daughter of Sir Thomas Berkeley, fourth Lord Berkeley, and wife of Richard Beauchamp, earl of Warwick. Perhaps Walton is tipping her the wink, that is, "God refuses no humble request, so you shouldn't either, should you?"

Be that as it may, a further possibility is worth countenancing with regard to *bone*. Around 1402 the successor to John Trevisa, the renowned translator of Higden's *Polychronicon* and Bartholomaus Anglicus's *De proprietatibus rerum* ("On the Properties of Things"), was appointed as vicar of Berkeley: the symmetrically named John Bonejohn (or Bonjon). He would have been vicar, therefore, when the Middle English translation of Boethius was being commissioned and completed.[3] In John Smyth of Nibley's account of Berkeley family history, it emerges, allegedly, that Bonejohn played a part in the pro-Elisabeth camp in the great litigious battle against James Berkeley, the nephew and male heir of Thomas IV. According to Smyth, John Bonejohn ("who proved a false preist [*sic*] to the heir male of his said lord") claimed under oath in front of the Mayor of Bristol that Thomas had (ca. 1402–03) enfeoffed him and others of "the Castle lordship and hundred of Berkeley and of all his lands within the County of Glouc.," and, along with other lands/properties, of the Manor of Walton.[4] It would appear, then, that Bonejohn was involved (or, at least, it was made out he was involved) in legal stratagems to sign over Berkeley lands to others in order to squeeze out the male heir in favor, presumably, of Elisabeth. Bonejohn's alleged oath-swearing in the pro-Elisabeth camp offers a tantalizing link between Bonejohn and Thomas's daughter, which is especially tempting when we bear in mind the dedication of the translation of Boethius to Elisabeth Berkeley (see below), and also those two *bone*s in the two acrostic signatory stanzas. Bearing in mind that this is an age in which surnames multiply promiscuously, we must wonder inevitably about some connexion between John Bonejohn and John Walton. Could they be the same man? Is it not a bit suspicious that twice, in such specifically signatory coded stanzas, *bone* is added in a rhetorically emphatic position, intriguingly unrequired by the exigencies of translation?

And so, the question of Bonejohn's *Boethius* arises. If such a possibility were hypothesized, what further comment might then be offered about those two stanzas? First, one might say that the inclusion of two surnames perhaps provides a signatory belt and braces—a horizontal and vertical marking of textual territory and petition. Second, perhaps it might be a petitioning that Bonejohn was trying to make to Elisabeth Berkeley or Thomas IV about the enfeoffment and benefits accruing from the Manor of Walton? Or, by encoding these two names into his text, he conceivably was showing his gratitude for the enfeoffment, or reminding his patron(s) of his loyal legal service in this matter, and thereby identifying his literary personality as a matter for her/them? This, of course, is all conjecture.

What about the connectability or otherwise of Walton and Bonejohn? The manuscripts that identify the author as John Walton, canon of Osney, are two in number. The colophons in Oxford, Balliol College, MS 316A and in Oxford, Christ Church, MS 151 state identically: "Explicit liber Boecij de consolacione philosophie de Latino in Anglicum translatus per Johannem Waltoun nuper canonicum de Oseneye anno domini millesimo cccc^{mo} decimo."[5] As far as I know, there is no evidence that Bonejohn was such a canon. However, were these two manuscripts just assuming in their colophons (without really knowing for sure) that this Walton had to be a canon of Osney? Colophon writers could be forgiven if they wrongly assumed that the John Walton who wrote such an imposing work were a suitably authoritative canon. Other manuscripts generally refer to a chaplain called John, without the Osney attribution. Ralph Hanna repeats that "one can develop a fair list of chaplains named John Walton."[6] But one might say that such a proliferation of John Waltons would be beside the point if the one John Walton who mattered also happened to be John Bonejohn. On the other hand, and more importantly perhaps, it is not helpful to a pro-Bonejohn case (and this article does not take a Bonejohannine position) that no surviving manuscript colophons name him. Nevertheless, one must still remember that a number of medieval writers took care to sign their names into their texts in order to preempt colophonic loss and misattribution. Is this oddity one such case?

Whether or not this proves to be the inaugural publication in International Bonejohn Studies is not currently decidable. It must be said that there is no compelling external evidence that the two men were the same. Still, there remain not only those two *bones* in the two most signatorially sensitized *loci* of this text but also Bonejohn's apparent declaration that he was enfeoffed with the Manor of Walton and the partisan litigious link with the work's dedicatee and patron.

Whatever the merits and demerits of the conjecture about Bonejohn, the two *bones* invite further comment. Let us return, then, to the last two lines of Stanza 1, 1m1: "Thus hath my disese distroyed al my delyte / And broght my blisse and my bone cheefe all bace." According to the *MED*, *bon-chef* commonly means "good luck" or "happiness," and such a meaning is certainly present here. Inasmuch as Walton is a translator of great lexical wit and hermeneutic suggestibility, it also can be suspected that he was aware of the semantic possibilities of playing with *bone* and *cheefe*. *Bone* carries connotations of "good" and "the Good." The word *chef* in the *MED*, numbers among its senses, "outcome of events" but, more commonly, "chief," "sovereign or dominant power," and "the most important or principal part or factor." In this Boethian text, it is by no means fanciful to see *bone cheefe* as a calque of *summum bonum*. For the Boethius-persona's *bone cheefe* to be *all bace* is thus a philosophically telling oxymoron: a degradation and misplacing of the greatest Good (commonly identified also as God in centuries of Boethian tradition). The truest and highest meaning and nature of *bone cheefe* as *summum bonum* may have been forgotten by the benighted Boethius-persona, but it is available to the alert reader able to see through the tell-tale calque to the *summum bonum* beyond. This is sophisticated Boethian lexical wit on the part of Walton.

How does this sit with the partnering line at the end of the translation stint, "For he refuseth neuere a lowely bone"? Here *bone* (*MED bon*) is a prayer to God, which also has connotations of the kind of boon or petition one might seek of an earthly patron or dignitary. This line advertises confidently and hopefully that God will never spurn a humble prayer/petition. While the first *bone* is stuck in the powerless earthly lowness of a sunken good/happiness (and an unnaturally mislocated *summum bonum*), the closing *bone* rises from earth through the powerful lowliness of irrefusably humble prayer and is acceded to by God, the source and occasion of *bone cheefe* without peer. The trajectory from the opening *bone* to the closing one reenacts the (thoroughly Christianized) progress of the soul from earthly misery to acceptance by God.

A further important context for these two acrostic stanzas recently has been given greater sharpness by Brian Donaghey, Irma Taavitseinen, and Erik Miller.[7] Their article offers the appealing prospect that in the early printed edition of Walton's *Boethius* the acrostic dedicatory verses, which contain Walton's and Elisabeth Berkeley's names, are authorial. They argue compellingly that the 1525 Tavistock edition of Walton's *Boethius* (*STC* no. 3200), published by the Benedictine monk Thomas Richard, used Copenhagen Royal Library MS Thott 304 as a copy text. Not only is there close textual correspondence between the two, but it is also highly evident that MS Thott 304 was marked up as Richard's copy text.[8] Unfortunately, the manuscript lacks the beginning and the ending of the work that is found in the 1525 edition and is therefore without the dedicatory verses that contain the acrostics **ELISABET BERKELEY** and **IOHANNES WALTWNEM**. Ian Doyle has gone so far, however, as to suggest that Thott was a presentation copy for Elisabeth Berkeley, in which case we may conceive of these verses as being authorial (and even if this was not the copy, it may be related to it).[9] The dedicatory verses, then, may be read more confidently in the light of the rest of the work and, of course, Walton's signatory acrostic stanzas at the beginning and end of the translation. It should be borne in mind also at this juncture that Walton may have been following a particular Berkeley dedicatory precedent: Lucy Lewis has argued convincingly that Thomas Usk's celebrated acrostic in his *Testament of Love* was written for Margaret de Lisle/Berkeley, Elisabeth's mother.[10]

Fascinating contextual light of a rather different nature is shed on the business of authorial naming by a particularly relevant vernacular text, which, appositely enough, is a near-contemporary anonymous Middle English prose rendering of book 1 of the *Consolatio*, *The Boke of Coumfort*.[11] The prologue to this remarkable and important work discusses how Boethius's many names are a faithful corollary of his merits and authority. The question of the extent to which Walton himself draws upon a repertoire of (nameable) selves, moralized or otherwise (Walton, Bonejohn, "Sapient Orpheus"[12]), is a topic in its own right. What is of greater interest for our purposes here, however, is another aspect of the same passage of this prologue which, in expounding the gospel, posits a profoundly significant relationship between human names and divine grace:

> it is furste to wite for to put lekynge in reders of hit, that the auttour of this forsaide boke was callid be dyvers names, and that for gret praisynge of him. ffor as the wers a man is, the more unacordyngely it is, that he have any name for name aftur the douet hit puttes substaunce in a man the weche is refte hym be wise. Wherefore he schal worthily lose his name, as be open ensample in the gospel of the ryche man, that was cladde in purpul and bise. ffor thorutgh synne

> he was to be beryde in helle, as he that hadde lost the substaunce of grace, that schulde have kept hym therfro. Crist rehersede of hym no name, as if he hadde none.[13]

This exposition seems to allude to Luke 10:20: "rejoice that your names are written in heaven."[14] Being named and being subject to the grace of God are both part of the same thing; so names and grace, in this Boethian text, are conditions or signs of each other. Something comparable is the case with the self-naming in Walton's *Boethius*. Walton signs himself *literally* (i.e., in letters) and devotionally into his work. His name is a locus of petition for grace in the text. Whether the human audience knows it or not, this acrostic self-offering is addressed to, and will be judged by, the Almighty:[15]

> Sith all þi werkes ben open and expresse
> Vnto þe presence of þe iuge on hye
> Þat all þing doth beholde plenerlye. (stanza 1002)

Let it not, furthermore, be forgotten that Walton sees his translating as a service to his Christian God:

> So þat in schenschip and confusioun
> Of all þis foule worldly wrecchydnesse,
> He helpe me in þis occupacioun.
> In honour of þat sofferayn blisfulnesse. (stanza 9)

So, naming oneself in due humility in a literary labor devoted to God constitutes a form of offering one's soul up to God in hope. Awareness of this is helpful for a fuller reading of both Walton's acrostic anagrammatic stanzas and (below) the acrostic dedicatory verses:

> Collectis insequentibus cuius libet linee primis litteris / non solum Translatoris sed & transferri procurantis / nomina cum cognominibus / inuestigare poteris
>
> NOMEN Transferri procurantis.
> **E**uer more exalted be thou lord on hy
> **L**awly wyche of thy benygnyte
> **I**n flesshe and blodde aperyng wyllyngly
> **S**o pyteously were peyned on the tre
> **A**nd sufferest / that greuous was to the
> **Be** bledde wyth al thy blodde for mannes sake

Euer more exalted be thy maieste
Thyn hert blodde / oure raunson woldest þ^{u} make.

COGNOMEN.
Blyseful lorde I pray the hertely
Er I depart of thys mortalyte
Reskewe me fro my perylous enemy
Kepyng me fro hys cursed cruelte
Eternally to set my thought in the
Lust of synnes fully to forsake
Endles god wyche art bothe one & iii
Ynto thy cure for euer I me betake.

NOMEN Translatoris.
I yelde yow thankes lady Sapience
Of that thys worke ys to an ende ybrought
Haue ye the worshippe & the recompence
And I no dele / I haue deserued nought
None other lust desyre I in my thought
Ne nought coueyt I but your Influence
Eternally / so that I may be brought
Souereyn lady into your presence.

COGNOMEN Translatoris.
Wyth al my hert to do your reuerence
And seruyse / suche as of me may be wrought
Lawly vnder youre obedyence
To plesen yow yf I suffysed ought
Wyth al my hert / as euer I haue besoght
No thyng coueyt I of youre excellence
Eternally but that I may be brought
My souereyn lady in to your presence.[16]

These highly crafted verses subtly modulate petitionary convention in a self-consciously Christian-Boethian manner. The **ELISABET BERKELEY** stanzas address not Elisabeth but Christ. They do invoke her, however, in the highest possible company rather than brazenly addressing her directly and asking for mere earthly favor. The second, **BERKELEY**, stanza asks for its speaker to be rescued from the devil and advertises a commitment of the soul to the care of Christ. This prayer, insofar as it is specially marked with Elisabeth's name, might conceivably have been designed by Walton to appeal to her as her own personalisable text to be used and reused afterwards for her devotions. The first of the two **IOHANNES WALTWNEM** stanzas then edges nearer to addressing Elisabeth Berkeley by giving thanks and the credit for the work to the authoritative feminine figure of Lady Sapience. Lady Sapience is a flattering possibility as a hyperbolic designation for Elisabeth Berkeley. More importantly, in Lady Sapience ideas converge that are key to our understanding of what Walton is endeavoring to do. First, as *Sapientia*, that is, Wisdom, she is a force that has its origins in God. Indeed, the second person of the Trinity, the subject of the first two stanzas, is, in medieval (and later) theological tradition, identified as the Wisdom that proceeds from God the Father. So, Lady Sapience has a special connection with the second person of the Trinity, proceeding from the first two stanzas. It is significant too that, in like vein, in his preface to books 4 and 5, Walton waxes petitionary about the relationship between wisdom and God as governing principles for his work:

> To þe þat art þe welle of sapience,
> All-myghti lord, þis labour I comyt. (stanza 582, lines 1–2)

She is, of course, also reminiscent of Lady Philosophy, but is necessarily greater, for *Sapientia* is anterior to the (mere) discipline of Philosophy, being its governing source and rationale.

In the **WALTWNEM** stanza there is a palpable, eloquent commitment by the supplicating speaker to Lady Sapience. Interestingly, given that this is dedicatory or petitionary discourse, there is on the part of the supplicant a noticeable avoidance of asking for favor or appearing venal. He covets not her excellence for himself ("No thyng coueyt I of youre excellence"; stanza 4, line 6) but only her influence (stanza 3, line 6)—and to be in her "presence," the latter signaling his social status as that of attendant and his epistemological status as object. Also, a key mercenary term is conspicuous for its absence or suppression from these verses. The final two stanzas have eight "-ought" rhymes, and time and time again a reader suspects that "bought" must be about to be used, but this never happens. The unuttered "bought" presumably suggests this petitioner's lack of venality. In similar vein "recompense," in the third line of the third stanza, is offered somewhat unexpectedly to Sapience herself: normally in petitionary verses, payment goes in the other direction. Here, however, because any success the work has is due to Sapience, the offering-back is humbly made, a suitably Boethian twist on the redressing of all good to divine Wisdom.

This highly rhetoricized and markedly "eloquent" paratextual commitment to Sapience fulfils *par excellence* the Ciceronian desideratum of *sapientia et eloquentia*. These verses are not merely eloquent words containing wise matter, which is normally the way in which texts follow this ideal. Here, the verses *are* eloquence specifically addressed to, and governed by, *Sapientia*.[17] This aim of deploying eloquence under Christian wisdom is, of course, a central concern of the whole work, as the *prefacio translatoris* clearly advertises:[18]

> [. . .] to god I praye.
> So help me wiþ hys inspiracioun
> Þat is of wisdom boþe lok and keye. (stanza 2, lines 6–8)

These dedicatory verses and Walton's prefaces harmonize with each other in a highly particular Christian reconciliation of wisdom and eloquence. But how do we see these acrostic dedicatory verses and the two acrostic stanzas at either end of the translation as partnering each other in complementary acrostic gestures of self-naming?

In Boethian discourse, a human name is a thing of transience, associated with fleeting fame and vain attachment to reputation and earthly honor. It is suitably Boethian, then, that in the devotional verses this author's name is committed to the Divine and to *Sapientia*. It is also suitably and subtly Boethian, that in the stanzas at the beginning and end of the translation, Walton's name is broken up "literally," that is, into its constituent letters, and scattered and concealed in the Boethian text itself, where it may now neither be heard nor seen by humans, but known only by God beyond the realm of fortune. In their mode of earthly existence, the anagrams are (unless spotted) an unuttered presence in the text. These signatures, however, are subject to being utterable beyond human textuality through grace in heaven (cf. *Boke of Coumfort*). This gives a twist to "Paul Zumthor's seminal teaching that [. . .] 'the poet is placed in his language rather than his language in him.'"[19] Here, the poet places and hides himself in his language, but he also transcends the norms of language. Finally, Laurence de Looze has made an intriguing comment on medieval anagrams, that, to a significant extent, "exploitation of the paradox of presence and absence in anagrammatic structures anticipates much recent post-structuralist thought on the impossibility of recovering a referent outside textuality."[20] This is an interesting point; but here, through the anagrammatic acrostics of Walton, the transcendental self-referent, committed to divine wisdom, may not be recoverable by human textuality, but it may be recoverable by God.

NOTES

*I am grateful for the helpful comments of Chris Given-Wilson during the preparation of this essay.

[1] For Walton, see Boethius, *De Consolatione Philosophiae*, trans. by John Walton, canon of Oseney, ed. Mark Science, Early English Text Society o.s. 170 (London: Humphrey Milford, Oxford University Press, 1927). For the Vulgate *Consolatio*, I have consulted *Sources of the "Boece,"* ed. Tim Machan (Athens: University of Georgia Press, 2005), 26–223 (esp. 26 and 220–22).

[2] See Ian Johnson, "New Evidence for the Authorship of Walton's Boethius," *Notes and Queries*, n.s., 43 (1996): 19–21. For discussion of authorial signatures, and their manifestations as anagrams and acrostics, see Erik S. Kooper, "Signature and Art and the Art of the Signature," in *Court and Poet: Selected Proceedings of the International Courtly Literature Society (Liverpool 1980)*, ed. Glyn S. Burgess, with the assistance of A. D. Deyermond et al. (Liverpool: Cairns, 1981), 223–32, and Laurence de Looze, "Signing Off in the Middle Ages: Medieval Textuality and Strategies of Authorial Self-Naming," in *Vox intexta: Orality and Textuality in the Middle Ages*, ed. A. N. Doane and Carol Braun Pasternak (Madison: University of Wisconsin Press, 1991), 162–78.

[3] See *De Consolatione Philosophiae*, ed. Science, xlvii, and also John Smyth's account in *The Berkeley Manuscripts: The Lives of the Berkeleys, Lords of the Honour, Castle and Manor of Berkeley in the County of Gloucester from 1066 to 1618, with a Description of the Hundred of Berkeley and of its Inhabitants by John Smyth of Nibley*, ed. Sir John Maclean, 3 vols. (Gloucester, 1883–85), 2:22. My discussion is generally indebted to the extremely useful and important article by Ralph Hanna III, "Sir Thomas Berkeley and His Patronage," *Speculum* 64 (1989): 878–916.

[4] See Smyth's account in *The Berkeley Manuscripts*, ed. Maclean, 2:22 and 44.

[5] *De Consolatione Philosophiae*, ed. Science, xlii.

[6] Hanna, "Sir Thomas Berkeley," 901–02n36, in which he is referring to a review in the *Times Literary Supplement.*

[7] Brian Donaghey, Irma Taavitseinen, and Erik Miller, "Walton's Boethius: From Manuscript to Print," *English Studies* 80 (1999): 398–407.

[8] Ibid., 406–07.

[9] Ibid., 407.

[10] Lucy Lewis, "The Identity of Margaret in Thomas Usk's *Testament of Love*," *Medium Ævum* 68 (1999): 63–72.

[11] "*The Boke of Coumfort of Bois* [Bodleian Library, Oxford Manuscript AUCT.F.3.5]: A Transcription with an Introduction," ed. Noel Harold Kaylor, Jr. and Philip Edward Phillips, in *New Directions in Boethian Studies*, Studies in Medieval Culture 65 (Kalamazoo: Medieval Institute Publications, 2006), 223–79. This is a reedition of "The Boke of Coumfort of Bois," ed. Noel Harold Kaylor, Jr., Jason Edward Streed, and William H. Watts, *CarmP* 2 (1993): 55–104.

[12] See Ian Johnson, "Walton's Sapient Orpheus," in *The Medieval Boethius: Studies in the Vernacular Translations of "De Consolatione Philosophiae,"* ed. A. J. Minnis (Cambridge: Brewer, 1987), 139–68.

[13] "*The Boke of Coumfort*," ed. Kaylor and Phillips, 226–27.

[14] Revised Standard Version.

[15] For further detail and discussion, see Johnson, "New Evidence," 20–21, and, by the same author, "Placing Walton's Boethius," in *Boethius in the Middle Ages: Latin and Vernacular Traditions of the "Consolatio philosophiae,"* ed. Maarten J. F. M. Hoenen and Lodi Nauta (Leiden: Brill, 1997), 217–42, esp. 234.

[16] *De Consolatione Philosophiae*, ed. Science, xliii–vliv.

[17] A further measure of Walton's considerable artifice is exemplified in the manner in which last three lines of stanza 4 closely rework the final three lines of the preceding **IOHANNES** stanza.

[18] For further discussion of this in Walton, see Johnson, "Walton's Sapient Orpheus," passim.

[19] De Looze, "Signing Off," 163.

[20] Ibid., 175.

AN EDITION OF AN ENGLISH MANUSCRIPT

Henry Somerset and His Translation of Boethius's *Consolation of Philosophy*

Kenneth Hawley

DONATED TO THE BRITISH MUSEUM by More Adey in 1922, two volumes now known as Additional Manuscripts 40693A and B preserve the work of a man cryptically identified on the title page as "His Grace / Hxxxxx Duke of xxxxxxxx."[1] Dated 1693, the first book holds two pages of introductory comments by the translator himself, as well as twenty-eight pages containing "The Preface to The Comforts & Consolations of Philosophy,"[2] an English version of Petrus Bertius's Latin biography, *The Life of Boethius*, which had been published in various forms in 1620, 1633, 1640, 1649, 1668, 1671, 1680, 1695, 1721, 1744, 1751, 1798, 1823, and 1860.[3] The second book holds the duke's prosimetric translation of *De consolatione philosophiae*. In his 1996 essay on "The Post-Medieval English Translations of the *De Consolatione Philosophiae* of Boethius," Brian Donaghey identifies this otherwise anonymous translator as Henry Somerset, duke of Beaufort (1629–1700).[4]

The Life of Henry Somerset

Molly McClain's 2001 biography of Henry Somerset, entitled *Beaufort: The Duke and His Duchess*, characterizes his translation of the *Consolation* "as a way of reconciling himself to the capricious whims of fortune."[5] As a teenager, Henry had lived at Raglan Castle, which his grandfather had developed "into a centre for Welsh Catholicism,"[6] and he witnessed there the dangerous consequences of his family's commitment to the royalist cause. In the summer of 1646, Raglan Castle was reduced to rubble by Parliamentary forces,[7] and the property of the Somersets was soon forfeit. Then, in December of 1646, Henry's grandfather died and left him everything, but it was years before Henry knew the truth about his inheritance.[8] In 1651, he was spending much of his time petitioning Parliament for the return of the seized family lands, eventually making a personal appeal to Oliver Cromwell.[9] Between these negotiations and his own efforts to buy such properties back from Parliament, Henry eventually reestablished his family's position in the region. However, when his staunchly royalist father was imprisoned from 1652–56, it was dutiful Henry's responsibility to manage everything. It was then that he learned that he was supposed to have inherited his grandfather's fortune, and it was not until 1657, after a long court battle, that Henry actually received the little that remained of his family's wealth.[10] Not only did he have to make a convincing case that the money and jewels should be returned to him, but he also had to work around his unhelpful father and negotiate with his disgruntled aunt, who had betrayed him for what riches she could gain for herself.[11] Most of what had rightfully belonged to his family, Henry was forced to purchase, and most of what should rightfully have been his, he never received.

As if this turmoil were not enough, Cromwell's death in 1658 prompted Henry to exercise prudence and sit out the controversial political struggle; however, in 1659, when his wife involved herself in correspondence regarding the return of Charles II, their estate at Badminton was searched and a number of their servants arrested.[12] Henry himself was sent to the Tower of London from August until November.[13] In 1660, however, Somerset fully supported Charles II and soon served as both lord-lieutenant and MP. His success on the political scene throughout the 1660s was routinely compromised, however, by his father's stubborn interference, by his family's suspiciously deep Catholic roots, and by his wife's impolitic missteps. In the 1670s, though, he accumulated both wealth and power, sitting on the Privy Council from 1672 until 1689.[14] It was in the late 1680s, then, after a season of relative success and with the ascendancy of William III, that Somerset had to confront "his history of political opportunism," whereby his station had been secured by his flexibility as "an earnest young royalist, a loyal Cromwellian and a dutiful king's man."[15] Henry stood firm, stopping short of proclaiming the rule of William and Mary "rightful and lawful"; moreover, the oath of allegiance that he eventually offered was not accompanied by an explicit abjuring of James II, and so he was branded a non-juror.[16]

Henry Somerset, duke of Beaufort, had already experienced a good deal of upheaval in his life, but by the summer of 1689, he was undone, "removed from his position as lord president of Wales and lord-lieutenant of Monmouthshire, Gloucestershire, Herefordshire and Bristol" as well as from his many leadership roles in the county.[17] No longer on the Privy Council, he could do nothing to help those on the local level, and so the loss of power was as complete as it was swift. Cautious, then, about being perceived as a conspirator backing the cause of James II, Somerset had his lawyer keep him informed "whenever his name appeared in correspondence seized by the government."[18] Such discretion was warranted, for in 1691, the duke of Beaufort did show up in some of the documents taken from the residence of Lord Preston—a fellow disgraced nobleman who, as it happens, would have his own translation of the *Consolation* published in the year of his death, 1695, just two years after Somerset's version was copied out in 1693.[19]

Bertius's *Life of Boethius* and the Consolations of Christianity

The first volume of Somerset's work opens with the two-page introduction entitled "The Translator's Preface," where he offers an explanation of the project and seems concerned that his readership may not realize how important his source material is, that they may fail to appreciate the great debt owed by so many to Boethius's influential work:

> It will no doubt seem very strange to see a Translation now come out of a Book written near 1200 years ago (for it is near so long since the Author dyed) when Tis impossible, but that whatever is good in him must have been suck't out & deliver'd to us by Authors that have written since, so that If the date be not consider'd, it will seem stolen from those that indeed borrow'd it from him.[20]

It is worth returning to the source, then, and making this great text available to an English-reading audience, and so Somerset offers his version of the *Consolation*. He has translated his author out of respect, as well as out of a sense of responsibility to an intellectual heritage that a general readership might otherwise not understand or appreciate: "That is one great Reason of the Translator's publishing it to do Justice to this great man, & shew to those, that are not Masters of ye Latin Tongue, to whom it is they owe what is deliver'd to them by others."[21] Obligated, then, as a mediator and as an educator, to show his English audience what Boethius has bequeathed to the ages, he introduces them not only to the *Consolation* but also to its author, filling the first volume of this translation project with his rendering of Bertius's *Life of Boethius*.

Somerset's Translation of *The Consolation of Philosophy*

Since Somerset's work has not received much critical attention,[22] any assessment of his place within the literary tradition of Boethius in English is preliminary; however, it is fitting here to consider briefly the translation itself and its contribution to the tradition. Somerset's prosimetric version offers almost all of the Boethian *metra* in rhymed couplets, employing occasional quatrains (rhymed ABAB) in five of the poems. His metrical scheme is pentameter in all but four of the poems, which instead are in tetrameter, though some thirteen lines here and there happen to be a foot long or a foot short, and three lines appear as odd, missing a rhyming line with which to form a couplet. The lines do not follow a strict iambic scheme, with gaps in the generally iambic patterns filled in with occasional spondaic, trochaic, or pyrrhic feet. It is also perhaps worth noting that in the four instances in which Somerset's poems contain fourteen lines, he does not opt to fashion them as sonnets. His approach to the poetic portions of the *Consolation* seems rather utilitarian, then, rather than particularly creative or literary, as the routine use of couplets apparently offered him sufficient flexibility for rendering the sense of the metrical passages. Far from merely servicable, however, Somerset's work surpasses the ambitious but largely unsuccessful all-verse translation by Coningsby from 1664.[23] It is also both more complete and less didactic than Elys's unfinished prosimetric version from 1674.[24] In fact, the scope and quality of Somerset's work are really more on par with Preston's 1695 translation, although the latter was published and distributed with some success, having been met with positive reviews and later reprinted in 1712.[25] Perhaps, though, this version that was originally signed "Hxxxxx Duke of xxxxxxxx" is in the tradition of the influential translation from 1609 by the similarly mysterious I.T., whose text was included in the Loeb edition on Boethius from 1918–73.[26] Somerset's translation is not only complete and free of interpolated commentary, but also quite accurate, readable, and clear. Moreover, while Colville's 1556 edition gave readers a Latin text in the margins,[27] Somerset's includes the Bertius preface—an important artifact in its own right. Altogether, then, his two-volume work befits a project meant "to do Justice to this great man, & shew to those, that are not Masters of ye Latin Tongue, to whom it is they owe what is deliver'd to them by others."[28]

Editorial Method

This edition of London British Library, MS Additional 40693B offers the *recto* and *verso* notations in brackets along the left margin throughout. The lines of verse are marked by bracketed numbers placed along the right margin at five-line intervals, while the end of each prose line has been identified in brackets and thus included within the text rather than in the margin. The spelling remains unchanged, but an italicized character (such as a second "m") indicates the expansion of a macron in the manuscript. Other anomalies or insertions are described in the footnotes.

NOTES

[1] Henry Somerset, *The Preface to The Comforts & Consolations of Philosophy* (London, British Library, MS Additional 40693A, 1693), 1. However, the title page for the volume containing Somerset's translation of the *Consolation* identifies the translator only with the line, "by xxxxx"; *A Translation of Flav. Annicius Manlius Torquatus Severinus Boethius's Comforts & Consolations of Philosophy* (London, British Library, MS Additional 40693B, 1693).

[2] The title page for Somerset's translation of the Bertius preface uses an ampersand ("Comforts & Consolations"), whereas the title provided at the top of the first page of the preface reads, "The Preface / To the Comforts or Consolations of Philosophy." *The Preface to The Comforts & Consolations of Philosophy*, 4.

[3] Special thanks to Brian Donaghey for his help with these publication dates for the Bertius preface, as well as for his prior work on this translator, for his careful review of this edition, and for his helpful advice on Somerset's concerns regarding the Socinians.

[4] Brian Donaghey, "The Post-Medieval English Translations of the *De Consolatione Philosophiae* of Boethius, 1500–1800," in *The Medieval Translator/Traduire au Moyen Age*, ed. Roger Ellis and René Tixier (Turnhout: Brepols, 1996), 302–21.

[5] Molly McClain, *Beaufort: The Duke and His Duchess* (New Haven: Yale University Press, 2001), 11.

[6] Ibid., 12.

[7] Ibid., 16.

[8] Ibid., 21.

[9] Ibid., 19.

[10] Ibid., 22.

[11] Ibid., 22–23.

[12] Ibid., 29–30.

[13] Ibid., 31.

[14] Ibid., 101.

[15] Ibid., 191.

[16] Ibid., 191.

[17] Ibid., 191.

[18] Ibid., 192–193.

[19] Richard Graham, *Anicius Manlius Severinus Boethius, of the "Consolation of Philosophy"* (London: F.D., 1695). Preston's political fortunes, like Somerset's, rose in the 1680s, as he ascended to the position of Envoy Extraordinary at the court of Louis XIV (1682–85) and to Secretary of State in 1688, only to be stripped of all such honors in 1689 and coerced into offering a confession that would free him from imprisonment in 1691. See Walter Edwards Houghton, Jr., *English Translations of Boethius's "De Consolatione Philosophiæ" in the Seventeenth Century* (PhD diss., Yale University, 1931), 148–49.

[20] Henry Somerset, "The Translator's Preface," in *The Preface to The Comforts and Consolations of Philosophy*, 2.

[21] Ibid., 3.

[22] My own work on this text began with a dissertation, "The Boethian Vision of Eternity

in Old, Middle, and Early Modern English Translations of *De Consolatione Philosophiæ*," (PhD diss., University of Kentucky, 2007) where the translation was discussed briefly in an appendix. Having already developed an online version of the Somerset manuscripts using digital images of the microfilm, I produced, with the generous guidance and input of Harold Kaylor and Brian Donaghey, this print edition of the translation, first published in the 2011 volume of *Carmina Philosophiae*, the journal of the International Boethius Society.

[23] Harry Coningsby, *The Consolation of Philosophy* (London: James Flesher, 1664). Coningsby's project can be considered ambitious in terms of its attempt to render the entire *Consolation* as poetry, not in the sense that Coningsby sought literary acclaim, for in his prefatory remarks, the translator explains that he "put the brave and stout BOETHIUS into an English dress, which though ruder and courser then it should have been, is so much the more like his own Condition, and gives himself satisfaction, though not others : a poor satisfaction and pitiful comfort to a lost Family; yet he leaves it as a Relique of his Honest Mind, reposing his trust in Almighty God, who when he pleases can raise up those are cast down lowest : at least by this Posterity will know how, and in what unhappy Times, and for what cause it was the Storm came upon him and ruined him, and learn to decline the fondness of this mutable World, and seek the never-fading Treasure," ix.

[24] Edmund Elys, trans., *Summum Bonum, or an Explication of the Divine Goodness, in the Words of the Most Renowned Boetius* (Oxford: H. Hail for Ric. Davis, 1674). One telling instance of Elys's didacticism is his note to the reader, which characterizes Boethius's "Notions of the SOVERAIGN GOOD" as ideas that are not the sole domain of Boethius himself or of his translators and commentators but rather are "Common to Us with All those that LOVE the LORD JESUS in *Syncerity*," viii.

[25] Houghton notes the initial publicity that Preston's work received from a review in *Miscellaneous Letters* published for the week of November 21–28, 1694: "The noble Author of this Translation has therefore mightily oblig'd the World in presenting us with this Version; nay he has put a great Obligation upon Boetius himself; for this is an excellent Proof that this Work is answerable to its Title, and that it affords Consolations in the most sad Circumstances"; *English Translations*, 165.

[26] I.T., *Five Books of Philosophical Comfort, Full of Christian Consolation* (1609), ed. William Anderson (Carbondale: Southern Illinois University Press, 1963). As editor William Anderson explains in his introduction, I.T. may be the initials for "John Thorpe (fl. 1570–1610) who was architect to Thomas Sackville, Earl of Dorset. . . . [or] John Thorie, a Fleming who was born in London in 1568. . . . [or] a Jesuit called Michael Walpole" who may have passed the work through the London press either by pseudonymous initials or via a surrogate," 15.

[27] Published originally by John Cawood in 1556 (and reprinted in 1561), Colville's text was edited by Ernest Bax in 1897. Strangely, though, while Bax's edition does include the original marginal notes, it does not provide the Latin parallel text provided in the 1556 and 1561 versions, thereby eliding the possible pedagogical purposes of the original *mise en page*. The facing-page layout was apparently arranged by the printer John Cawood in consultation with Colville, for Cawood's preface to the edition (which Bax provides in his 1897 text) explains that the Latin source came from Colville himself: "to the mergentes is added the Latin, to the end that suche as delyghte in the Latin tonge may rede the Latin, accordynge to the boke of the translatour, whiche was a very olde prynte."

[28] Henry Somerset, "The Translator's Preface," in *The Preface to The Comforts and Consolations of Philosophy*, 3.

Boethius's *Comforts and Consolations of Philosophy*
Henry Somerset, Duke of Beaufort
1693

British Library, MS Additional 40693B

Edited by
Kenneth Hawley

[02r] **First verse of the first Booke.**

Lo I, who once did pleasant verses write
Am now, alas, forc't sad one's to endite,
Which the tor'n muses dictate to my quill;
Who[1] with true teares, my elegies doe fill,
These friends, at Least, no terrour could o'recome,
But they would bee companions of my doome,
And beeing the glory of my ages spring,
To mee some comfort, in my old age bring,
W^{ch}, now, hastned with ills, hath seiz'd on mee
And greefe, it's proper age will have mee see.
My head is couer'd wth untimely snow,
And my Lanke skinne too wide for mee, doth show,
O happy death, that doth not us destroy,
In youthfull yeares, when wee are fill'd wth joy
But com'st, when call'd, to ease us of our greefe,
When nothing else, can well afford releefe;
But now, alas, shee turnes away her eare,
Though often call'd, how deafe shee doth appeare
To miserable mortalls? & deny's,
(Hard harte) to close up, willing watry eyes.
Whilst faithlesse fortune fauour'd mee, shee then
Had like to have ouerwhelm'd mee, when,
I Loathest was, but now, that shee doth know,
Her coming, would but ridde mee of my woe,

[1] "Who" underlined here; "And" provided in the left margin, adjacent to line 4, as a possible replacement.

Shee suffer's Life (growne wearisome) to raigne,
W^{ch} serueth only to prolong my paine;
[02v] O friends why did you mee so often happy call?
Who fell, stood on no stable heighth at all.

First Prose of the first Booke.

Whilst I was thus entertaining my sad thoughts, & setting [1] forth my complaint, in such dolefull verse, there seemed to [2] stand over my head a woman of a most reverend Looke and [3] behauiour, with eyes more fiery, & piercing then womens [4] usually are, shee had a uery Lively collour in her cheeks, [5] & a body that show'd to have it's full strength & vigour [6] unexhausted, though she seemed so full of age, as that [7] shee could not possibly bee of our time. her stature was [8] uncertaine, For sometimes shee restrain'd herselfe wthin [9] the ordinary Limits of a womans heigth, & sometimes [10] againe, her head seemed to touch the sky, & when shee [11] had a minde to Lift it higher, it penetrated the heavens, [12] & stole it selfe from the sight of men. Her garments were [13] composed of uery fine thread, so artificially wrought, that [14] they could not weare out, wch as I afterwards understood from [15] her, shee had woven with her owne hands, whose Lustre such [16] a duskynesse, as use's to come upon old smoaky pictures, [17] had ternish't, through a carelesse neglect. In the lowermost [18] hemme or border of wch there was woven a Greeke P & on [19] the toppe the greeke Letter Q and betweene those two [20] Letters, there were certaine stepps or staires marked out, [21] in the manner of a Ladder, by wch there was a way to climbe [22] from the bottome Letter, to the uppermost, but some rude [23] & violent hands had toren her garment, & carry'd away **[03r]** what peeces they could of it. In her right hand, shee [1] held some little bookes, & in her Left, a scepter, but [2] when shee saw the poeticall muses about my bed [3] dictating words to my complaints, being highly incens'd [4] shee could not forebeare crying out, wth eyes inflam'd wth [5] anger, who is it that hath sufferd these Litle stage= [6] =playing strumpets to approach this sick man? Who [7] do not only bring no remedys, to asswage his greefe, but [8] on the contrary feed & nourish it; with a pleasing poyson. [9] these are they, that with the unprofitable thornes & [10] briars of affections, choake up & destroy y^{e} plentifull [11] corne & fruite of reason, bringing men only to bee [12] acquainted with, & accustom'd to theire disease, not [13] freeing them from it. If they had only with theire [14] smooth flatteries seduced one of the ignorant & un= [15] =profitable vulgar, I could have boren it wth more [16] patience, since there I should not haue lost my paines [17] & Instructions, but to withdraw from mee one yt hath [18] bin educated & nursed up in my Eliatick & Accademick [19] Scooles? But get you gon, you Sirenes, charming [20] euen to destruction, & Leaue this man to bee cur'd, by [21] my precepts. At this reproofe, that crew of poeti= [22] =cal muses, casting downe their heads, & by theire blush= [23] =es confessing theire shame, departed sadly out of the [24] roome & I, whose eyes were so dimn'd with a flood of [25] teares, that I could not know who this woman was, [26] that assum'd so imperious an authority, remain'd [27] **[03v]** astonish't, & fixing my eyes upon the ground, began silently [1] to expect what shee would do. Then shee com*m*ing[2] neerer to mee, [2] sate her selfe downe upon my bed, & obseruing the sadnesse & [3] dejection of my Lookes, wch by reason of my greife were cast [4] down upon the ground, shee began in these words to com= [5] =plaine of the trouble & perturbation of my mind. [6]

2d Verse of the 1st Booke.

Alas how dull & stupid is hee growne?
How sadly meane & earthly cares do drowne
His drooping spirits, of theire Light bereft,
(Which hee ha's now for forraigne darknesse Left)
And doth as often that false guide pursue,
As th'winds of earthly thoughts his greife renew,
Hee who before was wont to soare, & fly
With greatest freedome through ye starry sky,
Searching all the curious hidden wayes
Of th'heavens, & even ye sunnes bright rayes,
Was us'd to view, & the pale frozen moone
Was us'd to visit, nor content alone
With that discovery, his active mind
Must the various courses also find
Of all the other severall Lesser starres
Through all theire orbes, & in theire golden carres
Triumphantly did ride & brauely brought
Them home his owne, & hee who also sought
[04r] With suitable successe the reason why,
The winds so much the rocky shores do ply,

[2] Here and throughout, the italicized second "m" indicates the expansion of a macron in the manuscript.

Of the enraged seas, what spirit move's
The stable earth, why welcome Phebus Loue's
To rise so bright & glorious in the east,
Sinking againe at night into the west=
=Terne maine, who furnishe's y^{e} pleasant howers
Of spring, & who y^{e} teaming earth wth flowers
Delightfully adornes, & makes the yeare
So full of grapes, in autumne to appeare,
Bring still us'd to search & dive into
Natures most hidden causes, & undo
The mistery, hee poore & meanely now
(His light being quite put out) is forc't to bow
His Loaded neck wch weighty chaines oppresse
Unto the foolish earth, whence no redresse
Can come, & where no man could euer finde
A cure, for the Least trouble, of his minde.

2^{d} Prose of the 1st Booke.

But (said shee) it is now rather time to apply a remedy [1] then to expostulate. Then Looking stedfastly upon mee [2] shee us'd these words: Are you then hee, y^{t} being suckled [3] & nurs'd up with our milke, & who with the nourishment [4] you had from Us, had attain'd a manly strength, & were [5] furnish't with such armour, of proofe, that (had you not [6] first volontarily throwne it away) would have defended [7] **[04v]** You against all stroakes of fortune whatsoeuer? do you [1] not know mee? Why are you silent? Is it shame & con= [2] =fusion, or astonishment that is the cause of it? I had [3] rather it were shame, but (by what I perceaue) it is a= [4] =stonishment, that stupify's you. Then seeing mee not [5] only silent, but absolutely dumb, shee put her hand gently [6] to my breast, & said, there is no danger (though) hee is [7] only in a Lethargy, the common disease of deluded minds, [8] hee ha's only a little forgot himselfe, hee will quickly come [9] to himselfe againe, if it bee true, that hee euer did indeed [10] know Us, wch that hee may, let us cleanse his eyes, that [11] are now clouded with the mist of worldly things; hauing [12] thus said, taking a pleate of her garment, shee with it [13] wiped away the teares, that my eyes were drown'd in. [14]

3^{d} Verse of the 1st Booke.

Then the darke mists forthwith my eyes forsooke,

And they as soone their wonted vigour tooke;
So, when the heauens are overcast
With clouds brought thither by a southerne blast
The Sunne lie's hid, & starres not being come
'T'afford theire Light, in that great plannets roome,
A dismall night ouer the earth is spread,
If Boreas then being rous'd off of the bed
Hee lies on, in his Thracian den, gets out
And hurrying all those swolne clouds about
Chaseth away that night, & restore's day,
(Which was imprison'd) Phebus doth display
[05r] His rayes more glorious then before, and
Brandishing his beames, make's people stand
Admiring, of that suddaine Light,
Which in an instant vanquish't night.

3d Prose of the 1st Booke

The clouds of my sadnesse being thus dispers't, I came a litle [1] to my selfe, & began to haue a minde to know the face of my [2] Physitian, & hauing to that end fixed my eyes upon her, whom [3] should I see, but my deare Nurse who had bred mee up from [4] my tendrest yeares (Philosophy) what is it then said I to [5] her, O thou mistresse of all vertues, that hath brought thee [6] downe from thy high seate into this solitary place of my exile? [7] Is it that thou ha'st a minde to bee inuolv'd in my guilt, and [8] haue thy share of the false accusations that are laid to my [9] charge? Were it just (said shee) that I should forsake my [10] scollar at such a time as this, & not beare my parte of the [11] burden, wch is Laid upon him, out of a hatred to my name. [12] Would it become Philosophy to suffer an innocent person to [13] bee unaccompany'd in such a journey? all the world would[3] conclude mee [14] guilty, & that I were startled at the accusations brought against [15] mee, as at a new thing, that I had not forseene? when alas, [16] 'tis knowne, that this is not the first time that wisdome hath [17] bin persecuted & slander'd by ill men. Have wee not had [18] many conflicts even before the times of Plato, with rashnesse [19] & folly, and did not his master Socrates is his dayes, by my [20] assistance, become victorious ouer an unjust death?

[3] "would" added here, inserted above "conclude" and marked with a subscript caret and a vertical line between "world" and "conclude" in the manuscript. Throughout, such insertions are indicated by the caret and vertical line.

whose [21] inheritance, whilst the Epicureans, the Stoicks, & y^{e} rest, would [22] haue deuided, & shared amongst themselues, & forced mee against [23] my will to haue gon with them, as parte of theire booty, in [24] **[05v]** Strugling, they tore the garment, I had made with my owne [1] hands, & taking euery one a parte of it, they went away, be= [2] =leeuing they carry'd mee entirely with them, & the foolish [3] vulgar, seeing them haue some raggs of mine, & therefore [4] thinking them to bee my followers, not a few were by that [5] mistake seduced & o'rethrowne. So that if thou ha'st not [6] bin acquainted with the exile of Anaxegorus, the poisoning of [7] Zeno, & the torments of Socrates, (they being forraigne, & remote, [8] both in relation to time & place) Yet thou cans't not but haue [9] heard of Canius of Seneca, & of Soranus, whose memorys are [10] both recent, & full of glory, whom nothing brought to y^{e} slaugh= [11] =ter, but that being bred up in our scooles & hauing suck't in [12] our principles, they appear'd unlike, & therefore were obnox= [13] =ious to the wicked. And it is no wonder to see Us tos't & tumbled [14] by the violence of tempests in the bitter sea of this world, when [15] our cheefest aime & designe is to displease wicked men, of whom [16] although the army bee uery greate & numerous, yet is to bee [17] contemn'd, it not being gouern'd by any certaine Leader, but [18] hurry'd to & fro, by the uncertainty of errour, & if at any [19] time it chances to take the feild, & come in array against Us, [20] (as being the stronger) Our Leader presently draw's his forces into [21] a strong hold, & whilst they busy & amuse themselues, in the [22] ouercomming & carrying away of Trifles, wee Laugh at their [23] folly, in being fond of those unvalewable toyes, being in our [24] strength secure, from the fury and tumults of the multitude, & [25] impregnably fortify'd against the assaults of madnesse & folly. [26]

4th Verse of the 1st Booke

Whoever is resolv'd & unconcerned can
Looke downe on fate, under his feete below
[06r] Who either fortune feele's unmou'd, that man,
Let stormes & tempests nere so roughly blow,
Seas threat the sky, nay should Vesuvius cast
Fire through it's broken chimneys, Lightning blast
All things about him, he'el'e his post maintaine,
And render all attempts against him vaine.
Wherefore are cruell tyrants feared then?
Who rage without a Power to hurt such men.

Hope nor feare nothing, & thou soone wilt show
How much without a power to hurt, they raue,
Thou wilt disarme them so, making them know
Thou dost not valew if they kill, or saue;
But hee that's base enough to hope or feare
And stand's not stedfast in a constant minde
Hath throwne away his sheeld & must then beare
The chaine wth wch their slaues they draw, & binde

4th Prose of the 1st Booke.

Are you sencible (said shee) of these things, do they make [1] an impression in your minde, or are you (as the greeke prouerb [2] hath it) as Litle concern'd, as an Asse is at ye hearing of a harpe? [3] Why do you weep? why do you shed so many teares? if you do [4] expect any helpe from yr Phisitian it is necessary you should [5] discouer yr disease; Then I taking courage, & gathering all [6] my strength together, began thus, Is it necessary for mee to [7] acquaint you with what is so notoriously knowne, as ye sharp= [8] =nesse & cruelty of fortune towards mee? doth not the very Lookes [9] of this place mooue you? Is this the Library you had chosen [10] as a certain mansion for yr selfe, in my house? where remaining [11] **[06v]** with mee, you did so often discourse to mee of the knowledge of [1] divine & humane things? was this my habit, or these my Lookes, [2] when I us'd with yr help to scrutanize & diue into the secrets [3] of nature? when you did endeauour to forme & suite my manners [4] and the whole gouernment of my Life after the example of that [5] heauenly order? are these the rewards of hauing follow'd and [6] obey'd you? You then confirm'd by the authority of yr owne [7] mouth, that sentence of Plato, that those Com*m*onwealths would [8] be happy where either the studdyers of wisdome rul'd; or [9] where the rulers hapned to studdy wisdome. You did also [10] by the mouth of the same person declare, that it was neces= [11] =sary that good men should desire the gouernment of ye Com*m*on= [12] =wealth, Least the gouernment of Cittys, being Left in ye hands [13] of ill men, they should introduce wickednesse, & bring destruc= [14] =tion upon the good. I following this authority, desired to [15] put that in practise for the publiq*ue*[4] good, wch I had Learn't [16] in private, & at Leasure, from you, You & hee that plac't [17] you in the minds of wise men, (God)

[4] Here and below, the italicized "ue" indicates the expansion of an abbreviation in the manuscript.

know & can beare mee [18] witnesse, that, that consideration alone, & a desire to do good [19] to good men, brought mee to bee a magistrate, & hence it is yt [20] there hath bin continuall disputes & quarrells betweene bad [21] men & mee, the satisfaction of my owne conscience, alwayes [22] making mee despise the anger of powerfull men, wheneuer [23] the maintaining of right was in question; How often [24] haue I resisted & withstood Conigastus, when hee invaded [25] the rights & fortunes of poore defencelesse people? How often [26] haue I hindred Triguillas provost of the Kings house from [27] compleating injuries hee had begun to do, & from enjoying the [28] benifit of those hee had already don? How often by [29] **[07r]** interposing my authority have I protected mistrable people, [1] whom, the unpunisht avarice of barberous men in power, did [2] continually vex wth calumnys & slanders. Neuer did any person [3] by what meanes soeuer draw mee from what I esteem'd just, to [4] do any injury. When I saw the fortunes & riches of ye Provinces [5] become a prey to the rapine of particular persons, or swept [6] away by publiq*ue* taxes & impositions, I was alwaies as much [7] concern'd for it, as those that suffer'd. When in the time of [8] that sore & bitter famine, there was establish't so greeuous a [9] coemption, as that it was apparent that the Province of [10] Compania, would bee greatly damnified, if not wholly ruin'd by [11] it, I took up the cudgells against the provost of ye Pretorium, [12] for the publiq*ue* good, contended with him before ye King concerning [13] it, & procur'd that it should not bee impos'd or exacted. The [14] wealth of Paulinus (a man that had bin Consul) I preseru'd [15] out of the jaws of the officers of the Kings pallace, who had [16] already in hope devour'd it. And Least the punishment of [17] a false accusation already judg'd, should fall wrongfully upon [18] Albinus another consular man, I expos'd my selfe to the hate [19] of Cyprian the informer. Was not this d'you thinke enough [20] to beget great animosities & hatred against mee? But as I procured [21] the ill will of these, one would thinke, I should haue bin ye more [22] secure from others, since for the Loue of justice I Lost that which [23] else would haue bin my security, the fauour of the courtiers, by [24] whose accusations, I am now condemn'd, one of which number, [25] namely Basilius, formerly turn'd out of the Kings seruice, [26] was forc'd by reason of his debts & pouerty to become my accuser, [27] and as for Orpilio & Gaudentius my two other accusers, they [28] were persons condemn'd to exile by the Kings sentence, for their [29] numberlesse treacheries, & frauds, but resoluing not to obey the [30] **[07v]** Kings decree, they tooke sanctuary, wch being made knowne to ye [1] King, hee commanded them to depart by a prefixt day out of Ravenna [2] upon paine of being marked in the foreheads, with hot irons, to w^ch [3] just seuerity what could have bin added? Yet these men the same [4] day, had theire accusations against mee receaued & credited, what [5] then shall wee say, did my ayme & studdys deserue this? or did the [6] precedent condemnation of those men render their accusations [7] just, & to bee credited? Is it possible, that fortune should not bee [8] asham'd of this? mee thinks if shee bee not so, for ye innocence [9] of the accused, yet shee should bee so at least for ye meanesse of [10] the accusers. But what is the crime wee are accus'd of? Wee [11] are said to haue desired the safety of the Senate, would you know [12] how? wee are accus'd to haue hindred the informer from carrying [13] those Letters, that would haue render'd the Senate guilty of high= [14] =treason. What is your opinion in this case, shall I deny the [15] crime for feare of shaming you, that bred mee? No, I did desire [16] the Senates safety, & shall neuer Leaue to do so, shall I confesse? [17] but the endeauours to preuent the accuser will hereafter cease. [18] Shall I call the desire of preseruing that noble order of men a [19] crime? truly by their decrees concerning mee, they haue made [20] it a kind of one. But folly & impudence, wch alwayes fight's w^th, [21] & is false to it selfe, cannot change the merit of things. neither [22] do I thinke it Lawfull for mee (according to the opinion of Socrates) [23] either to conceale the trueth, or to giue my assent to a lye. But [24] whether it be so or no, I leaue it to you, & to all wise men to judge, [25] the whole series of wch affaire, Least the truth of it should be hid [26] from posterity. I haue committed to writing, that it may be remembr'd. [27] As touching those forged Letters by wch I am accused, to haue hoped for [28] the liberty of Rome, what need I speake? the forgery of wch would haue [29] openly appeard, if I had had the Liberty (wch in all cases is allow'd, & [30] **[08r]** sway's most) to haue crosse examin'd my accusers. For indeed what [1] Liberty is there to bee hoped for? I would to God any were, I would [2] haue answer'd in Canius his words, who being examin'd by Cajus [3] Cæsar (Germanicus his sonne) concerning his being privy to a plot [4] against him, answer'd, If I had knowne it, you neuer had. In w^ch [5] thing sorrow hath not so stupify'd my scences as to make mee [6] complaine, that ill people dessigne, & Lay ambushes against vertue, [7] but I cannot but wonder how they come to bee able to effect what [8] they dessigne, for the willing & dessigning of an ill thing proceeds [9] from the deprauednesse of our nature, but to bee able to effect what [10] wee wickedly propose to our selues against innocency (God Looking [11] on) seemes monstrous & incredible. wch made one of your friends

[12] not improperly say, If there bee a God, how happen's all this [13] ill, if there bee none, how come's so much good? but it was [14] meete, that those wicked men that seeke the blood of all [15] good people, & the wholl Senate, should desire also my destruc= [16] =tion, whom they alwaies saw stickling for the defence of both. [17] But did wee deserue the like from the Senatours themselues? [18] You cannot but remember, for you were alwaies with mee, and [19] directed mee in whateuer I was to doe, or say, that at Verona [20] when the King being greedy of a generall slaughter & destruction, [21] did intend to extend Albinus his crime & Indictment of high [22] treason to the whole Senate, how I did with my owne hazzard de= [23] =fend the innocency of that whole body. You know I speake nothing [24] heere, but truth, & that to this hower I neuer brag'd of it. For [25] mee thinkes the inward satisfaction of ones owne conScience is [26] Lessen'd as often as any person by mentioning the good hee doth, [27] receaue's the reward of fame. But you see what euent my inno= [28] =cency hath, insteed of the rewards of true vertue; I receaue the [29] punishment of a false crime. Now what open confession or [30] undeniable proofes of the highest crimes did ever meete with [31] Judges so agreeing in severity, that either the errour of mans [32] judgement, frailty of his nature, or the uncertaine condition of all [33] **[08v]** mens fortune, did not relent & induce at least some of them to [1] pitty & compassion? If I had bin accused to haue design'd the [2] burning of Churches & holy places, & cutting ye throats of all the [3] preists, & of murdering all good men, Yet by the Law I ought not [4] to be punish't, except present, confessing, or convicted. Now, being [5] five hundred miles distant, without opportunity to defend my selfe, [6] I am proscrib'd & condemn'd to dye for my propension to preserue [7] the Senate. O men worthy to haue no man guilty of ye Like crime[5] [8] of wch they themselues confesse the dignity & worth, in going about [9] to darken it, by mingling with it for an allay some false accusations [10] of other crimes, falsely affirming that out of an ambition of being [11] in high places, & of possessing honours & dignities, I had fouled & [12] polluted my conscience with sacriledge, when (God know's) that [13] thou that art planted & fixed in mee has't long agoe driven out of [14] my mind all desire of earthly things, in whose presence, there is [15] no roome nor leaue for Sacriledge to enter, for thou didst continually [16] instill into my eares & thoughts that excellent saying of Pythagoras [17] Men shall serve God, not Gods. Nor was it convenient much lesse [18] necessary for mee to make use of the helpe of

[5] "hereafter," inserted here above "crime" but stricken through twice.

[6] "&" here at the end of the line mistakenly repeated at the beginning of the next line.

those vilest spirits, whom [19] thou hadst brought to that excellence as to bee like unto God, & besides, [20] the innocent & secret closet of my house & harte (my wife) & ye company [21] of my honest and faithull friends, together with my father in Law Symachus [22] both holly, & worthy even to bee held in equall veneration wth thy selfe, will [23] cleere mee from any Suspition of that nature. But O malitious [24] wickednesse, they that accuse mee make Phylosophy an accessary, &[6] [25] judge mee therefore to bee Likely to haue committed these crimes, [26] because I haue bin indued with thy precepts, & instructed in thy [27] manners. And thus it doth not only suffice, that the reverence of [28] thy name, doth not availe mee, but the prejudice of my accusation [29] must wound thee. And there is this accesse to my misfortunes, [30] that the generality of people do not consider the merit of things [31] in themselves, but the event of fortune, & judge hapy-nesse in [32] this world the only signe of innocence, & of Gods fauour and [33] **[09r]** protection, which is the cause that the good opinion of men is the [1] first thing that forsake's those that are unfortunate. I am Loath [2] to mention or call to mind, the seuerall unjust censures & slanders [3] cast upon mee by the people, only this I shall say, that it is the [4] highest degree of misfortune, & euen the worst that fortune can do [5] that when there is a crime Laied to the charge of miserable people, [6] they are thought really to deserue, what they are seene to suffer. [7] Yet behold mee thrust out of all my goods & possessions, & even [8] the company of good men, deprived of all honnours & dignities, [9] & for that reason of my good name also, suffring punishments [10] for my good deeds, Mee thinkes, I now see the receptacles & shops [11] of wicked men (where they forge theire mischeife) abound wth Ioy [12] & gladnesse. [Mee thinkes I see][7] the most desperate & Lost vil-laines [13] contriving new dessignes, & forging new accusations against [14] innocent people, Mee thinkes I see all good men in feare & [15] consterna-tion by the[8] terrour of my example, [Mee thinkes I see][9] wicked men incited [16] by impunity & rewards, to dare to performe all manner of Crimes, [17] & in*n*ocent[10] people not only deprived of security, but of Leaue to [18] defend themselues. Is it not then time to cry out. [19]

[7] "Mee thinkes I see" scratched out; "x" written above to identify the phrase with the "x" that is inserted between "example," and "wicked" a few lines below.

[8] "the" inserted here.

[9] "*" inserted here to mark where the phrase "Mee thinkes I see" from above should be relocated.

[10] Here and throughout, the italicized second "n" indicates the expansion of a macron in the manuscript.

5th Verse of the 1st Booke.

O maker of the heavenly Orbes
Who art still fixed to thy throne
Who with a Law the heavens curbes't
And turns't them with thy arme alone.
Thou mak'st sometimes the Moone to shine
And meeting at full her Brothers beames
Hide all those Lesser starres of thine
And sometimes stopping of the streames
Of Light, by beeing nearer to
Her Brother, her pale Light to Loose
[09v] And Hesper thou dos't order so
That hee the Evening first doth close,
Then rise's pale ith'morne agen
And the Sunns Lucifer is call'd
Thou mak'st the days bee shorter when
The winter make's the trees all bal'd
Thou dos't take back the houres of night
When the hot sum*m*er daye's appeare
And 'tis also by thy might
That all the seasons temper'd are.
Thou makest Zephirus to restore
The Leaues wch Boreas blew away
And makest Sirius, nurse that Store
Of Corne, whereof the seed Acture did Lay
Nothing's absolv'd from it's old Law
Nor euer act's out of it's Spheare
O, why, O Ruler, dos't not awe
And force mans nature so to steere.
Why dost thou suffer fortune so
Blindly, to order our affaires,
That innocents should only know[11]
The paines wch th'wicked[12] ought to beare.
For Whilst the bad sit on high thrones
And trample good men under feete

[11] "only know" underlined; "undergo" written above line 31 as an alternative.

[12] "punishments wch ill men" written above line 32 as a possible replacement for "paines wch th'wicked."

Whils't hidden vertues's Left forlorne
Or the reward of vice doth meete,
Theire perjuries do them no harme
Nor theire deceipts dawb'd 'ore wth Lies
[10r] For them, when need is, Kings doe arme,
And all theire Subjects with them rise.
O thou, that knit'st the bonds of things,
Looke downe, upon th' unhappy earth,
And what to men, such sorrow brings
Who are of it a parte by birth
Wee are sore shak't by fortunes stroake,
And in her Sea wee are so tos't,
That 'lesse by thee, her strength bee broke,
Wee must in it, of force bee Lost.
O, Rule us in such steddy course wee pray,
As thou the heauenly orbes dos't sway.

Prose the 5th of the 1st Booke

When I had with a continu'd Sorrow sob'd out these Verses, Shee [1] with a smiling countenance, not at all moou'd with my complaint, saide [2] thus. When I saw you so sad & shed so many teares, I presently knew [3] you to bee miserable, & a banish't man, but did not know how remote [4] your Exile was, 'till you y^{r} selfe told mee, but now I finde y^{o} are not [5] expell'd y^{r} Country, but of y^{r} selfe haue wander'd out of it. Or if you [6] had rather been thought to haue bin driven out, 'tis you haue driven [7] your selfe out. For it was neuer in the power of any other to do it. [8] For if you will but remember what countryman you are, you will finde [9] you are not a Citizen of that Comonwealth wch is Like Athens gouern'd [10] by a multitude, but of that Kingdome that is gouerne'd by God alone, [11] who doth not delight in the expulsion & banishment of his subjects, [12] but in the enjoyment of theire Company & the number of his Cityzens. [13] To bee gouern'd by whose reignes, & to obey whose justice, is y^{e} perfect= [14] =este freedome. You are not ignorant of the most antient and [15] firmest Law of that Kingdome, by wch it is ordain'd, that it [16] shall neuer bee Lawfull to banish any man out of it, that had [17] rather make his abode in it. So that whoeuer is once truely wthin [18] those walls, need neuer feare hee can deserue banishment. [19] **[10v]** But then whoeuer desist's from desiring to bee a citizen there, leaue's [1] also to deserue to bee one. Therefore 'tis not so much this place, as y^{r} [2] Lookes, that mooue mee, for 'tis not the walls of y^{r} Library richly adorn'd [3] with Ebony & crystall, that I looke after, but y^{r} mind, in wch I did not [4] place my bookes, but that wch only renderd my bookes of any valew, the [5] sentences, that were in them. You haue said a great deale & truly [6] of y^{r} owne merit towards the publike, and yet but a little in respect [7] of what you haue don. You haue mention'd what truly & w^{t} falsely [8] hath bin Laide to y^{r} charge. You haue also touch't upon the frauds [9] & deceipts of y^{r} accusers, wch even the com*m*on people are satisfy'd & [10] talke enough of. You have blam'd the unjust act of the Senate. You [11] haue complayn'd & show'd y^{r} concerne for the underseru'd prejudice [12] I have receau'd by y^{r} accusations. At Last you haue fallen seveerely [13] upon fortune, complaining that shee doth not giue just rewards to [14] peoples merits, and in the close your angry muse hath beg'd, that [15] the same peace & Order, wch gouerne's heauen, should gouerne the [16] earth, also. Now because so many tribulations haue assaulted y^{o} [17] together, & tumultuously moou'd y^{r} passions, & that greife, anger, [18] & sadness, haue so seiz'd upon you, as that I do not now looke upon [19] you in a temper to endure strong remedies, I shall for the present use [20] milder ones, wch may mollify & soften those passions (now swolne into [21] a hardnesse, by the flux of vexations & troubles into y^{r} mind) in such [22] a manner as that they may bee capable of receauing wth a more gentle [23] hand those strong remedys I shall hereafter apply. [24]

Verse the 6th of the 1st Booke

When the hot Sunne in Cancers house doth dwell
And that the planet wth that heate doth swell
Hee who to th'earth should Largely Lend his corne
Would finde himselfe deceaued in the returne
And must for akornes unto Oakes repaire.
Search not the wood for violets, when th'ayre
[11r] The Freezing North wind strongly doth possesse,
Nor thinke i'th'spring, wth cou'tous hand to presse
The ripen'd grapes, if wine th'art fond to haue,
To Autumne the God Bacchus that gift gaue,
To every time God hath it's charge assign'd
And not to change hee hath them all enjoyn'd
And hee who Leaue's that Order will not finde
That the event will answer to his minde.

Prose the 6th of the 1st Booke.

Suffer mee therefore in the first place with a few questions to sound & [1] find out the state & temper of yr mind, that I may judge what method it [2] will bee best to take in yr cure. Aske mee (said I) what you will, and [3] I will answer, then (said shee) tell mee, do you beleive this world is gov-ern'd [4] by meere chance, & accident, or do you thinke it hath a rationall gouernment? [5] I reply'd, I can no way thinke, that so certaine things, & so orderly [6] can bee mooued by rash chance & fortune, but know very well, that God, [7] who was the maker of it all, doth guide & gouerne his owne worke, the [8] trueth of wch opinion, I never shall bee beaten out of. So it is (said [9] shee) & you just now declared as much in yr verse. For where yo com= [10] =plain'd that man alone was not taken care & prouided for by Almighty [11] God yo did as good as say you doubted not but that all other things were [12] gouernd by reason. Now truly I cannot but admire, that holding fast so [13] true & sound an opinion, you can bee sick. But let us search deeper, [14] for certainely there is something wanting, thô I know not yet what it is. [15] Tell mee, since you do not doubt but that it is God that gouernes ye world, [16] what you conceaue hee gouerne's it by; I hardly (said I) understand yr [17] question, and therefore shall not take upon mee to giue yo an immediate [18] answer. I thought (reply'd shee) there was something wanting, by wch [19] breach & defect the disease of perurbation & disquietnesse hath got into [20] yr mind. But tell mee do you remember what is the end of all things, & [21] to what the dessigne & intention of nature tend's. I remember (said I) [22] to haue heard it, but sadnesse hath so dull'd my memory, that I cannot [23] **[11v]** at present call it to mind. Do you know (said shee) from whence all [1] things proceed? I do, (said I,) from God. Then how is it possible (said shee) [2] since you know the begining of things, that you should not know ye end? [3] But this is the custome of these perturbations of the mind, they haue [4] strength enough to remooue a man out of his place, but not wholly to [5] extirpate his knowledge, or teare him absolutely from himselfe: But [6] pray, answer mee one thing more, do you remember that you are a man? [7] How is it possible (said I) I should forget that? I do. Can you [8] then tell what man is (said shee)? Is your question (said I) whether [9] I know my selfe to bee a rationall & mortall creature? if it bee, [10] I do know & acknowledge my self to bee one. Did you neuer know [11] your selfe to bee any thing else? No, I reply'd. Now I know (said shee) [12] another maine cause of yr disease, (you have lost ye knowledge of your [13] selfe) wch hath giuen mee the meanes at least to giue an accompt of yr [14] Sicknesse, if it hath not open'd mee a doore for y^{r} recouery. For your [15] being blinded & confounded with the forgetting of y^{r} selfe, made you [16] greeue for y^{r} being banish't, & for the Losse of y^{r} goods, & because you [17] know not the end of things, you beleive wicked and dishonest people [18] to bee happy & powerfull, & because you haue forgot, how the world is [19] gouern'd, you conceaue things are hudled to & fro by the single guidance [20] of chance, & fortune. Great truly & dangerous are the causes of your [21] disease, enough not only to cause sicknesse, but death it selfe. But thanks [22] to the author of health, nature hath not yet quite abandon'd you. [23] There remaine's yet a roote of health in you, wch is the true opinion [24] you haue, that the gouerment of this world is not submitted to the [25] rashnesse of chance & accidents, but to the guidance of the divine [26] reason; feare therefore nothing, I do not doubt, but this small [27] sparke will produce the fire of Life in you. But because it is [28] not yet time to use stronger remedys, and that the nature of [29] mens minds is such, that as often as they cast off true opinions, [30] they take up false ones, from whence so great a mist of unquiet= [31] =nesse doth arise, as that it blind's & confound's theire insight [32] into things. I shall first endeauour wth slight remedys to attenu= [33] =ate that mist, to the end, that the darknesse of deceiving affections [34] being disperst, you may come to see & know the splendour of [35] true Light. [36]

[12r] Verse the 7th of the 1st Booke.

For when black clouds the heauens do benight
The starres & planets are bereft of Light
When the South winds the angry Seas imbroile
And make them foame as if they seem'd to boyle
(Although before so calme they did appeare
As that y^{r} face you might see shining there)
They then withstand y^{r} sight beeing thickly fraught
With mudde, wch th'winds haue from ye bottome brought
And as the rapid streames, wch from hills runne,
Are sometimes stop't by meeting wth a Stone,
So wilt thou bee obstructed in thy way
To trueth, if thou thy passions dost not sway,
Thou must then joyes, farre from thee stoutly drive,
Nor feare, nor hope, nor sorrow Leave alive
For where these are, ye mind quite clouded is
And (fetter'd) poorely faints in miseryes.

Second Booke
Prose the 1st

After this shee held for some time her peace, but when shee [1] perceau'd by my silence, my attention & readynesse to hearken to her, [2] shee began thus; If I am fully inform'd & do understand ye causes [3] **[12v]** and habit of your disease, you languish for the losse & Love of your [1] former fortune, whose change (for you thinke it one) hath ouerthrowne [2] the healthy state of your minde. I am very well acquainted with the [3] manyfold colours & deceipts of that Monster (fortune) & how shee use's [4] a most flattering familiarity & indearment, with those shee meanes [5] to cosen & beguile 'till at Last by a suddaine Leauing of them, shee plunge's [6] them into an insufferable greefe & torment, whose nature, conditions, [7] & merit, if you do but call to minde & consider, you will finde that you [8] neither euer had, nor haue now Lost any thing that was worth ye valewing, [9] but I thinke I shall not neede to take much paines to rubbe up your [10] memory in this particular, for you y^{r} selfe were us'd heretofore to treate [11] her as harshly as shee deseru'd, and to show by manly expressions (w^{ch} [12] you had learn't of us) that you did despise her, even when shee flatter'd & [13] fawn'd most upon you. But there is neuer any suddaine alteration [14] & change of condition, without some kind of perturbation of ye mind. & [15] hence it is, that you are a litle fallen from the former peace & tranquillity [16] of your thoughts. therefore it is time that I should give you some soft [17] & pleasant Iulep, that being swallow'd by you may make way for stronger [18] & more effectuall remedys. Wee will in the first place make use of a litle [19] Rhetorick, wch then only steer's a right course, when shee doth not forsake [20] our Lawes. and wee will now & then bring in Musick to help a gentlewoman [21] that attend's on us, & sing's sometimes Lighter, sometimes grauer ayres. [22] What is it then (O man) that hath throwne thee into this malencholly [23] & sadnesse, one would thinke thou hads't seene some new & extraordinary [24] thing. If you thinke fortune is chang'd towards you, you are deceau'd; [25] this was alwaies her nature & custome. Shee hath rather preseru'd [26] her wonted constancy towards thee in this change. Shee was the same [27] when shee flatter'd & sooth'd thee up with false happynesse. Thou art [28] now come to know the double face of this blind Goddesse. Shee that [29] hides and conceale's her selfe from others, discouer's & Laye's her selfe open [30] to thee. If thou likest her wayes well & good, thou has't liberty to [31] court her, do not complaine. If thou dos't obhorre her treachery &

per= [32] =fidiousnesse, despise & cast her off that play's so dangerously with thee. [33] For shee that is now cause of so much trouble & affliction to thee, ought to [34] haue produc't a contrary effect. Shee hath forsaken thee whom (no man [35] can euer bee secure) hee shall not bee forsaken by[13] It may bee thou esteemest [36] **[13r]** & valuest a happynesse that is so fleeting? and art fond of ye present [1] fortune though it bee not certaine to continue, & though at her going [2] away shee causeth so much sorrow & greefe? For since shee is not to [3] bee stop't at a mans pleasure, & that shee makes a man unhappy [4] when see goe's away, what is good fortune wch is alwayes upon ye wing [5] but a kind presage of misery to come? For t'is not enought to Looke [6] only upon what is just before our eyes, prudence measures y^{e} event [7] of things, and that same changing from one to another, make's, that [8] neither the flatteries of fortune are to bee desired, nor her threats [9] fear'd Lastly, it behooueth thee to suffer patiently, whateuer lyes with= [10] =in the verge & power of fortune, when once thou has't submitted thy [11] neck to her Yoke. And if you go about to prescribe Lawes of going [12] or staying to her, that you haue voluntarily chosen for y^{r} mistresse, [13] you become injurious & disobliging, & so by y^{r} impatience exasperate [14] & make that fortune worse, w^{ch} 'tis not in y^{r} power to avoid. If once [15] you hoist y^{r} sailes & commit them to the wind, you go not where you [16] will, but wither the winds will carry you. If you trust y^{r} seed to [17] the earth you must resolve to take y^{r} venture, whither the yeare bee [18] fertill or barren. You haue giuen y^{r} selfe up to Fortunes gouerment [19] & must obey the customes & humours of y^{r} mistresse. But you [20] haue a minde to stop the turning of the wheele, O foolishest of all [21] mindkinde, when once shee begins to stope, shee leaue's to bee fortune. [22]

Verse the 1st of the 2^{d} Booke:

Who whilst shee proudly sit's & (wth her hand
Turning our chances) show's th'unjust com*m*and
Shee hath o're mortalls, & violent as the Sea
Enrag'd tread's on the Necks of Kings, whom shee
Hath Late dethron'd, & flattering then
Rayse's the humble Lookes of conquer'd men
[13v] Doth from the wretched, turne away her eares
Nor mov'd at all is at their bitter teares,

[13] "bee" and "by" inserted on either side of "forsaken" here.

But Laughing at the paines shee make's them feele
Delight's herselfe, when by her strength they reele,
Showing her Minions that applaud her power
The pastime of a happy man, Lost in an hower.

Prose the 2^{d} of the 2^{d} Booke

But I would willingly plead a litle with you in the behalfe & in the [1] name of fortune & desire you would consider whither shee bee not in [2] the right. What reason has't thou (O man) to accuse mee euery day as [3] a guilty person? What injury is it I haue don you? What goods of [4] yours haue I taken away? Contend with mee before what judge [5] you please, concerning the possession of y^{r} goods and dignities, and if [6] you show they do, or did properly belong to any mortall man, I [7] will grant they were yours. When nature brought you forth out of [8] your mothers womb, and that you were naked & destitute of euery thing, [9] I tooke you up, maintein'd you out of my owne abundance, and w^{ch} [10] make's you now the more impatient, did out of my fauourable inclination [11] towards you, not only bring you up with all the kindnesse & indulgency [12] imaginable, but furnisht you with the plenty & affluence of all things [13] that Lay within my power, Now I haue a minde to withdraw my hand. [14] Thanke mee for what you haue enjoy'd, as hauing had the use of w^{t} [15] was not y^{r} owne, but complaine not as if you had Lost what was yours, [16] Why therefore dost thou greeue? I haue don thee no wrong. Richesse, [17] Honours, & all things of that nature are mine, the seruants know theire [18] mistresse, they come with mee, & when I retire, they departe also, This [19] I will boldly affirme, that had they bin really y^{rs}, you had neuer Lost them. [20] Am I the only person that am deny'd the Liberty to enjoy my owne right? [21] It is Lawfull for the heauens to produce cleere sunne shiny dayes, & to [22] hide them againe with darke nights. It is Lawfull for the earth to adorne [23] it selfe sometimes with pleasant flowers & fruite, & sometimes to bee [24] cloath'd with Ice & snow. The Sea hath the Liberty to bee sometimes [25] calme & smooth, & sometimes againe to bee tempestuous & rough, [26] **[14r]** Shall the unsatisfy'd couetousnesse of men tye mee (alone) to a con= [1] =stancy so much against my nature & custome. Thus do I exercise my [2] power & strength. This is my constant sport the constant game[14] I play at. I turne con= [3] =tinually a wheele about, & take delight in making the highest [4] things Lowest,

[14] "the constant game" inserted here.

& the Lowest highest; Mount if you please, but Let [5] it bee upon this condition, that you shall not thinke it an injury to [6] be throwne downe againe, when my game require's it. Is it possible [7] you should be unacquainted with my wayes & manners? Do you not [8] know how Crœsus King of the Lydians, who had bin before so formidable [9] to Cyrus was afterwards pittifully made his prisoner, & not only condem= [10] =ned to bee burnt, but actually comitted to the flames, & then sav'd by [11] a raine sent from heauen? Haue you not heard how Paulus y^{e} Roman [12] Consull, shed teares for the misfortunes of the King of Persia, whom [13] hee had himselfe taken. What are the Tragedians full of but exclamation [14] against fortune for subuerting with her suddaine stroaks the happyest [15] Kingdomes? Did you not learne in Greece when you were young that [16] there are two Tubbs in Iupiters porch or Lobby, whereof the one is fill'd [17] with good, & the other wth evill chances? What if you haue hapned [18] hitherto to haue the greatest share of the good? What if I haue not [19] quite forsaken you? What if this very mutability & changeablenesse [20] of my nature giue's you a just cause to hope for better things? Haue [21] you then reason to complaine? But howeuer that you may not bee [22] dismay'd, & desire, (thought plac't in a Kingdome common to all) to Live [23] after a different manner, & bee gouern'd by the dictates of y^{r} owne fancy, [24] harken to this. [25]

Verse the 2^{d} of the 2^{d} Booke.

Though full swolne plenty wth a Lavish hand
Give wealth & richesse equall to the sand
Which th'angry sea throwes up upon the shoare
When vex't by winds, or should send greater store
Then in a frosty night starres do appeare
Yet still complaints of mortalls you would heare
[14v] Though God should grant the couetous mans request
And, prodigall of gold, should fill his chest,
And give th'ambitious man his fill
Of honours, yet y'would find them gaping still
Thinking that nothing wch th'already haue
For couetousnesse deuoureth Like the graue
And still thirst's after more, what bridles can
Such fierce desires, within set bounds restraine
When by enjoyments, they more greedy grow,
And thirst encreaseth, e'uen, when gifts do flow,

Nor is hee rich, or happy, that hath store,
For hee that couet's, show's, hee yet want's more.

Prose the 3^{d} of the 2^{d} Booke

If fortune should thus plead her cause, I know not what you would bee [1] able to say for y^{r}selfe. If you haue any thing in defence of ye justnesse [2] of y^{r} quarrell, pray let's heare it, Wee giue you liberty to speake. [3] Then (said I) these are indeed specious things, sweetned & adorned[15] wth y^{e} flowers [4] & honey of musick & Rhetorick, but they only please whilst they are [5] hearing, & miserable people haue a deeper sence of the ills they suffer, [6] So that when theise things haue Left sounding in theire eares, greefe re= [7] =turnes in a[16] greater measure to possesse theire spirits. I grant it (said [8] shee) neither are these as yet administred to you, as absolute remedyes [9] for y^{r} disease, but as things that may a litle Lenify that rebellious [10] contumacy of y^{r} greefe, wch hinders y^{r} cure. and when I find it season= [11] =able I shall then apply things that shall go to the roote. In the meane [12] time Least you may haue forgotten what fortune hath don for you, Let [13] mee repeate a little to you the number of y^{r} felicitys, & the course of them. [14] I say nothing of the cheefest persons of the Cittys taking you into their care, [15] when you had Lost y^{r} Father, nor how you were chosen into the kindred & [16] relation of the Noblest families, & (what is the most valewable kind of [17] neerenesse in relation) were first deare before you became akin to them. [18] **[15r]** Who was there that seeing you surrounded with the splendour & Nobility [1] of y^{r} Father in Law, blest with the chastity of y^{r} wife, & strengthned wth a [2] masculine issue, did not esteeme & proclaime you the happyest man alive [3] I passe by (for I desire not to mention common things) your hauing [4] dignityes conferr'd upon you in y^{r} youth, that were deny'd to old men. I [5] haue a mind to come to the height & accomplishment of all y^{r} happynesse [6] If any product of mortall things haue any weight of happynesse in [7] it, can any misery of affliction make you forget that day, wherein [8] you saw y^{r} two Sonnes (made Consulls) conducted from your house by [9] such a multitude of Senatours, & with such generall acclamations of [10] the people, when they being sat in the court & in their currule seates, you [11] being the King's Orator did deserue & carry away the glory of wit & Eloquence [12] When in the cirque being plac't betweene thy sonnes (Consulls) thou didst

[15] "& adorned" inserted here.

[16] "a" inserted here.

[13] satisfie the expectation of the circling multitude, with tryumphant praise [14] & gifts? You gaue certainly some engagement to fortune, when shee courted [15] & made so much of you. For you receav'd that from her, that shee neuer [16] gaue to any other private man. Dare you venture to cast up y^{r} accompts [17] & reckon with fortune? This is the first time that e're shee Look't upon [18] you with an evill eye. If you consider & compare y^{r} happynesse wth [19] y^{r} misfortunes, you will not bee able to deny but that the first weigh's [20] downe the scale considerably. You ought therefore yet to accompt y^{r}selfe [21] happy. But if you therefore think y^{r} selfe unhappy, because those [22] things, wch caus'd your happynesse, are gon, you haue no reason now to think [23] y^{r} selfe miserable, since y^{r} misfortunes are passing away. Are you but [24] newly enter'd upon the stage of this Life? Is this the first time y^{o} haue [25] acted? How can you imagine there should bee any constancy in humane [26] things, when man himselfe is many times destroy'd & gon in an instant. [27] And although there were a certainty of fortunes continuance, Yet the [28] Last day of a mans Life, would bee also a kind of death to his fortune. [29] And what matter is it, whither you Leave her by dying, Or shee you, by [30] running away? [31]

Verse the 3^{d} of the 2^{d} Booke.

When Phebus 'gins his shining Light to spread
Changing the sky into a fiery red
[15v] The starres ore'come by the approching day
Pale & asham'd to make themselves away
When westerne gales haue fill'd ye spring wth flowers
A nipping frost all those faire hopes deuour's
Sometimes the sea doth a sweete calme enjoy
Sometimes the wind that calmenesse doth destroy.
Since all things heere to change are so enclin'd
And that no steddynesse in any thing you find
Why should you trust to slippery fortune then
Or to the fleeting goods posses't by men
When t'is ordain'd by a most firme decree
That no made thing im*m*utable shall bee.

Prose the 4th of the 2^{d} Booke.

What thou sai'st (said I) O nurse of all vertues is most true & I [1] cannot deny, but that the course of my prosperity hath bin as swift [2] & violent, as it hath bin short, but the remembrance of that giues [3] mee now the greater vexation, for in aduersity it is the most unhappy [4] kind of misfortune to haue bin happy. But (said shee) if you [5] undergo a punishment caus'd by an erroneous & false opinion of [6] your owne, there is no reason that it should bee imputed to ye things, [7] wherein you are mistaken. For if this empty name of good fortune & [8] felicity mooue you, pray let us reckon how much of that you still [9] possesse. For if that wch is the most pretious gift that it euer was in [10] the power of fortune to giue you, bee still preseru'd by the care [11] of heauen unhurt or violated, can you (when you still retaine the [12] best things) justly complaine of misfortune. Is not that pretious [13] honour & ornament of mankind (Symachus y^{r} father in Law a [14] man made up of wisdome & vertue, & one you would giue y^{r} Life [15] at any time to save) alive, & well, & being secure of his owne [16] **[16r]** condition bewaile's the wrongs are don to you? Do's not y^{r} wife liue, [1] a person of a great yet modest wit, & of eminent chastity, & to include [2] all her perfections in a[17] few words, Like her Father, shee Lives (I say) [3] & for you, alone, shee preserue's a Life, else growne hatefull to her, and [4] spends her time in teares & sorrow for want & desire of you, in w^{ch} [5] Last thing alone, I must allow, that y^{r} happynesse is diminisht. what [6] shall I say more? You haue two Sonnes that haue bin Consulls, in [7] whom there shine's the wit & Iudgment of theire Grandfather, and [8] Father. If therefore the cheefest care of mortalls is to preserue Life, [9] How happy are you (if you know y^{r} happynesse) who still possesse [10] things, that are dearer to you then Life it selfe? wherefore dry up [11] y^{r} teares, fortune hath not absolutely deseru'd y^{r} hatred, nor the [12] tempest hath not bin ouer outragious, since there still remain's such [13] holding ankors, as will neither suffer you to bee without present comfort, [14] nor probable hope for the time to come. And may they still continue [15] (said I) for as Long as they remaine, what euer happens I shall do well, [16] But yet you see how much of my happynesse is fled. Nay (said shee) [17] I haue got some ground since I haue brought you to confesse, that you [18] are not altogether unhappy. But I cannot endure y^{r} ouer great nicenesse, [19] that cannot beare the Losse of any parte of y^{r} happynesse wthout falling [20] into so excessive a greife & sorrow. For who is there so entirely happy [21] in all respects, as that hee doth not in something or other quarrell wth [22] his condition, for the state of humane things is neuer absolutely perfect, [23] &, at best, doubtfull; For either it neuer happens

[17] "a" inserted here.

to be compleat, or at [24] Least neuer continue's so. This man abounds in richesse, but is asham'd [25] of his ignoble blood; That man is Noble, but being of a small Estate, [26] doth rather wish hee were borne obscurely. Another that hath both, is [27] troubled for want of a good wife. A fourth is happy in a wife, but [28] destitute of children, take's paines to manage & improoue his estate [29] for the advantage of a Stranger. Another Blest wth children, weep's [30] & is afflicted for the death of this or that darling Sonne or Daughter [31] hee hath Lost. You see it is not easy for any man to bee pleas'd with [32] this condition of his fortune. For there is always either something y^t^ [33] not hauing try'd hee doth not know, or hauing try'd hee dislikes, and [34] wee may adde this, that in fortunate & happy men, there is so nice & [35] delicate a taste, that unlesse euery thing been to their minde, and not [36] imbitter'd with the least crosse accident, they are immediately disgusted [37] **[16v]** and cast downe. So litle a thing it is that will ouerthrow the [1] compleatnesse of the fortunatest mans felicity. How many doe [2] you thinke there are, that if they had the Least parte of that [3] happynesse remaines yet to you, would even thinke themselues [4] in heauen. That very place you call a prison, is to ye people [5] that inhabit it, theire beloued country. So true it is, that no [6] body is miserable, but hee that thinke's himselfe so. And on the [7] contrary, no body is happy but hee that is contented with his [8] fortune. what man is there so happy, that if hee once giue way [9] to impatience, doth not wish his condition alter'd? with how [10] much bitternesse is the sweete of humane felicity mingled. W^ch^ [11] if it chance to bee very pleasing to him that enjoye's it, Yet hee [12] cannot (do what hee can) stop it, if once it bee minded to bee gon. [13] It appear's then how miserable humane felicity it selfe is, w^ch^ [14] will neither continue with those that delight in it, Nor can [15] please, those that do not. Why then O Mortalls do you seeke [16] without, that happynesse that is plac't & can only bee found w^th^in [17] you? your errour & ignorance destroye's you. I will show you in [18] a few words the perfection of happynesse. Is there any thing [19] more pretious to you then y^r^selfe? you will tell mee, no. why [20] then if you possesse y^r^ selfe, you will enjoy that wch is dearest to [21] you, & that wch you can neuer Loose, nor fortune euer take away [22] from you. Now to the end you may bee convinc't & acknowledge [23] that happynesse doth not consist, in things subject to fortune, hear= [24] =ken to what I shall say. If happynesse bee the cheefest good in [25] nature, to those that are indu'd with reason, & that that cannot bee [26] the cheefest good wch may bee taken from one, because what cannot [27] bee taken away, doth excell it, it is manifest that the instability [28] of Fortune makes that it[18] can no way pretend to the making of a person happy. [29] Besides hee that suffers himselfe to bee carry'd away with this [30] deceitfull good fortune, either know's her to bee mutable, or doth [31] not, if hee doth not, what happynesse can there bee in so blind an [32] ignorance? if hee doth, hee must of necessity dread the Loosing of [33] that, wch hee know's may bee Lost, & what pleasure or happynesse can [34] there bee where there is so much feare? doth hee thinke the Losse of it, [35] not worth the being consider'd, if hee doth hee certainly esteem's it a [36] **[17r]** very small happynesse, the Losse of wch can bee borne with so much un= [1] =concerne & indifferency. Lastly Since the Soules of men are immortall [2] (as I know you are by demonstrations convinc't they are) & that it is [3] cleere that the happynesse wch fortune bestowe's ends wth ones Life, [4] it must necessarily follow (if that were properly to bee call'd happy= [5] =nesse) that all mankind would bee at Last miserable, since death [6] would put an end to theire happynesse. Now wee see how many haue [7] sought the fruit of true happynesse, not only through death, but [8] through a world of torments, then how can the present Life make [9] men happy, if the Losse of it doth not make them miserable. [10]

Verse the 4th of the 2^{d} Booke.

Hee that desire's to build a Lasting seate
That may the fury of the winds defy
And firmely stand thô floods & waves do beate
Against it's walls, & their foundations try
Hee must not proudly build his house too high
But tops of hills as well as Sands avoid
The first too much to winds expos'd will Lye
And these will sinke under so greate a Loade.
Thou therefore if thou dost desire to fly
The dangers to wch these are so expos'd
Choose thee an humble Seate that's firme & dry
And for defence by circling hills enclos'd
So shalt thou Laugh, when furious storms do roare
And threaten ruine to the Lofty piles
And being in thy Lowlynesse secure
Defeate[19] the weathers anger, wth thy Smiles.

[18] "makes that it" inserted here.

[19] "Defeate" underlined here; superscript "battle" inserted as another option, but the original "defeate" is repeated in the left margin.

[17v] Prose the 5th of the 2d Booke

But since I finde that these preparatory reasons begin to sinke [1] into you, I shall now venture to use stronger phisick, & come closer [2] to the businesse. Suppose the gifts of fortune, were not so momentary, [3] and so subject to change, What is there in them that can euer properly [4] bee call'd yours? Or that being considere'd & Look't into doth not grow [5] vile & of no valew? Is richesse to bee esteem'd for it's owne nature, or [6] upon the accompt of being yours, and in richesse what is most to bee [7] valu'd, gold, or a great masse of mony gathered together, but both [8] these bring more aduantage & honour in being spent then in being [9] Laid up, For avarice hath alwaies rendred men odious, as Liberality [10] hath made them renound & famous. If then what is giuen to a= [11] =nother, doth not remaine with the giuer, then mony is only to bee [12] valu'd when it is no more yours. But if all the mony that is [13] now scatter'd up & downe the world in the hands of severall people [14] were all in a heape in yr possession, then must of necessity all the [15] rest of the world bee poore & needy, & no person of any generosity [16] or good nature can esteeme himselfe happy, when hee make's so many [17] men miserable, and if that reflection doth not, at least the clamours [18] of so great a multitude will giue a great alloy to yr happynesse. [19] And to distribute yr richesse amongst others makes them (as I haue [20] already said) cease to bee yours, and consequently leaues you yr selfe [21] poore. O scanty, & indeed poore & necessitous richesse, wch many [22] cannot enjoy, & wch one enjoying, make's all others poore! Is it [23] the shining of pretious Stones that doth delight you? if so, pray [24] examine to whom that Lustre belong's, 'tis to the stones, not to [25] them that weare them, and therefore they that haue them, ought [26] not at all to prize themselues the more upon that accompt. But [27] I confesse I cannot but admire, what men finde to admire in them, [28] For that wch wants Life, & the joyning of the soule to the members of [29] the body (wch is that that ought to seeme fairest, & to be most admir'd [30] by a person indu'd with reason) though, compar'd with things of the [31] same nature, it haue somewhat a greater proportion of yr Last & Lowest [32] kind of beauty wherewith the Creatour hath adorn'd the universe. Yet [33] it being so much below our owne excellency it ought not at all to cause [34] **[18r]** our admiration. Is it the beauty of the feilds that pleases you? [1] why should they not (said I) since they are so faire a parte of Gods [2] creation, 'Tis in Like manner that the prospect of the sea when [3] it is smooth & calme delights us, and with the same[20] satisfaction and [4] content,

[20] "same" inserted here.

wee Looke upon the heauens, the Sunne, the starres & the [5] moone. Doth there any of these things (said shee) either belong [6] to, or concerne you? haue you the confidence to glory in ye beauty [7] of any of these things, are you the fairer for the vernall flowers [8] or the richer for the Summer fruits, why are you transported wth [9] vaine & idle joyes? Why do you embrace strange goods, as if they [10] were y^{r} owne? Fortune can neuer make those things yours, that [11] nature hath alienated from you. The fruits of the earth are wthout [12] doubt due to the nourishment of the beasts that inhabit it. & if [13] you only desire to satisfy the need of nature, you need not desire [14] the plenty that fortune brings. for nature is content wth a very [15] Litle. and if you will force a fulnesse upon her wth superfluous [16] things what you do to her of that kind, will at least bee unpleasant [17] if not noxious & hurtfull. Do you thinke it a fine thing to shine [18] in variety of clothes? but if there bee any thing in them that please's [19] the sight, to bee just, wee ought either to admire the art of y^{e} work= [20] =man that made them, or the Stuff whereof they are made. Or doth [21] the number of y^{r} retinue & attendance make you a happy man? [22] But if they are vitious & deboist, it doth not only reflect upon, but [23] may bee the ruine of theire master, if they are honest & good, why [24] should you rancke other peoples goodnesse & honesty amongst your [25] goods & richesse? By all this it doth appeare, that amongst all [26] those things that you accompt yours, there is not one thing really so. [27] in which since there is nothing worth the desiring, why should you [28] either greeue at the Losse of them, or rejoyce in the retaining them. [29] For admit they are faire in theire owne nature, what is that to you? [30] since, had they neuer bin y^{rs}, they had bin in themselues as faire. For [31] 'tis not their coming to bee a parte of y^{r} wealth that make's them [32] pretious, but because you judg'd them so, that you haue endeavour'd [33] to get them in amongst y^{r} wealth. But what is it that with all this [34] noyse you desire of fortune? Is it by plenty to fright away want? if [35] it bee, you take a wrong course, for you will want many helpes, to [36] keepe, & defend, such pretious things. For, it is most certaine, that [37] those stand in need of much, that haue much; & that they want least, [38] **[18v]** That measure theire abundance, by the necessity of nature, & not [1] by the superfluity of ambition & couetousnesse. Is it that there is [2] no good within you, that you take such paines to find it abroade [3] in externall things? how preposterous it is, that a man, that in [4] regard of his reason may bee call'd a divine creature should seeme [5] of no valew to himselfe, unlesse adorn'd with the possession of [6] inanimated things? other things are content with what's theire [7] owne, but you that are by the dignity of y^{r} soules made even Like [8] to God himselfe, must borrow ornaments from the meanest things [9] for y^{r} most excellent natures. Are not you aware of the injury you [10] do in this to y^{r} Creatour? Hee in his goodnesse, hath made mankind to [11] excelle all other creatures upon earth, & you will undervalew your [12] selfe so much, & so much debase y^{r} dignity, as to hide it under, and [13] preferre the meanest things before it. For if that wch is the good & [14] happynesse of any thing bee more pretious then the thing of wch it [15] is the good, wch it must bee since it is the thing it aspireth to, it fol= [16] =low's, that when you esteeme those vile & inanimated things y^{r} goods, [17] you do preferre them in y^{r} esteems before y^{r} selues. And indeed 'tis [18] not injust it should bee so, for this is the condition of humane nature, [19] That as, when it know's it selfe, it excell's all other things, So, when [20] it doth not, it prooue's worse & become's inferiour even to beasts. For [21] it is the nature of other creatures not to know themselues, but 'tis [22] a vice in man. Now how highly guilty are you of that vice & errour, [23] who thinke it possible for you to bee adorn'd with outward borrow'd [24] ornaments? & when all's don, it is in vaine, for if any thing Looke the [25] finer for the ornaments it hath on, 'tis the ornaments that ought to [26] haue the prayse of it, not hee that weare's them, & the thing that is [27] hid & cover'd by them still remaine's in it's owne uglynesse & deformity. [28] Besides I deny that any thing is a good, that is hurtfull to him that [29] hath it. Am I in the wrong? You will say no, But richesse & wealth [30] haue often brought hurt to those that enjoy'd them, for wicked men [31] coueting the gold & pretious Stones that they saw in others hands, and [32] thinking themselues only worthy of them, haue often Layd snares [33] into wch they haue made the owners of them fall. And you y^{r} selfe who [34] are now afraide of the sword & Speare, do not you thinke if you had [35] enter'd an empty pocketed traveller into the high way of this Life [36] you might now haue sung before the theeues? O pretious and [37] renown'd happynesse of mortall richesse wch you haue no sooner obtain'd [38] but you Leave to bee safe! [39]

[19r]

Verse the 5th of the 2^{d} Booke

Too happy was the former age
Which well content wth their owne feilds
Did Late at night hunger asswage
With Akornes such as each oake yeild's
Not being gi'n o're to dantyer fare

For wch men now take so much care
They knew not how to mix their wine
Nor poinant sauces how to make
Nor did they studdying to bee fine
Make wooll a Tyrian dye to take
Their sleepes were holsome on the grasse
Their drinke the streame as it did passe
The pleasant pine tree was their shade
The Sea as yet no Ship had bore
Nor had the merchants yet conveigh'd
Their choicest wares to foraigne shore
The Trumpetts & the Drums were still
And no man wish't another ill.
So farre they were from spilling blood,
When no reward it did procure,
That then each man made it his good,
To Live contented & secure.
O that those times might now returne
But wee alas Like Etna burne
[19v] With thirst of hauing, curst was hee
Who first div'd in & let us see
Those dangerous treasures in the womb,
Of th'earth, to wch before it was a tomb.

Prose the 6th of the 2d Booke

But what shall I say concerning dignity & power, wch you out of [1] ignorance of what is true dignity & power indeed do equall to the [2] heauens? wch if they happen into ill mens hands, what slaughters [3] & destructions do they not produce, such as no deluge nor ye flames [4] belch't out of Etna neuer caus'd? certainely I haue heard you your [5] selfe take notice, that the pride of former Consulls, was the cause yt [6] your predecessours, rather then suffer it, were content to abolish the [7] Consular Authority, though it had bin the begining of their freedome, [8] and was it not for the same reason, they had before that, cast out ye [9] Kingly name & power? And if sometimes (wch happens very seldome) [10] Honours are conferr'd on good men, what is it then, that is pleasing, [11] or satisfactory, but the honesty & goodnesse of the men so dignifyd? [12] So that 'tis not vertue that receaue's an advantage from power, but [13] Power from vertue. But Let us see what this your mighty coveted [14] Power &

Authority is. do you not consider (O earthly creatures) who it [15] is you seeme to gouerne, & to bee preferr'd before? For if you should [16] see one Mouse challenge a Power & Authority ouer the rest of his fellow [17] mice, would you not bee mou'd greatly to Laughter? & what is there [18] (if you consider the body) weaker then a man? whome the bite of a [19] Little fly or the sting of a Litle worme is able to destroy? Now [20] what power can any persons, Nay even fortune her selfe exercise, [21] ouer any thing but the body, or what is beneath it? can they so [22] much as pretend to haue any com*m*and ouer the free mind? Do you [23] thinke you can with any Authority whatsoeuer, remoue a mind [24] that's settled & constant to it's selfe, from it's owne quiet condition? [25] **[20r]** When a certaine tyrant by tortures endeauour'd to force a man [1] of setled principles to discouer a conspiracy against his person [2] together with the persons that were privy to it, hee manfully [3] bit of his tongue & spit it in the enraged Tyrants face, So that [4] the torture that the Tyrant intended to inflict as an effect of [5] his cruelty, that wise man turned into a proofe of his owne vertue. [6] and what is it that any may can do to another, that hee may [7] not suffer from another? Wee read that Busiredes that was us'd [8] to kill his guests, was himself kill'd by Hercules his Guest. [9] Regulus put many that hee had taken in Africa into fetters, & [10] was soone after himselfe put in chaines by those hee had ouercome. [11] and do you count it any power in a man, when hee cannot hinder [12] the same thing from bring don to him, that hee doth to another? [13] But besides all this, if there were really any naturall good inhe= [14] =rent in power, it would neuer come into ill mens hands, For [15] things of contrary natures neuer keepe company, or are consistent [16] together, Nature will not suffer contrarys to bee joyn'd in one. [17] Since therefore wee see that 'tis ill men that for the most parte [18] enjoy greatest dignities & preferments, it is manifest that they [19] are not in themselves a good, Since they indure to bee fastned to [20] & continue with ill men. And the same thing may bee said of all [21] the guifts of fortune, For generally they come in greater abundance [22] to ill men, then to good; This is also in my opinion worthy to bee [23] consider'd, that no body doubt's him to bee strong, in whom hee [24] hath seene strength, nor him to bee Swift, in whom hee hath [25] seene swiftnesse, So Musick make's Musitians, & Phisick Phisi= [26] =tians, & Rhetorick Rhethoricians, For the nature of euery [27] thing cause's it's proper effect in the subject it workes upon, [28] & neuer mingle's with it selfe in the effects of contrary things? [29] But richesse neuer yet quench't the thirst of avarice, & consequent= [30] =ly neuer made any man truly rich, not so much as in his fancy, [31] Nor power euer made that man ouercome himselfe that was bound [32] with the indissolu'ble chaines of vice & Lust, Nor dignity conferr'd [33] on ill men neuer made them Digni that is worthy as the Latin [34] word imply's, but rather discouer'd more of their unworthinesse. [35] **[20v]** From whence then doth this proceed? That you delight to giue [1] false names to things wch are so easily disproov'd by their Effects? [2] For neither those ought to bee call'd richesse, Nor these power & [3] dignity; Lastly wee may make the same conclusion of all [4] Fortune in generall, in wch it is apparent that there is nothing [5] worth the beeing desir'd or sought after, nor nothing of Naturall [6] goodnesse, Since it neither cleaue's alwaies to good men, Nor [7] make's them good to whom it cleaue's. [8]

Verse the 6th of the 2^{d} Booke.

How many ruines did that tyrant cause
Who treading under foote all sorte of Laws
Did Brother Senators & Mother kill
And wanting yet more Fuell to fulfill
His thirsty cruelty, did set on fire
The cheefest citty of the world, & higher
Yet in crimes could wade, & tearelesse read
A Lecture on his Mother's body (dead)
And unconcern'd attentively survey
Each Limb about her, when quite cold she Lay
Examining the beauty of each parte
With a most hard & unrelenting harte.
Yet this man did the greatest Scepter sway
That was on earth, & all men did obey
His boundlesse power, even from ye rising Sunne
Unto the place whereto his horses runne
And from the North unto ye South, hee did
Extend his power, Yet all this could not rid
[21r] Him of his madnese, what then doth power availe
If't could not o're himselfe make him prevaile
O wretched Fortune to us men, when power
Is joyn'd to rage, what will not they devoure?

Prose the 7th of the 2^{d} Booke.

You y^{r} selfe know (said I then) that it was not the ambition of [1] mortall things that sway'd mee in the desire of dignity & power, but [2] that[21] vertue might not remaine hid & conceal'd, and that is [3] the only thing (said shee) that can allure Soules, that haue indeed [4] worth in them, but haue not yet receau'd vertues Last touch, so as [5] to make them absolutely perfect (I meane) the desire of glory, & [6] of the good opinion of good men, & of those that haue deserv'd well of [7] the Com*m*onwealth, But Let us consider how slender a thing & how [8] void of weight even that is; All the circuit of the earth as you [9] haue bin taught by the demonstrations of Astronomers beare's [10] but the proportion of a single point to the bignesse of ye heauens, [11] that is, if compar'd with the Celestiall globe, would bee judg'd to bee [12] no bigger. of this small thing 'tis but the fourth parte (as wee are [13] assur'd by Ptolomy) that hath bin discover'd & is inhabited by us [14] knowne creatures, & if you take out of this fourth parte what the [15] seas & Lakes do couer, & robbe us of, together with the uninhabited [16] deserts & waste places, You'le finde but a very small space Left [17] for men to inhabite, and do you that are enclos'd within this Litle [18] point of a point think of the spreading of y^{r} name & renowne? [19] What Largenesse or magnificency can yor glory haue that is [20] bounded within such narrow & slender Limits? adde also to this, [21] that this Little enclosure & habitation is inhabited by severall [22] Nations that differ both in Language, Manners, & in the whole way [23] & order of their Lives to many of w^{ch}, what with ye difficulty of [24] travelling, the diversity of tongues, & the rarenesse of Traffick, the [25] fame of townes themselues cannot reach, much lesse that of private [26] **[21v]** Persons, Wee see that euen in the time of Cicero, as his owne booke [1] testifie's, the fame of the Roman Com*m*onwealth had not yet got ouer [2] Mount Caucasus, & yet was Rome then of many yeares standing, [3] & fear'd & redoubted by the Parthyans, & other Nations thereabouts. [4] Do you see then, what a narrow & slender glory you goe about to [5] propogate? Do you thinke that where the fame & glory of ye Roman [6] Empire could not reach, the fame of a private Roman will? Even [7] when the manners & principles of divers Nations do so disagree [8] that what is held worthy of praise with some, is held to deserue [9] the greatest punishment with others, in so much that the [10] character that recom*m*end's a man in one country & get's him [11] honour & Esteeme, doth not at all conduce

[21] "that" followed by "of" (which is stricken through twice).

towards it in another, [12] Every one therefore must bee content to haue his glory circumscrib'd [13] within the compasse of his acquaintance? & that renowned immor= [14] =tality of fame must bee restrain'd within the Limits of one Nation? [15] But how many renown'd persons hath the want of writers even [16] in their owne times buried in oblivion? But suppose there were [17] writers of their times that did them right, what would y^{t} availe [18] since a longer time, bury's the remembrance of them also, & of all [19] their writings, and yet you beleiue you haue made your selues [20] immortall, when once you thinke y^{r} fame will Last for some [21] ages to come, when as if you consider the infinite space of Eter= [22] =nity, you will finde, you had Little reason to rejoyce, or to bee [23] proud, though you were sure it would Last to the worlds end. For [24] one moment if compar'd with a hundred thousand yeares, hath [25] some proportion, thô a small one, because the time in both is [26] definite, but that very number of yeares, thô so vast a one, hold's [27] no proportion, nor can bee compared to what is eternall, and hath [28] no End. For thô amongst finite things, (thô neuer so different) [29] there may bee a comparison one with another, there can bee none [30] betweene a thing finite & infinite, wch make's, that, admit a [31] fame bee neuer so Lasting, yet being bounded within ye Limits [32] of time, (compared with unlimitted Eternity) it will not only seeme [33] Litle, but nothing at all. Besides you that so much consider [34] **[22r]** Fame must leaue the satisfaction of vertue, & a good conscience, [1] if you seeke y^{r} reward from the tongues & discourses of the vulgar, or [2] the generality of the people, & do y^{r} actions meerely for ostentation, [3] to wch purpose Let mee tell you a story of one that very handsomly [4] derided the vanity of that ayme; There was a certaine person [5] that, (seeing[22] a man out of vaine glory affect the name of a [6] Phylosopher, without beeing really so) began to set upon him [7] with contumelys & reproaches, adding that now hee would see [8] whether hee were really a Phylosopher or no, by his bearing [9] of injuries, the other, for a litle time forced himselfe to show [10] patience, but hauing upon that accompt silently borne the [11] affront, began presently to bragge & insult, saying, now at last [12] you perceaue I am a Phylosopher but he smartly reply'd, I [13] had (indeed) perceau'd it, if you had held y^{r} peace. But what is it [14] that Noble & worthy men meane (for of them I speake) that seeke [15] glory with vertue? what fame is it that euen they can ayme at, [16] after their deaths? For if (wch our reason forbids us to beleeue) men

[22] "seeing" followed by "of" (which is stricken through).

[17] dye body & soule, then there is no glory at all, Since hee whose it [18] is said to bee, is not at all; and, if the soule beeing free'd out of [19] the earthly prison of this body, fly's up to heauen then shee [20] will certainly despise all earthly things, since enjoying heauen [21] shee will rejoyce in being free from all things that sauour of the [22] earth. [23]

Verse the 7th of the 2^{d} Booke.

Whoeuer so much ouervalews Fame
As that hee thinkes the spreading of his name
The cheefest blisse, Let him but cast his eye
Upon the Large circumference o'th'skye
And then the straightnesse of the earth survey
Compar'd to that, then Let him truly say
[22v] What honour hee doth thinke t'his name can come
When's Acts can't make it fill that litle roome
When hee consider's this hee will bee more
Asham'd then hee exalted was before
To thinke that ever hee so high did prize
A Thing so litle in discerning Eyes.
How[23] vainly then do proud men strive t'advance
Their necks in the worlds yoake, when if they chance
To get renowne, & that Fames trumpet sound
Aloud their praises, through the earth, nay round
The habitable world, & that their names
And Familyes with Tytles shine, death claymes
A priviledge to contemne[24] this glory
Though it bee built up to the highest story,
And take's delight to throw it headlong downe
Confounding with the Noblest bloods the Clownes,
That's meanest, both in quality & Fame
Louing to make, of high, & low, the same.
Where shall wee find faithfull Fabritius' bones
What is become of Brutus, that did once
Rescue braue Rome out of the Tyrants jawes?
Where's Cato? hee that for the antient Lawes

[23] "How" underlined in the manuscript; another "How" added in the left margin as well.

[24] "despise" written above "contemne" as an alternative wording.

Of Rome did stand, against their potente foes?
All that is Left of them, that the world knows
Is a few words, by wch wee only know
Their names, not them, who are not happyer now
For our vaine talke, Or if you thinke their Life
Prolonged bee, by this, there is a knife
[23r] Will cut that thread, at farthest ye Last breath
O'th world must end that fame & bee their second death.

Prose the 8th of the 2^{d} Booke.

But least you should thinke I wage an irreconcilable warre against [1] Fortune, I must tell you that sometimes shee deserues uery well of [2] men, and that is, when shee Laye's her selfe open, & discouers her face, [3] & ownes her nature & conditions. It may bee you do not yet under= [4] =stand cleerely what I meane, 'tis strange, that what I so much [5] desire to make out, I should hardly find words to expresse. But [6] 'tis this, that I do really beleive, That fortune is more fauourable, [7] when it is that wch people call ill, then when it is that, wch they [8] call good, For when shee hath that smooth face, & seem's good [9] shee dissemble's horribly, & Lye's, The other when it come's speak's [10] the trueth, & show's how unconstant shee is. The first deceaues, [11] The second instruct's. The first makes those that enjoy her by her [12] seeming happynesse to beleeue a Lye. The second by showing the [13] frailty & uncertainty of that happynesse, teache's not to rely [14] upon it. So that you see that, alwaies waueing, floting heere & [15] there & ignorant of it's selfe; this sober, prudent, temperate, & [16] through the exercise of aduersity, wise. Lastly good Fortune by [17] her flatterys draw's men from the true good, & ill fortune for [18] the most parte bring's men back to true happynesse. Do you [19] thinke it a small aduantage that this so horrible & severe fortune [20] hath bestow'd upon you in discouering who are really y^{r} friends & [21] who not? Shee hath distinguish't the certaine Lookes of y^{r} Compa= [22] =nions, & acquaintance, from the doubtfull ones; going away shee [23] hath carry'd away her friends, & Left you yours; What would you [24] haue giuen to haue known this in y^{r} prosperity & whilst you [25] thought y^{r} selfe happy? Cease then to complaine of y^{r} richesse Lost, [26] you haue found that wch is the most pretious & most valewable kind [27] of riches, Friends that Love you. [28]

[23v]

Verse the 8th of the 2^{d} Booke.

'Tis Loue that make's th'inconstant world to Steere
A faithfull steddy course making the yeare
Vary it's seasons so as one the other
Constantly succeed's t'is that doth smother
The enmity t'wixt jarring seeds, & Cause
Them joyne in constant League, t'is by Loves Lawes
The Sunne doth warme the world, & giue us day
'Tis Love that makes the night the moone obey
'Tis Love that give's the Lawlesse Sea a bound
And keep's the harmelesse earth from being drown'd
'Tis Love & his dread Soueraignty
Make's by his power these differing things agree
To whose Com*m*ands heauen Earth & Sea submit
And should hee once his reignes of power remit
Or slacken, All these things that Loue unite's
And to their mutuall offices excite's
Would then, being in perpetuall jarre
On one another constantly make warre
And Striue who most should ruine & destroy
The fabricke of the world, making that joy
And Harmony to cease, wch Loue did cause,
'Tis Loue giue's strength unto those holy Lawes
That nations bind, not to invade & spoyle
Each others homes, content with their owne Soyle.
'Tis Loue Vnites the hartes of happy those
Whom sacred wedlock joyned, & doth dispose
[24r] Men to bee gouern'd by those faithfull rules
Which hee doth dictate in his holy scooles
O! happy were mankind, if that true Loue
Did Gouerne them, that gouernes heauen aboue.

End of the 2^{d} Booke

First Prose of the 3^{d} Booke

I was so rauish't wth ye melodious sweetnesse of her Verse, that [1] thô shee had made an end of singing, I remain'd some time [2] astonish't, & with open eares ready to haue heard more. But a [3] Litle after I broke silence, & said, O thou consolation & refreshm^{t} [4] of wearied minds, how much has't thou comforted & restored mee [5] by the weight of thy sentences, & the pleasantnesse of thy verse? [6] insomuch as that henceforward (I beleiue) I shall not think [7] my selfe unable to resist the stroaks of Fortune, & begin now no [8] only not to abhorre or feare, those harsher remedys, wch you said [9] just now were too sharpe for mee, but vehemently to desire to [10] know & to make use of them. I judg'd as much (said shee) when [11] I saw you so silent & attentive to my words, but expected 'till you [12] came into this temper of mind, or rather 'till I had brought y^{o} into [13] it. For those things that now remaine are, indeed, somewhat bitter [14] to the taste, but being swallow'd grow sweet & pleasant, But you [15] that declare y^{r} selfe already so desirous to heare these things, with [16] what easynesse would you bee transported, if you know whither [17] I intend by their meanes to Lead you. whither (said I)? to that [18] true blisse (said shee) that y^{r} heart doth but yet dreame of t*hat*[25] w^{ch}[26] [19] by reason of y^{r} sights being darkned with earthly things (wch are but [20] **[24v]** the shadows of that) you cannot yet behold. Do so then, I beseech [1] you (said I) & show mee quickly what that true felicity is. I shall [2] (said shee) for your sake very willingly do it. But I will first en= [3] =deauour to describe & set forth that false happynesse you are already [4] acquainted with, to the end, that, that being Look't into, & consider'd [5] you may, (turning y^{r} eyes on the other side) see the cleernesse of [6] true felicity. [7]

First Verse of the 3^{d} Booke.

Hee that would sow a fruitfull feild with corne
Must first take care to roote up every thorne
Destroy the bushes, & the ferne, that so
The graine wch hee into the earth doth throw
May not bee choak't, but plentiously appeare
With a Long stalke, & with a heavy Eare.
Hony is sweeter to the taste when wee

[25] "t" inserted here as an abbreviation for "that."

[26] "you" scratched out here but used below as the clause concludes.

Before haue eate some bitter thing, wee see
The Starres do seeme more radiant & more faire
When stormes haue Lately ceas't to vex ye Ayre
The day it selfe appeare's to bee more bright
When it hath newly chas't away the night
So shall you find good things will Enter straight
When you to earthly pleasures shutt the Gate.

2d Prose of the 3d Booke.

Then fixing her eyes upon the ground & hauing recollected her= [1] =selfe, shee began thus. The whole care & endeauours of Mortall men [2] about wch they beate their braines, & to wch they bend all their studdys [3] (though they proceed in it different wayes) is all directed to one & ye same [4] end, & that is, happyness & Felicity. [5] **[25r]** Now that is truely happynesse, wch when a man hath once obtain'd, [1] hee hath nothing Left to desire, & that is the cheefe & highest good, [2] conteining in it selfe all other goods, to wch, if there bee any thing [3] wanting, it cannot bee call'd the cheefe & Supreame good, there being [4] something beside it, that may bee wisht & desired. It is there= [5] =fore cleare & manifest, that happynesse is a State made perfect, [6] by the accumulation & meeting together of all goods. To this [7] State (as wee haue said) all Mortalls endeauour to arriue, thô by [8] different waies & meanes, For there is in all mens minds an innate [9] desire of obtaining & enjoying the cheefe & true good, though errour, [10] misleads them sometimes & carry's them after false ones, whereof, [11] some thinking that to want nothing, is the cheefe good, Labour so t[o][27] [12] abound in richchesse & wealth, others esteeming that to bee ye cheef= [13] =est good that seemes worthyest of Veneration & respect, endeauour [14] by the obtaining of honours to make themselues reuerenced and [15] respected by their fellow cityzens. Others there are, that place [16] the cheefe good in power & Authority, & these striue either to raigne [17] themselues, or to bee neare to those that do raigne. Some againe [18] thinke, that Fame & renowne, is the cheefest of goods, & those either [19] by their valours in the warres, or by their Arts & industry in peace, [20] hasten to get themselues a glorious name. Many there are that [21] measure happynesse by Ioy & mirth, and these thinke it ye happy= [22] =est thing to wallow in pleasure. There are also some

[27] Ascender on an "f" from line below obscures reading here, so that the "t" is clear but what should be an "o" is not.

that change [23] and mingle these ends & meanes (as for example) desire Richesse in [24] order to Power or Pleasure, & pursue Power in order to Richesse, or to y^{e} [25] exalting of their names; In these therefore & other Like things ye aimes [26] & designs of men are continually employd, and thus Nobility & ye fauour [27] & good will of the people, as giuing Fame & renowne, and a good wife & [28] children as yeilding pleasure & delight, are desired & sought after. For [29] as to that of friends, that is too sacred & too certaine a thing, to bee [30] reckon'd among the goods of fortune, it more properly belonging to [31] those of vertue, but all the rest is either pursued upon ye accompt [32] of Power, or delight. Now the goods of the Body are all desir'd in order [33] to these foremention'd ends, as strength & vigour, seemes to contribute [34] towards Power, Beauty & agility towards renowne, & health towards [35] pleasure. By all wch things it appeare's, that happynesse is the only [36] thing aymed at; For that wch any man seek's & preferr's before other [37] things hee doth certainly judge to bee the cheefest good, & that w^{ch} [38] is the cheefest good hee define's to bee happynesse, therefore hee [39] conclude's that State to bee happy, wch men seeke & preferre, before [40] all others, So that you haue now Laid before y^{r} eyes (as it were) [41] **[25v]** The modell or Scheame of all humaine Felicity, Richesse, honours, Power [1] Glory, & delight, All wch Epicurus considering, chose Pleasure for ye Soueraigne [2] good, for as much as that all the rest seem'd by ouermuch Sollicitude & care [3] to take away the mirth & Ioy of the heart. But Let us returne to what [4] men in generall ayme at, & designe to themselves, whose minds (althô [5] they are clouded by a darkenesse of memory) do notwithstanding, still [6] seeke & groape after the true & Soueraigne Good, but (as drunken men) [7] cannot finde the way hoame. Do those seeme to bee in an errour that [8] endeauour to want nothing? no certainly, For there is no State that can [9] bee styled so compleatly happy as that wch abounding in all good things, [10] & wanting nothing, is in, & to it selfe Sufficient. Do those mistake [11] that thinke that condition is best that seemes worthyest to bee honour'd [12] & esteemed? No certainly, For how can that bee vile & contemptible y^{t} [13] almost all mankinde endeauour's to obtaine? Is Power not to bee [14] numbred among those goods that make a man happy? Yes sure, For [15] how can that bee thought weake & to haue no strength, wch appeares [16] to prevaile aboue all other things? Is not Fame & Renowne to bee [17] valew'd? Yes certainly, For how can it bee denyed but that that wch is [18] most Excellent, is alwayes most famous & renown'd? 'tis needlesse to say [19] that happynesse is not Subject to greife, & Sadnesse, when even in the [20] Least things, wee see, that nothing is desir'd but what wee thinke [21] yeild's Ioy & content. These therefore are the things that men doe [22] most desire to obtaine, They therefore ayme at Richesse, honours, Rule, [23] Glory, & Pleasure, because by them they seeme to procure to themselues [24] abundance of Power, respect, renowne, & content; That therefore [25] must bee call'd good, that men by so many wayes & Studdies, do endeavour [26] to attaine, in which it doth appeare how great the strength of nature [27] is, Since so many various & disagreeing opinions, do joyne in the [28] choice of one end, wch is happynesse, or the cheifest Good. [29]

2^{d} Poeme of the 3^{d} Booke.

I'm therefore minded in delightfull verse,
And in slow straines of Musick to rehearse,
How powerfull nature hold's ye guiding reignes
Oth'World, & how shee gouerns & maintaines
[26r] The universe in it's due steddy course
Making all things obey her mighty force.
The Lybian Lyons that are kept in chaines
And calmely take their meate from feeders hands
Fearing their Masters heavy Lash, if they
Once come to bee but bloodyed wth a Prey
They presently resume their naturall rage
And nothing can their thirst of blood asswage,
They teare their chaines, & Barbarously fall
Upon their masters, first, then furiously, on all,
That cannot keep our of their furys reach,
The birds, that men take so much pains to teach
And feed in cages, if they once get free
(Although before they were fed carefully
With choysest meates, not knowing any want)
Will presently preferre ye woods (thô scant
Of entertainment for such Guests) & choose
Rather to want all other benefits, then Loose
That Liberty that nature gaue, & will rejoyce
In that bad change, stretching to heauen their voyce,
If you by force Lay hold upon the branch
Of a young Supple tree, you may perchance
Bow downe it's top unto the ground, but then

Let it once go, it take's it's place agen,
And towards heauen Looke's, The Sunne y^{t} seeme's
To fall at night in Westerne waves, redeeme's
Itselfe, e're morning, & a Secret way
Find's out, to get to th'east by breake of day,
[26v] All things endeauour to returne to their
Old course, & then they do most pleas'd appeare
When they are gotten hoame, & can enjoy
Their natures, without wch they haue no joy
Nor is there any order giuen to things
But that w^{ch} (taught by powerfull nature) bring's
The end to Suite wth the beginning, and
This doth procure the universe to stand.

Prose the 3^{d} of the 3^{d} Booke.

And you also earthly creatures, do (though it bee faintly), dreame [1] of your beginning, & Looke thô with a darkened & dimme Sight towards [2] that true end of happynesse & felicity, to which as to the cheefe good y^{e} [3] intention of nature Lead's you, & from wch ignorance & Errour do endea= [4] =vour to withdraw you. Consider then whether by the meanes of those [5] things by wch men thinke to gaine happynesse it is possible to obtaine [6] their designed end? For if many honours & such like things can bring a [7] man to that condition, that hee shall wante no good, Wee will then confesse, [8] that, by their enjoyment they may make some people happy, But if they [9] cannot effect what they promise, & that really they want many things, [10] that may bee style'd Goods, doth it not cleareły appeare that they only [11] beare a false show of happynesse? First then Let mee aske you y^{r}selfe [12] who not Long ago did flow & abound in richesse, did there neuer any [13] thing trouble you during that abundant wealth you did enjoy? truly [14] (said I) I must confesse I neuer can remember my mind so absolutely [15] at rest, but that still I had something that cros't & vexed mee. was there [16] not still something present that you could haue wish't away, or some= [17] =thing away that you could haue wish't present? (said shee) I confesse [18] (said I) there was. then (said shee) you desired the presence of this & the [19] absence of that, I did so (said I) But (said shee) whateuer one desire's, [20] one wants; So it is (said I) and whoeuer wants, is not sufficient to [21] himselfe, no more hee is not (said I) You then (said Shee) amidst y^{r} [22] richesse endured this want, I did (said I) Then richesse (said shee) [23] cannot make a man want nothing, & bee to himselfe sufficient, & yet [24] this was that, they seemed to promise. Besides, I thinke this very [25] considerable, that wealth hath nothing in it's owne nature, that can [26] **[27r]** prevent it's being taken away from those that possesse it, let them [1] bee neuer so unwilling to parte with it. I confesse it (said I) no [2] thanks to you (said shee) For wee see that daylie that whoeuer is the [3] stronger or the cunninger take's or gett's it away from ye weaker, or [4] Lesse cunning, For else there would not bee that number of Lawe Suites [5] whereof the Courts of Iustice are so full; If those that haue had [6] mony taken from them, or bin cheated were not forced to seeke there [7] to bee redrest? All this is true (said I) whoeuer therefore hath [8] mony (said shee) will need a guard from without to defend it? who [9] (said I) can deny that, But (said Shee) if hee had not that wealth [10] to Loose, hee would not need that guard, no doubt (said I) hee would [11] not. Why then (said shee) heere is the quite contrary of what was [12] expected; For wealth wch it was thought would remoue want, & make [13] it's possessors sufficient to themselues, & not to need the help of others, [14] on the contraryside make's them wante that forraigne aid of guards, [15] wch else they would not neede. But how is it that wealth drive's [16] away want? cannot rich men bee hungry? can they not thirst? & [17] drive away the cold.[28] But in this manner indeede, wante may bee [18] mitigated, & asswaged, but it is not thus, wholly, taken away. For [19] if this need that is still gaping after, & asking something bee fulfilled [20] by richesse, & other things, it must necessarily bee Graunted that there [21] is a need that want's such a fulfilling. I passe ouer in silence, that [22] to Nature a very Litle, to Avarice, nothing is enough. Since there= [23] =fore wealth cannot wholly take away want, but rather cause it, [24] what reason haue you to im*m*agine that richesse carry a Sufficiency along with them? [25]

Verse the 3^{d} of the 3^{d} Booke.

Although a rich man should behold
Rivers of his, running pure Gold
Yet would not all that pretious Store
Quench his dire thirst of hauing more,
And though hee should all Loaded bee
With choycest Pearles of the Red Sea,

[28] "drive away the cold" is underlined, and an "*" stands in the left margin, perhaps marking it for subsequent revision.

[27v] And with a hundred Oxen till
His fertill Feilds & all his Garners fill
Hee only Liuing would bee full of care
And (dead) 'tis others, must these richesse Share.

Prose the 4th of the 3^{d} Booke.

But Titles & Dignities render those honorable & respected that [1] enjoy them. Is there that force & strength in them as[29] that they plant [2] vertue, or driue out vice out of the minds of those that possesse them? Or [3] do they not oftener use to giue credit to wickednesse then to chase it away? [4] For which reason wee use to repine & bee troubled to see them generally [5] fall into the hands of the wickedest men insomuch as y^{t} Catullus thô [6] free saw Nonius sitting in State as Consull call'd him an impostume or [7] Sore of the Kings Euill. Do you not see by that, how much dishonor comes [8] to ill men by Titles & dignities? For their unworthynesse would bee Lesse [9] taken notice of if the Glory of their Tytles did not draw mens eyes upon [10] them. And you y^{r} selfe could neuer bee brought by the consideration & [11] apprehension of so many dangers threatned by King Theodorick, to bee [12] content to bee fellow Consull with Decoratus, because you had disco= [13] =ver'd in him the mind of a Villaine & of an informer. For how can [14] wee judge those render'd worthy of respect by honors, whom wee judge [15] absolutely unworthy of those honours? But if you see a man indu'd [16] with wisdome, you can neuer thinke him either unworthy of that [17] wisdome, or of reverence & respect; For there is that innate dignity [18] in vertue, that render's all men worthy that possesse it. w^{ch}, since [19] popular honours can not it is evident they haue no true & inherent [20] worth in them. In wch this is to bee obseru'd further; That since hee [21] is most abject, that is despised by most people, & that dignitiees and [22] honours cannot make men to bee reverenc't, but on the contrary [23] expose's the vices to ye eyes of more people who cannot but for that, [24] despise them, it follows that dignities contribute to most mens [25] dishonours. But it is againe true, that ill men are even wth those [26] dignities, for in revenge, they staine & blurre them as much. And [27] to the end that you may know that true honour & esteeme is not gain'd [28] by these shadowy tytles & dignitys, obserue, what I shall say. Let [29] a man that hath had the Honour to haue bin often Consull happen [30] to come into a Strange Nation, will that honour render him esteem'd [31]

29 "as" inserted here.

& reverenc't by those there? No; But if there were a naturall & inherent [32] **[28r]** Good in dignitys, no people whatsoeuer, would bee wanting in their dutys [1] of respect & reverence to it, As Fire to what parte of ye world soeuer it is [2] carry'd, will neuer cease to warme. But because in Dignitys there is [3] no proper innate strength & vertue, but only what the deceiptfull opinion [4] of men giues them, therefore they presently vanish, when they come to [5] bee consider'd by those that haue not that opinion of them. This as to [6] other nations, But even in those where they are obtain'd, do they Last [7] alwaies? The Pretorship that was before so great a Power, is now [8] a vaine & idle name, & become now only a heavy burden to the Revenue [9] of the Senate. Those that had heretofore the care comitted to them to [10] prouide corne for the people were held in great esteeme, & honour, Now [11] what is there[30] more abject then that office; For as I said just now, Those things [12] that haue no true & inherent beauty of their owne, Sometimes receaue [13] a Luster, & sometimes Loose it according to ye variety of mens opinions. [14] If then it is not in the power of dignity to make men reverenced, if [15] besides that, they are render'd by the coming into the hands of ill men [16] contemptible, if by the change of times, they Loose their Glory & Luster, [17] if in the opinion of Strangers, they are meane, & of no valew, what [18] is there in themselues of beauty to bee wish't, & sought after, or [19] what happynesse is in their power to afford to others? [20]

Verse the 4th of the 3^{d} Booke.

Though Nero did in Tyrian Purple shine
Adorn'd with pretious stones, Yet thô thus fine,
Hee hatefull did to all good men appeare,
Being both Luxurious & Severe,
Yet this man, did honours, on some bestow,
O'th Senatours, if wee may call them so.
But can you thinke those happy that receaue
Honours, wch th'vitious & ignoble giue?

[28v] Prose the 5th of the 3^{d} Booke.

But can Kingdomes & the Familiarity of Kings make a man [1] powerfull & mighty? why not? if they are Lasting. But how full are [2] former ages,

[30] "there" inserted here.

& euen this present one, of examples of Kings that haue [3] chang'd their condition, from being happy, to bee miserable? O [4] renown'd power & might that hath not strength enough to [5] preserue it selfe! But if this power of Kingdomes & Realmes [6] bee the conferer of happynesse, then certainly, where it is want= [7] =ing on any side, it diminishes the happynesse, & brings in[31] misery. [8] Now although the Empires of men stretch farre, Yet it is impossible, [9] but that there will bee some Nations ouer wch no one King will [10] haue rule, and there where that Power that makes men happy [11] end's, begin's that weakenesse, that make's them miserable. And [12] thus it will happen, that Kings will haue a greater share of misery, [13] then of happynesse. A Tyrant that had consider'd & found by [14] experience the danger of his condition uery properly compared [15] the feares of raigning to those of one that should see a Sword hang= [16] =ing ouer his head, continually threatning him with death. What [17] manner of thing then is this Power, that can neither driue away [18] the biting trouble of cares, nor avoid the goaring prickles of feare, [19] Those that enjoy it would willingly Liue secure, but cannot, & yet [20] they bragge & Glory in their Power? Now can you judge him power= [21] =full t*hat*[32] you see, would do a thing, & cannot? can you thinke him mighty [22] that stand's in need alwaies to bee surrounded with a Guard? Feares all [23] them whom hee terrefye's? as much, nay it may bee more then they do [24] him, who, that hee may seeme powerfull, is alwaies in the hands and [25] consequently in the power of a multitude of Seruants? And now, what [26] need I say any thing of those that are familiar with Kings, when I haue [27] show'd so Litle power, nay so much weaknesse to bee even in Kings [28] themselues? And when besides that, Kings do so often, whether their [29] Regall power continue or faile, throw these Fauourites downe to the [30] ground. Nero forced his Gouernour & familiar friend Seneca to choose [31] his manner of death. Antoninus exposed Papinian who had bin Long [32] one of the powerfullest men in his Court to the swords of his Soldiers, & both [33] these would willingly haue renounced their power, & one of them (to witt) [34] Seneca endeauour'd to get Leaue to giue his richesse to Nero, & to haue [35] gon himselfe volantarily into Exile, But the weight of their Masters [36] anger, brought so quick a ruine upon them, that neither could obtaine [37] what hee desired. What then is this Power, when those that enjoy [38] it, feare? which when you haue,

[31] "in" inserted here.

[32] "t" inserted as an abbreviation for "that."

you are not secure? & when you [39] [29r] would Lay downe, you cannot? are those friends any guard or Safety [1] to a man whom fortune & not vertue gaine's? No, For, hee whom fortune [2] made a Friend, misfortune will make an Enemy. And what greater & [3] more dangerous plague can there bee, then a familiar and Bosome Enemy? [4]

Verse the 5th of the 3d Booke.

Hee that desire's to bee thought Powerfull, must
Orecome his Passions, & his filthy Lust
Subdue, else, thô hee singly raigne
O're all the world, his Conquests are but vaine.
For hee that cannot vanquish foule desires
And keepe himselfe from passion, he aspire's
In vaine to bee thought mighty, being rul'd by Slaues,
Who masters them, brauely himselfe behaues.

Prose the 6th of the 3d Booke.

Now as to Glory & Fame, how deceiptfull & indeed how fowle and [1] contemptible is it, many times? For which reason the Tragedian, not [2] improperly cryes out, O Glory, Glory, what art thou to Thousands, but [3] a sweller & puffer up of eares, for many haue very wrongfully carry'd [4] away a great & glorious name by the false & mistaken opinions of the [5] vulgar, and what fouler & unjust thing can there bee imagined, [6] For whoeuer is cry'd up without cause, must needs blush at his owne [7] praises. But put the case, that they are really deseru'd being gain'd by merit, [8] what aduantage or delight will it bring to the conscience of a wise man [9] who doth not measure his good & happynesse by popular rumour, & [10] applause, but by the trueth & approbation of his owne conscience? [11] For & if it seeme a glorious & a hansome thing to haue spread & propo= [12] =gated ones name, it will follow that it is an ugly & inglorious thing [13] not to haue don it. Now since there must of necessity bee many Nations [14] (as I haue already shew'd) unto whom the Fame of one man cannot [15] **[29v]** haue arriv'd, it must follow, that hee whom you esteeme heere [1] glorious, in another parte of the world is without glory. And among [2] these I do not thinke popularity or vulgar applause so much as [3] worth the mentioning, Since it neither proceed's from judgement [4] nor is euer of any Long continuance. And now who is there that [5] doth not see how slender & empty a thing Nobility it selfe is? which [6] hauing relation to our Familys is forraigne to us, For Nobility is [7] properly an advantage deriv'd, or a praise coming to us from the [8] merrits of our Ancestors. But if it is the vogue & discourse of people [9] that render's a man famous, those only properly are so, of whose indi= [10] =uiduall & numericall persons the people talke, For anothers renowne [11] if you haue don nothing yr selfe to merit it, can neuer make you famous. [12] But if there bee a good in Nobility, I thinke it singly to bee this, that [13] by it, there seeme's to bee a necessity imposed upon men Nobly borne, not [14] to degenerate from the virtue of their ancestors. [15]

Verse the 6th of the 3d Booke.

All humane race from one beginning came
One is of all the Father, & did Frame
All things in heauen & earth, & gaue
To all things what they are, & haue
'Tis hee that giues the sunne his glorious beames
The Moone her hornes, to Starres their Lesser streames
Of Light, to the earth men, & did create
Bodys to th'soules hee gaue from his high seate.
If then all mortalls come of noble seede
And from the same originall proceede
Why do you boast the stock from whence yo spring
When 'tis not blood, but vertue, is the thing
Which make's a difference 'twixt yr birth
And that of others, For one selfe same earth
All men are made of, & hee's only base
Who foster's Low borne vice, in vertues place.

[30r] Prose the 7th of the 3d Booke.

But what shall I say of the Pleasures of the body, Of wch the pursuite [1] is full of anxiety & trouble, & the enjoyment of sorrow & repentence? How [2] many Loathsome & intollerable paines, are they us'd to bring (as a certaine [3] fruite of wickednesse) to the bodys of those that use them, whose motions [4] what they haue of pleasure & delight I know not, But this I know, that [5] whoeuer will call to minde the Lusts of his Life past, will find their end to [6] bee full of sorrow & affliction. And if such pleasures are able to make [7] men happy, I know no reason why beasts should not bee styled so, rather [8] then men, since their wholl businesse is to fulfill the Lusts & desires of [9] their bodys. The satisfaction of a wife & children were a very pleasant [10] & agreeable thing, if many times they were not so unnaturall as to [11] become the greatest torment of their fathers, the condition of w^{ch} [12] children (whatever it bee) how much trouble it create's it will[33] not bee need= [13] =full heere to tell you, who haue not only had the experience of it, but [14] are still doubtfull & concern'd about it, in so much as that I approue of [15] the opinion of my Euripides who said of one that wanted children, That [16] hee was become happy, by that misfortune. [17]

Verse the 7th of the 3^{d} Booke.

All worldly pleasure doth this mischeife bring
Unto th'enjoyers, that it Leaues a Sting
Behind, that's much more Lasting, Like the Bee
Who hauing given his hony, angerly
Doth fly away, & Leaue's wth those hee sting's, a paine
Which Longer then the taste of hony will remaine.

Prose the 8th of the 3^{d} Booke.

It is then undoubtedly manifest that all these things that I haue [1] mention'd are wayes, that rather Lead from happynesse, then to it, & con= [2] =sequently cannot afford to any that good they promise. Now besides how [3] intermixt & entangled they are with evills, I will immediately demonstrate; [4] For will you endeauour to get wealth? if you do, you must take it away [5] from those that haue it. Haue you a mind to shine with Tytles & dig= [6] =nitys? if you haue, You must Sue to those, that bestow them. And you [7] **[30v]** that desire to go before others in honour, must debase y^{r} selfe [1] by the meanesse of asking. Do you desire power? If you haue [2] it you expose y^{r} selfe to the snares & ambushes of those, that are [3] under you. Is it Glory you seeke? If so, whilst through dangers [4] and difficulties you pursue it, you leaue to bee safe. Would you [5] Live a voluptuous Life? who is there, that doth not scorne and [6] contemne to bee a slaue to the meanest & most fraile partes of [7] his body. And now you may see how Litle, & how slender a parte of [8] that litle they couet, who preferre the goods of the body, before their [9] reason. For can you exceed Elephants in bignesse? Bulls in strength? [10] Or Tygers in Swiftnesse? Looke upon the Largenesse, firmnesse & Swift= [11] =nesse of the Heauens, & cease at least to admire meane things. w^{ch} [12] heauens are

[33] "will" inserted here.

not more to bee admir'd for those qualitys, I haue men= [13] =tion'd, then for the reason & wisdome by wch they are rul'd & gouern'd. [14] Now the beauty of y^{r} Body, how swiftly passing & transitory is it? Euen [15] more flitting then the flowers of the spring. And if (as Aristotle says) [16] men did Looke with such peircing eyes as the beast wch they call a [17] Link is said to haue, So as that they could see through the things, that [18] now withstand their sight, would not that outwardly faire body of [19] Alcibiades, if its inside & bowells were Look'd into, appeare most Ugly [20] & foule. 'Tis not therefore y^{r} nature, but the weakenesse & infirmity of [21] those that Looke upon you, that make's you seeme hansome. But prize [22] and Esteeme the goods of y^{r} body as much as you please, prouided you [23] remember that whateuer of hansomnesse you Looke upon may bee [24] destroyed by a feauour in Lesse then three dayes. From all wch wee may [25] in shorte make this conclusion, that those things that cannot afford [26] those goods they promise, nor are perfect by the aggregation of all goods [27] together in one, are neither paths that Lead to happynesse, nor can [28] of themselues make men happy. [29]

Verse the 8th of the 3^{d} Booke.

O how doth ignorance the Steps misguide
Of wretched men, by putting them beside
The path that Leade's to truth? who do wee see
Going to seeke for Gold, in a greene tree,
Or Iewells in a Vine, who bait's for fish
Vpon the tops of mountaines to enrich
[31r] His feast withall? when you intend a Roe
Or Stagge to hunt, you do not use to goe
To th' + [34] fords? Men now are come to know
The creeks hid by the Sea when it doth flow
And by Laborious industry haue found
Where 'tis that Pearles, where Purple doth abound
What shores do most of tender fish afford,
And wch doth yeild that, wch the name of sword
For sharpnesse hath obtain'd, all this men know
But know not where their good is hid, but seeke below
On earth, what is aboue the heauens plac't,

[34] "+" and space left here, marking missing text and allowing room for an insertion for "Tyrrhena" later.

What should I wish worthy the deprau'd taste
Of such fond men? Let them bee restlesse till they gaine
Those goods, wch when they haue, may they judge vaine.

Prose the 9th of the 3^{d} Booke.

What I haue already said may suffice to giue you the picture of [1] false felicity, which if you haue clearly Look't upon & consider'd, it [2] will bee now fit according to the order I propose'd to my selfe, to show [3] you what true happynesse is. I am convinc't (said I) that it is not in [4] the Power of wealth to giue sufficiency, of Empire to giue Power, of Dig= [5] =nitys to giue Reverence & esteeme, of Glory to giue true Nobility, Nor of [6] Pleasures to giue perfect Ioy. And have you found out the cause of this [7] (said shee)? mee thinks (said I) I see as it were a glimpse of it, But I [8] would willingly know it more fully from you. The reason (said shee) is [9] manifest, For that wch is in it selfe by nature single & indiuisible, the errour [10] & folly of mankinde sever's & devide's, & brings us from what is entire & [11] truely perfect to runne after that wch is devided & imperfect. Do you [12] thinke that hee need's nothing, that want's power? I do not (said I) you are [13] right (said shee) For in whateuer any thing is weake, it will in that want an [14] outward helpe. 'tis true (said I) Sufficiency then & Power are one & the same [15] in nature. (said Shee) 'tis true (said I) Sufficiency then must bee added to [16] Power, to make it considerable? it appeare's so, (said I). [17] **[31v]** But what possesses all these together, do you think worthy to bee under= [1] =valew'd? or on the contrary to bee esteem'd of all things the most worthy? [2] It admit's (said I) of no dispute. What then if wee adde reuerence and [3] Esteeme to sufficiency & Power, so as to Looke upon them all as one thing, [4] what opinion will you then conceaue of it? shall you not then judge it [5] the brightest & most illustrious thing in the world? For you must [6] consider that what hath bin granted to need nothing, to bee most mighty [7] & most worthy of honour, if it bee not Illustrious by it's fame & renowne [8] (wch is a thing it cannot giue to it selfe, but depend's upon the good will [9] of others) it will bee upon that Scoare (though it haue the rest) ye Lesse [10] accompted of, & valew'd? certainly it will (said I) It follow's then (said [11] shee) that wee must joyne also renowne to the rest, to make up one thing [12] of them all, it doth so (said I) That then (said shee) that needs nothing [13] from without, that can do all things by it's owne strength, that is reve= [14] =renc't & famous, ought it not to bee the joyfullest & most contented thing [15] in the world? I cannot imagin (said I) how it is possible that any [16] thing of greife can euer come to what is thus quallyfy'd, therefore [17] it must bee confess't, that where those things are, & continue y^r thing [18] that enjoye's them ought to bee concluded most full of Ioy & content, & [19] it must for the same reason bee granted, That Power, Sufficiency, Renowne, [20] reuerence, & Ioy, are indeed different in name, but agree in Substance. It [21] doth (said I) necessarily follow, because they are singly incompleate. This [22] thing, therefore that is singly & simply one, the depravity of mans Nature [23] severs, and whilst it endeauours to gaine a parte of what is indeed w^thout [24] partes, it neuer gaine's the parte it aymes at. How (said I) do you meane [25] that? why (said shee) hee that seek's richesse out of his feare of penury [26] & want, Labours not for Power, & had rather bee obscure & of no accompt & [27] deny himselfe many naturall pleasures, then deminish ye heape of mony [28] hee hath Laid up. So that by this meanes, hee neuer attaines to a Sufficiency, [29] being destitute of power, Stung continually with care & trouble, cast [30] downe by his meanesse, & Lying hid in obscurity. Hee that ayme's solely [31] at might, Lauishe's away his wealth, despise's Pleasures, & valew's neither [32] Esteeme nor Glory, if it want Power. But to this man you see how many [33] things are wanting, for some times it happens, that hee even wants [34] necessaries, & is often vexed with trouble & unquietnesse, wch since hee [35] is not able to ouercome, hee Leaue's euen to bee powerfull, wch was the [36] thing hee courted. Wee may reason after the same manner concern= [37] =ing honours, Glory, & Pleasures, For since euery one of these, is the [38] same with the rest, that is, make's up one whole & indivisible thing [39] with them, hee that pursue's any one of them without the rest, cannot [40] obtaine euen that, that hee aime's at; But what (said I) would you [41] say if hee aim'd at them altogether? I would say (said shee) hee aymed [42] at the soueraigne happynesse, but do you thinke it possible hee should [43] finde it in these things that I haue show'd not to bee able to performe, [44] what they promise? by no meanes (I reply'd) certainly (said shee) [45] **[32r]** Happynesse is not to bee sought for in these things, though they seeme [1] to bee able to afford euery thing one desire's. I confesse it (said I) & there can [2] bee nothing truly so said. You haue then (said shee) before you, both ye Forme [3] & the causes of false felicity. Now turne back y^r eyes into y^r owne minde for [4] there you shall immediately see the true happynesse I promised. I were [5] (said I) worse then blinde if I did not already see what you haue made so [6] apparent, whilst you endeauour'd to Lay open the causes of false felicity, [7] For if I am not mistaken, that is true & perfect happynesse, that makes [8] a man powerfull, Sufficient, Reverenc't, Famous, & contented; and that w^ch [9] (what you may perceaue, I haue minded y^r discourse) can afford one of them, [10] they being not to bee seperated, affords them all, & that without any ye Least [11] doubt I know to bee true & compleate happynesse. O how happy are you [12] (said shee) since you are of that opinion, if you but adde what I am going to [13] tell you, what's that (said I) whether you thinke there is any thing in [14] these mortall & transitory things that can bring one to this Estate. I did[35] not [15] (said I) for you haue fully & in my opinion, demonstrated the contrary. These [16] things then seeme only to show us the shaddows of the true good, or to afford us [17] some imperfect ones, But the true & perfect good they cannot conferre upon [18] Us. I agree with you (said I) since then (said shee) you are come to know [19] what is true blisse, & what things do only falsely pretend to it, It remaine's [20] That you learne from whence to seeke that wch is true. Tis' that (said I) [21] that I haue Long impatiently desired & expected from you. But since [22] as our disciple Plato (said shee) hath it in his times[36], It is fit to im= [23] =plore the divine ayde even in the Least things, What do you thinke is [24] fit for us now to do, that wee may deserue to finde out that Seate of [25] the Soueraigne good? wee must invoke (said I) the Father of all things [26] without w^{ch}, nothing is well begun, You haue said right (said shee) & [27] immediately began to sing after this manner. [28]

Verse the 9th of the 3^{d} Booke.

O thou who do'st by eternall reason sway
The world thou mad'st, & mak'st ye heauens obey
Thy Pow're, thou that has't made ye times to runne
From age to age, since the first age begun,
And being still immutable aboue,
Mak'st all things that are under thee to moue,
Thou that in framing of all things, wer't mou'd
Not by e[x]ternall[37] causes, but ye Love to good,
[32v] That is inherent in thee without enuy's[38] gall
Or passion, Thou from thy originall
Dos't all things draw, & being thy selfe most faire
Of all, dos't in thy minde th'idea beare

[35] "did" underlined and marked with an "x" above, indicating that it should be revisited, perhaps to change it to the present tense.

[36] "times" here should be a reference to Plato's "timeo" or "Timaeus."

[37] The clear meaning here is "externall" rather than the original manuscript reading, "eternall." A faint "x" is visible in the manuscript, just above and between the "e" and "t."

[38] "enuy's" inserted here.

Of a faire world, & this by that doth frame
Giving com*m*and the partes should have ye same
Perfection, that the whole may perfect bee
And therefore mak'st the Elements agree
By contradiction[39] to support the whole
Making the moist & dry, the hot & cold
Temper each other so, as that the Fire
(W^{ch} purest is, & Light) should not aspire
Too high, nor too much weight bow downe
The earth, & make it in the waters drowne.
Thou dos't the soule of threefold nature (which
Doth all things moue) proportionably enrich
With members, that it being devided may
Moue in two Sphears, & then it selfe convey
Back to it selfe againe, & Fathoming
With profound thoughts ye heau'ns, may Likwise bring
The image of them hoame, Thou also dos't
Raise up Lesse soules, & (in Light charriots thrust)
Dost carry them on high & sow them in
Both heau'n & earth, & being conuerted then
By thy beningne Law, dos't by a Fire guide
Them back again, & make them wth thee 'bide
O Grant O Father, that my Soule may fly
Into that narrow Seate aboue, & by
Thy Grace and fauour may investigate
The spring & Fountaine of true good, & that
[33r] Having recouerd her Long wanted Sight
Shee fix her eyes on thee, who art the Light
And resting place of all good man, do thou
Disperse the clouds of earthly thoughts, & throw
Their weight quite downe, & on Us kindly shine
For th'art beginning, End, Guider, & way
To all that do thy just commands Obey.

Prose the 10th of the 3^{d} Booke.

Since therefore you haue seene the description of ye imperfect & of the

[39] "contradiction" underlined and marked with an "o" above, with "opposition" written beside this line in the left margin, perhaps as an alternate rendering.

perfect good, I thinke it now proper to show, wherein this perfection of [2] happynesse consist's, in order to wch I thinke it not unecessary first to enquire & [3] consider, whether, there bee really any such good (as you Lately defin'd) in [4] nature? Least wee unproffitably discourse, being carry'd by a vaine imma= [5] =gination beside the trueth of what really is; But that there is such a [6] thing, that is, (as it were) the Fountaine of all Goods, is not to bee doubted, [7] For whateuer is said to bee imperfect must bee proued so, by showing the [8] difference betwixt it, & what is perfect, to wit, what it wants of that [9] perfection, for wch reason it is evident that in[40] what kind soever there is some= [10] =thing imperfect, there must in the same bee of necessity, something that is [11] perfect. For taking away perfection, you cannot faine or imagine an im= [12] =perfection, for nature did not take it's beginning in Lame & unfinisht [13] things, but proceeding from what is whole & perfect, degenerates & fall's [14] into these Low & empty things, So that if there bee (as wee haue already [15] showne) an imperfect & fraile happynesse, it follow's that there must bee [16] also a happynesse, that is perfect, solide, & entire. It is most firmely (said I) [17] & most truly concluded. Now where that is, Let us consider. That God [18] who is the Prince of all things, is a Good the generall conceipt & appre= [19] =hension of all people doth sufficiently evince, For since nothing can [20] bee imagined that is better then hee, who can doubt that to bee a good, [21] then w^{ch}, nothing is better? and reason show's us that[41] God is so perfectly good that [22] wee cannot but bee convinc't that perfect good is in him. For if God were not [23] so, hee could not bee the Prince & cheefe of all things, for something that possest [24] a perfect good would be greater & worthyer then hee, & that thing would [25] consequently bee more antient then God, For wee haue already declar'd that [26] perfect things are first in nature before the imperfect, So that unlesse, wee [27] will reason to eternity, wee must confesse the high God, to bee fullest of the [28] cheefest & most perfect good. But wee haue already agreed that y^e cheefest [29] good is the true happynesse, it doth therefore follow, that the only true happy= [30] =nesse is in the most high God. I acknowledge it, (said I) nor do I see, how it [31] **[33v]** can admit of any dispute, But (said shee) Let mee intreat you to Let mee [1] know, how you do apprehend this, that I haue said of Almighty Gods being [2] fullest of the cheefe good, my reason of asking is, Least you should imagin

[40] "in" added here.

[41] "that" inserted here.

[3] that this Father of all things should haue receau'd that cheefe good (whereof [4] we haue show'd him to bee full) from without, or that hee possesse's it, as [5] a distinct substance from himselfe, wch were a great errour, For if you [6] conceau'd him to haue receau'd it from without, you might consequently [7] think that from whom hee receau'd it to bee worthyer then God, whom wee [8] do deseruedly confesse & acknowledge to bee the worthyest & most Excellent [9] of all things. But if this good that is in him by nature, bee apprehended by y^{r} [10] reason (because wee speake of God, as of the Prince of all things) to bee a [11] thing distinc't from him, Let any body faine (that can) who it was y^{t} joyn'd [12] these distinct things together? Lastly whateuer is distinc't from another, is [13] not a thing from wch it is distinct, wherefore, whateuer is by it's nature [14] distinct from the cheefe good, cannot bee the cheefe good, wch it were a Sinne [15] to thinke of God, then whom there can bee nothing more worthy, For it is im= [16] =possible that the nature of any thing should be better, then it's beginning, [17] therefore that, that is the beginning of all things, must be concluded by [18] right reason, to bee in it's whole substance, the most Soueraigne Good. But [19] it is already granted, that the Soveraigne Good is the only true happynesse [20] & felicity, it must therefore bee confes't, that God is that happynesse. I [21] cannot (said I) deny the premisses, & I do acknowledge, what you say to bee [22] rightly inferr'd from them. Now see (said shee) whether from hence also, it [23] bee not yet more firmly prou'd, that there cannot bee two Soueraigne Goods dis= [24] =tinc't from one another, For if they are different, it is plaine one cannot bee [25] t'other, wherfore neither can bee perfect, since one is wanting to the other, [26] But it is Evident that, that wch is not perfect, cannot bee the cheefe good, there= [27] =fore it is impossible that there should bee distinct Soueraigne goods, But wee [28] haue already gather'd both happynesse, & God to bee the Souereigne Good, it doth [29] therefore follow, That the high God is the cheefe happynesse. There can nothing [30] (said I) bee concluded that is in it's selfe nor in reason clearer, nor anything [31] bee imagin'd more worthy then God. Now therefore (said shee) as Geometrici= [32] =ans use (when they haue demonstrated their propositions) bring in something [33] wch they call ——— [42] & wch I will giue you as a Corollary (Viz ^{t}) [34] That since by the obtaining of happynesse, men are made happy, & that God is [35] happynesse, it is manifest that to enjoy God, make's men happy, & as by the [36] acquisition of Iustice, men

[42] A line drawn and space left here for a rendering of *porismata*; below, similar notation provided for a translation of *porisma* to be added later.

are Iust, & by attaining of wisedom, men are wise, [37] So by the same reason, those that enjoy God are Gods. Euery one then y[t] is happy [38] is a God. For though there bee in nature but one God, yet by participation nothing [39] hinder's but there may bee many; and this is (said I) a most faire and pretious [40] Corollary or —— Certainly (said shee) nothing is fairer or more [41] pretious. Then what in reason ought to be added to this, what is that (said I) It [42] is (said shee) that since happynesse seemes to containe in itselfe many things, whether [43] all those things do as so many members make up one body of Blisse & happynesse, [44] or whether there bee any one thing among them that of it selfe compleat's the [45] whole substance of happynesse, to w[ch] the rest do but relate? I should bee glad [46] (said I) that you would make this more plaine to mee, by once more [47] mentioning[43] & running ouer those things. Have wee not concluded [48] **[34r]** (said shee) that happynesse is a good? Yes (said I) & the cheefe good. [1] Adde then (said shee) that to all the rest, For that same happynesse [2] that is judged to bee absolute Sufficiency is also Soueraigne power, Reve= [3] =rence, Fame, Nobility, Pleasure &c[a] What then are all these goods [4] Viz: Sufficiency, Power, & the rest, as members of happynesse, or are [5] they related to happynesse as to their cheefe? I now understand [6] (said I) what you propose to bee search't into & consider'd, but I had [7] rather heare it declar'd by you. Take then (said shee) thus y[e] decision [8] of this question. If all these things were members of happynesse, [9] they would then differ from one another, For that is the nature of parts, [10] that being diuerse & distinct, they together compose one Body. But [11] all these things haue bin show'd to bee the same, therefore it follow's [12] they cannot bee members, For else happynesse that is a Body might bee [13] completed by one member, w[ch] were absurd. That is very cleare (said I) [14] But I expect to heare what remaine's. It is as cleare (said shee) that [15] all those other things do relate to happynesse, For therefore sufficiency [16] is desired because it is accompted a good, therefore Power is sought after [17] because it is esteem'd a good, the same may bee said of Honour, Fame, [18] pleasure & the rest; The reason then & cause of any things being desired [19] is because it is Look't upon as a good; For whateuer is neither in [20] reallity, nor in appearance a good, cannot be desired, & sought after. [21] But on the contrary t'is true that though things bee not by their Na= [22] =ture really goods, Yet if they seeme to bee so, they are often times [23] sought after, as if they were truly goods, So that

[43] "men=" on preceding line, but the full word "mentioning" on the next.

goodnesse is deser= [24] =uedly beleiu'd to bee the cheefe cause, why any thing is desired & [25] sought after. Now the thing for whose sake any thing is desired, is no [26] doubt, the most esteem'd, & most eagerly wish't for. As for example, [27] hee that desire's to ride for his health, doth not so much desire & intend [28] riding, as health, wch hee hopes will bee the effect of it. Since then all [29] things are sought after, because they are goods, or seeme, to be so, t'is [30] not so much those things, as good, that is desir'd of all. But that for [31] the sake of wch other things are desired, wee haue already granted to [32] bee happynesse, So then happynesse alone is the thing sought after, [33] From whence it doth cleerely appeare that happynesse & the cheefe [34] good, is one & the same thing in Substance. I do not (said I) see [35] how it can bee deny'd. But (said shee) wee haue already show'd that [36] God & true happynesse is one & the same thing, Wee may therefore safely [37] conclude that the substance of happynesse is to bee found in God, & no [38] where else. [39]

Verse the 10th of the 3^{d} Booke.

Hither then come you that are fondly caught
By cos'ning Lusts that haue detaind y^{r} thought
[34v] In wicked chaines, heere shall you find y^{r} rest
From Labours, heere you'le find a harbour blest
With quiet Safety, heer's the only true
Refuge for sinfull men, 'tis not Peru
With all it's Gold, not Tagus golden sand
Nor Hermus with his sparkling shining strand
Or Indus neighbour to the Sunne, that can
(Mingling the Emerauld wth the Pearle) a man
Free from his blindeness, but will yet still more
In darkenesse plunge him, then hee was before.
All that in despicable earth can moue
Your thoughts, is hid in holes, but that aboue
Which gouern's heauen auoid's all darke and
Obscure ruine of the Soule, & hee that can
Once come t'obserue that Light, will truly say
The Sunne is farre from bright, e'en at Noone day.

Prose the 11th of the 3^{d} Booke

I cannot (said I) but agree to what you say, seeing it so strongly [1] back'd with reason. What valew will you put upon it (said shee) [2] if by it I teach you to know the Soueraigne Good it selfe? an Infinite [3] one (said I) For then I must needs know God also, who is y[t] Soueraigne [4] good, This I shall not faile (said shee) to Lay open to you, if y[e] things [5] already concluded on, do but remaine in y[r] mind, they shall (said I) [6] Haue wee not demonstrated (said shee) that those severall things y[t] [7] are sought after by many are not really true & perfect goods, because [8] being distinct one from another, they may bee single, & one being w[th]out [9] the other cannot afford a full & absolute good? & that then it only [10] become's a true good when they are gather'd together, & are in effect one, [11] as when sufficiency is Power, honour, pleasure, &c: and so on y[e] contrary [12] Vice versa? For if all those things put together do not make up one thing, [13] they haue nothing in them singly, worth being desired? You haue (said I) [14] **[35r]** already demonstrated it, & it is no way to bee doubted. Those things then [1] (said shee) w[ch] when they are diuided & distinct, are not to bee esteem'd goods, [2] but when they grow to bee one thing, do become a good; are they not behold= [3] =ing to Unity for their being goods? It appeare's so (said I) But (said shee) [4] you grant that euery thing that is good is so, by the participation of [5] goodnesse, or do you not, I do (said I) then (said shee) you must grant by [6] the same reason that Vnity & goodnesse are the same thing. For the [7] substance must bee the same of things, that naturally do not differ [8] in the effect. I cannot (said I) deny it. Do you not know then (said shee) [9] that euery thing that is in being doth continue & subsist as Long as [10] it preserue's it's Vnity & remaine's one, and dye's & is dissolu'd when y[t] [11] Vnity is destroy'd, & that it cease's to bee one; As for Example, in Living [12] creatures, whilst the body & the Soule remaine together in one, it is [13] call'd a Liuing creature, but when that Unity is dissolu'd by their [14] seperation, it dye's, & is no more a Liuing creature. The body it selfe [15] whilst it remaines in one forme, by the joyning together of it's mem= [16] =bers, retaine's a humane shape, but if by the seuering of those parts [17] it's Unity is destroy'd, it Leaue's to bee what it was, & in y[e] same man= [18] =ner whoeuer will run ouer other things will find clearely that every [19] thing subsist's as Long as it continues one, & perishe's when it cease's [20] to bee one. It appeare's so to mee (said I) whateuer thing I consider. [21] Is there any thing (said shee[)][44] that act's according to nature) that neglects [22] & Leaue's it's owne preseruation, & desire's it's owne death & corruption?

[44] ")" missing in manuscript.

[23] If (said I) I consider Liuing creatures that haue a power in them to [24] will & Nill, I cannot find any, (no force being putt upon them from [25] without) that quit the desire of remaining in being, & absolutely[45] [26] hasten to their deaths; For all Liuing creatures Labour to preserue [27] their healths & safetyes, & do avoid (what they can) death & destruction. [28] But I am doubtfull what to say, as to herbs, Trees & such like unanimated [29] things; There is no reason for you to doubt concerning them (said shee) [30] Since you see Trees & herbs first choose to themselues convenient [31] places, where, as Long as their nature will endure, they are free from [32] the danger of being dry'd up, & dying. For some grow in the feilds, Some upon [33] hills, some in Marshes, others in Rocks, others on the dry sands, all w^ch^ [34] if you go about to transplant, into other places & Soyles of a different [35] nature, will dry up & wither. But nature giue's to euerything what is [36] conuenient for it selfe, & Labours to preserue it from dying as Long as [37] it hath power to Liue & to remaine. What shall I say more, You see they [38] all with their mouths (as it were) thrust into the ground suck in their [39] nourishment by their rootes, & so convey & disperse it throug their rind into [40] their Pith, & strength. You see that what is softest as the pith is hid in the [41] uery middle, & safest place, & couer'd without with firme wood to defend [42] it from hurts & bruises, & that againe fortyfy'd on the outside by a rugged [43] rind that is ablest to resist the injuries of the weather. Then consider [44] **[35v]** The care & diligence of nature to prouide that all things should by [1] their seed bee propogated & increas't, and by that meanes contriuing [2] that they should not only continue for a time, but from one generation [3] to another as Long as the world is to endure. and those things that are [4] beleeu'd absolutely inanimated, do they not also desire & take care to [5] hold what is their owne? For why else doth the Lightnesse of flames carry [6] them upwards, & weight keep downe the earth, But that those seuerall [7] places & motions are most agreeable to their natures? & so euery thing keep's [8] to what is most suitable & proper for it, as naturally as what is an Enemy [9] to it seek's to corrupt & destroy it. Those things that are hard, as Stones [10] keep their partes fast together, & by their firmnesse hinder themselues [11] from being easily broken & dissolv'd. Those things that are Liquid & thinne [12] as aire & water giue way without resistance, to any thing that would [13] devide & passe through

45 "absolutely" underlined, perhaps marked for revision in order to find a more fit rendering of *sponte*.

them, but then immediately returne againe to [14] their places & joyne. Fire refuseth all devision. For wee do not now speake [15] of the volantory actions & motions of a knowing Soule, but wee treate of [16] the naturall intention & tendency of things. As wee disgest our meate [17] without minding or thinking of it, & draw our breaths in our sleep, wth= [18] =out knowing it. For in beasts the desire of Liuing & continnuing doth [19] not proceed from the Will of their Soules, but from the principles and [20] instinct of nature. For many times the Will (mou'd by reason) choose's [21] death, wch nature feare's & abhorre's. And on the contrary side the Will [22] doth many times restraine & make men forbeare that act of generation, [23] wch nature alwaies desire's as the only meanes of making mortall things [24] to Last & endure. So that this Loue that euery thing beare's to it selfe, doth [25] not proceed from the motions of the Soule, but from the intention & instinct [26] of nature. For the prouidence of God hath giuen this gift to all things hee [27] hath created, that they all naturally desire to continue & Liue. There= [28] =fore you cannot doubt, but that euery thing that is naturall seek's it's [29] owne continuance, & to avoid it's destruction. I confesse (said I) I do [30] see it cleerely now, thô before it seem'd doubtfull to mee. But (said shee) [31] whateuer desire's to subsist & continue, desire's to bee one thing, For Unity [32] being taken away, it's uery beeing cease's, 'tis true (said I) all things [33] then (said shee) desire one thing, I agree, But that one thing (said shee) [34] wee haue show'd to bee same[46] as the cheefe good; All things therefore [35] desire the cheefe good, So that you may define that to bee ye cheefe good, [36] that is desired & sought after by all. There can nothing (said I) bee [37] imagin'd that is truer, for either all things will fall to nothing, being [38] destitute of that one, as of their head, & will bee tos't to & fro without [39] a ruler, or if there bee one thing, to wch all things tend & hasten, that [40] one thing must bee the cheefe & soueraigne good. Then (said shee) how [41] much do I rejoyce (O my schollar) that thou has't fixed this truth in [42] thy heart, But I find by this you haue discover'd what you said a [43] **[36r]** Litle while ago, you were ignorant of, what's that (said I)? What the [1] end of all things is, For that is the end of all things, wch all things desire & [2] seeke after. Which since wee haue show'd to bee the cheefe good, wee must [3] acknowledge That the cheefe & soueraigne good is the end of all things. [4]

[46] "t" inserted between "bee" and "same"—perhaps to indicate an abbreviation for "the."

Verse the 11th of the 3^{d} Booke.

Hee that would truth wth curious Studdy find
And in no odde by paths would bee misled
Hee must turne back his eyes into his mind
And draw back home those wandring thoughts y^{t} did
On other objects dwell, & teach his Soule
That it within those treasures doth possesse
(And might enjoy them there without controule)
That shee without doth seeke, & fondly misse.
And when the cloud of error's gon, hee'le find[47]
The sunne will not shine brighter then his mind
For 'twere injustice in Us once to thinke
That all the light of reason were put out,
In those, whose weight of body seeme's to sinke
Their minds into forgetfullnesse, for without doubt
Some Seedes of truth remaine, wch Studdy may
Draw forth, else how could you when ask't speake right
Of things, if that the roote of truth wch Lay
Before hid in y^{r} harte, gaue you not Light.
So Plato truly saith, that truth is not
Learnt by Us new, but as a thing forgot

[36v] Prose the 12th of the 3^{d} Booke.

I agree (said I) very much with Plato in his opinion, For y^{o} haue [1] already twice reuiu'd my memory concerning these things, first [2] when, by the infectious weight of my body, and secondly when by the [3] heavy oppres-sion of my greife, I had Lost the remembrance of them. [4] Then, (said shee), if you Looke back upon the things already granted, it [5] will not bee Long before you remember, what a litle while ago, y^{o} confes't [6] you were ignorant of; What's that (said I) By what Gouernment & Rule [7] the world is gouern'd, I do remember (said I) that I confest I was ignor= [8] =rant of it. & though I see a kind of glimpse of what you intend to say, [9] Yet I desire to heare it more plainly from you. That the world (said Shee) [10] is gouerne'd by Almighty God, you haue already declar'd to bee out of doubt. [11] I neither do, (said I) nor shall euer thinke that doubtfull, and I shall [12] breefly set forth upon what reasons, I ground my opinion.

[47] Lines 9 and 10 bracketed in right margin; this rhyming couplet follows two quatrains (lines 19 and 20 not bracketed, however).

The world con= [13] =sisting of so many severall & differing partes could neuer haue come [14] together into one Shape & forme, if some one thing had not joyn'd things [15] in themselues so different. And being joyn'd the diversity & disagreem^t [16] of their natures would quickly Sever & teare them asunder, if that one [17] thing that joyn'd, did not also keep them together, neither would nature [18] proceed in so certaine an order, nor produce such orderly & regular [19] motions as to time, place, Efficiency, Spaces, & qualities, if there were [20] not one that remaining stedfast order'd & disposed this variety and [21] change of motions. And this whateuer it is, by wch the things that are [22] created, are mov'd & do Subsist; I call by the name of God, wch is a [23] word us'd by all people. Then (said shee) since you are of this opinion [24] I thinke there will Litle remaine for mee to do, to bring you back whole [25] & happy into y^r owne country. But let us Looke back upon what wee [26] haue already premis'd; Haue wee not Show'd Sufficiency to bee in [27] happynesse? And haue wee not granted that God is happynesse? wee [28] haue. Then (said shee) if it bee so, hee will not need help from without [29] to gouerne the world. For if hee doth hee hath not an absolute Sufficiency. [30] That follows (said I) necessarily. Then (said shee) by himselfe alone hee [31] gouern's, & dispose's all things. It cannot (said I) bee deny'd. But [32] God (said shee) hath bin show'd to bee good it Selfe, I remember (said [33] I) hee hath, then (said shee) by that good hee gouern's all things, Since [34] hee who by himselfe gouern's all things is granted to bee that good. [35] and this is the[48] naile or pinne upon wch the frame of the world is kept firme [36] & Stable. I do fully agree to what you say (said I) and did before guesse [37] (though I was not absolutely assured of it) that you would make this [38] conclusion. I beleiue so (said shee) For I perceaue now you begin to [39] bend y^r Eyes more carefully towards the discerning of truths, But [40] howeuer what I shall further say to you, will not a Litle confirme you, [41] **[37r]** What's that (said I) Since God (said shee) is believe'd (& deseruedly) [1] to gouerne all things by the pinne or finger of his goodnesse, and that [2] all things (as I haue already taught) do naturally hasten to good, as to [3] their end, it can no way bee doubted but that they are volontarily gouernd [4] & do apply themselues willingly to obey the will of their King & Gouernour. [5] It must need's bee so (Said I) For else how could that Gouerment seeme [6] happy if it were

[48] "‸T" inserted between "is" and "the" to indicate a missing phrase, probably "as it were" or "so to speak."

a Yoke men Struggl'd to draw awry in, & not a place safe [7] in a calme obedience. There is nothing then (said shee) that keep's it's [8] nature, that endeauour's to oppose it selfe to God Nothing (said I) But [9] if it doth endeauour it (said Shee) will it availe any thing to oppose him, [10] whom by the right of happynesse and Blisse wee haue concluded to bee [11] most powerfull? without doubt (said I) it would not. There is there= [12] =fore nothing that will or can resist this cheefe & Soueraigne good. [13] There is not certainly (said I) Then the Soueraigne good (said Shee) is [14] that, that Gouern's all things Strongly, & dispose's all things sweetly. [15] 'Tis so (said I) & I am not only delighted with the summe of those [16] reasons you haue brought (wch are so convincing) but much more w^{th} [17] these Last words you haye utter'd, wch do absolutely make mee asham'd [18] of the folly of those I did at first barke out. You haue heard (said shee) [19] in the Fables of the Poets of the Gyants making Warre upon heauen, [20] but those were (as they deseru'd) ouerthrow'n & destroy'd by the benigne [21] Power of God. But shall wee strike those reasons themselues together [22] one against the other? it may bee from their meeting & conflict, there [23] may spring out some faire Sparkes of truth, as you please (said I) [24] no body (said shee) doubts, but that God is Omnipotent. No body [25] (said I) that hath his wits. But (said shee) there is nothing that [26] hee that is Omnipotent cannot do. Nothing (said I) can God then [27] do Evill? No (said I) Evill then is nothing (said shee) since hee cannot [28] do that to whom only nothing is impossible. Do you Laugh at mee [29] (said I) contriuing an inextricable Labarinth with y^{r} reasons, by [30] the meanes of w^{ch}, you may sometimes go in where you came out, [31] and sometimes go out where you come in? or do you go about to [32] frame by y^{r} words a wonderfull kind of circle to Environ the devine [33] singlenesse & simplicity with? For just now beginning wth happy= [34] =nesse you declared it to bee the Soueraigne Good & to reside in God [35] and that God, the cheefe good, & absolute happynesse, was one & the [36] same thing, out of wch you gaue this Litle conclusion as a guift [37] that no body could bee happy, but at the same time hee must [38] bee a God also. Againe you said that the very Forme of good was [39] the substance of God, & of happynesse, & you said, that, that was [40] the cheefe good, that was naturally desired & sought after by all [41] things, & that God ruled the Universe with the reignes of his [42] **[37v]** Goodnesse, and all things willingly Obey'd him, and that y^{e} Nature [1] of Evill was nothing, and all these things you made out by inbred [2] & Domestick Proofes drawen from one to another without fetch= [3] =ing any from without. I do not at all jest (said shee) or abuse [4] you, but haue show'd you the thing that is of the greatest conse= [5] =quence of all, but his helpe whom wee not Long ago, pray'd to. [6] For that is the quality of the Divine Substance that it neither [7] slide's into externall & Forraigne things, Nor receaue's any Forraigne [8] or strange thing into it's selfe, But (as Parmenides saith of [9] it) turneth the world & the moueable circle of things, remaining [10] it's selfe unmoueable. But if I haue used reasons taken from [11] within the thing I treated of, and not Sought for from abroad, [12] you need not admire at it, Since you may haue Learn't from [13] Plato, That the words & discourses one use's, ought to bee [14] neare akin to the matter & things wee speake of. [15]

Verse the 12th of the 3^{d} Booke.

Happy's that man that the cleere spring can see
Of good, & can himselfe set free
From bonds of heavy earth, that do withold
The mind from that blest sight, Orpheus of old
The Thracian Poet, hauing Lost his wife
Hauing expres't his sorrow to the Life
And cloath'd it in such charming verse that woods
Forgetting of their nature ranne, & rivers stood
Stocke still, to heare him, & Stagges to herd
With cruell Lyons, hares not bee affear'd
Oth'Sight of angry dogs, wch now appeas'd
By his smooth verse, Look't Louing & well pleas'd
Finding his hart still more & more inflam'd
With Loue, his powerfull verse hauing not tam'd
His Greife, thô it had all things else orecome
On earth, resolu'd, complaining of ye cruell doome
[38r] O'th'heauenly Gods, now to repaire
To Hell, to see if hee could there
With Flattering Songs, sung to his harpe obtaine
That pitty hee did Seeke, & in a straine
Deriu'd from the o're flowing well
Of his Great Mother Goddesse,[49] 'gan to tell

[49] "Calliope" indentified in left margin.

The Tale of his misfortunes, & his greife
Being doubled by his Loue, hee ask't releife
In teares, From those sterne Lords oth'Lower shades
The three headed Porter by his Verses Sway'd
Allow'd him entrance, & the furys that did there
Torment the wicked, now concern'd appeare
In pitty for him, Ixion doth not feele,
The dreadfull torment of his restlesse wheele,
And Tantalus forgetting of his thirst, doth scorne
To taste the flood, Tytius feele's not his Liver torne
By the Vulture, who being charm'd wth verse neglects his Prey[50]
At Last the Iudge of Soules to pitty mou'd, doth say
Wee are o'recome, Let us to Orpheus giue
His wife, & with him Let her henceforth Liue
As purchas't by his charming verse, but wee
Do this condition on our Grant impose, that shee
Shall not Looke back, untill she's out of hell
But those that thinke to giue Love Laws, know it not well[51]
Love's to it selfe the only Law, Orpheus alas!
When hee came neere, & was just going to passe
The Limits of the night, & hauing thither brought
His deere bought wife Euridice, & thought
All danger past, casting his carefull Eye
Behind, Ah! cruell Sight! hee there did Spye
[38v] His wife (hauing Look't back) returne; This fable may[52]
Teach you that aime y^{r} thoughts at ye cleare day
Of Soueraigne Good, For hee that once turn's back his Eye[53]
To th'Hell of Earthly things will presently
Loose all hee hath of pretious, from aboue
Stifling all heauenly Ioy, wth Earthly Love.

---

[50] "Prey" inserted above line 33 for lack of room at right margin.
[51] "well" inserted above line 40 for lack of room at right margin.
[52] "may" inserted above line 47 for lack of room at right margin.
[53] "Eye" inserted above line 49 for lack of room at right margin.

The Fourth Booke.

Prose 1st

When Philosophy had with a Reverend Look & a becoming [1] gravity & Sweetnesse deliver'd these things, I that was not quite [2] cur'd of my malancholly & sadnesse thus interrupted her, and pre= [3] =venting her from going on with something more, that shee [4] intended to haue said, O (said I) thou forerunner of the true [5] Light, the things that thou has't said do appeare both in their [6] divine selues, and by thy reasons cleere and undeniable & though [7] they were by reason of my greefe for the wrongs I haue receau'd [8] forgotten, yet I perceaue they were not wholly heretofore un= [9] =known to me. But this uery thing is the greatest cause [10] of my greefe & trouble. That since there is so Good and so just [11] a Ruler & disposer of all things, there should any Evills bee [12] comitted or being comitted, that they should go unpunisht, w^{ch} [13] thing aloane, how worthy it is to bee wondred at, I pray con= [14] =sider. And yet to this a greater is added; That wickedness [15] raigning & florishing, Virtue doth not only want it's due reward, [16] but is trodden under feete of ill men, and receaue's y^{e} punishment's [17] due to crimes. wch to be don, under the raigne of a God y^{t} knows [18] all, can all, & only wills, that wch is good, no body can sufficiently [19] admire, & deplore. It were indeed [(]said shee)[54] infinitely to bee [20] wondred at, & more horrible then any Monster, if it were as you [21] im*m*agine, that in so well ordered a house, of so greate a master & [22] father of the family, the vilest vessells should be worship't & esteem'd [23] **[39r]** and the most pretious ones dispis'd, durty'd & held of no accompt; [1] But 'tis not so; For if those conclusions wee made before, remaine [2] stedfastly with you, you will know by his very Authority, of whose [3] raigne & Gouerm^{t} wee speake, that the good are alwaies powerfull [4] and the bad alwaies weake & despicable, & that vices neuer are wth= [5] =out punishm^{t}; nor Virtues without reward, that to the good there [6] alwaies happens fortunate things, & to the bad alwaies unhappy & [7] many things of the Like nature, wch will silence y^{r} unjust complaints, [8] & confirme you in as strong resolutions. and since I haue already [9] shewed you what true happyness is, & where it reside's, hauing run [10] ouer all things that I thought necessary to premise, I shall now [11] shew you the way back to your owne hoame, and I will fix such wings [12] to y^{r} thoughts as will be able to carry them on high, to the end that [13] banishing all

[54] "(indeed said shee)" in the manuscript.

trouble & disquiet, you may returne by my guid= [14] =ance, (by the path I show you, & in the Charriot I furnish you wth) [15] sound & whole into y^{r} owne Country. [16]

Verse the 1st of the 4th Booke.

For I am owner of such wings as can
The highest heauen quickly reach, wch when
Your mind hath once put on, it will dispise
And hate the sordid earth, & quickly rise
Aboue the Region of the aire, & see
The clouds below it, & then passing by
The fiery orbe (that feele's it's heate encrease
By the swift motion of the sky) not cease,
'Till it get up into the houses that
Do beare the Starres, & ride in ye same Seate
With Phebus, or close companion bee
To Saturne, & there taking it's degree
Become a Knight of the bright Shining Starre
Of trueth, & hauing travell'd round as farre
As starry nights do reach, & hauing there
Remain'd a while, will Leaue y^{t} highest Spheare
[39v] And mounted on the Firmament will fly
'Till it be made partaker of the high
And dreadfull Light, where He reside's that's King
Of Kings, & supreame Lord of all holding
The Scepter of his might, & guiding reynes
Wherewth hee wisely gouerne's, & restraine's
The world, and (as the shining Iudge of things)
Sit's steady, thô his chariot haue wings)
When thou art thither brought, thoul't say
Forgetfullnesse 'till now, hath made mee stray,
For this, I now remember, is my hoame
Here was I borne, & since I am hither come
Againe, here Ile sett up my rest. If downe
From thence, thou hast a mind to Looke, upon
The early darkenesse thou has't Left, thoul't find
Those Tyrants banish't, that thou Left's behind.

Prose the 2^{d} of the 4th Booke.

Strange (said I) what greate things do you promise, and yet I do [1] not doubt but that you are able to performe all that you say. But [2] pray do not delay (now you have awakend mee & stirr'd up my expec= [3] =tation) to do it. First then (said shee) you must know that good men [4] are alwaies mighty, and that ill men are alwaies weake, & destitute [5] of all manner of strength, & power, the one parte of wch is demonstrated [6] from the other, For since good & evill are absolutely opposite, & con= [7] =trary the one to the other, if Good bee proued to conferre power and [8] Strength, it will follow consequently that Evill produce's weaknesse, [9] and if the frailty & weaknesse of ill bee made out, the firmnesse and [10] strength of Good will at the same time appeare. But that my [11] opinion may haue the more Authority, I will proceed both wayes, [12] confirming my Propositions, some times one way & some times [13] ye other; There are two things necessary to humane Actions, [14] to wit, Will & power, of wch if either be wanting, there can no action [15] bee perform'd. For if there be no will to a thing, no body will go about [16] what he hath no mind to effect, and if there be no power, the Will [17] **[40r]** is in vaine; wherefore if you see any body haue a mind to obtaine [1] a thing wch you see he doth not compasse, you cannot doubt, but that [2] hee wanted power; It is (said I) most cleare, & undeniable. But [3] (said shee) if you see him effect what he desire's, you will not then [4] doubt, his power & ability. No. But (said shee) in what euer a man [5] can do, in that hee is esteem'd to be strong, & powerfull, & in whateuer [6] he cannot, hee is to be judg'd weake; I confess it (said I) Do you not [7] remember (said shee) that it was concluded, upon the foregoing reasons [8] that the intention of all mens wills thô they take severall wayes to [9] compass it doth still naturally tend towards happyness. I do (said I) [10] and do you call to mind (said shee) that wee show'd Good & happyness [11] to be the same, and that therefore, Since happyness is aymed at by all; [12] it must follow that Good is so too. I need not (said I) call it to mind, [13] for it remaine's fixed there. All mankind then, as well the Good, as [14] the bad, striue and endeauour to attaine to the cheife good. It is cleare [15] (said I) they do. But it is certaine that the obtaining of good is [16] that, that make's men good; It is so (said I) Then it follow's that [17] good men obtaine what they desire; So it appeare's (said I) [18] But (said Shee) if ill people obtain'd that good they ayme at, they [19] could not be bad, it is so (said I) Since then (said shee) both ayme [20] at good, and these obtaine what they desire, & the others not, there [21] is no doubt, but that the good are powerfull, and the bad weake. [22] whoever (said I) doubt's it, must neither consider the nature of [23] things, nor the consequence, & strength of y^{r} reasons. Againe (said [24] shee) if there be two men who by nature haue the same inclination [25] & purpose, and one of the two is able to performe naturally what [26] he purpose's; and t'other being destitute of what properly belong's [27] to his nature, cannot fulfill his purpose, but barely imitate [28] him that doth, wch of these two will you judge to bee most powerfull? [29] though I guesse (said I) at what you meane, Yet I desire you [30] would make it a litle plainer; You will not [doubt][55] (said shee) but that y^{e} [31] motion of walking is naturall to men. I cannot (said I) and you [32] do (said shee) as litle doubt, but that the feete are the naturall [33] Instruments for that motion. I do (said I) Then (said shee) If one [34] hauing his feete is able to walke, & another that wanting those [35] (wch naturally he ought to haue) endeauoring to walke, is faine to [36] creep on his hands, wch of the two ought to bee esteem'd the more [37] able? You may go on (said I) with what you haue more to say, For [38] no man doubt's, but that he that hath his feete is abler to walke [39] then hee that hath none. But (said shee) the cheife & soveraigne [40] good, wch good & bad people both do ayme at, the good are able by [41] their virtues [42] **[40v]** (wch are the naturall instruments for that purpose) to obtaine. [1] and the bad do only by their various Lusts (wch are not the proper [2] instruments for the attaining of the cheife good) only endeauour [3] to obtaine it; Is it not so? it is (said I) and I now see plainly y^{e} [4] consequence that must follow. For out of what I haue granted [5] it must necessarily be concluded, that the good are mighty are [6] powerfull, & that the bad, are weake & impotent. You outrun [7] me very rightly (said shee) wch is, (to use the Physitians termes) [8] a sign of natures being restored, & able to resist the diesase, but [9] because I see you so ready, & willing to understand, I will bee [10] more Liberall of my reasons, then I was before. Obserue then [11] in the first place, how plainly the infirmity of the vitious, [12] doth appeare, who haue not the power, to attaine to that, to w^{ch} [13] the intention of their natures doth not only Leade, but in a man= [14] =ner compell them. what would they then do, if they were destitute [15] of that greate & almost invincible help, wch nature Lend's them? [16] consider then how greate weaknesse possess's wicked men, For 'tis [17] not slight & inconsiderable rewards, that they aime at, & cannot [18] obtaine, but 'tis the cheife & principall thing of all, that they [19] faile & miscarry in, neuer being able

[55] The context suggests that "doubt" has been accidentally omitted here.

to arriue at yt Soueraigne [20] good wch they Labour & designe day and night to compasse, in wch the [21] strength and power of good men doth Sufficiently appeare. For [22] as you must needs judge him most able in walking that can arriue [23] at the utmost period of his walke, you cannot but esteeme him most [24] mighty that attaineth to the end of all things, that are desirable, and [25] beyond wch there is nothing left to be desired, from wch, wee may con= [26] =clude, that wicked men on the contrary are destitute of all manner [27] of strength, for why do they leaue virtue & follow vice? is it because [28] they know not, what are true goods? If so, what is more weake [29] then the blindnesse of such ignorance. Or do they know what they [30] should follow, but are drawne aside by Lusts? their intemperance [31] making them so weake as that they are not able to wrestle wth and [32] resist vice? or do they not only knowingly but willingly forsake good, [33] give themselues up to vice? But so they do not only Leaue to be power= [34] =full, but to bee at all. For whoeuer Leaue's the com*m*on end, that every [35] thing that is, tend's to, Leave's at the same time to be. wch thô it [36] may seeme strange to some, to heare me call the bad (wch are ye great= [37] =est parte of mankind) no men, Yet 'tis a perfect truth. For I do not say [38] that bad men, are not bad men, but I do deny, that they are purely & [39] simply men. For as you may say of a carkasse that it is a dead man [40] and yet you cannot properly call it simply a man, So I will grant [41] **[41r]** the vitious to be bad men, but I cannot allow them to be purely & [1] simply men. For that properly is, that preserve's it's nature, & order, [2] and what falls from that, Leaves also to bee, its beeing consisting in & [3] being inseparable with it's nature. But you will say ill men can do [4] some things, I do not deny it, but that power of theirs proceed's from [5] their weaknesse, & frailty, not from strength, for they can do ill things, [6] wch they could not do, if they continued in the power & strength of [7] good men. wch power doth more plainly demonstrate that they can [8] do nothing, For if (as wee observ'd not Long since) evill is nothing, then [9] it is manifest that the bad that can only do evill, can in reallity do [10] nothing, and that you may understand what kind of strength this [11] power hath, You must call to mind, that wee haue agree'd that there [12] is nothing more strong & powerfull, then the cheife good; it is true [13] (said I) But (said shee) That soveraigne good cannot do evill. No more [14] it can't (said I) is there any body that think's, that ill men can do all [15] things? (said shee) No body (aid I) that is not mad. But they (said shee) [16] can do evill. I would to God (said I) they could not. Since then hee that [17] is powerfull, in the possession of all that is good, can only do all things, & [18] that those that are powerfull in Evill, cannot do all things, it is [19] manifest, that those that can do Evill, are the lesse powerfull, Adde [20] to this, that wee haue show'ne Power to be numbred among things [21] desirable, and that all things desireable are included in the cheife [22] good, as in that, that is cheife, & contain's in it selfe all goods, & that [23] the power to com*m*itt a crime cannot be included in what belongs to good. [24] It therefore follow's, that is not desirable. But all Power is desir= [25] =able, it is therefore cleere, That the power to do evill is no power. [26] Out of all w^{ch}, both the power of good men, & the weaknesse of bad, it [27] doth sufficiently appeare, (wch confirme's Plato's opinion to be most [28] true,) that wise men alone are able to do what they desire, that in= [29] =deed wicked men do what please's them, but neuer attaine w^{t} they [30] desire, foolishly im*m*agining, that pleasure & delight will afford them [31] that good, wch they can neuer that way obtaine, It being impossible [32] that vices should ever Leade to true happynesse. [33]

Verse 2^{d} of the 4th Booke.

Hee that could strip those Kings of their array
Who mounted on high Thrones do Scepters sway
[41v] And shining in their purple robes, surrounded are,
With angry guards, whose very Lookes do scare
Poore innocents, & nothing breath but rage,
When once those outward things wch did engage
Mens awe & reverence are gon, hee'd see those men
Within, beare chaines like Slaues, For on ye one
Side, Lust doth powre into their breast
Insatiable poison, anger all rest
Take's from their troubled thoughts, & raise's stormes
Not easily allay'd, or greefe, performe's
It's parte, & seizing on them, doth torment
Their minds, or slippery hopes the Like, thus rent
Are they in peeces by their passions sway
And must those greater Tyrants will's obey
Since then so many Tyrants reigne o're one
How can that man bee said, to Rule alone.

Prose the 3^{d} of the 4th Booke.

Do you not see in what a filthy mire those wicked men do [1] wallow, & on the contrary, with what brightness good men shine, [2] wch makes it apparent, that good men neuer want rewards, [3] nor bad men punishment. For in things that are don, there [4] can certainly be no fitter nor greater reward, then that for [5] the sake of wch, the things are don, as to those that runne a [6] race, the Goale or prize they runne for, is counted ye best [7] & fittest reward. But wee haue show'd yt true happynesse [8] is that good for the sake of wch all things are don. it follow's [9] therefore that, that good is the proper reward of all humane [10] actions. Now this good can neuer bee seperated from good men, [11] For if they had it not they could not properly bee call'd good, it is [12] then cleere, that goodnesse neuer want's it's rewards, Let ye bad [13] then [14] **[42r]** Rage as furiously, as they please, the wise & good mans [1] crowne will be sure to sit fast to his head, & neuer wither, [2] For anothers wickednesse, can neuer take away the just and [3] proper reward, that's due to ye vertuous, 'tis true, that if [4] one gloryed in a thing borrowed from without, it might bee [5] reassum'd by him that Lent it, or taken away by another [6] But since it is one's owne proper vertue & goodnesse that [7] conferre's this, no man shall euer want his reward, 'till hee [8] Leaue's to bee good. Lastly since all reward is therefore sought, [9] because 'tis thought a good, who can euer judge a good man to [10] want his reward, But what kind of reward? the greatest & [11] fullest imaginable; For remember that principall Corollary [12] I gaue you not Long ago, that since good is happyness, who= [13] =euer is good, of necessity must bee happy; But those that [14] are happy are Gods, there is then a reward of good men, such [15] as no time can weare out, no mans power diminish, nor no [16] mans wickedness deface, wch is to bee made Gods, wch being so, no [17] wise man can doubt of the inseperable punishment yt attend's [18] the wicked, For since good & euill as well as punishmt & reward [19] are absolute contraries, whateuer wee see happen in reward [20] to good, wee must conclude to bee answered on the contrary [21] side in punishmt to euill; As then goodnesse is a reward to the [22] good, So wickedness is a punishment to the euill, Now [23] whoeuer suffers a punishmt cannot doubt, but that hee [24] hath an euill upon him, if then they will consider & reflect [25] upon themselues, can they thinke themselues free from [26] paine & punishment, when they are not only affected but [27] infected with wickedness & vice, wch is the summe of all euills [28] See then what punishment doth accompany the wicked, by [29] comparing it with the reward of the uertuous; For you haue [30] already Learnt, that euery thing that Subsists is one, & that one [31] is good, So that it follow's, that whateuer Subsist's must bee [32] good, and that whateuer fall's from being good, fall's also from [33] it's very being, So that bad men Leaue to bee, but the Shape & [34] forme of their bodys, Showe's, that they were once men, wherefore [35] wee must conclude, that thô they retaine the outside, Yet by their [36] wickedness, they haue Lost the natures of men, And since vertue [37] and [38] **[42v]** Goodnesse alone can exalt a man aboue y^{e} Nature of men, it follow's [1] that wickedness & vice must cast him downe below the condition [2] of men, So that whomeuer you See transformed by vice, you can [3] no more esteeme a man, One that burne's with avarice & violent= [4] =ly take's away the Goods of other men you may Stile a Wolfe, [5] another that is continually Snarling, delight's in brawles and [6] contests, you may Liken to a Dog, a third that Studdys Slily by his [7] secret frauds to cheate and cozen, you may compare to a Fox, [8] Another rages furiously with anger, you may call him a Lyon, [9] Another is fearefull & cowardly? hee hath gott the Nature of a [10] hare, or hind? another is Slothfull, & Stupid? that man is [11] changed into an Asse. hee that is Light & inconstant & con= [12] =tinually changing his mind, is Litle different from a bird, [13] whoeuer wallows & is drown'd in filthy Lusts? may justly be [14] esteem'd a Swine. And thus whoeuer by forsaking goodness [15] Leaues to bee a man, (not being able to ascend into a divine [16] State & condition) is turned into a Beast. [17]

Verse 3^{d} of the 4th Booke

The Easterne winds hauing the wandring fleete
Of wise Vlisses, by their fury beate
Vpon the fatall Island wch belongs
To Circe (daughter of the Sunne) shee wth a Song
Fill's to her new come guests, inchanted cups
W^{ch} they no sooner greedily drinke up,
But by her powerfull magick skill they're charm'd
And into strange & various shapes transform'd,
The first is chang'd into an angry Bore,
The next doth, Like a cruell Lyon roare
(Of Marmorick) & hath both nayles & teeth
Like to that Beast, a third, going to weep
(Being turn'd into a Wolfe, doth houle,
Another Like an Indian Tygre bold=
[43r] =Ly walk's about the house, & thô Mercury[56]

[56] Lines 15–18 bracketed in right margin; these two couplets share the same rhyme and are perhaps marked for later revision.

Had in his pitty to Vlisses kept him free
Amidst so many dangers from y^{e} plague y^{t} shee
Intended him, Yet all his company
Had swill'd themselues wth y^{t} inchanted drinke,
Those, that were turn'd to Swine, begin to shrinke
From humane food, & greedily do fall
On graines & nasty trash, nothing at all
Remaine's now of their bodyes, or their voyce
(Only their thoughts) wch now (had they their choyce)
They would change too, but those they will retaine
To make them feele more sencibly their paine.
Yet all this misery is nothing, if compar'd
To Vice, For heere the body only far'd
The worse, the mind, still kept it selfe entire
And did not change, but to it's strength retire
For 'tis within that's hid the worthyest parte
Of man, now vice poysons the very harte,
And fill's the Soule, w^{ch}, how much it is, you'le find
When wth y^{r} body, you compare y^{r} mind.

Prose 4th of the 4th Booke.

I confess (said I) That it is not without reason that y^{o} declare [1] vitious men (althô they retaine the forme & shape of men) to bee [2] notwithstanding chang'd into Beasts. But I could wish their [3] wicked & cruell minds had not the power so much to rage to the [4] destruction of good men, neither haue they (said shee) as I shall [5] in due time demonstrate. and that if that power wch they are [6] thought to haue, were taken away, the punishm^{t} of ill men w^{d} [7] bee so much the Less; For (thô it may seeme strange) yet it is most [8] true, that ill men are more unhappy when they haue perform'd [9] what they desire, then when they are not able to performe it. [10] **[43v]** For if it be an unfortunate thing to will ill things, it is much more [1] so, to be able to do them, Since without that power (Let the Will be [2] neuer so bad) it would not produce an ill effect and since each [3] carry's a distinct misfortune with it, It doth consequently fol= [4] =low, That, that person lyes under a treble one, that wills, and [5] doth performe and ill thing; I grant it (said I) but do heartily [6] wish, that wicked men may quickly bee free'd from y^{e} misfortune. [7] that their power brings upon them. they will (said Shee) be freed [8] from it (it may bee) sooner then you desire, or they dreame of, for [9] there is nothing within the narrow Limitts of this Life, that an [10] immortall Soule can reasonably judge Long in coming, & their [11] great hopes, & high fabrick of crimes is many times thrown downe [12] & destroyed by a suddaine and unexpected end, wch puts a bound to [13] their misfortune. For if it be true that wickedness make's men [14] miserable, hee certainly is, that is Longest wicked, & consequently [15] the wicked would be yet more miserable, if death at Last did not [16] put a period to their wickedness. For if wee haue concluded rightly [17] of the misfortune of being bad, it is undoubtedly true that that [18] misery would be infinite if it were eternall. It is (said I) a [19] strange inference that you make & seemes hard to grant, But I [20] cannot say but that it follows from what wee haue already granted [21] you judge right (said shee) for whoeuer will not agree to y^e Conclu= [22] =sion must either show Something in the premises to bee false, or [23] that the propositions being granted, do not rightly ground the [24] inference, For else granting the premises you cannot deny the [25] conclusion. And what I am now going to say will not appeare [26] Lesse strange & wonderfull, & yet, out of what hath bin granted [27] doth as necessarily follow; what is that (said I) that those [28] wicked men (said Shee) are more happy that suffer punishment [29] then those that endure none, I do not meane (what may bee [30] obvious to euery mans thought) because ill manners use to be [31] corrected by $punishm^t$; & that some are brought by the feare of [32] paine to bee good, nor as it is an example that may deterre [33] others from vice, but really esteeme those wicked men more [34] unhappy that continue unpunish't, abstracting both from the [35] benefit they might make of that correction & y^e aduantage [36] that example might be to others. And in that other respect [37] can they (said I) bee thought so? haue wee not granted (said shee) [38] **[44r]** That the good are happy, & the bad miserable? wee haue (said I) then (said [1] shee) if to a man's misery there bee added something [2] of good, will not hee be happyer then one that is absolutely mi= [3] =serable, without any measure of good? hee will no doubt (said [4] I) what (said shee) if to this miserable person that want's all [5] manner of good, besides the ills make him unhappy there [6] were yet added another evill? would you not judge him more [7] unfortunate then hee whose misfortune is moderated by the [8] advantage of hauing his Share of something that's good? what [9] else (said I) but (said shee) the wicked where they are punish't [10] haue something of good added to them, to wit the punishment, w^{ch} [11] in relation to justice, is a good, and the wicked that are not pun= [12] =nish't, haue that evill added to them, to wit, impunity, wch in [13] respect of the injustice of it you cannot deny to be an evill, Ergo [14] &c: I cannot (said I) deny it. The wicked then (said shee) are [15] much more unfortunate that unjustly escape punishment, then [16] those that, justly beare it. For no man will doubt but that it is [17] just for the wicked to bee punish't, and consequently unjust [18] for them to escape it, Nor will any man deny what is just to bee [19] a good, nor injustice to be an evill. These, indeed, (said I) are the [20] consequences from our former conclusions, But pray do y^{o} Leaue [21] no punishm^{t} for the Soules, after the bodys are dead? Yes (said [22] shee) and those greate ones, whereof some I thinke to bee Ex= [23] =ercis'd with the utmost rigour of paine & torment, & others by [24] a purging clemency. But it is not my intent to discourse of [25] that now. That wch I haue hitherto don hath bin to show y^{t} [26] power, wch you held to be[57] unfit for the wicked, is really none, & that [27] those that you thought did escape unpunish't, carry their pun= [28] =nishm^{t} in their crimes, That the Licence, of the wicked, wch you [29] pray'd might not be Long, is, indeed of no continuance, that they [30] would be more unhappy, if it continu'd Longer, & most of all [31] if it neuer ended, that they are more unhappy when they escape [32] Iustice, then when they meete with just punishm^{ts}, wch in effect is [33] to say, they are then most punish't, when they seeme absolutely to [34] escape punishm^{t}. When (said I) I consider y^{r} reasons, I thinke [35] nothing truer then what you say; But if I turne back my eyes [36] upon the Iudgments of men, who is there that can endure to heare [37] these things, much less beleiue them? It is true (said shee) and y^{e} [38] reason is, because their eyes are so us'd to darkeness that they [39] **[44v]** cannot endure to lift them up against the Light of so shining [1] a truth, being like to those birds, whom the night makes see, & [2] the day blind's, For they not considering the order of things, but [3] their owne inordinate affections, Esteeme Licence & impunity [4] in crimes, a happy thing. But see what the eternall Law de= [5] =cree's, if you conforme your selfe to good things, you will not neede [6] any Iudge to giue you the reward, for you already haue it, in being [7] joyn'd to those good things. But if you bend y^{r} Studdys to ill things; [8] you need seeke no punisher from without, for you haue throwen [9] your selfe into that filth that is y^{r} punishment, wherein y^{o} [10] would see as much difference if you consider'd it aright, as [11] there is betweene being companion of the starres in the [12] firmament, & groueling on the filthy earth; But ye vulgar [13] doth not regard this, what then? shall wee adhere to those [14] that wee

[57] "to be" inserted here.

haue show'd to bee like unto beasts? what if one y[t] [15] had Lost his sight, should also forget, that euer he had eyes, [16] and therefore should thinke hee wanted nothing of humane [17] perfection, should wee therefore that see him, not thinke him [18] blinde? neither will they allow what is built upon as good & [19] strong reasons, to wit, that those are more unhappy that do, [20] then that receaue an injury. I would willingly heare those [21] reasons (said I) You will not deny (said shee) but that euery [22] wicked man, is worthy of punishment? No (said I) and that [23] wicked people are miserable hath sufficiently bin prou'd. [24] then you cannot doubt, but those that deserue punishm[t], are [25] miserable. I cannot (said I) then (said shee) if you Sate as [26] Iudge who would you thinke deseru'd punishm[t] the doer, or the [27] receauour of the injury? no doubt (said I) but I should giue [28] satisfaction to the receauour, by the punishm[t] of the doer, then [29] (said shee) you conclude the doer to be more miserable then the [30] receauour of the injury. it follow's rightly (said I) It appeare's [31] then by this, & other reasons from the same roote that Sinne by [32] it's owne nature make's men miserable, & that y[e] unhappynesse [33] is his that doth an injury, & not his that receaue's it. But yet [34] (said shee) Orators do seeme to be of another opinion, For they[58] [35] still go about to stirre up the pitty & compassion of the Iudges in [36] behalfe of those that haue suffer'd any greevious injury, Whereas [37] by right they should rather bring those wrong doers nakedly before [38] **[45r]** The Iudge as people do sick men to the phisitian stirring [1] up their pitty desiring them, they would in mercy endeauour [2] by punishment to cure the diseases of their wickednesse, w[ch] [3] if it were practis'd, the use of Aduocates would either bee [4] needlesse, or they would turne in pitty all accusers of the [5] wicked, w[ch] would bee much more proffitable & advantageous [6] to mankind, & the wicked men themselues, if it were possible, [7] for them to see through the Least crany, the vertue they haue [8] Left, & a meanes by punishment to do away the filth of their [9] vice, would refuse the help of any Advocate to defend them [10] and giue themselves freely up to their Iudges & accusers, & [11] this is the reason that in wise men there is no roome at all [12] Left for hate. For who is there but a foole that will hate a [13] good man? and to hate the wicked were wholy as unreasona= [14] =ble, since vice is a greater Sicknesse of the minde, then the [15] greatest wee pitty in the body. and since wee judge those that [16] haue a bodily

[58] The manuscript shows "go" stricken through twice here, apparently deleted since "still go" follows on the next line.

disease worthy rather of our compassion then [17] hatred, much more ought wee to commiserate the condition of [18] those, whose minds are sick & Languish of a disease, much [19] more cruell & dangerous then the plague itselfe, to wit, wickednesse. [20]

Verse the 4th of the 4th Booke

What is the good of stirring hatred up,
Or hastning Fate with yr owne hand, the cup
Of death y'are sure to drinke, hee of his owne
Accord, make's earnest haste to mow you downe,
Hee neuer stop's his winged horse,
What need then is there that you striue to force
[45v] What of it selfe will come, since that the Bore
The Lyon, Tyre, & innumerable more
of Beasts, & other mischeifs, seeke to spill
Mens blood, what need they one another kill,
Is it because their manners differ, that they must
Perish by one anothers swords, is that just
Cause, for such cruelty, would you proceed
With Equity? & giue to each that need
They do deserue? The Good then Loue,
And Let the bad your pitty moue.

Prose the 5th of the 4th Booke.

I haue heere seen (said I) the happynesse & misery that is [1] establish't in the merits of the good & of the wicked, But in the [2] very fortune of the same sort of people, I find something of [3] good & something of euill, For there is no wise man yt Like's [4] better to bee exiled poore & needy, then to remaine at home [5] flourishing & abounding in plenty, riches, power & strength, [6] since by the meanes of the Latter of these his wisdome would [7] appeare greater hauing the more witnesses to applaude it, and [8] consequently his happynesse in ruling would bee diffus'd, & taken [9] notice of both by the neighbouring & Forraigne countrys, Especi= [10] =ally, if imprisonmt; & other Legall punishments were inflicted [11] on the wicked, for whom they were first[59] intended, and to whom they [12] are justly due, Now that the contrary should happen, and that [13] the

[59] "first" inserted here.

good should suffer punishments due to crimes, and y^{e} bad [14] run away with the rewards due to vertue, is that wch I cannot [15] sufficiently admire at, therefore do extreamly desire to heare [16] from you the reason of so unjust a confusion. For I should not at [17] all wonder at it, if I beleiue'd things were thus jumbled together [18] **[46r]** by chance & accidents, But that wch cause's my astonishment is, [1] to see, that the just God (who rules all) doth sometimes bestow his [2] worldly fauours upon the good, & misfortunes upon the wicked, & againe [3] on the contrary misfortunes on the good, & prosperity on the wicked, of [4] wch proceeding, unless there can appeare some cause, pray in what [5] doth this gouerment seeme to differ from the hapning of things, by [6] chance; It is no wonder (said shee) that the greatest order im*m*agina= [7] =ble (when the reason of it is not knowne) should bee Look't upon as [8] rash & confus'd; But though you know not the cause, of y^{t} wonderfull [9] disposition of things, Yet satisfy & content y^{r} selfe, & do not doubt, [10] but that all things are rightly & justly ordered, Since they are [11] Gouern'd by so good and so just a Ruler. [12]

Verse the 5th of the 4th Booke

Hee that is unacquainted with the starre
That's call'd Arcturus, whose high Seate's not farre
From the cheefe Pole, & understand's not why
The Lazy Bo=otes, doth his charriot tye
From making haste; & afterwards at night
Drown in the Ocean his tardif Light,
And then as much too early in the morne
When few Looke out, the firmament adorne
Cannot but bee astonish't at the Lawes
And order of y^{e} heauenly Orbes, because
Hee know's them not, So when y^{e} Moone Look's pale
As if sh'were sick, some people judge her ayle
Proceed's from being inchanted, & do thinke
To free her from th' inchantm^{t} by the clinke
Of Brazen potts. But when th'wind feircely blowes
No man doth wonder if the Ocean flowes,
[46v] With violence against the Shore, nor that
The burning Sunne should wth such haste Lay flat
Mountaines of Snow that were by cold congeal'd
Since of these things the reason is reveal'd;

But when the causes hidden are aboue
It troubles mortall breasts, & doth much moue
The vulgar, who are alwaies apt to bee
Astonish't at what euer thing they see
And know no reason for, but were
Their ignorance once cur'd, nothing w^{d} strange appeare.

Prose the 6th of the 4th Booke.

It's true (said I) But it being y^{r} office to discouer ye hidden [1] causes of things, & to lay open those reasons that are couer'd [2] with too thick a mist for us to Looke through, I shall beg [3] of you, that you would unfold this wonder, that giue's mee so [4] much disturbance; You call mee (said shee smiling) to w^{t} [5] of all Questions I Looke upon to bee the hardest, & indeed, to w^{ch} [6] there is hardly any full & perfect answer to bee giuen; For the [7] matter is of such a nature, that, when one doubt is solu'd & [8] determin'd, innumerable others, like Hydras heads do arise, [9] of wch indeed there will bee no end, if they bee not supprest by [10] the heate & vigour of a piercing wit & judgment, For to this [11] belong's the enquiry concerning the singleness of Prouidence, [12] of the Series & course of Fate, of chance, Gods fore=knowledge,[60] & [13] predestination, & of Free=will, all wch of what weight & consequence [14] they are, do you y^{r} selfe judge, Yet because to know these things [15] may bee something of physick to you, I will endeauour (though [16] circumscrib'd within too narrow a Limit of time) to say something [17] of it, [18] **[47r]** But if you take any delight in the musick of Verse, You must bee [1] content a litle to forebeare that pleasure 'till I haue knit together & [2] put my reasons in some order & method. That as you please (said I) [3] Then taking her discourse (as it were) from a new beginning, [4] shee spoke after this manner. The generation of all things, and y^{e} [5] whole progresse of all mutable natures, and whateuer is any way [6] mou'd, receaue's it's causes, order, & forme from the steddy and [7] immutable mind of God; wch though in it selfe purely simple, Es= [8] =tablishe's a various method in the course of things, wch when it is [9] Look't upon in the purity of the diuine intelligence & understanding, [10] is called Prouidence; But when it relates to those things, wch it [11] doth moue, it is by the antients called Fate, wch two things will [12] easily bee allow'd to bee different & distant, by whoeuer doth but [13] consider the proper strength of each. For Prouidence, is that

[60] "fore=knowledge" and "Free=will" (below) hyphenated, not broken on a line.

[14] diuine reason it selfe residing in the cheefe prince, & beginning [15] of all things, wch disposeth all things; But Fate is y^{t} inherent [16] disposition remaining in the moueable things themselues, by [17] wch prouidence knitteth euery thing in it's due order & place. [18] Prouidence comprehend's all things though they bee various and [19] infinite. But Fate digest's & reduces each thing into motion [20] according to times, places, & formes, So that the prospect of all [21] that orderly course of things as in time they are to happen [22] brought together in one complex't veiw into the diuine mind [23] may bee stiled prouidence, and that same againe diuided and [24] digested into it's proper times & motions, may bee call'd Fate, w^{ch} [25] two things thô they bee different & distinct, yet one depend's upon [26] the other; For the fatall order or destiny proceed's from ye simplicity [27] or singlenesse of Prouidence. For as a workeman first conceaues in [28] his mind the Idea & forme of the thing hee is to make, & afterwards [29] put's it in Execution, & what hee had seene represented together [30] in one thought, hee now reduce's into it's temporall orders; So [31] Almighty God doth by Prouidence at once dispose & order all things [32] that are to bee don, But by Fate put's those things hee had Order'd [33] severally in Execution, in their due times, & circumstances. [34] **[47v]** So that, whether Fate bee exercised by certaine divine Spirits [1] waiting & attending as seruants upon Prouidence, or by ye helpe [2] of the Soule, or nature, or by the motions of the Starres, or by an [3] Angellicall virtue, or the various industry & diligence of divells, [4] or whether by any of these, or altogether the Series & Order of [5] Fate is woven; This is manifest, that the single & immoueable [6] forme & Idea of all things that are to bee don, is Prouidence, & [7] that the moueable weauing, & temporall order of those things [8] wch the Divine simplicity hath directed & ordered to bee don [9] is Fate; So that whateuer is Subject to fate, is subject also [10] to prouidence, to wch Fate it selfe is subject. But there are [11] Somethings that are under the disposall of prouidence, that [12] are aboue the course of Fate, wch are the things that are neare [13] to the first Godhead & being firmly Establish't are aboue the [14] Order of fatall mutability. For as in circles that turne about [15] the same point or center, that circle that is innermost and is [16] nearest to that point become's as it were a Center & Hinge for [17] the others that are further out to turne upon, & the outmost of [18] all wch hath a greater circumference, goe's so much a greater [19] compasse of ground by how much it is further off from ye middle [20] of that single point, and whateuer can joyne it selfe to y^{t} middle [21] so as to bee one with it, cease's to moue out of it's place, So in [22]

Like manner, what goe's furthest off & is at greatest distance [23] from the first thought of God is the more Subject to the weauings [24] of Fate & destiny, and that thing is least intangled & freest [25] from the Lome of Fate that can get neerest to that Hinge & center [26] of all things, and whateuer can cleaue to the firmnesse of [27] the Divine mind, being free from change or motion, will [28] absolutely surmount the necessity of Fate. So that as [29] reasoning & discourse is to the understanding w^{t} is begotten, [30] so what already is, & what time is to Eternity, & what [31] circle is to the middle point or center, that ye moueable [32] Series & course of fate is to the Stable singlenesse of Prouidence [33] and this is the Order by wch the heauens & the Starres do moue, [34] **[48r]** By wch the Elements do temper & moderate each other, & are [1] interchangeably transform'd, this is that renewe's againe all [2] things that grow, or are decay'd, by seeds of the Like nature, This [3] constrain's, by an indissoluable connexion of causes the actions [4] & fortunes of men, wch proceeding originally from unchangeable [5] prouidence, must of necessity bee themselues immutable. For [6] so things are indeed best gouern'd when the simplicity of prouidence [7] remaining immoueable in the mind of God produce's an inflex= [8] =ible order of causes, wch by it's steddynesse & immutability doth [9] restraine changeable things, wch else would fly up, & downe and [10] runne together promiscuously, as chance would guide them [11] and 'tis by this meanes, that thô all things seeme to you (who [12] are not able to see into & consider that Order) disturb'd and in [13] confusion, Yet there is that, that guide's & dispose's all things [14] to good, as to their certain end. For there is nothing y^{t} is don [15] for the sake of Evill, even by the wicked themselues, who (as I [16] haue sufficiently show'd) ayme at & seeke after good, but are [17] Led astray & seduced by Errour, but the order proceeding, from [18] the King of Soueraigne Good, doth not make any fall from their [19] beginning & principles; But you will say can there bee a [20] greater, or more unjust confusion in the order of things, [21] then that to good men sometimes there should happen [22] prosperous things, & sometimes aduersitys, & to[61] Evill men [23] sometimes their harts desires, & other times afflictions & [24] troubles? But first (said shee) do you thinke that men are so [25] penetrating & exact in their knowledge as that whoeuer [26] they Esteeme good or bad must of necessity bee so? when even [27] mens Iudgments so much disagree, as that some esteeme those [28] worthy of rewards that others think worthy

[61] "to" inserted here.

of punishment. [29] But let us grant that there may bee some, that can discerne [30] the good & the bad, But can they therefore see that inward [31] temper & constitution of the mind (to take the expression [32] from the comparison of Bodyes) wherein one differ's from another [33] will not that appeare as difficult a matter to one that doth [34] **[48v]** Not know it, as to judge why sweet things should be agreeable [1] to some sound bodys, and bitter things to others, and why of ye sick [2] some are help't by Soft and Smoothning remedys & some by Sharp [3] & harsh ones; But the Physitian who know's ye temper and [4] constitution of the body as well as the nature of the disease [5] doth not at all wonder at it; Now what is the health of ye Soule [6] but vertue & goodness, and what can bee it's disease but vice? [7] and who is the Ruler & Phisitian of mens minds but God, who is [8] the preseruer of the good & the expeller of evill? who Looking out [9] from the high Seate of his prouidence, see's & discouer's what is [10] conuenient for each person in particular, & accordingly giue's [11] what in his wisdome hee know's to bee properest for them, & [12] hence it come's that the fatall order & decree that's giuen by [13] him that know's what hee doth seeme's so wonderfull to those [14] that are ignorant, & to say something (as farre as humane [15] reason can go) towards the understanding & fathoming, of [16] the diuine depth (it may bee) of that person that you thinke [17] most just, & the most religious obseruer of Equity, Prouidence [18] (that is all knowing) hath another opinion. You see in our [19] freind Lucan, the victorious cause pleased the Gods, but y^e vanquish't [20] pleased Cato. And in whateuer you may see don in this world con= [21] =trary to yor Expectation & Iudgment, 'tis not but that the order [22] and direction is fit and Iust, thô to y^r perverse opinion it may [23] seeme otherwise. But suppose a man so really good, as that the [24] diuine knowledge, & humane opinion do agree concerning him [25] it may bee, howeuer hee may bee weake in his[62] mind, & want cou= [26] =rage & magnanimity, and if there hapned any greate affliction [27] to him, hee might perhaps bee driven to forsake his innocency [28] when hee saw it could not preserue him in prosperity. The good [29] & wise dispencer of Lots doth therefore Spare him, whome adversity [30] hee know's would make worse, because hee will not put him to [31] struggle & Labour knowing it would turne to his prejudice. Another [32] that is absolute in all vertues is so holy, & so neare to God, that pro= [33] =uidence think's it would bee a crime to let him suffer the Least [34] **[49r]** corporall $punishm^t$

[62] "his" inserted here.

or trouble. For (as one more excellent then I saith) [1] the whole body of such a man may bee made & built up of vertues. and [2] it happen's often that the Gouerm^{t} of affaires is put into good mens hands [3] that the exuberant malice of the wicked may bee abated or cutt short. [4] To others hee giue's a mix't Fortune according to the quality of their [5] minds, and some againe hee nip's, Least a Long prosperity should [6] make them proud & wanton, and others hee suffer's to bee exercised [7] by aduersity, that they may confirme & strengthen their courage [8] & vertue by the use of patience. Some there are that dread more [9] then they ought, what they are able to beare, and others that [10] despise more then they need to do, what they haue not courage [11] enough to endure; These God bring's by aduersities to know [12] themselues, many haue bought the Fame of this world at y^{e} [13] price of their Lives; and some haue by showing themselues not [14] to bee ouercome by torments manifested to ye world that vertue [15] is invincible, wch things, how rightly & fitly they are don, & how [16] much to the aduantage and good of those to whom they happen is [17] palpable & Evident; and 'tis from the same reason also, that [18] sometimes prosperity, & sometimes adversity doth happen to ill [19] men; For as to punishments, I think no body can wonder that they [20] should fall upon them, since all people judge that they deserue [21] them, and that wee see it proue's many times a meanes to de= [22] =terre others from the Like wickednesse, and to amend them, them= [23] =selues, and their prosperity teache's good & vertuous persons [24] what valew to put upon such like felicity, that they see y^{e} wicked [25] so often obtaine. Besides it is possible that the nature of some [26] people may bee so peevish & perverse that y^{e} scantynesse of [27] Estate may exasperate them more & runne them into greater [28] crimes. Others reflecting upon their present prosperity, & at the [29] same time considering their sinfull Liues may fall (it may bee) [30] into an apprehension of Loosing (as they are conscious they deserue [31] to do) what they find so much pleasure in the enjoym^{t} of, and for [32] that reason may mend their Liues for feare of Loosing their [33] good fortune. Some again the increase of their prosperity hath [34] precipitated into the ruine they did deserue. To others ye power [35] **[49v]** of punishing hath bin allow'd, that they might at the same time [1] exercise the good & bee the severer scourges to the wicked, For as [2] there is no League between good & bad, so the bad themselues [3] cannot agree one with y^{e} other, (wch cannot bee thought strange [4] when their consciences to make them many times judge & con= [5] =demne themselues for what they do) and thus that high & divine [6] prouidence, bring's to passe that wonder, of the bad, sometimes [7] making other bad men become good; For many times seeing [8] themselues suffer wrongs & oppressions from wicked men, & com= [9] =ming so, to hate their wickednesse, they returne back insencibly [10] into the way of vertue, whilst they studdy to bee unlike those [11] they hate, and 'tis that diuine strength & power alone that can [12] make euills turne into good, making such conuenient use of [13] what in it selfe is ill, or by it to produce at Least, a good Effect. [14] which show's that nothing is don without order & designe, & w^{t} [15] doth not seeme to continue in[63] the due order assign'd it, fall's into [16] another of more use and advantage towards the designed end [17] of good; For it is certaine that nothing in the Gouerment and [18] realme of Prouidence is Left to chance, But the right strong [19] God gouerne's all things in this world, thô it is not within the [20] reach of mans apprehension to find out, much Lesse within his [21] power by words to describe the Secret Engins & springs of the [22] divine worke. Let it suffice that wee are convinc't, That God [23] who created all natures, dispose's & direct's all things to good & [24] intending to bring all things to his Likenesse, doth by the Series [25] & course of a fatall necessity driue away all euill, from the [26] borders & Limitts of his Gouerment, in so much as that if you [27] do but Looke upon God's providence you will finde that thô [28] wee thinke the world so much abound's in Evills, there is really [29] (all things considered) no evill in it. But I see you begin to be [30] so burdned with the weight of this Question, & wearied with the [31] Length of my discourse, that you expect some refreshm^{t} from [32] Poetry take therefore this draught of it, by wch being refresh't [33] you may go on the more vigorously towards that wch is yet higher. [34]

[50r]
Verse the 6th of the 4th Booke.

If wise & diligent tho dos't desire[64]
To see the Goverm^{t} of the most high,
Looke up to th'heauens & thou wilt admire
How all things moue in perfect harmony
The Starres & Planets neuer interfere
But each distinctly doth his owne course steere
Preseruing still their antient League entire

[63] "in" added here above "continue."

[64] Lines 1–4 are bracketed in the right margin, perhaps highlighting them for later revision, since this quatrain begins a poem otherwise designed as a series of couplets.

The Sunne wth all his heate & scorching fire
Doth not disturbe the frozen Moone, ye Beare
That swiftly moueth in our hemisphere
And Steers her rapid Course about the top
O'th world, is neuer seene from thence to drop
Into the Westerne Sea, not coueting to steep
Her flames (as other starres do) in ye deep
And Briny Ocean, Hesper still forerunnes[65]
With news o'th morning, thus doth mutuall Loue
Make all those heauenly Starres & planets moue
In their due constant course, & banish farre
From that same starry country, cruell warre
This concord also doth the Elements vnite
Tempring the moist wth dry, wch else would fight
And makes the cold things willingly to joyne
With hott, & faithfully combine
For good of th'whole, this makes ye fire fly up
On high, & make's the heauy earth to stoope
[50v] Under it's weight, this makes ye Spring o'th yeare
Send forth sweet smells, The Summer ripe ye Eare
O'th corne, The Autumne plenteously abound
With mellow Fruit, The winter feed the ground
With raine, This is y^{t} temper, That doth giue
Both grouth & nourishm^{t} to things that Liue
Which were it gon, what flourishes w^{d} soone
Decay & dye, Meane while, on his high Throne
The greate creatour of all things doth sit
Who being the wise Iudge of what is fit
And, Iust, King, Lord, Fountaine, Ruler & Law
It selfe, holdeth the reigne's & keep's in awe
All hee hath made, giuing a Stop to things
Which hee had made to moue & rivetting
What hee see's Loose, For if wisely hee
Did not take care, tempring, to rectify
The motions of things, That wch is now restraind
By stable Order, & by that maintaind

[65] This line has been marked with an asterisk in the left margin, perhaps because it lacks a rhyming line with which to form a couplet.

Would quickly fall from it's Originall
And soone would grow degenerate, Now all
This doth proceed from the transcendent Loue
Hee beare's his creatures, whom hee makes to moue
Towards some good, as to their end, Else could
They not Subsist, but soone to nothing would
Reduce themselues, If euery earthly thing
Did not returne it's Love back to the Spring
[51r] From whence it hath it's beeing, thus wee see
Both Heauen, & Earth, maintaind by Charity.

Prose the 7th of the 4th Booke.

Do you perceaue now what follow's from all that wee haue [1] said? what (said I) That all Fortune whateuer (said shee) is good, [2] and how (said I) can that bee? why (said shee) Since all manner [3] of fortune, both prosperous, & adverse, happen's either for [4] the punishment & correction of the wicked, or for the [5] exercising or rewarding of the good, It is manifest that [6] it is good; Since it doth appeare alwaies either to bee just [7] or Usefull. Your reasons (said I) haue a greate deale of [8] trueth in them, and whether I consider the prouidence, or Fate [9] you haue described, I finde yr opinion Strongly grounded. But [10] Let us thô (if you please) place it among those that you said [11] a litle while ago, were not of the generally receau'd ones, why [12] (said shee) because (said I) it is a com*m*on thing for people [13] to say that some men haue ill fortune. would you then [14] haue mee (said shee) discourse more after ye manner of the [15] vulgar, Least I seeme to withdraw my selfe so much from [16] the Use & Custome of men? As you please (said I) Are you [17] not of Opinion (said shee) that whateuer is profitable & advan= [18] =tageous is good? I am (said I) But that Fortune, that doth [19] either exercise, or correct is profitable, I confesse it (said I) [20] it is therefore good no doubt It is (said I) But that (said shee) [21] is the fortune of them, who being Either in possession of Virtue [22] do wage warre against aduersity, or Leauing vice, do take up [23] the way of vertue, I cannot (said I) deny it. But (said shee) [24] That prosperity that is giuen to good people, for a recompence [25] and reward of their vertue, doth the vulgar Esteeme that ill [26] **[51v]** Fortune or no? By no meanes (said I) but (as it really is) [1] the best of all. What say you of the other fortune, wch thô [2] it bee harsh, restraineth by a just punishment the wicked, [3] doth the people thinke that good? No (said I) but on the [4] contrary the most wretched & miserable of all. Beware [5] then (said

Shee) Least following the opinions of ye people, [6] wee make conclusions wch will not bee receaued & allowed [7] of by the people? how so (said I) why (said Shee) out of [8] what is graunted it follow's, that all Fortune is good to [9] those that are either in possession of vertue, in the way to [10] vertue, or upon the point of attaining vertue, and that it [11] is alwaies bad to those that remaine in wickednesse? It is [12] (said I) most true, thô no man dare's confesse it, why so [13] (said shee)? A wise man ought no more to bee troubled [14] when hee is Led into the combat of fortune then a valiant [15] man is when hee heare's the signall of a Battle; For the [16] danger & difficultys to both are occasion to encrease their [17] Fame & Glory; to[66] The one by giuing him an opportunity to [18] Show his courage, & to the other by manifesting his wisdome [19] & vertue, For therefore it hath the name of vertue, be= [20] =cause by it's owne strength, it is able to preserue it selfe [21] from being ouercome by difficulties & adversitys. For [22] you that were put in the way of vertue did not come into [23] this world to flow in delights, nor to bee drown'd in pleasures, [24] but to grapple & fight with all Sortes of Fortune, thô neuer [25] so Extreame; Be therefore carefull to keepe the middle [26] way, That neither the adverse do oppresse, not ye prosperous [27] corrupt you. For whoeuer is exalted by the one, or cast downe [28] by the other will meete with contempt for reward of his [29] Labour. And 'tis in y^{r} owne power to make to your selfe [30] what fortune you please. For all that wch seem's adverse, [31] doth either Exercise, correct, or punish. [32]

[52r]

Verse the 7th of the 4th Booke.

The valiant Agamem*n*on did by ten
Yeares[67] warre, upon the men
Of Phrigia, (whom hee did destroy)
And by the burning of the Towne of Troy
Revenge th'Affront his Brother had receau'd
By being basely of his wife bereau'd
On wch designe, hee was so feircely bent
That for a wind, to second his intent
Being ready to begin that Enterprise
Hee did not stick (himselfe) to sacrifize

[66] "to" inserted here.

[67] "x" inserted here, perhaps to indicate a need for revision, since this line is shorter than the others.

His daughter to the Gods, wch did procure
That fauour from them, Vlisse's did endure
Greate sorrows, & shed bitter teares, for's Lost
Companions, But soone after, at the Cost
Of Gastly Poliphemus (who had drown'd
Them in his monstrous belly) a way found
To giue himselfe some comfort, in the cry
Of that vile Monster, whose one only Eye
Hee did thrust out, Hercules is fam'd
For his hard Labours, hauing bravely tam'd
The haughty Centaurs, & strip't of the Skin
Of a fierce Lyon, wch hee carry'd in
[52v] Remembrance of his Vict'ry, 'twa's hee kill'd
With certaine arrowes, that were Steel'd
The wicked Harpys, 'twas hee tooke away
The apples from the waking Dragon, at noone day.
Hee with his hand made weightier with Gold
On the three headed Cerberus Layd hold
And dragg'd him with a Triple chaine, he Slew
Cruell Diomedes, & after threw
Him to his yet more cruell horse for foode
Hee kill'd the Hydra wth its copious broode
Of heads, hauing the venom burn't & brought
Achelous (who in severall Shape's had fought
With him) at Last to hide his head for shame[68]
(Having i'th shape of Bull receau'd a maime
I'th horne) i'th riuer that doth beare his name
Hee threw Gyant Antheus (great in fame)
Downe on the Lybian Sand & by th'death
O'th Monster Cacus did appease the wroth
Of King Evander, & Lastly, had those shoulders
Mark't by Bores foame, that were to be upholders
O'th heauens, For 'twas the Last of his great
Actions, to support the mighty weight
O'th heauens on's neck, for wch Labour hee
Deseru'd that heauen his reward should bee.

[68] Lines 35–38 are bracketed in the right margin; these two couplets share the same rhyme.

[53r] Go then strong men, where this example Leades
Why do you turne y^{r} backs, when hee thus treads
The path of Vertue, & doth Stoutly fight
May justly challenge heauen as his right.

The Fifth Booke.

Prose the 1st.

When shee had Said this, Shee was turning her discourse [1] to other things wch shee had a mind to treate off, But I thus [2] interrupted her, The Exhortation you haue made (said I) [3] is extreamly good, & worthy of y^{r}selfe, But, I now find, what [4] you formerly told mee concerning this Question of Providence, [5] to be true (to wit) that it is + [69] in many more, for [6] now I cannot but aske of you whether you thinke there is [7] any such thing as chance, and if there bee, what kind of [8] thing it is? I am making what haste I can (said shee) [9] to performe my promise, and to Shew you a way back [10] into y^{r} owne country, and the things you aske, though the [11] knowledge of them bee very Usefull, Yet they will Lead us [12] out of the way wee were going, & I am afraid you will bee [13] so tired with rambling out of the roade, that you will not [14] haue strength enough Left to performe y^{r} necessary journey. [15] feare not that (said I) For it will bee a kind of resting my [16] selfe & a refreshment, to heare that wch I haue so great a [17] **[53v]** minde to know, and besides, when what you deliuer is made out [1] and stand's establish't on all sides there will bee no roome Left [2] for doubt in what's to follow. I will then proceed in that way [3] (said shee) and im*me*diately shee began to Speake thus. If any [4] one (said Shee) shall define chance to bee an Event hapning by [5] accidentall motions, and not produc't by any connexion of [6] causes, I shall make it appeare, that it is nothing but a meere [7] empty word, & quite beside the Signification of the Subject [8] matter. For since God restraine's every thing within a Certaine [9] Order, what roome is there Left for things to happen by acci= [10] =dent? For that nothing can receaue a beeing from nothing [11] is a most certaine truth, and that wch neuer was deny'd by [12] any of the antients (though they did not meane it in relation [13] to God the beginning & Efficient cause of all things; But of y^{e} [14] materiall Subject, that is, of the nature of all Formes. But [15] if a thing should happen proceeding from no Cause,

[69] The "+" and space here indicate where a rendering for *implicitam* would go, and perhaps something for *experior*.

it would [16] seeme to Spring out of nothing, wch (if it cannot bee) there [17] can consequently bee no such chance, as was before defin'd. [18] Then (said I) is there nothing that can properly bee call'd [19] chance or accident? or is there really Something, though not [20] understood by the Vulgar that those words do Signify? My [21] Aristotle (said Shee) in his Physicks, giues a Short, and [22] that wch come's very neare a true Definition of it. In [23] what manner (said I)? When (Saith Shee) Something is [24] don in order to one end, & that Some other thing happen's [25] from certaine other causes, that was not intended, it is [26] call'd chance, As for Example, If one digging his ground [27] in order to the Sowing of it, happen's to finde a bag of [28] Gold, this seeme's to happen by chance, But it is not [29] from nothing, For it hath it's proper causes of wch the [30] suddaine & unexpected meeting together is call'd chance [31] For if the husbandman had not digg'd the ground [32] **[54r]** And if the owner of the money had not hid it there the gold [1] would not haue bin found, Those then were the causes of [2] that accidentall chance wch is produced by the meeting [3] together of causes without the intention & designe of [4] those that put them on worke; For neither hee that [5] hid the gold, nor hee that digg'd the ground, intended [6] that finding of the money, but yet (as I said before) [7] because the one hid it, and the other dig'd, the money [8] was found. Let us then Define chance to bee the un= [9] =expected event of things produced by ye concur-rence [10] & meeting together of cause's & things don to another [11] end. Now that those causes do so meete together, pro= [12] =ceed's from that inevitable Order flowing & discending [13] from the fountaine of Gods prouidence, by wch hee di= [14] =rects and dispose's all things into their proper [15] times and places. [16]

Verse the 1st of the 5th Booke.

In the steepe Rocks of Achemene
Where 'tis the manner of the Men
By flying to maintaine a Fight[70]
Rounding their Enn'mys in their Flight
With Darts wch they do at them throw
Still as they greedily pursue
The Tygris & Euphrates Spring
Out of one head, & Severing
[54v] Their waters, make two Streames if then

[70] "Parthya" identified in the left margin.

They come to meete & joyne agen
In one, their waves will rudely beate
Against each others Streame, Ships meete
The truncks of Trees & other things
The Flood hath torne, & with it bring's
Will tumbling mix, as 'twere by chance
And do a thousand things as if the dance
Were Led by fortune, but still all
Those things are caused by the fall
O'the ground & rapidnesse o'th Streame
Although disorderly they seeme
To meete, So chance do's seeme to play
Our games, & by it's only Sway
To gouerne Us, But that alasse
It's mighty selfe, a bridle ha's
And's gouern'd by a Supreame Law
From wch it's selfe it can't withdraw.

Prose the 2^{d} of the 5th Booke

I do perceauce (said I) the truth of what you haue [1] said; But (pray) in this Series & concatenation of causes [2] that are Link't one to another do wee retaine y^{e} Liberty [3] of our wills, or doth that fatall chaine put also a force [4] **[55r]** upon the motions of mens minds? There is no doubt (said [1] shee) Free=will in men; For there neuer was any rationall [2] nature, but was indu'd with it, For that wch naturally [3] can make use of reason, hath a judgment by w^{ch}, it can [4] discerne things, & consequently know's what is fit to bee [5] desired, and what to bee avoyded, and what any body [6] knowe's is fit to bee desired his reason teache's him to [7] pursue, and on the contrary to fly, from that wch hee [8] judge's fit to bee avoided; So that whereuer there is [9] reason, there must bee a Liberty to will, & Nill; But [10] I do not hold that Liberty to bee alike in all, For in the [11] high & divine Substances the judgment is more cleare [12] & piercing, The Will more incorrupt, & the power more [13] efficatious, and in humane Souls, those of necessity [14] must bee freest that do employ themselues in the [15] contemplation of the divine minde, those Lesse free [16] that Let themselues downe to the consideration [17] & entertainm^{t} of Bodyes, and those yet Lesse that [18] are acted by earthly Springs & Sinews, But it is the [19] greatest & extreamest bondage, when being once giuen [20] to vice, they fall from the possession of their owne [21] reason, For as soone as they cast downe their eyes [22] from the shining Light of truth upon those Low [23] things they are presently blinded with the mist of [24] ignorance & destroy'd by pernicious affections, To wch [25] consenting, they encrease that Slavery, wch they had [26] brought upon themselues, & are in a manner depriv'd of [27] that Liberty they naturally had. All wch notwithstand= [28] =ing the Eye of Prouidence (that see's all things from [29] all Eternity) obserue's, & ordaine's what was predesti= [30] =nated to each persons merit. [31]

[55v]

Verse the 2d of the 5th Booke

Melliflueus Homer in his Verse of old
Exto'l'd the brightnesse of the Sun & told
Us that it all things saw wth it's pure Light
Yet notwithstanding all it's power & might
It cannot pierce with it's bright beames into
The bowells of the Earth, or Sea, but 'tis not so
With the Creatour of the world, For hee
Doth all things from aboue thrô all things see
Nor can the Earth wth all it's weight, nor might
With all her darkenesse obviate his Sight
Hee at one time, & in one Act doth See
All that e're was, or is, or e're shall bee
Since then 'tis hee alone, that doth see all
Wee ought him only the true Sun to call.

Prose the 3d of the 5th Booke

Behold (said I) I now Labour under a greater difficulty [1] what is that (said shee) For I do but guesse at what [2] trouble's you. It seeme's to mee (said I) repugnant and [3] a kind of contradiction to say that God foreknowes all [4] things, and that there should bee any Free=will. For [5] if God see's all things & cannot bee mistaken, That must [6] necessarily happen, that his prouidence hath foreseene, [7] So that since from all Eternity hee hath foreknowne [8] not only all mens actions, but also their Councells, wills [9] **[56r]** and intentions, there can no Liberty of Will remaine. [1] [71]For if the

[71] Here at the beginning of the line, a "^" indicates a place for an insertion, while "*" stands in the left margin to call attention to the omission of a rendering for "neque enim vel factum aliud ullum vel quaelibet exsistere poterit voluntas nisi quam nescia falli providentia divina praesenserit."

things may bee wrested otherwise then they [2] were foreseene, then there was no foreknowledge, of what [3] was to come, but rather a bare uncertaine conjecture [4] wch it were a Sinne to beleiue of God Almighty, Neither [5] do I approue of that reason by wch some think they are [6] able to Solue this difficulty, by saying that 'tis not there= [7] =fore that any thing happen's, because Gods prouidence [8] hath foreseene it, but rather on the contrary, that since [9] it was to happen, it could not Lye hid from Gods proui= [10] =dence, And that So it fall's back the other way, it being [11] not necessary that the things should happen that are [12] foreseene, but that whateuer happen's must bee fore= [13] =seene. As if men Labour'd to finde out wch were the [14] cause of the other, that is, whether the foreknowledge [15] is cause of the necessity of things to come, or the necessity [16] of things to come bee cause of the foreknowledge. But [17] I will endeauour to Show, that whateuer the Order of [18] causes bee, the hapning of things foreseene is necessary, [19] although the foreknowledge of things to come do not im= [20] =pose a necessity of their hapning. For if any body Sit's, [21] the opinion that hee doth Sit must necessarily bee true, [22] & on the contrary, if the opinion bee true that hee Sits, hee [23] must of necessity Sit, There is then in both, a necessity, in [24] the one of Sitting, & in the other of trueth, But it is not [25] therefore that the person Sit's, because the opinion is [26] true, but rather therefore the opinion is true, because [27] the person Sit's. So that thô the cause of the truth of the [28] assertion proceed's from one part, yet there is a com*m*on [29] necessity impos'd upon both, And So wee must reason [30] concerning prouidence, and things to come. For if in the [31] **[56v]** same manner, things do not happen, because they are [1] foreseene, but therefore are foreseene because they were to [2] happen, Yet notwithstanding there is a necessity both of [3] their being foreseene by God, & of their hapning, wch alone [4] is enough to take away Free=will. Now how preposterous [5] is it to Say that the euent of temporall things, should bee [6] the cause of an Eternall foreknowledge? For what is it [7] other to think that therefore, God foresees things to come, [8] because they are to come, then to imagine that what former= [9] =ly hath hapned hath bin the Cause of Gods high prouidence [10] To this adde, as what I know to bee must of necessity bee, So [11] what I know certainly will come, must of necessity come, [12] the event therefore of a thing foreknowne cannot bee [13] avoyded. Lastly, if any body thinke otherwise of a thing, [14] then, really is, it, is not only not a knowledge, but a [15] false & deceiptfull opinion farre different from the [16] trueth & certainty of knowledge. Wherefore if any [17] thing bee so to come, as that there is no certainty & [18] necessity of it's coming, how is it possible, that any [19] body should certainly know it will come. For as [20] knowledge hath in it no mixture at all of falsity, [21] So what conceaue's cannot be otherwise then as it [22] conceaue's. For that is the reason that knowledge [23] can neuer lye, because it is necessary that a thing [24] must bee, as knowledge apprehend's it. What then? [25] how doth God foreknow things that are uncertaine [26] to happen? For if hee doth judge that those things [27] will infallibly happen, w^{ch} 'tis possible may not [28] happen, hee is deceiu'd, w^{ch} 'tis not only a crime to [29] beleiue, but euen to mention of God Almighty. But [30] if hee see's them so as they are to happen, that is, [31] **[57r]** That hee know's they either may, or may not bee, what [1] is this knowledge, that comprehend's nothing in it, of [2] certaine or infallible? or what doth it differ from that [3] ridiculous Tiresian prophecy? What shall I say, will [4] either bee, or not bee? and what aduantage hath Gods [5] Prouidence aboue mans Opinion, if hee can only judge [6] as men do, that those things are uncertaine of w^{ch} [7] wee judge the euent to bee so? But if in that most [8] certaine fountaine of all things, there reside no= [9] =thing of uncertainty, the event of those things must [10] bee certaine, wch hee hath certainly knowne will hap= [11] =pen. Wherefore there is no liberty or freedome nei= [12] =ther in mens actions nor Councells, Since the divine [13] thought wch see's all things, doth by that constraine & [14] tye them to one Event. wch being once granted, what [15] a fall & ruine of humane things will follow, doth [16] sufficiently appeare. For in vaine then are rewards & [17] punishments propos'd & held forth to ye good & bad men, [18] wch they neither can deserue, or hope to obtaine by any [19] free or voluntary motion of their minds, and that will [20] seeme to bee then most unjust, wch now is judg'd to bee [21] most equitable, to wit, that the wicked should bee [22] punish't & the good rewarded, Since they would haue [23] nothing Left to the choice of their wills, but be forced [24] by a certaine & an inevitable necessity to do what [25] they are ordain'd to do; Neither ought Vices, or Vertues [26] to signify any thing, since there would bee a mix't [27] confusion of deserts without difference, then w^{ch}, there [28] can bee nothing more wicked or unjust imagined. For [29] Since all the order of things doth proceed from prouidence [30] it will follow that wee may[72] impute our vices to y^{e} Author [31] of all goodness, & there will bee noe reason for praying [32] for or against any thing, For to what end should one [33]

[72] "may" inserted here.

[57v] hope or pray for or against any thing, when the in= [1] =euitable course of destiny ouerule's all things? and [2] so, that not only commerce betweene God & man will[73] [3] be destroy'd, to wit, hope & prayer. For 'tis only [4] by them, & by the meanes of a just humility that [5] wee can hope to merit the inestimable treasure of [6] diuine Grace, & are able as it were to discourse with [7] God, & to bee admitted into that inaccessible Light, w^{ch} [8] cannot bee approched but by Prayer & supplication [9] wch if by a necessity of things to happen, shall bee [10] beleiued (as it would follow) to bee of no power and [11] efficacy, what way will there bee Left us by wch wee [12] can bee joyn'd & cleaue to that prince & cheife [13] fountaine of all things? But on the contrary there [14] will bee a necessity that all mankind should (as you [15] Sung not Long ago) fall from & bee disjoyn'd from the [16] originall Fountaine & beginning (God) [17]

Verse the 3^{d} of the 5th Booke

What jarring cause hath such division bred
'Twixt things by strict alliance joynd, w^{t} God
Hath made such a perpetuall Warre betweene
Two constant truths, that they should still haue been
Allow'd for such, assunder, but together mix't
Seeme so repugnant, how can this consist
With truths great Charracter? how can there bee
Discords 'twixt truths, wch alwaies must agree?
And both being certaine in themselues must needs
Cohere; & so they do, But that wch breed's
[58r] The difference is, the weaknesse of the mind
Which the dull Organs of the body blind
And Sadly stupify to that degree
It ha's not Light & strength enough to see
The Subtill knittings & connexion of
Such abstruse things, wch are so farre aboue
Its reach. But w^{t} is it that make's the minde
So earnestly endeauour how to finde
The hidden notions of truth? dos't know
What it impatiently desires? if so
Why doth it Labour so to finde that out
It know's? if not, why doth it go about

[73] "will" at the end of this line mistakenly repeated at the beginning of the next.

Blindly to search for what it doth not know?
Did euer any man in's wits pursue
Or yet desire a thing hee knew not? how
Doth hee know where to looke, or how to know
When hee hath found? is it not that the Soule
Before with flesh 'twas cumber'd did behold,
And know all things in God, who is the Soule
Of all, but clog'd with members, that controule
That knowledge, with a Mist they cast before
Her, doth not quite forget, but can no more
Distinguish euery parte? Hee therefore that
Doth seeke truth, neither know's nor hath forgot
Her wholly, But in grosse retaining what
Hee know's, seek's Studdying to recouer that
H'has Lost, & those forgotten partes restore
To what his memory perseru'd before.

[58v] Prose the 4th of the 5th Booke.

This dispute (said shee) concerning Prouidence is of an= [1] =tient standing, & much handled by Marcus Tullius in his [2] Booke of Divination, & hath by you y^{r} selfe bin Long [3] Sought after, but hath not yet by any of y^{rs} bin suffici= [4] =ently clear'd & the reason of that darkenesse & obscurity [5] is, that the motions of humane reasoning are no way [6] proportionate, and therefore cannot reach y^{e} singlenesse [7] & simplicity of Gods foreknowledge, wch if once we could [8] but apprehend as really it is in it selfe, there would [9] be no roome left for doubt, and this I shall endea= [10] =uour to Lay open, when I haue first dispatch'd & [11] remou'd out of the way those reasons wherewith you [12] seeme at present to bee mou'd; In the first place [13] then Let mee aske you why you do not thinke that [14] reason sufficient (of those that would Solace that [15] difficulty) who showing, that God's foreknowledge, [16] is not the Cause why things happen, do therefore [17] conclude that it doth not take away free will? For [18] can you draw an argument from any thing else of [19] the necessity of future things hapning, then that w^{t} [20] is foreseene cannot but happen? Now if Gods fore= [21] =knowledge doth impose no necessity upon future things [22] (as you seem'd just now to grant) how is it that the [23] volantary motions of things are forced to any certaine [24] event? For let us put the case by way of supposition [25] (to the end you may obserue what would follow) that [26] there is no foreknowledge, will then those things that [27] proceed from free will & choyce bee, upon that accompt [28] forced necessarily to happen? No. Let us againe Sup= [29] =pose that there is foreknowledge, but that it doth [30] impose no necessity upon actions, will not there then [31] remaine the same entire & absolute Liberty of y^{e} will [32] **[59r]** as if there were no foreknowledge? You'le say foreknowledge [1] thô it impose no necessity upon future things to happen, [2] Yet notwithstanding is a signe that of necessity they must [3] happen; But I answer, that so those things must how= [4] =euer haue hapned, althô there had bin no foreknowledge [5] For that wch is the signe of a thing, only show's what the [6] thing is, but doth not make the thing to bee, that it is [7] a Signe of. Wherefore you must first demonstrate, that [8] euery thing doth happen necessarily, before you can [9] make this foreknowledge appeare to bee a Signe of [10] that necessity, For else if there bee no necessity that [11] cannot bee a Signe of a thing that is not. So that if [12] you will haue y^{r} argument conclude & rest upon firme [13] & irrefragable reason, you must bring y^{r} proofes not from [14] Signes & things, sought for from without, but from Ne= [15] =cessary & proper causes within. But you will say how is [16] it possible that those things should not happen, that are [17] foreseene? to that wee need not beleeue that those things [18] that prouidence hath foreseene, will not happen, [19] But 'tis enough that wee thinke that, thô they happen, [20] they haue nothing in their owne natures to necessi= [21] =tate their hapning. wch from what I shall say will [22] easily appeare. For do wee not see things (of those [23] that are Subject to our eyes) whilst they are doing, as [24] for example, do wee not see a Coachmaker make & put [25] together his Coach, & other workemen make those [26] things that appertaine to their severall trades? Now [27] I aske, doth our Looking upon their doing those things, [28] force those things to bee don? Not at all. For ye Art [29] of those men would bee then in vaine; if looking on did [30] force things into those shapes. Some things therefore [31] that haue no necessity of being may be seene framing, and [32] ouerseeing that they are to bee, doth not (before they are) [33] propose any necessity upon them to bee. and there are [34] **[59v]** Some things, wch will certainly happen though they are [1] absolutely free from any necessity of hapning; For no [2] man I thinke will say but that those things that are now [3] made, were before they were made, certainly to bee those [4] things, then thô foreknowne, are free in their euents, for [5] as the knowledge of the things present, do impose no [6] necessity upon the present, So the foreknowledge of the [7] things to come, impose no necessity upon the things to [8] come. But this you'le say yet remaine's doubtfull

[9] whether there can bee any foreknowledge of things whose [10] causes are not necessary? & that you, that are of opinion, [11] that foreknowledge doth impose a necessity, do also [12] thinke there can bee no foreknowledge, if that necessity [13] bee wanting, Since that knowledge can comprehend no= [14] =thing but what is certaine, & that if what is uncertaine [15] to happen, bee foreseene as certaine, it would proue [16] an erronious opinion, not a knowledge, wch imply's [17] truth, For to think a thing otherwise then it is, is not at [18] all agreeable to the integrity of knowledge. Now the [19] cause of this Errour is, because you judge that those things [20] that any person know's, are knowne according to the [21] nature & strength of ye thing knowne, whereas it is [22] quite contrary, For every thing that is knowne is [23] rather apprehended according to the faculties & Capacity [24] of them that know it. As (to cleare it by one short [25] example) the same roundnesse of ye body is perceau'd [26] one way by the Sight, & another way by the touch, the [27] first remaining Stedfast, it also doth by the sending [28] emission of it's beames, See it all at once, The other [29] mouing & feeling about the whole circumference of [30] the round body, doth so discouer the roundnesse of it by [31] handling & touching the parts & man himselfe, is [32] Lookt upon & considered, one way by the Sences, another [33] way by the im*m*agination, a third way by reason, [34] **[60r]** and a fourth, by the divine intelligence, For the Sences [1] consider the figure constituted in the Subject matter, [2] the im*m*agination only the figure without matter; Reason [3] goe's beyond that, & consider's the Species it selfe, (wch is [4] in euery one aparte) by a generall & universall con= [5] =sideration; But the eye of the divine intelligence, goes [6] yet higher, & passing by the compasse of y^{e} universallity [7] Look's with the pure strength of it's thought upon the [8] very simple forme of man it selfe, In wch this is to [9] bee consider'd, that the Superiour strength of Compre= [10] =hension still include's the inferiour, [11] but the inferiour cannot rise up to reach the Superiour, For the sence [12] cannot go beyond matter, nor the imagination, See the [13] universall Species, Nor reason conceaue the Simple [14] forme, But the divine intelligence Looking as it were [15] from aboue (hauing comprehended the forme) judge's [16] & know's all that is under, but still in the same manner [17] as it comprehend's the forme it selfe, wch is after a way [18] that none of ye other can. For it know's the universall [19] Species, that is subject to the reach of reason, the [20] im*m*ateriall figure that is so to the imagination, and [21] the matter wch is subject to sence, without using either [22] reason, imagination or sence, but formally) as I may [23] so say) Looking & beholding all with one thought, & so, [24] reason, when it Look's upon

something that is univer= [25] =sall neither making Use of imagination, nor sence, [26] comprehend's both imaginable & sencible things, For [27] it is shee that defines a man, to bee a rationall two= [28] =footed creature, & yet euery body know's that man is [29] both an imaginable & sencible thing, thô shee neither [30] consider him by sence or imagination, but by an Exter= [31] =nall conception, And so the imagination thô it tooke [32] it's rise & originall of seeing & forming figures from the [33] sences, yet in the absense of Sence it comprehendeth [34] **[60v]** all Sencible things, not by a Sencible but an imaginary [1] way, of judging them. Do you not therefore See that [2] all things in knowing, Use rather their owne wayes & [3] faculty's then those of the things they know. & that not [4] without reason, For since all Iudgment consist's in the [5] act of him that judge's it is necessary that euery one [6] should do his owne worke by his owne power and [7] strength, and not by anothers. [8]

Verse the 4th of the 5th Booke

The Fame of the Learned Athens sometimes brought
Into their Porch Phylosophers that thought
The Soule had it's imaginations from
Th'impression of outward bodys bringing home
From thence, all that shee knew, just as wee see
Men use to take a borde, or table free
From all impressions, & then it carue
Such figures, or such Letters as do serue
T'expresse their thoughts, or as men write in Sand
(Such as the Sea make's smooth upon the Strand)
Such Letters as they please, but if the Soule
Doth not it selfe by it's owne strength unfold
And only passive lies, & useth not
It's owne free motions from within, but
[L]ike[74] an idle glasse only returne's ye shape
Of what is put before it, how can't reape
From thence that univerall knowledge, w^{ch}
It hath, seeing not things in grosse, but each
One singly in it selfe, whence come's that force

[74] "But" appears at the beginning of this line, underlined and marked with an "x" for deletion. Since the "but" at the end of line 14 is needed for a near rhyme with "not" above, the deletion of "But" here makes line 15 begin with a capitalized "Like."

Whereby it doth divide & sever course
[61r] From fine, in what it know's, & then agen
(As it see's cause) doth the divided joyne
Then taking a new way, sometimes doth Lift
It's head up to high things, then by as swift
A motion doth returne to minde the Low
Then turning in to'tselfe finde's meanes to know
The truth of things, & by that to disproue
What's false, all wch are things so farre aboue
What can bee fancy'd to proceed from bare
Impressions made by bodys, that 'tis cleare
They must haue a more powerfull cause, passion
'Tis true in Liuing bodys doth spurre on
The minde to exercise it's strength (as Light
Provoke's the eyes to exercise their sight
Or noise the eares to heare) by wch the minde
Being excited & stirr'd up, doth finde
It fit to call the vigour of it's inward Light
Unto Like motions, joyning the might
Of that into the notions it hath from
Without, & outward images to those at home.

Prose the 5th of the 5th Booke.

But if in bodys that are subject to the Sence of feeling, [1] although the objected qualities from without do moue [2] the Organs of the sences, and the passion of the body doth [3] go before the vigour & strength of the working Soule, and [4] provoke's it to an actuall thought, & doth so awaken & [5] excite the inward formes that Lay quiet & as it were asleep [6] **[61v]** if (I say) even in bodys to bee felt, the Soule hath not it's [1] impressions from, but barely is stirr'd by passion & by [2] it's owne strength judges's euen that passion wch is subject [3] to the body, how much lesse then do those that are free from [4] all Sences & affections of the body follow objects from without [5] in discerning of things, but accomplish all things by the [6] pure strength of their thought? Thus then there arise's [7] severall sortes of knowledges, according to the diversity [8] of the Substances that know. As for example, Oysters [9] Musells & such like Creatures that haue no motion, but [10] stick to & receaue their nourishm^{t} from rocks & stones, [11] haue nothing but sence destitute & void of all other kind [12] of knowledge in other creatures that moue, & in whom [13] there may bee perceau'd a capacity of desiring some [14] things & of avoyding others, there is imagination, [15] But reason belong's solely to mankind, as intelligence [16] doth to the divine nature. and from hence it is that [17] that knowledge most excell's the rest, wch of it's owne [18] nature doth not only know the highest & most pro= [19] =per object of it's owne knowledge, but likewise what [20] is subject to the knowledge of all the rest, But now [21] if sence & imagination should argue against reason [22] Saying that, that uniuersallity is nothing that reason [23] thinke's shee see's, for that what is sencible or imagi= [24] =nable cannot bee universall. then is either the [25] judment of reason true, & nothing is sencible, or if [26] there are many things knowne by reason to be subject [27] to sence & to im*m*agination, the conception of reason [28] is vaine & false, that consider's that as universall, [29] that is singular & sencible. If to this, reason should [30] answer, that shee doth in universallity comprehend & [31] see both what is sencible & what is imaginable, but [32] that the Sences & the[75] imagination cannot reach nor pretend [33] **[62r]** to the knowledge of universallity, because theirs cannot [1] go beyond Corporeall materiall figures, and that in the [2] knowledge of things it is fit to trust to the more perfect [3] judgment, In this controuersy & dispute should not [4] wee that are indued both with reason, imagination & [5] sence, giue it rather on reasons side? 'Tis in ye same [6] manner that humane reason, think's that the divine [7] intelligence doth not see future things, any other wise [8] then as shee doth, For thus you argue, if there are [9] things the event of wch is not necessary & certaine, it [10] cannot bee certainly knowne that they will happen, [11] & therefore there can bee no foreknowledge, of such [12] things, and if wee beleiue they do necessarily happen [13] there will nothing remaine voluntary, But all things [14] bee gouerne'd by inevitable destiny. But now if as [15] wee are indued with reason, wee could bee partakers [16] of the judgment of the diuine thought, as wee haue [17] already judg'd it fit for sence & imagination to submit [18] to reason, So wee should thinke it most just y^t^ humane [19] reason should yeild to the divine thought. Let us [20] then endeauour, if wee can, to get up to the pinacle of [21] that Soueraigne intelligence, for from thence reason [22] will bee able to see, what of itselfe it cannot, that is, [23] in what manner the certaine & definitiue foreknow= [24] =ledge of God see's those things, that haue no certaine [25] events, & that it is not opinion only, (wch might bee [26] subject to errours) but the Simplicity & purity of [27] Soueraigne unbounded knowledge, wch cannot Erre. [28]

[75] "the" added here.

Verse the 5th of the 5th Booke.

In how various Shapes & postures do
Those creatures that inhabite heere below
[62v] Passe up & downe the earth, some lye along
Stretch't out upon the ground from whence they sprung.[76]
And when they moue do wth their bodys sweep
The dust, making a track where they do creep
Like to a Litle furrow, others there are
Who wth their nimble wings beating the aire
Do wth an admirable Swiftnesse fly
In those wide spaces underneath the Sky,
Others do take delight to tread upon
The earth, & leaue impressions where they've gone
Choosing sometimes to ramble in the feild,
Sometimes the Shade that gloomy woods do yeild
But tho these creatures thus do disagree
In humours & in shape, yet this wee see
They are alike in, that their heads bow downe,
Towards the earth, wch do's their sences drowne
In stupid earthly dullnesse, only man
Lift's up his head, & doth uprightly stand
Scorning the earth, wch hee tread's under foote,
This posture of our bodys, ought to roote
All earthly thoughts out of our minds (unlesse
W'are mad) & teach us singly to addresse
Our selues to what's aboue, as the erect
Position of our bodys doth direct,
And not to suffer since our heads beare high
Our heauen born Soules in ye base earth shd Lye

[63r] Prose the 6th of the 5th Booke

Since then (as hath bin demonstrated) euery thing that [1] is knowne, is not knowne according to it's owne, but [2] according to the nature of those that know it, Let Us [3] Looke into (as farre as wee may) and consider the [4] estate & condition of the divine Substance, that wee [5] may by that understand what kind of knowledge [6] God's is; That God is eternall is

[76] "sprung." inserted above line 4 for lack of room at right margin.

unanimously [7] concluded by all rationall creatures; Let us then [8] consider what Eternity is, For that will both Lay [9] open to Us his Nature & his knowledge; Eternity [10] is the Entire & the (at once) perfect possession of [11] an euerlasting, & neuer ending Life, wch by ye Compa= [12] =ring of it with what is temporall, will the[77] more plain= [13] =ly appeare. For what euer Liveth in time, is at [14] present, & proceed's from time past, towards time to [15] come, & there is nothing establisht in time that can [16] possesse & embrace at once the whole space of his Life [17] For tomorrow hee is not yet arriued to, & yesterday hee [18] hath already Lost, So that in the Life of to day, you only [19] haue use in one moueable transitory moment. what= [20] =euer then Suffer's the condition of time, though (as Aristotle [21] thought of ye world) it should neuer haue had beginning, [22] nor neuer were to haue an end, But to haue a Life [23] stretch't out to infinity of time, Yet it would not bee that, [24] that ought justly to bee called eternall, For it would not [25] comprehend & embrace fully at one time, the whole Space [26] of that infinite Life, For what is to come it hath not yet, [27] and what's past & gon, it hath not; That then wch compre= [28] =hend's & enjoye's at one time, & together, the wholl full= [29] =nesse of a neuer ending Life, that neither hath any thing [30] absent of what is to come, Nor from whom any thing is [31] slipt away of what is past, that is justly & properly [32] **[63v]** held to be Eternall; and that thing must of necessity [1] bee[78] alwayes present, & competent to it's selfe, & haue the [2] infinity of moueable time alwaies before it's Eyes. and [3] therefore those were very much in the wrong, that [4] hearing that Plato was of opinion, that, this world neither [5] had a beginning, nor was to haue end, judg'd that the [6] made world would so, bee coeternall with it's maker. For [7] it is one thing to leade a neuer ending Life (such as Plato [8] giues to the world) and another thing to haue & embrace [9] at once, the full compleat presence of an euerlasting Life, [10] wch it is manifest is only proper to the divine thought. [11] And God ought not to bee thought antienter than ye things [12] hee hath made by quantity of time, But by the property [13] of his simple nature. For that infinite motion of Tem= [14] =porall things doth but endeauour to imitate the present [15] State (wee mentioned in God) of an immoueable Life, and [16] finding that[79] it cannot equall it, or come neare it, it falls from [17] immobility into motion,

[77] "the" inserted here.

[78] "bee" preceded on the previous line by another "bee" that is stricken through twice.

[79] "that" inserted here.

& from the simplicity & singlenesse [18] of presence, into the infinite quantity of time past & to [19] come, & not being able to possesse together at once ye whole [20] substance of it's selfe, because it would in some sorte seeme [21] neuer to cease to bee, it doth endeauour seemingly, and [22] weakely to im*m*itate that wch it cannot perfectly fulfill, & [23] expresse, tying it selfe to some kind of presence in this [24] Litle fleeting moment, wch because it beare's some show [25] of that permanent one in God, it make's whateuer it hap= [26] =pen's to, to seeme to haue some continuance & permanence [27] but because it cannot really remaine, it take's up an [28] infinite journey of time, & by that meanes continue's by [29] going a Life, whose fullnesse it could not possesse by re= [30] =maining & being permanent. Therefore if wee will giue [31] right names to things (following Plato) Let us call God [32] eternall, & the world perpetuall. Since then all knowledge [33] comprehend's things that are Subjected to it, according [34] **[64r]** to it's owne nature, and that God hath an Eternall [1] & presentary Estate, his knowledge must also surpasse [2] all motion of time, who being permanent & dwelling [3] in the simplicity of his presence, & comprehending [4] the infinite Spaces of time past, & to come, consider's [5] all things in his Simple and pure knowledge, as if they [6] were just now doing. If therefore you will figure [7] to y^r selfe that knowledge, by wch hee know's all things, [8] you must not Looke upon it as a foreknowledge of what's [9] to come, but as a knowledge of what is don in a neuer [10] ending instant that is allwaies present to him, and [11] therefore is not called previdence, but prouidence, [12] because it being plac't aboue all things, it hath as [13] it were a prospect, & from aboue Look's downe upon all [14] things, how then will you inferre that Almighty God [15] seeing things, make's them necessarily to bee don, any [16] more, then mens seeing things don, necessitates them [17] to bee don? For doth yor sight impose any necessity upon [18] those things to bee don, that you see present before [19] y^r Eyes? certainly no. Now compare the humane [20] present with the diuine, & you will finde, that as [21] you see somethings in y^r temporary present, So hee [22] doth all things in his Eternall one, wherefore this [23] divine foreknowledge, doth not at all change the [24] nature & property of things, For hee see's those things [25] present to him, that will happen in futurity of time, [26] neither doth hee mix and confound the x [80] of things [27] but at one sight see's as well those that do necessarily, [28] as those that do not necessarily happen; as you do

[80] The "x" and space here indicate where a rendering for "*iudicia*" would go.

see [29] men walke, & the Sunne rise, & thô at one sight you do [30] discerne them, Yet you judge one to bee voluntary, & the [31] other not to bee so. In the same manner Gods seeing [32] all things under him, doth not disturbe nor trouble the [33] quality of things, wch are indeed present as to him, but [34] **[64v]** future in relation to time, from whence it come's that [1] his, is not an opinion, but knowledge, grounded upon trueth, [2] by wch hee know's that thô Such a thing will happen, Yet [3] that there was no necessity that it should happen heere, [4] if you shall say, that what God see's will happen, can= [5] =not but happen, & that what cannot but happen, doth [6] of necessity happen, tying mee so to the word necessity, I [7] will confess (what is a most Solid & undeniable truth) but [8] what no body can see 'till hee bee a beholder of the divine [9] thought. For I will answer that it is indeed of necessity [10] to happen, as it hath relation to the diuine thought, [11] But as it is consider'd in it's owne nature, it is absolute= [12] =ly free from that necessity, For there are two necessitys, [13] one simply so as it is necessary that all men should bee [14] mortall, The other conditionall, if you know that any [15] walke's, it is necessary that hee should walke, For what[81] [16] =euer any body know's, cannot bee other then as hee know's [17] it to bee, But this conditionall doth not carry that Sim= [18] =ple necessity with it, For it is not it's proper nature, but [19] the adding of the condition, that make's that necessity, For [20] no necessity compell's a man to walke, that walkes volun= [21] =tarily, But when hee walke's, it is necessary that hee [22] do walke. and so if prouidence see's any thing present [23] it is necessary, that it bee, although it haue no necessity [24] in it of nature, but naturally might not haue beene. [25] Now God see's all things that are to proceed from free will [26] & choyce as if they were present, These then as they [27] relate to Gods sight, are don necessarily, because of the [28] condition of Gods knowledge annext, But considered [29] in themselues, Loose nothing of the absolute freedome [30] of their nature. All things then that God hath foreseene [31] will bee, without doubt must bee, But some of them [32] do not leaue to proceed from the Agents free will & choyce [33] & by their hapning, loose nothing of their nature, althô [34] before they were, they could not but happen. What availe's [35] **[65r]** then, that they are not necessary, if by reason of the con= [1] =dition of Gods knowledge they happen in euery respect [2] as if they had that necessity upon them? This, that [3] of those things that I mentioned just now, The sunne [4] rising, & a man walking,

[81] No "=" to indicate hyphenation at the end of this line.

the one had naturally a ne= [5] =cessity upon it of beeing before it was, & the other not, [6] and so those things also that are present before God [7] without doubt, are, but some of their beeings proceed [8] from the necessity of the things themselues, & others [9] from the power & choyce of those that do them. Wee [10] haue not therefore without reason saide, that these [11] Last, if they are consider'd in relation to the divine [12] knowledge, are necessary. But consider'd in themselues, [13] are free from all bonds of necessity, As all that lye's [14] open to Sence is universall in relation to reason, but [15] Looke upon it in it selfe, is Singular. But you'le say [16] if it bee in my power to alter my purpose, I may dis= [17] =appoint prouidence, altering perhaps, what shee fore= [18] knew; I answer, 'tis possible you may change y^{r} minde [19] & bend y^{r} purpose another way, But since prouidence [20] See's, as a thing present before it, without a possibility of [21] erring, both the power you haue to alter, & what use you [22] make of that power, it is as impossible to avoide that [23] foreknowledge, as it is to escape the Eyes of one that is [24] present, & Looking upon you, though you make use of y^{r} [25] will & power to turn y^{r} selfe to neuer so different actions, [26] What then you'le say, may I at my pleasure change the [27] foreknowledge of God, by willing now this, not that, & must [28] that as often alter it's knowledge? Not at all, For the divine [29] sight forerunne's what is to come, & recall's & bring's it [30] back to the presence that is proper for it's knowledge [31] and doth not change & alter as you fancy, But remain= [32] =ing firme it selfe, doth at one stroake in one act preuent [33] & comprehend their changes, wch presence of seeing & com= [34] =prehending all things, God hath not from the euent of the [35] things, But from the proper simplicity of his owne nature [36] **[65v]** out of w^{ch}, that difficulty is also Solu'd that you put not [1] Long since, that it was an unbeseeming thing & unworthy [2] of God, that future things should bee said to bee the Cause [3] of his knowledge; For this strength of knowledge com= [4] =prehending all things under[82] one present notion, Establishe's [5] the manner & meanes to all things, & oweth nothing to [6] Later things, wch being so, the Liberty of mens wills, re= [7] =maine's entire & untouch't, & those Lawes are not unjust [8] that propose rewards & punishments to wills that act [9] freely & without any manner of force or constraint [10] There remaine's also the alle knowing & consequently the fore= [11] =knowing God Spectatour & Ouerlooker of all things, who wth [12] the Eternall presence of his Sight, concurring with the future [13]

[82] "under" inserted here.

quality of our actions, doth dispence rewards to the good, & [14] punishments to the wicked, and 'tis not in vaine that wee [15] direct our hopes & prayers to God, wch when they are [16] as they[83] ought to bee, can neuer bee unsuccessfull. Abhorre [17] then vice, & respect vertue, & raise up y^{r} minds to righte= [18] =ous hopes, & send up y^{r} humble prayers on high, for [19] there is a greate necessity upon you to bee good, & not [20] to dissemble since you act before the eyes of a judge [21] that sees all things. [22]

[83] "as they" preceded on the previous line by another "as they" that is stricken through twice.

Selected Bibliography

THIS BIBLIOGRAPHY OFFERS a highly selective list of suggestions for further reading about Boethius and the vernacular traditions of the *De consolatione philosophiae*. The first section includes general studies devoted to Boethius, his life, and his influence, with particular emphasis on studies of the vernacular translations of the *Consolatio*. The second section includes a list of standard editions of the *Consolatio*. The third section includes checklists of the various translations treated in the volume, divided alphabetically by country and chronologically by date. The final section includes a list of bibliographical sources on Boethius. These suggestions for further reading are meant to augment the full-citation notes at the end of each chapter.

General Studies

Albesano, Silvia. *"Consolatio Philosophiae" volgare: volgarizzamenti e tradizioni discorsive nel Trecento italiano*. Heidelberg: Universitätsverlag Winter, 2006.

Black, Robert, and Gabriella Pomaro. *La "Consolazione della filosofia" nel Medioevo e nel Rinascimento italiano: Libri di scuola e glosse nei manoscritti fiorentini*. Florence: SISMEL-Edizioni del Galluzzo, 2000.

Brouwer, R. F. M. "Inleiding." In Boethius, *Der vertroosting van de filosofie*, translated by R. F. M. Browuer, 9–62. Amsterdam: Ambo, 2000.

Ceoletta, D. "Planude Traduttore di Boezio." In *Scritti in Onore di Caterina Vassalini*, edited by Luigi Barbesi, 157–64. Verona: Fiorini, 1974.

Courcelle, Pierre. *La "Consolation de Philosophie" dans la tradition littéraire: antécédents et posterité de Boèce*. Paris: Études augustiniennes, 1967.

Donaghey, Brian. "The Post-Medieval English Translations of the *De Consolatione Philosophiae* of Boethius, 1500–1800." In *The Medieval Translator/Traduire au Moyan Age*, edited by Roger Ellis and René Tixier, 302–21. Turnhout: Brepols, 1996.

Dwyer, Richard A. *Boethian Fictions: Narratives in the Medieval French

Versions of the "Consolatio Philosophiae." Cambridge, MA: Medieval Academy of America, 1976.

Galdi, Marco. *Saggi Boeziani.* Pisa: Giardini, 1938.

Geysbeek, P.G. Witsen. *Biographisch anthologisch en critisch woordenboek der Nederduitsche dichters: Deel 4, JAC–NYV.* Amsterdam: Schleijer, 1823.

Gibson, Margaret T., ed. *Boethius: His Life, Thought, and Influence.* Oxford: Blackwell, 1981.

Gibson, Margaret T., Lesley Smith, and Joseph Ziegler, eds. *Great Britain and Ireland.* Vol. 1 of *Codices Boethiani: A Conspectus of Manuscripts of the Works of Boethius.* 4 Vols. London: Warburg Institute, 1995.

Glei, Reinhold F., Nicola Kaminski, and Franz Lebsanft, eds. *Boethius Christianus? Transformationen der "Consolatio Philosophiae" in Mittelalter und Früher Neuzeit.* Berlin: Gruyter, 2010.

Goris, Mariken. "Boethius's *Consolatio Philosophiae* and the Early Printing Tradition." In *The Bookshop of the World: The Role of the Low Countries in the Book-trade, 1473–1941*, edited by Lotte Hellinga, Alastair Duke, Jacob Harskamp, and Theo Hermans, 49–54. 't Goy-Houten, Netherlands: HES & De Graaf, 2001.

Goris, Mariken, ed. *Boethius en het Nederlands: Studie naar en tekstuitgave van de Gentse Boethius (1485), Boek II.* Hilversum: Verloren, 2000.

Goris, Mariken and Lodi W. Nauta. "The Study of Boethius's *Consolatio* in the Low Countries Around 1500: The *Ghent Boethius* (1485) and the Commentary by Agricola/Murmellius (1514)." In *Northern Humanism in European Context, 1469–1625: From the "Adwert Academy" to Ubbo Emmius*, edited by F. Akkerman, A. J. Vanderjagt, and A. H. van der Laan, 109–30. Leiden: Brill, 1999.

Goris, Mariken and Wilma Wissink. "The Medieval Dutch Tradition of Boethius' *Consolatio Philosophiae.*" In *Boethius in the Middle Ages: Latin and Vernacular Traditions of the "Consolatio philosophiae,"* edited by Maarten J. F. M. Hoenen and Lodi Nauta, 127–28. Leiden: Brill, 1997.

Gruber, Joachim. *Kommentar zu Boethius, De Consolatione Philosophiae, 2: erweiterte Auflage.* Texte und Kommentare 9. Berlin: Gruyter, 2006.

Hermans, Theo. "Translation and Normativity." *Current Issues in Language and Society* 5, no. 1/2 (1998): 51–72.

Hoek, Jacobus Martinus. *De Middelnederlandse Vertalignen van Boethius' "De Consolatione Philosophiae" mete en overzicht van de andere Nederlanse en niet-Nederlanse veralingen.* Harderwijk: FLEVO, 1943.

Hoenen, Maarten J. F. M., and Lodi Nauta, eds. *Boethius in the Middle Ages: Latin and Vernacular Traditions of the "Consolatio philosophiae."* Leiden: Brill, 1997.

Kaylor, Noel Harold, and Philip Edward Phillips, eds. *A Companion to Boethius in the Middle Ages*. Brill's Companions to the Christian Tradition 30. Leiden: Brill, 2012.

Kaylor, Noel Harold, and Philip Edward Phillips, eds. *New Directions in Boethian Studies*. Studies in Medieval Culture 45. Kalamazoo: Medieval Institute Publications, 2007.

Kopanos, B. "Παραταχτιχα ζευγη στις μεταφράσεις του Μαξιμου Πλανουδη." ΕΕΦΣΘ 13 (1974): 21–34.

Lunardi, Serena. "'La victuoria de la terra dona lo cielo': l'interpretazione del metro IV, VII in un volgarizzamento italiano inedito alla 'Consolatio Philosophiae," *La parola del testo* 12 (2008): 117–63, especially 157–63.

Marenbon, John. *Boethius*. Great Medieval Thinkers. Oxford: Oxford University Press, 2003.

———, ed. *The Cambridge Companion to Boethius*. Cambridge: Cambridge University Press, 2009.

Megas, Anastasios. "Εισαγωγή." In Boethius, *Boethii De Philosophiae Consolatione in Linguam Graecam Translati*, translated by Maximos Planudes, edited by Anastasios Megas, 7–56. Thessalonicae: University Studio Press, 1996.

Milanesi, Carlo. *Il Boezio e l'Arrighetto: Volgarizzamenti del buon secolo, riveduti su' codici fiorentini*. Florence: Barbera, 1864.

Minnis, A.J., ed. *The Medieval Boethius: Studies in the Vernacular Traditions of "De Consolatione Philosophiae."* Cambridge: Brewer, 1987.

Papathomopoulos, Manolis. "Introduction." In Boethius, *Anicii Manlii Severini Boethii De Consolatione Philosophiae: Traduction Grecque de Maxime Planude*, edited by Manolis Papathomopoulos, xxiii–lxxiv. Athens: Academy of Athens, 1999.

Phillips, Philip Edward. "King Alfred the Great and the Victorian Translations of His Anglo-Saxon *Boethius*." In *Global Perspectives on Medieval English Literature, Language, and Culture*, edited by Noel Harold Kaylor, Jr. and Richard Scott Nokes, 155–73. Kalamazoo: Medieval Institute Publications, 2007.

Patch, Howard R. *The Tradition of Boethius*. Oxford: Oxford University Press, 1935.

Rand, Edward Kennard. *Founders of the Middle Ages*. Cambridge, MA:

Harvard University Press, 1928. Reprint, New York: Dover, 1957.

Schotman, J. W. "Inleiding." In Boethius, *Der vertroosting der wijsbegeerte*, translated by J. W. Schotman, vii–xxvi. Amsterdam: Wereld-Bibliotheek, 1924.

Smith, Lesley, and T. Christchev, eds. *Austria, Belgium, Luxembourg, The Netherlands, Sweden, Switzerland.* Vol. 2 of *Codices Boethiani.* Warburg Institute Surveys and Texts 27. London: Warburg Institute, 2001.

Stewart, Hugh Fraser. *Boethius: An Essay.* London: Blackwood, 1892. Reprint, New York: Franklin, 1974.

Sturlese, Loris. *Filosofia in volgare, Filosofia in volgare nel Medioevo.* Atti del convegno della S.I.S.P.M (Lecce, 27–29 settembre 2002). Edited by N. Bray and Loris Sturlese. Louvain-la-Neuve: Fédération internationale d'études médiévales, 2003.

Thomas, Antoine, and Mario Roques. "Traductions françaises de la *Consolatio Philosophiae* de Boèce." In *Histoire Littéraire de la France*, vol. 31, 419-88. Paris: Klincksieck, 1938.

Troncarelli, Fabio. "*Boezio.*" in *Lo spazio letterario del Medioevo, 2: Il Medioevo volgare*, vol. III, *La ricezione del testo*, ed. Piero Boitani, Mario Mancini, and Alberto Vàrvaro, 303–29. Roma: Salerno, 2003.

Van de Vyver, A. "Les Traductions du *De Consolatione Philosophiae* de Boèce en Littérature Comparée." *Humanisme et Renaissance* 6, no. 3 (1939): 247–73.

Zonta, Mauro. "Le origini letterarie e filosofiche delle versioni ebraiche del *De Consolatione philosophiae* di Boezio," in *Hebraica: Miscellanea di studi in onore di Sergio J. Sierra*, ed. F. Israel, A. M. Rabello, and A. M. Somekh, 571–604. Turin: Instituto di Studi Ebraici Scuola Rabbinica, 1998.

Standard Editions of the Latin *Consolatio*

Bieler, Ludwig, ed. *Philosophiae consolatio*, Corpus Christianorum Series Latina 94. Turnhout: Brepols, 1984.

Moreschini, Claudio, ed. *De consolatione philosophiae: Opuscula theologica.* Biblioteca Teubneriana. 2nd ed. Munich: Saur, 2005.

Peiper, Rudolphus, ed. *Anicii Manlii Severini Boetii Philosophiae Consolationis.* Leipzig: Teubner, 1871.

Tester, S. J., trans. "The Consolation of Philosophy." In Boethius, *The Theological Tractates; The Consolation of Philosophy*, translated by H. F. Stewart, E. K. Rand, and S. J. Tester. Loeb Classical Library 74, 130–435. Cambridge, MA: Harvard University Press, 1973.

Translations Discussed in the Individual Chapters

Dutch

[Thirteenth-Century Jacob of Maerlant] van Maerlant, Jacob. *Spiegel Historiael.* Edited by M. de Vries and E. Verwijs (Leiden, 1863).

[1466 Vilt] Utrecht, Universiteitsbibliotheek, Cod. 1335.

[1485 Anonymous Ghent] *Dat weerdich bouc boecius de consolatione philosophie.* Ghent: Arend de Keysere, 1485.

[1557 Coornhert] *Der vertroestringhe der Wyßheyt.* Translated by Dirck Volkertszoon Coornhert. Deventer: Symon Steinberghen, 1557.

[1585 Coornhert] *Boethius vande Vertroosting der wijsheyd: uijt 't Latijn op nieus vertaalt.* Translated by Dirck Volkertszoon Coornhert. Leyden: Christoffel Plantyn, 1585.

[1653 de Buck] *Troost-Medecijne-vvynkel der zedighe Wysheyt.* Translated by Nobertijn Adrianus de Buck. Bruges: Lucas vanden Kerchove, 1635.

[1654 van Hoogstraten] *Boethius van de verstroostingh der philosophie. Eerst vertaelt deur D.V. Coornhert. Nu op Nieuws oversien en in sijn Gedichten verandert.* Edited and translated by François van Hoogstraten. Dordrecht: Nicolaes Geerlingh, 1654.

[1686 Vollenhove (2m5)] Vollenhove, Joannes. *Poëzy.* Amsterdam: H. Boom en de weduwe van D. Boom, 1686.

[1703 and 1722 Gargon] *Vertroostinge der wysgeerte.* Translated by Mattheus Gargon. Amsterdam: Hendrik Bosch and Salomon Schouten, 1722.

[1809 Bilderdijk (meters)] Bilderdijk, Willem. *De Dichtwerken van Bilderdijk.* Volume 4. Haarlem: A. C. Kruseman, 1857.

[1833 Wiselius (1m6, 2m3, 5m2)] Wiselius, Sameul I. *Nieuwe Dichtbundel van Samuel Iperuszoon Wiselius.* Amsterdam: H. Garman, 1833.

[1924 Schotman] *Der vertroosting der wijsbegeerte.* Translated by Johan Wilhelm Schotman. Amsterdam: Wereld-Bibliotheek, 1952.

[1953 Suys-Reitsma] *Vertroosting der Wijsbegeerte.* Translated by Sophia Jacomina Suys-Reitsma. Amsterdam: N. V. de Arbeiderspers, 1953.

[1990 Brouwer] *Der vertroosting van de filosofie.* Translated by R. F. M. Brouwer. 3rd ed. Amsterdam: Ambo, 2010.

English[1]

[ca. 885–950 Old English Boethius] Godden, Malcolm R., and Susan Irvine, eds. *The Old English Boethius: An Edition of the Old English*

Versions of Boethius's "De Consolatione Philosophiae." 2 vols. Oxford: Oxford University Press, 2009.

[1380–85 Chaucer] Benson, Larry D., ed. "Boece." Translated by Geoffrey Chaucer. In *The Riverside Chaucer*, 395–469. 3rd ed. Boston: Houghton Mifflin, 1987.

[1410 Walton] Science, Mark, ed. *Boethius: De Consolatione Philosophiae.* Translated by John Walton. Early English Text Society o.s. 170. London: Oxford University Press, 1927.

[mid-/late 1400s Anonymous] Noel Harold Kaylor, Jr. and Philip Edward Phillips, eds. "*The Boke of Coumfort of Bois* [Bodleian Library, Oxford Manuscript AUCT.F.3.5]: A Transcription with Introduction," by Anonymous. In *New Directions in Boethian Studies*, edited by Noel Harold Kaylor, Jr. and Philip Edward Phillips, 223–279. Studies in Medieval Culture 45. Kalamazoo, MI: Medieval Institute Publications, 2007.

[1593 Elizabeth I] Kaylor, Noel Harold, Jr. and Philip Edward Phillips, eds. *The Consolation of Queen Elizabeth I: The Queen's Translation of Boethius's "De Consolatione Philosophiae"* (Public Record Office Manuscript SP 12/289). Introduction by Quan Manh Ha. Medieval and Renaissance Texts and Studies 366. Tempe: Arizona Center for Medieval and Renaissance Studies, 2009.

[ca. 1602 Bracegirdle] Kaylor, Noel Harold, Jr. and Jason Edward Streed, eds. *John Bracegirdle's "Psychopharmacon": A Translation of Boethius's "De Consolatione Philosophiae" (MS BL Additional 11401).* Medieval and Renaissance Texts and Studies 200. Tempe: Arizona Center for Medieval and Renaissance Studies, 1999.

[1609 I.T.] Anderson, William, ed. *Five Books of Philosophical Comfort, Full of Christian Consolation.* Translated by I.T. 1609. Carbondale: Southern Illinois University Press, 1963.

[1664 Conningsbye (Coningsby)] *The Consolation of Philosophy.* Translated by Harry Coningsby. London: James Flesher, 1664.

[1674 Elys (Anonymous)] *Summum Bonum, or an Explication of the Divine Goodness, in the Words of the Most Renowned Boetius.* Translated by Edmund Elys (Anonymous). Oxford: H. Hail for Ric. Davis, 1674.

[1695 Graham] *Anicius Manlius Severinus Boethius, of the* Consolation of Philosophy. Translated by Richard Graham. London: F.D., 1695.

[1693 Somerset] Hawley, Kenneth Carr, ed. "Boethius's *Comforts and Consolations of Philosophy* by Henry Somerset, Duke of Beaufort (1693), British Library, Additional MS 40693B." *CarmP* 20 (2011): 1–114.

[1717 Pope] "From Boetius, de cons. Philos." In *The Poems of Alexander Pope*, edited by John Butt, 115. New Haven: Yale University Press, 1963.

[1897 James] *The Consolation of Philosophy of Boethius.* Translated by H. R. James. London: Elliot Stock, 1897.

[1973 Tester] "The Consolation of Philosophy." Translated by S. J. Tester. In *Boethius. Tractates; The Consolation of Philosophy*, translated by H.F. Stewart, E.K. Rand, and S.J. Tester, Loeb Classical Library 74, 130-435. Cambridge, MA: Harvard University Press, 1973.

[1999 Walsh] *The Consolation of Philosophy.* Translated by P. G. Walsh. Oxford: Oxford University Press, 1999.

German

[ca. 1000 Notker] Tax, Petrus W., ed. *Notker der Deutsche: Boethius, "De consolatione Philosophiae," Buch IV/V.* Die Werke Notkers des Deutschen 3, Altdeutsche Textbibliothek 101. Tübingen: Niemeyer, 1990.

[ca. 1401 von Kastel][2]

[ca. 1450–1500 Münster Fragments] Bömer, Alois. "Fragmente einer gereimten deutschen Boethiusübersetzung." *Zeitschrift für deutsches Altertum und deutsche Literatur* 50 (1908): 149–58.

[ca. 1463/64 Lemgo][3]

[1477 von Wyle][4]

[ca. 1465 Erfurt][5]

[ca. 1462/63 or 1500 Humery][6]

[1473 Anonymous] Anonymous, trans. *Hic liber Boecii de consolatione philosophiae in textu latina alemannicaque lingua refertus ac translatus una cum apparatu & expositione beati Thome de aquino ordinis praedicatorum finit feliciter.* Nürnberg: Anton Koberger, 1473. n.p.

[ca. 1500 Anonymous] Anonymous, trans. *Boethius der Hochberumpt meister und poet von dem trost der weissheit.* Edited by Johann Schrott. Strassburg, ca. 1500. Reedit, Nürnberg: Anton von Koberger, 1473.

[1600 Hellwig (Helwig)] Johann Hellwig (Helwig). *Des Annici Manlii Torquatii Severini Boethii: V Bücher von Trost aus der Vernünft Lehre.* Nürnberg: Gedruckt bey Christophf Gerhard / In Verlegung Johann Taubers, 1660.

[1667 and 1697 von Rosenroth and van Helmont] Knorr von Rosenroth, Christian, and Franciscus Mercurius van Helmont. *Des Fûrtrefflichen Hochvveisen Severini Boetii, Weil. Bûrgermeisters zu Rom, Consolatio Philosophiae, oder Christlich-vernunfft-gemesser Trost und*

Unterricht in Widerwertigkeit und Bestûrtzung ûber dem vermeinten Wohl-oder Ubel-Stand der Bösen und Frommen: Verteutschet, und mit beygefügten kurtzen Anmerckungen ûber etliche dunckele Ort desselben zum andernmahl auffgeleget 1697. Lüneburg: Johann Georg Lippern, 1697.

[1717 F.R.] Roth-Scholz, Friedrich [F.R.]. *Fünf Bücher vom Troste der Weisheit in Widerwertigkeit aus dem Lateinischen übersetzt und mit kurzen Anmerkungen aus Licht gestellt von F.R.* Nürnberg, 1717.

[1724 Fahsius] Johann Just. Fahsius. *Der in seinem Gefängniss philosophirende Boëthius, das ist: des im 6ten Seculo hochberühmten römischen Bürgermeisters und königl. Ost-Gothischen Staats-Ministers Anicii Manlii Torquati Severini Boethii V. Bücher "De Consolatione Philosophiæ," oder Tröstung aus der Welt-Weissheit, usw.* Gosslat: Johann Christoph König, 1724.

[1753 Richter] Richter, M. Johann Gottfried, trans. *Des Anicius Manlius Troquatus Severinus Boethius: Fünf Bücher vom Philosophischen Trofte*. Leipzig: Johann Michael Teubner, 1753.

[1794 Freytag] Freytag, Friedrich Karl. *Trost der Philosophie aus Lateinischen des Boethius mit Anmerkungen und Nachrichten die Geschichte des Originals und das Leben des Verfassers betreffend von Fredrich Karl Freytag*. Riga: Johann Friedrich Hartknoch, 1794.

[1826 Wortberg] Wortberg, Lambert Ignaz. *Des römischen Consuls Anicius Manlius Torquatus Severinus Boethius Gesänge im Kerker (De Consolatione philosophiae) nachgebildet von L[ambert] I[gnaz] Wortberg*. Greifswalt, Barlini, Gesellius: Mauritius in Commission in der Maurituschen Buchhanlung 1826.

[1827 Weingärtner] Weingärtner, J.H., trans. *Fünf Bücher vom Troste der Philosophie: prosaisch und metrisch übersetzt und mit Anmerkungen eines Christen begleitet, von J.H. Weingärtner, Pfarrer*. Linz: Verlag der k.k. priv. academischen Kunst-, Musik- und Buchhandlung, 1827.

[1893 Scheven] Scheven, Richard, trans. *Die Tröstungen der Philosophie des Anicius Manlius Torquatus Severinus Boethius. Senator und Mitglied der obersten Rangklasse, gewesener ordentlicher römischer Konsul und Chef der Civilverwaltung, Patricius von Rom,* übersetzt von Richard Scheven. Leipzig: Philipp Reclam jun., 1893.

[1932 Gothein] Gothein, Eberhard, trans. *Anicius Manlius Severinus Boethius: Trost der Philosophie: Übersetzt von Eberhard Gothein*. Köln: Verlag die Runde, 1932.

[1934 Zimmermann] Zimmermann, Johannes, trans. *Boethius: Trost der Philosophie: Ausgewählt und Übersetzt von Dr. Johannes Zimmermann: Studienrat am Dreikönigsgymnasium in Köln.* Düsseldorf: Schwann, 1934.

[1939 Büchner] Büchner, Friedrich, trans. *Boethius: Trost der Philosophie: Deutsch von Karl Büchner.* Leipzig: Dieterich'schen Verlangsbuchhandlung, 1939.

[1956 Weiss] Weiss, Konrad, trans. *Die Gedichte aus der Tröstung der Philosophie des Boethius: Deutsch von Konrad Weiss.* Berlin: Suhrkamp, 1956.

[1959 Neitzke] Neitzke, Ernst, trans. *Boethius: Trost der Philosophie.* Stuttgart: Reclam-Verlag, 1959.

[1961 Endres] Endres, H.M., trans. *Boethius: Trost der Philosophie: Ins Deutsche übertragen und eingeleitet von H.M. Endres.* Munich: Wilhelm Goldmann, 1961.

[1981 Gegenschatz and Gigon] Gegenschatz, Ernst, and Olof Gigon, ed. and trans. *Boethius: Trost der Philosophie.* Munich: Deutscher Taschenbuch Verlag, 1981.

Greek

[ca. 1293–96 Planudes] Papathomopoulos, Manolis, ed. *Anicii Manlii Severini Boethii De Consolatione Philosophiae: Traduction Grecque de Maxime Planude* (Athens: Academy of Athens, 1999).

Hebrew

[1412 Benveniste] St. Petersburg, Oriental Institute, MS B 18.

[1423 Bonafoux] Sierra, Sergio Joseph, ed. *Sefer Di Konsolasioni Filosofya / Boezio De Consolatione Philosophiae; Traduzione Ebraica di 'Azaria Ben R. Joseph Ibn Abba Mari detto Bonafoux Bonfil Astruc 5183–1423,* trans. Bonafoux Bonfil Astruc. Turin: Instituto di Studi Ebraici Scuola Rabbinica, 1967.

Italian

[ca. thirteenth–fourteenth century, Giandino da Carmignano prose translation] Brunetti, Giuseppina. "Guinizzelli, il non più oscuro Maestro Giandino e il Boezio di Dante." In *Intorno a Guido Guinizzelli,* Atti della Giornata di Studi (Università di Zurigo, 16 giugno 2000), ed. Luciano Rossi and Sara Alloatti Boller, 155–91. Alessandria: Edizioni dell'Orso, 2002.

[ca. thirteenth–fourteenth century, Giandino da Carmignano prose translation] Brunetti, Giuseppina. "Preliminari all'edizione del volgarizzamento della *Consolatio Philosophiae* di Boezio attribuito al maestro Giandino da Carmignano," in *Studi sui volgarizzamenti italiani due-trecenteschi*, ed. Paolo Rinoldi and Gabriella Ronchi, 9–45. Roma: Viella, 2005.

[1322–32 Alberto della Piagentina prose and verse translation] Favero, Alessandra. *Nuovi studi sulla tradizione manoscritta e sul testo del volgarizzamento di Alberto della Piagentina del "De Consolatione Philosophiae" di Boezio*. PhD diss., Università degli Studi di Padova, 2002.

[1322–32 Alberto della Piagentina prose and verse translation] Favero, Alessandra. "La tradizione manoscritta del volgarizzamento di Alberto della Piagentina del 'De consolatione philosophiae' di Boezio." *Studi e problemi di critica testuale* 73 (2006): 61–116.

[ca. fourteenth century, Bonaventura da Demena prose translation] Babbi, Anna Maria. *"Consolatio Philosophiae," una versione veneta: Verona, Biblioteca Civica, ms. 212.* Milano: Franco Angeli, 1995.

[ca. fourteenth century, Anonymous prose and verse translation] Parodi, Ernesto Giacomo. "Studi liguri," *Archivio Glottologico Italiano* 14 (1898): 1–110.

[ca. fourteenth century, Anonymous prose and verse translation] Cropp, Glynnis M. "An Italian Translation of 'Le Livre de Boece de Consolacion,'" *CarmP* 11 (2002): 1–8.

[ca. fourteenth century, Partial translation] Napoli, Bibl. Nazionale, MS V.H. 57 (L'Aquila, c. XV ex).

Korean

[1990 Park] Boethius, *The Consolation of Philosophy*. Translated by Byung Duk Park. Seoul: Yookmoonsa, 1990.

[1993 Tjeng] Boethius, *The Consolation of Philosophy*. Translated by Father Eui Chai Tjeng. Seoul: St. Paul, 1993.

Polish

[1694 Bardziński] Bardziński, Jan Alan, trans. *Skuteczny na wszelkie przygody nieszczęśliwe sposób, wszystkim w utrapieniu zostajacym podany, to jest, Pociecha Filozofiey, niegdy od An. Man. Torq. Seweryna Boecyusza napisana, teraz przez W. X. Jana Alana Bardzińskiego, S. Theologiey Lektora, Przeora Łęczyckiego Zakonu Kaznodziejskiego, przetłumaczona.* W Thoruniu: nakladem Jana Christiana Laurera, 1694.

[1738 Wielopolski] Wielopolski, Karol, trans. *Konsolacya Philozophyi Boecyusza.* Warszawa: Collegium Scholarum Piarum, 1738.

[1926 Jachimowski] Jachimowski, Tadeusz, trans. *Boecjusz: O pociechach filozofji ksiąg pięcioro oraz Traktaty teologiczne.* Pisma Ojców Kościoła 5. Poznań: Fiszer i Majewski, 1926.

[1962 Olszewski] Olszewski, Witold, trans. *Boecjusz: O pocieszeniu jakie daje filozofia.* Warszawa: PWN, 1962.

[2006 Kurylewicz] Kurylewicz, Antczak, trans. *Boecjusz, O pocieszeniu, jakie daje filozofia.* Kęty: Wydawnictwo Marek Derewiecki, 2006.

Bibliographies

Gruber, Joachim. "Boethius, 1925–1998." *Lustrum: Internationale Forschungsberichte aus deim Bereich des klassichen Altertums* 39 (1997): 307–83; 40 (1998): 199–259; and 52 (2010): 161–80.

Kaylor, Noel Harold, Jr. *The Medieval Consolation of Philosophy: An Annotated Bibliography.* New York: Garland, 1992.

Obertello, Luca. *Severino Boezio.* Volume 2 [Bibliography]. Genoa: Accademia Ligure di Scienze e Lettere, 1974.

Phillips, Philip Edward. "Anicius Manlius Severinus Boethius: A Chronology and Selected Annotated Bibliography." In *A Companion to Boethius in the Middle Ages*, ed. Noel Harold Kaylor, Jr. and Philip Edward Phillips, Brill's Companions to the Christian Tradition 30, 551–89. Leiden: Brill, 2012.

NOTES

[1] A comprehensive checklist of English translations is included as an appendix in the article on the English Tradition.

[2] See, for example, Christine Hehle, "Boethius's Influence on German Literature to *c.* 1500," in *A Companion to Boethius in the Middle Ages*, ed. Noel Harold Kaylor, Jr. and Philip Edward Phillips, Brill Companions to the Christian Tradition 30 (Leiden: Brill, 2012), 255–318.

[3] Ibid.

[4] Ibid.

[5] Ibid.

[6] Ibid.

Notes on Contributors

Jonathan Davis-Secord (PhD, University of Notre Dame, 2008) is Assistant Professor of English at the University of New Mexico. He is an Anglo-Saxonist specializing in the interaction of language and culture, and his recent publications include: "Rhetoric and Politics in Archbishop Wulfstan's Old English Homilies," in *Anglia*; "Rhythm and Music: The Sequences of Notker Balbulus," in *The Journal of Medieval Latin* (forthcoming); and "Sequences and Intellectual Identity at Winchester," in *Latinity and Identity in Anglo-Saxon England*, edited by Rebecca Stephenson and Emily Thornbury (forthcoming).

Marina Gorlach (PhD, Ben-Gurion University, Israel, 2000) is Associate Professor of English at Metropolitan State College of Denver. She specializes in linguistics and is the author of *Phrasal Construction and Resultativeness in English* (2004).

Kenneth Hawley (PhD, University of Kentucky, 2007) is Associate Professor of English at Lubbock Christian University, where he teaches early British literature and honors world literature. He contributed to the Electronic Beowulf and Electronic Boethius projects while at Kentucky and has continued to study the English tradition of *De consolatione philosophiae*. He is the editor of the *IBS Newsletter* website (http://boethius.blogspot.com) and coeditor of the interdisciplinary journal *Carmina Philosophiae*.

Ian Johnson (PhD, University of Bristol, 1990) is Senior Lecturer of English at the University of St. Andrews in Scotland. He has published widely on Middle English literature, with particular interests in Latin and vernacular traditions of medieval literary theory. He is also interested in conceptions and practices of translation in the Middle Ages, Geoffrey Chaucer, Boethius, and Boethianism (especially English versions of *De consolatione philosophiae*), and the Middle English tradition of *Vitae Christi*.

Ji-Soo Kang (PhD, University of Washington, 1993) is Professor of English at Inha University in Incheon, Korea, where she teaches medieval and Renaissance English literature. Her recent research interests are in medieval women writers as well as the uses of the vernacular in the later Middle Ages. Her publications include essays on Korean translations of English literature and English translations of Korean literature.

Noel Harold Kaylor, Jr. (PhD, Vanderbilt University, 1985) is Professor of English at Troy University, where he teaches medieval English literature and German language and literature. He is the Executive Director of the International Boethius Society and coeditor of its interdisciplinary journal, *Carmina Philosophiae*. He is author of *The Medieval Consolation of Philosophy* (1992) and coeditor of *New Directions in Boethian Studies* (2007), *Global Perspectives on Medieval English Literature, Language, and Culture* (2007), *The Consolation of Queen Elizabeth I* (2009), and *A Companion to Boethius in the Middle Ages* (2012).

Peter King (PhD, Princeton University, 1982) is Professor of Philosophy and Medieval Studies at the University of Toronto. He has published widely on medieval philosophy, especially on Augustine, Boethius, Anselm, Abelard, Duns Scotus, and Jean Buridan. He is the translator of *Jean Burden's Logic* (1985), *Augustine: Against the Academicians and The Teacher* (1995), and *Augustine: On the Free Choice of the Will, On Grace and Free Choice, and Other Writings* (2010). He has recently completed a critical edition of the commentary on the Περὶ Ἑρμηνείας by a student of Abelard's.

Serena Lunardi (PhD, Université de Siena, 2009) is a Postdoctoral Fellow at the Université de Genève, Switzerland. She specializes in medieval Italian and French literature. Her recent publications include articles on the translations of the *De consolatione philosophiae* produced in Italy between the thirteenth and fifteenth centuries and on the Old French fabliaux and their manuscript tradition.

John Magee (PhD, University of Toronto, 1986) is Professor of Classics and Medieval Studies at the University of Toronto. He studied at the University of California at Berkeley and University of Toronto and has taught at Columbia University and University of Toronto. His general research interests are in late ancient philosophy and philosophical commentators, and in textual criticism. He has published extensively on Boethius in particular and recently completed a critical edition of his Περὶ Ἑρμηνείας commentaries and an English translation of Calcidius.

Philip Edward Phillips (PhD, Vanderbilt University, 1996) is Professor of English and Associate Dean of the University Honors College at Middle Tennessee State University, where he teaches early European literature. He is the Secretary of the International Boethius Society and former coeditor of its interdisciplinary journal, *Carmina Philosophiae*. He is author of *John Milton's Epic Invocations* (2000); editor of *Prison Narratives from Boethius to Zana* (2014); and coeditor of *New Directions in Boethian Studies* (2007), *The Consolation of Queen Elizabeth I* (2009), and *A Companion to Boethius in the Middle Ages* (2012).

Jefferey H. Taylor (PhD, Southern Illinois University at Carbondale, 1994) is Professor of English at Metropolitan State University of Denver. He specializes in medieval and Renaissance English literature. He is author of *Four Levels of Meaning in the York Cycle of Mystery Plays* (2006) and coauthor, with Leslie A. Taylor, of a forthcoming book on Boethius in the Renaissance.

Leslie A. Taylor (PhD, Southern Illinois University at Carbondale, 1997) is an independent scholar who specializes in classical and Renaissance literature. Her coauthored book with Jefferey H. Taylor on *Boethius in the Renaissance* is forthcoming.

Władysław Witalisz (PhD, Jagiellonian University, 1996) is Professor of English at the Jagiellonian University in Kraków, where he teaches medieval and Renaissance English literature and serves as Dean of Studies at the Faculty of Philology. He is the author of *The Trojan Mirror—Middle English Narratives of Troy as Books of Princely Advice* (2011) and coeditor of Cracow Studies in English Language, Literature and Culture (Peter Lang).

General Index

Typeset in 11/13 Adobe Garamond Pro

Medieval Institute Publications
College of Arts and Sciences
Western Michigan University
1903 W. Michigan Avenue
Kalamazoo, MI 49008-5432
http:/ /www.wmich.edu/medieval/mip

WESTERN MICHIGAN UNIVERSITY